"The best tutorial I've seen yet on the Internet. . . . Gilster has done millions of newcomers a great service. . . ."
Knight Ridder News

". . . probably the most descriptive and useful strategy we've seen in print for getting on the Internet. . . ."
Jack Rickard
Boardwatch Magazine

". . . the one I turn to first . . ."
Daniel Akst
Los Angeles Times

"This is an Internet reference work whose time has come . . . a 'must have' for all online users. . . ."
Online Newsletter

". . . Makes you feel as if you were looking over Gilster's shoulder."
Joshua Quittner
Newsday

". . . Everything non-techies need to know. . . ."
U.S. News & World Report

"Must-have . . . Excellent . . ."
Mondo 2000

"At last I have found the perfect book . . . ."
Peter McWilliams
United Press

THE NEW INTERNET
NAVIGATOR™

THE NEW INTERNET NAVIGATOR™

Paul Gilster

Mark Ammerman '95

John Wiley & Sons, Inc.

NEW YORK • CHICHESTER • BRISBANE • TORONTO • SINGAPORE

Publisher: Katherine Schowalter
Editor: Philip Sutherland
Assistant Editor: Allison Roarty
Managing Editor: Frank Grazioli
Text Design & Composition: North Market Street Graphics, Lancaster, PA

This publication is designed to provide accurate and authoritative information in regard to the subject matter covered. It is sold with the understanding that the publisher is not engaged in rendering legal, accounting, or other professional service. If legal advice or other expert assistance is required, the services of a competent professional person should be sought.

Library of Congress Cataloging-in-Publication Data
Gilster, Paul,
    The new Internet Navigator / Paul Gilster.
        p.   cm.
    Includes index.
    ISBN 0-471-12694-2 (pbk. : acid-free paper)
    1. Internet (Computer network) I. Title.
TK5105.875.I57G563 1995
005.7'136—dc20
                            95-32589
                              CIP

Printed in the UK by The Bath Press, Somerset
10 9 8 7 6 5 4 3 2 1

For Eloise

"Whispering I knew not what of wild and sweet,
Like that strange song I heard Apollo sing,
While Ilion like a mist rose into towers."

Tennyson

Contents

Chapter 9   The Art of the List **273**

Appendix   **Dial-Up Internet Service Providers and Public Access Unix Sites**   **599**

Foreword

Unlike frontiers with well-defined and precisely fixed boundaries, the Internet frontier is in a constant state of flux and renewal. As quickly as the frontier is settled, new islands, oceans, and even whole continents become a part of it. As a virtual space of software, networking, and computers, the Internet is infinitely renewable and infinitely adaptable, and it grows and changes every day.

The increasingly eclectic character of the Internet and its penetration into almost every corner of the globe have created a rich and often unpredictable environment in which common interests and experience are sometimes more important than the geopolitical and social boundaries that separate its users. This mix of diversity and cohesion has created a collection of global villages with the unusual property that many people on the Internet live in more than one global village at a time.

The scope, complexity, and richness of the system we have today was not predicted. Looking at the Internet of 1995 even with 1990 eyes (let alone from the vantage point of 1973), one can only wonder at this (r)evolution. And (r)evolution is the right term. Just as complex life forms arise from simpler ones, genetic experiment by genetic experiment, the Internet is an evolving and organic virtual environment. But it is also a revolution because, viewed from the present, it is transforming our culture.

The extraordinary freedom of expression and accessibility of information on the Internet is revolutionary. In a way, the Internet has made every author a publisher and given new meaning to the phrase desktop publishing. Our social and business practices are becoming visibly affected. Our educational system may undergo a profound sea change as tools for producing and sharing knowledge blend with new ways of drawing students into learning experiences. Already, legislators are wondering what to make of an on-line electorate. There are, of course, downsides to the flood of information on the Internet. The most obvious is the difficulty of simply *finding* items in the vast seas of available material. Consumers of information or their proxies (*knowbots*) have had to become truly selective and thoughtful voyagers, ceaselessly sorting through and evaluating the information available to them as they sail the electronic oceans and cast their nets and troll for valuable content. Indeed, like gold in the ocean, the valuable content of the Internet is enormous in quantity but hard to find, and more of it is created daily. Browsing is giving way to efforts to index and catalog a burgeoning sea of information and creating new business opportunities in the process.

We already know there are some unwelcome side effects, such as *flaming*, which seems to be exacerbated by a medium of communications that often invites instant responses rather than thoughtful correspondence. Many are troubled by the very freedom of expression the Internet invites and supports. There have been calls for some form of censorship or at least access controls for minors who have access to the Internet. Others decry the use of the network as a rallying point for groups whose opinions and attitudes, in their view, seem antisocial, destructive, or even treasonous. The technical and legal framework of Internet operation will have to cope with the turmoil of rapid growth through its own process of evolution. But much of what users *will* find, offered as a labor of love and sharing, is of extraordinary quality and value. We can doubtless look forward to extensions of the Internet that will lead to richer, more expressive modes of communication—including enhanced sound, graphics, and video—just as we hope that users will avail themselves of these tools in humane and intelligent ways.

The World Wide Web has burst on the Internet in a cascading explosion of new applications, reducing the apparent complexity of finding and using Internet-based information while increasing the richness of its texture. WWW has augmented the Internet and will almost certainly continue to evolve toward richer capabilities. The recent demonstration of dynamic software exchange from server to client or the reverse (such as Sun Microsystems' Hot Java) suggests that flexibility will become ever easier to provide. "Oh, you don't have a viewer for the material I just found for you? Here, take this piece of software and run it."

The late Ithiel de sola Pool called these electronic and computer-based tools the "technologies of freedom." Of course, that, too, has its downside. Hidden in that phrase is all the good and the not-so-good of the human animal. Charity and fellowship will cross paths with the coarse and the venal, but that is the price we pay for freedom of information.

Long-term citizens of the network are struggling with the side effects of growth from the small-town, collegial atmosphere of the early days to the clamor of a seemingly boundary-less megalopolis. As business uses of the Internet mature, far more attention is being paid to security, privacy, and authenticity of transactions taking place in the Internet environment. The virtual communities found in the Internet make me think of Stephen Hawking's description of the universe at the subnuclear level. The seemingly placid vacuum of space is in fact a roiling mass of energy in which particle pairs form and merge in fleeting femto-seconds. These vacuum fluctuations have no energy limits, and an entire universe, such as the one we know, could possibly arise as a consequence. The Internet seems to me a bit like that, vibrant with the energy and the ideas of millions of producers and consumers. Communities will form and coalesce, with some subsiding and many persisting and evolving.

To take just one example, consider one interesting effect of the Internet—the growing worldwide use of English. Other languages *are* used on the Internet, and there has been recent work to improve the technical standards for e-mail and other communications protocols to accommodate more than the use of the ASCII (English-language-based) character set encoding. Indeed, two phenomena are discernible. English is widely used, but other languages are becoming increasingly common. Many offerings found on the net are multilingual ("Press this button for English, this one for French, and that one for Japanese."). While *lingua anglica* becomes commonplace on the Net, I believe we will also preserve and even extend the appreciation and use of other languages. The Internet will preserve and extend the richness of our global, cultural heritage.

In this book, Paul Gilster has done a remarkable job of describing the dynamic, daily growth and change that characterizes the Internet. He has also ably summarized the important points in the history of the system, and suggested the breadth and diversity of the communities that use it today. And, perhaps most important, he has amassed a truly astonishing list of resources and service providers. I learned of many new ones, so his new editions are finding welcome space in my reference collection.

As Gilster points out, any medium such as print has the simultaneous blessing and curse of a fixed nature. The Internet is changing so rapidly that anything written about it in immutable form is bound to be out of date. This book, however, unlocks many doors and leads you to sources of information on the Internet that you can use to stay up to date. By decoding the argot of the Internet and empowering its readers to become modern day Lewises and Clarks, this book will show you how the Internet offers an endless journey of discovery along its infinitely changing frontier. You'll be welcome there.

Vinton G. Cerf
Annandale, Virginia
July 1995

Preface to the Third Edition

When you're shooting at a moving target, the usual technique is to lead just enough so that your shot hits the place where the target *will* be; obviously, your timing had better be good. The Internet is a moving target, but trying to lead it can be a confounding experience. The changes we've seen since the second edition of *The Internet Navigator* have been so immense, and ongoing, that there have been days when I thought the network was totally out of control. Master one set of tools and another arose. Teach the basics of Mosaic, and pretty soon everyone was trying Netscape. Master Netscape, and the Net begins to buzz with talk of third-generation systems like Sun Microsystems' Hot Java, and Silicon Graphics' WebSpace. Where does it all end?

But there is a ready answer, and it's a positive one. While we can't know the minutiae of how technology will evolve six months, or six years, from now, we can state an unequivocal fact: the Internet is getting easier to use with every passing day. The huge user revolution that has occurred within the last two years has had two major effects. First, it has brought a population of home and small business users onto the Internet for the first time. Second, it has energized service providers, in the heat of competition, to lower the cost of the essential SLIP and PPP connections that make it possible to use graphical Internet tools. Two years ago, Mosaic wasn't available to most new users because they didn't have the kind of connection it demanded. Today, Mosaic, Netscape, the other Web browsers and a host of shareware, freeware, and commercial tools are providing ever new and ever easier to use graphical environments that have people exploring this exciting realm.

It was clear in approaching this third edition that I needed to reflect this sea-change in access methods. *The Internet Navigator* has always been written for the modem user who, for most of the Internet's life, was limited to a character-based interface through a Unix shell account. In many parts of the world, this is still the major means of access, and these users will find that this book continues to speak to them and to illustrate how they can use the network. But I've also moved into the SLIP/PPP realm with a host of examples and illustrations of the various graphical client programs at work. The idea is not to insist that you use a particular software program for your Net access, but rather, to say that no matter which tool you use, the underlying Net remains the same. Master Internet principles, then, and your choice of tools is yours.

Even as the access methods we use on the Internet have changed, so too has the nature of what we find there. The World Wide Web has grown at rates that have astonished even the most optimistic network aficionados. And, just as important, a host of new search tools has arisen that make using the Web a productive, rather than a fascinating but generally fruitless, experience. With business-building Web sites, individuals setting up their own home pages, and magazines and newspapers coming on-line in abundance, surely it's the Web that is now the dominant form of access, and the one that will shape, for better or worse, what the Internet will become.

This book, then, attempts to reflect these changes while retaining its initial charter of speaking to modem users of all persuasions. You'll find Unix commands here as well as the addresses for obtaining graphical client programs. Illustrations include a variety of different client programs and reflect both Microsoft Windows as well as Macintosh operating parameters (although considering the market dominance of Windows, I have leaned more often toward that system for figures, even if the Macintosh remains an excellent Internet tool). I've also tried to keep a sense of balance; we don't want to become so caught up in sight and sound that we forget the value of on-line text and the need to build up libraries of the written word. Current trends in this regard seem positive.

The Internet remains a place of endless fascination. What I find most enjoyable about it is that study repays your efforts; the more you learn, the more you can find out. We are heading toward a network that will have a profound impact on how we access information on a day-by-day basis; a searchable archive of news stories lets us look at the day's events with the ability to place them in context; a Web page that plays audio files lets us link sound to our data; a repository of historical information provides an opportunity for scholars and others to study and relate their findings.

We are seeing an explosion in content that is daily making the Internet a more valuable reference engine. My hope is that by reading this book, people will be disposed to use the network within the parameters of its long-established culture. If you draw ideas, facts, and inspiration from the Net, do your best to give information back to it, whether it be through a USENET posting helping someone out, or a Web page of your own, or a contribution to a mailing list in the field of your choice. This voluntary activation of intellectual resources has always kept the Internet vibrant. The influx of new Internet users has the opportunity of adding to that priceless exchange of ideas.

Acknowledgments

Space forbids listing everyone who has written to me over the course of the past few years about *The Internet Navigator* (and thank heaven for Eudora, the mail program that lets me manage all this material!). Suffice it to say that I have appreciated the ideas, suggestions, and comments from readers around the world, and hope that this new addition will generate equally helpful correspondents.

I have been pleased and honored since the first edition to have had a foreword written by Vinton Cerf, the man I admire above all others in the Internet business. On the editorial front, thanks go to Phil Sutherland and Allison Roarty at John Wiley & Sons, Inc., who have helped shepherd this new edition through the production process, as have Frank Grazioli, Sue Curtin, and my excellent copy editor, Janice Borzendowski, who somehow made sense out of all my notations, inserts, and commentary on the original text. Thanks, too, to Bob Ipsen and Jeff DeMarrais for handling and explaining a marketing process that is well beyond the range of this reclusive writer. The original editor of this book, and the man responsible for its seeing the light of day, was Paul Farrell, whom I am pleased to call a friend. I count myself lucky to have had the chance to work with such a fine team.

THE NEW INTERNET NAVIGATOR™

A Wild Surmise

John Keats didn't know anything about computers, and he wasn't much on history, either. He evidently thought Cortez discovered the Pacific Ocean, when in fact it was Balboa. But in a poem written 180 years ago, Keats captured the essence of what the newcomer experiences when confronted with the Internet. Listen to him as he compares a translation of Homer by George Chapman to that first glimpse of the Pacific:

> Much have I travelled in the realms of gold,
>   And many goodly states and kingdoms seen;
>   Round many western islands have I been
> Which bards in fealty to Apollo hold.
> Oft of one wide expanse had I been told
>   That deep-browed Homer ruled as his demesne;
>   Yet did I never breathe its pure serene
> Till I heard Chapman speak out loud and bold:
> Then felt I like some watcher of the skies
>   When a new planet swims into his ken;
> Or like stout Cortez, when with eagle eyes
>   He stared at the Pacific—and all his men
> Looked at each other with a wild surmise—
>   Silent, upon a peak in Darien.[1]

A wild surmise indeed. To realize upon seeing the Pacific that there was yet another ocean to cross must have struck early explorers with the force of thunder. In the late twentieth century, the sensation Keats so exquisitely depicts is alive and well, thanks to computer networking. The Internet, a worldwide, interconnecting, communicating amalgam of more than 40 thousand networks, between 20 and 30 million users, and a growth rate that makes attempts to quantify it in print necessarily obsolete, inspires just that sense of awe.[2] The moment you run your first World Wide Web session, clicking on a network resource to travel to it, or use FTP to retrieve a file from another continent, you know the boundaries that separate us are being redefined.

But how do you know what to do? Unlike commercial on-line services, the Internet provides few pointers. Users logging on through a Unix-based service provider work with a cryptic prompt as simple, and in some ways as profound, as a Japanese watercolor's brushstroke. Others, using a form of connection called a SLIP/PPP account, take advantage of graphical client programs that let them perform network tasks. You can make your modem take you around the world in seconds, retrieving files, reading mail, subscribing to electronic journals, using remote databases, but you have to know where you're going and the commands you'll need once you're there. That's what this book is about—it's a guide to navigating the Internet, assembled with the modem user in mind.

Destinations You Haven't Thought Of

There can be no all-inclusive printed directory of the Internet. Those who write about this globe-spanning network are destined to labor forever behind the technological wave. Simply put, the Internet is changing so rapidly, with so many new databases, services, addresses, and projects, that it can't be neatly encapsulated in any one set of commands or maxims. The more you use the Internet, the more you will realize that each day is a learning process.

Each discovery leads to another, for the Internet is self-referential. A casual reference on a mailing list may point to a hitherto unknown resource on a computer in a distant city. A file on that computer may remind you of the existence of a USENET newsgroup which, once subscribed to, updates you on new Internet services. A link on a World Wide Web page leads you to another link located halfway around the world. You will seldom find yourself exactly where you planned when you embark on an Internet voyage.

This book will construct a set of strategies that will allow you to get started. It provides mapping to put you in the neighborhood of your destination, just as early maps of the New World sketched out the coast of Cuba, or Hispaniola, or Virginia, but left it to later cartographers to refine their work. Even today, maps are continually being fine-tuned as more precise methods of measurement are developed. So too on the Internet, new directories are coming into being that attempt to solve the problem of locating resources—the InterNIC, or Internet Network Information Center, is but one such attempt. On-line searching tools like Lycos and the World Wide Web Worm let us find resources by entering keywords. These and many other tools will be explored in subsequent chapters.

Let me make one point clear at the outset. Some of the destinations you read about in this book will have subtly changed by the time you try to access them. Perhaps a login command has been replaced with another, or a sign-on sequence now sports a new menu. In some cases, the service itself may have moved to a new address. Such changes can be harrowing to the newcomer, but if you follow the principles outlined in this book, you should be able to understand what has happened and to proceed. Above all, realize that you must be both attentive and creative in your dealings with a network as powerful, and elastic, as the Internet.

Let me give you a glimpse of the kind of destinations available to you on the Internet. In the examples that follow, don't worry about the addresses specified; a note at the end of the chapter explains how to read them, and the book itself is dedicated to teaching you how to use them. Bear with me, then, as we take a whirlwind tour of the Net.

Internet Echoes from All Over

There are millions of Internet destinations. Network links remain largely a phenomenon of the developed world, but even Eastern Europe, South America, and Africa are beginning to sprout network nodes. Traffic on Internet mailing lists regularly reveals addresses from countries only now establishing their connectivity, and the clear benefits of network access in terms of tying together the academic, scientific, and government communities of developing areas ensures this trend will only accelerate. After a short time on-line, you begin to take international connectivity almost for granted.

A newsgroup on the USENET network, called misc.test, exists so that people who send test messages don't tie up the daily reading of newsgroups with greater content. A number of sites around the world monitor this newsgroup, and if you send a test message on it, you'll receive a set of replies, letting you know your message was indeed received and where.

When I posted a test message on misc.test, the replies began immediately. The first was from the University of Zurich in Switzerland. Next was Ingres Corporation in Alameda, California, acknowledging reception of my two-line message "General Test." After that was a Free-Net in Youngstown, Ohio; Free-Nets provide community services and offer Internet gateways to their local audience. I heard from a site in Lyon, France, as well as Harper Community College in Palatine, Illinois. Lund, Sweden responded, and so too did Network Architecture Consulting, a firm in Fremont, California. I received mail from a commercial site in Hollywood, California (just below the Hollywood sign, said the message), and from the University of Natal in Durban, South Africa.

The Internet crosses borders and oceans with daredevil ease. There is no greater challenge to a parochial outlook than a day or two monitoring message traffic in this ongoing worldwide conversation.

Searching TIME Magazine for News

In the past year, numerous magazine and newspaper publishers have moved onto the Internet, but few have approached the sophisticated level reached by *TIME*. When you use a World Wide Web browser like Netscape to go to the *TIME* magazine site (http://www.timeinc.com/time/timehomepage.html), you will encounter current and past issues in hypertext format. Click on the item you want to see and it will be presented on-screen. You can see an example of this in Figure 1.1.

If I wanted to see the article called "The Man Who Would Be Deficit Buster," I would simply move my mouse cursor to the underlined term "Congress" and click on that word. The presence of underlining tells me that this is a hyperlink; once I click on it, I will be taken to the underlying file.

TIME has done its Internet service right. Not only can you explore the text of the magazine, reading it on-line or searching it by keyword, but you can also enter a series of bulletin boards where current issues are discussed. *TIME* also provides a synopsis of daily news, and links to audio and video clips, as well as cover and interior graphics—you can even call up "spiked" stories, those that never saw print in the magazine itself. All of this traffic flows over the global system of hypermedia called the World Wide Web, where the Internet's growth has become the most vibrant in recent months.

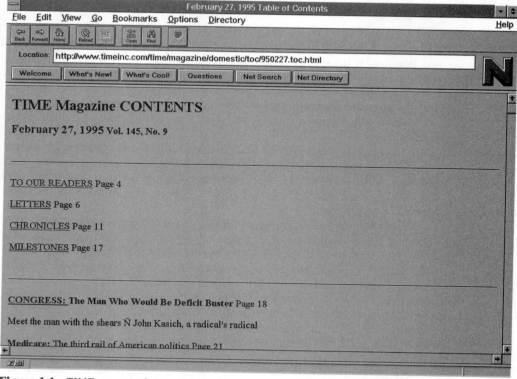

Figure 1.1 *TIME* magazine's Internet site allows you to read and search the magazine on-line.

Via the Internet to the Asteroids

What seems outlandish when you begin your Internet journeys becomes commonplace with experience. Yet in all the time I've been making these voyages, I've never lost a sense of wonder at the bounty available on the network. Take images, for example. You'll find plentiful files in a variety of formats and subject matter, ranging from museum exhibits on the Vatican library to photographs of landscapes and people. One of my favorite sites is a NASA archive containing imagery from agency missions, including photos of Jupiter, Venus, and the Space Shuttle.

An asteroid named Toutatis, for example, made a close pass to the Earth on December 8, 1992, closing to within 2.2 million miles. NASA's Deep Space Network site in Goldstone, California bounced radar off the asteroid, creating a set of images which can be retrieved on-line. By using the Internet procedure known as anonymous FTP, you can log on to the computer at this site (its Internet address is ftp://explorer.arc.nasa.gov) to download this material. There is also a text file, toutatis.txt, which presents the captions for these photographs. Figure 1.2 shows the images.

Whether you're interested in photos from Viking, Voyager, Magellan, or a host of other astronomical vistas, NASA's site contains a wealth of imagery.

FTP, as you'll quickly learn, is a primary tool for Internet exploration. Using FTP, dial-up users can move into remote computers, change directories and examine their

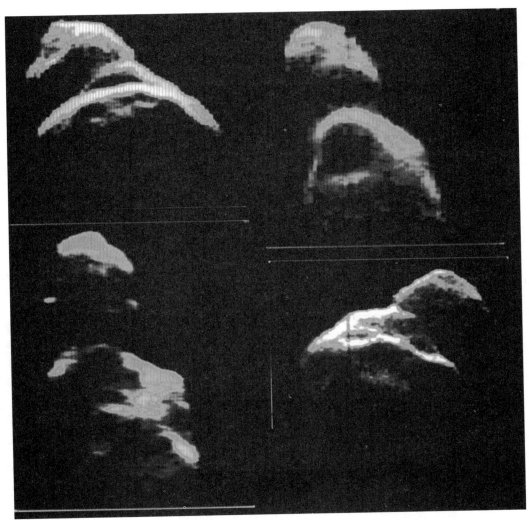

Figure 1.2   Images from NASA of the asteroid Toutatis.

contents, and transfer copies of their holdings to their service provider's computer. From there, they can download the files they've chosen onto their own hard disks. We'll go through the procedures for FTP and use it frequently to retrieve documents as we build an Internet file library.

Finding a Map of Finland

When my son needed a topographical map of Finland for a school report, it seemed a simple enough project, but the problem was time. It was too late to head for the library. Fortunately, I recalled a computer site in Finland—ftp://garbo.wwasa.fi at the University of Vaasa—that maintained GIF files. GIF is a format used to encode many of the images found on the Internet (the Toutatis pictures discussed earlier were downloaded as GIF files, and then run through a file viewer for presentation). Could the computer at Vaasa help?

FTP is fast. Enter the appropriate commands and you're there before you know it. Searching through the directories in Finland, I found a directory called *pc/gif*. Moving to it, I requested a listing of its contents, selected a file called suomi.gif, and moved it to the computer I dial in to here in Raleigh, North Carolina. I then downloaded it to my PC and printed a copy on my laser printer. Problem solved. The map is shown in Figure 1.3.

Like many things on the Internet, FTP access can be handled in a variety of ways. When I brought the Finland map to my service provider's site and then downloaded it to my own computer, I was using a form of Internet access called a *shell account*. I could also have used so-called SLIP/PPP access, which would have allowed me to take advantage of a graphical FTP program with pull-down menus and point-and-click commands. Figure 1.4 shows an FTP session using WS_FTP, a graphical client that allows me to use point-and-click mouse commands. Here, I am looking at the same site in Finland, browsing through the various files available in its directories.

I could even have used a World Wide Web browser like Mosaic or Netscape to handle the same chores through its interface. As you'll see, the Internet challenges you to come up with the best out of a variety of possible solutions to any network problem.

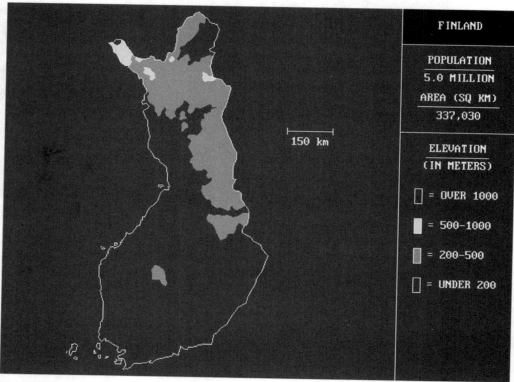

Figure 1.3   A map of Finland, direct from the source.

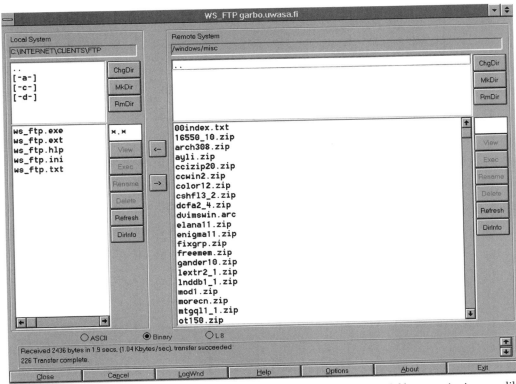

Figure 1.4 A graphical client like WS_FTP lets you see the directories and files at a site in a readily understood format.

Software in Profusion

Multiply the number of FTP sites around the world by the number of available files and you quickly realize there is software out there by the gigabyte, waiting to be accessed. There are collections of shareware and public domain software, not to mention text files on a wide variety of subjects, so extensive as to boggle the mind. Looking for telecommunications programs, I turned to the huge archive at Washington University in St. Louis, at the address ftp://wuarchive.wustl.edu. Like the Finnish computer, this site is accessible by anonymous FTP.

Figure 1.5 shows a screen from a recent visit to Washington University. It may give you some idea of the scope of the contents there. Note that each of these entries has a name, listed on the far right. There's a section on PostScript, one on the communications program Qmodem, one on security, and one on spreadsheets. At the far left, you'll see that each entry is prefixed with the letter **d.** Every entry so marked is itself a directory, containing an abundance of software. We are looking at a single, tiny corner of a vast software archive. It is but one of many such archives on the Internet. Later in this book, we'll examine the tools you need to retrieve this software.

```
drwxr-xr-x   2 root      archive     1536 Jun 18 02:38 postscript
drwxr-xr-x   2 root      archive      512 Jun 18 02:39 preprocess
drwxr-xr-x   2 root      archive     3584 Jun 29 00:32 printer
drwxr-xr-x   2 root      archive     1024 Jun 18 02:39 procomm
drwxr-xr-x   2 root      archive      512 Jun 18 02:39 prodigy
drwxr-xr-x   2 root      archive     1024 Jun 18 02:39 progjourn
drwxr-xr-x   2 root      archive      512 Jun 18 02:39 prolog
drwxr-xr-x   2 root      archive     2048 Jul  1 00:28 qbasic
drwxr-xr-x   2 root      archive     1024 Jun 18 02:39 qedit
drwxr-xr-x   2 root      archive      512 Jun 18 02:39 qemm
drwxr-xr-x   2 root      archive     1024 Jun 18 02:39 qmodem
drwxr-xr-x   2 root      archive      512 Jun 18 02:39 qpascal
drwxr-xr-x   2 root      archive     1024 Jun 18 02:39 qtrdeck
drwxr-xr-x   2 root      archive      512 Jun 18 02:39 ramdisk
drwxr-xr-x   2 root      archive     2048 Jun 18 02:39 rbbs-pc
drwxr-xr-x   2 root      archive      512 Jun 18 02:39 satellite
drwxr-xr-x   2 root      archive     4608 Jul  1 00:28 screen
drwxr-xr-x   2 root      archive      512 Jun 18 02:39 security
drwxr-xr-x   2 root      archive      512 Jun 18 02:39 simulation
drwxr-xr-x   2 root      archive      512 Jun 18 02:39 small-c
drwxr-xr-x   2 root      archive      512 Jun 18 02:39 smalltalk
drwxr-xr-x   2 root      archive      512 Jun 18 02:39 snobol4
drwxr-xr-x   2 root      archive     1536 Jun 18 02:39 sound
drwxr-xr-x   2 root      archive     1024 Jun 18 02:39 spreadsheet
```

Figure 1.5   A world of software awaits in Internet-linked machines.

My Kingdom for a Network

Recalling details from texts you read long ago is difficult for those not blessed with an acute memory. So, when a friend and I recently fell into a discussion about Shakespeare, and he quoted the famous line "My kingdom for a horse!," we began trying to remember the surrounding lines. The play, *Richard III*, features one of history's most controversial monarchs, characterized by Shakespeare as a scoundrel, but now undergoing a rehabilitation in some quarters. What did Shakespeare have him say in that famous scene on Bosworth Field as his kingdom fell apart around him?

A Gopher at wiretap.spies.com provided the answer. There, the complete works of Shakespeare are available on-line. Gopher is a program that allows you to make simple menu choices to find information; Gopher also allows you to search the files you are looking through for specific information. In Figure 1.6, we see the result of going to the wiretap.spies.com site, calling up *Richard III*, and searching under the words kingdom for. As you can see, Gopher has taken us right to the lines in question.

Burrowing into the InterNIC

Is there any logic to the Internet? It can be hard to find, for although resources may exist in profusion, they may be hidden from us by the proliferation of network sites. That makes resource discovery a major theme of the network, and later chapters will cover the wide range of tools available.

One place we can turn to for help is an information repository known as the Inter-NIC. The InterNIC's resources, like so many other information banks on the Internet,

```
/kingdom for
...skipping
          [Alarums. Enter KING RICHARD III]

KING RICHARD III        A horse! a horse! my kingdom for a horse!

CATESBY Withdraw, my lord; I'll help you to a horse.

KING RICHARD III        Slave, I have set my life upon a cast,
        And I will stand the hazard of the die:
        I think there be six Richmonds in the field;
        Five have I slain to-day instead of him.
        A horse! a horse! my kingdom for a horse!

        [Exeunt]




        KING RICHARD III


ACT V
--More--[98%] Press space to continue, 'q' to quit
```

Figure 1.6   Part of Shakespeare's *Richard III* discovered with a Gopher.

can be accessed by a wide variety of tools. In Figure 1.7, I have entered via the World Wide Web, using the Mosaic browsing program. The URL is http://www.internic.net /ds/dsdirofdirs/html (URLs will be explained shortly).

Through the resources of the InterNIC site, I can examine network statistics, look up information about service providers in my area, print out documentation about the history of the Net, and explore the various kinds of connectivity available to me. There are links to a wide variety of other information sources as well, all of them accessible by clicking on the item with a mouse.

And the InterNIC is hardly alone. In the past six months, a number of sites have come on-line with the express purpose of making the chore of finding resources easier. There's Yahoo, a site where resources are listed by topic; this model is also followed at EINet Galaxy. Even keyword searches are available for interesting Web destinations, at sites such as Carnegie Mellon's Lycos, the World Wide Web Worm, and InfoSeek. We'll examine these and make the on-line journey to several of them in Chapter 14.

Rocky Mountain High

A program called Telnet lets us take the controls of computers worldwide. Each machine we access will make different options available. Some are full featured indeed, as in the case of the CARL System, the Colorado Alliance of Research Libraries' contribution to data proliferation. Take a glance at the menu in Figure 1.8 and you'll realize how abundant the information is on this system. I got there simply by entering a Telnet command: telnet pac.carl.org.

It's not a bad list—there are library catalogs, including government publications, as well as a range of databases and an on-line encyclopedia, among other entries. The ERIC database of education resources is a frequently tapped source. Some of CARL's services require an account, but many are available for public access.

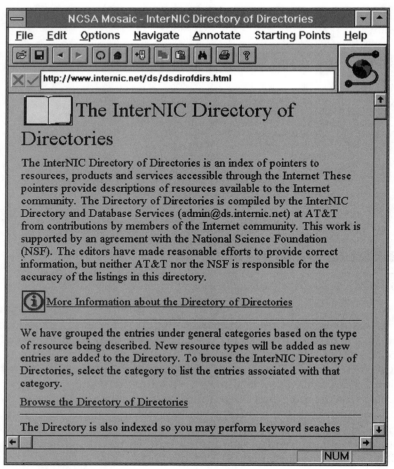

Figure 1.7 Comprehensive sites like the InterNIC's can help you find information when you need it.

USENET for the Facts

USENET is a worldwide collection of electronic conversations, spread over some 11 thousand different topics. You can sign up for as many groups as you please, reading and posting replies to articles as you go. Pretty soon the experience becomes addictive, as you check in through your newsreader software each day to see who has posted what. For keeping up with developments in a particular field or just exchanging ideas with people who have related interests, USENET is hard to beat. It's also a terrific resource for facts.

USENET newsgroups follow a long-established convention of collecting the basic questions asked by newcomers into documents called Frequently Asked Questions lists. Such a document, called a FAQ for short, eventually becomes a compilation of basic information about the topic in question. In Figure 1.9, you see the beginning of one such

```
CARL offers access to the following groups of databases:


    1. Library Catalogs
            (including Government Publications)

    2. Current Article Indexes and Access
            (including UnCover and ERIC)

    3. Information Databases
            (including Encyclopedia)

    4. Other Library Systems

    5. Library and System News



Enter the NUMBER of your choice, and press the <RETURN> key >>
```

Figure 1.8   The Colorado Association of Research Libraries offers plentiful information sources.

FAQ, written for a newsgroup called misc.invest.funds. The newsgroup exists for people who are interested in investing through mutual funds. I am viewing it through a newsreader program called WinVN, distributed as freeware on the Net.

Notice that this document has grown beyond a simple how-to primer for using the newsgroup itself. If you ever wondered how a signature guarantee worked or why you needed it when changing your account information, the data can be found further down in this document. You can also check out such terms as closed-end fund, net asset value, capital gain distributions, and more. After a while, it becomes clear that you don't necessarily have to follow a particular newsgroup to get something out of it. By browsing through FAQs on different topics, you can get a quick refresher course on the major issues. FAQs of all descriptions are regularly posted in the USENET newsgroup news.answers.

E-Mail in an Emergency

When an earthquake wrought devastation in Kobe, Japan on January 17, 1995, the Internet came to the rescue for an Australian living in that city. Graeme Robinson is a teacher of English who moved to Osaka, some 30 kilometers east of Kobe, in 1993. Shortly after the earthquake hit at 5:45 A.M. local time, a pyjama-clad Robinson found himself out on the street with a host of other citizens, trying to find out just what had happened.

Although the buildings in his neighborhood were largely unscathed, Robinson began to worry about the news reports that would soon be reaching his parents and friends in Australia. Local telephone lines quickly became jammed, making it impossible to connect, but the local line to his Internet service provider was still functioning, and Robinson sat down with his laptop computer to send messages to friends in Sydney, asking them to relay news of his well-being to his brother and other family members.

"In those first several days, the e-mails flew thick and fast between myself and the two friends' computers who are connected to a dial-up server in Sydney," Robinson said. "Gradually more of my circle of friends visited one or other of these friends and sent off

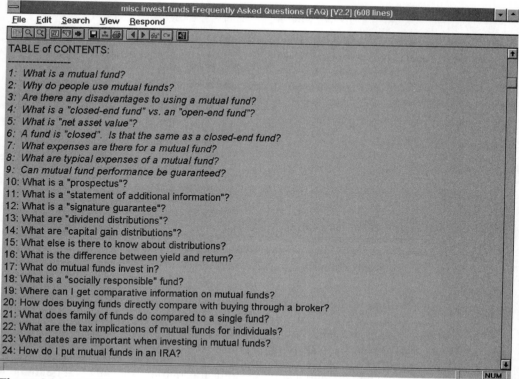

Figure 1.9 USENET newsgroups carry background information about numerous topics in their Frequently Asked Questions documents.

messages of support." Soon, the word was out that Robinson was safe. "We were now receiving e-mail not just from the two friends in Sydney I usually have contact with but also from other friends and family via computers in Melbourne and elsewhere." In a pinch, as Robinson learned, the Internet can be a true lifeline.

To New Zealand by Way of USENET

From Japan let's turn south. Intrigued since childhood with New Zealand, I used to try to keep up with Kiwi news by means of a shortwave receiver and Radio New Zealand, which was almost impossible to catch except at late hours. Now I keep up by USENET, where a newsgroup called soc.culture.new-zealand carries on a lively discussion of topics related to the North and South Islands. A major bonus of this newsgroup is the presence of one Brian M. Harmer of Victoria University of Wellington. The indefatigable Harmer updates the list frequently with a digest of local news events drawn from his morning paper.

Figure 1.10 shows the New Zealand news accessed over the World Wide Web through Netscape. Many Internet resources are beginning to show this kind of cross-referencing, making themselves available through a variety of means. Here, I can click on a date to call up the news from that day.

On-Line to Ancient Greece

Electronic books offer certain advantages over their hard-copy brethren. While you can't hold them in your lap for idle browsing, they're nonetheless excellent for text searching. Do you want to find every reference to fate in Sophocles' Oedipus Trilogy? With an ASCII text file of the material, it's a simple matter to load Sophocles' work into a text editor and use its find function to track down the word. No wonder CD-ROMs full of text material are becoming common. An electronic version of *Roget's Thesaurus* allows you to locate the word you need almost instantly. An electronic encyclopedia makes it possible to search for cross-linkages between referenced citations. Commonplace reference books suddenly spring into three-dimensional life.

Project Gutenberg, run by Michael Hart at Illinois Benedictine College in Lisle, Illinois, is an attempt to make ASCII texts of classic works available to as wide an audience as possible. Using FTP, I frequently visit the archive site at ftp://mrcnext.cso.uiuc.edu, heeding the system's request not to tap the service between 10 A.M. and 5 P.M. local time. There, I can find and download documents from *Paradise Lost* to *Aesop's Fables*, from *Alice in Wonderland* to *The Federalist Papers*, along with recent references like the *CIA World Factbook* and *The Hackers' Dictionary*. We'll examine Project Gutenberg, along with several other text projects, in Chapter 10.

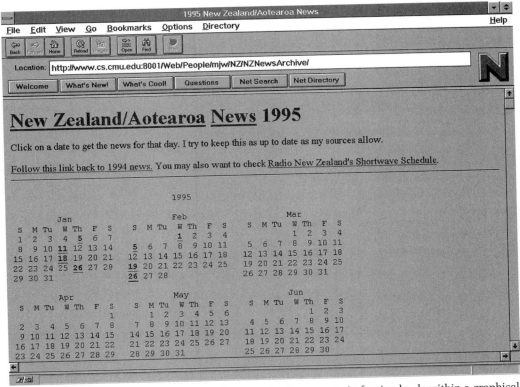

Figure 1.10   A World Wide Web browser lets you check on events in foreign lands within a graphical environment.

A Nice Day for Networking

The University of Illinois at Urbana-Champaign can help if you're looking for a weather forecast. The Daily Planet is menu-driven, providing current weather information and forecasts in a strictly noncommercial setting. Figure 1.11 illustrates the range of information available here, from current maps and satellite images to global climate data. You can access the World Wide Web site at this address: http://www.atmos.uiuc.edu/.

The Overstuffed Mailbox

USENET isn't the only way to keep up with network news. The Internet is also densely populated with mailing lists, whose contributions are sent into the electronic mailboxes of subscribers daily. Every day, when I sign on, I have messages about subjects I've culled from a list of thousands. There are astronomy postings, physics musings and discussions, a genial argument about Anglo-Saxon poetry, and a wild and woolly debate about the future of the Internet and the National Research and Education Network. And, every now and then, I receive messages about the formation of new lists, to which I can subscribe or not, as the inclination moves me.

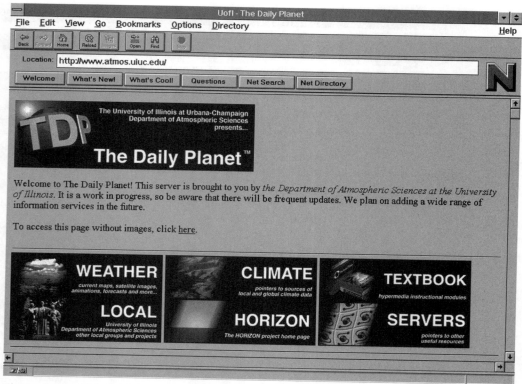

Figure 1.11   A World Wide Web site with plentiful weather information.

One of my interests being film and its history, I take particular pleasure in a mailing list on film, television, and popular culture. It's a lively list, populated with people discussing reviews of films, books and documentaries, with news of courses and conferences on the subject. Many mailing lists are run by automated programs called listservs. To subscribe, I sent a message to this address:

```
mailto:listserv@uicvm.bitnet
```

My message contained the message **subscribe h-film paul gilster.** The listserv added me as a new subscriber.

By now, you should be getting the idea. The problem with the Internet is its vastness; a description could start almost anywhere. Every time you sign on, there are new services available and new databases to explore. Mailing lists seem to pop up overnight, and with the current trend toward commercial use of the network, services like ClariNet and Msen Reuters News Service are turning your electronic mailbox into a digital newspaper, with stories chosen according to profiles you select. On-line journals are changing the boundaries of the publishing industry, making retrieval of past issues as simple as querying the proper server computer. Newsletters on a wide variety of subjects have begun to appear; their numbers can only increase. Believe it or not, there's even an Internet radio program, available through the network itself. And video isn't far behind.

The Internet Catch

There's also a catch. Many of the best resources for accessing and using the Internet are found on-line. The development of the new InterNIC as a central repository for Internet materials ensures there will always be a place to turn when problems arise. Across the Internet, there are lists of access providers, suggestions on how to use everything from e-mail to remote databases, tutorials, lists of frequently asked questions, newsgroups for beginners. If you spend some time reading through just a fraction of this material, you will quickly become proficient at using the network.

The Internet catch: How do you learn what you need to know about the Internet? You read the Internet materials that can help you. How do you obtain the Internet materials that can help you? You have to be on the Internet.

That's why I wrote this book. I fumbled around making every mistake possible as I first tried to gain access to, then learn how to use, the Internet. This is the book I wish I had had available to me when I began my first voyages. If it can help you as you set sail, I will be gratified indeed.

How Addresses Are Specified in This Book

Unlike previous editions of *The Internet Navigator,* this new edition follows the Uniform Resource Locator (URL) format for specifying how to locate information. URLs were developed as part of the specification for the World Wide Web; they provide a way to point to a resource, no matter where it is located on the Internet or how it is accessed, in an efficient manner.

To understand how to read a URL, first look at the following example:

```
ftp://ftp.ncsa.uiuc.edu/Web/Mosaic/Windows/mos20a9.exe
```

This is the specification for a particular file. Begin at the left and read straight across.

- The first thing you see is the access method, in this case, FTP. This is followed by a colon and two slashes.
- Next you see the address of the site: ftp.ncsa.uiuc.edu.
- The site is followed by the directory tree that leads you to the file in question. You see that you must change to the /Web/Mosaic/Windows directory.
- Finally, you find the file you're after: mos20a9.exe.

I have chosen to use the URL method because it is so much more economical than previous listings. In earlier editions, I would have listed the same file this way:

Address: ftp.ncsa.uiuc.edu
Directory: /Web/Mosaic/Windows
File: mos20a9.exe

As you can see, this method takes up a good deal of extra space, whereas the URL can list the same file in one line.

URLs differ depending upon the kind of resource being accessed, but they can be used to specify any kind of file. As you read through this book, I will, on a case by case basis, explain how to interpret URLs of a particular kind, to make sure you get the hang of it. But here is a quick rundown, showing you a sample URL for each major Internet protocol. If you are unsure of what these protocols mean at present, don't worry; my job in each chapter will be to explain the Internet tools and how to use them. I will, however, list some URLs in the early chapters for reference; later, when you know how to access them, you will want to come back and explore some of the sites listed.

TELNET
telnet://locis.loc.gov/
This means that you open up a Telnet connection to the address locis.loc.gov.

GOPHER
gopher://gopher.interpath.net/
The resource is Gopher; the address is gopher.interpath.net.

WORLD WIDE WEB
http://www.einet.net/galaxy.html
Using a World Wide Web browser, access the site www.einet.net; the document you want to retrieve is galaxy.html.

ELECTRONIC MAIL
mailto:info@cix.org
Send mail to the address info@cix.org.

USENET NEWSGROUPS
news:alt.internet.services

More on all these URLs and how to use them as we proceed. Once you've become accustomed to URLs, I think you'll wind up using them in your own Internet work. And as you'll see, they play a major role in the hypertext system behind the World Wide Web.

Chapter 1 Notes

1. "On First Looking into Chapman's Homer." From *The New Oxford Book of English Verse*, chosen and edited by Helen Gardner. New York: Oxford University Press, 1972.
2. Tracking Internet growth is a full-time task in itself. You will find much help in this endeavor at the InterNIC—the Internet Network Information Center, discussed in Chapter 2. Another helpful source is *Matrix News*, a regular electronic magazine that tracks network growth statistics. Information on how to gain access to this journal is provided in Chapter 2.

2

The Internet Defined

The Internet is a vast, sprawling network that reaches into computer sites worldwide. By its very nature, this interlinked web of networks defies attempts at quantification. Some sources cite Internet penetration into over 100 countries, with 50 thousand separate networks containing more than 5 million host computers and more than 30 million users.[1] A recent survey attempted to pin down network growth by querying domains all over the Internet. Its results: roughly 22 million active Internet users, including providers of services and those who use tools like Mosaic, Telnet, and FTP to access them.[2] All of which points to the elastic nature of these computations. It's easy to become confused when estimates about the Internet's growth are proliferating almost as fast as new host computers on the network itself.

But if we don't know for sure how many people are using the Internet, we can at least point with reasonable accuracy to its history. By 1985, approximately 100 networks formed the Internet. By 1989, that number had risen to 500. The Network Information Center of the Defense Data Network found 2,218 networks connected as of January 1990. By June 1991, the National Science Foundation Network Information Center (NSFNET) pegged it at close to 4 thousand, and, as we've seen, connections now top ten times that amount. If we extrapolate based on current numbers, the Internet would be reaching 40 million people by year's end, 100 million by 1998. Its current growth rate is 100 percent yearly. Figure 2.1 shows in graphical form the surge in Internet growth since 1990, a set of numbers that has already been superceded since this book went to press.

Couple that information with an estimated 120–150 million personal computers in use worldwide and you've created a situation with dramatic possibilities. Few of the desktop computers in the average home, for example, are networked together. But many home and business computer users would like to access the Internet's rich resources. The solution: a modem and a dial-up account.

Until a few years ago, it was difficult to access the Internet on a dial-up basis, but the increase in Internet service providers has improved that situation. The appendix of this book bears witness to the surge in the connectivity business, with providers coming on-line throughout the world, and mushrooming particularly in the United States, Canada,

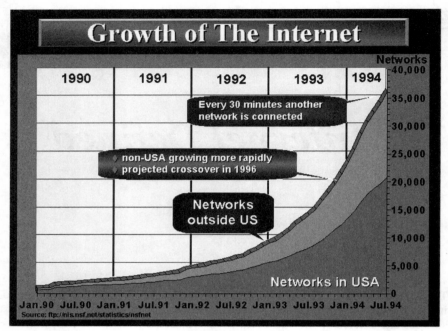

Figure 2.1   A graph of Internet growth courtesy of the Internet Society.

and Europe. Most of these are full-service companies whose only job description is to connect people to the Internet. But commercial on-line services like CompuServe and America Online have also taken the Internet plunge. In April 1995, CompuServe opened up Point-to-Point Protocol access to all its nodes, meaning that you could call a Compu-Serve access number and achieve a direct Internet connection. Previously, CompuServe had made basic Internet services like File Transfer Protocol (for downloading files) and USENET newsgroups (worldwide discussions on almost any topic) available through a gateway system to its users.

America Online has joined the fray with conspicuous energy. Already offering electronic mail and USENET access, the service moved quickly toward providing World Wide Web capability, even as Prodigy had done by introducing its own Web browser in 1995. The World Wide Web, which allows you to click on hypermedia links to see data, no matter where it is located around the globe, is obviously a major driver for many of the Internet's new users. In fact, World Wide Web use is, if anything, growing faster than the Internet itself. Some 30 thousand Web sites are now accessible, while the growth of new pages is said to have reached 20 percent per month. No matter who you talk to— commercial on-line services or Unix-based Internet access providers—the growth in the individual user market has been intense, and shows no signs of abating.

Equally impressive is the change in access methods. When this book's first edition appeared, it was designed for people who used so-called shell accounts to access the Internet. Working from a basic command prompt, users needed to enter commands to run programs on their service providers' machines; the method is fast and it works, but you can't use visually appealing tools like Mosaic and Netscape with such a connection.

As interest in connecting Internet resources through a graphical interface with pull-down menus and mice soared, more and more providers began to drop their prices for the kind of connections that would let you use such programs. SLIP (Serial Line Internet Protocol) and PPP (Point-to-Point Protocol) prices plummeted, and more and more users learned that a wide range of graphical tools existed by which they could use the network. Today, both methods of access exist side by side, but the trend toward graphics seems unstoppable.

A Brief History of the Internet

The Internet's beginnings gave no hint that it would evolve into a publicly accessible network. Like many other great ideas, the "network of networks" grew out of a project that began with far different intent: a network called ARPANET, designed and developed in 1969 by Bolt, Beranek, and Newman under contract to the Advanced Research Projects Agency of the U.S. Department of Defense (ARPA).

The ARPANET was a network connecting university, military, and defense contractors; it was established to aid researchers in the process of sharing information, and not coincidentally to study computer-based command and control for the U.S. military. From humble beginnings—the ARPANET's founders originally contemplated letting only researchers log on and run programs on remote computers—the network grew. They soon added file transfer capabilities, electronic mail, and mailing lists to keep people interested in common subjects in communication.

But even as the ARPANET grew, other networks were under development, and it became clear that new methods of communicating would be necessary. As early as 1973, in an era of mainframe computing a decade before the desktop PC revolution took hold, ARPA, under its new acronym DARPA (Defense Advanced Project Agency)[3] began a program called the Internetting Project. The goal was to examine packet switching by radio and satellite in two networks linked to ARPANET. Central to this concept of internetting is the need to overcome the different methods each network uses to move its information. When properly implemented, so-called *gateways* can be used to connect networks, passing traffic seamlessly from one to the other.[4]

Finding the Right Protocol

Making internetwork links work requires the right protocol. In computer parlance, a *protocol* is simply a set of conventions that determines how data will be exchanged between different programs. Protocols specify how a network is to move messages and handle errors; using them allows the creation of standards separate from a particular hardware system. DECnet, for example, is a protocol used by networks running Digital Equipment Corporation computers; Novell, a familiar name in office networking, is another example of a protocol standard that allows computers to work together. Everything from the speed of the communicated data to the addressing schemes used to move individual message traffic is factored in the protocols used by a given network.

The Internet uses a protocol called TCP/IP, which stands for Transmission Control Protocol/Internet Protocol. IP is responsible for network addressing, while TCP ensures that messages are delivered to the correct location. These powerful protocols were developed in 1974 by Robert Kahn, a major figure in ARPANET development, and now president of the Corporation for National Research Initiatives (CNRI), and computer scientist Vinton G. Cerf, former president of the Internet Society and senior vice-president of data network architecture at MCI. Their pioneering work created the mechanisms by which the Internet could appear. In fact, if we are looking for a quick definition of the Internet, we can simply say that it is a network of networks that run the TCP/IP protocol suite.

If you will fall into the habit of thinking of the Internet as a metanetwork—a network made up of interconnecting networks—you will grasp the dispersed, decentralized nature of this enterprise. Around the world, connecting through special computers called *routers* and *hubs*, computers from different manufacturers running a whole range of operating systems can communicate with each other. Digital Equipment Corporation minicomputers can talk to Sun Microsystems workstations. Standalone PCs and Macintoshes can talk to Intel machines on office networks; they, in turn, can reach large-scale regional networks, which connect their high-speed circuits over a grid called a *backbone.*

You should realize that TCP/IP is not the only protocol for connecting a variety of different networks. The Internet is actually a multiprotocol network, integrating other standards into its operations. Among these is Open Systems Interconnection, or OSI. Developed by the International Organization for Standardization (ISO), OSI was once popular in Europe, although its fortunes have sharply declined. Systems using other protocols however, connect through gateways to the Internet; BITNET, for example, is a network that communicates using its own standards, but which is at least partially accessible to the Internet through such linkages. And the Unix-to-Unix Copy Program (UUCP) network connects thousands of computers by dial-up telephone lines; its electronic mail destinations are likewise available to the Internet user. Nonetheless, the momentum behind TCP/IP is such that most BITNET traffic now moves over the Internet itself, even as the USENET newsgroups distributed over UUCP links are widely propagated by TCP/IP. For all intents and purposes, you as a user will find tapping such external networks is transparent.

The Internet vs. Commercial Online Services

Commercial on-line services like GEnie and DELPHI take an entirely different approach to distributing information. If you have been a user of one or more of these systems and now want to dial in to the Internet, you must master the differences between the two models. CompuServe, for example, manages its huge user base through a centralized set of computers. When you call in to local telephone numbers around the world to gain access to the system, you are connecting ultimately to a centralized set of resources. More telling is the fact that the commercial operation is managed from the top as a business. There is a company behind CompuServe, just as there is behind America Online.

Not so with the Internet, which has grown up free of both the advantages and problems caused by management from the top. This is why, when you connect to the Internet, you must choose from among a wide range of service options (we examine these in the next chapter). No central sign-up facility exists for the Internet; rather, you make contact with a service provider who allows you to gain access to the network through local computers. The consequences of this decentralization on network resources are likewise strong. What you find on the Internet depends on the decisions of thousands of system administrators around the world. No single company has made an overall decision about network design, which makes mastering the search tools we will examine later a critical part of your explorations.

What Is Packet Switching?

Consider the great problem of networking diverse computer systems. We would like to move a stream of data from one computer across a communications link to others. How does the data get there, and how can we ensure that when it does so, it arrives in precisely the condition it was when it left? Can we be sure that our addressing scheme works, and that, in the event of a network failure, our data will be rerouted so that it reaches its destination? These are problems that network protocols must address. The Internet uses a scheme called *packet switching* to solve them.

Packet switching takes data and assembles it into parts, giving each segment a header with the necessary routing information. Computers on the network examine these headers and move the data packet along to the next site. Each time, the packet gets closer to its destination. A major bonus of packet switching is that the computers routing this data can select alternate routes when a given link fails (remember, this system was developed by researchers who were considering how to ensure reliable communications when parts of the network were destroyed in a nuclear conflagration). Another bonus: The computers at either end of a packet network connection can operate at different speeds; the network itself acts as a buffer to adjust for the difference.

You may also have run across the term *circuit switching*. Think of one-to-one contact here. If you set up a data session between two computers using ordinary telephone lines, placing a call whenever you need to move data, you would be using circuit switching. The method is useful when you need to connect computers to transfer large amounts of information. But because it requires you to set up a circuit dedicated to an exclusive use each time you use it, circuit switching is unable to handle the massive amounts of diverse data carried by the Internet. Complex applications requiring contact with multiple computers must rely on the packet switching model.

The Internet Emerges

In 1983, the U.S. Defense Communications Agency mandated TCP/IP for all ARPANET hosts. In doing so, it established a standard by which the Internet could grow. From this point forward, it would be possible to add more gateways, connecting more networks, while the original core networks remained intact. Most people date the true arrival of the Internet at 1983, the year when the original ARPANET was split into MILNET—to be used for unclassified military communications—and the ARPANET—for continuing research into networking. But, as early as 1980,[5] CSNET, a network linking computer science departments in several states, became the first autonomous network DARPA allowed to connect to the ARPANET.

CSNET eventually merged with BITNET in 1989. The ARPANET itself was decommissioned in June 1990, its functions absorbed into the broader structure of the Internet. But the two networks had established a workable principle: let networks communicate by a set of protocols, with new networks being added to an ever-growing metanetwork communicating through gateways. That principle would be advanced yet again by the National Science Foundation, which assumed much of ARPANET's functionality within a new network of its own.

Connecting Supercomputers

That network, the National Science Foundation Network, or NSFNET, grew out of a particular networking need. NSF wanted to connect its six supercomputer centers around the country, and began a network program to link the sites to the scientific community. TCP/IP would be the protocol of choice. By 1986, NSF had expanded these efforts into a backbone network. It also helped fund regional networks whose purpose was to connect universities to NSFNET to give researchers access to supercomputers.

The original NSFNET backbone connected six sites by 56-kilobits-per-second (Kbps) data circuits, a topology that quickly became overloaded as traffic increased. This backbone carried some 115 million packets per month in the first half of 1988.[6] In 1987, NSF awarded a contract to Merit, Inc. (the Michigan Education and Research Infrastructure Triad), working in partnership with MCI Corporation and IBM, to manage and operate the NSFNET backbone, as well as to continue its development. The growing backbone now connected some 13 sites, six of them supercomputer centers, the others regional networks.

By July 1988, the network comprised 13 nodes using T1 connections at 1.5 megabits per second (Mbps). Traffic flow quickly expanded to fill the communications channels, averaging a 20-percent-per-month growth rate between July 1988 and July 1989. A fourteenth node was added, and connections were put in place for FIX East and FIX West (FIX stands for Federal Interagency eXchange), which are governmental interagency connection points. FIX West is located at the NASA Ames Research Center near San Francisco; FIX East is near the University of Maryland.

In September 1990, the National Science Foundation announced the formation of Advanced Network & Services, Inc. ANS was the creation of Merit, IBM, and MCI. The three proposed its formation to provide structure to the NSFNET operation. Operating under contract to Merit, ANS would operate the T1 backbone for NSFNET and build a new T3 (45 Mbps) backbone to supersede it.

The T3 backbone became an operational reality on December 2, 1992, creating a 700-fold increase in power since the 56-Kbps days. T3 speeds carry data at the equivalent of 1,400 pages of single-spaced, typed text per second.[7] These remarkable numbers were no less noteworthy than the traffic figures behind them. NSFNET traffic had grown from 195 million packets in August 1988, to almost 24 billion by November 1992. In that month the network reached the billion-packet-a-day mark, and network traffic growth continued at a rate of 11 percent per month.

With the T3 backbone functioning, a new arrangement was developed that would allow ANS to operate two separate networks over the same equipment. NSFNET itself would continue to support institutions reliant on government subsidies for their connections. But ANS would also create a subsidiary called ANS CO+RE which would support commercial users of the network. Thus the development of a commercially viable Internet. Out of the regional networks whose growth had been stimulated by the NSF, commercial operations sprang into being. From NYSERNet came Performance Systems International, while CERFnet grew out of work performed by General Atomics, the firm that runs the San Diego Supercomputer Center. JVNCnet offered commercial services through GES, Inc., while UUNET Technologies created Alternet. Today, Internet service providers are springing up in cities around the world, offering access for everything from large corporate accounts to the individual dial-up users for whom this book is written.

NSFNET is no longer the backbone for Internet traffic in the United States, having been decommissioned in April, 1995. Today, the role of the backbone has been taken by internetMCI, operating with SprintLink and ANSNET (along with UUNET and PSINet) to offer wide-area connectivity. As we'll see, this change has had a profound impact on how companies conduct business on the Net. ANS, meanwhile, was acquired in late 1994 by America Online, an indication of how the lines of demarcation between Internet services and other forms of commercial on-line service are beginning to blur.

Add to this complicated picture the varying conditions of the so-called mid-level networks. Some are operated by their states, as is PREPnet in Pennsylvania. Others are run by university consortia operating large regional networks, such as MIDnet. Some of the regionals are run commercially, as is CERFnet, while others are managed by university computer scientists. NSF has encouraged regional networks to connect to new sites even as it maintained the general expectation that the regionals would become financially independent, weaning themselves of NSF support. At the same time, the regionals have also been encouraged to offer network services as a way of achieving that independence.

It could be said that it was the emergence of NSFNET that marked the emergence of the Internet as a mature networking medium; at the very least, NSFNET's work demonstrated the demand for this new form of communications in our colleges and universities. Commercial electronic mail linkages to the network soon followed. In 1990, an experimental mail relay was established at the Corporation for National Research Initiatives which linked MCI Mail, the worldwide e-mail messaging service, with the Internet. Today, almost all commercial e-mail carriers in the United States are connected, as are the major commercial on-line services. The Internet's momentum has reached a point where any messaging system, to be competitive, must offer a gateway to it, creating a common access channel through which people worldwide can communicate.

Figure 2.2 gives you an idea of how remarkably the surge in commercial Net sites has changed the demographics of the Internet. Although these figures, the latest available in graphical form, are from 1993, they illustrate the clear preponderance of commercial sites in a network which had, until not long ago, been firmly in the hands of government and educational interests.

Throughout this book, I intend to point you to resources that may be of interest, all of which are located on the Internet itself. Let's get started with the first such pointer. These three excellent articles fill in detailed information about the development of the Internet. The first two are the work of Vinton Cerf, who was, as was once said of Averell Harriman, "present at the creation." The third is by author Bruce Sterling, who first

What You Need: Supplemental Information about the Internet's History

The Documents: "A Brief History of the Internet and Related Networks," by Vinton Cerf; "How the Internet Came to Be," by Vinton Cerf as told to Bernard Aboba; and "A Short History of the Internet," by Bruce Sterling.

Where to Get Them: At a Gopher maintained by the Internet Society. The address is:

gopher://gopher.isoc.org:70/11/internet/history/

Chapter 12 explains Gopher usage. Once you've mastered the system, you can use this address to get the needed files. They'll form the beginnings of an on-line file library.

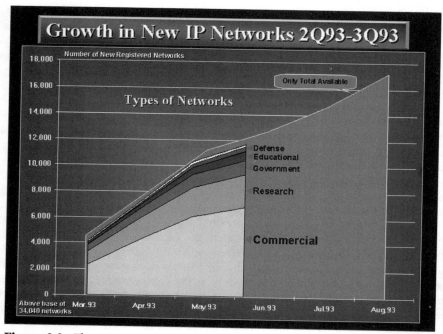

Figure 2.2 The rise in commercial activity on the Internet, which has continued unabated since this graph was composed. Source: The Internet Society.

published it in *The Magazine of Fantasy and Science Fiction.* And what better venue could there be? As you'll see, the Internet is a classic case of science fiction becoming science fact.

The Structure of the Internet

A strict definition is useful for describing what the Internet has become. In his book *The Matrix: Computer Networks and Conferencing Systems Worldwide* (Digital Press, 1990), John S. Quarterman describes the Internet as "an internetwork of many networks all running the TCP/IP protocol suite . . . , connected through gateways, and sharing common name and address spaces."[8]

There you have an operating definition: The Internet is held together by TCP/IP. What then of networks operating under different protocols which, however, can be contacted through the Internet? BITNET, an academic network many of whose resources are reachable through an Internet connection, isn't a part of the Internet because it uses its own protocols. So does UUCP, the Unix-to-Unix Copy Program where USENET began. USENET newsgroups are commonly read by people on the Internet, but because it propagates by different protocols, it's not, strictly speaking, *on the Internet.*

What should we make of such distinctions? They have value in helping us understand what we're dealing with, to be sure, but for the purpose of hands-on network use, let's broaden our scope to what Quarterman, following the lead of science fiction novelist William Gibson, calls the Matrix. Quarterman again: "The Matrix is a worldwide metanetwork of connected computer networks and conferencing systems that provides unique services that are like, yet unlike, those of telephones, post offices, and libraries."[9]

Most of us will continue to refer to this metanetwork as the Internet, though in the back of our minds we have Quarterman's distinctions in mind. What we mean is access to the Internet and the various networks it comprises, including its gateways into networks that run under widely different protocols. For me, for example, BITNET is invaluable; I probably spend more time reading BITNET mailing lists than any other on-line activity. I don't need a separate network connection to mine its riches, but I concede that the technology behind it is considerably different from that which drives the Internet proper. Even here, however, the distinctions blur. Much BITNET traffic is now being carried over TCP/IP linkages, considerably enhancing its speed. And Internet users can also access close to three-quarters of the BITNET mailing lists by reading USENET newsgroups, which mirror them.

When we get down to examining individual network resources, we'll see that a wide range of skills must be employed to use them. I can search for information in a variety of ways on the Internet, including through the use of a developing generation of resource discovery tools. But searching an Internet database through techniques such as Wide Area Information Servers (WAIS) is vastly different from using the BITNET protocols to rummage through files on one of its server computers. Don't be surprised by this; it's the necessary result of the Internet's (and related networks') diversity. We are not yet at a sufficiently advanced state of technology where rival approaches to presenting information have been subsumed under a single user interface. Nor are we likely to be there soon, although World Wide Web URLs are a step in that direction.

An Internet Cartography

Early explorers of the New World constructed their first maps by following alien coastlines, tracing out river mouths, bays, and harbors as their ships proceeded. The only way to assemble a complete picture, even of a small section of coast, was to sail its entire length. Later, charts could be compared with the work of other navigators, until, out of shared experience, more accurate maps emerged. Even now, maps are under constant refinement, as satellite observations allow cartographers to measure distance and size to an extent hitherto considered impossible. Other kinds of maps also preoccupy us, for humans are mapping creatures. Thus we map the structure of galaxies, of chemical compounds, and, audaciously, the hidden coding of the human genome, perhaps the greatest challenge of all.

Each mapping project proceeds with its own set of assumptions and difficulties. Surprisingly, mapping the Internet takes us into the realm of metaphysics. We can trace network connections throughout the world, even as we realize that the network's constantly changing parameters ensure that no printed map, not even an electronic one posted online, can be completely up to date. But given a chart of major network connections, applying it to on-line navigation is another challenge. Maps show distance and proximity to other land masses. Yet how do we measure distance in a network where it's as simple for me to send and receive mail from Taiwan as it is to read a campus directory at the University of North Carolina at Chapel Hill? How much does distance actually count in the electronic world?

As opposed to conventional geographic maps, which reveal the shapes and contours of land masses and oceans, an Internet map is like a diagram of a brain. What we see as we draw the various local and regional networks together with the high-speed backbone networks that link them is a set of clusters, places where connectivity is widespread. The map becomes hard to read; even computer scientists call this phenomenon a *cloud* of connections, because it becomes impossible to trace each pathway in the interweaving cyberspace. Move away from the densest intersections and network pathways begin to emerge from the cloud; as we move to less-networked areas—South America, say, or West Africa—each linkage becomes distinct.

A network map without connection overlays is easiest to decipher. Figure 2.3 shows a map prepared by Lawrence H. Landweber, founder of CSNET and president of the Internet Society; the map is used with their permission. This world view can't be considered an Internet map alone; it also displays the status of other networks, including BITNET, UUCP, and FidoNet, each of which runs under a different set of networking protocols than the Internet's TCP/IP. But because network linkages between the Internet and these other networks are so well established that Internet users routinely move between them, it seems reasonable to include them.

The map has changed significantly since the first edition of this book in 1993. In those days, huge swatches of the earth's surface showed BITNET connectivity but lacked access to the Internet, while an enormous area in central Asia, China, Africa, and

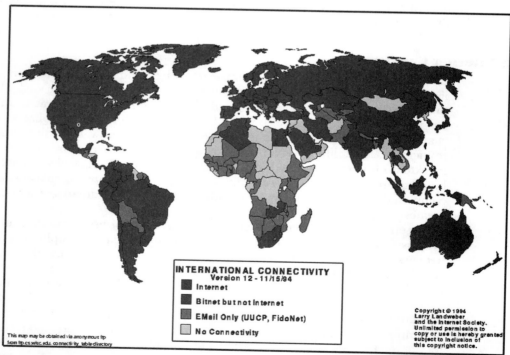

Figure 2.3 International network connections are shown in this map prepared by Lawrence H. Landweber and the Internet Society.

South America received e-mail only, through the UUCP protocols or bulletin board systems like FidoNet. The former Soviet Union was listed as a BITNET-only country. Today, with the exception of Africa, the bulk of the world's population lives in countries where the Internet has taken hold (although the map does not illustrate the extent of its penetration in each country). In South America, only Bolivia and Paraguay show e-mail only connectivity, while e-mail connections have moved in greater numbers into west and south Africa. Russia and the former Soviet republics are now on the Internet, as is China. The only areas of nonconnectivity are in Africa, in a broad stretch north from Zaire through Libya to the Mediterranean littoral and in Mauretania and scattered states on the west coast. Mongolia, Burma, and Laos are joined by Iraq, as well as North Korea, in having no connectivity through e-mail or any other form of networking.

At the end of this chapter, you'll find a list of domain names, also compiled by Landweber, along with information about the status of the named country in terms of network linkages. The information presented in each column shows connections, sites, and protocols available.

When *Matrix News*, a monthly newsletter covering the Internet and developments in other networks, set out to survey the state of the Internet, it uncovered some interesting geographical facts.[10] U.S. bases at the South Pole exchange electronic mail with the various networks through a satellite link to a NASA computer in Florida; otherwise, the most southerly network connection is Hobart, Tasmania. The northernmost network appearance seems to be a node on the NASA Science Network in Thule, Greenland; the second, a UUCP connection in Atqasuk, Alaska. Iceland's most northerly site is at Kopasker, with Internet and UUCP connections. The network connection farthest west in longitude is Hawaii; easternmost is Fiji, at the Department of Mathematics at the University of the South Pacific in Suva, which maintains UUCP links to New Zealand. Russia's easternmost network connection is at Magadan, running both FidoNet and UUCP; even Sakhalin Island appears on a network map with UUCP connections.

The constantly changing dimensions of the Internet and related networks make this kind of mapping an ongoing process. In March 1993, *Matrix News* estimated there were some 2,152,000 host computers between the Internet, BITNET, FidoNet, UUCP, and various corporate IP connections. This led to its estimate of 18,150,000 users worldwide in some 130 countries.

By late 1993, *Matrix News* was prepared to update these numbers to a whopping 29 million users in the worldwide matrix. Between the various networks, some 3.6 million hosts were found to be on-line. Interestingly, the newsletter also made several estimates on the number of users of commercial services. A conservative estimate showed just more than 1 million users between Prodigy, CompuServe, GEnie, AT&T Mail, and other such systems; a more liberal estimate ratcheted that number to over 5 million. The large discrepancies are the result of problems in gathering information; many administrators at such systems refuse to announce the total number of accounts. *Matrix News* found some 34.6 million electronic mail users throughout the connected network structure. The newsletter's carefully compiled study, produced in its December 1993 issue, deserves credence; its estimate for an Internet growth rate of 80 percent a year must be measured against other, perhaps more fanciful estimates, of 15 percent growth per month.

In late 1994, John Quarterman's company, Matrix Information and Directory Services, conducted a survey that queried most of the domains representing organizations on the Internet. The survey divides Internet use into three camps:

- A *core Internet,* consisting of those people and machines that actually provide interactive services, like Telnet and FTP. Quarterman estimated the size of this group at 7.8 million people and 2.5 million computers.
- A *consumer Internet,* consisting of those people that use the interactive services supplied by the core Internet. The estimate here is for 13.5 million users and 3.5 million computers. This counts, for example, anyone who can use Mosaic to browse the World Wide Web, or download a file via FTP.
- *The Matrix,* which refers to all users who can exchange electronic mail with other users. These are people who lack interactive access, but who can communicate and use basic Internet services by mail. This number is now pegged at 27.5 million, a decrease from Quarterman's earlier numbers, but one that seems to reflect a more rigorous methodology.

Many Internet writers have proceeded under the assumption that each host connects 10 users, but Quarterman thinks the figure errs on the high side, while many host computers turn out to be out of service at any particular time. In fact, in his recent survey, Quarterman found that only some 30 percent of host computers respond to queries at any given time, leading to the assumption that the Internet population may be consistently overestimated. We can't really know the answer to these questions, but a reality check is probably in order, given the intense media hype that has characterized the Internet in recent months. But wherever you start, the numbers do seem to be growing exponentially. Quarterman now believes that the Internet is doubling in size each year.

If you are interested in tracking such issues, a subscription to *Matrix News* is a good idea. You can reach the publication at:

MATRIX INFORMATION AND DIRECTORY SERVICES, INC.
1106 Clayton Lane, Suite 500W
Austin, TX 78723
Voice: 512-451-7602
Fax: 512-452-0127
mailto:mids@tic.com
http://www.tic.com
gopher://gopher.tic.com
ftp://ftp.tic.com

Matrix Information and Directory Services also publishes *Matrix Maps Quarterly,* displaying and comparing networks in terms of locations, hosts, servers, users, and a variety of other measures.

It's a vast and evolving structure, this Internet, an interlinked entity made of fiber-optic and copper cable and microwave links, reaching all the way from the depths of the world's fastest supercomputers to 1200 bps dial-up modems moving electronic mail traffic into some of the world's poorest countries. Clearly, a directory of all its constituent networks would be a massive volume which would quickly pass out of date. Users interested in tracking down network structure will, however, be interested in Tracy L. LaQuey's *The User's Directory of Computer Networks* (Digital Press, 1990) as well as John S. Quarterman's *The Matrix* (Digital Press, 1990); both are excellent starting points. I also recommend the Internet book with the unpronounceable name. It's *!%@:: A Directory of Electronic Mail Addressing and Networks,* by Donnalyn Frey and Rick Adams

(O'Reilly & Assoc., 1994). And anyone seriously attempting to monitor network growth will learn that an active on-line presence is critical.

The Big Three Internet Applications

As Douglas Comer points out in his *Internetworking with TCP/IP. Vol 1: Principles, Protocols, and Architecture,* what you as an end user see of the TCP/IP protocols is a set of application programs that enable you to use the network to good advantage.[11] You and I don't need to know the intricacies of how TCP/IP functions, though if you're curious, there's no better or more respected guide than Comer's work. But running the programs themselves is not difficult, as we'll see.

Users of dial-up computer services, like users of bulletin board systems (BBS) and commercial on-line services, have come to expect certain capabilities from their providers, which the Internet provides in its own way through TCP/IP. Here is how the Internet delivers these basic functions.

ELECTRONIC MAIL

Electronic mail is the most elementary service, and for many users, the most useful. Many people on the Internet have used nothing but electronic mail and still find the network indispensable. You can send messages to one or more people, deliver text files, retrieve information by automated computer programs like LISTSERV (through a gateway to BITNET), and more. While access to all three of the major Internet services is vastly preferable, it's possible to do quite a lot with electronic mail alone.

Not all that long ago, e-mail gateways were the only access to the Internet provided by the big commercial on-line services. In those days, working with an Internet connection through e-mail alone was a fascinating task. It turns out you can do quite a lot with nothing more than a mailbox, including running everything from WAIS and Gopher searches to pulling down World Wide Web pages. We examine how to do these tasks and more in Chapter 8. Those whose Internet access comes through bulletin board systems, or is otherwise restricted to mail only, will find that Chapter 8 provides a way to stay active on the Internet despite the built-in limitations of the mail gateway. To be sure, you'll want to upgrade as soon as you can to full Internet access through a service provider who offers the complete range of tools, but Chapter 8 can tide you over until then.

But let's not underestimate e-mail in its simplest form, as a carrier of digital messages between two people or a mailing list of those interested in the same subject. You'll soon find that you're using e-mail every day, corresponding with people near and far; after a month or two, you'll wonder how you got along without it. Ironically, in the early days of the ARPANET, electronic mail was considered an insignificant add-in to network capabilities. No one anticipated the high volume of traffic that began to flow as scientists exchanged ideas with geographically distant colleagues. Today electronic mail is taken for granted, from small companies with office networks to giant corporations linking remote offices worldwide. Its growth has been just as strong on the commercial networks, many of whose members maintain accounts solely for the e-mail connectivity they provide.

FILE TRANSFER

Moving files between computers is one of the handiest features of the networking revolution. If you can find something you can use—and if it's made publicly available, as are thousands of computer files on the Internet—you can transfer it to your computer. The process is called *file transfer protocol*, or FTP. You access documents made available to the public through a procedure called *anonymous FTP*. This procedure allows you to log on to remote computers and use the resources in directories the administrators have made available to the public. Anonymous FTP will be a major tool as we retrieve files and build an Internet library later in this book.

With FTP procedures, the Internet gets challenging indeed. Instead of consulting a single library source, as on CompuServe or America Online, for a catalog of files, you are faced with thousands of computer sites offering programs and text files. To track down the program you need easily, you should learn about the access tools we'll discuss later. With them, you can locate programs, then use FTP to download them to your own machine.

REMOTE LOGIN

Remote login, otherwise known as Telnet, provides the ability to connect to a remote computer and work with it on an interactive basis. Again, the Internet opens the doors to a worldwide computing environment, on many of whose connected machines are services, databases, and other resources that can be examined and manipulated. By using Telnet, you can log on to the library catalogs of distant universities, look for information about everything from the formation of distant galaxies to recipes for potato soup, and examine Supreme Court decisions or the lyrics of popular songs. All the while, your computer will act as a terminal of the remote computer, which will respond to your command. In many cases, menu-driven systems at the other end make interactive sessions intuitive, but some systems are considerably easier to work with than others.

Internet Terminology

Note that when the network called the Internet is referred to in print, it always has a capital I. But you may also see abundant references, if you prowl your bookseller's shelves for computer books or read the computer press, to general terms such as internets, internetting, and internetworking. Remember that TCP/IP can pass information among computers that aren't on *the* Internet. Your company, for example, might have local area networks in a number of sites. At some point, it would make sense for management to link those LANs together. One way of linking them is through TCP/IP. Your company would have established an *internet*, but you're not on *the Internet* unless you decide to be.

Public Packet Switching Networks

We have already discussed packet switching, and how it assembles messages into segments, each of which contains the necessary addressing information to ensure safe delivery. The ARPANET was the first major packet-switched network, running on an experimental basis for the use of DARPA contractors and not open to the general public. But as a dial-up modem user, you have probably encountered another form of packet switching, as used by networks like BT Tymnet or SprintNet. These public networks allow you to contact distant computers with a local telephone call; they then route your computer traffic to the appropriate destination.

The birth of these public packet networks came about because of ARPANET's work. Two companies formed in the early 1970s—Packet Communications Inc. (PCI), created by former BBN employees, and Telenet Communications Inc., which BBN itself formed—were the early players in this rapidly evolving field. And while PCI didn't last long, Telenet was to grow into a public network that would eventually be purchased by a subsidiary of GTE. By 1987, Telenet offered some 18 thousand local telephone numbers nationwide and access from 70 foreign countries. Now known as SprintNet, Telenet has continued to flourish, its growth paralleled by the development of other public packet networks. BT Tymnet is now owned by MCI and called Xstream, while CompuServe maintains its own network—CompuServe Packet Network—which can be used to connect to a number of computer services.

Let's consider what packet switching does for dial-up telecommunications users. If you're calling a local bulletin board system, or BBS, your call moves through standard, voice-grade telephone lines. This is not a problem when calling locally, but calling a BBS half a continent away costs you long-distance charges. One reason public packet networks make sense is that they allow you to call a local number that connects you to a computer known as a *node*, which routes your call through the packet network's system to its destination. Your on-line charges decrease and you have access to a wide range of services.

Another reason for using packet networks is the stability of the X.25 protocol, which retains its integrity even when line conditions are less than optimum; your chances of getting accurate data thereby increase. Most callers to commercial services such as CompuServe, GEnie, BIX, and DELPHI use packet networks to place their calls, and a number of Internet service providers are also available through the packet network, as we'll see in Chapter 3. Packet-switching networks bill the on-line services themselves for your connect time, so the bill you receive from the service includes network charges.

Although X.25 and TCP/IP are different protocols, the idea behind packet switching remains the same—route data to its destination by sorting it into clearly addressed packets which can move from machine to machine until delivered. If you do access the Internet via a public packet network, your traffic to and from your service provider will be handled by the public network's packet-switching protocols. But the traffic going between the Internet and your service provider's equipment will be managed by the Internet's TCP/IP protocols.

Put another way, the service provider's computer carries an IP (Internet Protocol) address—it is part of the functioning Internet. You can use that computer in a dial-up session to perform Internet functions, but your own computer, lacking an IP address of its own, is not itself on the Internet. As we'll see in Chapter 3, there are ways to provide a dial-up connection that include an IP address—they're called SLIP and PPP. The great shift in Internet access is occurring with these two methods, for the price of SLIP/PPP accounts has dropped enormously in the past two years. Intriguingly, CompuServe announced in early 1995 that it was bringing PPP access to the local numbers it makes available to users worldwide; America Online is likewise moving in the direction of a direct IP connection. This being the case, the old model of the X.25 network carrying your data to your commercial service is beginning to break down. We are moving into an era of direct Internet connections by modem, opening up client software like Mosaic and Netscape to a new generation of users.

How Data Moves—Transmission Media

It's easy to imagine a computer network in terms you may have encountered in a business office: computers connected by cables, moving information back and forth behind the scenes while users work at keyboards. In fact, however, the Internet's connectivity can't be visualized as a network of wires or even fiber-optic cabling alone. Digital data moves through special hardware devices called *routers* which connect networks and use sophisticated algorithms to choose the best route for network traffic.

How does the packetized data flow? Perhaps it moves through telephone lines, standard dial-up or leased lines, perhaps by satellite networks. And that's not all. Traffic can also flow through microwave radio transmission, fiber-optic cable connections, and even so-called *packet radio*. Let's look at each possibility.

DIAL-UP LINES

The telephone line running into your house is a dial-up line; the connection you make when calling a number lasts only until you hang up. A dial-up link between two networks could be established for data transfer and then closed back down. The lowering cost of long-distance service has made this a workable alternative for people running small office networks. And as we'll see in Chapter 3, it's possible to call into an Internet site and access Internet services—even to become an on-line IP site yourself—using dial-up connections alone.

LEASED LINES

A leased line works differently. It's established as a full-time connection, always available for traffic flow between sites; leased lines are frequently called *dedicated lines*. Leased lines for digital data transmission come in various grades ranging from a speed of 2.5 kilobits per second to 45 megabits per second. T1 service boasts a transmission rate of 1.544 megabits per second. A T3 link is faster still, moving data at 45 megabits per second, and OC3 technology takes that rate to 155 megabits per second.

MICROWAVE

Microwave equipment can link networks without wires, using a transmitter to send data to a receiving antenna at the destination. Between the two are repeaters, whose job is to receive the signal, amplify it, and pass it along to the next station. The spacing between repeaters can vary depending on terrain since microwave is a line-of-sight medium.

SATELLITE COMMUNICATIONS

From geosynchronous orbits 22,500 miles above the equator, communications satellites offer advantages in the realm of very long distance communication. Transponders aboard the satellites receive signals from ground stations and rebroadcast them back to Earth. A *very small aperture terminal*, or VSAT, is the receiving antenna.

DATA BY RADIO

RadioMail Corp. uses a wireless modem to connect to wireless networks like RAM Mobile Data or ARDIS, linking you to Internet mail while you're on the road. SkyTel Corp. pagers, meanwhile, can now receive electronic mail from the Internet as well as such services as AT&T Mail and MCI Mail. Notable Technologies offers a display pager with Internet address and e-mail forwarding service. Meanwhile, Microsoft and the parent of SkyTel, Mobil Telecommunication Technologies Corp., are cooperating to build a

$150 million system called Nationwide Wireless Network that will allow users to send and receive messages using pagers or the small computers called Personal Digital Assistants. Look for further developments in packet radio from Motorola, Ardis, RAM Mobile Data, and Metricom.

NEARnet: A Representative Network

Let's take a look at a representative network, a mid-level regional funded initially by NSFNET, to see how it operates. Founded in 1988 by Boston University, Harvard, and the Massachusetts Institute of Technology, the New England Academic and Research Network includes member organizations from New England's universities, technology industries, and both government and private agencies. The network is now part of BBN Planet, run by Bolt Beranek and Newman Inc. in Cambridge, Massachusetts, the private sector contractor that built the original ARPANET, and that until recently housed the NFSNET's Network Service Center, or NNSC. NEARnet offers its members leased-line and microwave connectivity, as well as supporting dial-up access using the SLIP (Serial Line Internet Protocols) we will discuss in the next chapter.

We can represent such a network on a map in one of two ways. Figure 2.4 depicts the more familiar structure, superimposing network lines upon recognizable geographical features. As you can see, NEARnet connects sites throughout the New England states. Figure 2.5 is a map showing the network topology of NEARnet. In many respects, this form of map is both more accurate and more revealing, for it depicts the routes information takes and highlights the major member organizations. Naturally, since the Internet is a network of networks, we should look for connectivity points with the outside world, depicted on this map as ellipses, the oval shapes containing a network name. We can see that NEARnet connects through MIT to ESnet, AlterNet, and NSFNET, for example, and through Bolt Beranek and Newman in Massachusetts to DSInet.

As the major provider of Internet services to New England, NEARnet has also explored commercial routing for its member organizations. Through an agreement with ANS CO+RE Systems and the Commercial Internet Exchange, NEARnet offers the ability to pursue commercial activities like sales and technical support. Traffic is carried over the ANS CO+RE backbone network service either directly to the destination or to the Commercial Internet Exchange for interchange with other commercial network service providers.

Note what's happening on the NEARnet map. The NEARnet member organizations, only a few of which are shown here, link to the major network nodes at BBN, MIT, Boston University, and Harvard through a variety of physical media. As the map shows, there is a 10 Mbps microwave link between MIT and Boston University; indeed, the major nodes all connect to each other by microwave. Also available are T1 (1.544 Mbps) leased lines, like those connecting Boston University with the Naval Undersea Warfare Center in Rhode Island, or the one that connects Boston University with the University of Hartford. T3 (45 Mbps) connections feed NEARnet traffic onto the NSFNET backbone out of MIT, while T1 lines shunt traffic to Alternet and ESnet; 56 Kb leased lines connect a host of businesses, like Aware, Inc. and Phoenix Technologies, Ltd., to MIT. Dial-up connections provide network links for smaller businesses, linking their local area networks via dial-up routers to NEARnet. At the same time, NEARnet provides SLIP connections, using 9600 bps modems to move traffic. These connections are shown on the map as a series of dots.

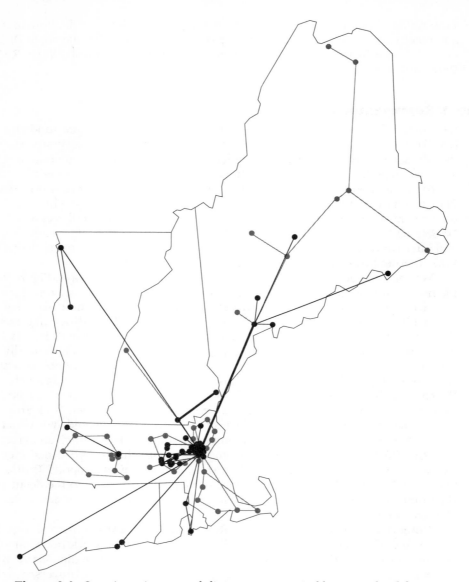

Figure 2.4 Superimposing network lines upon recognizable geographical features. Map courtesy of NEARnet.

Perhaps now you can understand why network connections are sometimes referred to as a cloud. Given this matrix of interconnecting networks and independently routed data packets, we can't resolve traffic with a fine degree of detail. But the beauty of the procedure is that we don't need to. The important thing for the user at, say, Wellesley College, is that he or she have access to the same Internet resources as users anywhere

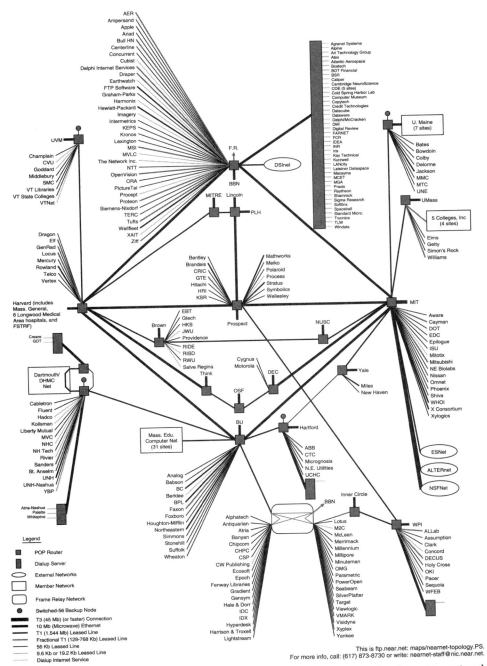

Figure 2.5 A map showing the network topology of NEARnet, an example of a major regional network.

else in the world; and indeed, Wellesley is as accessible as anywhere else on the Internet. Its faculty and students don't have to know a complicated network topology to make this work. Even if we tried to work out the precise path a given packet took on its route to a distant computer—out of MIT to NSFNET, perhaps, thence across the ocean to NORDU-net, and so on—we probably couldn't pin it down with any degree of reliability. The point is, it works, thanks to the magic of TCP/IP.

Managing the Internet

Does anyone actually manage the Internet, or does it just happen? Sketched out in its most elementary form, there is an underlying system of networks, called the *backbone*. In the United States, the largest of these is MCI's internetMCI. The Commercial Internet Exchange presides over a healthy and growing backbone of commercial providers. Mid-level networks are regional in nature, connecting one or more states to the high-speed backbone. On the local level, institutional networks are linked to the regional networks which, in turn, give them access to the traffic flow of the backbone. Overseas, we can include EBONE, the pan-European IP backbone network, as well as NORDUnet, DANTE, and EUnet, which are providing broad European connectivity.

Each of these networks is responsible for the traffic that flows within it and can route that traffic as necessary. If two computers located within the same university need to exchange information, for example, there is no need for that traffic to flow out of the local network. The same principle applies to the regional networks. If an Internet user wants to send electronic mail to someone at an address connected to the same regional network, that traffic would stay within the regional network and would not need to cross the network backbone. This has had significant ramifications, as we'll see when we discuss the issue of commercialization of the Internet.

A related operating principle is that each network bears the responsibility for connecting to the network at the next higher level. Let us go back to the example of the university and assume its computer science department chooses to gain Internet access. There is no central body the department must contact to achieve its new status. Instead, someone will make arrangements with the appropriate service provider. Meanwhile, the department remains autonomous. Its responsibilities include providing information about the computers it maintains to the next higher level of the network. The routing and addressing information within the local network remains in the hands of local administrators.[12]

Who pays for all this? Each network system is responsible for its own funding, just as each system must develop its own administrative procedures. This, more than anything, accounts for the rapid increase in Internet communications. Whether the Internet is growing at 15 percent per month or 100 percent per year, the growth can be accounted for only by realizing that networks joining the Internet retain control of their own administration. The political dilemmas that might arise are thus muted, while the benefits of connectivity loom large.

Because there is no single service provider, agencies fund their own networks, each of which is considered a part of the overall Internet. We also find private backbone systems, frequently offering commercial access to the Internet to the growing number of corporations and private individuals interested in going on-line. Many regional networks have been created through initial funding from the National Science Foundation, with the understanding that the emerging networks become self-supporting entities. The result is a series of self-administering networks whose funding, management, and policies differ widely from each other. Some networks, for example, allow commercial traffic while others specifically forbid it.

Internet Addressing

Considering the vast number of networks connecting to form the Internet, how can all those information packets in search of a destination be sure they're going to the right address? How, for that matter, can we specify an Internet address so that it makes sense not only to the machines routing it, but also to the end users of the system? Let's examine how Internet addressing works.

At each step of the Internet hierarchy, a participating network is responsible for maintaining its own organization. In addressing terms, this means each network-linked organization maintains a database of the computers it connects to the network. The numbers used to identify Internet computers are called *IP addresses*. Each machine on the Internet has a unique IP address.

An IP address contains four numbers connected by periods: 92.33.33.22 is an IP address; so is 138.40.11.1. The numbers farthest to the left are the broadest, representing a larger network and then, working to the right, increasingly specific network information until we arrive at a particular computer.

Let's say you wanted to reach a computer at Washington & Lee University in Lexington, Virginia. Perhaps you could track down its IP address, 137.113.10.35. But the immediate problem with IP addresses is that they're lengthy and difficult to remember. To provide a bit of mnemonic help, computers came to be identified with particular names. The computer just mentioned is also known as liberty.uc.wlu.edu. Now we've got some information that's easier to work with, because the consistent nature of these names provides us with a ready way to identify what they refer to. You type a name, and the routers that handle network flow supply the equivalent numbers.

The Domain Name System (DNS) that describes computers and the organizations they support works in opposite fashion to numerical IP addressing. Whereas an IP address presents its most *general* information at the far left, names are chosen with the most *specific* information at the left. Consider a machine I frequently work on which is called mercury. Users at my service provider normally have this sequence as part of their address: mercury.interpath.net. At the left is the name of the computer: mercury. The following term, interpath, is the name of the network I connect to, which serves North Carolina statewide. Its status as a network is shown by the final word in the address, net, which is the top-level domain for this address. Again, in the world of Internet names (but not IP numbers), moving from left to right takes us from greater to lesser specificity.

A brief aside: You will find that computers tend to be given names with a certain whimsical similarity. My former address was on a machine called rock, which was part of a (now defunct) statewide network called CONCERT-CONNECT. With the musical theme already established, CONCERT maintained other computers with names like banjo and jazz. And music, of course, is but one possibility. You'll encounter computers named after colors, movie stars, cooking tools, or flowers. The possibilities are endless.

Domain names tell you a great deal about a given address, as should be obvious from the following breakdown:

com　　These are U.S. commercial domains, indicating they're a corporate or company site. allen.com, for example, is the name of the high-tech marketing firm Allen Marketing Group in Raleigh, North Carolina.

edu　　Found in U.S. addresses, edu denotes a university or college. wisc.edu stands for the University of Wisconsin.

gov　　The domain name for a U.S. government site. nih.gov is the National Institutes of Health.

mil　　A U.S. military site. ddn.mil is the Defense Data Network, run by Government Systems, Inc. in Chantilly, Virginia.

net　　Refers to an administrative organization for a network, as in the name inter-path.net mentioned previously.

org　　Organizations, usually private, that don't fit the above categories. Thus the Internet Society is isoc.org.

While .com, .edu, .gov and .mil apply solely to U.S. organizations, individual countries have their own top-level domain names. Thus .de is the domain name for Germany, .ch for Switzerland, .it for Italy, and there is also a .us domain for the United States. The address of an Internet resource tool in Germany is archie.th-darmstadt.de, while another such tool in New Zealand is archie.nz. At the end of this chapter, you'll find a complete listing of country domain names, along with information about the status of networking in each country.

Reaching a specific user at a given computer address is a matter of adding that person's user name to the address. My Internet mailbox address, then, is gilster@ interpath.net. gilster is my user name at Interpath, which is connected to the address of the machine where my account is located by the @, or at, symbol.

Now that we have domain names, are IP addresses obsolete? Hardly. The numbers allow computers on the network to return information about the addresses in question. When you specify a particular computer by using a domain name, such as quake. think.com, an appropriate translation into an IP address will be made for you by a computer in the relevant area, or domain. This computer, called a *nameserver*, will return the proper IP address for the computer you're trying to reach. Depending on the location of the machine you're searching for and its geographical relation to you, such requests may go through one or more nameservers before targeting the final address. The beauty of the system is twofold:

1. You don't have to handle any of these transactions, because they take place automatically.
2. As opposed to a central list of Internet addresses (which, incidentally, used to be the way addressing was managed), the Domain Name System allows the Internet to grow with far less organizational overhead.

Acceptable Use and How It Has Changed

The question of what can and can't be done on the Internet has always been tricky. The ARPANET, after all, was designed with an explicit mission—to provide an experimental platform for designing computer networks that could undergo various calamities and still function. The redundancy of routing options that gets your electronic mail message through derives from the recognition that networks would have to possess "self-healing" characteristics if they were to work unimpeded when partially shut down. Hence the Internet's ability to send information packets by whatever route necessary to ensure their delivery.

The later involvement of the National Science Foundation, and its key role in propagating regional networks, defined the network's charter in support of research and education. It would be reasonable to expect the NSFNET backbone to carry traffic from a university's computer science department, for example, but unreasonable to expect it to furnish the data highway for a large corporation doing commercial work via the Internet. Accordingly, a set of core principles regarding NSFNET usage grew up and was codified in the form of NSFNET's Acceptable Use Policy. Figure 2.6 shows what it had to say.

A careful reading of this document will show that commercial use was not forbidden *ipso facto;* in fact, paragraph 1 explicitly exempts "research arms of for-profit firms when engaged in open scholarly communication and research." But the document rules out ". . . extensive use for private or personal business."

Exactly how these lines were drawn could be problematic. Perhaps your company produced a software product used in mapping molecular structures. And perhaps that product was about to be released in a version that would present significant new features. Presumably, your decision to use the Internet to acquaint interested parties—particularly those in the academic and research communities—with such a product would not be in violation of the NSFNET policy. But using NSFNET as a medium for general advertising certainly would have violated the spirit of that policy, as would commercial activities such as invoicing. In between was a wide and murky area about which controversy continued to swirl.

But note this twist: NSFNET's policy restricted use of the NSFNET backbone only. In fact, connecting networks, according to NSF, ". . . will formulate their own use policies." So a key question became, What kind of traffic were we talking about, and did it cross the NSF backbone on its way to its destination?

Because of the rapid growth in commercial traffic, some method had to be found to promote traffic without the restrictions of the NSFNET backbone. This is why the Commercial Internet Exchange, or CIX, was created. CIX was founded by Performance Systems International, Inc. (Reston, Virginia), operators of PSINet, UUNET Technologies Inc. (Falls Church, Virginia), which operates AlterNet, and General Atomics (San Diego, California), which operates CERFnet. According to a CIX Association, Inc. press release, "The CIX founders and all new members are Public Data Internetwork (PDI) Service Providers cooperating to provide a nonrestrictive packet interchange for TCP/IP and OSI traffic."

In Elmsford, New York, Advanced Network and Services, Inc., operators of ANSnet, provided the only network connected to all the major mid-level and regional networks that NSF financed. But ANS, which, as described earlier, was itself a partnership of IBM Corporation, MCI Communications Corporation, and Merit Inc., also ran a commercial backbone service called ANS CO+RE. In this way, regional networks sponsored by the NSF could send and receive commercial traffic across the gateways provided by ANS (not without some controversy regarding ANS' competitive position *vis a vis* the CIX providers). Considering this connection, and the commercial linkages developed through CIX, it became clear that commercial usage of the network was not only acceptable, it was mushrooming as companies became aware of the Internet's possibilities.

```
                THE NSFNET BACKBONE SERVICES ACCEPTABLE USE POLICY

GENERAL PRINCIPLE:

(1) NSFNET Backbone services are provided to support open research and education
    in and among US research and instructional institutions, plus research arms of
    for-profit firms when engaged in open scholarly communication and research.
    Use for other purposes is not acceptable.

SPECIFICALLY ACCEPTABLE USES:

(2) Communication with foreign researchers and educators in connection with
    research or instruction, as long as any network that the foreign user employs
    for such communication provides reciprocal access to US researchers and
    educators.

(3) Communication and exchange for professional development, to maintain
    currency, or to debate issues in a field or subfield of knowledge.

(4) Use for disciplinary-society, university-association, government-advisory,
    or standards activities related to the user's research and instructional
    activities.

(5) Use in applying for or administering grants or contracts for research or
    instruction, but not for other fundraising or public relations activities.

(6) Any other administrative communications or activities in direct support
    of research and instruction.

(7) Announcements of new products or services for use in research or instruction,
    but not advertising of any kind.

(8) Any traffic originating from a network of another member agency of the
    Federal Networking Council if the traffic meets the acceptable use policy
    of that agency.

(9) Communication incidental to otherwise acceptable use, except for illegal
    or specifically unacceptable use.

UNACCEPTABLE USES:

(10) Use for for-profit activities (consulting for pay, sales or administration
     of campus stores, sale of tickets to sports events, and so on) or use by
     for-profit institutions unless covered by the General Principle or as a
     specifically acceptable use.

(11) Extensive use for private or personal business.

This statement applies to use of the NSFNET Backbone only.  NSF expects that
connecting networks will formulate their own use policies.  The NSF Division
of Networking and Communications Research and Infrastructure will resolve any
questions about this Policy or its interpretation.

                                                          2/92
```

Figure 2.6 NSFNET's Acceptable Use Policy. Now an historical curiosity, this document once set limits on business use of the Internet.

Today, commercialization of the Internet is a *fait accompli*. Not only were IBM and MCI deeply involved in ANS, but ANS itself has now been purchased by America Online, a striking symbol of the merging of commercial on-line services into the global Internet. MCI has been a major player in Infonet, a company offering global Internet connectivity, and is now developing internetMCI, the company's bid to acquire a larger chunk of the lucrative access business. Both MCI and Infonet are involved in Government Systems, Inc., the company in Chantilly, Virginia that operates the Defense Data Network Network Information Center.

Not to be outdone, US Sprint, a member of the Commercial Internet Exchange, now offers SprintLink, described as the first TCP/IP-based data transmission service offered by a national long-distance carrier. Current planning involves linking Sprint-Link with the company's SprintNet service. European commercial service, meanwhile, is surging, and the Internet Initiative Japan (IIJ) actively supports commercial networking.

As of mid-1995, the NSF has removed its funding for the existing NSFNET backbone. In its place, commercial service providers will take over the responsibility of maintaining high-speed network communications. Not that NSF is leaving the networking realm altogether. MCI operates its Very High Speed Backbone, connecting the supercomputer sites with which its work began to experimental network access points for continuing research. The whole issue of commercialization has thus been rendered moot. The best advice I've heard regarding commercialization comes from John Curran, network analyst at the Network Information Center at NEARnet, in a posting on USENET. The group alt.internet.services had been discussing these issues, and Curran, after summarizing the situation, added this:

> What does this all mean? It means that you will find folks who think that the Internet is only for research and education, folks who think that the Internet is a wide-open highway for commercial use, and folks who think something in between. What's most amazing is that they're all correct, due to the eclectic nature of the Internet infrastructure."

These diverse viewpoints are gradually giving way to an understanding that, with the demise of the NSFNET, the Internet is now open for business.[13]

Key Internet Organizations

Despite its decentralized nature, the Internet and its activities are coordinated to a greater or lesser extent by a number of organizations. These are names you'll encounter frequently as you prowl the Internet.

The Internet Society

One of the most helpful things you can do for yourself if you plan to become a regular Internet user is to join the Internet Society. This organization was founded to promote the growth of the Internet into a global research and information infrastructure. Quoting from a descriptive document sent out by the Society:

> Its principal purpose is to maintain and extend the development and availability of the Internet and its associated technologies and applications—both as an end in itself, and as a means

of enabling organizations, professions, and individuals worldwide to more effectively collaborate, cooperate, and innovate in their respective fields and interests.[14]

Critical in this mission are the following two goals:

- development, maintenance, evolution, and dissemination of standards for the Internet and its internetworking technologies and applications;
- growth and evolution of the Internet architecture.

The Internet Society publishes *On the Internet,* a major source for Internet information. Dues are $35 per year for individual membership ($25 per year for student members). For information about the Internet Society, write to:

INTERNET SOCIETY
12020 Sunrise Valley Drive, Suite 210
Reston, VA 22091
Voice: 703-648-9888 or 800-468-9507 (USA only)
Fax: 703-648-9887
mailto:membership@isoc.org (individual membership)
mailto:org-membership@isoc.org (organization membership)
gopher://gopher.isoc.org/
ftp://ftp.isoc.org/isoc/
http://www.isoc.org/

Figure 2.7 shows the Internet Society's home page on the World Wide Web.

Internet Architecture Board

As part of its mission, the Internet Society, or ISOC, has incorporated the Internet Activities Board, now known as the Internet Architecture Board (IAB), under its auspices. The IAB has coordinated research and development of the TCP/IP protocols and helped to provide research advice to the Internet community. IAB was formed in 1983 following the reorganization of DARPA's Internet Configuration Control Board. Its early goals were to encourage research into TCP/IP and the Internet, and it gradually evolved into an independent organization. Today, IAB oversees the standards-supporting activities of the Internet Society. IAB works, naturally, with TCP/IP, but also with a wide variety of protocols involved in computer messaging, data interchange, and resource discovery, including gateways to link TCP/IP networks to other kinds of systems.

IAB relies on several task forces central to the evolution of Internet technology. A brief description of each follows.

THE INTERNET ENGINEERING TASK FORCE (IETF)

Composed solely of volunteers who meet thrice yearly, the IETF is responsible for approving standards for Internet protocols and architecture. Its working groups specialize in problem areas as they arise. The mission of IETF is to develop and approve solutions to the operational and technical problems that arise on the Internet. The IETF makes its recommendations to the Internet Engineering Steering Group (IESG) regarding the standardization of protocols and protocol usage in the Internet. It also provides a valuable forum within which vendors, researchers, users, network managers, and

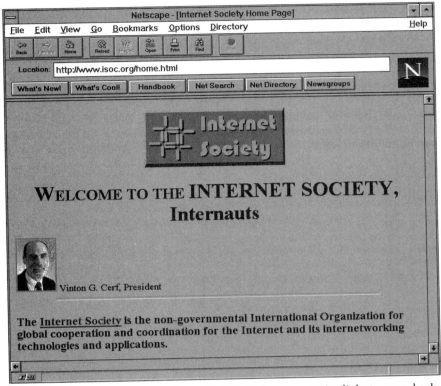

Figure 2.7 The Internet Society's World Wide Web page contains links to many background documents about the Internet.

other interested parties may meet and discuss the issues. There is no formal membership in the IETF. Meetings are open to all, with contributors keeping in touch between sessions through working group mailing lists.

For further information, contact:

IETF SECRETARIAT
CNRI
1895 Preston White Dr., Suite 100
Reston, VA 22091
Voice: 703-620-8990
Fax: 703-620-0913
mailto://ietf-info@cnri.reston.va.us

THE INTERNET RESEARCH TASK FORCE (IRTF)

Consider the Internet Research Task Force the research wing of the IAB. This group focuses on developing technologies that may be required in the future. This long-term orientation currently includes research groups working on such issues as resource discovery, privacy and security, and library use of the Internet. For further information, contact:

USC/INFORMATION SCIENCES INSTITUTE
4676 Admiralty Way
Marina del Rey, CA 90292-6695
Voice: 310-822-1511
Fax: 310-823-6714

INTERNET ASSIGNED NUMBERS AUTHORITY (IANA)

The IANA, operated by the University of Southern California's Information Sciences Institute, records protocol identifiers in network-accessible databases and Requests for Comments documents (see the upcoming section). IANA maintains a registry for all identifiers associated with Internet protocols. This provides a standard way for systems to refer to network resources.

INTERNET COMPUTER EMERGENCY RESPONSE TEAM (CERT)

The Internet CERT specializes in network security issues. The largely volunteer organization attempts to coordinate network responses to security problems. For further information, contact:

CERT COORDINATION CENTER
Software Engineering Institute
Carnegie Mellon University
Pittsburgh, PA 15213-3890
Voice: 412-268-7090
Fax: 412-268-6989
mailto:cert@cert.org
ftp://info.cert.org/

FARNET

The Federation of American Research Networks was established in 1987, creating a nonprofit corporation with a mission to promote the use and improvement of computer networks in research and education. Members include local, state, regional, national, and international network service providers, as well as nonprofit and commercial corporations, universities, supercomputer centers, and other organizations. FARNET offers educational programs for members, works with network organizations to improve information services, and provides a forum for the discussion of technical and policy issues. Its monthly on-line newsletter keeps members abreast of its activities. For further information, contact:

FARNET
1511 K St. NW, Suite 1165
Washington, DC 20005
Voice: 202-637-9557
http://www.farnet.org

COALITION FOR NETWORKED INFORMATION (CNI)

Founded in 1990, the CNI has created a task force of 191 organizations that explore issues of information management and their impact upon society. Members include universities, publishers, computer companies, library organizations, and network service providers. Of particular interest is the Coalition's TopNode Directory of Network Directories and Resource Guides, which has grown out of the need to promote collaboration between library and information technology groups. For further information, contact:

COALITION FOR NETWORKED INFORMATION
21 Dupont Circle
Washington, DC 20036
Voice: 202-296-5098
Fax: 202-872-0884
ftp://ftp.cni.org/
gopher://gopher.cni.org:70/
http://www.cni.org/CNI.homepage.html
CNI's Assistant Executive Director is Joan K. Lippincott
mailto:joan@cni.org

You can see CNI's online information source in Figure 2.8. And to examine the TopNode Project, use Telnet to a.cni.org. Log in as brsuser.

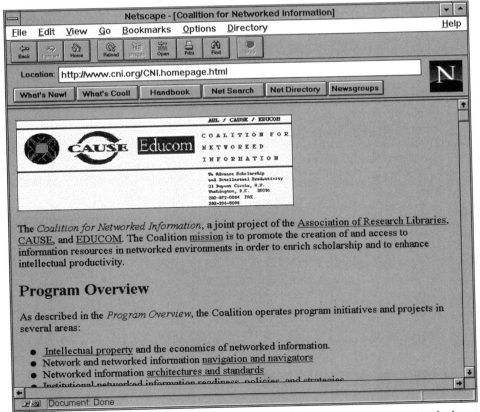

Figure 2.8 The home page at the Coalition for Networked Information puts you in the heart of educational networked computing.

COALITION FOR RESEARCH & EDUCATION NETWORKING (CREN)

BITNET is operated by this organization, with user support and information services provided through the BITNET Network Information Center (BITNIC). An organization that wishes to participate in BITNET must take out a membership in CREN. For further information, contact:

COALITION FOR RESEARCH & EDUCATION NETWORKING
1112 Sixteenth St. NW, Suite 600
Washington, DC 20036
Voice: 202-872-4200
Fax: 202-872-4318
http://www.cren.net/

CLEARINGHOUSE FOR NETWORKED
INFORMATION DISCOVERY AND RETRIEVAL

In April 1992, the National Science Foundation awarded a three-year cooperative agreement to help establish a center supporting the development of wide-area information retrieval tools. These user-friendly systems, like World Wide Web, Wide Area Information Servers (WAIS), and Gopher, are making it possible for Internet users to locate information and retrieve it. They and other software programs now under development are actively supported by CNIDR (pronounced snyder), which provides a repository for such systems, and which is also active in the development of standards, as well as the continuing education of new users.

CNIDR's initial funding from NSF and the MCNC Center for Communications in Research Triangle Park, North Carolina is supported by funding from other government agencies as well as a consortium of public and private participants. And although it has not been in operation long, this support center should draw increasing attention as the critical role of information discovery becomes apparent. With over 40 thousand networks now feeding data into the worldwide Internet, knowing where to look becomes a critical issue. Tools like WAIS, Gopher, and the rest, all discussed in later chapters, are essential agents in acquiring a mastery of the Internet.

For more information, contact:

CNIDR
MCNC Center for Communications
P.O. Box 12889
Research Triangle Park, NC 27709-2889
Voice: 919-248-1499
mailto:info@cnidr.org
ftp://ftp.cnidr.org/
http://www.cnidr.org/

COMMERCIAL INTERNET EXCHANGE

When commercial organizations wanted to use the Internet for business purposes, they had to cope with the problem of NSFNET's Acceptable Use Policy, which prohibited network traffic for such uses. The Commercial Internet Exchange grew out of this need; it is an association of regional and national networks that have agreed to route commercial traffic to each other without using the NSFNET backbone. As we saw earlier, the CIX has been a major force in the evolution of commercial activity on the Internet.

For more information, contact:

COMMERCIAL INTERNET EXCHANGE
3110 Fairview Park Dr., Suite 590
Falls Church, VA 22042
Voice: 303-482-2150
Fax: 303-482-2884
mailto:info@cix.org

EDUCOM

A nonprofit consortium of colleges, universities, and other institutions that focuses on the application of technology to higher education.

EDUCOM
1112 Sixteenth St. NW, Suite 600
Washington, DC 20036
Voice: 202-872-4200
Fax: 202-872-4318
mailto:info@bitnic.educom.edu
http://educom.edu/

FEDERAL NETWORKING COUNCIL

This consortium of U.S. government agencies involved in networking, which includes such major movers as ARPA, the National Science Foundation, the Department of Energy (ESnet), and NASA (NASA Science Internet), has been established to foster collaboration in providing network services to the various research communities. The Council has also provided funding for the administration and operational needs of the Internet Architecture Board and the Internet Engineering Task Force. For further information: gopher://nsipo.arc.nasa.gov/11/

TERENA

TERENA is an association of network organizations and users in Europe whose goal is to boost networking cooperation and support the spread of the medium. A supporter of the Open Systems Interconnection (OSI) protocols, TERENA has also moved to incorporate TCP/IP, and today stands as the European body most similar to the Internet Engineering Task Force.

TERENA makes electronic copies of its publications available over the Internet. For further information, contact TERENA at:

TERENA SECRETARIAT
Singel 466-468
NL-1017 AW AMSTERDAM
Voice: +31 20 639 1131
Fax: +31 20 639 3289

mailto:secretariat@terena.nl
gopher://gopher.terena.nl/
http://www.terena.nl/

RIPE

Reseaux IP Europeens is a collaborative organization of European Internet service providers whose aim is to provide technical and administrative coordination towards the creation of a European-wide network. Created in 1989, RIPE now boasts more than 60 member organizations; more than 1 million computers throughout Europe are accessible through the network's RIPE coordinates. RIPE is the major body behind TCP/IP development in Europe; it has been incorporated into TERENA.

A particularly valuable collection of documentation is maintained at the RIPE Network Coordination Center, which is accessible via a variety of network tools. A menu-driven service allows users to read documents and retrieve them by electronic mail. You can reach the NCC by Telnet to info.ripe.net. All RIPE documents and the full set of Internet RFCs are available via anonymous FTP from ftp.ripe.net, and the same documents can be retrieved through a Gopher interface at gopher.ripe.net; WAIS and World Wide Web access are also available. You can see RIPE's home page in Figure 2.9.

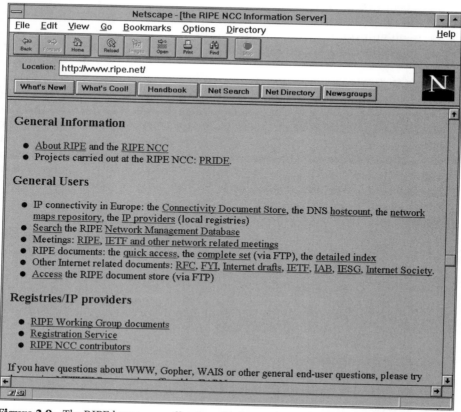

Figure 2.9   The RIPE home page offers broad information about access providers in Europe.

For further information about RIPE, contact:

RIPE NCC
Kruislaan 409
NL-1098 SJ Amsterdam
The Netherlands
Voice: +31 20 592 5065
Fax: +31 20 592 5090
mailto:ncc@ripe.net
http://www.ripe.net/

CCIRN

The Coordinating Committee for Intercontinental Research Networks has a lofty aim—
to establish a global research network by coordinating existing network activities inter-
nationally. The ocean-spanning nature of CCIRN was clear from its first meeting in
1987, when William Bostwick, chairman of the Federal Research Internet Coordinating
Committee, was chosen as co-chairman along with RARE's secretary-general, James
Hutton. With initial membership from European network organizations, U.S. governmental agencies, and the Internet Architecture Board, among others, the CCIRN quickly
expanded, and now includes members in Eastern Europe, South America, and the
Pacific Rim.

Internet Documentation

Although you'll never have to wade into Internet technical details unless you want to, it's
helpful to know something about them. A number of useful documents are available,
some called Requests for Comments, others called FYI, or For Your Information documents, that provide background information helpful to any new user.

Requests for Comments (RFCs)

TCP/IP is controlled by the Internet Society through both the IAB and the IETF. A series
of Requests for Comments (RFCs) has been established, containing documentation
about TCP/IP and the Internet at large. RFCs are managed by the IAB and can be
obtained by electronic mail or by file transfer protocol (FTP).
   Who writes RFCs? Anyone can put an RFC together, commenting on a particular
issue or developing a standard he or she would like to see discussed. The proposed RFC
is then reviewed by the RFC editor. If accepted, it is assigned an RFC number. These documents, begun in 1969 and steadily growing, are managed by editor Jon Postel at the
Information Sciences Institute of the University of Southern California.
   RFCs and the FYI documents discussed next are available at numerous sites.
Although we have not discussed electronic mail yet, the following provides a way to keep
up with RFCs now. You may want to return to this section after you've used e-mail so
you can send for the relevant material.
   RFCs are under active development and are available by File Transfer Protocol
(FTP), Gopher, and WWW from on-line repositories around the world. The Network
Information Centers discussed in the next few pages are all repositories of RFCs and a
great deal of other helpful documents. Many sites also provide for automated retrieval

What You Need: A Way to Find RFCs

The Document: Where and How to Get New RFCs

How to Get It: Send electronic mail to rfc-info@isi.edu. In the subject field, enter **Accessing RFCs.** The message should consist of only one line, starting at the far left margin. It should read exactly as follows:

Help: Help

You can also retrieve a fuller manual containing the complete list of options at the site. To do so, send a message to the same address, reading as follows:

Help: Manual

of RFCs by e-mail, so if your only Internet access is by a mail gateway, you can still use it to find what you need.

The document cited here contains full information about FTP sites where you can find RFCs and other documents. The major ones are these:

ftp://ds.internic.net/

ftp://nis.nsf.net/

ftp://nisc.jvnc.net/

ftp://ftp.isi.edu/

ftp://wuarchive.wustl.edu/

ftp://src.doc.ic.ac.uk/

ftp://ftp.ncren.net/

ftp://ftp.sesqui.net/

ftp://nis.garr.it/

FYIs

FYI is a familiar acronym; it stands for For Your Information. A subset of the RFCs, the FYIs are documents that provide useful background information about the Internet. However, the FYI documents are generally written with a broader audience in mind, and many documents available at the various FYI sites target beginners. You'll find both an RFC and an FYI number on these documents because, properly speaking, FYIs are a subset of the RFC materials and hence are included in a complete listing of RFCs. You retrieve FYIs just as you do RFCs—by locating an appropriate site and using File Transfer Protocol, electronic mail, or any of the other Internet access tools available.

STDs

STDs—the abbreviation means standards—are another subset of the RFC materials. STDs identify those RFCs that document Internet standards. Like FYIs, STDs possess both an RFC number and an STD number. You find them the same way you find RFCs. Figure 2.10 shows the format typical of such Internet documents.

```
Network Working Group                                    D. Crocker
Request for Comments: 1775                    Brandenburg Consulting
Category: Informational                                  March 1995


                       To Be "On" the Internet

Status of this Memo

   This memo provides information for the Internet community.  This memo
   does not specify an Internet standard of any kind.  Distribution of
   this memo is unlimited.


Abstract

   The Internet permits different levels of access for consumers and
   providers of service.  The nature of those differences is quite
   important in the capabilities They afford.  Hence, it is appropriate
   to provide terminology that distinguishes among the range, so that
   the Internet community can gain some clarity when distinguishing
   whether a user (or an organization) is "on" the Internet.  This
   document suggests four terms, for distinguishing the major classes of
   access.


1.   INTRODUCTION

   The Internet is many things to many people.  It began as a technology
   and has grown into a global service.  With the growth has come
   increased complexity in details of the technology and service,
   resulting in confusion when trying to determine whether a given user
   is "on" the Internet.  Who is on the Internet?  What capabilities do
   they have?  This note is an attempt to aid Internet consumers and
   providers in determining the basic types of end-user access that
   distinguish critical differences in Internet attachment.

   The list was developed primarily for the perspective of users, rather
   than for the technical community. The definitions in this list take
   the perspective that users are primarily interested in application
   services.   A curious implication is that some of the definitions do
   not rely on the direct use of the underlying Internet connectivity
   protocols, TCP/IP.  For many technical discussions, therefore, these
   terms will not be appropriate.




                                                            [Page 1]
Crocker
```

Figure 2.10   RFC 1775 shows the typical RFC format; this one is about Internet access providers.

2.   LABELS FOR INTERNET ACCESS

   The following definitions move from "most" to "least" Internet
   access, from the perspective of the user (consumer). The first term
   is primarily applicable to Internet service providers. The remaining
   terms are primarily applicable to consumers of Internet service.

   FULL ACCESS

      This is a permanent (full-time) Internet attachment running
      TCP/IP, primarily appropriate for allowing the Internet community
      to access application servers, operated by Internet service
      providers. Machines with Full access are directly visible to
      others attached to the Internet, such as through the Internet
      Protocol's ICMP Echo (ping) facility. The core of the Internet
      comprises those machines with Full access.

   CLIENT ACCESS

      The user runs applications that employ Internet application
      protocols directly on their own computer platform, but might not
      be running underlying Internet protocols (TCP/IP), might not have
      full-time access, such as through dial-up, or might have
      constrained access, such as through a firewall. When active,
      Client users might be visible to the general Internet, but such
      visibility cannot be predicted. For example, this means that most
      Client access users will not be detected during an empirical
      probing of systems "on" the Internet at any given moment, such as
      through the ICMP Echo facility.

   MEDIATED ACCESS

      The user runs no Internet applications on their own platform. An
      Internet service provider runs applications that use Internet
      protocols on the provider's platform, for the user. User has
      simplified access to the provider, such as dial-up terminal
      connectivity. For Mediated access, the user is on the Internet,
      but their computer platform is not. Instead, it is the computer
      of the mediating service (provider) which is on the Internet.

   MESSAGING ACCESS

      The user has no Internet access, except through electronic mail
      and through netnews, such as Usenet or a bulletin board service.
      Since messaging services can be used as a high-latency -- i.e.,
      slow -- transport service, the use of this level of access for
      mail-enabled services can be quite powerful, though not
      interactive.

Figure 2.10   (*Continued*)

Internet Monthly Reports

Keeping up with a rapidly moving target like the Internet isn't easy, but Internet Monthly Reports (IMRs) can help. They're distributed by a mailing list and can also be retrieved by FTP from various sites, as well as through electronic mail, Gopher, and WWW, much in the fashion of RFCs. Events of significance in the various networks making up the Internet appear here, as well as reports on ongoing research and engineering projects, and a calendar of Internet events.

What You Need: A List of Ways to Retrieve Internet Monthly Reports

The Document: Ways to Get IMRs

How to Get It: Send electronic mail to rfc-info@isi.edu. In the subject field, enter **Getting Imrs.** The message should read:

help: help

The best way to proceed is to access the ISI site at the following address:

ftp://ftp.isi.edu/in-notes/imr

But as the document accessed previously will show, you can also use electronic mail alone to retrieve IMRs. This document will also explain how to sign on to the mailing list to receive the Internet Monthly Reports automatically.

Network Information Centers

Network Information Centers (NICs) exist to provide documentation and useful information about the Internet to users. Their role is all the more important given the lack of Internet centralization. By locating abundant information sources in a single site, the Network Information Centers make it possible to find out quickly what is available on the Internet about basic topics. This role becomes even more critical given that the Internet is now moving away from its strictly academic and research focus to comprise users from all walks of life. Here are some of the major NICs.

BITNET Network Information Center

Although it's not part of the Internet because it runs its own protocols on top of TCP/IP, BITNET is a valuable resource that Internet users can reach through electronic mail gateways. Its Network Information Center, called BITNIC, was established by EDUCOM, a consortium of universities, colleges, and other institutions promoting computer networking technologies and now functions within CREN. The holdings at BITNIC are essential for anyone planning to take advantage of BITNET. They include general introductions to using the BITNET system, lists of BITNET servers for particular kinds of information, documents about network etiquette and history, and planning for BITNET's future as it integrates its operations with the TCP/IP protocols.

CORPORATION FOR RESEARCH AND EDUCATION NETWORKING (CREN)
1112 16th St. NW, Suite 600
Washington, DC 20036
Voice: 202-872-4318
mailto://info@bitnic.educom.edu

Defense Data Network Network Information Center

The DDN NIC is the Internet Registrar for domains and network numbers for MILNET; it also maintains a WHOIS database for MILNET users, a kind of on-line directory we'll look closely at later. Like the other NICs, the DDN provides a wealth of publicly accessible files through its anonymous FTP address at nic.ddn.mil. Soon, I'll show you how to use such addresses to retrieve a great deal of valuable information. Information is also available through electronic mail. Send to service@nic.ddn.mil. If you type nothing in the subject field of the letter and just the word help as the message, the NIC will send you information on how to get other documents by e-mail.

GOVERNMENT SYSTEMS, INC.
14200 Park Meadow Dr., Suite 200
Chantilly, VA 22021
Voice: 703-802-4535
Fax: 703-802-8376
mailto:hostmaster@nic.ddn.mil
ftp://nic.ddn.mil/

InterNIC

The Internet Network Information Center consists of two organizations known collectively as the InterNIC. Among the many information services provided here are the complete RFC documents and materials relating to the work of the Internet Society and the IETF. The Internet Monthly Report is available, as are many other documents. The InterNIC also provides a new directory and database service operated by AT&T. This so-called Directory of Directories is being established to serve as a pointer to resources on the Internet, and includes FTP sites, lists of servers, lists of directories, library catalogs, and data archives. AT&T also plans to provide its own directory services to users and organizations. Finally, the InterNIC serves as the registrar for domains and network numbers for the Internet at large (a function formerly managed at the DDN Network Information Center).

To reach the InterNIC from the top, you can try several methods:

INTERNIC
Voice: 800-444-4345; 619-455-4600
Fax: 619-455-4640
mailto:info@internic.net
telnet://internic.net/
ftp://ftp.internic.net/
gopher://gopher.internic.net/

Keeping up with Internet resources is difficult; so many things are happening so fast that it's easy to lose track. I firmly recommend you take advantage of a USENET newsgroup that sprang up out of work performed at the InterNIC.

What You Need: Access to comp.internet.net-happenings, a newsgroup containing news about new network sites.

How to Get It: Use your newsreader program to access the newsgroup. We will discuss news-readers in Chapter 11. Whenever you log on to your service provider, your newsreader will show you the messages that have accumulated since you last read through the newsgroup.

Figure 2.11 shows the InterNIC's home page on the World Wide Web. The InterNIC replaces the NSF Network Service Center, whose services have been transferred to the InterNIC team. Three organizations manage the InterNIC, with responsibilities broken down as follows.

REGISTRATION SERVICES

This is where IP addresses and domain names for the Internet are assigned. The RIPE NCC performs the same function in Europe. Provided by Network Solutions, Inc. of Herndon, Virginia.

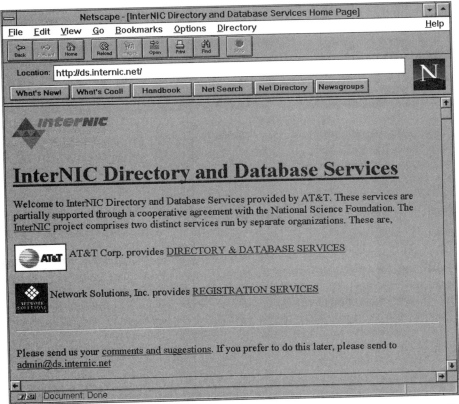

Figure 2.11 The home page for INTERNIC Directory and Database Services, a core site for Internet information gathering.

NETWORK SOLUTIONS, INC.
Attn: InterNIC Registration Services
505 Huntmar Park Dr.
Herndon, VA 22070
Voice: 703-742-4777
mailto:hostmaster@rs.internic.net
ftp://rs.internic.net/
telnet://rs.internic.net/

DIRECTORY AND DATABASE SERVICES

Provided by AT&T.

DIRECTORY AND DATABASE SERVICES
5000 Hadley Road, Room 2F25
South Plainfield, NJ 07080
Voice: 908-668-6587
mailto:admin@ds.internic.net
ftp://ds.internic.net/
http://ds.internic.net/

SURAnet NETWORK INFORMATION CENTER (BBN PLANET, SOUTHEAST REGION)

An excellent archive of network information.

SURAnet
8400 Baltimore Blvd.
College Park, MD 20740-2498
Voice: 301-982-4600
Fax: 301-982-4605
mailto:info@sura.net
ftp://ftp.sura.net
http://www.sura.net/

Merit Network Information Center

Newsletters and a variety of Internet documents are found at this site, which offers a wide-ranging data depository.

MERIT NETWORK INC.
4251 Plymouth Rd.
Arbor Lakes Bldg. #1, Suite C
Ann Arbor, MI 48109-2785
Voice: 313-936-3000
Fax: 313-936-3185
mailto:nic-info@nic.merit.edu (send **help** command)
ftp://nic.merit.edu/
gopher://nic.merit.edu/

NASA Network Applications and Information Center

This is the top-level network information center for the NASA Science Internet. In addition to its function as a support site for NASA networking, it also acts as a referral center for NASA's information resources.

NAIC
NASA Ames Research Center
M/S 204-14
Moffett Field, CA 94035-1000
Voice: 800-858-9947
Fax: 415-604-0978
mailto:naic@nasa.gov/
telnet://naic.nasa.gov/ (log in as **gopher**)
gopher://naic.nasa.gov/
ftp://naic.nasa.gov/
http://naic.nasa.gov/naic/

International Connectivity List

Larry Landweber tracks Internet connectivity worldwide from his position at the Computer Science Department at the University of Wisconsin in Madison. The following list summarizes Internet and other network connections. Note that you can retrieve updated versions of this list (and of the world network map shown earlier) by using the FTP address given in Figure 2.12.

Chapter 2 Notes

1. As compared to the 20 thousand networks, with 2.5 million host computers and 20 million users, cited less than one year ago in the second edition.
2. John Quarterman is the principal exponent of this view, and his painstaking work cannot be taken lightly. Whereas others have been content to ratchet up user estimates with abandon, Quarterman has based his views on surveys conducted with a rigorous methodology. We may not be able to say precisely how many people are using the Internet at any given time, but Quarterman's work is a useful check against overly optimistic guesses.
3. DARPA is again ARPA, as of early 1993.
4. Vinton Cerf's "How the Internet Came to Be" is a wonderful account of the early years of the network (http://www.isoc.org).
5. Malamud, Carl, *Exploring the Internet*. Englewood Cliffs, NJ: Prentice Hall PTR, 1992, p. 355.
6. These figures are from Eric M. Aupperle's "Changing Eras: Evolution of the NSFNET." *Internet Society News* Vol. 1., No. 4, Winter 1993, p. 3.
7. From Merit press release, December 2, 1992.
8. J.S. Quarterman, *The Matrix: Computer Networks and Conferencing Systems Worldwide*, Burlington, MA: Digital Press, 1990, p. 278. Quarterman's book, though dated, remains a major source for obtaining an overall view of networks throughout the world.
9. *Ibid.*, p. xxiii.
10. *Matrix News*, Vol. 3, No. 3, March 1993.
11. Comer, Douglas E, *Internetworking with TCP/IP*. Vol. 1: *Principles, Protocols, and Architecture*. 2d ed. Englewood Cliffs, NJ: Prentice Hall, 1991, p. 1. Comer's work is regarded as the seminal study of TCP/IP, its growth and development, and its current status.

INTERNATIONAL CONNECTIVITY
Version 13 - February 15, 1995

Please send corrections, information and/or comments to:

Larry Landweber
Computer Sciences Dept.
University of Wisconsin - Madison
1210 W. Dayton St.
Madison, WI 53706
lhl@cs.wisc.edu
FAX 1-608-265-2635

Include details, e.g., on connections, sites, contacts, protocols, etc.

Thanks to the many people from around the world who have provided information. This version (postscript, ditroff, text forms, maps in postscript) and earlier versions may also be obtained by anonymous ftp from ftp.cs.wisc.edu in the connectivity_table directory.

In the following, "BITNET" is used generically to refer to BITNET plus similar networks around the world (e.g., EARN, NET-NORTH, GULFNET, etc.).

SUMMARY

NUMBER OF ENTITIES WITH INTERNATIONAL NETWORK CONNECTIVITY = 168
NUMBER OF ENTITIES WITHOUT INTERNATIONAL NETWORK CONNECTIVITY = 70

BITNET
        Col. 2 (Entities with international BITNET links.)
        b: minimal, one to Ævedomestic BITNET sites, 21 entities
        B: widespread, more than Ævedomestic BITNET sites, 27 entities

IP INTERNET
        Col. 3 (Entities with international IP Internet links.)
        I: = operational, accessible from entire open IP Internet, 86 entities

UUCP
        Col. 4 (Entities with domestic UUCP sites which are connected
        to the Global Multiprotocol Open Internet.)
        u: minimal, one to Ævedomestic UUCP sites, 61 entities
        U: widespread, more than Ævedomestic UUCP sites, 80 entities

FIDONET
        Col. 5 (Entities with domestic FIDONET sites which are
        connected to the Global Multiprotocol Open Internet)
        f: minimal, one to Ævedomestic FIDONET sites, 29 entities
        F: widespread, more than Ævedomestic FIDONET sites, 69 entities

        An entity is a geographical area that has an ISO two letter
        country code (ISO 3166). These country codes are included in
        the Table below for each entity (Cols 8-9). Note that the ISO
        codes do not always agree with the top level DNS (Domain Name)
        code(s) used for a particular entity.

        Haiti's u entry is based on a ccmail email link. Restricted access
        or dial-up IP links exist to Lebanon, Senegal, Mali, Burkina Faso,
        Guinea, and Niger. These are not included in the table.

```
        ----    AF      Afghanistan (Islamic Republic of)
        ----    AL      Albania (Republic of)
        -I--    DZ      Algeria (People's Democratic Republic of)
        ----    AS      American Samoa
```

Figure 2.12   Larry Landweber's International Connectivity List.

```
----  AD   Andorra (Principality of)
---f  AO   Angola (People's Republic of)
----  AI   Anguilla
-I--  AQ   Antarctica
--u-  AG   Antigua and Barbuda
BIUF  AR   Argentina (Argentine Republic)
-IU-  AM   Armenia
---f  AW   Aruba
-IUF  AU   Australia
BIUF  AT   Austria (Republic of)
b-U-  AZ   Azerbaijan
--u-  BS   Bahamas (Commonwealth of the)
b---  BH   Bahrain (State of)
--U-  BD   Bangladesh (People's Republic of)
-Iu-  BB   Barbados
bIUF  BY   Belarus
BIUF  BE   Belgium (Kingdom of)
--U-  BZ   Belize
----  BJ   Benin (People's Republic of)
-IUF  BM   Bermuda
----  BT   Bhutan (Kingdom of)
--UF  BO   Bolivia (Republic of)
--u-  BA   Bosnia-Herzegovina
--uf  BW   Botswana (Republic of)
----  BV   Bouvet Island
BIUF  BR   Brazil (Federative Republic of)
----  IO   British Indian Ocean Territory
----  BN   Brunei Darussalam
bIUF  BG   Bulgaria (Republic of)
--U-  BF   Burkina Faso (formerly Upper Volta)
----  BI   Burundi (Republic of)
----  KH   Cambodia
--Uf  CM   Cameroon (Republic of)
BIUF  CA   Canada
----  CV   Cape Verde (Republic of)
----  KY   Cayman Islands
----  CF   Central African Republic
----  TD   Chad (Republic of)
BIUF  CL   Chile (Republic of)
-IuF  CN   China (People's Republic of)
----  CX   Christmas Island (Indian Ocean)
----  CC   Cocos (Keeling) Islands
bIu-  CO   Colombia (Republic of)
----  KM   Comoros (Islamic Federal Republic of the)
--U-  CG   Congo (Republic of the)
--u-  CK   Cook Islands
-Iuf  CR   Costa Rica (Republic of)
--Uf  CI   Cote d'Ivoire (Republic of)
-IuF  HR   Croatia
--U-  CU   Cuba (Republic of)
bI-f  CY   Cyprus (Republic of)
bIUF  CZ   Czech Republic
bIUF  DK   Denmark (Kingdom of)
----  DJ   Djibouti (Republic of)
----  DM   Dominica (Commonwealth of)
--Uf  DO   Dominican Republic
----  TP   East Timor
-Iu-  EC   Ecuador (Republic of)
bIU-  EG   Egypt (Arab Republic of)
--u-  SV   El Salvador (Republic of)
----  GQ   Equatorial Guinea (Republic of)
---f  ER   Eritrea
-IUF  EE   Estonia (Republic of)
```

Figure 2.12   (*Continued*)

```
---f  ET   Ethiopia (People's Democratic Republic of)
----  FK   Falkland Islands (Malvinas)
-Iu-  FO   Faroe Islands
-Iu-  FJ   Fiji (Republic of)
BIUF  FI   Finland (Republic of)
bIUF  FR   France (French Republic)
--u-  GF   French Guiana
--u-  PF   French Polynesia
----  TF   French Southern Territories
----  GA   Gabon (Gabonese Republic)
---f  GM   Gambia (Republic of the)
--UF  GE   Georgia (Republic of)
BIUF  DE   Germany (Federal Republic of)
--uF  GH   Ghana (Republic of )
----  GI   Gibraltar
BIUF  GR   Greece (Hellenic Republic)
-I-f  GL   Greenland
--u-  GD   Grenada
b-uf  GP   Guadeloupe (French Department of)
-I-F  GU   Guam
--u-  GT   Guatemala (Republic of)
--u-  GN   Guinea (Republic of)
----  GW   Guinea-Bissau (Republic of)
--u-  GY   Guyana (Republic of)
--u-  HT   Haiti (Republic of)
----  HM   Heard and McDonald Islands
----  HN   Honduras (Republic of)
BI-F  HK   Hong Kong
BIUF  HU   Hungary (Republic of)
-IUF  IS   Iceland (Republic of)
bIUF  IN   India (Republic of)
-IUF  ID   Indonesia (Republic of)
bI--  IR   Iran (Islamic Republic of)
----  IQ   Iraq (Republic of)
BIUF  IE   Ireland
BIUF  IL   Israel (State of)
BIUF  IT   Italy (Italian Republic)
-Iu-  JM   Jamaica
BIUF  JP   Japan
---f  JO   Jordan (Hashemite Kingdom of)
-IUF  KZ   Kazakhstan
---F  KE   Kenya (Republic of)
--u-  KI   Kiribati (Republic of)
----  KP   Korea (Democratic People's Republic of)
BIUF  KR   Korea (Republic of )
-I--  KW   Kuwait (State of)
--U-  KG   Kyrgyz Republic
----  LA   Lao People's Democratic Republic
-IUF  LV   Latvia (Republic of)
--U-  LB   Lebanon (Lebanese Republic)
--u-  LS   Lesotho (Kingdom of)
----  LR   Liberia (Republic of)
----  LY   Libyan Arab Jamahiriya
-I-F  LI   Liechtenstein (Principality of)
-IUF  LT   Lithuania
bIUF  LU   Luxembourg (Grand Duchy of)
-I-F  MO   Macau (Ao-me'n)
--u-  MK   Macedonia (Former Yugoslav Republic of)
--U-  MG   Madagascar (Democratic Republic of)
---f  MW   Malawi (Republic of)
bIUF  MY   Malaysia
----  MV   Maldives (Republic of)
--U-  ML   Mali (Republic of)
```

Figure 2.12 (*Continued*)

```
--u-   MT    Malta (Republic of)
--u-   MH    Marshall Islands (Republic of the)
----   MQ    Martinique (French Department of)
----   MR    Mauritania (Islamic Republic of)
--uf   MU    Mauritius
----   YT    Mayotte
BIuF   MX    Mexico (United Mexican States)
----   FM    Micronesia (Federated States of)
-IuF   MD    Moldova (Republic of)
-I--   MC    Monaco (Principality of)
----   MN    Mongolia
----   MS    Montserrat
--Uf   MA    Morocco (Kingdom of)
--Uf   MZ    Mozambique (People's Republic of)
----   MM    Myanmar (Union of)
--U-   NA    Namibia (Republic of)
--u-   NR    Nauru (Republic of)
--u-   NP    Nepal (Kingdom of)
BIUF   NL    Netherlands (Kingdom of the)
--u-   AN    Netherlands Antilles
----   NT    Neutral Zone (between Saudi Arabia and Iraq)
--U-   NC    New Caledonia
-IUF   NZ    New Zealand
-Iu-   NI    Nicaragua (Republic of)
--U-   NE    Niger (Republic of the)
--Uf   NG    Nigeria (Federal Republic of)
--u-   NU    Niue
----   NF    Norfolk Island
----   MP    Northern Mariana Islands (Commonwealth of the)
bIUF   NO    Norway (Kingdom of)
----   OM    Oman (Sultanate of)
--U-   PK    Pakistan (Islamic Republic of)
----   PW    Palau (Republic of)
-IuF   PA    Panama (Republic of)
--u-   PG    Papua New Guinea
--u-   PY    Paraguay (Republic of)
-IUf   PE    Peru (Republic of)
-IuF   PH    Philippines (Republic of the)
----   PN    Pitcairn
BIUF   PL    Poland (Republic of)
bIUF   PT    Portugal (Portuguese Republic)
bIUF   PR    Puerto Rico
----   QA    Qatar (State of)
-Iu-   RE    Re'union (French Department of)
BIuF   RO    Romania
bIUF   RU    Russian Federation
----   RW    Rwanda (Rwandese Republic)
----   SH    Saint Helena
----   KN    Saint Kitts and Nevis
--u-   LC    Saint Lucia
----   PM    Saint Pierre and Miquelon (French Department of)
--u-   VC    Saint Vincent and the Grenadines
--u-   WS    Samoa (Independent State of)
----   SM    San Marino (Republic of)
----   ST    Sao Tome and Principe (Democratic Republic of)
B---   SA    Saudi Arabia (Kingdom of)
--Uf   SN    Senegal (Republic of)
--u-   SC    Seychelles (Republic of)
----   SL    Sierra Leone (Republic of)
bIuF   SG    Singapore (Republic of)
-IUF   SK    Slovakia
-IUF   SI    Slovenia
--u-   SB    Solomon Islands
```

Figure 2.12   *(Continued)*

```
---- SO   Somalia (Somali Democratic Republic)
-IUF ZA   South Africa (Republic of)
BIUF ES   Spain (Kingdom of)
--U- LK   Sri Lanka (Democratic Socialist Republic of)
---- SD   Sudan (Democratic Republic of the)
--u- SR   Suriname (Republic of)
-I-- SJ   Svalbard and Jan Mayen Islands
--u- SZ   Swaziland (Kingdom of)
BIUF SE   Sweden (Kingdom of)
BIUF CH   Switzerland (Swiss Confederation)
---- SY   Syria (Syrian Arab Republic)
BIuF TW   Taiwan, Province of China
--uf TJ   Tajikistan
---f TZ   Tanzania (United Republic of)
-IUF TH   Thailand (Kingdom of)
--u- TG   Togo (Togolese Republic)
---- TK   Tokelau
--u- TO   Tonga (Kingdom of)
--u- TT   Trinidad and Tobago (Republic of)
-IUf TN   Tunisia
BI-F TR   Turkey (Republic of)
--u- TM   Turkmenistan
---- TC   Turks and Caicos Islands
--u- TV   Tuvalu
---f UG   Uganda (Republic of)
-IUF UA   Ukraine
---- AE   United Arab Emirates
bIUF GB   United Kingdom (United Kingdom of Great Britain and Northern Ireland)
BIUF US   United States (United States of America)
---- UM   United States Minor Outlying Islands
-IUF UY   Uruguay (Eastern Republic of)
--UF UZ   Uzbekistan
--u- VU   Vanuatu (Republic of, formerly New Hebrides)
---- VA   Vatican City State (Holy See)
-IUF VE   Venezuela (Republic of)
--U- VN   Vietnam (Socialist Republic of)
---- VG   Virgin Islands (British)
---f VI   Virgin Islands (U.S.)
---- WF   Wallis and Futuna Islands
---- EH   Western Sahara
---- YE   Yemen (Republic of)
--uf YU   Yugoslavia (Socialist Federal Republic of)
---- ZR   Zaire (Republic of)
-I-f ZM   Zambia (Republic of)
--uf ZW   Zimbabwe (Republic of)
```

Figure 2.12   *(Continued)*

12. This discussion of network administration owes much to Jay Habegger, who discusses the subject in "Understanding the Technical and Administrative Organization of the Internet." *Telecommunications*, April 1992, pp. 12–14.
13. You'll likely be surprised, as I was, at how much information you begin to acquire simply by following Internet postings like the one from which I've quoted. The ultimate goal of a guide like this one is to make you self-sufficient in terms of information, so that your Internet presence keeps you abreast of what you need to know.
14. This and other information about the Internet Society comes from a Frequently Asked Questions document available on the Society's Gopher. The address is: gopher://gopher.isoc.org:70/00/isoc/faq/what-is-ISOC.txt

3

Signing On to the Internet

Access to the Internet has changed markedly in the last few years. Until recently, most modem users signed on through a Unix shell account, a method of connecting, as I will explain shortly, that provides a perfectly workable Internet interface, albeit a character-based one. You functioned by entering commands at a system prompt, and let your service provider's computer carry out those tasks by running software under the Unix operating system. Of course, that meant learning a bit of Unix, but the commands are not difficult, and the number of them necessary for a reasonably active network presence is small.

Today, more and more providers are offering, in addition to shell accounts, so-called SLIP (Serial Line Internet Protocol) or PPP (Point-to-Point Protocol) accounts. Using these, the modem user can run the basic TCP/IP software, called a *stack*, on his or her own machine. Numerous benefits are thus achieved, perhaps the greatest of which is the ability to run graphical client programs like Mosaic and Netscape. Indeed, a wide range of freeware and shareware software is available for SLIP/PPP users; this form of connection doesn't limit you to what's on your service provider's machine, but lets you choose what you want to use to access the Net.

Mosaic helped to launch this change. A full-featured World Wide Web browser, it's also software that provides access to major Internet tools like Gopher and FTP. In that sense, it and browsers like it come close to being all-purpose Internet interfaces; they certainly point to a graphical future in which commands are stored in pull-down menus, icons provide helpful guidance through client software's capabilities, and users point and click their way across the Internet. And as more and more people wanted to use Mosaic and other graphical tools, the price of SLIP/PPP access dropped like a stone. In my area, the cost difference between a shell account and SLIP/PPP has all but vanished.

The key point to remember is that, whatever method of access you use, the underlying Internet remains the same. To use it effectively, you must remove the notion of one-stop shopping from your thinking. True, you'll be dialing in to a single telephone number to gain access to one computer as your first step. At that point, however, all resemblances between the Internet and the commercial on-line services evaporate. You will use your initial computer contact only as the first step in a worldwide journey, although it will always provide a useful home base, and it will be the site where your mail is delivered and stored, and where any files you choose to retrieve are kept. You might consider your home directory on a service provider's computer the analog to Balboa's base camp. From it, you have a glimpse of the broad Pacific.

Just a few years ago, Internet access for dial-up users was hard to acquire because there were few commercial providers. Unless you already worked for a company with network access, or had a compliant friend who was willing to let you use his or her account, you were simply out of luck. The Internet was for network users only, and the individual user with a standalone computer and modem was shut out. A different kind of service had grown up for such people—the commercial networks such as CompuServe, Prodigy, and America Online. Dial-up users, it was assumed, would stay within those confines while the Internet served the networks.

Today, all that has changed, and a growing number of companies offering dial-up access have emerged. Each of these companies lets you use computer space on their machines. That space is your foothold on the network. From there, you are in position to explore the worldwide Internet.

Opening up the Internet to the individual user brings an unprecedented expansion to the network's population, and with it, the inevitable conflicts that occur when a relatively parochial, tightly knit community must suddenly mingle with hordes of newcomers. These issues will continue to dog the Internet, but growth always brings with it a measure of frustration along with new opportunities. I have no doubt that the great rush to the network will pay off for all concerned, if we are all patient enough to help each other learn. If you'll examine the list of service providers in the glossary, you'll see that the Internet access business is vibrant. The wave of new users is by no means over.

Dial-Up Connectivity and the Client/Server Model

Dial-up connections come in several flavors. To illustrate the differences, I'm going to go through the various ways people access the Internet, both by modem and through direct network connections to office Local Area Networks and the like. This chapter will explain the differences between these access methods, by way of showing you what your dial-up connection is doing to put you on the Internet. You'll find that the full range of Internet tools—electronic mail, File Transfer Protocol, Telnet, Gopher, WAIS (Wide Area Information Servers), USENET newsgroups, and the World Wide Web—is available to you no matter which of the access models you follow (although some commercial services, as we'll see, aren't fully up to speed yet with some of the Internet tools).

If any of the access methods can be used for Internet work, what's the major difference between them? For the end user, the major answer is that some modes of access don't allow you to use the client programs of your choice. Clients are programs on computers that perform network tasks. An FTP client, for example, is a program that allows me to run FTP sessions to remote sites to download files. A Telnet client is a program that lets me log on to a remote computer and use its resources, such as searching a library catalog. Each of the Internet services we'll examine in this book is run through a client of one kind or another. But people who use shell accounts can only run the clients available on their service provider's computer. That's because a shell account doesn't give you a true network presence; it only lets you perform your work on a computer that already has such a presence. Whereas SLIP and PPP connections and, of course, full network connections through dedicated phone lines, do let you run whichever client program you choose on your machine.

Just what are these clients? The client/server model operates this way: Client programs request information from *servers,* which are programs running on other computers. There are numerous clients in varying degrees of complexity. A Macintosh user with full connectivity might use a client called WAIS for Macintosh to gain access to a wide range of Internet databases. The client makes the process of data retrieval more intuitive than it would otherwise be by providing a helpful interface that prompts the user what to do. Clients like this are available for computers ranging from MS-DOS and Windows machines to Sun workstations, from VAX computers to NeXT machines and Macintoshes.

Not all of these client programs are available to shell account users. Because they are limited to running programs on their service provider's computer, they must use the clients available *on that system.* The clients they run are character-based, which means that while they can display text on-screen, they can't handle graphics. Shell accounts are set up this way because the remote computer is treating the computer on the other end of the line as a terminal, with limited display capabilities. Don't assume that character-based clients aren't powerful; in most cases, they perform very well, making a shell account a viable way of tapping the Internet's resources. We'll see terminal-based clients in each chapter, although I'll also point out the difference by showing you a graphical client that can run the same application. Thus we'll see alternative ways of accessing the World Wide Web through programs like lynx and Netscape, and we'll sift through gigantic amounts of data using a client called archie and several graphical equivalents called Wsarchie and Anarchie. You can do everything you need to do on the network with a shell account, but if it's graphics you're after and an intuitive interface, then a SLIP or PPP connection is what you're going to want to acquire.

Take a look at Figure 3.1, which shows the World Wide Web as accessed through the character-based lynx client. Here I'm examining a terrific site at the Massachusetts Institute of Technology, one that contains the complete works of a number of authors from ancient Greece and Rome on-line. Notice that the display includes no graphics; it's all straight text characters.

Now take a look at Figure 3.2, which shows the same site viewed through the graphical client called Netscape. Not only do you get graphics, but also on-screen formatting that reminds me of a typeset document. To move about in this document, I point to an underlined link and click. With the character-based browser, I would move an on-screen pointer to get the same result.

Think of clients as the tools through which you perform your Internet chores. If you want to get something done, you need to run a client to do it. And clients are accessible in a wide variety of ways. Shell users run the clients available at their service provider's site. SLIP or PPP users run the clients they've chosen, from the vast number of shareware and freeware programs available on the network, and the growing number of commercial products. Those with direct network connections do the same thing SLIP or PPP users do, only they don't need a modem to make the connection to the Internet.

And there's yet another option. If you're a shell account user and can't find the client you need on your local machine, you can often find a client that is publicly accessible through Telnet. For example, a client at Thinking Machines Corporation lets us examine the same set of databases that the Windows-based EINet WinWAIS client does, though without the latter program's elegance and power. Although this client is not running on our local service provider's computer, it is still accessible by using Telnet to reach the

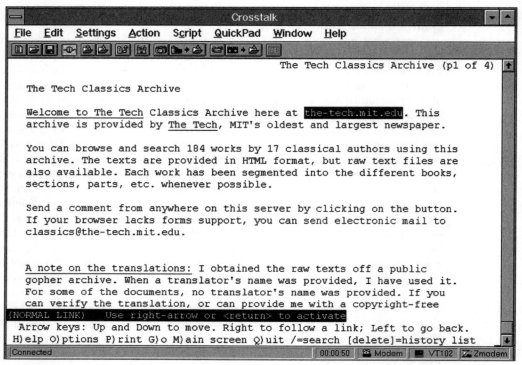

Figure 3.1   Viewing a World Wide Web site through a character-based browser.

Thinking Machines site; other clients are frequently made available in the same way, and we'll look at several.

You can always use a public site if necessary, but first check to see that your service provider doesn't have the client available locally. This minimizes the workload placed upon the network. Users of commercial services like CompuServe will find some services accessible only through Telnet; archie, for example, can be reached at a number of Telnet sites, although there is no client available through CompuServe's WinCIM interface that allows an archie search on the company's own computers. As we go through the Internet tools, I'll list public sites where clients are available.

Terminal Emulation and the Shell Account

Why can't you run all available client software with a shell account? The answer has to do with the nature of the connection. When you place a call to a service provider, you won't necessarily know (unless you ask) what kind of computer you're dialing in to. Whatever it is, your computer has to find some way of talking to it. A mainframe computer, for example, is used to dealing with terminals, which are simply screens that reflect what the mainframe is doing; terminals offer only limited functionality. You may hear such terminals referred to as *dumb terminals* because of this lack of processing muscle. Such a terminal usually contains a video display unit, a keyboard, and the circuitry to communicate with the computer to which it is connected. It can send what you

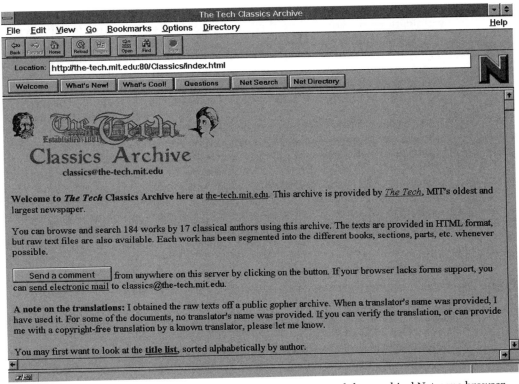

Figure 3.2 Viewing the same site with a SLIP/PPP connection and the graphical Netscape browser.

type and display what the main computer returns. Personal computers, on the other hand, offer greater processing power; they can be *smart* terminals.

The problem is, we can't always use the smarts inside our desktop machines when we make this kind of connection. Because we're not actually networked into the service provider's computer, it regards us as a terminal. To get anything to happen, our computer must emulate a terminal so the remote *host* will know what's going on. This process, called *terminal emulation,* is established through software settings. Interfaces run by terminal emulation don't always have to be dull, however. America Online, for example, has done a good job of providing a graphical interface that simplifies basic tasks for its users, and CompuServe's CIM products do the same for that network. But most Internet access providers offer the kind of straightforward, no-nonsense interface discussed here in their shell accounts, and that means learning the necessary commands and doing without graphics.

Terminal emulation is a critical feature of good communications software. It allows us, even as we pretend to be dumb terminals, to use some nonterminal features such as the ability to capture data and download files. The character-based client programs examined in this book can all be accessed over a shell account if you set your software to emulate VT-100 (VT-102 will work just as well), a terminal emulation mode tuned for Digital Equipment Corporation's computers, and widely used no matter where you go on the Internet.

Figure 3.3 shows the settings screen for Crosstalk for Windows 2.0, a popular communications program. Note that the figure shows a menu for terminal emulators.

A wide range of emulators is available. A familiar one is ANSI PC, which is commonly used to connect to bulletin board systems running on IBM-compatible platforms. There are emulators for Digital Equipment Corporation's computers, from V-T52 to VT-320, as well as emulators for Hewlett-Packard, IBM, WYSE, and others. You can't see the full list in Figure 3.3 because the menu has to be scrolled to display all the choices.

Signing On—A Personal Odyssey

Commercial access to the Internet has improved so dramatically in the past five years that newcomers will be startled to learn that there was a time when the process was excruciating, although many early treatments of the subject made it sound like a snap. "Need access? Just ask your system administrator," they blithely said, assuming you wouldn't ask if you weren't already working on a network in the first place. And indeed, if you were already on a network, the advice was sound. Many people to this day don't realize they can connect through their work site and that, in such cases, a simple request is usually enough to get them up and running.

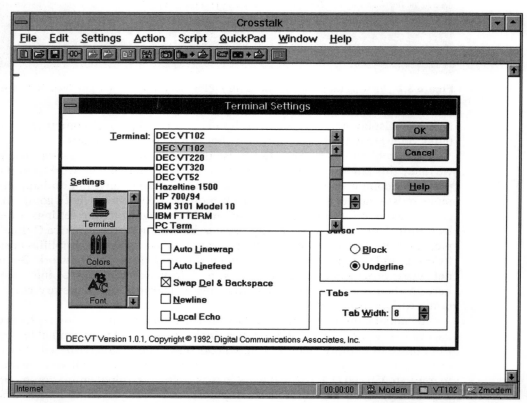

Figure 3.3 Crosstalk for Windows, terminal emulation choices from its Settings menu.

But it was a different story for anyone who was trying to log on by modem from a standalone computer. For me, logging on to the Internet became something of a crusade, deepening into obsession as I continued to run into a stone wall. Years ago, I made the mistake of asking this question: "I work out of a home office. I don't have Internet access and I don't have a system administrator. What do I do?" I asked people in my area and looked for answers on various on-line services. I peppered local bulletin boards for advice and called computer gurus in Research Triangle Park, pestering some poor souls for months.

The result? "Try the universities," some said. I called Duke, UNC, North Carolina State; access there was restricted and no one I spoke with knew how to get it. Maybe if I was a student. Unfortunately, my years at UNC had ended in the mid-1970s. "Call some of the big corporations," I was told. "Someone out there might be able to get you an account." I didn't know what I was doing, but I began to make these calls. Most people didn't know what I was talking about. Those who did seemed incredulous that I would ask. "Network connections are private," they said. Network connections private? If that doesn't give you something to think about, what does?

The Internet is not CompuServe or Prodigy. Lacking any central organization, the network has no billing address. You can't make a phone call to a network office and say, "Sign me up." You'll also get confused by the plethora of possibilities some of the people who are already on the network will tell you about. "Do you want a full connection?" they'll ask, and you reply, "Sure," not understanding why you would want anything else. "The best we can do is SLIP," you may hear. SLIP? What does it mean? And why do these people I'm talking to have nothing better to offer? Is SLIP some kind of restricted access?

It wouldn't be until CONCERT-CONNECT came along that I made my real plunge into the Internet. CONCERT-CONNECT was a service provider which, among other options, made possible local dial-up access to the Internet. It brought order into the North Carolina Internet scene by offering a flat rate per month, allowing you to log on to the computers at MCNC (formerly the Microelectronics Center of North Carolina, now known solely by its acronym, as are many computer organizations). The flat rate was attractive, as were the services; not just USENET newsgroups, but FTP and Telnet as well; not just electronic mail, but the whole panoply of features that make the Internet so fascinating.

Today, CONCERT-CONNECT is gone. In its place are a growing number of Internet service providers, each offering dial-up access. Many also offer more advanced forms of network connection, including the aforementioned SLIP and other forms of direct links all the way up to high-speed dedicated T1 and T3 lines. My new service provider is Interpath, a division of Capitol Broadcasting Corp., here in Raleigh. Interpath is representative of the new breed of service provider, offering network connections to a great variety of customers from individual home users to the largest businesses.

What a change. In every state, service providers are springing up; indeed, Internet access is becoming a growth industry, bidding fair to create a price war that will be followed by an inevitable period of consolidation. For you, the individual or small business user, the good news is that prices are dropping across the board. CONCERT-CONNECT once charged $175 per month for SLIP access; Interpath is now offering comparable service for $37.50, and regular dial-up access is cheaper still. If it's a full-service access provider you're looking for, finding one will keep getting easier. No provider in your area? There will be soon.

Even more options are appearing from the ranks of the commercial on-line services like CompuServe and America Online. In fact, all of the major on-line services now offer some form of Internet connectivity, while local bulletin board systems are opening up mail gateways and sometimes USENET access for their patrons. DELPHI and BIX moved early into the Internet world with both FTP and Telnet links in addition to electronic mail. America Online has widened its once mail-only gateway with a host of new services including the USENET newsgroups and access to Gopher, a system of menued information; its World Wide Web access will be in place by the time you read this; Prodigy's already is. CompuServe has not only offered FTP, Telnet, e-mail, and USENET; it has also made Point-to-Point Protocol access available at all its network nodes, meaning you can run client software on your own machines over a CompuServe handled TCP/IP connection. Watch for other announcements from the commercial services; they know that Internet access has become the hottest ticket in town, and they want to share in the action as the networks grow together into a true global matrix.

We will work our way up the access ladder to show you what options are available. If you are already on the Internet, you won't need to read the following unless you just want to understand why your non-networked friends seem so impatient when you talk about what you do on the network.

Using a Local Bulletin Board

The first misconception faced by Internet newcomers isn't about the Internet at all; it's about Unix. Unix is an operating system that runs on computers at a wide variety of academic and research sites around the world. Because of its built-in communications capabilities, it has been used for years to carry mail and move messages by way of a cooperative, wide-area network called UUCP. USENET news, the bulletin board style messaging service covered in Chapter 11, grew up in this Unix environment, and thus many novices assume Unix is *ipso facto* the language of the Internet community. USENET is often the first Internet-reachable tool many novices encounter, usually through a local bulletin board system (BBS) running Unix and offering the capability of logging on to some or all of its newsgroups.

We now have several Unix-based bulletin boards in my area. With any of them, you can log on and read USENET postings, responding to them as you please; you can also send electronic mail. Figure 3.4 shows the sign-on screen for one such bulletin board, a Raleigh BBS called Computer Business System. After calling its number, this is what is displayed after a brief log-in message.

Ah, the Internet Catch again. Here we have a tool that will guide you into your first glimpse of the Internet, but in true Unix fashion, it's cryptic. You have to prowl around, in this case entering a **?**, to find out what's available. By working through the help system, the new user discovers how to access USENET newsgroups. Figure 3.5 shows the section of the Help menu that's applicable.

Entering **new** at the prompt displays messages that have come in since your last login. The **read** command will also suffice if you want to examine other messages. The help message says we can change the message base by entering the number of the board at the main prompt, although how we learn which number to enter isn't yet clear. The **join** command lets us add USENET newsgroups, and so on. Note, too, that we're presented with mail options. The other major form of connectivity that such bulletin boards provide is an electronic mail address for Internet access.

```
*   Please enter your account name and password.

*   Accounts names on this system single words, rather than the first and last
    name. For example,

        Login or NEW: jsmith
        Password:

*   If you do not have an account, type NEW to sign up.

Login or NEW: paulg
Password:

    Logging in: paulg

Previous login: 13-Jan-93


No mail

[#1: General Forum]
9:53a (?=help!) -
```

Figure 3.4   The sign-on screen from a BBS.

We could continue working through the menus, but it would be pointless to do so, because local bulletin board connections are frequently modified by their system operators, and they often have their own software quirks. You have to explore your area to find which BBS systems have some kind of connectivity, and then call to see what's available.

The downside to connectivity such as this, in addition to not offering FTP and Telnet, is that such systems are usually available only through a limited number of tele-

```
MAIL    - Send electronic mail between users. Once in MAIL, either enter the
          user's name you want to contact, or SEND and then the user's name. If
          you have mail, the system will tell you.  MAIL supports aliasing and a
          carbon-copy feature.

NEW     - Read all new messages (since your last call) on all forums.

OFF     - Another way to LOGOUT.

PLAN    - To augment information displayed with the FINGER command, type PLAN to
          enter a message that can be seen by other users when someone FINGERs
          you.

POST    - Enter a message on BBS. Select a relevant subject for your message.
          Type your message, ending it with /ex. Then SAVE. See HELP EDITOR for
          information on how to use the editor.

READ    - Read messages on BBS. To change the message base ("forum"), type the
          number of the board at the main prompt.
```

Figure 3.5   A help screen on a typical BBS.

phone lines. Prepare yourself for busy signals when you're trying to sign on to read your favorite newsgroups. Many local BBS systems, too, carry only a fraction of the total available number of newsgroups, so you may have to lobby the system operator to add a group you're particularly interested in.

But don't overlook the tremendous upside of these systems. Although they're still relatively rare, a growing number of BBSs with USENET hooks are becoming activated as interest in Internet-related activities grows. For a great many people, a local BBS will be the first glimpse of the worldwide community of users that is the Internet. These callers will have the chance to learn gradually, working through the USENET newsgroups and asking questions of local people and their own system operator as they go. The system operators of these bulletin boards have a great deal to do with the recent explosion of interest in the Internet.

Next-Generation Bulletin Board Systems

In recent months, more and more BBS packages running a variety of operating systems have appeared with Internet links, often electronic mail, but now including expanded access to network resources like FTP, Telnet, and even, experimentally, the World Wide Web. The example if Figure 3.6 shows the main screen at Micro Message Service, a BBS here in Raleigh that includes, as do most BBS systems, file libraries, links to the worldwide FidoNet echo conferencing system, and the usual utilities. But look further, for Micro Message Service also has Internet links aplenty. You can see the Internet menu in Figure 3.7.

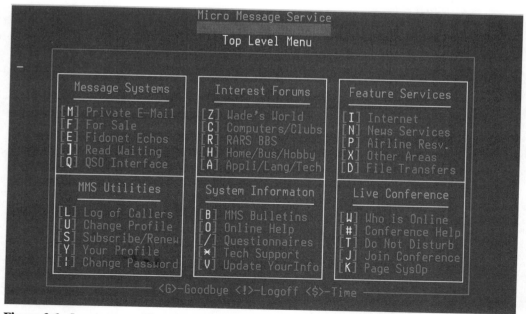

Figure 3.6 Logging on at Micro Message Service, a BBS in Raleigh, North Carolina with a wide range of Internet capabilities.

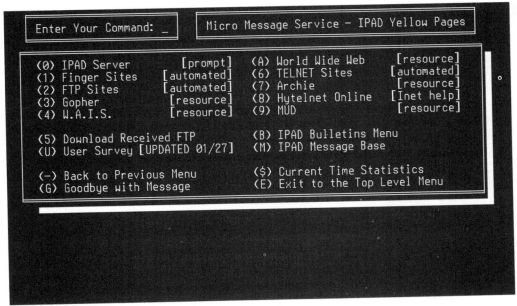

```
 ┌────────────────────────────────┐ ┌──────────────────────────────────────┐
 │ Enter Your Command:  _         │ │ Micro Message Service - IPAD Yellow Pages │
 └────────────────────────────────┘ └──────────────────────────────────────┘
 ┌─────────────────────────────────────────────────────────────────────────┐
 │  (0) IPAD Server       [prompt]      (A) World Wide Web    [resource]     │
 │  (1) Finger Sites      [automated]   (6) TELNET Sites      [automated]    │
 │  (2) FTP Sites         [automated]   (7) Archie            [resource]     │
 │  (3) Gopher            [resource]    (8) Hytelnet Online   [Inet help]    │
 │  (4) W.A.I.S.          [resource]    (9) MUD               [resource]     │
 │                                                                           │
 │  (5) Download Received FTP           (B) IPAD Bulletins Menu              │
 │  (U) User Survey [UPDATED 01/27]     (M) IPAD Message Base                │
 │                                                                           │
 │  (-) Back to Previous Menu           ($) Current Time Statistics          │
 │  (G) Goodbye with Message            (E) Exit to the Top Level Menu       │
 └─────────────────────────────────────────────────────────────────────────┘
```

Figure 3.7 The main Internet screen at Micro Message Service.

Notice the range here, which formerly would have been out of reach of a local **BBS** system like Micro Message Service. We can use not only Telnet, Gopher, WAIS, FTP, archie, and finger, but **SLIP/PPP** access is soon to be implemented (we'll discuss why this is important later in this chapter). Along with it, World Wide Web access through **Mosaic** is on the horizon, while both USENET and Internet Relay Chat (IRC) are already available. Micro Message Service is using an access tool known as the Internet Protocol Adapter (IPAD) to work this magic; at the time of this writing, IPAD remained experimental, but Micro Message Service was one of four BBS systems chosen to perform alpha testing.

Today's BBS systems tend to offer a variety of display options. You can stick with straight VT-100 emulation, or you can turn on ANSI graphics by choosing that option from your communications software. Another possibility is RIP (Remote Imaging Protocol), a graphics display engine from TeleGrafix Communications, Inc. RIPterm, the company's terminal package, allows you, once equipped with the proper software on your own computer, to work with a more graphical interface which can use a mouse and point-and-click commands.

BBS packages now proliferate; space prohibits discussing them all. You will see systems from Galacticomm (The Major BBS), which includes RIP support, and Searchlight BBS (from Searchlight Software), also including RIP. Digital Dynamics produces a RIP-supporting BBS system called Synchronet BBS, while Dynamis Software's Tera BBS brings a complete mouse-driven environment to the Unix operating system. Other systems include WWIV (WWIV Software Services) and PC Board. Whatever software your local BBS is running, you're likely to find that Internet access is becoming an option on more and more menus. Keep your eye on this fast-changing Internet access option.

Finding Local Bulletin Boards

How can you find local bulletin boards with e-mail access, USENET newsgroups, and more? It can be a tough proposition unless you keep your ear to the ground. If a computer user group in your area is tracking bulletin board activity, they may provide a list of local boards. In my area, an umbrella organization called the Triangle Computer Society maintains a monthly listing of all active boards; your area may also boast such a group. Ask questions in the computer community, at retail stores, and on any bulletin boards you already frequent. And don't forget your newsstand. *Boardwatch Magazine, CONNECT,* and *Online Access* all track on-line developments; although these magazines have been heavily BBS-oriented in the past, they're expanding their coverage of the Internet and, in particular, the links between local BBSs and the Net. New journals are certain to arise as well.

You could also tap into NixPub, a useful list of open-access Unix sites worldwide. Compiled by Phil Eschallier, NixPub is a superb resource, and represents the kind of thing the Internet does best—the open contribution of information to help others. Of course, NixPub is also a prime example of the Internet Catch at work. How do you get it? Through the Internet. What's one way to access the Internet? By using the Nix-Pub list.

So, while the following tells you where to find the list on-line, you will also find information from the most recent version (at the time of this printing) of the NixPub list in the appendix. Later, we will examine the tools that can help you get it for yourself on-line. When you do that, you can update your information as new lists appear.

What You Need: A List of Public Access Unix Sites

The Document: The NixPub List

How to Get It:
- Use anonymous FTP. The URL is: ftp://vfi.paramax.com/pub/pubnet/. There are actually two NixPub files, one the long listing (which is what I advise you to get) and the second a condensed version. The file names are nixpub.long and nixpub.short. We discuss anonymous FTP in Chapter 5.
- Use electronic mail. Send a message to mail-server@bts.com. The body of your message should contain the following: **get pub nixpub.long** or **get pub nixpub.short.** If you want to subscribe to the NixPub electronic mailing list, and receive future versions in your mailbox automatically, send mail to the same address with this text: **subscribe nixpub-list** *your_name.* We discuss how to use electronic mail in Chapter 7.
- Find the list on USENET. It is posted regularly to the newsgroups comp.misc, comp.bbs.misc, and alt.bbs. We discuss USENET in Chapter 11.

The Free-Net Advantage

A Free-Net is a superb idea; if there were more of them, Internet access wouldn't be as complicated as it sometimes is today. A Free-Net, created by volunteers and maintained by people who believe in networking, is a computer system with two goals: to broaden a community's access base to local computing resources, and to provide hooks into the broader world of networking. To do this, Free-Nets tap Internet connections, and that means they're a way for users to log on without the usual hassles. Access is usually restricted to electronic mail and some Telnet capabilities. On the plus side, Free-Nets generally provide easy-to-use menus.

The idea behind Free-Nets is to make telecommunications resources available to all; audience building is what this initiative is all about. Think of National Public Radio (absent any federal funding); then apply the concept to computing. Free-Nets are the brainchild of the National Public Telecomputing Network, or NPTN, which is based in Cleveland, Ohio. By helping organizers in various parts of the United States, NPTN hopes to construct a network similar to what its media-based counterparts have created, only with the added resources of computing power to spread information. A key word is cybercasting, the dissemination of network services to NPTN affiliates around the country, supplementing local data with high-quality information feeds for all.

Free-Nets, though, aren't yet common. Perhaps the best known is the Cleveland Free-Net, which was the testbed for the concept, and remains a driving force behind Free-Net development nationally. The Cleveland Free-Net is accessible through the Internet, as are its relatives such as Tri-State Online and the Heartland Free-Net. Keep a lookout in your area for Free-Net development. These systems can get you up and running on the Internet faster than any other. Figure 3.8 shows what the Cleveland Free-Net looks like when you sign on from the Internet. The screen will be slightly different when you call directly to the site.

The Free-Net concept involves community access and involvement, so it's no surprise to find a heavy emphasis on making the system workable for computer novices. Look at the basic menus of the Cleveland Free-Net shown in Figure 3.9 and you'll see what I mean. They're based on the concept of the town hall, with the various services broken out as menu options. The metaphor is that of a town itself; you move through an on-line city, making choices as you go.

Choice 14, for example, *The Communications Center*, breaks into a submenu which offers access to electronic mail, other computer systems, and file transfer options. You also have access to university library systems, databases on agriculture, space science, weather, oceanography, and geography, not to mention USENET news and a host of other features. The menu system is simple to use, but as you begin to find your way around the Internet, mastering the commands on whatever system you use to access its resources, you may find yourself wishing for a leaner interface. Nonetheless, it's hard to imagine an easier introduction to the Internet for the novice than a Free-Net. The only problem: Unless you have a local Free-Net, tapping Free-Net resources isn't going to be workable unless you're already on the Internet. So find out what's happening in your area about Free-Nets; a complete list of Free-Nets, as compiled by the National Public Telecomputing Network, is found in the appendix, along with full contact information by telephone, modem and Telnet.

Keeping Up with Free-Nets

Because new Free-Nets are coming on-line all the time, you will want to keep up with their activity. Using the methods you will learn later in this book, you can do so by using anonymous FTP to a site that contains Free-Net materials.

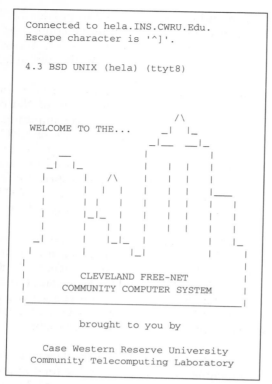

Figure 3.8 The introductory screen to the Cleveland Free-Net.

What You Need: Up-to-Date, Renewable Free-Net Information

How to Get It: Use anonymous FTP. The URL is:

ftp://nptn.org/pub/nptn.info/

Here you will find several files of interest: nptn.affil-organ.list is a list of Free-Nets now in service; another file, starting.Free-Net, explains how Free-Nets are created; and a third, cpc-us.txt, is a discussion by Tom Grundner about the philosophy behind the Free-Net concept.

Commercial On-Line Services

Here we need to be careful with terminology. Commercial on-line services refers to operations like CompuServe, DELPHI, and America Online. Before the Internet became a viable option, these and other services were the primary destination of the modem user who wanted to tap into extensive text databases, retrieve stock quotes, make computerized airline reservations, or join worldwide discussion groups. And, as we have already seen, these services are not the same animal to which I refer as an Internet service provider.

```
< CLEVELAND FREE-NET DIRECTORY >

 1 The Administration Building
 2 The Post Office
 3 Public Square
 4 The Courthouse & Government Center
 5 The Arts Building
 6 Science and Technology Center
 7 The Medical Arts Building
 8 The Schoolhouse (Academy One)
 9 The Community Center & Recreation Area
10 The Business and Industrial Park
11 The Library
12 University Circle
13 The Teleport
14 The Communications Center
15 NPTN/USA TODAY HEADLINE NEWS
16 < SPECIAL FEATURES >
------------------------------------------------
h=Help, x=Exit Free-Net, "go help"=extended help

Your Choice ==
```

Figure 3.9   An upper-level menu on the Cleveland Free-Net.

The difference? Local service providers offer you a way to get onto the Internet by dialing in to their own computers, which are, in turn, linked directly to the Internet. When you called CompuServe or DELPHI, on the other hand, historically, you were connecting to an on-line service's mainframe computer, and using whatever features it made available for its members. These commercial services, until recently, were a world unto themselves. CompuServe members didn't run into BIX members, and GEnie participants usually didn't log on to DELPHI.

All that is changing rapidly, however, as the idea of Internet access takes hold. Today, all the major commercial on-line services have set up connections of some kind to the Internet. These connections began with electronic mail gateways, but soon grew to include other service options as well. CompuServe now offers FTP, Telnet, and USENET newsgroups through its CIM software, and its recent roll-out of Point-to-Point Protocol access means that users can now count on their CompuServe account to give them access to the World Wide Web. America Online and Prodigy have similarly opened up links to the Web, while firming up other Internet tools; America Online was quick to get into this arena with early offerings of Gopher and USENET. DELPHI and BIX have offered full FTP and Telnet capabilities for some time now.

And even if your service offers little more than electronic mail to the Internet, you can still do a lot with it, including requesting and receiving programs and other files (they're sent to you in the form of messages, which you must run through decoding routines to restore to their natural state), following mailing lists and their wide range of discussions, and retrieving a wealth of valuable background information about the Internet. An e-mail link and a little ingenuity can produce startling results—you can even search directories and hunt down programs at remote sites by using the mail versions of Internet tools like archie and WAIS.

Chapter 8 focuses on using the Internet through e-mail alone. Some of the workarounds are cumbersome, but the results may allow you to do everything you need to do.

Nonetheless, as you explore the increasingly wide range of Internet options made available through your account, you'll probably want to move beyond the world of e-mail and into the broader connectivity now provided by these companies. That being said, let's take a look at how two major firms are offering Internet access through their previously closed systems.

CompuServe as Internet Service Provider

CompuServe's collection of on-line databases, user forums, and wide variety of news and information sources has made it one of the premium commercial services. Like most such companies, CompuServe began its Internet access with an electronic mail connection through a gateway, prompting many users to experiment with the broad range of services accessible through mail alone. But links to FTP and Telnet soon followed, all of them managed through the CompuServe Information Manager (CIM) interface. The recent announcement of Point-to-Point Protocol access further widens CompuServe's scope, since it allows any user who chooses them to run third-party programs like Mosaic rather than CIM.

But it's safe to say that the average CompuServe user will enter the Internet through the CIM gateway, at least until he or she develops the necessary experience to venture further onto the Net. In Figure 3.10, you can see the result of giving the **GO FTP** command to move to CompuServe's file transfer area.

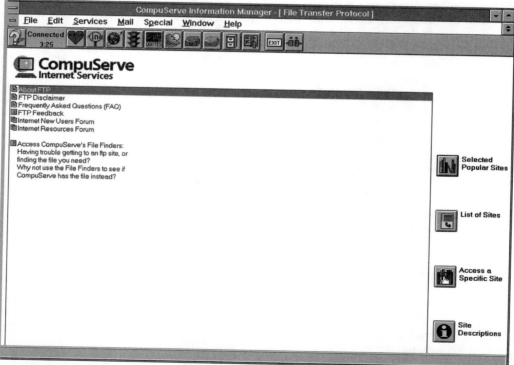

Figure 3.10   CompuServe's file transfer area allows you to download files from the Internet.

As you can see, a number of background documents are provided to bring the Compu-Serve user up to speed on how to use this area, while accessing a site involves clicking on an icon labeled Access a Specific Site. Taking that option, you will see the screen in Figure 3.11. Here we can enter the necessary site information to open a connection to any of the thousands of computers that make files available to the public on the Internet.

The thing to notice about these figures is the CIM interface itself (in this case, you are seeing WinCIM, the version for Microsoft Windows, but a Macintosh version exists as well). Here we are using terminal emulation, but of a different kind than the VT-100 emulation previously discussed. The remote computer is working with the software on our own system to draw a screen that is relatively painless to use. Its pull-down menus, icons, and mouse support allow us to click on what we want to do or see, making net-work exploration easier for the novice. The downside of such software is that it slows operations. I can move through a file download session much faster with a straight Unix shell account than through WinCIM.

The engaging thing about the CIM interface is that it is shared by so many people. For the novice, moving onto the Internet using CIM is made somewhat less intimidating, because users know they are working with the same interface that everyone else on CompuServe is seeing. When network glitches arise, as they invariably do, sorting them out on one of the user forums is thus simplified. And CompuServe maintains two forums for that purpose. The first is the Internet New User's Forum, where questions

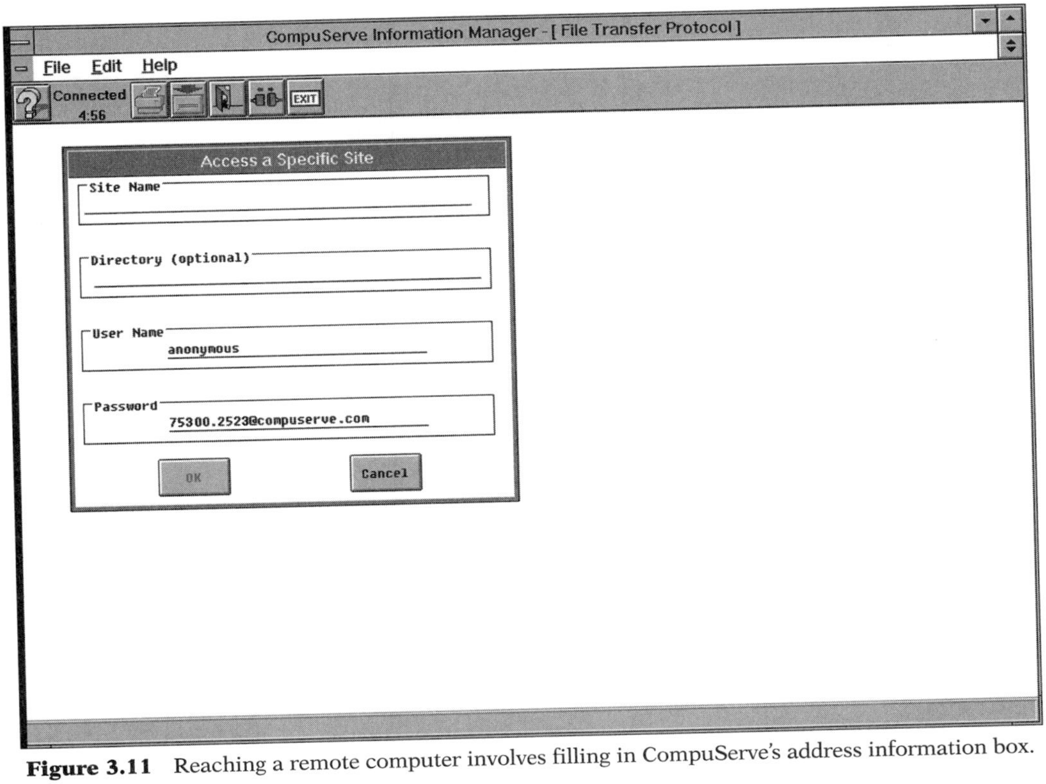

Figure 3.11 Reaching a remote computer involves filling in CompuServe's address information box.

about the Internet itself and questions of access may be asked of an audience comprised of old network hands and newcomers alike. The second, the Internet Resources Forum, is designed to categorize Internet offerings, helping users to find what they need through an extensive file library. Either can be reached by giving the **GO INTERNET** command.

CompuServe users can also use Telnet, an Internet protocol that allows you to take the controls of a remote computer to use the resources available there. When you give the **GO TELNET** command on CompuServe, you are shown a dialog box in which you can enter the address of the computer you want to contact. By entering that information, you can be whisked off to that computer to run the software available there. In Figure 3.12, I have set up a Telnet session with the Library of Congress. I can use this session to search the catalog of this mammoth collection, or to examine other data catalogs available at the site. When I am through, I use the remote computer's sign-off command, which is shown on its menu system, to return to CompuServe.

With USENET access likewise provided, CompuServe offers a great many of the tools the Internet requires through a usable and friendly interface. You will pay $4.80 an hour to access the entire range of these services, including Point-to-Point Protocol (the latter running under different software than WinCIM). CompuServe also requires a monthly fee of $8.95. Network novices will thus find CompuServe a good place to learn the ropes, while those who plan to use the Internet extensively will want to compare prices with local access providers, many of whom offer a flat rate plan that CompuServe

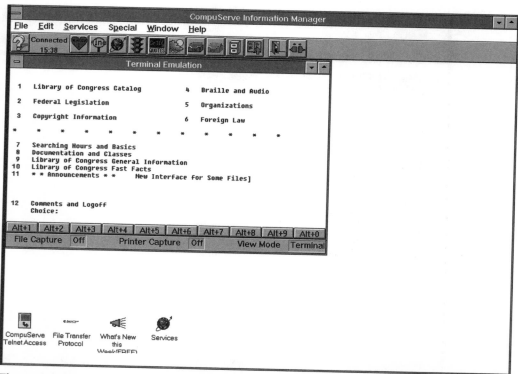

Figure 3.12 CompuServe sets up Telnet sessions in a box within its CIM interface.

has not yet implemented. As usual, the key is to weigh cost against services; for many, the additional access to CompuServe's own resources and the availability of the Internet support forums will justify paying a higher charge. And by making PPP access available at all its nodes, CompuServe certainly provides ready access for people whose jobs require extensive traveling.

What You Need: Further Information about CompuServe

Where to Get It: Call 800-848-8199

America Online as an Internet Gateway

Like CompuServe, America Online moved quickly into the Internet business by offering its large consumer base an electronic mail gateway to the Internet. The company then shored up its position by offering USENET newsgroups to its customers, along with access to the menued systems of information called Gophers. You can also tap a system of databases called Wide Area Information Servers through America Online. Figure 3.13 shows you the main Internet screen. Notice that several background documents about the Internet are provided, along with access options shown in the form of icons.

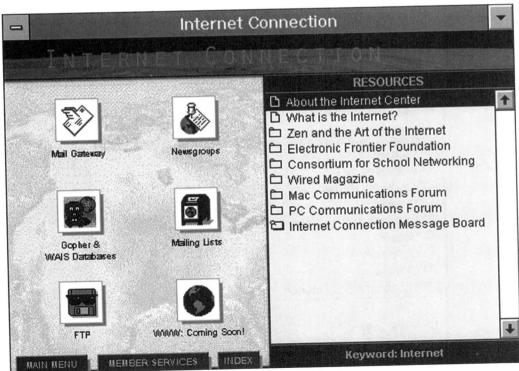

Figure 3.13   America Online's main Internet screen; note the use of icons.

Like CompuServe's, the America Online interface makes liberal use of pull-down menus and icons. An additional benefit of using such an interface is that its designers have tried to categorize network resources. In Figure 3.14, for example, you can see the screen that appears when you click on the Gopher & WAIS icon. Notice that information is shown broken out by category, so that you can home in on what you want to see.

One of the major problems about using the Internet is the fact that its resources are so hard to find. You know that with gigabytes of data on-line, there has to be something that meets your need to learn more about geology, for example, but where do you look? We'll see in later chapters that a variety of search and browsing tools exist, but newcomers will find the America Online interface an easy way to get started. Figure 3.15 shows a Gopher specializing in geology that I uncovered by moving through the topics on the initial Gopher & WAIS screen.

The downside of structured menus of information is that you are dependent upon what the composer of the menu has chosen to show you. As we'll see, Internet search tools can help us move beyond this problem by letting us use keywords to search a large number of filenames or Gopher menu items. Whether you will find the restrictions of working with a predetermined menu too confining depends upon your information needs. Certainly America Online makes it possible to experience many of the Internet's major tools to find out whether you will need a broader network presence. Its $9.95 per month tariff includes five free hours, with additional hours billed at $2.95 each.

And it's likewise true that America Online is planning to expand its presence. In February 1995, the company announced that it had closed its acquisition of the assets of

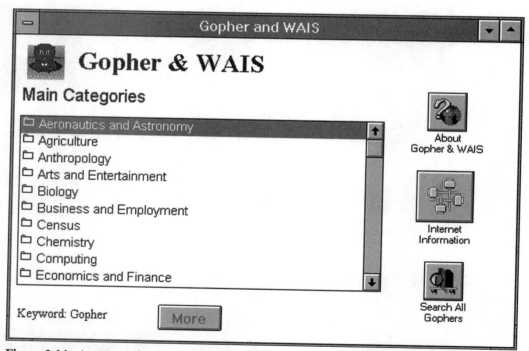

Figure 3.14 America Online breaks Gopher and WAIS information down by category, although its listing is representative rather than complete.

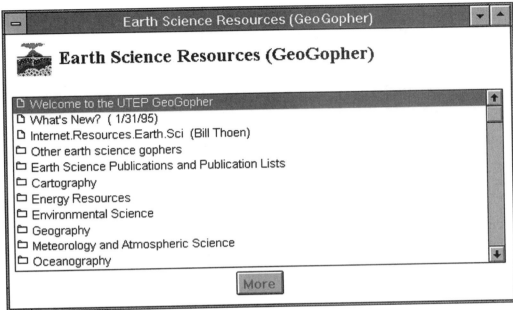

Figure 3.15 A specialized Gopher found by browsing the categories on America Online.

Advanced Network & Services, Inc. (ANS), the company that created the Internet backbone. The $35 million deal is proof that America Online intends to expand its Internet connectivity significantly, with a movement into the World Wide Web and other Internet resources all but assured.

What You Need: More Information about America Online

How to Get It: Call 800-827-6364

The Changing Nature of Commercial Online Services

When Prodigy Services Company announced it had launched AstraNet, an independent service that offers content on the World Wide Web, it became clear that all the major commercial services had taken the Internet seriously. AstraNet is already accessible to anyone with World Wide Web access (http://www.astranet.com); you can see it in Figure 3.16. Prodigy has also developed its own World Wide Web browser that will allow

What You Need: More Information about Prodigy's Internet services

How to Get It: Call 800-776-3449

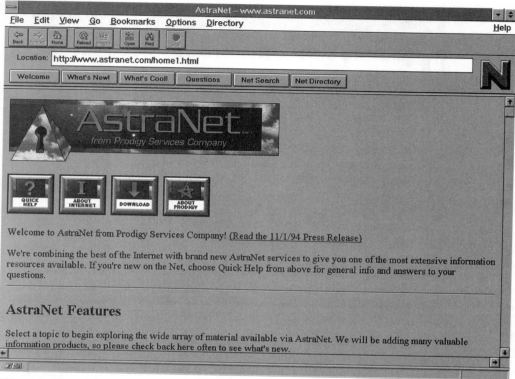

Figure 3.16 Prodigy's AstraNet is a foothold on the World Wide Web that the company plans to expand.

Prodigy members to access not just AstraNet, but the rest of the Web, through an interactive, visual environment.

DELPHI and BIX were the first two commercial on-line services to offer full Internet access, by which I mean not only electronic mail, but file transfer through FTP, Telnet, Gopher, and the complete range of Internet tools. Access has been text-based, though, preventing you from using browsing tools like Mosaic, but DELPHI is working on the development of a Windows-based interface that will bring graphical features to its service. At the time of this writing, BIX and DELPHI were in the process of merging their services, one of presumably a number of changes that will occur under new owner Rupert Murdoch.

What is intriguing about the onset of the commercial services is the degree to which they alter our conventional view of Internet access. Several years ago, the CompuServes

What You Need: More Information about DELPHI/BIX

How to Get It: Call 617-491-3342

and America Onlines of this world were closed systems. If you were a member of one, you couldn't send mail to another. By firming up Internet options, these services become visible in a new light. They can be seen as part of a worldwide system of connecting information providers, and their content, as much as their access capability, is what distinguishes them from the competition. It is not unreasonable to suppose that the great battle between Internet services will be fought over who can enrich the network's content; after all, within a few years, getting the data pipeline to most locations will be a *fait accompli*. Each provider will try to outdo the other in terms of price and value-added services, while all the time battling with the local and national Internet providers whose sole mission is connectivity through a variety of interfaces. The commercial services, of course, will be accessible through the Internet, as opposed to the strictly local Points of Presence they now use for most of their customers.

While I use a local service provider for the bulk of my Internet work, I maintain accounts on the commercial services because of their databases and the targeted nature of their forums and special interest groups. Because they are moderated, these electronic discussion areas often keep conversations on topic better than the more free-form newsgroups of USENET; they therefore provide a valuable adjunct to what is already available on the Internet itself. Rather than independent bastions of connectivity, then, the commercial services begin to resemble something like television networks, each with its own set of programming, all flowing over the same communications medium. This is surely the model that we will follow as the Internet expands into tomorrow's information infrastructure.

Commercial Dial-Up Providers

We're victims of our own terminology. Isn't dialing up what you do with a local bulletin board in the first place? Aren't you using your modem to place a call, and isn't that what dialing up means? You'd think so. But we have to distinguish between calling a bulletin board system and calling in to a full-fledged service provider. Most bulletin boards have their own agenda, which may or may not include some kind of hooks into USENET, Internet mail, and other services. Bulletin boards may or may not charge a usage fee.

Think of a *service provider* as someone who makes Internet access a business. This access may come in several guises, as we'll see, and the range of capabilities is up to you, your provider, and your wallet, but moving to this level is almost guaranteed to give you greater functionality and, if you choose, access to things like FTP, Telnet and graphical tools like Netscape.

Running a Shell Account

A shell account connection to the Internet is relatively straightforward. You use your modem to place a call to a computer that already has network access. You log on to this remote system and perform your Internet work with its help. The number of service providers offering such connections is growing rapidly, and the cost is reasonable. Usually, you can get by for $20 to $30 per month, sometimes with a per-hour fee tacked on, sometimes not.

Consider The World, run by Software Tool & Die in Brookline, Massachusetts. The World offers a full panoply of Internet services, including electronic mail, FTP for file transfers, Telnet for remote login to distant computers, USENET newsgroups, and in general, the whole range of Internet features covered later in this book. The World is a local call from Boston, but Software Tool & Die has also made arrangements for connections through CompuServe Packet Network, which means you can call a local number and pay an hourly access fee that's a lot lower than you'd pay through long-distance charges.

The World offers several rate packages. You can pay $5 per month and $2 per hour, or $20 per month and an additional $1 per hour for any time over the 20-hour limit. The charge for access through the CompuServe network is an additional $5.60 per hour. Disk storage in varying amounts is also provided depending on which plan you choose.

Shell account usage is best illustrated by examining what happens when you download a file from the Internet through the mediation of a service provider. Compare the situation with what happens when you download a file from a commercial on-line service. When you call a commercial service such as CompuServe or America Online, your work will involve a direct connection between you and the host computers. Ask to download a file and the file will be sent directly to you, ending on your hard disk. You can watch the modem lights flicker to signal the incoming data.

This is not the case with a shell account connection to the Internet. Here, when you download a file through FTP procedures, the file is downloaded not to your computer but to *the computer to which you are connected, that is, the service provider's computer.* When I go into a remote computer using Telnet through my connection at Interpath in Raleigh, I am tapping my provider's resources to help me do my work. The file I retrieve doesn't come directly to me (the modem's lights don't flash); rather, it's sent directly to the Interpath computer over high-speed links and is stored on disk there. I must then download it to my own computer, flashing modem lights and all. So the file transfer process is a two-step procedure. Understand this paradigm or a shell account won't make sense to you.

SLIP/PPP—Graphical Internet Access

The appearance of Mosaic, a graphical World Wide Web browser, brought unprecedented attention to the idea of moving through the Internet by pointing and clicking at resources, rather than entering commands. Mosaic and the next-generation Netscape product changed the nature of the Internet game. Before, a shell account was the soundest route to the Internet for individual users and small businesses alike. But because shell users aren't actually on the Internet, they can't run the graphical client programs that have become so popular. For that, you need a way to move data packets directly between the Internet and your own computer, thus allowing you to run any client programs you choose.

Serial Line Internet Protocol (SLIP) and Point-to-Point Protocol (PPP) are, as you have seen, the two methods for doing this. While you're still dialing up a remote computer, you're able to use software on your own machine—called a TCP/IP stack—to handle the complicated protocols that make the Internet function. The model is completely different from what you saw with a shell account. The FTP session that used to be a two-part process—download the file to your service provider, and thence to your own computer—now takes place in one step, with the data coming directly to your machine. All other Internet protocols work in a similar way, giving you total control over how you manage your own network connection.

A variety of TCP/IP stacks exist, and as a new SLIP/PPP user, you may at first be intimidated by the question of which one to use; for that matter, you will also need software to make the telephone connection with your provider. But in truth, many of the service providers who have traditionally offered shell account access are now moving into the SLIP/PPP environment. The best answer to which stack to use, then, is to take your service provider's suggestion. These companies are in the business of offering Internet connectivity; they will provide software packages that are known to work with their systems.

Several TCP/IP stacks in particular stand out as you evaluate the options. You may want to know about these, because no matter what your service provider offers by way of software, you'll find it interesting to compare the clients that other developers make available. I started my own SLIP/PPP work with NetManage Chameleon, but later moved on to Trumpet International's Trumpet Winsock, a shareware program that does everything I need it to do. Here is some information about good choices for Microsoft Windows machines and Macintoshes.

TRUMPET WINSOCK 2.0
TRUMPET SOFTWARE INTERNATIONAL PTY LTD.
GPO Box 1649
Hobart, Tasmania
Australia 7001
Voice: +61-02-450220 (international); 002-450220 (Australia)
Fax: +61-02-450210 (international); 002-450210 (Australia)
mailto:tech-support@trumpet.com.au

If you're planning to experiment with different TCP/IP stacks, this is the place to begin. Trumpet Winsock is shareware; if you like the program, you send the author a $25 registration fee. Having worked with a number of TCP/IP stacks in the Windows environment, I've found that Trumpet Winsock delivers excellent performance at a fraction of the cost. Of course, the package does not include the kind of technical support you would expect from a commercial vendor, nor is Trumpet Winsock a full-featured package of client programs like Chameleon. Nonetheless, I think the more experimentally minded will find this software well worth a look. Here's how to get it.

What You Need: Trumpet Winsock 2.0

Where to Get It: The software is available at numerous sites around the Internet. Try the following URLs:

ftp://ftp.utas.edu.au/pc/trumpet/winsock/

ftp://ftp.trumpet.com.au/ftp/pub/winsock/

ftp://ftp.cica.indiana.edu/pub/pc/win3/winsock/

At the time of this writing, the filename was twsk20a.zip.

INTERNET CHAMELEON 4.1
NETMANAGE INC.
10725 N. De Anza Blvd.
Cupertino, CA 95014
Voice: 408-973-7171
Fax: 408-257-6405
mailto: support@netmanage.com

At a list price of $199, this Windows-based stack and suite of software applications has proven a popular way to connect to the Internet. An interesting addition to the newest version of Chameleon is called Instant Internet, which simplifies the configuration process enormously by offering scripts for connection to access providers like Alternet, CERFnet, IBM Internet, InterRamp (from PSINet), and Portal.

SUPERTCP PRO
FRONTIER TECHNOLOGIES CORP.
10201 N. Port Washington Rd.
Mequon, WS 53092
Voice: 800-929-3054 or 414-241-4555
Fax: 414-241-7084
mailto: supertcppro @frontiertech.com

Frontier's SuperTCP Pro sells for $595, which includes a program called WinTapestry, a full-featured World Wide Web browser that contains integrated FTP, Telnet, and Gopher, thus placing it squarely into competition with browsers like Netscape. E-mail clients for electronic mail and USENET news are also provided. Frontier has also announced the $149 SuperHighway Access for Windows 4.0, which includes a variety of client programs and an easy-to-use installation procedure.

MacTCP

This is the TCP/IP stack for the Macintosh, and the good news about it is that it is now built into the Mac's operating system. Since System 7.5, Apple has been building MacTCP in (we're seeing the same trend in the Windows world, where both Microsoft's new version of Windows and IBM's OS/2 Warp are being shipped with built-in TCP/IP connectivity).

If you don't already own MacTCP, you can get a copy direct from Apple Computer by upgrading to System 7.5. At the time of this writing, the version in use was 2.0.6. You can also contact the Apple Programmers & Developers Association (APDA) at 800-282-2732 to order MacTCP; in addition, many mail-order dealers sell the product. Because Apple is the supplier for MacTCP, all Macintosh Internet applications will work with it.

If you're a Mac user, of course, your service provider will include MacTCP in the software provided when you open your account. And a good service provider will also offer a complete set of instructions on how to set up that account, along with the relevant information that will need to be entered into the TCP/IP software for the connection to work. Nothing proves the value of a good help desk than SLIP/PPP, which can be complicated to install but well worth the effort. Once it's up and running, you shouldn't need to tinker with the stack again.

By providing a halfway station between dedicated Internet access through a leased telephone line and dial-up capabilities, SLIP and PPP give you most of the benefits of high-speed access, though, naturally, at a slower rate of data transmission. And because you can run client software on your machine, you can take advantage of the huge collection of shareware and freeware client programs that are freely available on the Internet. If you read, for example, about a new client that helps you search databases, like the EINet WinWAIS program we'll examine in Chapter 13, you can locate a copy online, download it directly to your computer, and run it there. If you don't like it, nothing is lost; if it works for you, you can pay the shareware fee (if there is one) and proceed in a graphical environment that will make the character-based shell account seem lean.

Using such clients can be of large or little benefit depending upon your needs. You may find that Internet access, even using terminal emulation in a shell account, can provide so many possibilities that it will suffice. In my own work, I frequently use my shell account when I need to go quickly to a given resource and get back out again; shell accounts often run faster than their SLIP/PPP counterparts because of the heavily graphical nature of the SLIP/PPP client software. But if getting client software up and running is a major issue for you, then a SLIP/PPP connection will make sense. Graphical browsers like Mosaic and Netscape may be enough on their own to tempt you into the universe of SLIP/PPP. We'll discuss both graphical and character-based tools as we make our way through the network.

The Evolving User Interface

While SLIP/PPP accounts make it possible to use client programs with graphical features, it's also true that the need for a friendly front end to the Internet has come to preoccupy commercial service providers of all stripes. We've already seen that both CompuServe and America Online have used terminal emulation to produce graphical interfaces that take away the burden of having to memorize complicated command statements. In like manner, other national providers have moved to broaden the network's appeal to a less technologically savvy audience. For many people, it's not so much how the interface is generated that matters as what they can do with that interface. Let's now take a look at three such providers and what they can offer.

THE PIPELINE:
THE INTERNET THROUGH WINDOWS

Recently acquired by service provider Performance Systems International, The Pipeline is a New York-based graphical front end to the Internet. With its new national availability through PSI's network, the service provides access to all major Internet features, from electronic mail to Telnet to FTP, through a Windows-based software package that lets users read mail and USENET news on-line or off. The interface offers pull-down menus and mouse support; an added benefit is its ability to let you perform several Internet activities simultaneously in different Windows. Pipeline founder James Gleick is the author of *Chaos: Making a New Science*, and *Genius*, a life of physicist Richard Feynman. Scientifically sophisticated, Gleick nonetheless understood that although the Internet is a remarkable resource, it can frustrate and intimidate the nontechnical person.

Out of frustration grows opportunity. Figure 3.17 shows you the introductory screen at The Pipeline. Noteworthy here is the way the software breaks down the Internet activ-

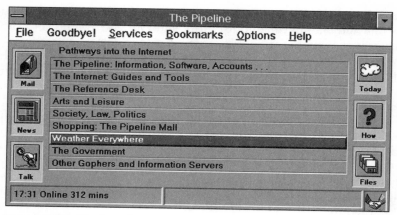

Figure 3.17   The introductory screen at The Pipeline shows how pull-down menus and icons can simplify your Internet choices.

ities from the top: You see information listed by topic, and can point and click to move to submenus laden with further information. Also, notice the icons for electronic mail, newsgroups, and other features, which quickly take you to The Pipeline software interface for their respective services. No manual is required to work through the intuitive screens.

Typical of The Pipeline's organizing capabilities is the screen shown in Figure 3.18, which depicts a series of electronic journals available over the network. Find these one by one and you will spend quite a bit of time. Here, we see a great range of journals clustering under the initial letter s. Moving between them with the mouse is easy. If you are interested in an interface that fully shields you from Internet complexities, The Pipeline just may be the ticket.

As for PSI itself, the network provides its services under the trade name InterRamp, offering direct dial-up access to network nodes in over 80 cities as of early 1995. You can sign up for 14.4 Kbps modem service or 64 Kbps through the new ISDN service, which provides high-speed performance with TCP/IP connections (the latter requires ordering ISDN circuits from your local telephone carrier). We're now seeing the service provider war extended firmly into the national arena, as companies vie for a position that offers easy access to the Internet along with the software to make that access usable.

The Pipeline costs $15 per month for five hours, or $20 per month for 20 hours of use, with additional time billed at $2.50 per hour; $35 per month buys unlimited access. For more information about The Pipeline, contact the company at this address:

THE PIPELINE
150 Broadway, Suite 1710
New York, NY 10038
Voice: 212-267-3636
Fax: 212-267-4380
mailto:info@pipeline.com

NETCRUISER: THE INTERNET VIA NETCOM

The movement of Internet access from the local and regional level to nationwide capabilities is nowhere made more striking than by looking at NETCOM. Here is an Internet

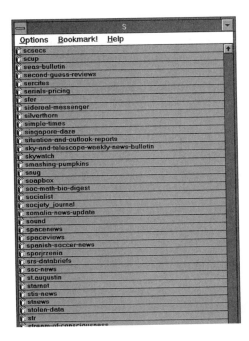

Figure 3.18 Examining some of the numerous electronic journals available over the Internet.

provider with local numbers throughout the United States and a software front end, called NetCruiser, that simplifies Internet access. The software attempts to answer the Internet's biggest question—how do you know what to do and where to go once you do get on-line?—by providing a map from which you can select a range of resources, from FTP to Gopher, from Telnet to the World Wide Web. All of this is handled in a point-and-click environment.

NETCOM's offering also demonstrates how radically the price structure of Internet access is changing. Users get 40 hours of on-line time for $19.95 per month (there is a $25 start-up fee). Configuring the system is painless, since the software is expressly designed to work with the NETCOM network and no other, and the installation is completely automated. The downside to NetCruiser is this very integration with NETCOM's network; you are unable to run other client software while using the interface. NETCOM is in the process of adding this capability to future releases of NetCruiser, however, which should address the problem. Opening up access tools to other client programs means you can use programs like Netscape and Mosaic rather than being tied to one provider's browsing tools.

For more information about NetCruiser, contact NETCOM at the following address:

NETCOM ON-LINE COMMUNICATIONS SERVICE INC.
3031 Tisch Way, Second Fl.
San Jose, CA 95128
Voice: 800-501-8649 or 408-983-5950
Fax: 408-983-1537
mailto:info@netcom.com

MCI's Nationwide Internet Access

The role of the long-distance carriers in Internet connectivity is an interesting one. They, after all, provide the long-haul infrastructure that allows us to communicate; their interest in acquiring a stake in the Internet connectivity business is clear. Through its internetMCI program, MCI has provided access to the Internet at a rate of $9.95 per month for the first five hours of local access, and $2.50 for every additional hour. In addition, 800 service is available for $6.50 per hour for those who are on the road. The company provides a Windows-based access product that includes Netscape Communications' browser software and simplified configuration.

In Figure 3.19, you see the internetMCI World Wide Web site, which you can use to access further information about the network's offerings. As you can see, access to a

Figure 3.19   internetMCI's World Wide Web page, a starting point for information about the long-distance company's access service.

number of information sources is provided, including network directories and USENET newsgroups. MCI has also unveiled an on-line marketplace, accessible through its Web server, where a number of companies have opened up digital storefronts.

With Internet patriarch Vinton Cerf on its team, MCI's move onto the Internet is a serious bid with wide ramifications. It's noteworthy, too, that AT&T has announced plans to work with Microsoft in providing access for the new Microsoft Network. Clearly, the move toward widespread Internet connectivity—ultimately being as commonplace as phone access itself—is proceeding apace. What a change this represents from the situation only a few years ago, when access was limited to universities, major corporations, and research laboratories!

For more information about MCI's Internet offerings, you can reach the company at the following address:

INTERNET**MCI**
MCI Center
Three Ravine Dr.
Atlanta, GA 30346
Voice: 800-779-0949 or 800-955-5210
http://www.internetmci.com/

Public Access Internet Providers

The number of service providers continues to increase as the Internet evolves. You'll need a way to keep up with them, and fortunately, a useful directory exists. The directory is called the *Public Dialup Internet Access List (PDIAL)*, and it's compiled by Peter Kaminski, a software developer in the San Francisco Bay area. The material listed in the appendix draws heavily on both Kaminski's work as well as the NixPub list. Look there for information about service providers you can use. The latest list can be found on-line. Here's how to obtain it.

What You Need: An Updated List of Internet Service Providers

The Document: The Public Dialup Internet Access List

How to Get It: Send electronic mail to info-deli-server@pdial.com. In the subject field of the message, enter **send pdial.** If you wish to receive future editions as they appear, send e-mail with the subject **subscribe pdial** to the same address. You can also retrieve the PDIAL list by sending e-mail to mail-server@rtfm.mit.edu. In your message, put the command **send usenet/news.answers/pdial.** This is a query to the archive of the news.answers newsgroup on USENET, where the PDIAL list is frequently posted. PDIAL is also posted regularly to the newsgroups alt.internet.access.wanted, alt.bbs.lists, alt.online-service and ba.internet.

Long-Distance Options

It wasn't that long ago that services such as The World were relatively unknown to the modem-using public, but today, these providers are spreading widely. Like The World, many are available through Public Data Networks (PDNs) like CompuServe Packet Network or BT Tymnet for those who are not within range of a local call. A PDN provides a local number through which, by paying a usage-related fee, you can call the service provider's number and pay significantly less than you would through standard long-distance. PDNs are in the business of moving data packets, and by taking advantage of their offerings, you can cut your on-line costs by a wide margin. The following are the major public data networks.

XSTREAM

Now run by MCI, the former BT Tymnet offers local access in more than 1,100 cities and 100 foreign countries. Call 800-937-2862 (or 610-666-1770 outside the U.S.) for information and local access numbers. This is a voice call, not a modem transaction.

Alternatively, if you already know a local access number, you can call by modem. Set your modem to 7 data bits, even parity, 1 stop to make this call (7–E–1). After the modem at the other end answers, enter **a** (no **RETURN** after the **a**). At the please log in prompt, enter **information.** You'll then be given everything you need to know about the service and you can search for access codes useful to you. Choose #1, *Direct Dial & Outdial Worldwide Access* at the main menu. Figure 3.20 shows the secondary menu you'll be presented with.

As you can see, this database is searchable, and can quickly help you determine the Xstream number nearest you.

```
                   DIRECT DIAL & OUTDIAL ACCESS INFORMATION


    MCI provides local dial-up access 24 hours a day to our Network in over
    1000 US cities and in over 100 international locations.  Industry standard
    modem technology may vary in some locations. Please select an option from
    the following menu:

    Please select an option from the following menu:

         1.   Access Location Index and Country Abbreviations
         2.   Worldwide Access numbers
         3.   Access Numbers for a Specific State or Country
         4.   Access Numbers for a Specific Speed or Service
         5.   Regional Bell Operating Company (RBOC) Access Numbers
         6.   Access Change Notification
         9.   Search by City, State or Area Code

    If you need assistance, type <H>elp.  To return to the previous menu, type <U>p.
    To return to the main menu, type <T>op.  When you are finished, type <Q>uit.

    Type the number or letter of the desired option at the Select prompt.

    Command:
```

Figure 3.20   MCI's menu for access information.

COMPUSERVE PACKET NETWORK

Another widely used network is run by CompuServe, the CompuServe Packet Network, or CPN. Despite some misconceptions, you don't have to be a CompuServe member to use this network. You can obtain further information and local access numbers by dialing 800-848-8199 for a voice call.

And, just as with TYMNET, you can access CPN numbers by modem. Set your modem to 7–E–1. Dial a local access number and press the **RETURN** key. Enter **phones** at the Host Name: prompt. You'll see the information shown in Figure 3.21.

SPRINTNET

If you're interested in looking up access numbers from Sprint by modem, the number is 800-546-1000. Callers using 1200 bps should press **RETURN** three times after the modem answers; 2400 bps callers should enter **@RETURN RETURN**. You'll then be prompted for your area code and local exchange, after which a prompt will appear. Enter **mail** at the @ prompt, **phones** at the User Name? prompt, and **phones** at the Password? prompt. Figure 3.22 shows the introductory screen to SprintNet, while Figure 3.23 shows the menu you will eventually reach.

PSINET

You can obtain information for this network by calling 800-827-7482 or 703-709-0300 by voice. Alternatively, you can send electronic mail (Chapter 7 will show you how) to all-info@psi.com. You can also retrieve a list of local access numbers by sending mail to numbers-info@psi.com.

```
Host Name:  PHONES

FINDCIS                    PHN-1

Welcome to the CompuServe Phone Number Access area; a free service of the
CompuServe Information Service. This area gives you access numbers for the
CompuServe Information Service and allows you to report any problems you may
be encountering with an access number.

*** For 9600bps access, CompuServe supports CCITT standard V.32/V.42 only. ***

Press <CR> for more !

FINDCIS                    PHN-1
   1 Find Access Numbers
   2 Report Access Number Problems
   3 International Access Information

Last page, enter choice 1
```

Figure 3.21   The CompuServe phone number access area.

```
Welcome to Sprint's online directory of SprintNet local access telephone numbers.

SprintNet's Dial Access Services provide you access to the SprintNet global data
network 24 hours a day for reliable data transmission across town and worldwide.
You can access the network with a local phone call from thousands of cities and
towns or by using SprintNet In-WATS service. The network is also accessible from
over 100 international locations.

Depend on SprintNet's Dial Access Services for:

* dial-up flexibility with access on demand
* error protected network transmission and
* 24-hour customer service and network management

For customer service, call toll-free 1-800/877-5045.(option #5). From overseas
locations with non-WATS access, call 404/859-7700.
```

Figure 3.22   SprintNet's introductory screen.

```
US SPRINT'S ONLINE

            LOCAL ACCESS TELEPHONE NUMBERS DIRECTORY

            1. Domestic Asynchronous Dial Service
            2. International Asynchronous Dial Service
            3. Domestic X.25 Dial Service
            4. New Access Centers and Recent Changes
            5. Product and Service Information
            6. Exit the Phones Directory


Please enter your selection (1-6):
```

Figure 3.23   Looking up access numbers via Sprint.

Full Access: The Internet's Holy Grail

And so we arrive by circuitous path to the ultimate Internet step, full connectivity, or what is otherwise known as "being on the Net." This is the domain of large institutions, corporations, educational organizations, and the like, which lease a telephone line and use additional hardware to maintain a network connection. Such organizations generally bring a large number of their computers onto the network. Each machine hooks up to the company network and then to the Internet. Obviously, all the client software options you hear about are accessible to you when running in full-access mode. But at this level, you're a long way from the home user dialing in with a modem and a PC on the desktop.

4

Introduction to Unix

The early explorers of the New World could not have anticipated the kind of peoples they would encounter. A linguist trained in European languages could do explorers no good when they confronted native tribes speaking in dialects unlike anything they had heard before. But people make contact one word at a time, and language is something that's best acquired through experience. Like the early navigators, those who learn the ways of the Internet will pick up words and phrases as they go. Computer jargon runs rampant on the network—a sea of acronyms and strange abbreviations to be mastered gradually. A welter of operating systems, each with its own set of commands, is in use at various network sites.

Do you really need to master an operating system to work on the Internet? The answer depends upon how deeply you have decided to delve into this new terrain, and upon what kind of access you have acquired to make your explorations. One of the beauties of a SLIP/PPP connection is that you will not come face to face with the Unix shell. The way SLIP/PPP works, you place your call to your service provider's computer and, when your machine has connected to it, the necessary transactions take place behind the scenes. Your job is then to click on the application you choose to run—e-mail, Telnet, FTP, a Web browser—and the client software will launch. Everything you do can take place within a friendly graphical shell, so that mastering the Internet is not conceptually different from mastering a new software tool, like a word processor or a spreadsheet.

Shell users, on the other hand, will need some Unix to make their way forward. That's because, when they log on, they encounter a Unix system (in most cases), waiting for them to enter a command to accomplish network functions. As with travel to any foreign country, the more of the local language you pick up, the more rewarding the trip will be. It makes sense, then, for shell users to acquire a certain proficiency in basic Unix operations, because they can make your journey easier and provide a set of tools for manipulating the information you'll discover. And even SLIP/PPP users can benefit. After all, when they log on to remote sites, many of the Unix commands will be useful for moving about in the remote system's directories. We'll see that point illustrated in Chapter 5, on FTP.

Using Unix—at first an alien tongue, then, with experience, a logical and powerful language—you will be able to draw from the Internet the information you need, download it to your own computer, and send it by electronic mail to other users. Unix will also make you proficient in file management, a necessary skill when conserving disk space is a priority. Many services charge you for using more than a set amount of storage space on their machines, so you'll want to know how to delete unnecessary files, rename others and arrange what's left.

Why Unix?

First, a necessary qualification. Although people frequently associate the operating system called Unix with the Internet, Unix is no more an official language of the network than is VMS, the operating system driving Digital Equipment Corporation's VAX computers or, for that matter, VM, the IBM mainframe language. It is true, however, that many people first come to the Internet through Unix implementations. This is because DARPA was concerned with making its TCP/IP protocols available for widespread use in the research community. Since university computer science departments commonly used Unix, and in particular the Unix variant known as Berkeley Unix (developed at the University of California at Berkeley), DARPA funded the integration of TCP/IP into the Berkeley Unix system.

Today, Unix is the *lingua franca* of the Internet world through a shell account (even though some systems use VMS), and as such, it tends to be intimidating. Like MS-DOS, Unix presents you with a prompt, usually % or something similar, and then waits for you to act. My service provider, the North Carolina company called Interpath, offers me an inscrutable : (colon) prompt. It takes only a few minutes of trying out commands and getting nowhere before you look back on the menu structure of the average BBS or commercial service with great fondness. Doesn't the Internet have any menus? If not, why not?

Easy-to-use menu structures are beginning to be common on the Internet, even among the ranks of shell providers; they're complemented by the new graphical interfaces provided through terminal emulation in products like NetCruiser and The Pipeline. But many providers remain who offer only a Unix prompt as their key interface. We're still contending with the fact that this network grew out of a research and academic environment where user friendliness settled in late as a goal. Then, too, there are many destinations on the Internet, so many that, in some ways, a menu structure can become confining. You have to have the right menu choices to be able to go where you want to go. The following will help you get your bearings by exploring the Unix terrain.

Of Interfaces and Complexity

Unix is unique in that the program that determines its interface runs like an application, like any other program. Therefore, you may choose from a variety of user interfaces. The Unix interface is known as a *shell*. A shell is a program that accepts keyboard commands, interprets them, and takes action based upon them.

The shell discussed in the following is the C Shell, also known as csh. When you log on to a service provider, you may be asked which shell you prefer. Besides csh, there may be choices like the Bourne Shell, or sh, which uses a $ as its user prompt. This was the original Unix shell; it comes with all Unix systems. Other shells include tcsh, bash, and ksh. In this book, I am using the csh shell to illustrate basic Internet procedures. The C Shell uses the percent sign (%) as its user prompt instead of the dollar sign ($); it's the standard shell of Berkeley Unix.

What you see as your command prompt isn't critical. In fact, it's possible the command prompt will be customized by your service provider. For example, my account at Interpath gives me the following prompt:

```
mercury:
```

where mercury is the name of the computer I log on to; this is the prompt even though the shell here is csh, and we would expect the percent sign (%). On the other hand, my account at The World in Brookline Massachusetts, uses this prompt:

```
world%
```

Again, I am set up to use csh at The World; the prompt has simply been customized by the service provider.

Access Assumptions

For the purposes of this chapter, I am assuming you are dialing in to a service provider who makes a standard Unix shell account available. The examples shown in the following pages operate under this assumption. If you are not—say, for example, you use The Pipeline or NetCruiser for graphical access, or a SLIP/PPP account that uses graphical client programs—you will find much of the command complexity has been removed from your networking. You'll still proceed with many of the Internet functions discussed here, but they'll be easier to accomplish than by working through a Unix shell. And if you run a SLIP/PPP connection, your file management chores will be handled by the same operating system tools you've been using all along on your computer.

If you're accessing the Internet through one of the major commercial on-line services, like CompuServe or America Online, you'll need to master your system's command structure. Remember, each of the interface options provided by these systems is different, just as the proprietary interfaces provided by The Pipeline and NetCruiser are different, so you need to learn what the local rules of the road are through practice and by reading. A little work should get you up to speed, because these graphical front ends are designed to be intuitive. If your entry is through DELPHI, however, you do have one additional layer of complexity to contend with, even though the system does operate through a menu structure. Because of its reliance upon VMS as its underlying computer implementation, DELPHI requires that you modify certain commands to make it do what you want it to do. This will show up particularly in Chapter 5, when we move files with FTP.

But no matter what form of access you use, you'll want to pay attention to this chapter, because when you use Telnet to manipulate a computer at a remote site, you may well need some of these commands. The Internet provides you with the chance to take the controls of various machines around the network, and not all of them will be intuitive in their basic design. If you learn the core principles of Unix, you'll be able to adapt to these machines easier. You'll also learn, by working with Unix, that while using menus is simpler than entering commands, a Unix prompt does give you remarkable speed and flexibility.

The Smattering of Unix You'll Need

Surely you've operated a word processor well enough to write and print out a letter, or a report for your school or business. You didn't have to learn a programming language to do it, either, because the program's own interface shielded you from all the problems. Unix doesn't shield you as completely from a computer's inner workings, but the good news is you don't have to learn much of it. You will return to certain core commands again and again as you familiarize yourself with your service provider's system. But the great bulk of Unix can safely be left behind. Learn what you need; learn more only if you choose.

The following set of Unix commands is provided only as a reference. In the chapters that follow, with each step you take into unexplored Internet terrain, you will see what to type and what to expect. You may want to return to this chapter on occasion as you work your way through basic operations like directory listings and file deletion. Above all, don't be afraid to use an operating system that is admittedly powerful, but on the level of its basic commands, not at all difficult to master.

Understanding Unix Files

Unix filenames must follow certain conventions.

- You should not start a filename with a dash (-) or a plus sign (+).
- You may, however, use a dash (-) or plus sign (+) inside the filename. Any combination of alphabetic characters, digits, periods (.), underscores (_) or dashes, and pluses can make up a Unix filename.
- Unix is case-sensitive. This is an important consideration; often users of other systems forget about it, and don't understand why they can't access a Unix file called WORK.DOC, for example, by asking for work.doc. So remember, case counts. The file Network.Txt is a different file from network.txt.

Unix Directory Structure

Like any operating system, Unix attempts to create order out of the data on your hard disk. An MS-DOS user will have no problem with the Unix directory structure because it was the model for the MS-DOS system of directories and subdirectories, as well as for Digital's VMS system, so its impact has been wide. But note one crucial difference: Unix directory path separators are forward slashes, not the backslashes DOS users have become accustomed to. In other words, a DOS directory named *windows\xtalk* would appear in Unix as *windows/xtalk*. The backslash is the only difference, but it's an important one.

When you establish an account with an Internet system provider (and most providers of dial-up access use Unix as their operating system), the system administrator at the service provider's site will set up a directory for you to use. This directory is called your *home directory*. Consider it a starting point for your Unix explorations, and hence your first beachhead into the Internet. There will also be a set of subdirectories available for your use which contain other data related to your account. At Interpath, for example, when I save a mail message, it's sent to a subdirectory called *Mail.* When I save USENET postings, they go to a subdirectory called *News.*

Basic Unix Commands

Take a look now at some basic Unix commands. What's not clear quickly should become so through practice. Some of these commands you won't need to use right away. Others you'll want to experiment with to get the feel of the operating system. You'll put your service provider's Unix to major use in downloading files (covered in Chapter 5), managing your disk space by deleting (or compressing) the files you save there, and moving and renaming files. These commands will help you manage such tasks.

cat *filename*   Displays a file on-screen. This is handy if the file is less than one screen long, or if you prefer to display a long file continuously and capture it with your software's capture buffer. But because the text scrolls through without interruption, you'll also find the **more** command (described later) useful; it provides page breaks.

cd   Changes your current working directory. Entering it without any specifications causes the system to return you to your home directory.

Unix distinguishes between absolute and relative path names. An absolute path name begins with a slash and includes the complete path starting with the root directory; */home/gilster/Mail,* for example, is an absolute path name. To reach it, I would type **cd /home/gilster/Mail** (note the uppercase on Mail!).

If I were already in the *gilster* subdirectory, however, I could switch to the *Mail* subdirectory by typing a relative path name; **cd Mail** would take me there. Note that the relative path name does not require the complete path statement, as it works in relation to the current working directory. Also note that it requires no slash.

cp   Copies a file. Thus **cp internet.intro internet.start** copies the file internet.intro to a new file called internet.start.

help   Don't miss this command. It calls up a screen of help information when you get lost. (Note: Not every system will have this function installed. Try yours and see if it's there).

logout   Logs off the system.

ls   Lists files and directories. **ls** can be tightened up to include more specific commands. Thus **ls -l** lists directories and files in a longer format which includes the type of the file and other information.

Figure 4.1 shows what the **ls -l** command looked like on a particular day at my Interpath account.

Another useful **ls** variant is the recursive **ls -lR,** which provides a listing of all files in all directories.

man   This is another command that may or may not be installed on your system. The *Unix User's Manual Reference Guide* is a large document that can be stored on disk and kept available on-line. If you need detailed help with a particular com-

```
% ls -l
total 240
drwx------   2 gilster        512 Mar 29 13:05 Mail/
drwx--S---   4 gilster        512 Mar 27 09:33 News/
-rw-r--r--   1 gilster    8442288 Mar 10 08:11 core
-rw-------   1 gilster        625 Mar 15 08:54 date
-rw-------   1 gilster        526 Mar 11 09:47 dial
drwxr-sr-x   2 gilster        512 Jan  9  1992 ftp/
-rw-------   1 gilster       6724 Mar 24 16:24 mbox
-rw-------   1 gilster       5326 Mar 29 13:04 michnet
-rw-------   1 gilster       4094 Mar 27 08:32 nobody1
-rw-------   1 gilster        197 Mar 19 09:16 sig
-rw-------   1 gilster     122423 Mar 27 08:49 world.ps.Z
-rw-------   1 gilster        691 Mar 27 09:04 xmodem.log
```

Figure 4.1   An **ls -l** directory listing.

mand, you can get it by entering **man** followed by the name of the command in question. Thus **man ls** gives you useful information about the **ls** command. Figure 4.2 shows an example of the **man** command at work.

Be advised: The *Unix User's Manual Reference Guide* is written by programmers, and it's pretty heavy stuff. Fortunately, the commands about which you need detailed information, such as **mail** and **ftp,** will be covered in detail in later chapters, so you won't need the **man** command often.

mkdir *name*   Creates a new subdirectory. You choose the name; thus **mkdir letters** creates a subdirectory named *letters*.

```
mercury: man ls

LS (1V)                    USER COMMANDS                      LS (1V)

NAME
     ls - list the contents of a directory

SYNOPSIS
     ls [ -aAcCdfFgilLqrRstul ] filename ...

SYSTEM V SYNOPSIS
     /usr/5bin/ls [ -abcCdfFgilLmnopqrRstux ] filename ...

AVAILABILITY
     The System V version of this command is available  with  the
     System V software installation option.  Refer to Installing
     SunOS 4.1 for information on how to install  optional
     software.

DESCRIPTION
     For each filename which is a directory, ls  lists  the  con-
     tents of  the  directory; for each filename which is a file,
     ls repeats its name and any other information requested.  By
--More--(8%)
```

Figure 4.2   A manual page for **ls.**

more	Allows you to display a file one screen at a time. If, for example, you wanted to read the file letter.txt, you would enter **more letter.txt** to activate the program. You would then see a prompt at the end of every page. To move to the next page, use the **spacebar**. A carriage return only moves the text forward one line at a time. Figure 4.3 shows an example of a file being read with **more**, as viewed in Crosstalk, a telecommunications program.
mv	Renames a file. You might, for example, not want to keep a file called net.gloss.txt in quite so verbose a form. So entering **mv net.gloss.txt gloss.doc** would change the longer title to the simple name gloss.doc.
pwd	Shows the name of the current directory.
rm	Removes, or erases, files. You'll use this one a lot. **rm letter.doc** gets rid of the file letter.doc. When you set up an account with a service provider, your account will include storage limitations which you can't exceed. Use the **rm** command to keep the files in your directories pared down to size.
rmdir	Deletes a directory. **rmdir letters** deletes the directory *letters*. The directory must be empty for this command to work.

```
Crosstalk
 File   Edit   Settings   Action   Script   QuickPad   Window   Help

mercury: more macweb.doc
From AROARTY@support.jwiley.com Wed Jan  4 11:08:26 1995
Date: 03 Jan 95 11:22:21 EST
From: AROARTY@support.jwiley.com
To: Paul A Gilster - Computer Focus <gilster@mercury.interpath.net>
Subject: SOFT> New Version of MacWeb Rel

---------- Forwarded message ----------
Date: Tue, 20 Dec 94 13:33:35 EST
SENDER: Cynthia Williams <cwilliams@interramp.com>
Subject: New Version of MacWeb Released

Following is a summary announcement about a significant new release of
MacWeb, the Macintosh-based Web browser from EINet.  If you would like to
receive a full copy of this news release, please contact:

Cynthia Williams
207/871-1260
cwilliams@interramp.com

EINET'S NEW MACWEB IS FASTER AND MORE
POWERFUL, WITH GREATER FLEXIBILITY
--More--(17%)
Connected                    00:00:32  Modem  VT102  Zmodem
```

Figure 4.3 A file being read using the more command.

Having looked at these basic Unix commands, perhaps you see the fundamental difference between a shell account and SLIP/PPP. With the former, you perform your file maintenance on your service provider's computer; space has been allocated for you on that computer to handle the basic chores, and to store your files. Files that you download from network sites wind up at your service provider's site, and you decide what to do with them from there. With SLIP/PPP, file maintenance takes place on your own computer. Your network connection is a complete one, in which data packets travel all the way to your machine, and any files you download come straight to your hard disk.

pico: An Easy-to-Use Text Editor

Sometimes we find it helpful to be able to use a text editor in Unix for basic file chores. Perhaps you've stored a document in your home directory and would like to search it for a particular expression. Or you would like to compose a short article and send it along to various correspondents without going through the hassle of writing it first on your own computer's word processing program and then uploading it to your service provider's machine.

Another popular use for a text editor would be in the creation of such small documents as signature files, which you can append to the end of any electronic mail messages you send. You can also create .plan and .project files for your home directory which would be viewable by anyone who gave the **finger** command to your network mailbox address.

pico is a Unix text editor that allows you to handle these chores. Although not as feature-rich as the vi editor we discuss later, pico is much easier to use because its interface provides basic commands along the bottom of the screen. If pico looks familiar to you, it may be because you have seen it in the pine mail program (we discuss pine in Chapter 7). pico is a major reason why pine is considered so user-friendly.

Calling Up pico

From the system prompt, enter the command **pico**. The basic screen for editing, as viewed through Crosstalk, appears in Figure 4.4. You will notice that the bulk of the screen is blank; pico has set up a fresh palette for you to use in creating a document. On the other hand, there will be times when you want to edit an existing document. To do so, use the command **pico** *filename*, which will cause the editor to appear with the file already inserted and ready to edit. To call up a file while you are already in pico, use the **Ctrl-R** (retrieve) command, which inserts the file into the pico screen; **Ctrl-r** is also acceptable—pico is not case-sensitive.

Creating a Document

pico makes few demands upon you when it comes time to enter text. When you begin typing, the editor will wrap your text to the next line; you don't have to use the **RETURN** key to do this. As you write, you can move back and forth in the document using the cursor, or arrow keys. A variety of other keys are available for quick movement in a document. **Ctrl-A**, for example, moves you to the beginning of a line, while **Ctrl-E** moves you to its end. The **DELETE** key is available for erasing characters, and you have the ability to search documents as well as to cut and paste text.

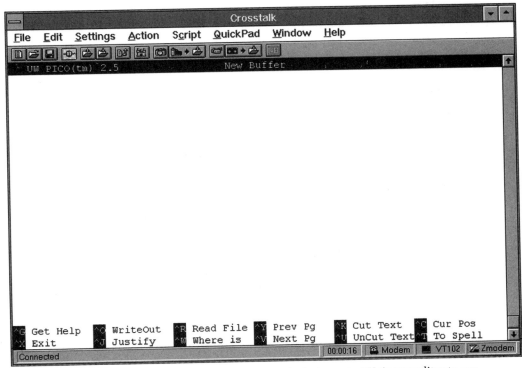

Figure 4.4   pico's clean design and menu structure make it the easiest Unix text editor to use.

Searching for Files

If you forget which files are in your home directory, you can ask pico to show you a display. Press **Ctrl-O** from the main pico menu to access a submenu, which will allow you to choose **Ctrl-T**. You will be shown a screen containing the files and directories in your home directory. You can move the highlight bar between files and subdirectories as needed.

pico's Cursor Movement Commands

Many of pico's commands use the **Ctrl** key in combination with another key. You hold down the **Ctrl** key and press the other key shown. Other commands use the arrow keys.

Up Arrow	Moves the cursor up one line.
Down Arrow	Moves the cursor down one line.
Right Arrow	Moves the cursor one character to the right.
Left Arrow	Moves the cursor one character to the left.
Ctrl-A	Moves the cursor to the beginning of the current line of text.
Ctrl-B	Moves the cursor back one character. The **Left Arrow** key does the same thing.

Ctrl-C	Causes pico to display a message showing you your current position in the file.
Ctrl-E	Moves the cursor to the end of the current line.
Ctrl-F	Moves the cursor forward one character. The **Right Arrow** key has the same function.
Ctrl-N	Moves to next line.
Ctrl-P	Moves to previous line.
Ctrl-V	Moves forward one page of text.
Ctrl-Y	Moves backward one page of text.

Editing Commands for pico

Editing operations in pico also use **Ctrl** plus letter key combinations. Here are the major commands.

Ctrl-D	Deletes the character to the right of the cursor.
Ctrl-H	Deletes the character to the left of the cursor.
Ctrl-J	Justifies the text in the current paragraph, making all right-hand margins even.
Ctrl-K	Deletes the entire line in which the cursor is located.
Ctrl-U	Undeletes the last deleted line at the cursor position.

Cut and Paste Operations

You can use the **Ctrl-K** command to perform basic cut and paste functions, pico is limited in this regard, but the fact that it retains deleted text in a buffer means that you can move that text to a new position. Here's how: Use **Ctrl-K** to delete a line. Then move the cursor to the place where you want to insert the text and press **Ctrl-U** to paste the line into that position.

Checking a pico File for Spelling

pico includes a simple spell checker program. Use **Ctrl-T** to invoke it. When you do so, the program will check the words in your file. Any words that are not in its dictionary will appear, along with a prompt that allows you to make corrections. You make changes by altering the text and then pressing the **RETURN** key. Remember: There will be many words, such as proper nouns, that are not necessarily going to be in pico's dictionary. If you want to leave the word intact, just press a **RETURN** and proceed.

Inserting Text in pico

In addition to writing text in a pico file, you can insert a text file into the current document. To insert a previously existing file into pico, use the **Ctrl-R** command. A prompt will ask you for the name of the file you wish to insert. Type the name followed by a **RETURN.** At this point, the file will be inserted at the current cursor position.

Searching for Text

You can use the **Ctrl-W** command to search for words inside the file you are currently editing. You will be asked to supply a search term; simply enter the word or string of characters for which you want to search and press a **RETURN**. pico will begin searching at the current position of the cursor and will search forward, returning to the beginning of the file to complete the search if necessary.

Saving Your File

You can save the file you have been editing with the **Ctr-O** command. pico will prompt you for a filename. Enter the name you choose and press the **RETURN** key.

pico's Help Screens

You can call up a useful list of commands in pico by using the **Ctrl-G** command. Leave help mode by pressing **Ctrl-X**.

Exiting pico

Ctrl-X is the command to exit pico. When you press this command, you will be given the option of saving the changes you have made to a current file, giving it a name, and saving it. At this point you will be returned to the system prompt.

Using the vi Text Editor

Another common Unix tool is a text editor called vi. With pico available, you may wonder why you would ever want to use vi; after all, pico presents an interface that helps to guide you through its capabilities, whereas vi is as inscrutable as the Sphinx. Unfortunately, although acceptance of pico is growing rapidly, the most commonly supported text tool is still vi. That means your service provider may not make pico available, and if that is the case, you will need to master enough of vi's commands to perform the occasional file editing operation.

Starting vi

Launching vi by entering **vi** plus a **RETURN** at your service provider's prompt will call the program up on the screen with a field for your data entry. If you launch the program with a filename, as in vi letter.doc, vi will appear with the document available for editing.

One confusing thing about this text editor is that it works with two modes. When you start the program, you are in *command mode,* and any keystrokes you enter will be interpreted as commands to the editor rather than as text. Common command mode operations are opening and saving files, moving the cursor to new positions within the file, and performing a variety of editing chores. To actually write text, you need to enter *insert mode.*

Changing Modes in vi

To switch into insert mode from command mode, you can use a variety of commands. Press an **a** to begin inserting text after the cursor. Pressing an **i** will allow you to begin inserting text before the cursor. Here are several other commands to move into insert mode:

A   Begin inserting text at the end of the line.

I   Begin inserting text at the beginning of the line.

o   Begin inserting text on a new line below the current line.

O   Begin inserting text on a new line above the current line.

To switch from insert mode back to command mode, press the **ESC** key. Your biggest source of confusion with vi will come when switching back and forth between modes as you enter text and then need to perform editing operations. One of the dubious charms of vi is that it gives absolutely no indication of which mode you are in at the time.

Moving the Cursor

The vi screen includes tilde (~) characters which run along the left-hand side. The presence of these characters indicates lines without text, spaces, or **RETURN**s.

Here are the vi commands for cursor movement. Remember that these require you to be in command mode at the time. Again, you can move to command mode at any time by pressing the **ESC** key.

Up Arrow   Moves up one line. You can also use the **k** key.

Down Arrow   Moves down one line. You can also use the **j** key.

Left Arrow   Moves left one character. You can also use the **h** key.

Right Arrow   Moves right one character. You can also use the **l** key.

b   Moves left one word.

w   Moves right one word.

0   Moves to the beginning of the line.

$ Moves to the end of the line.

You can also move forward and backward one screen at a time, as follows:

Ctrl-B   Moves back one screen.

Ctrl-F   Moves forward one screen at a time.

vi is loaded with commands. You can, for example, move down half a screen at a time using the **Ctrl-D** command. To move up half a screen, use the **Ctrl-U** command. Space forbids going into the more arcane vi commands; if you become obsessed with vi, a comprehensive Unix text will provide the complete command set. There is also a book from O'Reilly & Associates called *Learning the vi Editor*, by Linda Lamb. Now in its fifth edition, this text offers a complete explanation of vi's more advanced tools. The commands listed here are intended only to cover the most common file operations.

Deleting Text with vi

Editing text is a difficult proposition with vi because of the need to move frequently between command and insert mode. This limitation shows up dramatically when you attempt to delete or change text in a document. To do this, you must first switch into command mode by pressing the **ESC** key. At this point, you will use the **d** command to perform vi's delete command options. You may also use the **x** key for certain operations. As with all of vi's commands, there are numerous possibilities.

x	Deletes the character at the cursor.
X	Deletes the character in front of the cursor.
dw	Deletes the word to the right.
db	Deletes the word to the left.
d0	Deletes to the beginning of the line.
d$	Deletes to the end of the line.
dd	Deletes the entire current line.
dG	Deletes to the end of the file.

Searching for Text

vi makes it possible to search for particular strings of text inside a document. In command mode, you can use the */text* command to find a particular text string. Thus, to search for the name Paracelsus in a document, go into command mode and enter the command **/paracelsus**. This command will cause vi to search forward for the string specified. If you would like to search backward in the file, use the *?text* command.

One of vi's most useful tools is its ability to search and replace; the editor will find the text you specify and then replace it with whatever you choose. You can do this with the following command:

```
:%s/text/newtext/
```

followed by a **RETURN**.

Suppose I want to find every instance of the word Canterbury and replace it with Winchester. I could do it thus:

```
:%s/canterbury/winchester/
```

Saving and Quitting in vi

You must be in command mode to exit vi. After editing a file, use the **:x** command to save it and quit vi. If you want to save the file without quitting vi, you can use the **:w** command. You can use **:q** to quit if you haven't made any changes to the file, and **:q!** to quit if you have made changes but decided not to keep them.

Of Challenges and Minimalism

How much Unix you decide to master is your own call. Newcomers with graphical access may well decide to put off Unix work until they have had the chance to find their way around the Internet; many will decide to avoid Unix altogether. But I think this would ultimately be a mistake. It's all well and good to remove some of the barriers that keep people from using the Internet. But gaining a mastery of the network, as opposed to being an occasional visitor, really requires reaching a deeper level of understanding, of the kind that Unix, as one example, can help provide. The Internet is steeped in Unix and, as previously mentioned, you will likely encounter it throughout your network travels as you explore remote sites. A basic proficiency, then, makes sense.

It's also true that Unix, and the Internet itself, are simply demanding media. We can go out of our way to make tools accessible, but we can't ultimately hide all the network's complexity without sharply curtailing its functionality. Put another way, the more you learn to work with advanced tools—and that includes the widespread Unix operating system—the more things you will be able to do in your network travels. No one will demand that you master Unix, but I think the curious people who want to know not only how to use something but why it works the way it does will inevitably gravitate toward Unix. The great conductor Pierre Boulez once said of current trends toward minimalism in music that he thought the human mind was capable of understanding at deeper levels than the minimalists gave it credit for. The same remark could apply to Unix—a bit of study may surprise you in terms of what you can learn.

5

FTP:
Files by the Gigabyte

The best way to learn the Internet is through hands-on experience, which is why we'll begin our discussion of FTP, or File Transfer Protocol, right away. FTP is a way of sending files between computers. One great benefit of the TCP/IP protocols is their ability to give computers using different operating systems a common set of tools, the implements out of which the worldwide internetworking process called the Internet has evolved. That means it doesn't matter if you are using an Apple Macintosh logged on to a Sun Microsystems workstation using Unix at your service provider's site, and want to tap into a remote IBM mainframe computer using VM. Using the FTP protocol, you can get the file you need with a few simple commands.

And just as the Internet itself uses a common set of tools to facilitate file transfer, you will have a toolbox of your own available. If you operate through a shell account, you can use the FTP program available on your service provider's machine; this chapter will show you how. If you use a graphical interface through a service like CompuServe or NETCOM's NetCruiser, you will access the same files through the systems' own procedures, which involve pulling down the relevant menu and choosing file transfer options. And if you work with a SLIP/PPP connection, you will have any number of FTP programs available; in this chapter, I'll show you several, and demonstrate how they work. The point is, you're performing the same function through a wide range of tools, and while I can't demonstrate every single program that handles FTP, I can give you the principles at work, as illustrated by representative examples, and you can apply them to the interface you are using.

Don't be put off by FTP. You can use it even if your only contact with the Internet is through an electronic mail gateway from a local BBS or a commercial on-line service. Although you won't have the ability to run interactive FTP sessions, going into a remote computer in real time and prowling around in its directories, you will be able to locate the file you need and have it sent to you through electronic mail. The process is complex and can be slow; in fact, it sometimes fails altogether. But persistence pays, and Chapter 8 will show you how to set up such a mail delivery, and what to do when it doesn't function. One way or another, you can find what you need on the Internet, as long as you remain undaunted.

For the purposes of this book, FTP is a major tool. As you go through topics from USENET to Gopher, from database access to BITNET mailing lists, you will learn how to use the Internet itself to generate further information on each of these topics. In many cases, you will be directed to information available as text files on remote computers, which you'll access through the FTP protocol. Intimidating at first, this process quickly becomes second nature, and you'll soon be zipping around the world with ease. The variety of software and text available is staggering.

We're talking gigabytes of information here. A gigabyte is approximately equal to 1 billion bytes, meaning one gigabyte equals some 1 thousand megabytes. The archie program, which we'll look at shortly, tracks a huge number of sites around the Internet which you, as a public access user, can tap. But even archie's listings are limited, because millions of computers are out there on the network, many of them not covered by archie's data sweeps, and many of these likewise offer interesting files. Estimates of the amount of information available on the Internet now reach well into the terabyte range—a terabyte is equal to 1 thousand gigabytes, or 1 million Mb of data. Granted, there is a great deal of overlap when a successful program appears on directory listings at multiple sites, and a successful program can be propagated throughout the network in a matter of hours. But it's clear that ongoing software development and the posting of unique resources in a wide variety of data formats will keep the FTP sites of the world a fascinating and ever-changing landscape to explore.

Shareware and Public Domain Software

You won't find commercial software at FTP archive sites because licensing agreements prohibit it from being posted publicly. But you will find shareware and software that's in the public domain. The two differ: Public domain software is free, while shareware requires you to pay the author if, after a trial period, you decide to keep and use the program. You'll also find so-called freeware, software on which the author retains copyright, but which he or she allows you to use for free. The shareware movement has produced some remarkably successful programs; among them are Procomm, a telecommunications program; PC-File, a database that was one of the earliest shareware programs to be marketed; and PC-Write, a full-featured word processor. Notice, too, how adventure games like DOOM have captured a worldwide audience by mastering the shareware concept. You can find DOOM and numerous related game programs on the Internet, along with programs to teach you Italian, play chess, draw blueprints, plan your spring garden, catalog your collection of CDs and arrange your finances. As the Internet grows out of adolescence into maturity, the shareware scene appears more vibrant than ever.

The traditional method of dissemination for these programs has been the computer bulletin board. Consumer-driven on-line services have long recognized the importance of software to their user bases. Each provides extensive program libraries, often broken out by specific area of interest, so users can download programs they need. And the mushrooming growth of private bulletin board systems (BBSs) throughout the world has provided thousands of new repositories for shareware and public domain programs. Exec-PC is a case in point. The Wisconsin-based BBS maintains well over half a million files in its libraries, and has now opened up access to the Internet.

The Internet adds an interesting twist to the shareware story. In the Unix world, there exists a long tradition of free software development, as exemplified by the continuing work on a project called the Free Software Foundation. FSF's head, Richard Stallman, is of the opinion that software should be shared by the user community. Huge amounts of free software have been produced by programmers associated with Stallman, and the Foundation has been instrumental in developing GNU (Gnu's Not Unix), an operating system designed as a free work-alike for Unix. GNU EMACS and GNU C are well-distributed software tools written as part of the overall GNU project.

You probably will not use GNU or its associated utilities, not unless you get involved with networked workstations, but you should understand that the vigorous free software movement on the Internet is in many respects more vocal than the comparable scene on the PC/Macintosh side of the world. Whereas shareware, the idea of paying for software after a trial use, has become common among commercial service users, there is still a powerful user community insisting on software's free distribution on the Internet. The difference between free software and shareware is that free programs are usually made available on the Internet in the form of *source code* (the program language before it has been compiled into machine instructions that the computer executes). Such code is distributed without charge by the academics and programmers who created it. And while support issues have always dogged the users of such software, it is interesting to see that some third-party organizations have begun to appear to offer technical services for users of operating systems like GNU. Cygnus Support Inc., for example, charges a yearly fee for supporting GNU and other programs.

Unlike the commercial services, the Internet is a vast and unruly landscape. There are few menus to guide the traveler, and even at the largest archival sites, software can be challenging to locate by type or description. Also unlike America Online or CompuServe, the Internet's libraries contain a much higher proportion of professional materials. You'll certainly find Procomm, PC-Write, and the rest of the PC shareware panoply here, but you'll also encounter the client software that drives networked computers of various descriptions and allows them to tap into Internet resources. You'll find archival sites for magazines and newsletters, scientific documents, and maps. You'll find the textual treasures of Project Gutenberg and the Online Book Initiative, electronic editions of classic works of literature. And, of course, you'll find the client programs that SLIP/PPP users can tap to run network functions like FTP and Telnet.

Make no mistake about it, the latter are among the most significant network tools you will encounter on the network. Add a direct TCP/IP connection to your computer through SLIP/PPP and you have at your fingertips a whole range of client programs, from the superb WS_FTP file retrieval program we discuss later in this chapter, to World Wide Web browsers like Netscape and Mosaic. And client programs can be extremely specialized as well. Tools exist for database searching on the specialized server system known as Wide Area Information Servers, or WAIS. There are client programs to run finger queries (finger is a way to check a user's status on-line, and to generate additional information about him or her). You can use client software to examine a Gopher site or to read USENET news, and if you don't like the client you're using, you can go back on the Internet and try one of the rival programs. The best clients are, in most cases, freeware or shareware.

The Internet is a vast realm, most of it uncharted because it is growing too fast for maps to be current. But the tools for exploring the network are growing in sophistication. With software available at numerous sites, you'll learn to move around the globe to collect what you need.

The process will be fundamentally different from what dial-up users are accustomed to. You will not tap bulletin board systems but networked computers, using the FTP capabilities provided by TCP/IP. Instead of keeping a list of telephone numbers and dialing up BBSs in sequence, you'll call one number—your access provider's—and move out from there by FTP, using your network presence and related software to reach your destinations.

Description of Archive Sites

As compared to a BBS, run by one or more operators, or a commercial on-line service, run by a company whose business is providing connectivity for the public, Internet FTP sites usually have other things to do. They're working computer systems at a variety of locations worldwide. While their resources, or at least some of them, have been made available for FTP purposes, meaning anyone can go into their archives and download files, they are not designed for the general public, nor are they necessarily user friendly. You won't find, for example, an FTP site with an easy-to-use interface like CompuServe Information Manager, or a logical menu structure like DELPHI's.

That means a bit more work, but the sheer immensity of the resources available is compelling enough to encourage us up the learning curve. But first, a matter of terminology. Throughout this book you will use *anonymous FTP* as you log on to remote sites and pull down information. Anonymous FTP is the ability to log on and retrieve publicly accessible files without any special permission to do so. You'll enter **anonymous** when asked for a name, clueing in the remote computer that you are logging on to a part of the disk reserved for public use.

You can see why this would be necessary. Because so many of these systems are providing services to organizations ranging from research laboratories to medical clinics, from military bases to universities, it would present enormous security challenges simply to leave the computer open to FTP without any kind of restriction. A hard disk or an entire computer can be devoted to public information, but the anonymous FTP protocol ensures that you have available the part of their resources the people at the host computer site are willing to share.

Some of these sites are treasure troves. Washington University in St. Louis, for example, offers a huge repository of software and information. Here you find not just public domain and shareware programs, but a wealth of other data including USENET newsgroups (similar to CompuServe Forums and GEnie RoundTables, as you'll see in Chapter 11). There are many Macintosh programs; the complete source code to TeX, a powerful text formatter, as well as the X-windowing system, which is widely used on Unix computers. There's a clone of Unix for IBM-compatible PCs, and a collection of Graphics Interchange Format (GIF) pictures. No matter what your own computer, there's something for you here.

Washington University (wuarchive.wustl.edu) isn't much like a dial-up commercial service; neither is the site at ftp.uu.net where UUNET Technologies of Falls Church, Virginia maintains thousands of files, nor the oak.oakland.edu archive covering a multitude of software programs for various operating systems. Macintosh users aren't left out of the picture, either; plentiful material resides at such addresses as ftp.apple.com, mac.archive.umich.edu, and sumex-aim.standford.edu. Amiga and Atari users can find much to occupy their attention at mars.ee.msstate.edu.

Perhaps the most obvious difference between such Internet archival sites and the libraries of the commercial vendors will be in the nature of their software. Whereas a commercial service will focus on the most popular available personal computers—those using MS-DOS and Macintosh software—because these represent the dominant equipment base of its user population, an Internet archival site is likely to include a much broader range of materials. You know about Unix software at Washington University, but you'll also find tools for VAX users (VMS is their operating system), IBM minicomputers and mainframe computers, and more. Look for Sun Micro-systems material, for example, at titan.cs.rice.edu, while OS/2 is supported at ftp-os2.cdrom.com. You can expect to see a lot of things that won't interest the average modem user along with a wealth of programs, graphics, and text materials that certainly will.

There's still another difference between the commercial on-line services' libraries and the FTP sites of the Internet. CompuServe's forums, for example, are run by system operators (sysops) who are paid by CompuServe. The job of the sysop is to keep a close check on the files uploaded to the libraries, to make sure they contain no viruses, to ensure that they work, and to determine that they're worthwhile. A good sysop also makes sure the programs are current versions. Software at FTP sites, on the other hand, may or may not receive this kind of careful scrutiny. There are so many FTP sites out there, with holdings so diverse, that there is no way to be sure how carefully a particular site has checked a given program.

Assume you've heard about a great new communications program. On CompuServe, you'd log on to a particular forum, perhaps the IBM Communications Forum. There you'd leave a message asking about the program. Because CompuServe offers a central repository for files and messages, others could respond and tell you in which library to look for your program. You could be assured you had the latest version in most cases merely by downloading the most recently dated copy of the program. Updates and new version announcements would generally be made in the same forum, so you could keep up with program developments without difficulty.

The Internet is more challenging. Finding the program requires you to scan a wide range of FTP sites for what you want, using tools like archie, which is discussed later in this chapter. Unfortunately, archie does not rank its findings by version number or date. Once you've found the program, usually at any number of sites, you must look carefully to determine which version you're getting; and in some cases, it may be impossible to tell without actually downloading the program. Keeping up with updates is likewise decentralized. The best avenue is to subscribe to an appropriate newsgroup on USENET, watching for news of your program. Ultimately, you will have the same software up and running, but it often takes more ingenuity to achieve the same end on the Internet than on the commercial service.

Internet users, then, must learn to take advantage of the self-referential nature of this metanetwork. A good networker will constantly update information and learn new tricks by following USENET newsgroups, reading mail, and using FTP to pull in publicly available materials. A premise of this book is that the Internet is a moving target, whose constantly shifting parameters impel us to compile our own up-to-date libraries of information. Books are not yet obsolete, nor will they ever be. But supplementing books, constantly revising data, building electronic Alexandrias immune from damage caused by the loss of a single site, is what the Internet does best.

Courtesy When Using FTP

It's time to try out FTP. But first, a word about network courtesy. If we barge into the computers at UUNET or Washington University, or any other working site for that matter, without regard to the effect we're having on local operations, we're committing a newcomer's blunder. The Internet's wide reaches are filled with people trying to get things done. While it's exciting to have software archives accessible at so many different sites, it should also give us pause. With network usage comes network responsibility, and overuse of a privilege can cause the entire user community to suffer.

Basic courtesy, then, involves minimizing the amount of resource drain we put on the Internet. FTP sessions should be run only *after working hours*. And if you fail to take into account the Internet's wide reach, you'll be making a mistake. Sure, it's simple to tie into a computer in Finland, but if it's early morning where you are on the California coast, it's late afternoon in Finland and people are trying to get work done. Base your calling on *the local time at the site you're planning to reach*. Plan on calling between 1900 and 0600 hours *at the site*.

FTP through a Shell Account

With that in mind, let's now retrieve some information. The format outlined here is the one used in the rest of the book for FTP procedures. Refer back to this section if you have trouble later on, as the basic file transfer and downloading instructions are contained here. And if you're using DELPHI, be sure to read the special FTP procedures necessary with that system. We will discuss them later in this chapter.

I've chosen a file containing an index of materials available on one prominent network site, the SURAnet Network Information Center in College Park, Maryland. It's a useful list because it illustrates the resources available at a single network location. A network information center, or NIC, is itself a valuable resource, offering a variety of information about the services available on-line. As we explore the Internet, we'll find many NICs that offer useful material which they make available by anonymous FTP.

We'll get an ASCII file; ASCII stands for the American Standard Code for Information Interchange. To say that a file is in ASCII format has important implications. It means that nothing in the file deviates from this standard; the file is therefore readable by virtually any computer. Contrast this with, say, a WordPerfect file that contains all the

What You Need: An Index of Files at a Network NIC

The Document: A Directory Listing

How to Get It: Via anonymous FTP. Use the following URL:

ftp://ftp.sura.net/pub/nic/00-README.FIRST

Remember how URLs work. What this URL means is:

1. Use FTP to reach the site ftp.sura.net.
2. Change directories to the *pub/nic* directory.
3. Retrieve the file named 00-README.FIRST.

formatting codes and other information specific to that word processor. You could download it, but you wouldn't be able to do anything with it unless you had a copy of WordPerfect and could load it into the word processor. ASCII can be viewed by just about anybody. If English is the standard language of commerce worldwide, ASCII is the standard language of computing.

Remember, you want to handle this file transaction after business hours at the site, so check the clock. The following is the FTP procedure in a nutshell. At your service provider's command prompt, enter the **ftp** command, followed by the destination. Figure 5.1 shows what you'll see on-screen. Commands I've entered are shown in bold type. Notice that the term ftp is part of the address: Thus, our actual command is **ftp ftp.sura.net.**

In the example that follows, I am showing you an FTP session as seen through a Unix shell account. Later in this chapter, I will show you FTP through a SLIP/PPP connection, with graphical client software. Whichever kind of connection you are running, I advocate looking through the shell procedure first, as it makes clear what is happening at every step of the connection. The SLIP/PPP connection uses a client program that shields you from some of this complexity, but at the same time, it conceals the negotiation between computers that makes FTP happen. It is this negotiation that I want to show you now.

As you can see, we've logged on by sending the word **anonymous** when prompted for a name, sending our complete user name as the password. The password doesn't show up in this transaction because it's blanked as you type, but note that we're

```
% ftp ftp.sura.net
Connected to nic.sura.net.
220 nic.sura.net FTP server
Name (ftp.sura.net:gilster): anonymous
331 Guest login ok, send e-mail address as password.
Password:
230-    SURAnet ftp server running wuarchive experimental ftpd
230-
230-Welcome to the SURAnet ftp server.  If you have any problems with
230-the server please mail the to systems@sura.net. If you do have problems,
230-please try using a dash (-) as the first character of your password
230- -- this will turn off the continuation messages that may be confusing
230-your ftp client.
230-
230-Nifty feature:
230-
230-    Compressed files may be uncompressed by attempting to get the
230-name without the .Z.  Example: to get zen-1.0.tar.Z uncompressed one
230-would get zen-1.0.tar.
230-
230-    Entire hierarchies may also be tarred and optionally compressed.
230-To get, for example, the sendmail hierarchy tarred & compressed, one would
230-get sendmail.tar.Z.
230-
230-
230 Guest login ok, access restrictions apply.
ftp>dir
```

Figure 5.1 Logging on at the SURAnet NIC.

prompted to enter it by the phrase **Guest login ok, send e-mail address as password.**
I then entered **gilster@interpath.net** as my password. We then see a sign-on message
followed by the FTP prompt. At the prompt, I asked for a directory listing by entering the
command **dir.** Figure 5.2 shows the listing.

Many of the things we tend to look for at FTP sites will be found in directories called
pub; in this case, we need to move to a subdirectory attached to *pub* called *nic;* in other
words, our target is *pub/nic.* Let's check there for the file in question. We'll switch to that
directory by entering **cd pub/nic** and again run a **dir** command, as shown in Figure 5.3.

The file we want is 00-README.FIRST. Note the capital letters—remember, Unix is
case-sensitive! To retrieve this file, we'll use the **get** command. The transfer will take
place with the following screen information presented:

```
ftp>get 00-README.FIRST
200 PORT command successful.
150 Opening ASCII mode data connection for 00-README.FIRST (9977 bytes).
226 Transfer complete.
local: 00-README.FIRST remote: 00-README.FIRST
10164 bytes received in 0.22 seconds (45 Kbytes/s)
ftp>bye
221 Goodbye.
```

As you can see, after the file was retrieved I entered the **bye** command to log off.

Note how quick the transfer was. The first thing that strikes modem users about FTP
is that they've never seen bytes fly through a connection as quickly as they move through
the Internet's high-speed hookups. There's a big difference between a standard twisted-
pair telephone connection like the one running into your home and a high-speed T3 line
linking supercomputer sites on the backbone, which moves data at 45 Mbps (45
megabits per second). According to Merit Network Inc., a statewide network in Michigan, which helped implement the upgrade from T1 to T3, 45 Mbps is like moving all the
information in a 20-volume encyclopedia in less than 23 seconds.[1]

Your modem connected to a commercial provider can't move quite that fast; it's
probably a 9600 bps (bits per second) modem, or perhaps a 14,400 bps model. At 9600
bps, you're moving data at roughly 960 characters per second; a 14,400 bps modem
should produce up to 1,400 characters per second, although actual rates depend upon

```
ftp> dir
200 PORT command successful.
150 Opening ASCII mode data connection for /bin/ls.
total 968
drwxrwx--x   3 0         120         512 Aug  5  1994 bin
drwxrwxr-x   2 0         120         512 May 10  1994 etc
drwxrwxr-x   3 0         120         512 Mar 23 17:36 incoming
drwxrwxr-x   2 0         120        8192 Feb 15  1992 lost+found
-rw-rw-r--   1 0         120      470823 Apr  4 00:00 ls-1R
drwxrwxr-x  20 0         120         512 Dec 21 13:45 pub
226 Transfer complete.
385 bytes received in 0.0093 seconds (40 Kbytes/s)
ftp> cd pub/nic
```

Figure 5.2   A directory listing at the SURAnet NIC.

```
ftp>dir
200 PORT command successful.
150 Opening ASCII mode data connection for /bin/ls.
total 4702
-rw-rw-r--   1 mtaranto 120      1384 Jan  7 16:30 .message
-rw-r--r--   1 mtaranto 120      9977 Feb 10 15:01 00-README.FIRST
-rw-rw-r--   1 mtaranto 120     47592 Mar  5  1992 BIG-LAN-FAQ
-rw-r--r--   1 mtaranto 120      4266 Dec  8 21:38 ERIC.sites
-rw-r--r--   1 mtaranto 120      3938 Feb 10 14:55 NIC.WORKSHOP.INFO
drwxr-sr-x   2 mtaranto 120       512 Jul 22  1992 NREN
-rw-r--r--   1 mtaranto 120      2351 Oct 19 18:05 NSFNET.acceptable.use
-rw-rw-r--   2 root     120      2565 Oct 14 13:03 SURAnet.acceptable.use
-rw-rw-r--   1 mtaranto 120     85677 May 11  1992 agricultural.list
-rw-rw-r--   1 mtaranto 120     27840 Apr 17  1992 archie.manual
-rw-r--r--   1 mtaranto 120     30500 Oct 14 17:17 bbs.list.10-14
-rw-r--r--   1 mtaranto 120      3030 Nov 11 19:42 bible.resources
-rw-r--r--   1 mtaranto 120      1347 Nov 12 14:05 bionet.list
-rw-r--r--   1 mtaranto 120     41580 Dec  8 21:09 cwis.list
drwxrwsr-x   3 mtaranto 120       512 Apr 28  1992 directory.services
-rw-rw-r--   1 plieb    120      1904 Jan  6  1992 farnet-recommendations
-rw-r--r--   1 mtaranto 120     15968 Oct 28 16:21 holocaust.archive
-rw-r--r--   1 mtaranto 120      2985 Jan 29 19:58 how.to.get.SURAnet.guide
-rw-r--r--   1 mtaranto 120    137525 Feb 10 14:31 infoguide.2-93.txt
-rw-rw-r--   1 mtaranto 120    360853 Aug 20  1992 interest.groups.Z
-rw-r--r--   1 mtaranto 120    879381 Dec  9 13:09 interest.groups.txt
drwxr-sr-x   3 mtaranto 120       512 Jan  5 16:06 internet.literature
-rw-r--r--   1 mtaranto 120     15682 Dec  8 21:18 library.conferences
-rw-r--r--   1 mtaranto 120     69341 Oct  9 16:32 medical.resources.10-9
-rw-r--r--   1 mtaranto 120     15474 Nov 11 19:14 network.law.info
drwxrwsr-x   2 mtaranto 120       512 Apr 14  1992 network.service.guides
-rw-r--r--   1 mtaranto 120     20553 Oct  9 15:54 nnews.9-92
-rw-rw-r--   1 mtaranto 120      6194 Feb 21  1992 obi.directory.index
-rw-r--r--   1 mtaranto 120     39945 Aug 24  1992 search.techniques
drwxr-sr-x   2 1077     120      1024 Nov 12 15:17 training
-rw-rw-r--   1 root     120      6170 Jan  3  1992 wholeguide-help.txt
-rw-rw-r--   1 root     120    499902 Feb  4  1992 wholeguide.txt
226 Transfer complete.
2343 bytes received in 0.58 seconds (4 Kbytes/s)
```

Figure 5.3   The *pub/nic* directory at SURAnet.

such external factors as line noise. Our modems are designed to be effective over voice-grade telephone lines, and must cope with their limitations.

Internet file transfers take advantage of a ride on broadband fiber-optic cables using sophisticated routers to move local network traffic onto the broader backbone; no wonder they're fast. To get used to the Internet, you should remember the varying nature of the communications links it encompasses. Dial-up modems connect some computers to the network, but so do dedicated leased lines, moving traffic at much higher speeds. Some Internet traffic moves by satellite links, some by microwave, and much of it by way of fiber optics. The genius of TCP/IP, of course, is that it can work with such diverse communications capabilities and interconnect them all.

What we've just seen, then, is the two-part FTP process involved in a shell account. First, the network moves the file to your service provider's computer, using the high-speed links of the Internet itself. The second step, not yet illustrated in these pages, will be the transfer of the file from your service provider's computer to your own. The latter will occur at the speeds dictated by your modem, and the line conditions that influence its performance. Had we been using a SLIP/PPP connection for the above transfer, the entire process would have occurred between your computer and the remote site, and the speed of the transmission would have been dependent upon your modem as it retrieved the file to your machine.

Digression: A Bit More Unix

Remember that the blink of an eye that it took to bring your file from SURAnet to your service provider's computer does not mean that it is now on *your* computer. How-ever, because the file is available through your provider, you can examine it with a series of standard Unix commands. To make sure it's there, enter **ls** at your command prompt, and you should see the filename, along with whatever else is currently in your home directory. I see the following when I type the **ls** command at my account at Interpath:

```
% ls
00-README.FIRST News/ ftp/
Mail/ core xmodem.log
```

Examine this listing for a moment. There's our file, 00-README.FIRST. Along with it is the name of another file, called xmodem.log, which is a record of the uploads and down-loads I've done by way of the Xmodem file transfer protocol to this computer.

Note, though, that some of the entries are followed by a slash (/). This indicates they are not files but subdirectories. We can change, for example, to the *News* subdi-rectory by entering **cd News.** Here, too, we must remember that Unix is case-sensitive; entering **cd news** (small n) will simply cause the system to tell you no such directory exists. We can enter **cd** to return to the home directory. This wouldn't work in DOS, where entering **cd** with no further commands produces only another display of the command prompt. In Unix, the **cd** command changes the working directory to your home directory.

Note that Unix uses a slash (/) in path names for directories; thus */home/gilster* is a statement of the subdirectory *gilster*'s location branching off from the directory *home* which, in turn, branches off from the root directory, known solely by its slash as /. You can change between directories with the **cd** command. If you get lost doing so, a **pwd** command displays the absolute path name for the current working directory. Remem-ber, too, that entering **ls -l** will give you an expanded listing of the directory.

```
-rw-------  1 gilster   11332 Feb 17 11:15 00-README.FIRST
drwx------  2 gilster     512 Feb 17 13:31 Mail/
drwx--S---  4 gilster     512 Feb 16 13:33 News/
-rw-r--r--  1 gilster 8610224 Jan 13 14:47 core
drwxr-sr-x  2 gilster     512 Jan  9 1992 ftp/
-rw-------  1 gilster  172942 Feb 17 11:18 xmodem.log
```

With that bit of Unix directory lore as reminder, let's take a look at the name of our retrieved file. 00-README.FIRST is glaringly different from the name of a standard

DOS file. With DOS, you're limited to an eight-character (or less) filename along with a three-character extension, in the form MYFILE.DOS (this is why DOS users have become so adept at expressive three-letter extension names—they have no choice). FILE.TXT, FILE.DOC, FILE.NTS, and so on, are all legitimate DOS file names. So, for that matter, is the DOS equivalent of the file we just downloaded, which could have been something like 00readme.1st.

Unix clearly has different conventions. It does not limit you to eight-character names, for one thing. And, unlike DOS, a filename can contain more than a single period (.). Thus you could have a file called test.ltr.fax in Unix, but a DOS file named tst.ltr.fx is impermissible. DOS uses the period for one purpose only: to separate the base name from the extension.

Is 00-README.FIRST a useful document? Let's read it by using the Unix **more** command, which you can invoke at your service provider's prompt, as shown in Figure 5.4. Here we have the first page of the document, broken at the bottom of the screen. As you saw in Chapter 4, the **more** command allows you to page through the file one screen at a time, pressing the **SPACEBAR** at the end of each screen to advance to the next page. Accustomed to pressing the **RETURN** key to move between pages on commercial on-line systems, dial-up users are frustrated when they try this with Unix, since the more program will simply advance the text one line at a time with a **RETURN** key command. It will take you a long time to read any file that way! (A **q** command, incidentally, takes you out of more and back to the system command prompt at any point during your reading; you don't have to page through the entire file.)

```
% more 00README.FIRST
Welcome to the SURAnet Network Information Center,

        In this directory you will find many materials useful to the
new user of the Internet. Sub-directories have been created which
contain information on Directory Services, "Zen and the Art of the
Internet", copies of all the sessions from Richard Smith's "Navigating
the Internet: An Interactive Workshop", and several "How to Guides" for
better network navigation.  These sub-directories are entitled
directory.services, ZEN, NREN, training, and network.service.guides.
The structure of "nic" directory and sub-directories follows:

nic
-rw-rw-r--    1 mtaranto 120         6122 Jun 29 13:46 00-README.FIRST
-rw-rw-r--    1 mtaranto 120        47592 Mar  5 17:04 BIG-LAN-FAQ
-rw-rw-r--    1 root     120       216594 Jan  3 15:43 Internet-Tour.txt
drwxr-sr-x    2 mtaranto 120          512 Jul 22 13:37 NREN
drwxr-sr-x    2 mtaranto 120          512 Jun 29 13:17 ZEN
-rw-rw-r--    2 root     120         2555 Jan  3 15:43 acceptable.use.policy
-rw-rw-r--    1 mtaranto 120        85677 May 11 17:29 agricultural.list
-rw-rw-r--    1 mtaranto 120        27840 Apr 17 14:10 archie.manual
-rw-r--r--    1 mtaranto 120        23501 Jun 26 15:16 bbs.list.XX-XX
-rw-r--r--    1 mtaranto 120         3030 Nov 11 19:42 bible.resources
--More--(11%)
```

Figure 5.4 The 00-README.FIRST file, read on-line with the **more** command.

The NIC Goldmine

Note in Figure 5.4 that the more program indicates we have a good bit of the file to go. You might want to page through this file to get an idea of the resources available to you here. The index includes a readout by means of **ls -lR** (a command that generates not only a fuller directory listing of the current directory, but a list of the contents of all subdirectories as well) of what's in the NIC computers at SURAnet. Figure 5.5 gives you an idea.

There are numerous files in the working directory, which is what you'll find yourself in when you log on by FTP. But notice too that there are subdirectories, marked with their distinctive stamp drwxr-sr-x. The files, in contrast, are marked -rw-r-r-. A regular file when listed this way always shows up with a dash (-) in front of its listing; a d always signifies a directory. The first character in each line of the listing, then, identifies whether it's a file or a directory. The remaining characters contain security information, or *permissions*, explaining who can access the file. We will not discuss Unix file permissions in this book. For more on Unix permissions, and on Unix in general, see *Unix Unbound* by Harley Hahn (McGraw Hill, 1994). You may also want to consult *UNIX Power Tools*, by Jerry Peak, Tim O'Reilly, and Mike Loukides (O'Reilly/Bantam, 1993) for a superb collection of Unix tips and techniques. And an excellent short take on Unix is *Learning the UNIX Operating System*, by Grace Todino, John Strang, and Jerry Peak (O'Reilly & Assoc., 1993).

NICs, as you can see from the file descriptions in Figure 5.5, go out of their way to provide useful information to their users. A number of how-to guides are presented here, along with useful overall documents like the one called Internet-Tour.txt. The following is its file listing:

```
drwxrwsr-x   2 mtaranto 120        512 Apr 14  1992 network.service.guides
-rw-r--r--   1 mtaranto 120      20553 Oct  9 15:54 nnews.9-92
-rw-rw-r--   1 mtaranto 120       6194 Feb 21  1992 obi.directory.index
-rw-r--r--   1 mtaranto 120      39945 Aug 24 15:00 search.techniques
drwxr-sr-x   2 1077     120       1024 Nov 12 15:17 training
-rw-rw-r--   1 root     120       6170 Jan  3  1992 wholeguide-help.txt
-rw-rw-r--   1 root     120     499902 Feb  4  1992 wholeguide.txt


NREN directory

-rw-r--r--   1 mtaranto 120       8225 Jun 29  1992 GPO.bill.6-92
-rw-r--r--   1 mtaranto 120       9848 Jul 22 13:06 GPO.questions
-rw-r--r--   1 mtaranto 120      36482 Jul  7  1992 iita.1992


directory.services directory

-rw-rw-r--   1 mtaranto 120        310 Apr  9  1992 00README
-rw-rw-r--   1 mtaranto 120      25161 Apr  9  1992 FINGER.protocol.info
-rw-rw-r--   1 mtaranto 120       1036 Apr  9  1992 KNOWBOT.email.directory
-rw-rw-r--   1 mtaranto 120        816 Apr  9  1992 NETMAILHOSTS.database
--More--(60%)
```

Figure 5.5 A glimpse of the Internet background information available at a Network Information Center.

```
-rw-rw-r-- 1 root 120 216594 Jan 3 15:43 Internet-Tour.txt
```

The file size is shown to the left of the date of this file's last modification; it's 216,594 bytes, so we're dealing with a big file. Next to this is the title itself.

A number of interesting files are to be found at SURAnet, some of which we'll call upon later as we build up a network library. One called networking.terms looks helpful; it contains basic terminology for people new to the Internet. Another is netiquette.txt; it's the Miss Manners document of the network, especially useful for people who have logged on but who don't yet know what is and is not acceptable. And note the subdirectories here; one is filled with information on the NREN, the proposed National Research and Education Network that will eventually become the U.S. part of the Internet for the American research and education community. There's a subdirectory called *Network Service Guides,* and another called *ZEN,* which contains a popular network document known as *Zen and the Art of the Internet.* It provides much useful background material.

Given the huge number of FTP sites around the globe, how do you know which one you want to visit? In general, you'll find sites on a case by case basis as you explore the Net, reading about programs that have been made available, and getting tips from other users through USENET and electronic mail. But it would help to know about a comprehensive list of sites.

What You Need: A List of FTP Sites

The Document: The multipart FTP Sitelist

How to Get It: Use anonymous FTP to the following URL:

ftp://rtfm.mit.edu/pub/usenet/news.answers/ftp-list/sitelist/

The files start with a document named part1 and continue through multiple parts up to (at the time of this writing) part20. You can use the **mget** command described on page 134 to get multiple files with one command.

Using DELPHI to Run an FTP Session

DELPHI is based on computers using the VMS operating system, which runs on Digital Equipment Corporation equipment. This can pose problems for FTP sessions, and if you are using DELPHI or any other VMS system to manage your file transfer work, you should consider several alternative actions if the transfer does not work out as planned. There are two areas of concern:

- Changing directories may require you to add quotation marks to be effective. If you try the command **cd pub/nic**, for example, and it fails to work, try **cd "pub/nic"**.
- Retrieving a file may also fail when you're using FTP from a VMS system. If this occurs, try enclosing the filename in quotes. Thus, if **get 00-README.FIRST** fails, try **get "00-README.FIRST"**.

Getting Files to Your Computer

Before we move on to look at another network information center, let's do something about that index file, 00-README.FIRST. We want to get it onto our own computer because a printout would be a helpful document to keep. First we will change its Unix-style filename into something shorter, so we don't have to wrestle with so many characters. The command is simple: **mv.**

```
% mv 00-README.FIRST read.me
```

You can run another directory display by using **ls** to be sure the command took. The **mv** command is called move because it does just that: It moves the data in one file to another, and then deletes the original file.

Downloading the File with Xmodem

Now we can download the file to our computer. Here the terms begin to seem a bit more familiar. We can use the file transfer protocol Xmodem to download the file. Xmodem, created by telecommunications guru Ward Christensen, is one of a number of error-checking protocols familiar to users of commercial on-line systems; others include Ymodem, Kermit, and Zmodem. I'll rely on Xmodem for our task here because it's so widely distributed throughout the on-line world, and most users of commercial services are familiar with it. You'll also find it installed on virtually any service provider's computers. And it's hard to name a communications software package that doesn't include Xmodem.

Xmodem operates by transferring files in 128-byte blocks, adding an extra bit called the checksum to each block. The extra bit is useful; it allows the receiving computer to determine whether the transmission was accurate (if not, the protocol causes the receiving machine to request a retransmittal of the data packet). In this way, despite the perils of line noise or other communications difficulties, even large, complex files can be transmitted safely to their destination.

Using Xmodem by way of a Unix shell account requires calling up the Xmodem program from the command prompt and specifying the parameters and filename. Typically, the program will support Xmodem and Xmodem/CRC (CRC stands for cyclic redundancy check, which increases error-checking efficiency), as well as Ymodem and Ymodem-G. More on each of these as we go through the Xmodem command options.

We can perform a simple file transfer like the one in question by entering the command shown in the following:

```
% xmodem st read.me
XMODEM Version 3.9 (November 1990)—Unix-Microcomputer File Transfer Facility
File read.me Ready to SEND in binary mode
Estimated File Size 12K, 89 Sectors, 11332 Bytes
Estimated transmission time 14 seconds
Send several Control-X characters to cancel
```

As you see, the result is a message from the computer telling us the estimated file size, number of sectors and bytes in the file, and an estimated transmission time. At this point, the service provider's computer is waiting for you to begin receiving the file. You specify the appropriate protocol (Xmodem) in your communications software, enter a filename for the incoming file, and start the download procedure as prompted.

The way Xmodem is implemented on your system may vary. If you try the **xmodem** command and nothing happens, try the **sx** command. In other words, to move the read.me file, we would send the command **sx -a read.me**. In this case, the **-a** is used because we are retrieving an ASCII file. We would use **-b** if our file were binary in nature, like a picture or a program file.

Downloading with Zmodem

We can also use Zmodem to achieve the same result; in fact, Zmodem is preferable, because it is widely used and faster than Xmodem. To transfer the read.me file with Zmodem, we simply change one letter. Our command becomes **sz -a read.me**. And again, if we were going to receive a binary file, we would change the suffix to a **b,** thus, **sz -b** *filename.*

Uploading Files

There doubtless will be occasions when you want to upload a file to your service provider's computer. You may, for example, want to compose a lengthy message to some-one without trying to use the on-line Unix text editors to do so. In this case, the command is simple. You would use **rz -a** to upload an ASCII file, and **rz -b** to upload a binary file. Thus, to upload letter.doc to my service provider's machine, my command is **rz -a letter.doc**.

If I were using Xmodem to do the same thing, I could simply make a one-letter sub-stitution. Thus, **rx -a** would send an ASCII file; **rx -b** would send a binary file. Remember that, whichever protocol you choose for file transfer, you must have set your communi-cations software to use that protocol. Being set for Zmodem in your communications program and telling your service provider to receive in Xmodem simply won't work.

Translating ASCII for Your Computer

You've just downloaded a text, or ASCII, file using a binary download protocol. There are other ways you could have retrieved the file, including the simplest: using the Unix **cat** command to cause the file to scroll without page breaks, and capturing the results by turning on your communications program's capture buffer. But using Xmodem makes a great deal of sense, even when you're dealing with ASCII. The reason: The download is more accurate, because Xmodem checks for errors and corrects them when it finds them. Make it a habit to use error-checking protocols no matter what kind of file you want to retrieve.

But there's more to this story. I said earlier that ASCII is a file standard. This may have been overly optimistic. In fact, not all ASCII characters are standardized. In par-ticular, computer systems don't always have the same ideas about how to end a line of text. An MS-DOS computer ends lines with a carriage return (CR) and line feed (LF). These characters, CR and LF, are ASCII codes 13 and 10. Macintoshes use only the car-riage return to end a line. Unix systems use only the line feed.

Can you see the problem? A Macintosh doesn't know what to do with the line feed character at the end of every line of a PC file. Open a PC text file on a Macintosh and it displays these characters; it cannot interpret them. On a Unix system, the text file you upload from your MS-DOS computer has an extra carriage return for every line. Retrieve a file from a Unix system, on the other hand, and the MS-DOS user has to create the standard carriage return/line feed pairs MS-DOS expects, while the Macintosh user needs the carriage return characters the Mac likes.

Problems like these can be handled by invoking command line parameters. You've already used parameters; the command **sz -b** involves them. **sz -b** stands for send by way of Zmodem in binary format. By varying the parameters after the **sz** command, you can handle a wide range of possibilities, including uploading as well as downloading to the service provider's computer. Several of these parameters can be useful, depending on the type of computer you're using. What follows are the parameters for Xmodem to illustrate the options available.

Xmodem Parameters

The basic **xmodem** command structure is:

```
xmodem [parameter] filename.
```

rb   Receive Binary. Here you're sending, rather than receiving files. **rb** means that files are to be placed on the service provider's computer without any conversion. Xmodem destroys existing files of the same name, so be careful. You might upload if you're planning to send a previously prepared file to someone as a message.

rt   Receive Text. This process converts an incoming file in MS-DOS format to a form more familiar to Unix. The CR-LF pairs are converted to the Unix line feed-only format. The result is a file that Unix editors can use.

ra   Receive Apple. This does the same thing as **rt** but for files sent from Apple Macintosh computers. It translates the CR characters in the incoming file into Unix line feeds.

sb   Send Binary. Here, files are sent from your service provider's computer to you without conversion, just as they exist on the Unix disk.

st   Send Text. This translates the Unix line feed characters into the CR/LF pairs MS-DOS wants in a text file.

sa   Send Apple. Does the same thing as the **st** parameter, but converts Unix line feed characters into CR characters.

Other Xmodem Options

The following options should give you every tool you need to get a file from your service provider's computer to your own. I generally work with Ymodem because I transfer more than one file at a time on most occasions; when I download a series of files, I'll specify **xmodem sbyk** *filename1 filename2*, etc. I then sit back and let my communications software, Crosstalk for Windows, handle the transfer.

y   Although still invoked through the **xmodem** command, the **y** option (**xmodem y**) selects the Ymodem batch protocol for sending files. Ymodem uses CRC error checking and can transfer multiple files. Because it transmits data in 1 K blocks (Xmodem uses 128-byte blocks), Ymodem can be significantly faster than

Xmodem, although it doesn't function nearly as well when you're working with a poor telephone connection.

g   Selects Ymodem-G, a variant of Ymodem that sends files in a continuous stream. Ymodem-G works only with error-free connections because it contains no built-in error correction. But if you have an error-correcting modem, it can transfer files quickly.

m   Uses the Modem7 batch protocol for sending files. This means a list of files specified on the command line will be sent in sequence. This batch protocol is used automatically if the sending program requests it. Use Modem7 only if Ymodem batch protocols aren't available in your communications program.

k   Uses the Xmodem-1 K mode for sending files. By using 1 K packets, speed can be increased, but as with Ymodem, excessive transmission retries due to line noise or other errors can significantly slow operations.

c   Uses CRC error checking when receiving files. CRC is automatically selected for transmission if the receiving modem program requests it.

l   Do not write to the log file. A file called xmodem.log in your directory area is normally appended to whenever you use Xmodem to handle a file upload or download (you saw an example when I listed the files in my home directory). You may never need to use this file, but it can be useful if you're having problems with file transfers because it records when things went wrong.

w   Wait 15 seconds before beginning the start-up handshake. The handshake is a set of control signals between computer and modem that verifies all is ready for the transfer to begin. You may want to use **w** to force this delay if the handshaking process is causing characters to appear that hinder your own typing as you prepare for the transfer.

Retrieving Three Useful Files

You've now had an opportunity to see how the file transfer process works, from using FTP to gain access to the resources of a remote computer, transferring the file to your service provider's computer, and then downloading it to your own using Xmodem. Let's now get in some practice.

We'll use the **cd** command to change directories. It is best to go one directory at a time, in order to minimize the potential for typing mistakes. In the case of the first file shown, sign on by means of FTP, as shown in Figure 5.6, and then issue a **cd pub** command. When you're in the *pub* directory, you can issue a **cd Net_info** command to change to that directory (note the underscore, and be sure to pay attention to case!). Go one subdirectory at a time until you're in the directory called *EFF_Net_Guide.* That's where the file is.

And as before, we'll retrieve the files with the **get** command. Thus, **get internet-cmc**, and so on. You can then download them to your computer using xmodem, sz, or sx.

What to Do When You Can't Find What You Need

Change is a constant on the Internet, a fact that is never more obvious than when you're dealing with FTP sites. And this creates a problem for users, because system administrators often change the directory structures at their sites. You read about a great resource and then try to find it, only to discover that the directory you had hoped to find it in does not exist. Or perhaps the directory is still there but the file has been renamed. What to do?

Ingenuity is the answer. That and a bit of perseverance. First of all, many FTP sites contain files called README in their root directories that explain what the current directory structure is, and tell you where to find major documents or programs that have been shifted. You can also look for files called INDEX, or ls-lR. The latter is the output of the **ls-lR** command that lists the files in all directories at the site (be careful about ls-lR files, though; they can be huge, and downloading one can quickly use up your disk allotment. It always pays to check the size of any file you want to download before you actually perform the procedure. Give the **ls -l** command to produce a complete directory listing, with file size information included).

And often, a given site will make it clear that you can find what you need in a particular place. Take a look at Figure 5.7, for example, which shows you how a system administrator can construct a signpost to guide you home. In this case, administrators at the ftp.eff.org site we looked at previously was aware of the fact that the site's EFF Guide was a well-regarded network document. Anxious to keep people apprised of its whereabouts, they set up the message shown in Figure 5.7 so that it would appear when anyone accessed the *pub* directory.

What You Need: Several Documents Containing Directories of Internet Information

The Documents: Eff's Guide to the Internet, by Adam Gaffin; Information Sources: The Internet and Computer-Mediated Communication, by John December; and the MaasInfo Directories, by Robert E. Maas.

How to Get Them: By using anonymous FTP. We will use three different sites, so this will be good practice. To get Eff's Guide to the Internet, use the following URL:

ftp://ftp.eff.org/pub/Net_info/EFF_Net_Guide/netguide.eff

To get Information Sources: The Internet and Computer-Mediated Communication, use this URL:

ftp://ftp.rpi.edu/pub/communications/internet-cmc

To get the MaasInfo Directories, use these URLs:

ftp://ftp.unt.edu/articles/maas/maasinfo.docindex
ftp://ftp.unt.edu/articles/maas/maasinfo.topindex

If you're having trouble mastering URLs, go back and look at the procedure we followed when downloading the 00-README.FIRST file. Remember, work from left to right, first contacting the site using the FTP command, then working through the directory structure to reach the file in question.

```
% ftp ftp.eff.org
Connected to ftp.eff.org.
220 ftp.eff.org FTP server (Version wu-2.4(2) Thu Apr 28 17:19:59 EDT 1994) ready.
Name (ftp.eff.org:gilster): anonymous
331 Guest login ok, send your complete e-mail address as password.
Password:
230-Please read the file README
230-  it was last modified on Mon Mar  6 18:00:07 1995 - 29 days ago
230-Please read the file README.CDCI_author
230-  it was last modified on Tue Mar 14 10:59:12 1995 - 21 days ago
230-Please read the file README.WWW
230-  it was last modified on Thu Sep 15 16:34:52 1994 - 201 days ago
230-Please read the file README.eff.org
230-  it was last modified on Fri Sep 30 17:25:06 1994 - 186 days ago
230-Please read the file README.incoming
230-  it was last modified on Sat Feb 26 19:07:43 1994 - 402 days ago
230-Please read the file README.sysops
230-  it was last modified on Fri Mar 17 16:40:08 1995 - 18 days ago
230 Guest login ok, access restrictions apply.
ftp> cd pub
```

Figure 5.6   Change directories one at a time to avoid confusion.

Nonetheless, disappearing files and directories are a fact of Internet life. The files I just recommended have proven stable for several years now; they are well established and seem likely to stay put. But the day will come when you look up a file in an Internet directory and simply can't find it, despite looking at the site's index file. The only thing to do in that case is to use the various Internet search tools. We discuss the first of these, archie, later in this chapter.

Basic FTP Principles Applied

So far we've had it easy. The file transfers we've managed all involved ASCII data. But FTP procedures can be a bit more complex than that. What if we want to transfer a binary file, for example, or retrieve more than a single file with one set of commands? These things are workable, but we have to know how to find our way around inside the computer at the end of the connection.

Binary vs. ASCII Files

We've been looking at ASCII files—straight text—and haven't attempted to download software programs or, for that matter, text files that have been compressed to save on storage space. It's a simple process to make the necessary changes in our FTP settings, but before we do, let's take a closer look at what the differences between ASCII and binary files are.

When we speak of 7-bit ASCII files, which is the format in which electronic mail normally moves over the Internet, we're referring to seven bits of data being sent as a group; 128 possible combinations arise from our use of the ASCII standard, allowing us to assign some of them to letters—upper- and lower-case—and others to the necessary symbols we use in writing, such as punctuation marks, or various symbols that appear

```
250- ****************************************************************************
250- ** NOTE! Please review the material in the /pub/Alerts directory.
250- ****************************************************************************
250- Looking for EFF'S GUIDE TO THE INTERNET (formerly Big Dummy's Guide)?
250- Do this, EXACTLY as shown here, to get the regular text version:
250-     cd Net_info
250-     cd EFF_Net_Guide
250-     ls
250-     ascii
250-     get netguide.eff
250-     get netguide.faq
250- if "cd" doesn't work, try replacing it with "chdir".  Not all ftpware
250- works the same. The "ls" command will show you the other files there.
250- ****************************************************************************
250- See the file README.changes for chronological update on what's new.
250- ****************************************************************************
```

Figure 5.7   Notes like these allow system administrators to tell users where to find information.

in our text. And it's common parlance to speak of such files as text files, as opposed to the binary format of software programs, and so on:

In reality, an ASCII file binary file is just as digital as a binary file, but by convention, we use the term binary to refer to 8-bit files, where eight binary numbers are sent as a cluster. If we go from seven to eight binary numbers, we increase our list of possible combinations to 256. This extra range of numbers lacks a standard set of uses, unlike the 128 numbers of ASCII; software programs use these upper combinations for whatever purposes the programmer has in mind. Thus, if I choose to send a word processor file in binary format, I am including the upper-level number combinations, each of which is particularized according to the word processing program I use.

Now, when we're using FTP to transfer files, we need to tell the remote system what kind of file we want to move. If it's a binary file—a graphics image, a spreadsheet in native format, a word processing file with control codes for underlining, bolding, and so forth, we can announce this intention by giving the binary command. In a shell account, the way to do this is to type **binary** at the system prompt after you have logged on to the remote site. The process looks like this:

```
ftp> binary
200 Type set to I
```

At this point, you are ready to proceed with the transfer of the binary file. The procedure is exactly the same as moving an ASCII file, once you've told the system what you're doing. The statement "Type set to I" in the example refers to Image format, simply another way of specifying a binary transfer. If you change back to ASCII by giving the **ascii** command, you will see the statement "Type set to A" for ASCII. FTP defaults to ASCII, so changing the setting to binary for the transfer of such files is a necessity.

SLIP/PPP users can change their settings in much the same way, although rather than typing in the **binary** command, they will find graphical ways of doing the same thing, such as highlighting a button or making a menu setting change. And some SLIP/PPP client programs, such as Fetch for the Macintosh, handle the file recognition chore automatically, so that the whole question of which kind of file you're downloading is not critical. This is one of the additional advantages of the SLIP/PPP environment.

The FTP Command Structure

While using FTP, you'll have the opportunity to tap resources in computers around the world. These may range from Unix-driven workstations to Digital's VAX/VMS computers, from IBM-compatible PCs running MS-DOS, to Apple Macintoshes, and IBM mainframes. The directory structures of some remote systems may require you to experiment with commands to see which work. Entering **cd ..** will generally move you up through the directory tree to the previous directory. But on a VMS system, you may have to use **cdup**. Changing directories with **cd** works with an IBM system running the VM operating system, but instead of changing directories, it actually changes disks.

This may sound intimidating. After all, it took a while to learn to drive that desktop personal computer. But you do not have to master mainframe-style operating systems to get the most out of the Internet. FTP's command structure does almost everything for you; the only help it doesn't provide is converting the output of a remote system into a uniform notation. But you'll almost always be doing one of two things with FTP—looking for a specific file whose name you already know, or asking for a directory listing in a remote computer to confirm a filename before retrieving it.

Let's make sure, then, that you understand the operating parameters of FTP itself. The following describes the major commands you'll be working with.

ascii	The default setting. This allows you to transfer ASCII text files. Bear in mind that if you change this setting and subsequently want to transfer an ASCII file, you must reset the option by typing **ascii** at the prompt.
binary	The proper mode for transfer of a binary file, such as a program or a compressed file. Once **binary** is set, all subsequent transfers occur in binary mode unless the user specifies otherwise.
bye	Ends the FTP session with the remote server, taking you out of the FTP program and back to your system's command prompt.
cd *directory*	Changes the directory on the remote computer.
cdup	Changes to the parent of the current working directory on a remote VMS machine.
dir	Lists contents of the current directory in the remote machine.
get *filename*	Retrieves the file you specify and stores it on your service provider's machine.
help	Lists the major FTP commands on-screen.
ls	Lists contents of the current directory in the remote machine.
mget *filenames*	Retrieves the listed filenames from the remote computer. Used to retrieve multiple files.
pwd	Prints the name of the current working directory on the remote machine.
status	Allows you to check your file type, to verify whether you're currently set for ASCII or binary data transfers.

And here's a useful thing to know. If you're involved in an FTP session with a remote computer and find a file you simply want to look at, you can page through it by using the **get** command with a variant. For example, to read the file bogart.doc on-line (without actually transferring it), give this command:

```
get bogart.doc "|more"
```

The file will be presented on-screen using the more program, so that you can page through it at your leisure. This is a helpful way to learn which files you truly want to retrieve, and which you'd just as soon leave on the remote computer. But use this option with discretion. When you are engaged in an FTP session, the connection is "live" the entire time you are logged in; this means that you are taking up a slot that another user could need to perform his or her own work. Viewing a great number of files on-screen at an FTP site isn't the way to go; use this method only for a quick, targeted look at a specific file. If you want to examine more, download them and look at them at your leisure on your own machine, or on your service provider's computer. You can always go back to the FTP site to get more if the need arises.

A Closer Look at File Retrieval

File transfer commands under FTP are simple. You use the **get** command to retrieve the file you want. The following command, for example, pulls in a file called working.groups:

```
ftp> get working.groups
```

You can rename the file on the fly if you choose. The command

```
ftp> get working.groups work.doc
```

will transfer the file to your service provider's computer and also rename it work.doc.

Why would you want to change a file's name as you download it? The answer has to do with the different kinds of computers you can access through FTP. Unix allows you to have lengthy program names, as we saw in Chapter 4, and these can be very descriptive. On the other hand, MS-DOS limits you to eight-character names (or fewer) with three-character extensions. Thus it makes sense to rename a lengthy Unix file to something your MS-DOS system can work with, rather than letting your communications program truncate the filename to something that is too inscrutable to understand.

Retrieving Multiple Files

The command **mget** handles the transfer of multiple files. You can use wild-card commands to pull such files in. Thus the command **mget book*** will retrieve every file beginning with the four letters book and having any further characters. book1.doc would be retrieved, as would bookbinding.txt. The wild-card character *, operates exactly as it does in the DOS environment. It can stand for one or more characters. The ?, available on Unix systems, is another wild card. As in DOS, it can stand for any one character. Thus the command **mget paper?.doc** will pull in paper1.doc, paper2.doc, and so on, but will not retrieve paperback.doc. However, the command **mget paper*.doc** would bring in all these files.

Of course, wild-card strategies only apply in particular situations. Perhaps you prefer to get several unrelated files with dissimilar names. To do so, the command is **mget** *filename1 filename2*, and so on. The system will prompt you for each file you want to transfer, as shown in Figure 5.8.

NcFTP: An Alternate Take on File Transfer

If it strikes you that the Internet was not created for normal people, you're more or less right. Academic computer specialists don't have the same concerns that you and I have about making user interfaces easy to use; Unix is proof of that. But although mastering FTP is essential to success on the Internet, you should also be aware of a new method of file transfer called NcFTP, which provides a front end to the standard FTP process. Produced by Mike Gleason, NcFTP brings a graceful simplicity to moving files.

What can NcFTP do you for you that FTP can't? For one thing, NcFTP can log you in at a remote site automatically, supplying your e-mail address as your password (which is what you do manually with FTP). Because its configuration is preserved in a file called .netrc, you can add a variety of defaults, including lists of FTP sites you frequent regularly. Perhaps most useful to any regular FTP user is NcFTP's ability to page through remote file listings. Trying to read what's available in a lengthy directory full of entries normally calls for capturing screen output, or else redirecting it to a file. You will have no need to take such measures with NcFTP.

Using NcFTP to Log In

Let's use NcFTP now to log in to a remote computer and retrieve one of the Internet's most useful files, Scott Yanoff's *Special Internet Connections* list. Updated biweekly, the list covers everything from anonymous FTP sites to Telnet destinations, from electronic mail to finger servers. It's a great way to keep up with what's happening around the network as new sites come on-line.

Let's now retrieve this file using NcFTP. Here is how to set up the session:

```
ftp> mget infosource_contents INDEX
mget infosource_contents? y
200 PORT command successful.
150 Opening ASCII mode data connection for infosource_contents (52068 bytes).
226 Transfer complete.
local: infosource_contents remote: infosource_contents
52836 bytes received in 1.8 seconds (29 Kbytes/s)
mget INDEX? y
200 PORT command successful.
150 Opening ASCII mode data connection for INDEX (25718 bytes).
226 Transfer complete.
local: INDEX remote: INDEX
26308 bytes received in 0.85 seconds (30 Kbytes/s)
```

Figure 5.8   Prompting for multiple files using **mget**.

```
% ncftp csd4.csd.uwm.edu
NcFTP 1.6.7 (February 20, 1994) by Mike Gleason, NCEMRSoft.
Tip: If you don't want a .ncrecent file in your home directory, put the command
'#unset recent-list' in your .ncftprc file.
ncftp>
```

As you can see, we receive a note from Mike Gleason of NCEMRSoft, followed by a new prompt: ncftp>.

But notice what has happened, or rather, what hasn't happened. We've gone straight to the ncftp> prompt without any intervening requests for log-in information. NcFTP has logged us in at the site, supplying anonymous as our login, and our electronic mail address as our password. We're ready to do whatever we need to do with no further effort.

What You Need: Special Internet Connections, by Scott Yanoff

Where to Get It: Use anonymous FTP. The URL is

ftp://csd4.csd.uwm.edu/pub/inet.services.txt

Changing Directories with NcFTP

Changing directories is also different. To move to the *pub* directory with regular FTP, I would enter the command **cd pub**. Not so with NcFTP, whose guiding principle is to reduce workload on the user. All we need to do here is enter the directory name at the prompt:

```
ncftp> pub
This directory contains public files for anonymous users. Files may be read, but
not written (use "incoming" for writing new files).

csd4.csd.uwm.edu:/pub
ncftp>"
```

We now receive a brief statement about the directory, a listing of the directory name, and the basic ncftp> prompt.

Now for the best part. We want to look through this directory to be sure the file we need is here. Normally, we would use the **dir** command, and the results would scroll across our screen. But with NcFTP we can use the command **pdir**. The files will begin filling our screen, as we would expect:

```
ncftp>pdir
total 1061
-rwxr-xr-x 1 925    -2    7361 Mar 11 12:52 .cache
-rw-r--r-- 1 925    -2   21585 Mar 10 20:05 .cache+
-rw-r--r-- 1 501    -2    7701 Nov 5 1991 .ftp.help
-r--r--r-- 1 root   system  135 Dec 6 08:48 .message
```

and so on. But look what happens at the bottom of the page:

```
drwxr--r-x 5 1302   -2    512   Oct 22 15:53 Psychology
drwxr-xr-x 2 4502   -2    512   Oct 10 18:52 Satellite
```

```
drwxr-xr-x 2 1512   -2    512    Mar 8 11:14 agesa
-rw-r--r-- 1 4502   -2   88491  Feb 25 22:03 ajs.tif
-More-
```

As you can see, we're now in the realm of normal pager commands; we can press the **SPACEBAR** to move on through the directory. This feature alone makes NcFTP worth adding to your toolbox.

Retrieving the File

We find the file we need several pages down in the listings:

```
-rwxrwxr-x 1 4494 -2 45181 Mar 2 10:30 inet.services.txt
```

To receive it, we use the standard **get** command:

```
ncftp> get inet.services.txt
Receiving file:inet.services.txt
100% 0           45181 bytes. ETA: 0:00
inet.services.txt: 45181 bytes received in 4.25 seconds, 10.38 K/s.
```

Notice carefully what has happened now. After we have given the **get** command, we receive a statement—the name of the file we are retrieving. Notice that right below it is a percentage figure, which currently shows 100%. As the file is being received, this figure will change, reflecting the status of the file transfer. Finally, we are given the results of the transfer in the bottom line.

There is no question that throughout the Internet we are moving gradually in the direction of greater user friendliness. NcFTP is proof positive. On one level, we have a tool that is simple to implement and use. On another, we have the ability to edit the .netrc file to add default FTP sites and, in general, to tailor what we do with the program. The scope of NcFTP's options is wide. The best way to study them in detail is to look at the NcFTP manual page. To do so, enter the command **man ncftp** at your service provider's prompt. If NcFTP is not available on your system, ask your service provider to add it.

FTP through a SLIP/PPP Account

The command structure we use to make FTP transfers work underlies all transactions, no matter what interface we call into view. The beauty of a SLIP/PPP connection, however, is that it allows us to run client programs on our own machines, adding greatly to the level of user friendliness by giving us menus and other graphical niceties. Moreover, SLIP/PPP means we can choose whichever client programs we want to run our session.

Take a look at Figure 5.9, which shows an FTP session in progress with The Internet Society's FTP site; this is a good source for background information about the Internet. Examine the figure with care. On the left is a listing of the files in the current directory on my hard disk. On the right, and taking up the bulk of the display, is the listing of files at the remote site. The directories available are listed in the box at the top right (and notice the scroll bar, indicating the presence of yet further directories). The files in each directory are laid out in the box below. Double-click on a directory and you are taken to it, with its files displayed.

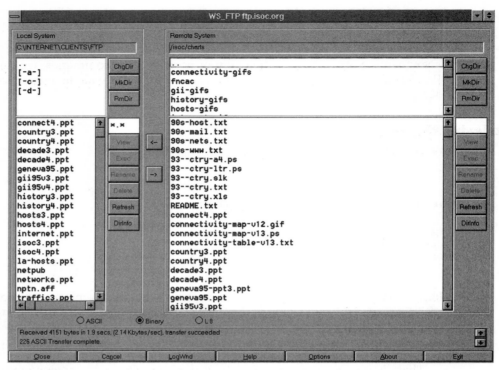

Figure 5.9 A graphical program helps you visualize the relationship between files on the remote computer and those on your own.

File transfer is straightforward. I highlight the file I want to retrieve and then click on the left-pointing arrow; in graphical terms, I am telling the remote computer that I want to move that file onto my own hard disk. A progress box then appears, as shown in Figure 5.10.

Everything about WS_FTP, the program running this transaction, is intuitive; it renders an FTP session a matter of clicking on the appropriate buttons, and makes surveying a remote site's directories a simple matter. And because you can save session profiles, you can readily set up the sites you want to visit the most so that going to them requires only clicking on the right profile.

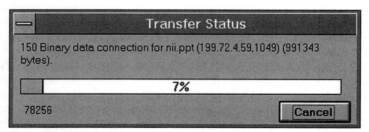

Figure 5.10 The progress box indicates the status of an ongoing file transfer.

File Compression and Unpacking

Anyone who has worked with a hard disk knows what happens when you think you've got your storage problem licked. That big new disk with seemingly inexhaustible storage space quickly becomes filled; before long, you're casting longing glances at computer catalogs, wondering how soon you'll be able to upgrade to yet another, bigger disk.

And if you've logged much time on local bulletin board systems or commercial on-line services, you know that computer systems big and small all suffer from the same problem. To get around the problem, most BBS sysops use file compression. By squeezing extraneous information out of their text, data, and program files, they can store more files on disk. This is frequently the way administrators at FTP sites handle the situation, too, using compression programs not only to shrink files but to combine multiple files into a single archive. A good file compression routine can reduce a file to 40 percent or less of its original size.

How do you know when you're dealing with a compressed file at an FTP site? Look at the file extension. Each extension tells you how the file was compressed and, therefore, what tool you will need to decompress it. Most of the decompression tools are themselves found at FTP sites around the Internet; they're also easy to locate on commercial on-line services like CompuServe and America Online. The extensions you will most often find with FTP files are these (I also include the programs necessary to decompress them, shown by computer type following each entry):

.arc   This denotes the ARC program from System Enhancement Associates, one of the first compression programs to achieve wide popularity, although it's now a system in eclipse; another compression program that uses this scheme is PKARC.
  DOS: arc602.exe; pk361.exe
  Macintosh: ArcMac1.3c
  Windows: winzip56.exe

.arj   The ARJ program from Robert Jung compresses files, while ARN is the comparable decompressor.
  DOS: arj241a.exe
  Macintosh: unarjmac
  Windows: winzip56.exe
  Unix: unarj241

.cpt   Files compressed with the Macintosh-specific Compact Pro compression program use this extension.
  DOS: ext_pc10.arj
  Macintosh: Compact Pro 1.34

.exe   Although the extension makes you think of a ready-to-use executable file, .exe can also denote a self-extracting archive. To unpack the contents, you run the file like any other program. Self-extracting files make file extracting a simple process.

.gz   The compression and decompression tool from the Free Software Foundation.
  DOS: gzip124.exe
  Macintosh: MacGzip0.2
  Windows: winzip56.exe
  Unix: gzip124

.hqx   This is the marker for a file that is in BinHex format. The BinHex standard allows Macintosh files to be accessed regardless of the type of computer involved.
    DOS: binhex.exe
    Macintosh: BinHex4.0
    Unix: mcvert

.lha   Produced by the LHA program from Haruyasa Yoshizaki.
    DOS: lha255b.exe
    Macintosh: MacLHA 2.13
    Windows: winzip56.exe
    Unix: lha1.01

.lzh   Produced by the LHA program.
    DOS: lh113c.exe
    Macintosh: MacLHA 2.13
    Windows: winzip56.exe
    Unix: lharc102

.pak   Compression and decompression.
    DOS: pak251.exe

.shar   This is a Unix tool for file compression.
    Unix: unshar

.sea   A self-extracting archive created by any of a variety of programs for the Macintosh.

.sit   A Macintosh file that has been compressed by Aladdin's StuffIt utility, or the related StuffIt Lite or StuffIt Deluxe programs.
    DOS: unstuff.exe
    Macintosh: StuffItLite

.sqz   A Dos program that compresses and uncompresses software.
    DOS: sqz1083.exe

.tar   Unix systems use tar to pack collections of files in the same master file. The .Z compression system is then used to compress the entire package.
    DOS: tar4dos.zip, tarread.arc,
    extar10.zip
    Windows: winzip56.exe
    Macintosh: Tar 4.0b
    Unix: tar

.taz   A tar file compressed in the .Z format.

.uue   A binary file encoded into straight ASCII by the uuencode program.
    DOS: toaduu21.zip
    Macintosh: uutool2.3.2
    Unix: uudecode

.Z   A file compressed with the Unix compress program uses this extension; .Z also denotes files compressed with the gzip program.
    DOS: comp430d.zip
    Windows: winzip56.exe
    Macintosh: MacCompress3.2
    Unix: compress, uncompress, u16.zip

.zip   Denotes files compressed with PKZIP, from PKware, Inc. The decompression
program is PKUNZIP.
DOS: pkz204g.exe
Windows: winzip56.exe
Macintosh: ZipIt1.2.6
Unix: unzip512

.zoo   File compression and decompression.
DOS: zoo210.exe
Macintosh: MacBooz2.1
Unix: zoo210

This list shows the major compression extensions, but there are a number of other schemes as well. If you would like a complete list, along with file sites where you can find each of these programs, an FTP site can come to your rescue.

What You Need: A Directory to File Compression Programs by David Lemson

Where to Get It: ftp://ftp.cso.uiuc.edu/doc/pcnet/compression

This document will give you specific sites where you can download any of the decompression programs you will need.

Uncompressing a File

Let's now look at an actual compressed file. This file is the mother lode of mailing list directories, the so-called List of Lists, a file you'll want to keep for future reference when we move to BITNET as well as Internet-based mailing lists.

What You Need: A Directory of Mailing Lists

The Document: The List of Lists

How to Get It: Through anonymous FTP. The URL is:

ftp://ftp.sura.net/pub/nic/interest.groups.Z

Note: You don't necessarily have to take the compressed file route. The same file is available as interest-groups.txt in a straight ASCII version. If your service provider does not make the compress program available, you can always download the uncompressed version of the file.

On the other hand, your download time will be significantly less when you use compression. So, if you would prefer to download the compressed version and uncompress it on your own computer, you can acquire a utility program that includes both compress and decompress features for DOS. The file, comp430d.zip, can be found by running a search with archie. Later in this chapter, we'll do just that, so you can add this utility to your collection of tools. And if you're a Microsoft Windows user, WinZip is the program you need. It contains a wide variety of compression and decompression tools, and is the easiest of all such programs to use.

Although the file you are interested in is a text file, the fact that it has been compressed means you must treat it as a binary file, and set the binary flag to download it. You do that simply by entering **binary** at the ftp> prompt. A **dir** command shows all the files in that directory. You then can change to the *nic* directory using the **cd** command, and retrieve the file with the **get interest.groups.Z** command. You sign off from the session by entering **bye.** A graphical client would make this procedure even easier.

Now you need to uncompress this file. There are two ways to proceed. If you're using a shell account, you can perform the decompression on your service provider's machine. Remember, the computer you are logging on to is one that contains a wide range of software tools, usually Unix programs designed to handle your network chores. The file will have been retrieved to your home directory on that machine. To unpack it, simply give the following command at the system prompt:

```
uncompress interest.groups.Z
```

This lets the Unix uncompress program go to work and unpack your file. A measure of the significance of the compression process is the total size of the compressed file, which was 360,853 bytes, versus the size of the complete, uncompressed text, some 879,381 bytes. Clearly, file compression can save a lot of space on disk.

Naturally, you don't want to use up your allotment of disk space and tax the patience of the system administrator. So why not download this file to your own computer, and then remove it from your service provider's machine? The **xmodem** command can handle the chore:

```
% xmodem sb interest.groups
```

Or you could use **sz -b:**

```
% sz -b interest.groups
```

It's a long download, but it's worth the effort, considering how useful this directory can be. When the download is complete, be sure to erase the file from your service provider's computer. The command **rm interest.groups** will do the trick. Note, by the way, that when the uncompress routine did its work, it removed the old .Z file, replacing it with the newly uncompressed file.

If you're running a SLIP/PPP account, you won't have to go through the two-step FTP process. The interest.groups.Z file will have moved by FTP directly to your own computer. On your machine, you will need to unpack it, using a decompression program like the comp430d.zip package, WinZip (for Microsoft Windows), or MacCompress3.2.

tar Files and How to Use Them

The compress utility, as we've seen, squeezes the fat out of files to make more room for other files on disk. But another type of compression is needed. PKZIP, for example, can squeeze single files and archive multiple ones. The tar utility creates file archives out of multiple files in Unix. A file created with tar is easy to identify because it has the .tar extension. Thus we have recipes.tar, a file whose name tells us it's an archive of multiple recipe files.

An archive can also be compressed. If we want to shrink our recipes.tar archive, we can enter the command **compress recipes.tar**. The result is another file with an unwieldy name: recipes.tar.Z. But despite its multiple extensions, recipes.tar.Z is easy to decode. The .Z at the far right tells us the first thing we must do to get at this file is to uncompress it. The second thing is to unpack the archive of the resulting recipes.tar file (a file with a .tar extension is commonly called a *tarfile*). This is handled by invoking tar with options. There are two tar commands you'll need to know.

tar -xf Extract all the files in the archive. Thus, to extract everything in recipes.tar, you enter **tar -xf recipes.tar**.

tar -tf List the contents of the tar file. To see the contents of recipes.tar, then, you enter **tar -tf recipes.tar**.

Using archie to Track Down Files

One problem arises immediately as we look into FTP. If this is a way of downloading files, how do we know where to look for those files in the first place? With commercial systems, it's easy: call up the local access number and get on-line, move to the file libraries, and browse. The Internet lacks that kind of organization. There's no central repository, no library area clearly set aside for users. Internet rookies have to be aggressive to find what they're looking for, and that often means asking questions, making mistakes, digging for information.

This is where archie comes in. A retrieval tool, archie helps you find the file you need, no matter which FTP site happens to make it available on the network. And as you'll see in later chapters, it's one of a string of search and discovery tools now being fine-tuned to help the Internet navigator.

Originally developed by computer scientists at McGill University in Montreal, the archie system is now a product of Bunyip Information Systems in the same city.[2] archie stores information on what is available at FTP sites in regularly updated servers. You or I can query these databases to find out quickly where a given file is. Finding files on the Internet would be a dicey proposition without archie.

Using archie is simple. You use Telnet to log on to an archie server and search the database, or you use an archie client, either on your service provider's system or your own.

McGill University is where it all began. However, there are numerous Telnet sites for archie. For example, the InterNIC maintains archie at ds.internic.net. You would reach this address by using Telnet; the command would be **telnet ds.internic.net**. We'll cover Telnet procedures shortly; the idea is that they allow you to log on to a remote computer and use its resources. Throughout the archie system, sites around the world store information about the contents of Internet sites, performing a portion of their search work every night, so that the entire archie database is eventually updated about once every 30 days.

The collected information is a powerful Internet resource, and it is one you can examine. archie allows you to do this by searching for entries containing a particular search string, and it can provide other information that is useful in the hunt for specific files. Figure 5.11 shows you the introductory screen you'll see when you log on through

```
SunOS UNIX (finsun)


login: archie
Password:
Last login: Fri Apr 14 16:05:08 from ecn01.cineca.it
SunOS Release 4.1.3_U1 (FINSUN) #14: Wed Feb 8 09:55:53 EET 1995
!       CSC - Tieteellinen laskenta Oy    !    Teknillinen korkeakoulu      !
!       PL 405 Tietotie 6                 !    Atk - keskus Otakaari 1      !
!       FIN-02101  ESPOO                  !    FIN-02150  ESPOO             !
Q---------------------------------------Q-------------------------------Q
! Neuvonta    : 90-457 2821, neuvoja@csc.fi ! Opastusj{rjestelm{t komennoilla: !
! Käyttöluvat: 90-457 2075, usermgr@csc.fi !    'gopher' ja 'help'            !
! Keskus     : 90-457 1                    ! Asiantuntija- ja ohjelmistolista:!
! Fax        : 90-457 2302                 !    'help ohjelmistolista'         !
! Valvonta Nmt: 949 - 465 293, oper@csc.fi !                                  !
Q---------------------------------------------------------------------------Q
! CSC:n ja TKK:n valokuituyhteyksiss{ olleet ongelmat ovat johtuneet Cypressin!
! verkkoliittym{n viallisesta toiminnasta. Cypressin tietoliikenne kulkee     !
! toistaiseksi CSC:n ethernetverkon kautta, kunnes vika saadaan korjattua.    !
Q---------------------------------------------------------------------------Q


                        Welcome to Archie!
                           Vers 3.3


archie.funet.fi  is now in a temporary home at finsun.csc.fi. We are
constructing a new home for it. In case of problems you could
try archie.luth.se or archie.doc.ic.ac.uk instead.


# Bunyip Information Systems, Inc., 1993, 1994, 1995


# Terminal type set to `vt100 24 80'.
# `erase' character is `^?'.
# `search' (type string) has the value `sub'.
FUNET-archie>
```

Figure 5.11 Logging on to archie in Finland.

Telnet to the archie server in Finland. The command is **telnet archie.funet.fi**. (log on as **archie**). Using a client on your own system, however, is a better way to access archie. Your service provider probably has one set up for your use; or if you use a SLIP/PPP account, you can take advantage of graphical client programs to perform the same chores.

A variety of commands are available at the prompt. I used the **list** command to see how many sites were currently tracked here, and received a scrolling melange of hundreds of entries. Clearly, there's no shortage of material for software hunters.

archie Servers

Numerous archie servers exist. The list follows in Table 5.1.

Which archie to Use?

Given that archie servers are located around the world, and that your Internet access is international in scope, you may be tempted to access an archie server in some exotic land. Resist the temptation. A cardinal principle in your Internet travels should be: *Don't be wasteful of network resources.* Why route your work through Australia when there's a server in the adjacent state? The resources of archie servers aren't infinite, and if people work with servers nearest to them, the result is a more distributed workload for the system. Responsiveness drops when a single server becomes overloaded, which is why you may be informed that a given server is working up to capacity and cannot handle your request at the moment.

Table 5.1 archie Servers Worldwide

SERVER ADDRESS	LOCATION	COUNTRY
archie.au	University of Melbourne	Australia
archie.univie.ac.at	University of Vienna	Austria
archie.bunyip.com	Bunyip Information Systems, Inc.	Canada
archie.cs.mcgill.ca	McGill University	Canada
archie.uqam.ca	University of Quebec	Canada
archie.funet.fi	Finnish University and Research Network	Finland
archie.univ-rennes1.fr	——————	France
archie.th-darmstadt.de	Technische Hochschule, Darmstadt	Germany
archie.ac.il	Hebrew University, Jerusalem	Israel
archie.unipi.it	University of Pisa	Italy
archie.wide.ad.jp	WIDE Project, Tokyo	Japan
archie.kornet.nm.kr	KORNET	Korea
archie.sogang.ac.kr	Sogang University	Korea
archie.uninett.no	Trondheim	Norway
archie.icm.edu.pl	Warsaw University	Poland
archie.rediris.es	RedIRIS, Madrid	Spain
archie.luth.se	University of Lulea	Sweden
archie.switch.ch	SWITCH, Zurich	Switzerland
archie.ncu.edu.tw	National Central University, Chung-li	Taiwan
archie.doc.ic.ac.uk	Imperial College, London	United Kingdom
archie.hensa.ac.uk	University of Kent at Canterbury	United Kingdom
archie.sura.net	BBN Planet Southeast	USA
archie.internic.net	AT&T InterNIC	USA
archie.rutgers.edu	Rutgers University, NJ	USA
archie.ans.net	Advanced Network & Services; Elmsford, NY	USA

Note: The load on archie servers has become intense. You are now more likely than ever to run into a prompt like the following:

```
% telnet archie.sura.net
Trying 128.167.254.195...
Connected to yog-sothoth.sura.net.
Escape character is '^]'.
telnetd: All network ports in use.
Connection closed by foreign host.
```

Network congestion is the culprit, and the only recourse is to try another server, or to wait a short while and try this one again. You will run into fewer problems with network overload if you try to time your archie sessions for periods after business hours at the server site. Presumably, fewer people will then be trying to log on.

A Sample archie Search by Telnet

We use the **find** command to search archie; the syntax is simply **find** *search-term*, where *searchterm* is whatever you're looking for. You can also use the older **prog** command if you choose. I'm interested in shortwave radio, for example, so let's see if we can find any sites that contain files on the subject. I'll send the **find radio** command to the server at SURAnet (it's the nearest server to me, based in Maryland), assuming that the term *shortwave* may be too precise for the database index. Figure 5.12 shows a fragment of what I receive.

This is only a segment of the list, but it imparts the flavor of the archie search. As you can see, it has given me a list of FTP sites that contain material indexed under the term *radio*. Exactly how relevant those sites will be to my search for shortwave information remains to be seen; I would next need to use FTP to go to the sites and check out what files they had available.

Tightening Up Search Terms

Is archie always this unspecific? Not really. Suppose I needed a specific file. I know there's a shareware program, called GEOCLOCK, that calculates the sun's position over the earth and produces a constantly updated map. Such a map is useful for shortwave listeners, because the best times for picking up low-power, difficult-to-hear stations are when the sunrise or sunset line is passing right over them. I'd like to find this program and download it for evaluation, so I will give archie the job of finding it. The command will be **find geoclock.** Figure 5.13 shows the result. As you can see, we have here a listing of sites containing files that include the search term, *geoclock*, in their name.

Now we face an interesting dilemma. If you have been around computers for long, you've noticed that filenames are often anything but intuitive. If every instance of the program GEOCLOCK were listed as geoclock.zip or geoclock.exe, that would be one thing. But what if the program were stored as geoclk.exe? Our search wouldn't have turned it up. What we need is a way to change the terms of the archie search to find those instances of the program that are not so obviously listed. archie obliges by providing a series of search parameters that can be controlled by our commands. We can change the search type with the following command:

```
set search searchtype
```

```
Host funet.fi      (130.230.1.1)
Last updated 09:56 13 Apr 1995

    Location: /internet-drafts
       FILE     -rw-r--r--    2263 bytes  01:00 14 Aug 1994   draft-adamson-ipng-ra
dio-req-00.txt

Host ftp.univ-rennes1.fr     (129.20.254.1)
Last updated 08:44 11 Apr 1995

    Location: /reseau/internet/internet-drafts
       FILE     -r--r--r--    2263 bytes  20:25 11 Aug 1994   draft-adamson-ipng-ra
dio-req-00.txt

Host ftp.luth.se     (130.240.16.39)
Last updated 08:53 13 Apr 1995

    Location: /pub/docs/internet-drafts
       FILE     -r--r--r--    2263 bytes  20:00 11 Aug 1994   draft-adamson-ipng-ra
dio-req-00.txt

Host ftp.rrzn.uni-hannover.de     (130.75.2.2)
Last updated 07:20 12 Apr 1995

    Location: /pub/info/internet-docs/internet-drafts
       FILE     -rw-r--r--    2263 bytes  14:05  8 Aug 1994   draft-adamson-ipng-ra
dio-req-00.txt

Host ftp.crim.ca     (192.26.210.1)
Last updated 04:58 14 Apr 1995

    Location: /Internet/Internet-Drafts
       FILE     -rw-r--r--    2263 bytes  20:00  7 Aug 1994   draft-adamson-ipng-ra
dio-req-00.txt

Host ftp.vse.cz     (146.102.16.9)
Last updated 03:57 12 Apr 1995

    Location: /pub/docs/internet-drafts
       FILE     -r--r--r--    2263 bytes  19:00  7 Aug 1994   draft-adamson-ipng-ra
dio-req-00.tx
```

Figure 5.12 Results of an archie search under the term *radio*.

(where *searchtype* is a variable that determines how archie looks for information). Here are the command possibilities:

exact   An exact match to the filename.

regex   Treats the search string as a Unix regular expression to match file-names. For more on Unix regular expressions, see Harley Hahns *Unix Unbound* (Osborne McGraw-Hill, 1994).

```
Host cranach.rz.tu-ilmenau.de      (141.24.8.28)
Last updated 09:02 11 Apr 1995

     Location: /pub/msdos/comp.binaries
        DIRECTORY      drwxr-xr-x       512 bytes   07:08 17 Oct 1994   geoclock

Host ftp.rc.tudelft.nl    (130.161.180.86)
Last updated 09:58 13 Apr 1995

     Location: /pub/pc/msdos/misc
        FILE     -rw-r--r--   180518 bytes  18:00 29 Nov 1993   geoclock.exe

Host cranach.rz.tu-ilmenau.de      (141.24.8.28)
Last updated 09:02 11 Apr 1995

     Location: /pub/msdos/ham/erlangen_mirror/diverses
        FILE     -r--r--r--    74793 bytes  18:00  9 May 1993   geoclock.zip

Host nic.funet.fi    (128.214.248.6)
Last updated 05:21 12 Apr 1995

     Location: /pub/dx/software/msdos/solar
        FILE     -rw-r--r--   307089 bytes  21:00  9 Apr 1991   geoclock.lzh
```

Figure 5.13   Results of a search using the **set search sub** command.

sub	The search string will find a hit if the filename in question contains it *as a part of* its name. This is a much broader form of search than the two previously listed.
subcase	While **sub** is not sensitive to case, **subcase** is. Thus, using this setting will cause your search string to find a hit only if the filename contains it as part of its name, and only if the case matches the case of the substring.
exact_sub	Searches for an exact hit. If archie finds no matches, it will then try the substring search strategy.
exact_subcase	Searches using the *exact* strategy; but if this fails, the search switches to a subcase, or case-sensitive substring, search.
exact_regex	Begins with the exact search method, but switches to *regex* if no matches are found.

With these capabilities in mind, we can see that archie provides for a wide variety of searches. At the archie> prompt, we can enter the search type we require (although you should check when you log on to an archie server what type is established as the default at the site—it's often **sub**).

Ponder what would have happened to our search for GEOCLOCK if we had used the **exact** search type. In that case, we wouldn't have retrieved any of the files we found with the **sub** setting, because the search term, *geoclock*, is not exactly the same as the file geoclock.zip, even though the latter contains the former as part of its name. You will find that the **sub** setting is the easiest one to use, and the one most likely to provide the results you need. But if you do know an exact filename is stored on a computer somewhere, you can give the **set search exact** command before running the search to find it.

Directories vs. Files

archie is doubly useful because it doesn't just find files, it also finds directories. Assume, for example, that we're searching for a Spanish language tutorial. It would be of considerable interest to learn that a directory meeting our search terms existed, because it would imply abundant resources for us to explore. We can consider this possibility by looking through the archie archives under the term *spanish*. After running this search, we come up with seven possibilities (I started with the **exact** setting on), about which we notice something interesting. Look at what I retrieved in Figure 5.14.

What stands out in this list is the fact that all of these entries are directories. In the last entry, for example, we're directed to a directory called */pub/doc/dictionaries/ wordlists*. We don't know exactly what's in that directory, but if we use FTP to access the site, we can then run a **dir** command to view what's there.

If we reset the search terms, entering **set search sub**, we can generate a broader list of actual files. We will also see that one difference between using **sub** and **exact** as search types is that **exact** searches take less time to run; the search is less intensive because the pattern matching is so precise. When I ran the search again using **sub** as a search type, I pulled up some of the hits shown in Figure 5.15. As we see, these are files rather than directories, and while we don't know for sure what they are, we're clearly homing in on the tutorial we need. We can now use FTP to the site to examine each file in turn.

Using Whatis

archie maintains a software description database that holds the names and descriptions of software packages. This database can also be searched by using the **whatis** command. You'll get back a filename and a short description of that file. The database is useful when you're looking for something but don't know which programs might be able to help. You'll probably use the **whatis** command first in many cases, turning then to the standard **find** command once you know the name of the file you're interested in.

We might, for example, need to find a conversion program that would switch ASCII text into a format usable by PostScript. To find it, we could use the **find postscript** command, but asking archie for anything with PostScript in the file description could lead to a very long list. Better to be specific, using the **whatis** command to ask for conversion programs. Let's try the command **whatis converter**. Figure 5.16 shows a shortened version of what we'll see on-screen.

Clearly, the file a2ps is just what we're after. Having located it through this shortcut, we can now use the standard **find** command to track it down; **find a2ps** yields eight locations for this file, such as:

```
Host ftp.uni-trier.de (136.199.8.81)
Last updated 01:36 11 Apr 1995
     Location: /pub/unix/systems/linux/SLT/g1
        FILE    -rw-r--r-- 15761 bytes 07:51 25 Feb 1994 a2ps-bin.tgz
     Location: /pub/unix/systems/linux/SLT/g1.old
        FILE    -rw-r--r-- 15761 bytes 07:51 25 Feb 1994 a2ps-bin.tgz
```

```
Host epas.utoronto.ca      (128.100.160.1)
Last updated 05:38 14 Apr 1995

     Location: /pub/cch
        DIRECTORY      drwxr-xr-x       512 bytes   13:50 22 Jan 1995   spanish

Host idea.sec.dsi.unimi.it     (149.132.3.1)
Last updated 04:21 12 Apr 1995

     Location: /.1/security/src/dictionaries
        DIRECTORY      drwxr-xr-x      1024 bytes   11:53 28 Dec 1994   spanish

Host gopher.eunet.es     (193.127.1.2)
Last updated 09:23 11 Apr 1995

     Location: /pub/unix/text/TeX
        DIRECTORY      drwxr-xr-x       512 bytes   11:43 21 Nov 1994   spanish

Host ftp.denet.dk     (129.142.6.74)
Last updated 06:19 13 Apr 1995

     Location: /pub/wordlists
        DIRECTORY      drwxr-xr-x       512 bytes   09:08 26 Sep 1994   spanish

Host ftp.informatik.tu-muenchen.de     (131.159.0.198)
Last updated 04:26 12 Apr 1995

     Location: /pub/comp/platforms/pc/msdos/patches/msdos
        DIRECTORY      dr-xr-xr-x         0 bytes   02:58 14 Jul 1994   spanish

Host luna.gui.uva.es     (157.88.111.241)
Last updated 04:55 12 Apr 1995

     Location: /pub/pc/microsoft
        DIRECTORY      dr-xr-xr-x      1024 bytes   19:00  5 Jul 1994   spanish

Host ftp.uni-trier.de     (136.199.8.81)
Last updated 01:36 11 Apr 1995

     Location: /pub/unix/security/dictionaries
        DIRECTORY      drwxr-xr-x       512 bytes   09:11 28 Jun 1994   spanish

Host brother.cc.monash.edu.au     (130.194.11.1)
Last updated 13:18 13 Apr 1995

     Location: /pub/celia
        DIRECTORY      drwxr-xr-x       512 bytes   20:00 14 Jun 1994   spanish

Host ftp.informatik.uni-hildesheim.de     (147.172.48.223)
Last updated 07:36 12 Apr 1995

     Location: /pub/security/ftp.dsi.unimi.it/src/dictionaries
        DIRECTORY      drwxrwxr-x       512 bytes   18:00 12 May 1994   spanish

Host coli.uni-sb.de     (134.96.68.11)
Last updated 01:31 11 Apr 1995

     Location: /pub2/cs.tu-berlin.de/mirrors/apple/dts/mac/sys.soft.intl
        DIRECTORY      drwxrwxr-x       512 bytes   19:00 13 Oct 1992   spanish

Host ftp.inf.tu-dresden.de     (141.76.1.11)
Last updated 08:33 12 Apr 1995

     Location: /pub/doc/dictionaries/wordlists
        DIRECTORY      drwxr-xr-x       512 bytes   18:00 11 Aug 1992   spanish
```

Figure 5.14 Results of a search for a Spanish language tutorial.

```
Host ftp.cwi.nl     (192.16.191.128)
Last updated 10:14 13 Apr 1995

    Location: /pub/jack/spunk/info/intro
       FILE     -rw-r--r--    1661 bytes  06:46 23 Feb 1995  spanish

Host ftp.tu-graz.ac.at    (129.27.2.4)
Last updated 11:40 13 Apr 1995

    Location: /.1/pub/Linux/distributions/debian/debian-0.91/dist/packages/words
       FILE     -rw-r--r--  248198 bytes  21:00 29 Jan 1994  wspanish.deb

Host coli.uni-sb.de    (134.96.68.11)
Last updated 01:31 11 Apr 1995

    Location: /pub2/cs.tu-berlin.de/demo
       FILE     -rw-rw-r--     579 bytes  19:00  1 Feb 1993  spanish_lang.intro
       FILE     -rw-rw-r--   66176 bytes  19:00  1 Feb 1993  spanish_lang.bin

    Location: /pub2/cs.tu-berlin.de/mirrors/apple/dts/mac/sys.soft.intl
       DIRECTORY    drwxrwxr-x     512 bytes  19:00 13 Oct 1992  spanish
```

Figure 5.15   Results of a tightened search for the Spanish language tutorial.

archie's descriptive index is helpful, but it can be deceptive. Because the index for the whatis function and the (separate) archival index for the **find** command are not simultaneously updated, you may find yourself with a hit using **whatis**, but when you try to locate it, archie seems to have no record of it. What has doubtless happened is in the time between updates, the file in question has been deleted from the system. The only thing to do in such a case is to keep searching for other files that meet your criteria.

All in all, the **whatis** command is limited. It depends on the people who place files at various sites to submit complete descriptions of those files, and this is often not the case. Bunyip Information Systems is now moving in the direction of *templates*, which

```
archie> whatis converter

8to1                  SUN raster file color to mono converter
a2ps                  ASCII to PostScript converter
conv                  Simple numeric base converter
cvtbase               Generalized base converter
ditroff-to-dvi        Device-independent troff (ditroff) to TeX DVI converter
dvi2ps                DVI to PostScript converter
dvips                 DVI to PostScript converter
epsonps               Epson to PostScript converte
f2ps                  A FIG to PostScript converter
fig2ps                A FIG to PostScript converter
gif2ps                A GIF to PostScript converter
```

Figure 5.16   A **whatis** search for a Postscript conversion program.

can be used to record information such as date of last update for a given file. The widespread use of templates would significantly increase the usefulness of archie as a search tool.

The following describes a number of other archie commands.

bye   Logs you off the system. You can also use **quit** or **exit**.

help   Produces a short help screen; subtopics are available.

list   Tells which FTP sites are listed in the archie database.

mail   Lets you send the output of your search to a user. Include an e-mail address.

servers   Lists publicly available archie servers known to the site you are using.

site   Lists the files at an archive site. Thus **site uts.mcc.ac.uk** produces every-thing available at that location.

Putting an archie Client to Work

Is there an archie client on your service provider's machine? If you're not sure, enter **archie** at the command prompt and see what happens. You should get a list of archie commands usable at the prompt. These commands let you precisely modify the output you'll get from the program, helping you gain control over your search. The most signif-icant of these commands are described in the following. The syntax is simple: **archie** *[options] searchterm*, where the search term, as with a Telnet archie search, is what-ever you are looking for. Note that you're using **archie** as a command here instead of **find**, the command used in Telnet sessions.

-c   Sets up a case-sensitive substring search. This lets you search for embedded terms using case distinctions; thus, you could search for cello.exe while excluding CELLO.EXE. Note that this kind of search is the same as entering **set search subcase** with a Telnet connection.

-e   Matches the search term exactly. This is the default setting, and the equivalent to using a **set search exact** command with a Telnet connection to an archie server.

-h *hostname*   Using **-h**, you can specify a server host for your search. Thus, **archie -h archie.ans.net** tells the client to use the server at ANS to run its search.

-l   Lists one match per line. Use this only if you need to receive results that you plan to process with other Unix tools. The equiv-alent Telnet command is **set output_format machine**.

-L   Lists servers known to the archie client, as well as the server the client defaults to when it searches.

-m *number of hits*   One of the key options in your arsenal. You can use **-m** to set the number of items the archie search will return. Thus, **-m30** returns 30 hits. You can do the same thing through Telnet with the command **set maxhits 30**. Using this command is a good way to minimize the information flow to find what you need quickly.

-N	Sets the so-called niceness level. This allows you to adjust how fast your search proceeds. Choose a niceness level between 0 and 35,765 (the default is 0). The higher the number, the more likely it is your search will be moved to the back of the queue to allow other searches to proceed first.
-o *filename*	Stores the results of your search in a file. This practice is highly recommended, as it will prevent results from scrolling quickly off your screen. Thus, **archie graphics -o universe txt**.
-r	Searches using Unix regular expressions, allowing a high degree of flexibility in search strategy. The comparable command with an archie server through Telnet is **set search regex**.
-s	Creates a case-insensitive substring, meaning you can search for embedded terms without regard to upper- or lowercase. With a Telnet connection you would use **set search sub**, which is actually the default setting for archie version 3.0.
-t	**-t** is a sort command, allowing you to arrange output by time and date, with the most recent date first. The equivalent command with Telnet is **set sortby time**.
-V	Causes archie to insert a statement reminding you that it is working. It looks like this:

```
Searching..
```

A typical archie client search statement might look like this:

```
archie -s -m25 belloc -o belloc.doc
```

Here, we are looking for a file whose name we suspect contains the letters belloc. We don't know what extension it might have, so we choose **-s** to run a substring search without regard to case. We also limit our number of hits to 25, a manageable amount, and send the output to a file called belloc.doc, for examination later.

The **whatis** command, by the way, is not available through the line-oriented archie client for Unix, but this limitation is more than made up for by the client's ease of use. If you have a client on your service provider's computer, you should definitely plan on using it rather than going through Telnet, even though Telnet operations offer a wider range of switches. The archie client is your fastest method of archie access.

Using an archie Client to Retrieve the Compression Utilities

Let's run a quick search to find the useful tool winzip56.exe, which includes both compress and decompress routines; this allows us to pack and unpack .Z files on our own machines. WinZip also includes a full range of file compression utilities, allowing you to use almost all of the options discussed earlier in this chapter. Our archie command will be as follows:

```
archie -m20 winzip56.exe -o compress.doc
```

The command accepts the default search strategy, since we know the precise file title already, and asks archie to limit itself to 20 hits. We then direct the program to send the output to a file called compress.doc. Here are a few of the hits thus generated. We can now use anonymous FTP to retrieve the file from any of these sites. But try running the archie search first for practice.

```
Host plaza.aarnet.edu.au
    Location: /micros/pc/SimTel/win3/archiver
        FILE -r--r--r-- 294736 Feb 4 15:06 winzip56.exe
    Location: /micros/pc/garbo/windows/util
        FILE -r--r--r-- 294736 Feb 24 07:14 winzip56.exe

Host brother.cc.monash.edu.au
    Location: /pub/win3/util
        FILE -rw-rw-r-- 294736 Feb 28 21:35 winzip56.exe

Host bode.ee.ualberta.ca
    Location: /pub/dos/win3/local-winsock/util
        FILE -rw-r--r-- 294736 Mar 19 21:34 winzip56.exe

Host ftp.vse.cz
    Location: /pub/msdos/simtel-win3/archiver
        FILE -r--r--r-- 294736 Feb 4 15:06 winzip56.exe

Host sun0.urz.uni-heidelberg.de
    Location: /pub/simtel_win3/archiver
        FILE -rw-rw-r-- 294736 Feb 4 16:06 winzip56.exe

Host ftp.uni-kl.de
    Location: /pub3/pc/win/archives
        FILE -rw-rw-r-- 294736 Mar 2 01:53 winzip56.exe

Host ftp.msc.cornell.edu
    Location: /incoming
        FILE -rw-rw-r-- 294736 Mar 2 04:57 winzip56.exe

Host ftp.loria.fr
    Location: /pub/pc/cica/util
        FILE -r--r--r-- 294736 Feb 25 12:47 winzip56.exe

Host ftp.cyf-kr.edu.pl
    Location: /pub/mirror/simtel/win3/archiver
        FILE -rw-r--r-- 294736 Feb 4 15:06 winzip56.exe

Host ftp.sunet.se
    Location: /pub/pc/mirror/SimTel/win3/archiver
        FILE -r--r--r-- 294736 Feb 4 15:06 winzip56.exe
    Location: /pub/pc/windows/mirror-cica/util
        FILE -r--r--r-- 294736 Feb 25 12:47 winzip56.exe
```

What would we do if winzip56.exe underwent a version change? Our exact strategy would no longer work, but we could still search using a substring approach. A simple command might be **archie -s winzip**. This would look for any file with the substring **winzip** and any further extensions. Of course, we would also be more likely to retrieve extraneous material from this search.

Looking for Macintosh versions of the compression utilities? See Chapter 8, where we discuss how to retrieve them by electronic mail.

archie with a Graphical Client

archie is a classic case of command line complexity. To use it properly, you must master the necessary commands; they are at once obscure yet powerful, for they give you considerable control over your search parameters. When you move into the **SLIP/PPP** environment, you will be able to take advantage of client software like Wsarchie for Microsoft Windows, and Anarchie for the Macintosh. Both provide graphical interfaces that ease the complex task of locating files at FTP sites.

Figure 5.17 shows you an example of Wsarchie at work. In the example, I am searching for the Wsarchie program itself. The program could hardly be easier to use; the method is to enter your search term in the Search for field, while choosing an archie server in the box immediately below. And notice how a graphical client handles the question of search types. Rather than requiring you to enter commands, Wsarchie provides you with a series of search options; click on the button you want. In this case, I have

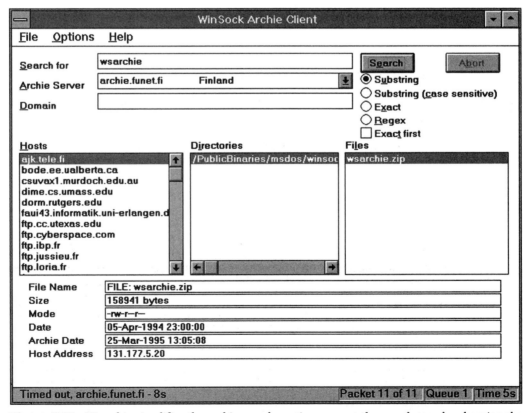

Figure 5.17 Wsarchie simplifies the archie search routine; you set the search type by choosing the right button for the job.

chosen to search with the **sub** setting, because I don't necessarily know the exact name of the file in question.

Notice how the results are laid out. The panel to the left contains the sites where hits have been found. The highlighted, or current, site is ajk.tele.fi; I could move the highlight around as necessary to see what's in each site (and the scroll bar is available to look through those sites that have scrolled off at the bottom). The directory is shown in the center box, while the filename is shown to the right. Full file information, including filename, file size, and more is provided at the bottom left of the screen. A good client program provides you with connectivity options to other clients as well. Wsarchie, for example, allows you to configure it so that when you double-click on the file you want, it launches WS_FTP to retrieve it.

Figure 5.18 shows a fine program for the Macintosh called Anarchie. Of all the archie clients, I find anarchie the easiest to use. Like Wsarchie, it makes it possible to double-click on the item you want and FTP directly to the site. In the figure, I am examining the results of a search for the program Anarchie itself. As with Wsarchie, I have chosen a server, in this case the one at archie.sura.net, and have given a search term using the **sub** search type. As you can see from the figure, there are a number of places from which you can download the program.

It would be helpful to have a site at which to examine the various archie clients to see which is best for your use.

What You Need: A Site for archie Clients

Where to Look: In addition to the major file archives like ftp://wuarchive.wustl.edu and ftp://oak.oakland.edu, try the following URLs:

ftp://ftp.cs.mcgill.ca/pub/archie/clients/

ftp://ftp.cs.widener.edu/pub/archie/

anarchie from archie.unl.edu

Name	Size	Date	Zone	Host	Path
anarchie	-	7/30/94	1	ftp.cac.psu.edu	/pub/mac/comm/anarchie
anarchie-100.hqx	92k	12/3/93	1	ftp.wustl.edu	/systems/mac/info-mac/comm/net/an
anarchie-110.hqx	141k	2/18/94	1	ftp.germany.eu.net	/pub/comp/macintosh/comm/anarchie-
Anarchie-113.sit.hqx	173k	6/28/94	1	freebsd.cdrom.com	/.13/mac/MacSciTech/comm/Anarchie
anarchie-12.hqx	187k	6/6/94	1	ftp.cc.utexas.edu	/microlib/mac/tcpip/anarchie-12.hqx
anarchie-120.hqx	186k	6/5/94	1	sumex-aim.stanford.edu	/info-mac/comm/tcp/anarchie-120.hqx
Anarchie-121.hqx	187k	7/30/94	1	ftp.cac.psu.edu	/pub/mac/comm/anarchie/Anarchie-12
anarchie-121.hqx	187k	7/10/94	1	mrcnext.cso.uiuc.edu	/pub/info-mac/comm/tcp/anarchie-121
anarchie-121.hqx	187k	7/10/94	1	ftp.halcyon.com	/disk2/tidbits/tisk/tcp/anarchie-121.h
anarchie-121.sea.hqx	210k	7/14/94	1	casbah.acns.nwu.edu	/pub/newswatcher/helpers/anarchie-1:
anarchie.sea	356k	9/4/94	1	ftp.halcyon.com	/disk2/tidbits/select/anarchie.sea
anarchie1.00.sit.hqx	92k	12/4/93	1	ftp.wustl.edu	/systems/mac/umich.edu/util/comm/a
anarchie1.21.sit.hqx	187k	7/20/94	1	freebsd.cdrom.com	/.13/mac/umich/util/comm/anarchie1
ANARCHIE121_SIT.HQX;1	1k	8/24/94	1	enh.nist.gov	/MAC.DIR;1/ANARCHIE121_SIT.HQX;1

Figure 5.18 Anarchie at work, combining full archie search capabilities with FTP file transfers.

Chapter 5 Notes

1. Merit press release, December 2, 1992.
2. Bunyip Information Systems may be contacted at:

310 St.-Catherine St. West, Suite 202
Montreal, Quebec
Canada H2X 2A1
Voice: 514-875-8611
Fax: 514-875-8134

Thanks to Peter Deutsch for background information about archie and thoughts about where it is heading.

6

Telnet Shrinks the World

Telnet is an Internet tool that allows you to log on to remote computers and manipulate them to retrieve data. By entering commands at the system prompt (or using a graphical client program), you instruct your service provider's computer to make a connection with another computer somewhere on the network. You log on to that machine, usually by providing a user identification name and a password. Services that are publicly available often prompt you with the correct log-on sequence, or in many cases the sequence is available through listings of Internet resources like the one you will find in this book in Chapter 16. Once logged on, you can take advantage of the services offered at the remote site.

What's available through Telnet? The variety is impressive. Many universities, for example, make campus information available over publicly accessible Campus Wide Information Systems (CWIS). You can use these to find out what's happening at schools around the world, to search directories to find student and faculty addresses, and, often, to take advantage of services like library catalog searches. When you use Telnet it's as easy to track down a book at the University of Hong Kong as it is at the school around the block.

Database resources are out there as well, many of them openly accessible. The Advanced Technology Information Network, for example, is designed to provide information about agricultural markets in California as well as useful data for exporters. HPCwire tracks high-performance computing developments and includes newsletters on computing topics. NYSERNet/PSI's Online X.500 Directory provides address information for personnel at major organizations throughout the United States. The Dartmouth Dante Project makes the corpus of The Divine Comedy available to scholars, along with centuries of scholarly commentary. The Louis Harris Data Center maintains Harris polling information back to 1960 on a wide variety of topics, constituting a treasure trove of data for sociologists. And there are a growing number of commercial sites as well.

You can see by this diversity that the range of Telnet-accessible resources is broad. The emphasis, as you would expect, has thus far been on scientific topics, but the success of scholarly endeavors such as the Dartmouth Dante Project ensures there will be growing participation from the humanities as well. Telnet thus ranks as a powerful Internet tool, and its ability to allow users of diverse computer systems to tap distant databases is a vindication of the internetworking concept that TCP/IP made possible.

Telnet vs. Dial-Up Systems

In order to place Telnet in context, it's useful to contrast it to dial-up bulletin board systems. If you call up local bulletin boards, you understand that each offers its own set of features and is slanted toward a particular user community. To tap into a wide variety of bulletin board systems, you must call each in turn, perhaps using a packet network to cut costs. Each call, however, involves choosing a particular BBS and making a call to it. Once logged on to a system, you are, in effect, in an electronic building, one filled with a variety of rooms, but one whose only exit is through the door from which you entered.

When you use Telnet to access a distant computer, you've also entered an electronic building filled with many rooms. But when you've concluded your stay at one address, you need not go off-line, choose another telephone number, and make another call. Instead, your connection to your service provider remains intact. You are returned to its system prompt, from which you can use Telnet again to log on to a different computer. Your modem remains on-line the entire time, but your electronic presence moves from computer to computer on the Internet, using your service provider's machine as its electronic home base. It's possible in this way to move around the world by means of Telnet at a rapid clip, exploring resources, checking catalogs, and gathering information.

Through Telnet to the Gateway City

Let's take a look at Telnet in action by logging on to Washington University's World Window, a gateway offering a unique battery of Internet functions under a simple menu structure. To reach this data storehouse, we enter the **telnet** command followed by the address of the site. The address is library wustl.edu. Here is the first thing you'll see when you enter this command.

```
% telnet library.wustl.edu
Trying 128.252.173.4...
Connected to library.wustl.edu.
Escape character is '^]'.
```

The URL format for Telnet sessions is straightforward. In this example, the URL would be as follows:

```
telnet://library.wustl.edu
```

Just as with FTP sessions, when you see the colon followed by the double-slash, you know that the initial term refers to the tool you are using—in this case, Telnet—while the information following the double-slash tells you the address of the site you are contacting. As has been the case throughout this book, when I am referring to a specific address, I will give it; when I am referring to contacting that address through a particular protocol like Telnet, I will use a URL.

The Log-In Screen

Let's examine this screen carefully. After giving the **telnet** command and the address of our requested site, we see the message Trying 128.252.173.4. . . . This is the IP, or Internet Protocol, address of the computer in question. Remember that Internet computers use addresses with four numbers joined by periods. These numbers are filed with the InterNIC; each identifies a unique computer on the Internet.

We also know that computers can be identified by names. In this case, the name library.wustl.edu has been mapped to the corresponding IP number. Both are addresses, and both refer to the same computer.

Note the statement: Escape character is '^]'. This is a useful bit of information. During a Telnet session, it's possible something will go wrong. Because Telnet makes it possible to log on to many different kinds of computer systems, we may lose track of where we are and be unable to get out. Telnet incorporates an escape routine that can be activated by pressing the keys shown. The ^ symbol should be interpreted as the control key. Thus, ^] means "press the control key at the same time you press the] key"; it can also be written as **Ctrl-].** This will return you to a Telnet prompt, at which you can enter the command **quit** to exit. You will see an example later in this chapter.

We're now taken to the screen shown in Figure 6.1, which presents the World Window logo and asks us to enter a terminal type, or else press a **RETURN** to accept the default VT-220 emulation. If your communications software is set for VT-100, you can press a **RETURN** now.

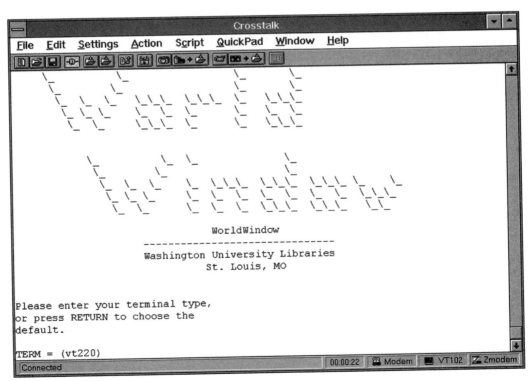

Figure 6.1 Signing in at Washington University.

Remember, the remote computer needs to know how to send data to us. By asking us for your terminal type, the computer is determining what kind of special features it can present, from color or graphics to full-screen editing and command keys. The statement TERM = (VT-220): suggests an answer. By enclosing VT-220 in parentheses, the machine is telling us this is the default choice. If you enter a carriage return here, you announce your intention to use VT-220 as your default terminal emulation. You can accept this default or use VT-100; either will let your computer function as if it were a Digital Equipment Corporation terminal, a standard for terminal-based communications.

A Remote Menu Structure

Once we've told the remote computer how to display its data, the computer presents the menu shown here:

```
WorldWindow     Washington University Libraries, St. Louis, MO   04/17/95 10:22

Welcome to WorldWindow, the WU Libraries' Electronic Information Gateway! Some
services are only available to authorized users and require that you log in with
a username and password. If you do not have a username and password, just press
RETURN and you will receive access to all public services.


                         Username [         ]
                         Password [         ]
```

This is an important set of information. Telnet sites vary in terms of how they handle their log-in procedures. In this case, we learn that some of the facilities here are restricted, presumably to students and faculty at the university. However, the subset of public services is available if we will simply press a **RETURN** as we go through the Username and Password fields. Always examine initial Telnet screens like this one with care, as they often provide clues on how to use the system.

We can now move to the main menu at World Window, as shown in Figure 6.2. A quick glance through this menu may reveal why Washington University Services is a popular Telnet destination. University libraries in this country and abroad are available for searching, as are a number of publicly accessible databases, Campus Wide Information Systems, Gophers, and more. The menu system makes it possible to reach these destinations without difficulty.

Learning the Commands

Examine now the bottom of the main menu screen, where you'll find a place to enter commands. Of these, perhaps the most important is the **?** command, which pulls up a help menu. We're now on foreign turf. It would be pointless to go through every command available at Washington University, because you will encounter a wide range of systems using Telnet, and many use their own command structure. So the first rule is: always determine how to call up a help menu. Doing this will help you to navigate diverse computers.

Notice, however, that the World Window system isn't terribly difficult to use. We can use the **Up** and **Down Arrow** keys to select an item, pressing a **RETURN** to activate it. Figure 6.3, for example, shows what happens when we examine item 1, *LUISPLUS (WU Libraries' Catalog & Journal Indexes)*. Now we are in a search screen with a different set of commands. By reading carefully, we can deduce the basic principles of searching the

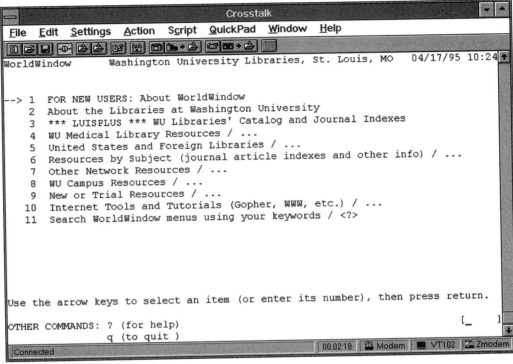

Figure 6.2 The main menu at World Window.

library catalog. Notice that we are again prompted for further information; the system tells us that pressing a **RETURN** will call up news about the catalog and the other library sources that can be consulted.

We can also examine a range of other Internet sources through the World Window site. Figure 6.4, for example, shows you an example of the system's range. Like many good Internet sites, this one contains abundant local information, but includes links to data far afield. Major Internet search tools like WAIS and World Wide Web are provided here, along with on-line publications including a dictionary.

A Telnet Jump to Another Site

Moving through the menus at World Window, we will encounter numerous sites of interest. Figure 6.5, for example, shows us a menu of scientific databases and other materials. World Window is packed with such resources.

Our Telnet voyages will often show the same strengths and weaknesses. The Internet is rich in public-domain information, much of it scientific and technical in nature, as we would expect given its origins. The concentration of material in the "soft sciences"—psychology, for example—is growing, as is that in the humanities. But because the Net's earliest implementers were government-sponsored, and thus encouraged to share their information through the new medium, we continue to see numerous federal sites, and comparatively little by the way of commercial database activity. All this will change as

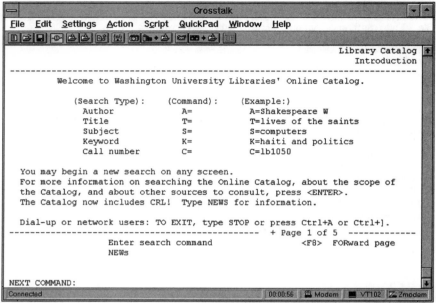

Figure 6.3 Moving to a library search screen at Washington University.

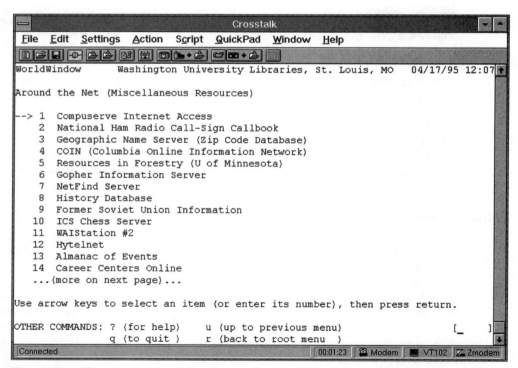

Figure 6.4 Like many sites, World Window reaches across the Internet to link distant data.

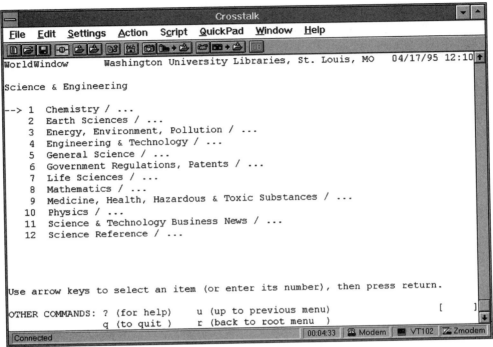

Figure 6.5 Scientific materials are abundantly available on the Internet.

the Net moves toward new authentication, security, and billing capabilities. We discuss these necessary developments in Chapter 16.

We can also move through World Window's menu to other Telnet sites. In doing so, we run into an interesting fact about Telnet connections. They often (but not always) require some kind of login, but the login to publicly accessible sites is generally available, either through a resource list distributed on the Internet, or through prompts from the menu system you are using. In Figure 6.6, for example, you can see how World Window prompts me to use a stock market service available through its menus. By pressing a **RETURN** here, I would be sent out on another Telnet session to the remote site.

The log-in procedure isn't complicated, but you do have to know what you are up to or it won't work. World Window thus tells me exactly what to expect so I can get on-line. When I follow these procedures, I find myself at the main screen at the site, as shown in Figure 6.7.

Telnet is taking us on quite a journey. We've accessed computers at Washington University in St. Louis, using its menu structure to find our way around the available services. And then, when we chose a menu item, we were propelled, again through Telnet (only this time Telnet as mediated by Washington University's computers) into yet another database. In this way, a menu at one Internet site can actively call up a network connection to another site.

Realize, then, that *such menus are not static entities—they often point to network connections.* You could also reach the above site by using Telnet to access it directly once you learned its name or IP address.

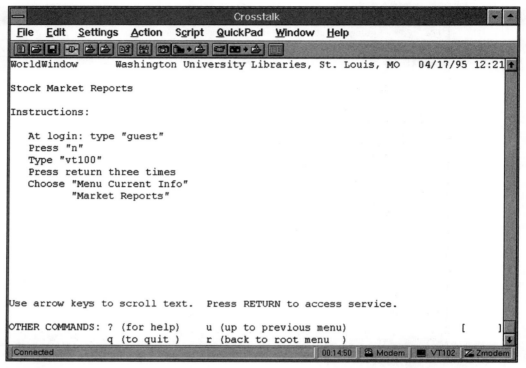

Figure 6.6 A Telnet session can involve logging on to yet another Telnet site; when this occurs, the system you are on will usually provide log-in information.

Exiting a Telnet Session

Intrigued? I would imagine so. This is Telnet showing off, demonstrating how nimble a person with the basic Telnet know-how can be at moving around the world at light-speed, through fiber-optic cables and microwave transmissions to find information. In this exercise I've traveled from Raleigh to Washington University to a major business database, all in one telephone connection, using publicly available sources to find what I need.

But as mentioned before, you must know how to exit. The process is relatively routine, as long as you remember how Telnet operates. If, for example, you examined the main menu at Washington University, exiting would be simple. The menu says **q (to quit)** and that's exactly what entering this command will do, returning you to your service provider's system prompt.

Things get a little stickier, however, if you get stuck and have to invoke the **Ctrl-]** sequence to quit your Telnet session. Rather than returning you to the friendly local prompt, this command takes you back to the command prompt for the Telnet program itself. You must enter **quit** at this point to return to your system prompt.

```
telnet> quit
Connection closed.
```

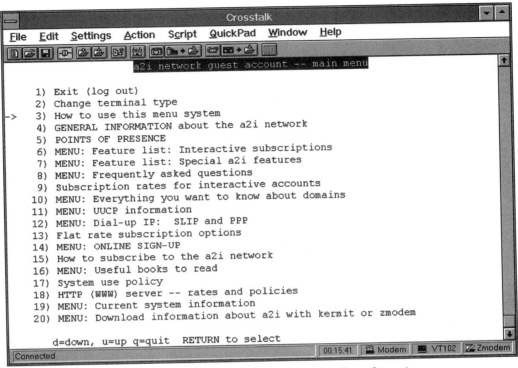

Figure 6.7 A completed login at the a2i site, containing stock market information.

A Graphical Telnet Session

Let's try to run a Telnet session through a graphical Telnet client. I've worked with most of the clients now available in both the Windows and Macintosh environments and can't say I'm impressed with any but the simplest. And perhaps that makes sense; after all, when you're dealing with a Telnet session, what you're doing is working with commands on a remote computer. Hence the significant issues of user interface and intuitive command structure depend more upon the machine you've contacted—and how it has been programmed—than upon the client on your machine. But a good client can still simplify things by putting the session into a point-and-click environment, with readily available menu commands.

Trumptel, or Trumpet Telnet, as it's otherwise known, is a handy client that comes from Peter Tattam in Tasmania, the creator of the Trumpet for Windows News Reader and Trumpet Winsock, a TCP/IP stack that we discussed in Chapter 3. In Figure 6.8, I'm using Trumptel to connect to the site at the Colorado Association of Research Libraries. The address is pac.carl.org. From there, I've contacted the UnCover system (this is made available as a menu choice at CARL) to run a search. Some 1,400 periodicals may be searched at this site.

The main menu for UnCover presents search possibilities. I'm able to search by keyword, author, or journal title. Entering the keywords *global warming*, I call up the screen of results shown in Figure 6.9. Here, I have formed a database on the subject that con-

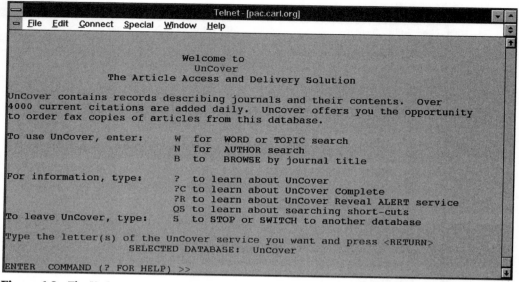

Figure 6.8 The UnCover system, available through the Colorado Association of Research Libraries.

tains 1,711 entries, and am looking at the first screen of hits. To reduce the number of hits, I could also have added a second search term, thus refining my search by area, or data, or journal. As you can see, the journal entries are sorted by date. As I move through them, I move forward to more recent articles. This kind of sorting would be more useful if the system presented recent articles first, which is why it makes sense to refine your search—to pare the list of hits down to a manageable number.

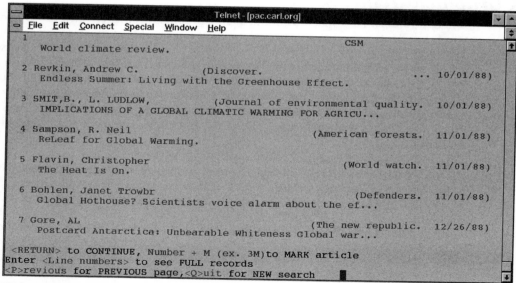

Figure 6.9 Results of a search through the UnCover database on the keywords global warming.

But UnCover is nonetheless useful. Armed with this list of hits, I can get a quick overview of scholarship on the subject. Moreover, I can zero in on any of the hits to find out more about it. If I want a copy of the document, I can enter its number to call up the screen shown in Figure 6.10. By pressing a **RETURN** from this screen, I can move through the payment options. A variety of them exist; those with accounts on the UnCover system can retrieve these documents at lower cost. Full information about obtaining accounts is available from the initial UnCover screen.

To use Trumptel, I need only double-click on its icon, calling up the program and the dialog box shown in Figure 6.11. In this box, I have already entered the destination site. Clicking on OK will launch the session, from which point I am completely in the hands of the remote computer. This can get interesting; the CARL system isn't completely clear on some of its levels about how to exit, but if you read the instructions carefully as you log on, you'll learn that you can usually get out by sending the **//exit** command (note the twin slashes).

One nice thing about using a graphical client like this is that it makes basic operations, like cut and paste, a routine matter. I call down the Edit menu to perform these chores, thus lifting information as needed off the on-line screen. I also have excellent control over fonts. Figure 6.12 shows you the screen from which I can edit the screen display. Font style and size are readily configurable from this screen.

Interested in Trumptel? You can retrieve it on-line.

What You Need: Trumpet Telnet

Where to Get It: ftp://ftp.trumpet.com.au/pub/beta/trmptel/

At the time of this writing, the filename was ttel0_07.zip.

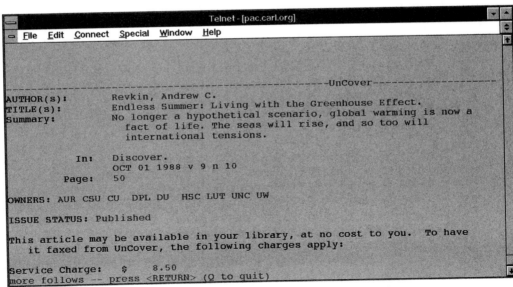

Figure 6.10 To retrieve the full text of a document, you can request that it be sent to you.

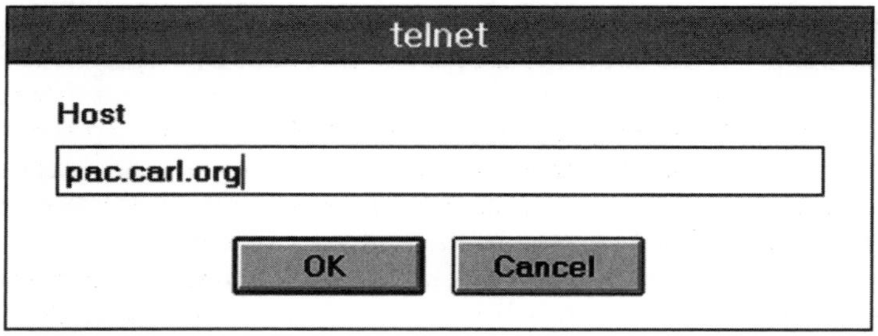

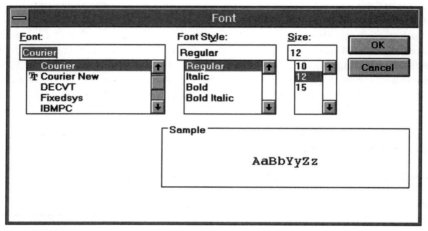

Figure 6.11   TrumpTel's open connection box.

Figure 6.12   Settings fonts within Trumptel involves changing the settings in this box.

And if you're a Macintosh user, you'll find a good client in NCSA Telnet, a program from the same site where Mosaic and other significant software tools have been developed, the National Center for Supercomputing Applications in Urbana-Champaign, Illinois. In Figure 6.13, you can see NCSA Telnet at work; here, I am accessing a commercial site at marketplace.com.

This is an on-line catalog, containing a variety of shopping possibilities provided through MarketBase Systems of Santa Barbara, California. In the center of the log-in screen, you can see a URL showing a World Wide Web address. This is a symptom of what is gradually happening to many Telnet sites. The World Wide Web has become so widespread that services that formerly would have been handled exclusively through Telnet are now migrating to the Web. But those without graphical Web capability may choose to run their sessions through Telnet just as readily. This site also maintains a Gopher server.

Figure 6.14 shows part of the directory at the MarketBase site. By using a keyword search, I can move through the various businesses that make products available here. To receive detailed information about the categories, I would simply enter the name of the

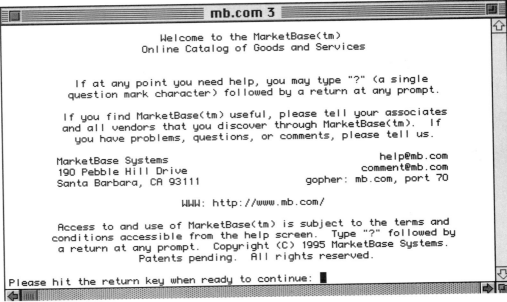

Figure 6.13   Looking at a commercial site through NCSA Telnet.

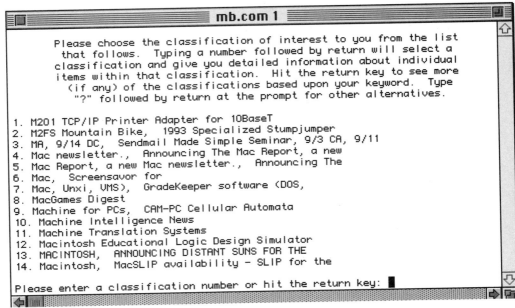

Figure 6.14   A section of the directory at the MarketBase site.

item I wanted to see. MarketBase is an example of commercial interests using Internet resources to sell products; it will be interesting to see how much of its business results from the various access options it now makes available. A look at the percentage of users accessing the site through Telnet versus the World Wide Web would be intriguing.

NCSA Telnet is an excellent choice for Macintosh users wanting to use Telnet resources. Here's how to get it:

What You Need: NCSA Telnet, a Telnet Client for the Mac

How to Get It: From the following URL:

ftp://ftp.ncsa.uiuc.edu/Telnet/Mac/Telnet2.7/2.7b1/

Two files are available at this URL. The first is Telnet2.7b1-fat.sit.hqx. This file contains code for the Power Mac computer. The second is Telnet2.7b1-68K.sit.hqx. This contains the program in the form used by conventional 68 K Macintoshes.

The Telnet Command Structure

Let's go back now to the Unix Telnet program. To get into it, you can enter the command **telnet** without any further specification at the system prompt. You'll be placed in Telnet's command mode, shown by the prompt telnet>. Chances are you will not have much need to use Telnet in command mode, other than to quit from it if you've had to escape from a remote login that was going awry. But there are actually a number of commands available at the telnet> prompt. The following lists some of the things you can do.

RETURN	Pressing the **RETURN** key without any command takes you out of command mode and returns you to your Telnet connection to the remote computer.
close	Ends the current Telnet connection.
display	Shows operating parameters for the current session.
mode	Allows you to enter line-by-line or character-at-a-time mode.
open	Connects to a remote site.

On the important **open** command we must pause. Note that you have two ways to reach a remote computer:

- You can give the **telnet** command along with the name of the remote site. Thus, **telnet library.wustl.edu** takes you to World Window at the university; it's a straight shot from your service provider's command prompt.
- You can use the **telnet** command by itself at the system prompt. This places you in Telnet command mode; the prompt becomes telnet>. You can follow this with the **open** command and the site specification: **open library.wustl.edu.** The results are the same.

quit   Exits Telnet.

set   Allows you to set a variety of operating parameters. You can enter **set ?** in command mode to receive a list of the possibilities. Of particular interest to us is the **set escape** command. Why? Because **set escape** changes the escape character.

The default escape character is **Ctrl-],** which moves you into command mode during your Telnet session. Most of the time you can leave the default setting in place, as you won't have any need to change it. However, it is possible that a more complicated Telnet session could require a different escape character.

Remember that Telnet can involve more than one remote computer. In the example of World Window, you saw that a variety of databases and other services are accessible through the system's menu structure. If you choose one of these, your Telnet connection will have several branches—from your computer to your service provider's computer, then to Washington University, and then to the service you chose at the menu. Your Telnet session will be hopping from site to site. The speed of Telnet makes this kind of connection workable, but it does present a practical challenge.

Suppose, for example, you have made a Telnet connection to a remote computer, followed by another Telnet jump from there to a third. Let's say something went wrong that made you want to exit from the database you're using at the third site and return to the second. If you were to use the standard escape sequence while connected in this way, you would wind up not at the second site's computer, but back in your own service provider's machine; the whole piggy-backed structure would vanish, and you'd have to set up the entire set of connections again.

The **set escape** command allows you to declare a different escape character for each leg of the electronic journey. By choosing which escape character to enter, you give yourself the flexibility to enter into command mode at the connected sites you choose. You do this by entering the command **set escape** followed by the appropriate character. Thus, **set escape ^q** establishes **Ctrl-q** as the escape key for that leg. Note that you do this *after you have already established a connection.*

Let's assume your first Telnet site is Washington University's World Window. Your escape character on the first leg to Washington University is the default, **Ctrl-].** You change that by going into command mode *after* you log on at Washington University, entering a new escape sequence, say, **set escape ^q** (you type the caret, or **^,** character, then the **q**). Having done so, you now opt for a menu item taking you to the Science and Technology Information System (STIS) at the National Science Foundation in Washington, DC. Once connected to STIS, your escape sequence again defaults to **Ctrl-].** To go into command mode at Washington University, you enter **Ctrl-].** To go into command mode at your home site, you'd enter **Ctrl-q.**

Here are the rest of the Telnet command options:

status   Prints status information about your connection.

toggle   Toggles operating parameters for Telnet.

z   Puts the Telnet connection in the background, returning you to your local Unix shell. At this point, you can run any Unix commands you choose. To resume the remote connection, use the **fg** command from the system prompt: % **fg.** This reactivates Telnet and allows you to resume your connection. Note:

Not all Unix shells support this feature, which is known as *job control*. It's handy if you want to perform a few quick chores without ending your connection.

? Prints help information.

Using Computer Ports

When more than one service is provided on a given computer, port assignments must be made for each. This is done by assigning a specific port number to each service. Think of it this way: A server is actually a software application that runs on a computer—it's not the computer itself. That means a computer can offer more than one server, and most do, not just for Telnet but for many other applications as well. The server has a particular port assignment to differentiate it from other servers. In this case, the word port refers to a software designation that keeps traffic properly routed. It has nothing to do with hardware ports.

For a client program to access the proper server in such an environment, it must specify which port it wants to use. You can spot such servers quickly; their addresses consist of the computer information followed by a port number. Examples are easy to find. If we were looking around the Internet to find schedules for professional sports teams, we'd encounter a server providing baseball scores: telnet://culine.colorado.edu:862. The number 862 is this server's port address. Figure 6.15 shows what it offers.

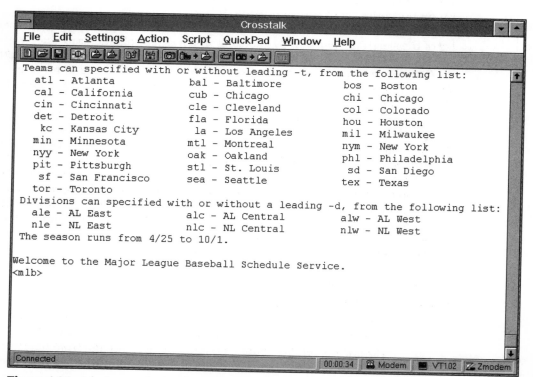

Figure 6.15   A look at professional sports schedules.

As you can see, you're offered a list of Major League baseball teams and the chance to generate schedule information for each. On-line help is provided, and by using it, you know that you can create a list of any team's full schedule for the year. Figure 6.16 shows an example.

The baseball server at this site is only one of several; in fact, this computer also offers hockey, basketball, and football schedules. To separate these services, the system administrators have given each a separate port assignment. National Hockey League schedules are found at the same address with a different port number: telnet://culine.colorado.edu:860. Basketball is at telnet://culine.colorado.edu:859, and football at telnet://culine.colorado.edu:863. This is how port assignments can separate specialized traffic from other Telnet operations. Just remember to add the number to the address.

Telnet and "Big Blue Iron"

The term "Big Iron" usually refers to big computers—mainframes come to mind, and particularly IBM mainframes. These machines can pose problems for us, because the terminals they're used to dealing with don't work like any others. IBM's 3270 terminals generally function by having users fill in blanks on the screen, entering information in a variety of fields. They also use special keys called *programmed function* or PF keys. To work with such terminals, we need a terminal emulator that can interpret what the 3270 system needs and allow our keyboards to work within its parameters.

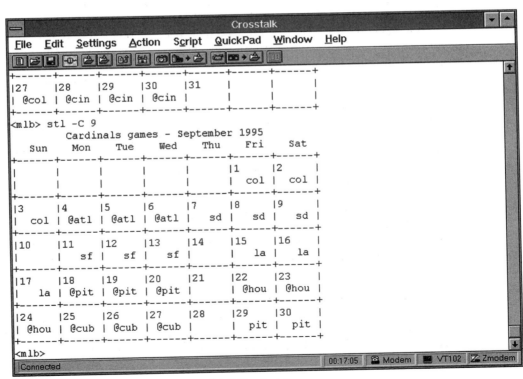

Figure 6.16   A segment of the Cardinals' 1995 schedule.

This is where the tn3270 application comes in. It's a version of Telnet that includes the appropriate 3270 emulation. In most cases, you'll never need to use tn3270. Often, the IBM computer you connect to will handle the appropriate terminal emulation automatically. But in some cases, tn3270 will be a necessity. Some systems will not work with standard Telnet because of their reliance on 3270 features. For these systems, the only way you can establish a connection is with tn3270.

Fortunately, doing so is as easy as using Telnet itself. The University of North Carolina at Chapel Hill maintains a database of material from the Harris organization relating to poll results. Over 750 Harris polls are located here; all of them are searchable. This useful archive is stored on an IBM computer which we reach by using tn3270. If we try to connect with regular telnet, the result is a hung system:

```
% telnet uncvm1.oit.unc.edu
Trying 152.2.21.5 ...
Connected to uncvm1.oit.unc.edu.
Escape character is '^]'.
```

This looks fine, but nothing more happens, and we'll eventually have to use a **Ctrl-]** sequence to get back to the Telnet prompt, and then to our system prompt. Using tn3270 works better, as shown in Figure 6.17. We're informed immediately as to the nature of the computer we're using; the message banner tells us it's an IBM 3090.

This sounds imposing. In fact, the publicly available systems you're going to be dealing with are generally much easier to run than specialized setups that are off-limits to outsiders. A good thing, too, for 3270 emulation can be tricky business, and can depend on how special keys have been mapped onto your keyboard. For our purposes, a few tips should provide all you need to use these systems, and you can rely on on-line help to provide more clues in the specific situations you find yourself in.

Let's examine the log-on screen in Figure 6.17 for further information. You're asked for a user identification and password. The appropriate ID is irss1; the password is irss. (This is information you would have to learn before calling the system; it's available in a variety of sources including Chapter 16 of this book.) But note: Data entry is a bit different here. Rather than entering your user ID, pressing the **RETURN** key, and then entering your password, you can enter the user ID and use the **TAB** key to move to the next field before entering the password. The 3270 is a full-screen application, meaning it expects you to move around on the screen for data entry, often using the **TAB** key.

When we have entered the password, pressing the **TAB** key takes us to the COMMAND line. Fortunately, the system has prompted us for what to do next. Pressing **RETURN** here takes us to a screen of introductory information, shown in Figure 6.18.

Again, we're prompted for what to do next. Passing through the menu chain, we arrive at a menu that prompts us to search in the extensive data holdings here, as shown in Figure 6.19.

What matters here is not the methodology of this particular database, but the way the 3270 system works with input and output. You'll notice as you go through such a system that the screen does not scroll upward a line at a time. Instead, the screen goes blank and then reappears. You'll also notice that some keys don't work as advertised.

```
% tn3270 uncvm1.oit.unc.edu
Trying...
Connected to uncvm1.oit.unc.edu.


VM/XA SP 2.1 ONLINE-PRESS ENTER KEY TO BEGIN SESSION


VM/XA SP 2.1 ONLINE


   UU      UU  NN      NN    CCCCC         OOOOO    IIIIII  TTTTTTTT
   UU      UU  NNN     NN   CCCCCCC       OO   OO     II       TT
   UU      UU  NNN     NN  CC      CC    OO     OO    II       TT
   UU      UU  NN N    NN  CC            OO     OO    II       TT
   UU      UU  NN  N   NN  CC            OO     OO    II       TT
   UU      UU  NN   N  NN  CC            OO     OO    II       TT
   UU      UU  NN    NNN   CC      CC    OO     OO    II       TT
    UUUUUUU    NN      NN   CCCCCCC       OO   OO     II       TT
     UUUUU     NN      NN    CCCCC         OOOOO    IIIIII     TT


        UNIVERSITY OF NORTH CAROLINA    IBM 3090 COMPUTING SYSTEM
                     VM/XA SP   2.1   (9104)




Fill in your USERID and PASSWORD and press ENTER
(Your password will not appear when you type it)
USERID   ===   _____
PASSWORD ===
Type VMEXIT on AND line to leave VM/XA
COMMAND   ===

                                                    RUNNING   UNCVM1
```

Figure 6.17 Signing on at UNC-Chapel Hill.

Take your function keys. The bottom of the screen in Figure 6.18 gives you a set of commands. **f1=Help** seems like a straightforward statement. But it may be that when you press the **F1** function key to generate help, you simply get an error message. If that happens, try using the **ESC** key in combination with a number. Thus, instead of using **F1** for the help screen, it might work to hold down the **ESC** key and press **1** at the same time. One or the other of these methods should produce results. And as we saw earlier, these keys can then be used for help or, in this case, to choose a database and to search it, which is how **F2** and **F3** are used here.

This discussion is necessarily vague because it's impossible to specify which keys will have exactly what function on your system. tn3270 relies on a file called map3270 to list how the various keys are mapped to your keyboard. In the absence of a universal method, key assignments vary from one system to another. This often calls for a fair amount of trial and error, and you can wind up, as with Telnet, stuck inside a remote computer without knowing how to get out.

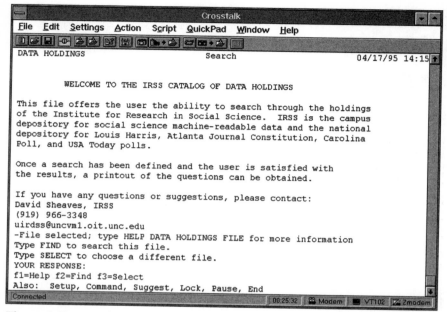

Figure 6.18   Introductory information at the Institute for Research in Social Science.

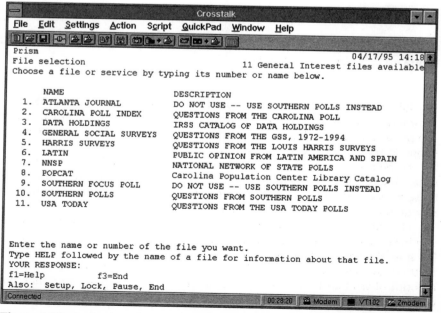

Figure 6.19   An Institute for Research in Social Science catalog screen.

This is where you need the escape sequence, which will take you to command mode. Try **Ctrl-C** if **Ctrl-]** doesn't work. As with Telnet, the escape sequence deposits you at a prompt, after which you can exit.

```
tn3270> quit
Connection closed.
```

On the other hand, as you can see from the screens at UNC, systems designed to be useful to users usually try to give you enough information on-screen to help you get around. If the screen gets filled up with information (and this can easily happen with 3270 emulation), try **Ctrl-Z** or **Ctrl-Home** to clear it.

7

A World of Electronic Mail

Electronic mail is a core Internet application. Using e-mail, you can communicate with people all over the world, often receiving replies the same day. Your messages are stored in the recipient's mailbox until they are read, so there's little risk of their being overlooked. You can include previous messages in what you write; you can send your mail to one person or a group of users. And because mail management involves no more than mastering a few basic commands, you can gain control over the influx quickly as your daily mail count grows, saving what you need, discarding the rest. Electronic mail is fast, powerful, and addictive; once you've worked with it, you'll wonder how you got along without it.

What appears in my own mailbox changes frequently, as I move into and out of various mailing lists and develop on-line relationships with more and more people. Whether near or far, my correspondents and I have one thing in common: We've learned that an electronic mailbox is a tool that can be customized to meet a wide variety of interests and needs. To make it all work, you have to know the options available to you. Proper navigation techniques are just as important with electronic mail as with any other part of the Internet.

In this chapter, we'll discuss what electronic mail can do for you and how you can use a mail program to continue your on-line explorations. Because Internet addresses are the first thing users see, we'll take the mystery out of these cryptic runes, and then move on to a sample log-in session, working through the primary commands in a Unix program called pine. We'll also examine the most basic mail tool of all, the no-frills Unix mail. We graduate to Eudora, a powerful mail program for the SLIP/PPP user. No matter which mail program you choose to use, I guarantee that your Internet mailbox will soon become one of your most valuable assets.

Shattering the Borders

Many people use mail as their *only* Internet application, not realizing how much else is available, or finding that the power of e-mail meets their current needs. Get involved with a number of on-line correspondents and your electronic mailbox can quickly grow to gigantic proportions, particularly when you subscribe to the mailing lists and other resources that are described later.

Fortunately, the Internet could not grow to its present complexity without providing tools that make mail management feasible. Many such tools—the lug wrenches and precision screwdrivers of electronic-file maintenance—are there, in varying degrees of power and user-friendliness. But using electronic mail doesn't have to be complicated. A practical knowledge of a few simple programs is all it takes to participate. And the scope of e-mail is wide.

Mail can reach out beyond the Internet itself. You might think of the Internet as the core medium you can use to contact a wide variety of other networks (which use different protocols than the Internet's TCP/IP to provide their own kinds of information and connectivity). If you use local bulletin board systems to exchange messages and download files, you're probably familiar with FidoNet, which allows your local system to be connected with thousands of other computers by telephone link. FidoNet is often a user's first stop on the road to the Internet. By making a local telephone call, users can read and respond to messages that may have been written a city or a continent away.

Then there's BITNET, an academic and research network whose mail distribution features are explored more fully in another chapter. There's UUCP, which stands for Unix-to-Unix Copy Program; its store and forward capabilities keep USENET humming, running newsgroups on countless subjects. There are the big commercial providers, such as CompuServe, GEnie, and America Online, not to mention dedicated e-mail specialists like MCI Mail. Users of all these services are available for electronic mail correspondence through your Internet connection, and the Internet's ever-widening series of gateways ensures that connectivity with other providers will only grow.

So the first caveat is this: If you use any other information provider—even if you're an old hand—you must change your thinking as you approach the Internet. You're used to sending a message to a limited audience—people who have accounts with a particular provider. But Internet communications ignore such borders. Get used to a communications medium where the transfer of information occurs not just between fellow members of one networked group, but between networks worldwide, no matter what their protocols. And remember, users of those other networks can just as readily get back to you.

A Word to Users of Commercial On-Line Services

If you are sending electronic mail to the Internet from a commercial service like CompuServe or America Online, you will not be able to use the Unix mail program. Nor will you be able to work with pine, Eudora, or any of the other mail programs available through a full service Internet provider. The commands in this chapter will therefore be irrelevant. You will need to work through the mail system provided by your service—instead of worrying about the various Unix programs, you need to know how to handle CompuServe Mail, or DELPHI Mail, or whatever service you use. Because of the number of such on-line offerings, space does not make it possible to go into them all here. You should spend time brushing up on your system's commands, an effort that will pay off soon, as we will see in the next chapter.

But don't dismiss the rest of this chapter. For the great consolidation that is occurring between conventional on-line services and the Internet holds out promise that our tools will also begin to merge. Already, CompuServe is offering Point-to-Point Protocol access at its nodes, meaning that users can activate a PPP connection and use client programs like Eudora. America Online's purchase of Advanced Network & Services is likewise a step in the direction of merging the different kinds of connectivity. Perhaps the best advice I can give is to use your provider's mail system, master it thoroughly, and be alert to news of changing options. The fuller featured the mail program you can work with, the more able you will be to take maximum advantage of this priceless Internet tool.

Electronic Mail Defined

Electronic mail provides the ability to send messages by computer. A letter routed electronically has enormous advantages over conventional mail, not the least of which is the speed of its delivery. Internet regulars say it all when they refer to the U.S. Postal Service as "snail mail." Indeed, after only a few days of mastering electronic mail, it seems hard to imagine the era when the mailbox at the end of the driveway was the only way we could communicate with people who were far away. Dazzled by the possibilities of the new medium, we want the rest of the world to operate as smoothly, as usefully, as our electronic mailbox.

Unlike a letter printed on paper, an electronic mail message can be stored on your computer disk. You can handle it like any other file, pulling it into your word processor for editing or printing, or perhaps forwarding it to another person you think would be interested. People who are novices at electronic mail are often surprised at the high rate of return they receive on their Internet mail. The reason is obvious: People find it easier to use a brief computer command to package and send a message than to look up a person's address, print out the letter, address an envelope, and send the whole thing off with a stamp.

The concept of electronic mail is taking time to penetrate the general population. Although office-based computer networks are now the norm, many fail to take advantage of e-mail to send messages between workers. And while users of commercial on-line services may have some experience with the medium, most have not glimpsed the full power of e-mail, nor have they guessed that e-mail is headed toward an even brighter future, connecting not just the users of one computer system, but crossing electronic frontiers to reach users across the way. All that is coming, and much of it is here right now.

Every morning when I dial in to the Internet, a mailbox stuffed with messages is waiting for me. Discussing the ins and outs of the writing trade with a fellow practitioner is something I now do at the keyboard. Because my phone is often busy, there's no reason to leave messages on my voice mail system; my correspondents know I'll quickly see any message they leave by e-mail. Is there a hot new restaurant in town? Someone is sure to tell me. Has a nearby company produced an unbeatable software product? My e-mail will soon have news of it. Is a new site available for file downloads? One way or another, e-mail will tell the tale.

But the great thing about this electronic version of the post office is that it's immune to distance. The message left for me this morning at a terminal in Edinburgh, Scotland is already in my mailbox in Raleigh by the time I log on. My response is automatic: By replying to the missive with a simple command, all necessary routing information is added to my message, and it takes but a keystroke to send it flying by high-speed network to its destination. The message I received last week from New Zealand keeping me up on news in Wellington could as easily have come from Duke University, a mere 20 miles down the road, so transparent is the Internet's mail function.

And there's more, considerably more. Maybe I need to get word to a group of friends that a new market for telecommunications writers is about to open up. Rather than writing a series of letters to various correspondents, I can write one e-mail message and direct it to multiple sites. The recipients can read my message at their leisure and then respond to it. We've set up a circle of interested parties, moving from one to many and back to one, all without the hassle of printing out multiple copies and mailing them.

Nor is e-mail limited to textual data, even if most of the messages I send are composed of nothing but words. When the occasion arises that I need to send a binary file— a spreadsheet from Excel, a word processor program from WordPerfect, a shareware program for a friend to evaluate—I can do so by using MIME. Multipurpose Internet Mail Extensions is a new standard that helps to surmount the text-only barrier that has always stood between the Internet and the transmission of such attachments. Today, I can ship a completely formatted computer column to an editor as a word processor file, with all codes native to that program maintained, so that on his or her end, the column can be called up with every bit of formatting intact. All the new mail readers and new versions of the old incorporate this feature; both pine and Eudora, as we'll see, use it.

More than any other medium, e-mail lets you master your own schedule. Writers work on deadline, and the process of composition is susceptible to all kinds of jars—the muse is sensitive and often obstinate. A ringing telephone is intrusive; answering it, I must break my chain of thought and shift attention to an entirely new subject. E-mail, however, lets me handle business when I have time. I can save my correspondence for later in the morning if I choose, preserving those productive early hours for writing. Then, ready for a break, I can respond to ten e-mail messages as a second pot of coffee is brewing.

As with all computer subjects, a high-tech name describes such processes—*asynchronous communications*. The terms means that electronic mail uncouples you from the normal messaging train. Call a phone number and encounter a busy signal—you've run into a brick wall, until you dial back, sometimes repeatedly, and make connections. Dial that same number and reach a voice mailbox and you're into the realm of the asynchronous. Processes don't have to occur simultaneously with this kind of communication; you can leave a message and the person in question will call back when time allows. Electronic mail provides that same service, only the rate of return on e-mail, at least in my experience, is vastly superior to voice mail. Maybe e-mail is just more enjoyable.

Electronic Mail Programs

The Internet is so huge that no one scheme works on all systems. We're not talking about MS-DOS here, nor a single Macintosh on a desktop, but a network comprising a wide variety of operating systems. You may be running an IBM-compatible computer, trained in DOS software applications. Maybe you're dialing in with an Amiga or a Mac. One way or another, you need to be able to deal with the various devices that make up the Internet. Fortunately, most of the dial-up service providers are using Unix as their operating system, and that gives shell account users a common language with which to work. It also gives them a core program.

We will work with the Unix mail program in our first log-on sessions. We will then move to an increasingly popular program called pine, which goes beyond the spartan mail interface to offer useful screen help and a variety of interesting features. Finally, we'll examine Eudora, the best program for mail management I know. Your choice will depend upon your temperament. I use mail for short notes and Eudora for the bulk of my work. A little experience with each will soon reveal which holds the most appeal for you.

Bear this in mind: When you dial in to the Internet, you're going through several layers of complexity you don't face when dialing a commercial on-line service. It's easy for me to call up CompuServe and start interacting with its host computers in Columbus. I type a command, which gets sent to the host, which then does something about it, and gets back to my computer. In this way, I can do various CompuServ-ish things such as sending e-mail, participating in forum discussions, conferencing, checking the weather patterns, and using on-line databases.

The same paradigm holds with an Internet account, except there is a wide variety of host computers. The physical location where the message is stored is the host computer you're accessing, only now there's no centralized set of tools for use throughout the network. If you have a shell account, you will use whichever software programs are available on the machine at your service provider's site—this is why I begin with the Unix mail program, as it's well nigh universal. Both pine and elm are likewise spreading throughout the Internet world; few service providers worth their salt will have neither of them. SLIP/PPP users have more latitude at choosing the mail program that best meets their needs; they can shop around on the network looking for interesting software. My guess, though, is that they'll wind up with Eudora.

Unix Mail Programs

Numerous Unix programs exist to handle Internet mail. Most of them sport odd, Zen-like names of the kind favored by the Unix community: elm, pine, mush. The tendency toward bizarre cryptography persists in the Unix world, as we'll see when we cover newsreaders for USENET, which sport such descriptive monikers as trn and nn. If you want to learn more about Unix alternatives to mail, a document available on USENET called *Unix EMail Software—A Survey* works through the options from the standpoint of a systems administrator, the person who is responsible for setting up a Unix system to communicate with the outside world.

What should a mail program be able to do? The primary functions are obvious: It should make reading your mail intuitive and logical. It should make it easy to reply to messages in your mailbox, and it should provide general housekeeping chores like save and delete functions, forwarding capabilities, insertion of text files into your messages, and more. The user interface you select for your mail will gradually become second nature, but don't fail to explore the options available. Let's now look at the simplest option, the Unix program called mail.

What You Need: A Document on Mail Programs

The Document: Unix EMail Software—A Survey, by Chris Lewis

How to Get It: In one of several USENET newsgroups: news.answers, news.admin.misc, comp.mail.misc, comp.answers, where it appears as a regular posting. We'll discuss how to sign up for such groups in Chapter 11.

Putting Mail to Work

To activate mail, you need to be at your service provider's command prompt. If you have any messages waiting for you when you log on, you'll see the following:

```
You have mail.
```

The message tells you one or more messages are waiting in your mailbox.

But assuming you're coming to electronic mail for the first time, at the command prompt you will see:

```
No mail for username
```

where *username* is your user identification on the system.

Here's an example of mail's entry screen when you have messages waiting.

```
% mail
Mail version SMI 4.0 Thu Jul 23 13:52:20 PDT 1992   Type ? for help.
"/usr/spool/mail/gilster": 8 messages 8 new
>N  1 NACSPNS@ncsuadm.acs.ncsu.edu Fri Apr 21 17:32 15/708 Re: Re: Re: Re: R
 N  2 pag@world.std.com Fri Apr 21 17:44 18/1103 Reading E-Mail
 N  3 dfor8320@uriacc.uri.edu Fri Apr 21 20:09 46/2360 Last chance for COTIM!
 N  4 pbalsamo@ruacad.ac.runet.edu Fri Apr 21 20:46 36/1670 thanks
 N  5 NACSPNS@ncsuadm.acs.ncsu.edu Sat Apr 22 07:02 18/943 Birthdays
 N  6 pbalsamo@ruacad.ac.runet.edu Sat Apr 22 08:50 178/7248 another try
 N  7 aa@SERVER.INDO.NET.ID Sun Apr 23 22:57 54/3092 Billing Systems
 N  8 mailserv@ds2.internic.net Mon Apr 24 08:54 72/2667 Your request
&
```

The prompt you see following the messages is the & symbol, called an ampersand. This prompt tells you the system is now waiting for your command; mail is active and ready.

The information in the top two lines tells us that eight messages have been received, and that all eight are new (I'm seeing them for the first time). We also receive the useful information that help is available by pressing the **?** key. We'll look at help options in a moment. Next is a statement of the current mailbox in use; in this case, it's the file /usr/spool/mail/gilster.

Examining Your Mailbox

We're then given a listing of the messages in the mailbox. Note that the messages are numbered. In the example, the letters to the left of the message entries tell us something about the status of the message they mark. Messages marked N are new; you haven't yet looked at either their summary line or their text. A message marked with U is one you didn't look at even though it was in your mailbox the last time you checked. U thus stands for unread; you saw the summary line last time but didn't read the message. A P signifies a message that has been preserved; you've elected to leave it in your mailbox even though you've already read it at least once.

Notice that a greater than, or >, symbol points to message 1, flagging this as the current message. Any commands you give will take effect on the current message unless you specify a different message. You'll always find the > marker pointing to your first new message or, in the absence of new mail, to the first message in your mailbox that's unread.

After the message status and number, you're given the address from which each message was sent. Depending on circumstances, this may not be the originating address, but may be the address of a mailer that routed the message between you and the original sender. Date and time information appear next. If you look closely, you'll find the messages are listed in the order in which they were received. Following the date and time is a set of numbers separated by a slash. This shows the number of lines and characters in the message, a figure that includes the header information. The subject appears last.

Reading the Mail

To begin reading the current message, you can simply press the **RETURN** key. The message will appear, as in Figure 7.1. If the message runs to more than one screen, you can press the **SPACEBAR** to advance to the next screen. Pressing the **RETURN** key will only advance one line at a time—definitely *not* the way you want to read your mail.

What if you choose not to read the current message? In the preceding case, to read the fourth message, simply enter the number **4.** The message will then be displayed. Thus:

```
&  4  [RETURN]
```

From which I retrieve the message in Figure 7.2.

The following is a list of some basic mail commands you'll use daily as you read through your mailbox.

[RETURN]   Displays next message.

p   Displays current message.

-   Displays previous message.

```
Message  1:
From NACSPNS@ncsuadm.acs.ncsu.edu Fri Apr 21 17:32:51 1995
Received: from CCVS2.CC.NCSU.EDU (ccvs2.cc.ncsu.edu [152.1.13.21]) by mercury.i0
Message-Id: <199504212132.RAA11417@mercury.interpath.net>
Received: from NCSUADM.NCSU.EDU (MAILER) by NCSUVAX (MX V4.1 VAX) with BSMTP;
         Fri, 21 Apr 1995 17:30:35 EDT
Date: Fri, 21 Apr 95 17:33 EDT
From: NACSPNS@ncsuadm.acs.ncsu.edu
To: Paul A Gilster - Computer Focus <gilster@MERCURY.INTERPATH.NET>
Subject: Re: Re: Re: Re: Re: Re: Re: Your books
Status: R

Pablo:
Perfecto! I have Wednesday, May 3, on my calendar for lunch con
Pablo. Ben's?
Lisita

&
```

Figure 7.1   A basic electronic mail message.

```
Message  4:
From pbalsamo@ruacad.ac.runet.edu Fri Apr 21 20:46:00 1995
Received: from enterprise.interpath.net (root@enterprise.interpath.net [199.72.0
Received: from ruacad.ac.runet.edu (ruacad-gw.runet.edu [137.45.128.4]) by ente0
Received: (from pbalsamo@localhost) by ruacad.ac.runet.edu (8.6.9/8.6.9) id UAA0
From: Peter Balsamo <pbalsamo@ruacad.ac.runet.edu>
Message-Id: <199504220046.UAA11710@ruacad.ac.runet.edu>
Subject: thanks
To: gilster@interpath.net (Paul A. Gilster)
Date: Fri, 21 Apr 1995 20:46:39 -0400 (EDT)
In-Reply-To: <199504212040.QAA13239@redstone.interpath.net> from "Paul A. Gilstm
X-Mailer: ELM [version 2.4 PL24]
MIME-Version: 1.0
Content-Type: text/plain; charset=US-ASCII
Content-Transfer-Encoding: 7
Content-Length: 578
Status: R


Paul -- thanks so much for sending me your comments about the combination
media/guided study project.....i am still not sure if and when it will go,
but i will give it a shot.

take care.   peter
```

Figure 7.2   A message retrieved by choosing a message number.

h   Displays list of headers.

d   Deletes current message.

u   Undeletes current message.

Saving Messages

The mail program doesn't throw away messages unless you give it a specific command to do so. Messages are saved automatically into a file called mbox after being read. When you've read your mail and taken no further action, you'll receive notice of this fact. If I read through nine messages and then exited mail for example, I'd see the following:

Saved nine messages in /home/gilster/mbox

Again, the /home/gilster/mbox statement simply tells me where the mbox file is located. I could go back and reread these messages, or perform any of the other mail commands on them, by the expedient of reinvoking the mail program and specifying that I wanted to read the messages currently saved in mbox. How? Read on.

Reading Saved Messages

Getting at mbox requires you to add a parameter to the **mail** command that invokes the program. Entering **mail -f mbox** brings mbox up on-screen, where it will appear exactly as your first list of headers in the mail program did. If I enter this command at my prompt, here's what I get:

```
% mail -f mbox
Mail version SMI 4.0 Thu Jul 23 13:52:20 PDT 1992 Type ? for help.
"mbox": 8 messages
>    1 pag@world.std.com Wed Apr 19 11:31 19/1123 Reading E-Mail
     2 AROARTY@support.jwiley.com Wed Apr 19 11:41 45/1975 Internet Navigator 3e
     3 NACSPNS@ncsuadm.acs.ncsu.edu Wed Apr 19 12:08 41/2407 Re: Re: Re: Your books
     4 cryan@cryan.pdial.interpath.net Wed Apr 19 13:55 59/3053 Internet Access Article
     5 dfor8320@uriacc.uri.edu Wed Apr 19 15:26 62/3099 Last chance for COTIM-95!
     6 winnet@merlin.magic.mb.ca Wed Apr 19 15:29 50/2340 Re: Review Copy of Newest
     7 skoster@INTER.NL.NET Thu Apr 20 06:02 78/3560 forum on B to B marketing
     8 midnight@HALCYON.COM Thu Apr 20 06:41 93/4536 forum on B to B marketing
&
```

With any saved text, the standard **mail** commands function just as they do when handling your new messages.

A brief word about your mailbox. Many new users don't realize mbox is there and, as you would imagine, it can grow to remarkable size in a fairly short time. Unix users have a limited amount of disk space allocated to them; pushing the envelope past the point that will keep your administrator happy is bad policy. But rather than deleting the entire mbox file (which you could do if you so desired), why not simply edit it periodically and throw out what you don't need?

File management is the idea, and the following **mail** commands walk you through the tools available. Learn them so you can keep your mailbox tidy.

Saving Messages to a File

If a particular message strikes your fancy, it's easy enough to save it to a separate file. Use the **s** command to do the job, paired with a filename of your choice. Because I write a newspaper column, for example, it's frequently necessary for me to save a provocative message for later consideration. I typically type **s column,** which tells the system to save the current message in a file called column.

Each time I do this, the message is appended onto the existing column file, which I usually let grow to 10 or 12 messages before I print it out for scrutiny. Multiple messages can be handled the same way by specifying their message numbers. Thus **s 2 7 8 column** saves the designated messages to my column file in sequence.

Deleting Mail

The **d** command can be used to delete the current message. As I work through my new messages, for example, I'll use a **d** to delete the message I've just read, assuming I've decided not to save it. Alternatively, you can delete one or more messages from the mail prompt by specifying them: **d 1 2 6** deletes the messages in question. Fortunately for those of us who are sometimes too quick on the keyboard, there's also a **u** command to take care of undeleting a file. The problem is that you can only undelete a file during the current mail session. Once you've given the command to exit mail, it's too late.

Assume I've just read a message and have thoughtlessly pressed the **d** key to send the message into limbo. The command **u** will bring it back.

Setting Up Folders

If you're like me, you may receive a wide variety of incoming e-mail, much of it in the form of mailing list material from people you don't correspond with personally, the rest in the form of letters directed specifically to you. To organize the e-mail load, consider setting up folders for your regular correspondents and areas of particular interest in mailing lists. That way, when you want to save something and examine it later, you'll have a specific place to look for it. You can respond to, add and delete files from your folder as easily as you can from the mailbox itself.

Folders are easy to establish. Use the **s** *filename* command to save the desired messages in a file. To manage the file, mail offers a **folder** command. Think of a folder as a message file that mail can manipulate with its standard commands. To move into it, you simply enter **folder** *filename,* which will load the messages in that folder into mail; this works the same way as calling up your mbox file.

What is the difference between saving to a regular file and saving to a folder? My column file is something I want to save for my own use, and I'm not worried about answering the messages in it or forwarding them to anyone else. Once I've saved messages to it, I'm content to manage column simply by downloading it regularly to my computer.

Folders, on the other hand, are meant to be handled by the mail program. The message that came in this morning might have a question you need to investigate before answering. Filing it in a folder would allow you to store it until you had discovered the right answer. Then, by using the **folder** command, you could use mail's command structure to respond to the message. Think of folders as containing mail that's still active, messages you may yet want to respond to or manipulate.

Changing folders is simply a matter of invoking the **folder** command with the new filename. A folder called ansible is where I store messages about science fiction, as sent to me from an on-line newsletter of the same name. The folder camelot is set aside for matters Arthurian, as routed to me from a site in Edinburgh by a list called Camelot. Discussions of food and wine from the Foodwine mailing list reside in a folder called, not surprisingly, foodwine.

Responding to Messages

Responding to a message is simple. After reading it, use the **r** command (remember, your command operates on the current message). A lowercase **r** replies to the sender of the message only. An uppercase **R** replies to the sender and anyone else who received the letter. (As we'll see shortly, electronic mail can be sent to a wide group of people simultaneously.)

You'll immediately be asked for a subject. Try to be descriptive, but remember that you have limited space to work with, and you want the subject field to make some sense. Having typed it in, you're ready to start your message. The bad news is that mail's editing functions will likely disappoint you. Perhaps you've been writing letters with Word-Perfect in the office, or composing that new novel with Microsoft Word for Windows. If so, prepare yourself for culture shock when you start writing with mail.

Just remember this. All you need to do at this point is type in your message. You must press **RETURN** at the end of each line. Work about two-thirds of the way across the screen before doing so and check the line for errors before you press **RETURN**. You'll notice that if you made a mistake in line 3 and you've already moved on to line 5, pressing the **Up Arrow** key will not get you back to line 3. You can, however, work backward using the **BACKSPACE** key to correct an error on the current line. This is where pine shows its superiority. It uses a full-screen editor, allowing you to move the cursor as necessary to edit your file; mail, alas, forces you to edit one line at a time.

Figure 7.3 shows a sample message, along with my reply to it. Note that at the end of the message, we're back at the mail command prompt. That's where the action starts.

Notice also in the example in Figure 7.3 that it wasn't necessary to supply an address, nor to give a subject. mail does this automatically, letting us concentrate on what we have to say. A single period (.) ends our message and sends it on its way. Now we can move on to the next message.

Aborting a Message

Sometimes you regret saying something even as you write it, and decide not to send your message. If this happens, you can abort the message in mid-composition with **Ctrl-C** (hold down the **Control** key and press the letter **c**). You'll be prompted for whether you truly want to abort the message. A second **Ctrl-C** aborts it.

The following shows what the process looks like. I began to write a letter, and then changed my mind:

```
% mail pag@world.std.com
Subject: Project On the Rocks
Sorry the project didn't work out. I wonder, though, if you should
```

```
From NACSPNS@ncsuadm.acs.ncsu.edu Thu Apr 20 16:40:39 1995
Received: from enterprise.interpath.net (root@enterprise.interpath.net [199.72.0
From: NACSPNS@ncsuadm.acs.ncsu.edu
Received: from CCVS2.CC.NCSU.EDU (ccvs2.cc.ncsu.edu [152.1.13.21]) by enterpris0
Message-Id: <199504202040.QAA13662@enterprise.interpath.net>
Received: from NCSUADM.NCSU.EDU (MAILER) by NCSUVAX (MX V4.1 VAX) with BSMTP;
          Thu, 20 Apr 1995 16:38:14 EDT
Date: Thu, 20 Apr
To: gilster@INTERPATH.NET
Subject: E-mail
Status: R

Hola Pablo:
I've heard never to say in e-mail what you don't want to read in the newspaper.
How is it that unauthorized users get access to your e-mail?
Lisita

& r
To: NACSPNS@ncsuadm.acs.ncsu.edu
Subject: Re:  E-mail

Lisita,

Usually, they don't.  But it's always possible for someone at a service provider
site to see what you've written, so you can never be 100% sure.  The rule holds:
don't send anything in e-mail that you consider confidential.

Pablo
.
EOT
&
```

Figure 7.3   A message and a response.

```
have                                          <Here I hit Ctrl-C
(Interrupt-one more to kill letter)
                                  <I hit Ctrl-C again
%                                 <And I'm back to the prompt
```

You can, incidentally, also abort a message with the ~q command. More about this and related commands later.

Getting the Headers Back

As you work through your messages, it will occasionally be useful to get an overall view of what's in your mailbox. Maybe you've decided to go back in and delete unnecessary messages, or you want to move immediately to a particular message. The **h** command at the mail prompt will restore your list of message headers.

The Extremely Useful :n Command

You're reading through a long message and suddenly realize you don't have the remotest interest in it. Nonetheless, every time you get to the bottom of the screen, there's more message to go. What can you do?

Fortunately, the mail program provides for this eventuality. If you're stuck in a long message, enter **:n** and you will be returned to the mail prompt (&). NOTE: You don't have to press the **RETURN** key after the **:n** command; it will take effect as soon as you enter it. At the mail prompt, you can use the **d** command to delete the message and move on to the next, or exit mail altogether.

Sending New Messages

The best way to learn mail is to send practice messages to yourself. You can send a new message using the sequence **mail *login@address*** at the system prompt. Thus, to send myself a message, I'd enter **mail gilster@interpath.net,** after which I'd be prompted for a subject. After entering the subject, I type in my text. When finished, a single period (.) followed by another **RETURN** ends the message and sends it on its way.

```
% mail gilster@interpath.net
Subject: Learning the Ropes
Mail is easy to send; it's more difficult to manage.
```

All of which is to remind you that message management is the core of effective electronic mail.

The message you just sent should blast its way right through your system and pop up in your mailbox. Mail can be sent either from the & prompt (from inside mail) or from the system command prompt; it's your choice.

Looking for Help

Remember that mail provides a help function, invoked by pressing the **?** key. Figure 7.4 shows what I see on-screen at Interpath when I press this key at the mail command prompt.

The commands in Figure 7.4 are not the complete set. If you want to see the whole list, you can tap into the on-line manual that Unix systems make available. Enter **man mail** to call up this storehouse of information as it pertains to the mail program. The

```
cd [directory]            chdir to directory or home if none given
d [message list]          delete messages
e [message list]          edit messages
f [message list]          show from lines of messages
h                         print out active message headers
m [userlist]              mail to specific users
n                         goto and type next message
p [message list]          print messages
pre [message list]        make messages go back to system mailbox
q                         quit,saving unresolved messages in mbox
r [message list]          reply to sender (only) of messages
R [message list]          reply to sender and all recipients of messages
s [message list] file     append messages to file
t [message list]          type messages (same as print)
top [message list]        show top lines of messages
u [message list]          undelete messages
v [message list]          edit messages with display editor
w [message list] file     append messages to file, without from line
x                         quit, do not change system mailbox
z[-]                      display next [previous] page of headers
!                         shell escape

A [message list] consists of integers, ranges of same, or user names separated
by spaces.  If omitted, Mail uses the current message.
```

Figure 7.4   A help screen in the mail program.

output will be presented a screen at a time, allowing you to page through it. This is convenient if you have time to read the manual on-line, but a printout of the commands is preferable if your problem is complicated.

Using the Tilde Escape Commands

Let's talk about forwarding messages for a moment. You're reading your messages and come across one you'd like to pass along to a co-worker. This happens all the time, for the networks are so big that we're constantly running across items of use to others. Recently a friend wanted to know how to get the manual pages for mail to scroll. Normally, the manual is set up so that you'll get its pages a screenful at a time, pressing the **SPACEBAR** to move to the next screen. My friend wanted to scroll the output and capture the result to disk, after which he would print it out.

I sent e-mail to the system administrator, who quickly sent the solution. You can save the mail section to a file with the command **man mail > *filename*.** I was then able to send to my friend the administrator's message embedded in a message of my own by using a series of special commands. These commands are preceded by the tilde character (~), common in the Spanish language where its presence above a letter indicates special pronounciation.

For our purposes, the tilde commands (sometimes called *tilde escapes*) help us with the process of sending messages. Here's how they worked in this case: Starting a new message, I explained to my friend that I would include in the text the information he'd requested, in the form of a message sent to me from the system administrator. I then typed **~m,** a command that told mail to insert the system administrator's message into my letter. I added a few more comments at the end and sent the message on its way.

Keep in mind that your command acts on the current message, and in the case of inserting a previous message, it will insert whichever message is current. It's easy to perform the insertion, only to find to your dismay that you've enclosed the wrong letter. Needless to say, this could lead to some embarrassment. So be certain of what's current, or else insert the appropriate message number!

Figure 7.5 shows what mail looks like as you proceed to insert your text. Note that I've used the **~m** command to insert message #8 in my mbox queue into my message. What I see is the statement Interpolating: 8, as the host computer puts the message where I want it. At the (continue) prompt, I finish my message and sign it. Then I use the . command followed by a **RETURN** to send it. Figure 7.6 shows what the finished message will look like on the receiving end.

The tilde escape commands you'll need most are the following (remember you can generate the complete list with a **man mail** command).

~c	Allows you to send a "carbon copy" of the message to another recipient.
~b	Allows "blind" carbon copies.
~v	Starts the vi editor.
~p	Displays the entire letter for review.
~h	Lists message headings, which can then be changed.
~r	Inserts a file into your letter.
~q	Cancels the letter you're writing.
~m	Includes the current message in your letter.
~f	Includes the current message in your letter.

```
% mail nacspns@ncsuadm.acs.ncsu.edu
Subject: Inserted Message
Lisita,

This is an example of an inserted message.  I'm sending a copy of
the message just sent to me by the mail server at the InterNIC.  It
gives you information about how to obtain files from this site.

~m 8
Interpolating: 8
(continue)

Let me know if this reaches you.

Pablo
.
EOT
&
```

Figure 7.5 A message with another inserted inside it.

```
To: nacspns@ncsuadm.acs.ncsu.edu
Subject: Inserted Message

Lisita,

This is an example of an inserted message.  I'm sending you a copy of the message
just sent to me by the mail server at the InterNIC.  It gives you information
about how to obtain files from this site.

        From mailserv@ds2.internic.net Mon Apr 24 08:54:55 1995
        Received: from ds2.internic.net (ds2.internic.net [192.20.239.132]) by 0
        Message-Id: <199504241254.IAA22172@mercury.interpath.net>
        Date: Mon, 24 Apr 95 09:00:06 EDT
        To: gilster@mercury.interpath.net
        From: AT&T-InterNIC Mail Server <mailserv@ds2.internic.net>
        Subject: Your request
        Status: R

        AT&T InterNIC Directory and Database Mail Server 1.0 [ds2]

        Request arrived - Mon Apr 24 08:36:50 EST 1995
        Request processed - Mon Apr 24 09:00:05 EDT

        Processing mail headers ...

        Processing message contents...

        Command: file /ls-1R
        => FILE:  /ls-1R

        Mail server completed processing message contents


Let me know if this reaches you.

Pablo
.
```

Figure 7.6   The final message with insertion.

You'll note two sequences for inserting a message. The **~m** I used inserts a tab character in front of each line of the insert, which is what I wanted since I was quoting someone else's message, and the offset made that more clear. Using the **~f** command instead will insert the same text, but without the leading tabs.

Another important point: *You must always insert the tilde escape commands at the far left margin of the page.* Otherwise, they won't work.

The following sections provide a closer look at the tilde escape commands.

CARBON COPIES

What if I want to send mail to more than one user? mail lets you create a Cc: field in the outgoing message area. Anyone you list on this line will receive a copy of the same message. Use the **~c** command anywhere in the message (but as with all the tilde escape commands, be sure you enter it at the left margin). Entering **~c gilster@interpath.net** sends me a copy of the message you're currently writing. On the other hand, if you don't want the message to be circulated elsewhere, just press the **RETURN** key at this line.

You may find Cc: set up as a default on your system, so that the mail program prompts for carbon copies whenever you compose a letter. If you'd prefer to have this option activated, a line can be added to .mailrc, a Unix file containing defaults for your mail system; you can do this with either the vi text editor or with pico.

Another form of carbon copy is accessible through the **~b** command. It creates so-called blind carbon copies which go out to a list of recipients just like the conventional copies; the difference is, people who receive blind carbons don't know who else received the message. The sequence **~b** creates the blind carbon capability.

The following is an example of setting up a blind carbon (the same procedure applies for a regular carbon copy):

```
% mail pag@world.std.com
Subject: Meeting Announcement
~b stroud@med.unc.edu
Don't forget the July 16th meeting at The Columns!
.
%
```

Note how this works. After entering the subject, I include a **~b** command followed (after a single space) by the address of the person to whom I want to send a blind carbon copy. The address must be on the same line for this to work—don't enter the tilde escape command and then press **RETURN.**

CALLING UP AN EDITOR

As you work with mail's command structure, you may sometimes find yourself wishing for more features, particularly the ability to go back and rewrite that awkward sentence in the second paragraph, or to fix that misspelled word in line 3. This is where the **~v** command comes into play. Inserting the command at the far left of the screen while you're composing e-mail will call up the vi editor program. The lines you've already typed will appear in vi, ready to be edited, and you can add additional material as you choose. When you finish writing, exit vi by entering **ESC** followed by **:wq** and a **RETURN,** and you will return to the mail program. You'll then need to type a period (.) to send your message on its way.

The following example shows what a mail message looks like as I begin to compose, and then switch into vi:

```
% mail pag@world.std.com
Subject: Showing Off vi
This is designed to illustrate what happens when you use the ~v command
to switch into the vi text editor. I will insert ~v on the far left
margin on the line immediately below.
~v
```

By adding a **RETURN** after the **~v,** I move directly into the vi editor. What I have composed so far is already on-screen and is shown in Figure 7.7. I can now edit what I've already written or add to it.

```
"/tmp/Re14248" 3 lines, 179 characters
This is designed to illustrate what happens whenyou use the ~v command
to switch into the vi text editor.  I will insert~v on the far left
margin on the line immediately below.
~
~
~
~
~
~
~
~
~
~
~
~
~
~
~
~
~
~
~
"/tmp/Re14248" 3 lines, 179 characters
```

Figure 7.7 Working on a message with the vi editor.

The command structure of vi is discussed in Chapter 4. But remember that you can use the **man** command for further information. Thus, **man vi** will call up the basic commands; they're not intuitive, but you'll learn them fairly quickly as you put them to use. I think you'll agree that basic text editors are not a strong point of Unix systems.

PREVIEWING THE RESULTS

I can't stress enough that you must review the results of your tilde escape commands. Inserting the wrong letter into a sensitive missive can lead to problems. Fortunately, mail contains another command, **~p** which allows you to preview the message. Assume I've just inserted a file into a letter I'm composing. By typing **~p** at the left margin, I get a preview, as the mail program scrolls through the letter. When it finishes scrolling, I can either add to the letter or send the letter as is. But now I'm assured it is correct.

CHANGING HEADERS

Another tilde escape command, **~h,** is useful for those times when you're involved in a sequence of back and forth mail conversations. Maybe you began an on-line messaging session with a letter whose subject was "Concert Last Night," in which you solicited opinions on how the local symphony performed. After that subject played itself out, you and your correspondent moved on in a series of e-mail exchanges to discuss his job prospects, the firing of the new supervisor, and the Yankees-Red Sox game last Saturday. As you read and replied to your correspondent's letters, all the mail was still going out and coming back under the heading "Concert Last Night."

You could, of course, simply send a new message with a new subject. But why go to the trouble? Reading the current message, you can go to the left margin and do a **~h** command. Now you'll be prompted as shown in Figure 7.8.

Note what happened here. When I typed the **~h** command, I was prompted with the headers of the message as they were presently constituted. I could use the **RETURN** key to cycle through them until I came to the subject header, which was the one I had decided to change. I backspaced to remove the original header and supplanted it with a new one. I was then given the (continue) prompt, at which point I used a single period followed by a **RETURN** to send the letter.

MAILING FILES

As you become more proficient with on-line commands, you'll use mail's forwarding capabilities more and more. A friend of mine shares my interest in portable computing, but because of a busy work schedule, she had not been following events in the industry as closely as she would have liked. Having just completed a column on the subject, I wanted to pass it along, so I saved the column as a file and moved it into the mail program. There, I began a message to her and used the **~r** command to insert the file into the message. Since my file was called column.210, I sent it with the command **~r column.210**. Figure 7.9 shows what this looked like.

Again, I see a statement that my file has been added into the message ("column.210"); the number of lines and characters in the message are also included. I add after this a final comment and send the message with a period (.). On the receiving end, my correspondent sees what is shown in Figure 7.10 (I deleted the superfluous header information).

```
% mail nacspns@ncsuadm.acs.ncsu.edu
Subject: Changing Headers

Lisa:

You're going through all this mail wondering when I'm going
to get to the good stuff!  I'm going to keep you wondering.
For now, this is nothing more than an example of how
to change headers.  If I do it right, you won't see
anything in the Subject field except 'New Title.'  Let
me know if it works.

Paul
~h
To: nacspns@ncsuadm.acs.ncsu.edu
Subject: New Title
Cc:
Bcc:
(continue)
.
```

Figure 7.8 Changing message headers.

```
% mail nacspns@ncsuadm.acs.ncsu.edu
Subject: Recent Computer Column

Lisa:

Here's a computer column I wrote recently.  I'm sending it
to demonstrate how to enclose a file within a letter..

Paul

~r column.210
"column.210" 127/7213
Let me know if this gets through OK.
.
```

Figure 7.9 Mailing a file to another user.

CREATING A SIGNATURE FILE

As you begin to accumulate e-mail in your mailbox, you'll notice that many correspondents use electronic signatures. Some of these are relatively spare, including no more than a name and phone number. Some can be quite elaborate, with inset ASCII figures and quotations from various sources. Sometimes, in fact, the signature section of a message can be longer than the message itself. But it's not considered good Internet form to work with overly long signatures, which take up unnecessary storage space. So if you're thinking of creating a signature of your own, keep it to the point. Four lines is a reasonable size.

Here's a sample of a signature that could be attached to any electronic message I send:

```
Paul A. Gilster      gilster@interpath.net      CompuServe 73537,656
          919-782-5947 (voice)      919-782-7024 (fax)
"Few things are harder to put up with than the annoyance of a good example."
                                              -Mark Twain
```

```
Lisa:

Here's a computer column I wrote recently.  I'm sending it
to demonstrate how to enclose a file within a letter.

Paul


     The word out of Las Vegas, where an estimated 195,000
attended the annual Comdex computer show, is that mobile
computing ruled the roost.  Its prevalence was inevitable,
given the fact that computing is about to enter a second,
and far more problematic, wave of growth.  Getting
corporations up to speed on distributed computing was the
theme of the '80s.  Now computers must move into the field...
[and so on].
```

Figure 7.10 The letter with a portion of the inserted file.

To create an electronic signature, you can use mail's **~r** command to insert the appropriate text. The idea is to compose your signature box as you want it to appear and then save it as an ASCII file on your system. Then, as you compose a letter, you can use an **~r** command at the end to insert the signature into the message. Other mail programs, as you'll see, make this process somewhat easier.

EXITING LETTERS

As mentioned before, a **Ctrl-C** aborts the message in progress; a second one returns you to the mail program's prompt. But there's another way of exiting that may save you trouble, particularly in those cases where you have composed a partial letter and would like to continue it later. The **~q** command makes this possible. Entering it at the far left margin while you're composing a letter will save the letter you're composing in a file named dead.letter. This is helpful, because now you can go back and finish the letter at a later time. Unlike the mbox file, dead.letter doesn't accumulate abandoned mail. The next time you cancel a letter, the old letter is replaced by the new cancellation.

Handling Longer Messages

Simple messages are one thing, but what if you need to send something more meaty? The easiest solution may be to write your message out in your favorite word processor, save it as a straight ASCII file, and send it along to your recipient. If you're using a shell account, this involves uploading the file to your host system first.

We covered file downloading and uploading in Chapter 5 on FTP procedures. You could, for example, compose a file called story.doc. Saving it as an ASCII file, you could upload it to your service provider's computer through the command **rz *filename.***

Once the file is present at your service provider, using mail to send it along to your recipient is a simple matter. The format is **mail address <*filename.*** Thus, **mail nacspns@ncsuadm.acs.ncsu.edu <burgundy.txt** sends my file on Burgundian vineyards to the address listed.

Setting Up an Alias

There's no need to work with complicated addresses even though you're using a fairly austere program like mail. It's easy to set up a shortened address which you can use over and over again. This can be a real time-saver, since entering an address like gilster@interpath.net every time you want to write this person, and making the inevitable typing mistakes, can be a pain in the neck. How to proceed? The Unix file .mailrc is where you need to make the changes. You can edit this file with the editor you use on your system, which, at least for starters, will probably be pico.

If you enter a quick **ls** command at your service provider's command prompt (asking to see a directory listing), you won't see .mailrc. That's because it's a hidden file. But enter an **ls -a** command and you'll see it and other hidden files. Look at the difference between the two commands on my system. First, here's an **ls**:

```
% ls
Mail/    core    mbox        xmodem.log
News/    ftp/    world.ps.Z
%
```

The names with the backslash trailing them are directories; those that stand alone are files. Now we'll do an **ls -a:**

```
% ls -a
./        .gopherrc*      .newsrc     Mail/       world.ps.Z
../       .gopherrc~*     .oldnewsrc  News/       xmodem.log
.article  .letter         .pnewsexpert core
.cshrc*   .login          .rnlast     ftp/
.elm/     .mailrc         .rnsoft     mbox
%
```

As you can see, the **ls -a** list is a good bit longer, showing more files and directories. Among the files is the one we're looking for .mailrc. Figure 7.11 shows what .mailrc looks like when called up into the pico editor. I've just added an alias comment.

The idea behind the alias is this: From now on, the line **alias lisa "<NACSPNS@ ncsuadm.acs.ncsu.edu>"** will allow me to reach this person simply by entering **mail lisa** instead of entering the whole address. The alias is handy for frequent correspondents and makes the job of using mail that much easier. pine, incidentally, makes this whole process more intuitive by providing you with an address book that does much of this automatically. We'll look at pine shortly.

Keeping Your Mailbox Tidy

You'll use the mail program to keep your mailbox tidy. That's an easy lesson to learn. Leaving town for what was to have been a short holiday, I was unavoidably detained for over a week. When I returned and logged on to my Internet account, I found 632 mes-

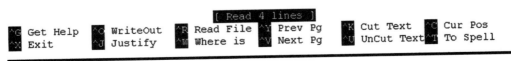

```
  UW PICO(tm) 2.5                    File: .mailrc

set crt=24
set autoprint
alias lisa "<nacspns@ncsuadm.acs.ncsu.edu>"
```

```
                          [ Read 4 lines ]
^G Get Help   ^O WriteOut   ^R Read File  ^Y Prev Pg  ^K Cut Text   ^C Cur Pos
^X Exit       ^J Justify    ^W Where is   ^V Next Pg  ^U UnCut Text ^T To Spell
```

Figure 7.11   Editing .mailrc with the pico editor.

sages waiting for me in my mailbox! This is what people mean by "information glut," and it can make dealing with mail an odious proposition unless you know how to handle the overload.

The solution to a mailbox groaning with the weight of hundreds of messages is obvious: Read the headers and decide which messages look interesting to you. Scuttle the rest. You already know how to delete files, so a quick **d 4** can dispatch message 4 with a minimum of fuss. Entering **d 6 8 23-29** gets rid of those messages, and so on. Note that you can specify a range of messages for deletion.

Be ruthless. You can, of course, work through your messages one by one, but 632 messages in one mailbox makes that a losing proposition. A better way is to jump around. Entering the number of the message that interests you lets you read it. To check the headers again, it's a simple matter to return to mail's command prompt (&) at the end of a message and enter an **h,** which puts the headers back up for your perusal. In this way, culling messages of questionable interest, you can pare your mailbox down to size.

Exiting mail

Enter **q** when you've finished reading a particular message and you'll be returned to the & prompt. A second **q** will then exit the mail program altogether, returning you to the main system prompt. When you do this, all unread mail will be saved in your system mailbox. Any mail that you left undeleted will be saved in the mbox file in your home directory.

There's also another way to leave mail. Using the **x** command, you can leave mail without making any changes to your files. This method also preserves any deleted messages.

Internet Addressing—The Long Way Home

We have now taken a long, hard look at mail, examining the functions any good mail reader should make available, and practicing them within a bare-bones Unix program. Next, I want to contrast the mail program with pine, to show you a completely different approach to mail management. But before we move on, it's time to examine Internet addresses and how they work within a message. Otherwise, you may feel intimidated when you see an address embedded within a long message header full of inscrutable information. Take a look, for example, at Figure 7.12, which is an actual message right out of my mailbox. Note that the message header is considerably longer than the message itself.

Let's take this message header apart. If you look at the top line, marked From:, you'll see the Internet address nacspns@ncsuadm.acs.ncsu.edu. We examined domain names in Chapter 2, and this one isn't too difficult to figure out. The .edu statement at the far right tells us it's from an educational institution; ncsu is North Carolina State University in Raleigh; ncsuadm and acs refer to computers and departments at the university. nacspns is the user name of my contact at the site. Remember the principle: Internet addresses go from the most specific—the user name—to the most general. As you can see, the name and address are followed by the date and time the message was sent.

What does Received: stand for? If you're a technological purist and insist on knowing through which portals a message has passed, these references provide your clues. In this case, the message was routed from North Carolina State University in Raleigh (and

```
From NACSPNS@ncsuadm.acs.ncsu.edu Fri Apr 21 14:00:49 1995
Received: from CCVS2.CC.NCSU.EDU (ccvs2.cc.ncsu.edu [152.1.13.21]) by mercury.i0
Message-Id: <199504211800.OAA25042@mercury.interpath.net>
Received: from NCSUADM.NCSU.EDU (MAILER) by NCSUVAX (MX V4.1 VAX) with BSMTP;
          Fri, 21 Apr 1995 13:58:31 EDT
Date: Fri, 21 Apr 95 14:01 EDT
From: NACSPNS@ncsuadm.acs.ncsu.edu
To: Paul A Gilster - Computer Focus <gilster@MERCURY.INTERPATH.NET>
Subject: Re: Hangchow
Status: R


Pablo:


Thanks for lunch!


Lisita


&
```

Figure 7.12 Headers can sometimes overwhelm the message they identify.

you can track its progress through the ccvs2 machine there in the second line) and passed along to my account at Interpath through a machine called mercury. This information falls into the "nice to know" category; you'll have no need to work with it. In fact, many mail programs simply filter it out; it is of little use to learn that a message was passed through particular computers en route, as long as you are able to read the message and respond to it.

The date appears next—this is the date and time the message was actually sent, as opposed to when it first entered the system (the date and time shown in the first line). The From: address is the address you should reply to. In this case, it's the same as the address in the first line, but in many cases, a message may contain an address that shows you where the mail is coming from, as opposed to who sent it.

Message-ID: Every message identification number is unique, but like routing information, it's of use to Unix wizards and no one else. To: is obvious—it's the address of the recipient and is followed by the subject of the communication in question. If you see a header marked Cc:, it's a listing of additional addresses where the message has gone. The good news is that even the simplest mail programs take care of the necessary routing information. Usually, all you'll want to do is check the From: and Subject: headers as you glance through your mailbox to find out which messages are really worth reading.

You'll occasionally encounter a different kind of tag, an exclamation point (!), which Unix purists refer to as a "bang." It might look like this: uunet!check-mate!crk. When you see the exclamation point, you know you are dealing with a UUCP account. None of this matters to you, the end user, unless you have two address possibilities. Because many UUCP sites are now listing Internet domain names, it's best to try the Internet addressing scheme when you're trying to reach someone. UUCP routing is more restrictive and can fail when a machine somewhere along the line goes down.

Internet routing strategies sound complicated, and they are if you examine them from the level of a network administrator. But mastering their intricacies demands nothing more than a few basic principles, knowledge of which can connect you to Internet sites worldwide and to a host of other computer networks. The most exciting thing about Internet e-mail for dial-up users is that this network is now linking up so seamlessly with other networks, including the big commercial providers, that someday you may be able to do everything on-line with a single network address, instead of the variety some of us now use.

Every day, for example, I read and respond to my Internet mail before moving on to check the various newsgroups I use to keep up on events in the computer industry and elsewhere. Later in the day, I'll use the Internet's Telnet capabilities (discussed in Chapter 6), to log on to BIX, a popular on-line service known for the high level of computer expertise available on it. Checking my mail and messages there, I'll move on to Compu-Serve, where an active user group now follows Internet developments and participates in network exploration through FTP and Telnet linkages.

Telnet features and file downloading are not electronic mail, of course, and the commercial networks vary in their ability to exchange messages one to one. But the trend is clear. Right now we sail through islands of computer connectivity, pausing where we find something interesting, then moving on to the next island for a fresh look. We're moving toward the gradual firming up of trade routes between those islands; someday, it may not matter whether you consider your primary account to be on the Internet or on CompuServe or America Online or MCI Mail. Through information gateways, your explorations will be worldwide.

The next chapter specifically addresses how to use Internet mail gateways from commercial providers. If your sole entry into the Internet is through a bulletin board by means of e-mail, be sure to read that chapter.

Hitting a Brick Wall

It's not surprising that sometimes, despite your best efforts, things go awry with electronic mail. Because they're complicated, e-mail addresses can fall victim to typographical errors. For that matter, you may simply have your information wrong, and get the address confused, giving someone the wrong domain name or mistaking his or her user name at the site. The Internet mail system will bounce the message right back to you. Along with the failed mail will be a message advising you on the nature of the problem. Figure 7.13 shows what happened to me when I got the user name wrong and sent to a nonexistent address.

What to do when you have a message returned? The example in Figure 7.13 involved an addressing error. The host computers were unable to locate the person I was mailing to. My mistake, but at least the mail came back. I realized the message had not been delivered, and was then able to contact the person in question to correct the addressing problem. This kind of mistake can occur with people we already correspond with. Used to entering the **r** command to reply and letting mail supply the correct address, we forget what that address is when we decide to send new mail to the same user.

Mail sometimes disappears for other reasons. Remember, an active Internet user receives a large number of messages every day. Perhaps the subject on your message wasn't as clear as it should have been; a busy person might simply delete such mail without realizing what it was. Don't assume bad motives on the part of those who don't respond to their mail. We all do our best, but I can tell you how easy it is to overlook a particular message when you're not looking out for it in the first place. If the message is important, resend it. And be sure to make your subject heading germane.

```
rom daemon Fri Apr 21 14:39:26 1995
Received: from localhost (localhost) by mercury.interpath.net (8.6.9/8.6.9) wit0
Date: Fri, 21 Apr 1995 14:39:26 -0400
From: Mail Delivery Subsystem <MAILER-DAEMON>
Subject: Returned mail: User unknown
Message-Id: <199504211839.OAA27612@mercury.interpath.net>
To: gilster
MIME-Version: 1.0
Content-Type: multipart/mixed; boundary="OAA27612.798489566/mercury.interpath.n"
Status: R

This is a MIME-encapsulated message

--OAA27612.798489566/mercury.interpath.net

The original message was received at Fri, 21 Apr 1995 14:39:24 -0400
from gilster@localhost

    ----- The following addresses had delivery problems -----
narlot@world.std.com   (unrecoverable error)

    ----- Tra
... while talking to world.std.com.:
>>> RCPT To:<narlot@world.std.com>
<<< 550 <narlot@world.std.com>... User unknown
550 narlot@world.std.com... User unknown

    ----- Original message follows -----

--OAA27612.798489566/mercury.interpath.net
Content-Type: message/rfc822

Return-Path: gilster
Received: (from gilster@localhost) by mercury.interpath.net (8.6.9/8.6.9) id OA0
Date: Fri, 21 Apr 1995 14:39:24 -0400
From: Paul A Gilster - Computer Focus <gilster>
Message-Id: <199504211839.OAA27609@mercury.interpath.net>
To: narlot@world.std.com
Subject: Test Message

Test.  Please ignore.

--OAA27612.798489566/mercury.interpath.net--

&
```

Figure 7.13   Results of a mistaken address entry.

pine—Making Mail Easy

Developed by the University of Washington, pine is an easy-to-use mail program that provides on-line help and requires little expertise. We've already examined the text editor called pico. When you use pine, you will be working with the same editing commands, thus simplifying your use of both programs (pico in fact, stands for pine composer, showing the close linkage between the two applications). In most cases, you will find that your commands are single keystrokes or combinations of the **Ctrl** key and a letter key. Conveniently, the basic commands are given along the bottom of the screen, eliminating the need to memorize them.

Invoking pine

To call up pine, simply type the command **pine** at your service provider's command prompt:

```
% pine
```

The initial, main menu screen is shown in Figure 7.14. In this figure, you will notice that pine has found a message in my inbox, as shown along the highlighted bar at the top of the screen. This number, of course, will vary depending upon how many messages have accumulated when you log on.

pine operates by storing mail in folders; these are simply areas where the program keeps messages of various kinds. When you first run pine, for example, the program will ask you whether it can create a folder named for the current month. In that folder, it will store copies of all the messages you send during the month. You can accept this choice by pressing the **y** key when prompted to do so.

Your incoming mail is placed in a folder called *INBOX*, and it is in this folder that you are automatically placed when you call up the program. Notice the highlight bar in Figure 7.14, which sits atop a line marked like this:

```
L    FOLDER LIST      - Select a folder to view
```

```
 PINE 3.91    MAIN MENU                            Folder: INBOX  1 Message


         ?      HELP               -  Get help using Pine

         C      COMPOSE MESSAGE    -  Compose and send a message

         I      FOLDER INDEX       -  View messages in current folder

         L      FOLDER LIST        -  Select a folder to view

         A      ADDRESS BOOK       -  Update address book

         S      SETUP              -  Configure or update Pine

         Q      QUIT               -  Exit the Pine program



    Copyright 1989-1994.  PINE is a trademark of the University of Washington.
                    [Folder "INBOX" opened with 1 message]
 ? Help                        P PrevCmd                    R RelNotes
 O OTHER CMDS L [ListFldrs]  N NextCmd                      K KBLock
```

Figure 7.14 The main menu screen in pine.

By pressing the **RETURN** key with the highlight on this line, we will call up a list of folders available to us. We can achieve the same result with the **L** command. Here are the results of using this command at my account at Interpath.

```
INBOX           sent-mail           saved-messages          mac.doc
sent-mail-mar-1995
```

These folders store old messages I have sent, as well as archive any messages I have decided to save. The reason there are no folders older than these is that pine periodically gives you the option of deleting old folders in order to conserve disk space. It's always a good idea to clear any folders you won't be needing.

Note that at any time you can create a new folder simply by typing the **a** command. This makes it easy to sort and store messages in a logical manner. You can do the same thing in mail by using the **s** *filename* command to save the message in question. The **folder** *filename* command is how you change folders with mail. By making folder management a prompted operation with menus, pine simplifies the process.

Case in pine Commands

You have learned to be worried about case when dealing with Unix, and pine is a Unix program. But within pine, there is no need to worry. Whether you type an **L** to call up the folder list or an **l** (lowercase), the result will be the same. If you examine the commands shown in Figure 7.14 along the bottom of the screen, you will see that they are all given as capitals. But feel free to use either upper- or lowercase depending on which is most comfortable to you. And look for items in brackets. When you see **[y]**, for example, it means a **y** is the default choice. Pressing a **RETURN** is how you accept a default.

Composing a Message

The **c** command is used to write a message. When you press a **c** (or a **C**) at pine's main menu screen, you will see the screen shown in Figure 7.15. Note that the cursor appears at the top of the screen, in the To: field. Here you would enter the address of the person to whom you were writing. By pressing either the **TAB** or the **Down Arrow** key, you can move to the next field, marked Cc:, which allows you to list addresses for other people to whom you might like to send the same message. The Attchmnt: field, which we will examine shortly, allows you to include a separate file in your message. The Subject: field, of course, is the place to enter the subject of your message. As with mail, you want to be sure that your subject is a careful statement of what is in your message.

The top of the composition screen is called the *header;* it comprises everything above the line marked *Message Text.* Once you have completed the information in the header, you can press the **TAB** or **Down Arrow** key again to move to the second part of the screen, where you will write the body of the text. Because pine uses pico as its editor, composing your message is a simple process. You do not need to add a **RETURN** at the end of each line, because pine uses automatic word wrap. The only place you will need to place a **RETURN** is at the end of paragraphs; placing two spaces between paragraphs makes for greater ease in reading.

When you have finished a message, the **Ctrl-x** command sends it. You will notice this command marked at the bottom of the screen as **^X,** which is saying the same thing; the **^** character is frequently used to stand for the **Ctrl** key. You hold down the **Ctrl** key

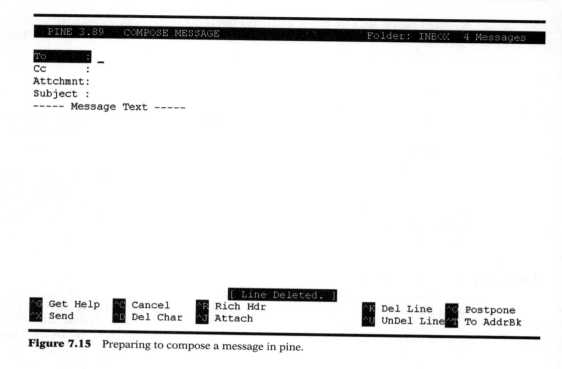

Figure 7.15   Preparing to compose a message in pine.

and type the letter **x** or **X.** When you press this combination after writing a message, you will see this at the bottom of the screen:

```
Send message? [y] :
```

The **y** in brackets is the default; you can press a **y** or a **RETURN** to accept it and send the message. If you change your mind, pressing an **n** causes pine to take you back to the editing screen to make any further changes or additions to your message.

Sending a Practice Message

Get in some practice with pine by sending a sample message to yourself. From the main menu screen, press a **c** to call up the editor. In the To: field, enter your own Internet address. If you make any typing mistakes, you can use the **BACKSPACE** key to change your text before proceeding to the next field. Because this is a test message, leave the Cc: and Attchmnt: fields blank; pine will still process the message without them. Remember: The **TAB** or the **Down Arrow** key moves you between fields. In the Subject: field, enter a title of your choice.

Type as you please, adding whatever text you'd like. And note this interesting fact: pine uses a full-screen editor. If you look back over your text and realize you have made a mistake, all you need to do is to move the cursor back to that point and make the changes. We'll examine the editing keys in a moment; right now, simply realize that, whereas mail did not allow you to go back and edit previous lines of text, pine makes it easy. The benefits of a full-screen editor are obvious, and they alone may make you decide to choose pine as your mail program.

When your message is complete, press a **Ctrl-x** to send it on its way. When prompted, press the **y** key to finish the transaction. As you saw previously, you could also press an **n** if you chose to go back and add more text, or edit the text you already had. And there is a third option. If you choose to abandon the message, a **Ctrl-c** will do so. When you press a **Ctrl-c** in pine's editing field, you will see this prompt:

```
Cancelling will abandon your mail message. Cancel? [n] :
```

Pressing a **y** will cancel the message; the default is an **n,** which leaves the message on-screen for further action.

Notice that throughout this process, you have had a series of commands at the bottom of the screen. You are prompted that a **Ctrl-g,** for example, will call up a help screen pine's help functions are first-rate); a **Ctrl-j** will justify the margins of your text. If you take full advantage of these built-in aids, you will find that pine is perhaps the easiest to use of all the Unix mail programs.

Editing Messages with pine

The pico editor used by pine makes text creation and editing relatively straight-forward. As we would expect, the arrow keys can move us up or down from line to line in the message we are editing. The **Right Arrow** and **Left Arrow** keys perform the same functions within a single line. These text movement commands are simple, but they are augmented by a powerful set of editing commands which we will now consider. You will master these commands with a little practice.

Ctrl-d	Deletes the current character. In other words, move the cursor to the character you want to delete, then press **Ctrl-d** to delete it.
Ctrl-h	Deletes the character before the current one.
Ctrl-j	Justifies the right-hand margins in the paragraph you are currently working on.
Ctrl-k	Deletes the current line.
Ctrl-u	Undeletes the last deleted line.
BACKSPACE	Deletes the character to the left of the cursor.

Inserting Files into a Message

The ability to include a separate file in a message is a useful one. Perhaps you would like to transmit the text of a report you have written to your home office, or send a lengthy letter to a friend. While pico makes text creation easy, it is no substitute for a full-fledged word processor. You could, therefore, write your document off-line and simply upload it to your service provider's computer, using the file transfer techniques we discussed in Chapter 5.

Once your file is in your home directory, you can call up pine and begin to compose a message. From within that message, the **Ctrl-r** command will allow you to insert the file directly into **pine.** Decide where you would like the inserted text to begin and place the cursor at that position. When you press **Ctrl-r,** you will be prompted as follows:

```
Insert file:
```

Enter the name of the file you want to insert and press a **RETURN** to insert it. You will see the text appear on your screen. Now you can either add more text manually or proceed to send the file using the **Ctrl-x** command.

You will notice that when you enter the **Ctrl-r** command to insert a file, the prompts at the bottom of the screen change. Instead of the normal editing commands, you now get a much shortened menu listing just three: **Ctrl-g** for help; **Ctrl-c** for cancelling the file insertion; and **Ctrl-t,** which is cryptically labelled *To Files*. The latter is helpful if you have forgotten the name of the file you want to insert. When you press **Ctrl-t** at the file insertion point, pine will call up a listing of the files in your home directory and the sub-directories that branch off from it. You are also able to move between directories, and to check the contents of each, with the arrow keys.

Attaching Files to a Message

Although it might sound like the same operation, attaching a file is different from inserting one. The primary difference is that inserting a file requires that the file be a text document. When you attach a file, you can include other kinds of files. Perhaps you have a software program you'd like to pass along to a friend. Using the file attachment option, you could send this with a message explaining what it was.

To attach a file to a message, move the cursor to the Attchmnt: field. Once it is there, press the **Ctrl-j** command. The following prompt will appear:

```
File to attach:
```

Enter the name of the file you would like to attach to the message and press a **RETURN,** which will incorporate the file. pine will now give you a second prompt:

```
Attachment comment:
```

You can enter anything you would like to say about the file. The Attchmnt: field will now change to reflect the added document. Here, for example, is what it showed when I sent a document with the comment "test document."

```
Attchmnt: 1. /interpath/users/gilster/errata.doc (3.1 KB) "test document"
```

As opposed to file insertion, where you actually see the text of the inserted file appear within your message, an attachment will not appear on-screen other than as listed in the Attchmnt: field. The message can now be sent, along with its attached file, using the normal pine methods.

pine's Spell Checker

We've all gotten used to using spell checkers to catch our more egregious mistakes. pine incorporates a spell checker that can do the same thing for your outgoing e-mail. Once you have finished writing a message, you can call up the spell checker by entering the **Ctrl-t** command.

Here is how to use the **Ctrl-t** command. When you have finished writing your message, move the cursor back to the beginning of the message. Then give the **Ctrl-t** command, followed by a **RETURN**. The spell checker will display the following prompt as it works:

```
[ Checking Spelling... ]
```

It will then fasten on any problems it finds in your document. Here, for example, is what pine did when it ran into the term fax in a message I was sending:

```
Edit a replacement: Fax
```

The spell checker's dictionary doesn't include the term fax, and pine is offering to let me change the word, which it assumes is a mistake.

Of course, we know that fax is correct, and would like to leave the word as it is. To do so, I press the **RETURN** key at this point, and the spell checker continues its work. If I wanted to make a correction, I would do so and press the **RETURN** key when I was done. pine will automatically insert the correction at the point in the text where the misspelled word appeared.

When pine has gone through your entire document, you will receive the following prompt:

```
[ Done checking spelling ]
```

You are now placed back in the editor and can send your message.

Reading Mail with pine

Let's go back to examine the opening screen in pine. Take another look at Figure 7.14 and notice that the main actions are laid out for you. The highlight bar is sitting on the **L** option, which displays a list of the folders pine is currently using; but you can also choose **c** to compose a message, **i** to retrieve an index of the messages in your inbox, an **a** to go directly to the address book, an **s** to configure pine, and a **q** to leave the program altogether. Also useful is the **?** command, which takes you to pine's help facility.

To read messages, choose the **i** command from the main menu screen. This will take you to the index screen and present you with information about what is available. Figure 7.16 illustrates a typical index screen, as called up in my own mailbox (here, I'm showing you pine as viewed through the Crosstalk communications program). This screen is your launching pad for electronic mail; here you will select the messages you want to read and delete those you don't; from here, you will move to the actual messages for a closer look.

We now know to look at the bottom of the screen for useful information about commands. And as before, we can see that the commands available change depending on what we are doing at the time; the help information, in other words, is context-sensitive—it knows what we are doing and what we're likely to need. We also see that the highlight bar is currently sitting on top of the first message in the inbox. We are given information about the message headers and also data about the message itself. Here is a typical message header:

```
N 13 Apr 11 Gleason Sackman (11,742) Wash. Post article/Internet Pers. Fin
```

We begin at the left as we read this inbox information. The number tells us that this is the thirteenth message in our inbox. The N preceding this tells us that the message is new; it has arrived since the last time we read mail messages. When we see a blank in

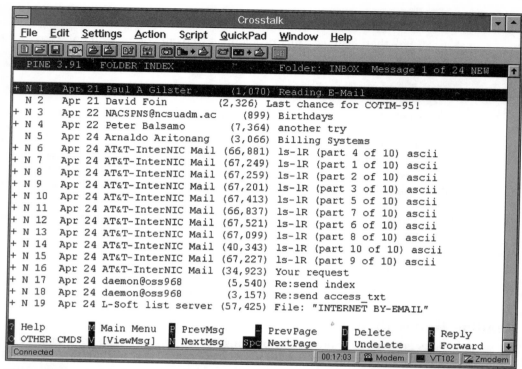

Figure 7.16   pine's index screen lists the contents of your inbox.

this position while reading the index screen, we are looking at a message that has previously been read. A **D** indicates the message has already been marked for deletion. If the message has already been answered, there will be an **A** in this position. A plus character (+) indicates a message that had been sent directly to my account, as opposed, for example, to being sent as part of a larger mailing list.

Following this, we have the date, which is followed by the address of the sender. The size of the message then appears (this one is 11,742 bytes long), and the final statement is the subject. To read any message, simply move the highlight bar, using the **Up** or **Down Arrow** key, to the message in question and press a **RETURN**. The message will then be displayed. Figure 7.17 shows a typical message.

Notice how pine has structured its screen. At the top, you are given the necessary address information, along with the date and time of the message, the address of the sender, and the person to whom the message was sent. This message has been sent by request from an automated server (it's an extremely helpful document, by the way).

As before, commands are shown along the bottom of the screen; notice in particular that you can use the **SPACEBAR** to move to the next page of a multipage message. And notice that you can delete a message from within the message itself by choosing the **d** command. You may choose to read your mail this way, calling up each message, and deleting messages as you go, perhaps responding to them first, or saving some into a folder of saved messages. As you can see, it is also possible to undelete a message by

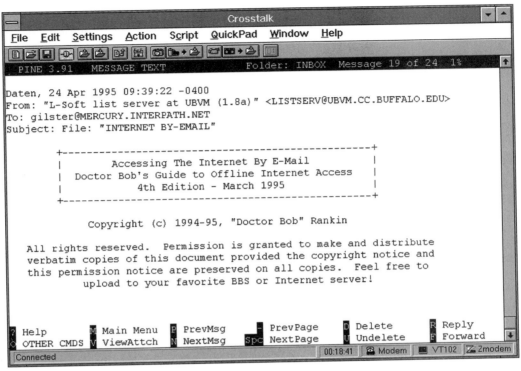

Figure 7.17   A message as displayed in pine.

using the **u** command; this command works, however, only during the current editing session. The dash (-) command is likewise useful; it moves you to the previous page of the message in question. An **n** moves you to the next message, while a **p** displays the previous message.

Responding to a Message

The **r** command is used to respond to a message in pine. When you use it, you will receive the following prompt:

```
Include original message in Reply? (y/n/^C) [n]:
```

As you can see, the default (shown by the brackets) is **n** for no. However, you have two other choices. A **y** will cause the original message to appear in your response, which can be helpful in reminding your correspondent about what he or she said. And a **Ctrl-c** will cancel the message entirely.

If there is an address in the Reply to: field of the original message, you will then receive a second prompt:

```
Use "Reply to:" address instead of "From:" address? (y/n/^C) [y]:
```

Here, as you can see, the default is **y** for yes. And finally, if you are responding to a mailing list as opposed to a single individual, you will see this prompt:

```
Reply to all recipients? (y/n/^C) [n]:
```

The **n** is the default; if you choose it, your reply will only go to the person whose name is in the From: field of the message.

When you have answered the necessary prompts, pine will call up a response screen, allowing you to enter your message. Here, for example, is the header information from a typical message response (in this case, to a mailing list message).

```
To      : Gleason Sackman <sackman@plains.nodak.edu>
Cc      :
Attchmnt:
Subject : Re: Wash. Post article/Internet Pers. Finance Resources (fwd)
----- Message Text -----
```

Your message will go below the ----Message Text---- line, just as it did when we were composing original messages earlier. You simple enter the message, without worrying about word wrap, until it is complete. Again, using a **RETURN** between paragraphs inserts a blank space and makes reading the message much easier.

Whenever using pine, examine the bottom of the screen to remind yourself of the commands available. A **Ctrl-x** sends the message, while a **Ctrl-c** cancels it. And, of course, you have the usual options you learned while composing messages earlier, including the ability to incorporate a file into a message, or to add a file as an attachment to it. Once you have finished the message and sent it on its way, however, the message is gone. Be sure to think carefully about what you send, as you can't retrieve a message that has already gone out the door.

Message Deletion

The **d** command deletes messages; using it will cause pine to delete the current message and take you to the next one available. When you delete a message, a D appears beside that message on the index screen. Remember: You can still undelete such a message with the **u** command, but you will be unable to do so once you have ended the current pine session. And notice this: The **d** command will work either from the index screen or from within a message itself.

Proper mail management, as you learned when you studied the mail program, requires that you delete messages as you read them, unless you have decided to save or forward a message. Your mailbox will become unmanageably large without such supervision, and you may be subject to additional storage charges from your service provider.

Saving a Message

pine makes it easy to hold on to messages for later use. To do so, use the **s** key. This creates the following prompt on-screen:

```
SAVE to folder [saved-messages] :
```

Because pine stores its messages in folders, you are being asked which folder you would like to keep the message in. Here you have several choices. The default folder, as you can see from the bracketed information, is called *saved-messages*. You can press the **RETURN** key to accept this choice. Or, if you'd prefer to create a new folder, you can do so now by entering a new name. pine will prompt you this way (I have just told pine to put my messages in a folder called *questions*):

```
Folder "questions" doesn't exist. Create? (y/n/^C) [y]:
```

Answering a **y** will create the new folder. The message in question will then be saved to this folder.

But perhaps you would prefer to save the message to a separate file outside of pine. To do so, use the **e** command; this will export the message into your home directory. You can use the **e** command from the index screen by placing the highlight over the message you would like to save before using it. In either case, you will receive this prompt:

```
File (in home directory) to save message text in:
```

Enter a filename here and press the **RETURN** key. The file will now be found in your home directory, and can be downloaded for subsequent use. But don't forget to remove it from your service provider's hard disk once you've acted upon it!

Forwarding a Message

pine makes it easy to forward messages to another person. You can do this by using the **f** command, either from the index screen or while reading the message. A new message composition screen will then appear, containing the message you would like to forward, and giving you the opportunity to enter the address of the person to whom you want to forward it. You might enter a brief comment before the forwarded message to let your recipient know what it is all about.

Basic Folder Commands

You've already seen that you can use the **l** command to call up a screen that shows your folders; you can choose a folder by moving the highlight bar with the arrow keys until you reach the one you want to open; pressing a **RETURN** at this point will open the folder. What you will see is a screen similar to the index screen we've already examined; the difference is that the material shown on the screen will correspond to what was stored in the folder you've opened.

Want to move a message from one folder to another? You can do so with the **s** command. Remember that a prompt appears when you use **s,** asking you for the folder you would like to send the message to:

```
SAVE to folder [saved-messages]:
```

You can now enter a folder name or create a new folder by typing in the name of the folder you would like to create.

Here are the folder commands you will find useful:

a   Adds a new folder.

d   Deletes a folder and everything in it.

g   Moves to a specific folder and opens it.

r   Renames a folder.

w   Searches for a folder.

pine's Address Book

Now we come to one of pine's nicest features. pine makes an address book available that totally simplifies the process of setting up aliases for frequent correspondents and recording addresses. You will remember that with the mail program, we had to go into pico and call up the .mailrc file to do this, typing in a very precise sequence of information. And even when we had done so, what we wound up with was an alias—that is, I could type **mail lisa** to send a message, and mail would supply the address. But mail couldn't be configured to record an address with a keystroke, and it certainly couldn't set up a sorted field of your most used addresses, which pine can do and more.

From the main menu, choose **a** to open up the address book. In Figure 7.18, you see the results of doing this at my account at Interpath. Going from left to right, you will see an alias or nickname, which is all I need to enter into pine's To: field while typing a message; when I follow it with a **RETURN,** the nickname is transformed into a complete

```
   PINE 3.89    ADDRESS BOOK                    Folder: INBOX   Message 2 of 3 NEW

  paul              Farrell, Paul              pfarrell@jwiley.com
  lissa             gilster, lissa            GILSTER@CCIT.ARIZONA.EDU
  duane             Hall, Duane               Duane.Hall@lambada.oit.u
  howard            Harawitz, Howard          harawitz@fox.nstn.ns.ca
  hart              Hart, Michael             hart@vmd.cso.uiuc.edu
  microsoft         Kaski, Becky              rebeccak@microsoft.com
  joe               Lazzaro, Joseph           lazzaro@bix.com
  jayne             Levin, Jayne              helen@access.digex.net
  joel              maloff, joel              jmaloff@aol.com
  pease             Pease, Paul               ppease@netcom.com
  richard           Richard Scoville          rscovill@rock.concert.ne
  rick              Smith, Rick               rsmith@interpath.net
  lisa              Stroud, Lisa              NACSPNS%NCSUADM.BITNET@V
  vic               sussman, vic              vic@access.digex.net
  sas               Swain, Wink               saswes@unx.sas.com
  bix               Taylor, Christine         ctaylor@bix.com
  walnut            velte, jack               velte@cdrom.com
  david             Warlick, David            dwarlick@dpi1.dpi.nc.gov
  delphi            Williams, Russell         rusty@delphi.com

  ? Help         M MainMenu    P PrevField   - PrevPage    D Delete      S CreateList
  O OTHER CMDS   E [Edit]      N NextField  Spc NextPage   A Add         Z AddToList
```

Figure 7.18   A pine address book.

address. The person to whose nickname the alias refers is listed in the middle column, while the corresponding Internet address for each nickname is at the right. It is also possible to create a distribution list, so that you can send e-mail to more than one person at a time by using a single nickname.

Once you have gone into the address book, you can press the **a** key again to add a new name to it. A prompt will appear asking for the name of the person you want to add:

```
New full name (last, first) :
```

Fill in the name, last name first, with a comma between the names, and press a **RETURN.** When you do so, a new prompt appears:

```
Enter new nickname (one word and easy to remember) :
```

This is the opportunity for you to add the nickname of your choice. Notice that it should be one word only; after all, the whole point of this exercise is to make it easy to enter names. Once you have entered the nickname, a final prompt appears:

```
Enter new e-mail address :
```

Here you simply add the complete Internet address of the person in question. From now on, that person is listed in your address book, and sending mail is a snap.

What if you would like to send mail to a large group of people? A distribution list can be created in much the same way. Use the **s** command while in the address book to do so. This will create a prompt like the following:

```
Long name/description of new list:
```

You can enter whatever description you choose for the distribution list you are creating. Press a **RETURN** to get the next prompt:

```
Enter list nickname (one word and easy to remember) :
```

This, of course, is equivalent to the nickname prompt, which you set up for a distribution list just as you did for a single person. Insert the nickname of your choice and press a **RETURN.** The final prompt asks for the addresses you want to place in the distribution list:

```
Enter 1st address or blank when done :
```

Go through the process, adding the addresses you want to include, and pressing a final **RETURN** when you're ready to exit.

And here's a feature I use all the time. You can add addresses while you're reading your mail, without making a first stop at the main menu screen. Perhaps you are reading a message and realize that you would like to add its sender to your address book. Use the **t** command to do so. A new prompt appears:

```
Enter nick name :
```

Go through the process as before, following the nickname with a **RETURN,** and being prompted for a full name. The final prompt will include the person's e-mail address, with the information already entered. You simply press a **RETURN** to accept it. The entry now appears in your address book. And note: You can perform the same operation from the index screen by using the **t** command; just remember to place the highlight bar over the message whose sender you would like to add to your address book.

Setting Up a Signature File in pine

As with mail, we would like to create a signature file that will automatically be appended to the end of any message we send. Fortunately, pine makes this considerably easier to do than mail. All we need to do is to create a file called .signature (note the period in front of the name). You can do this with the pico text editor. Your signature should contain your electronic mail address and other information, including, perhaps, a favorite quotation. The signature will be inserted with no further action on your part every time you compose or reply to a message.

Exiting pine

You can exit pine from the main menu or the index screen simply by entering the **q** command. pine will send this message:

```
Really quit pine? (y/n/^C) [y]:
```

A **y** quits the program; an **n** takes you back to where you were, as does a **Ctrl-c.**

Managing Mail with Eudora

SLIP/PPP users have a distinct advantage over shell account people; they can use a superb program for electronic mail called Eudora. A product of QUALCOMM Inc., Eudora is available in two versions: a free program widely available over the Internet, and a commercial product with a variety of additional features. When you've examined these features, which include a number of filtering options that allow you to take real control over your mailbox, you'll probably opt for the commercial product. But there's no better way to find out than by using the freeware version of Eudora, which is a powerful and easy-to-use mail program in its own right. Versions exist both for the PC and the Macintosh, though the program was originally developed for the Mac, and remains the best choice for that platform.

But first things first. Where do you get Eudora?

What You Need: A Copy of Eudora

Where to Find It: If you're interested in Eudora for IBM-compatible equipment, proceed to the following URL:

ftp://ftp.qualcomm.com/quest/eudora/windows/1.4/eudor144.exe

Also pick up the documentation at this URL:

ftp://ftp.qualcomm.com/quest/eudora/windows/documentation

If you need the Macintosh version, use this URL:

ftp://ftp.qualcomm.com/quest/mac/eudora/2.0/

Full instructions for installation are provided with the software. The one caveat I have is that you must take care with the initial configuration, so that your mail winds up being routed correctly to your computer. Take a look at Figure 7.19. This is the Configuration dialog box, called up by pulling down the Special menu from the menu bar and choosing the Configuration option.

Notice the top field, called POP Account. This cryptic item should be filled in by consulting the information provided by your service provider when you signed up for your account. Service providers always give their clients an information sheet with the basic settings for activating their SLIP/PPP functions; if you have any doubt about what this value is, call your provider.

Post Office Protocol

But we need to pause on the issue of Post Office Protocol to examine just how mail travels through a SLIP/PPP connection, because the model is considerably different than with a shell account. The shell user works with a mail program on-line. That program uses an Internet protocol called SMTP—Simple Mail Transport Protocol—which has become the worldwide standard for the transmission of electronic mail. SMTP governs the formatting of electronic mail as 7-bit ASCII text; we can send binary files—programs, word processor files, spreadsheets—through such mail, but we have to code them into ASCII first, and decode them at the other end. More on the latter issue, and on how to circumvent it, in a moment.

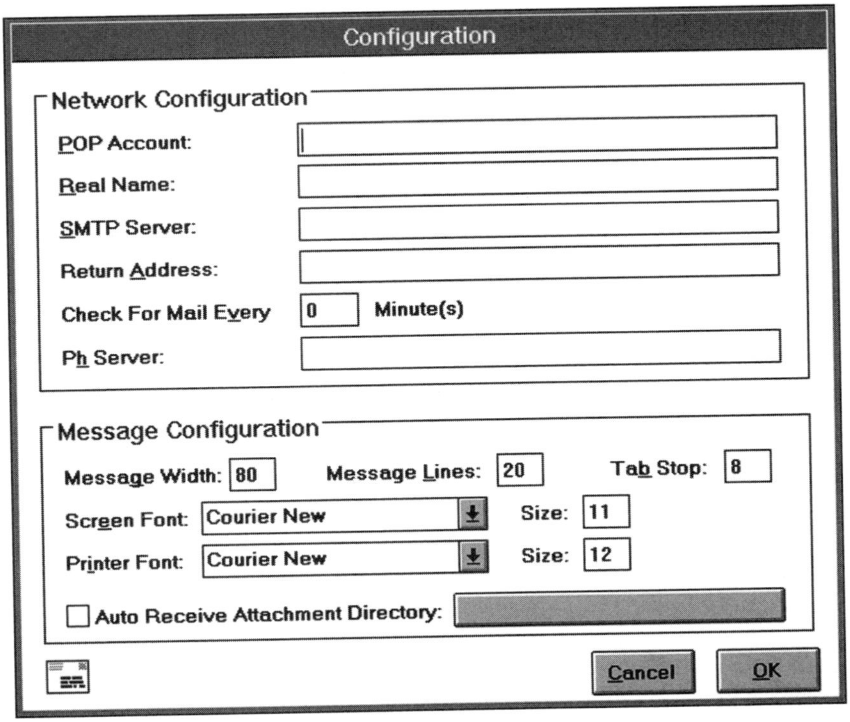

Figure 7.19 Eudora's configuration screen.

When you use Eudora, you're also working with SMTP, but in a different way. Remember, while your service provider's computer maintains an Internet presence 24 hours per day, your own machine probably doesn't; simple cost factors dictate that most of us will sign on to do our network chores and then log off again, being mindful of the time we are using on the system. We need, then, a mail system that can work with users who log on for short periods and then log off again, a system that will queue incoming messages and hold them for those users, transmitting them in a burst when the user signs on and requests them. This is what POP—Post Office Protocol—can do.

The model is this: incoming mail winds up on your service provider's computer, in this case, a POP server that holds the mail for you. When you use Eudora to sign on to your account, the program will request the queued messages, which will then be sent by the POP server. Once the messages are on your machine, Eudora then offers a wide range of options for managing your mail. Usefully, you can sign off from your account and work with your mail off-line, taking as much time as necessary for replies, and performing other functions, such as adding files into your responses or creating new mail with Eudora's shortcut features. When you're ready to send your mail, you call your service provider again and tell Eudora to upload your mail.

When you send mail from your computer onto the Internet, the model is somewhat different. There is no need for your service provider to queue your outgoing mail, so it is handled directly by an SMTP server, which then sends it out onto the network. Remember, SMTP functions best when the computers running it are available to manage mail chores full-time. Post Office Protocol is for asynchronous mail communication, of the kind you run by necessity when you log on through a modem.

If you will refer back to the screen shown in Figure 7.19, then, you will see that the field for POP server specifies for Eudora which computer it should log on to for downloading your mail. You can also fill in several other fields: your real name, and the address of your provider's SMTP server. In many cases, you can leave the SMTP field blank, because the same machine is used for both POP and SMTP functions. But check with your service provider's information sheet to make sure that this is the case. Note as well that Eudora allows you to enter a return address in the field of that name. This allows you to work with multiple accounts, if you prefer to have your mail appear with a different address than the one used in your SLIP/PPP account.

Reading Mail with Eudora

Once you have installed Eudora, the easiest way to learn it is to put it to use reading your mail. The process is simple:

1. Pull down the File menu.
2. Click the Check Mail option.
3. In the dialog box that appears, enter your account password.
4. Click on OK.

You should now see a progress window appear as Eudora logs on to the POP server and begins to download your mail. When the process is complete, you will see a screen full of messages, like the one shown in Figure 7.20. As you can see, the display is not dissimilar from what you see when you use pine to read your mail. The name of the sender

● H.Gibson	05:57 PM 5/26/95	2 Internet Guide
● Edupage	09:41 AM 5/25/95	13 Edupage 5/25/95
● Phil Kemelor	04:01 PM 5/26/95	3 CHANGE: NRCH - Hospital Information Systems I
● Ronald W Crawfor	04:52 PM 5/26/95	3 NEW: TCAN - Texas Counseling Association Netw
● Mustafa Akgul	04:59 PM 5/26/95	4 NEW: WOMEN - Women's Issues and Gender Discus
● Brian Smithson	05:04 PM 5/26/95	3 CHANGE: xpress-list on new host
● Edupage	10:01 AM 5/26/95	13 Edupage -- 5/25/95
● MarcusK583@AOL.C	12:14 PM 5/27/95	2 Reference Works
● TobyFDL@aol.com	08:43 AM 5/28/95	2 Internet Providers
● PNEWS	11:43 PM 5/27/95	4 NEW: PNEWS-L - Progressive News and Views
● Gregory Monahan	11:14 PM 5/27/95	3 SEARCH: Lists for Notebuilder users?
● DAVE	11:15 PM 5/27/95	3 NEW: SWFLBIZ - Southwest Florida Business-to-
● Brian Smithson	11:02 PM 5/27/95	3 CHANGE: ultralite-list on new host
● James Adams	11:33 PM 5/27/95	3 NEW: PRCL-L - Preaching the Revised Common Le
● Paul Lufkin	11:47 PM 5/27/95	3 NEW: CSAR - Computers in Search and Rescue
● bruce searles	11:09 PM 5/27/95	4 NEW: PPM-L - Extracorporeal Technology
● PNEWS	11:37 PM 5/27/95	4 NEW: PAIN-L - Pain List
● Jacob Richman	11:05 PM 5/27/95	3 CHANGE: CJI - Computer Jobs in Israel
● Melissa Bishop	11:22 PM 5/27/95	3 NEW: MBishop+DOLLS - Ragdolls
● Brian Smithson	10:56 PM 5/27/95	3 CHANGE: metacard-list on new host
● Brian Smithson	10:59 PM 5/27/95	3 CHANGE: zoomer-list on new host
● Linda Henneman	10:23 PM 5/28/95	3 CHANGE: FRUGAL-L - Discussion on Frugality
● Tod Maffin	10:28 PM 5/28/95	5 NEW: synod-list - Anglican General Synod news
● Edupage	08:20 PM 5/28/95	11 Edupage 5/28/95

Figure 7.20   Incoming mail waiting to be read in Eudora.

is shown, as is the date and time, followed, on the right, by the Subject: field of the message. To read a message is simple:

- Double-click on the subject field.

The message will now appear in its own window.

Responding to Messages

Eudora makes it easy to respond to any message. With the message on-screen, move to the Message menu and choose Reply. Eudora will display a new message window with the full text of the message already inserted, preceded by the greater than (>) character on each line. Following Internet conventions, this character is used to show text that is being quoted. As mentioned before, it is always a good idea to quote text from the message you are responding to; this gives your recipient the chance to refresh his or her memory about what it is you are talking about.

Of course, it's seldom necessary to quote the entire message; instead, we want to single out the particular part of the message we want to respond to and display it, while cutting the rest of the message, which is likely to be extraneous. Figure 7.21 shows this process in action. Here, I have a message on-screen and have begun to reply to it. Notice the text shown with the brackets, indicating it is quoted from the previous message.

You also can see my text following the quoted material; it appears without the leading > character. Once I've finished with my response, I can send the message by clicking on either the Queue or the Send button as I choose. Read on.

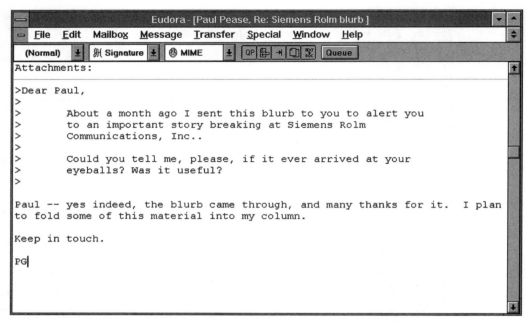

Figure 7.21   Responding to a mail message; note the quoted material at the top.

To Queue or to Send Immediately?

By default, Eudora is set to allow you to send messages immediately. If you examine the main Eudora screen, you will see a Send button on the right-hand side of the icon bar. Figure 7.22 shows the icon bar, with the Send button, and the other items on the Eudora screen for reference.

When you've finished responding to a message, you can simply click on the Send button and the message will be forwarded to the Internet via your service provider's SMTP server. A progress bar will appear showing you the transmittal of the message.

But in most cases, this is not how you will want to send your message. After all, as a SLIP/PPP user, you would like to take advantage of Eudora's ability to queue your messages and upload them in a single burst, thus cutting down your connect time. Messages can be sent to your Out mailbox instead of being sent immediately to the network; from there, they can be uploaded the next time you log on to your service provider. But to enable this option for regular use, you need to make a change to Eudora's configuration. This is done in the following way:

1. Pull down the Special menu and choose the Switches option.
2. In the resulting Switches box, turn off the Immediate Send option by clicking on the Immediate Send box.

Figure 7.22   Eudora's icon bar, showing the Send button and other features.

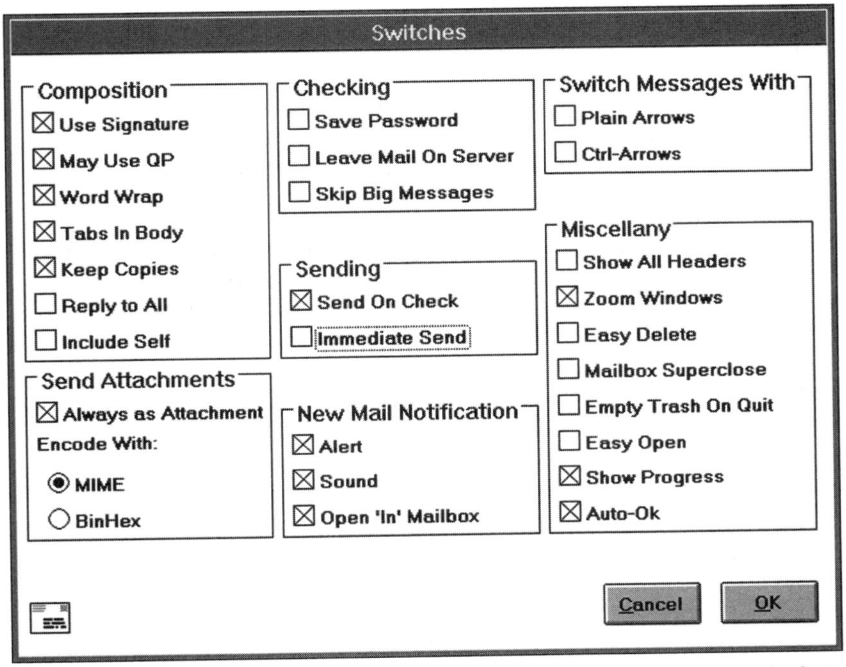

Figure 7.23 Eudora's Switches box; note the Send on Check item, which is checked to allow for the queueing of messages.

You can see this process in Figure 7.23. The figure shows the Switches dialog box with various Eudora options made available for configuration. Notice that the Immediate Send box is left empty, while the Send on Check box is marked.

When you return to the main Eudora screen, you will find that the Send button on the icon bar has been replaced by a Queue button. From this point on, when you compose a message or reply to one, you will be able to click the Queue button to send the message to the Out mailbox, for delivery at a later time. When you are ready to send queued messages, simply connect to your service provider's machine. There, you can:

1. Pull down the File menu.
2. Click on Send Queued Messages.

All the messages in your Out mailbox will be sent on their way.

Forwarding a Message

One of the pleasures of a good mail reader is that it makes it so easy to manipulate your mail. How many times have you received a paper document through the Postal Service and thought how useful it would be to pass it along to someone else? But passing it along involved faxing it, or physically stuffing it in an envelope and putting a stamp on it. Like as not, the letter you wanted to forward stayed on your desk. With electronic mail, it's a simple matter to make sure that doesn't happen. Eudora can forward your mail to others with ease.

With the message in question displayed on the screen, follow these steps to forward a message:

1. From the Message menu, choose the Forward command.
2. Fill in the address of the person to whom you want to forward this mail.
3. Edit the text as required and add your own comment if you wish.

You can also use Eudora's Redirect function to do much the same thing. Perhaps you've received a message that really belongs to someone else; perhaps you know it would interest them more than you, or that they would be a more logical recipient for the message than yourself. In that case, choose the Redirect option from the Message menu instead of Forward. The message will appear in a new message window, allowing you to type in the address of the recipient in the header. The address in the From: field will remain that of the original sender, and no brackets will be used to mark the original text as with forwarded messages.

Deleting a Message

Once you've read the mail, you'll want to delete any messages you've chosen not to save. Eudora sets up a two-step process for message deletion that ensures you don't accidentally delete a message you actually need. The number of times this has saved my bacon scarcely bears recounting; suffice it to say that the ability to call up a message you thought was gone is one of the more inspired features of this software. You see, when you delete a message from Eudora by choosing Delete from the Message menu, the message is not actually deleted—instead, it's transferred to the Trash mailbox. The Trash mailbox functions like any other mailbox; it's a place to store your mail until such time as you decide to dispose of it.

I generally let my deleted messages build up to a certain point and then delete them for good. To do this, choose the Empty Trash option on the Special menu. Once a message is deleted from the Trash mailbox, it's gone for good. You'll also be prompted if you decide to delete a message that you haven't read; Eudora will query to make sure that you really want to get rid of the message. If you choose not to see such warning messages, you can change the default settings in Eudora's configuration menu, available through the Switches selection on the Special menu.

Creating a Message with Eudora

Perhaps you're a first-time mail user who has just set up an account, and you don't have any messages waiting in Eudora's In mailbox. In that case, it would make sense to send yourself a message so you can see how Eudora will process it. Sending mail is likewise intuitive:

1. Pull down the Message menu.
2. Select New Message.

A message window will appear, as shown in Figure 7.24.

The window should include your return address information where mine is shown in the figure. Notice that the cursor automatically moves to the To: field, to allow for the insertion of your recipient's address. To send mail to yourself, simply enter your own address in this field. You can then fill out the Subject field as well, using the subject of

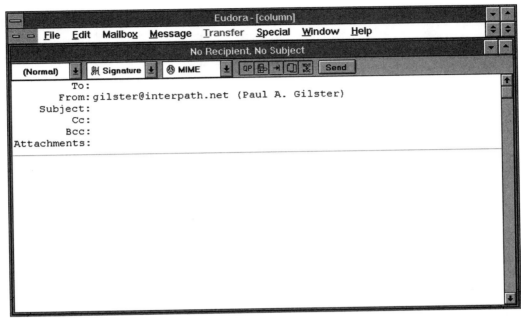

Figure 7.24   Creating a new message in Eudora.

your choice; use the TAB key to move between fields. Eudora also provides three additional fields:

Cc: Sends a copy of the message to the address(es) you specify here.

Bcc: Sends a blind carbon—that is, a copy without any information about the other people to whom you've sent the message—to the addresses you specify.

Attachment: Allows you to provide a filename of any file you choose to send with your message. This is a particularly useful field with Eudora, because as you'll see in a moment, the program allows you to send not only straight ASCII files, but also files in a variety of formats.

Once you have moved through these fields (and only the To: and Subject: fields need be filled in), you can then use the **TAB** key once again to move into the text entry section of the message window. There you can enter your message. Figure 7.25 shows a completed message, ready to be sent.

Having entered the necessary information and text, I'm ready to send this message. There are two ways to do it:

Queue   I can queue the message by pressing the **Queue** button at the top right of the screen. This will simply add the message to any others that are waiting to be sent, and will send them all in a burst once I log on to my service provider's

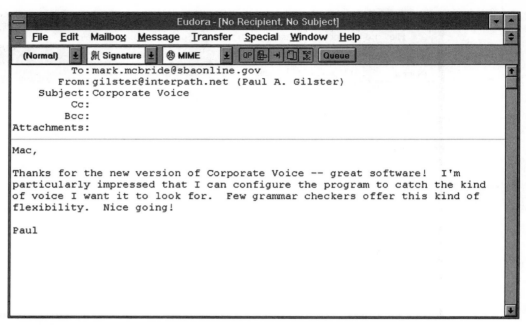

Figure 7.25   A completed message, with all necessary fields completed.

machine. As mentioned, to send queued messages, I would log on, pull down Eudora's File menu, and click on the Send Queued Messages item.

Send   I can send the message immediately by clicking the Send button. The Send button will, in this case, appear instead of the Queue button, depending on your configuration. The choice is yours, but I find that using the Queue is the only reasonable alternative for the SLIP/PPP user, who needs to send and receive mail in bursts to economize.

Setting Up a Signature File

Your signature file is one of the more important additions to any mail reader you choose; after all, it identifies you and supplies information that someone reading your posts may need to know, such as your telephone number, or a favorite quotation, or a description of what it is you do. Business people use their signatures as a mild form of advertising, along the lines of a business card; if they answer a posting on a newsgroup, say, in a way that wins approval, the recipient of their message may note their name and company. Thus you'll find signatures not only on electronic mail, but also on USENET messages (and, as with mail readers, News Readers can be configured to display them automatically, as we'll see in Chapter 11).

To set up a signature in Eudora, perform the following steps:

1. From the Window menu, choose the Signature option.
2. When the Signature window appears, fill it in as you choose.
3. Close the Signature window by double-clicking the close box in the top left corner.

Figure 7.26 shows a typical signature as filled in in this window.

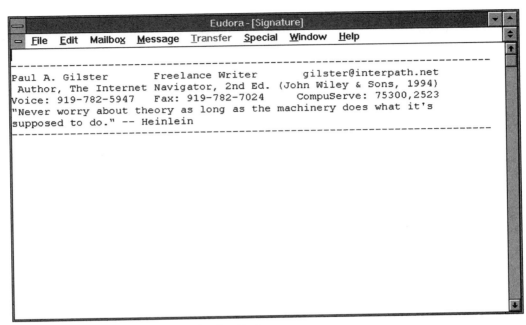

Figure 7.26   A signature file created within Eudora.

MIME: Sending Binary Files with Eudora

It happens all the time. You're working on a report in your word processor and want to deliver it as soon as possible to your boss. You could take it in to work the next day, but if you have an e-mail address, you could simply ship it off to the office via the Internet. And then something makes you pause.

That something is the fact that the Internet, using SMTP, moves e-mail as 7-bit ASCII data. Sending data this way allows you a total of 128 characters, which gives you plenty of room for such necessary things as the complete lower- and uppercase alphabet, numbers, punctuation marks, and a variety of symbols. And the system works great for sending straight textual mail; obviously, you can send messages through the simplest Internet mail program, like the Unix mail program itself, or pine.

But a word processor file, to use but one example, contains a lot of additional information besides the text that you've written on-screen. You may not see it as you type, but the word processor is inserting a great deal of formatting information into the file, all the other digital data it needs to display your file as you want to see it. This information is specific to the software program you are using at the time, and because there are no standards for these codes, there is no universal way of reading them through conventional mail. If you simply take, say, a Microsoft Word file and send it as e-mail, your recipient will receive a jumble of characters, many of which won't make any sense, and the formatting information is likely to be lost.

Convert the file to straight ASCII to send it? If you do, you lose the formatting, although the text survives. No, the answer is something called MIME—Multipurpose Internet Mail Extensions. MIME allows you to send and receive digitized files like your word processor document, or a spreadsheet, or a photograph, even an executable program. The only catch is that, to use MIME, you and your recipient must use a MIME-compliant mail program. Fortunately, pine supports MIME, as does Eudora. Indeed, the need to send binary information all but ensures that any modern mail reader will now include MIME capability.

To send a mail message with a MIME attachment, do the following:

1. Compose your message using the methods just described, including address and subject information.
2. Check to be sure that the Attachment Type box is set for MIME. As shown in Figure 7.22, the Attachment Type box is located in the icon bar at the top of the Eudora screen.
3. From the Message menu, choose the Attach Document item.
4. In the file dialog box that appears, choose the file you want to include as your attachment.
5. Click on OK to attach it to the message.

Your attachment will not appear in the text of the message itself; rather, it will show up in the Attachments: field of the message header, where its complete path will be shown.

If your recipient uses Eudora, he or she will be prompted for a place to put the incoming attached text; or, depending on how the program is configured, attachments can be set up to automatically go to a chosen directory. If your recipient is using a different mail program, the attached file will be found at the end of the message in MIME format, and may need decoding or not, depending upon the capabilities of the recipient's mail program. In any case, the file has successfully crossed the Internet with the necessary formatting or other binary information. Once you've tried sending binary data with Eudora, you'll begin to use this feature often.

Using Eudora's Mailboxes

Eudora's greatest benefit, it seems to me, is its ability to manage your mail in electronic areas called mailboxes. You can set up as many mailboxes as you choose, and can divide these mailboxes further into individual topics or categories. Eudora works with several mailboxes all the time—new mail always winds up in your In mailbox, while any messages you queue are sent to your Out mailbox, and a Trash mailbox holds messages you have read and discarded, until such time as you decide to delete them permanently. But by allowing you full control over the creation of new mailboxes, Eudora significantly enhances your ability to turn electronic mail into a productive tool.

Other mail programs—pine, for example—are as easy to use as Eudora, but none offers the degree of control over mail management. And, particularly if you begin to log on to mailing lists and receive a great deal of incoming mail, you will find that the biggest problem with mail is not so much reading it, as knowing what to do with it once you have. True, many of your messages can be read, responded to, and discarded. But others are more problematic. One may demand some thought before you answer it, and perhaps a check with key reference sources. Another may be from a mailing list, and represent an excellent compilation of material you'd like to keep. Where to put all the information? If you've designed your mailboxes carefully, you will be able to transfer documents to the appropriate place.

It's easy to create a mailbox. Perform the following steps:

1. Pull down the Mailbox menu and choose the New item.
2. Enter the name of the mailbox you want to create.
3. Click on OK to create the mailbox.

You can see the new mailbox dialog box in Figure 7.27.

Eudora allows you to set up hierarchies of mailboxes by creating folders. A mail folder is used to house one or more mailboxes; it can also hold other folders, so that you can have a nested hierarchy of mailboxes depending upon how you choose to categorize your information. Folders are created in virtually the same way mailboxes are. If you will examine Figure 7.27 again, you will see that there is a box labelled Make it a Folder on the new mailbox dialog window. By clicking this box, you set up a folder rather than a mailbox.

All this begins to get confusing: Which is a mailbox, which a folder, and which is inside which? Fortunately, Eudora includes a Mailboxes window that helps you get things organized. Using this window, which is shown in Figure 7.28, you can create new mailboxes and change the organizational structure of those you already have. Mailboxes can be moved from one folder to another or renamed as necessary. In my own work, I've found that these functions are critical; proper information management is rarely a static process, but changes as your work changes.

To call the Mailboxes window up on your screen, choose the Mailboxes item on the Windows menu and the box will appear. In the example shown, I have set up a series of mailboxes and folders as an illustration of how you can organize your mail. I have the ability to rename, remove, or create any mailbox I choose.

While full instructions on using the mailbox feature are provided with Eudora's documentation, the easiest way to get up to speed with mailboxes is to create a few and use them. It's easy to do this, because Eudora lets you create a mailbox on the fly; this way, rather than imposing a structure from the top down, you can simply build up your mail folders as you read mail. Here's how:

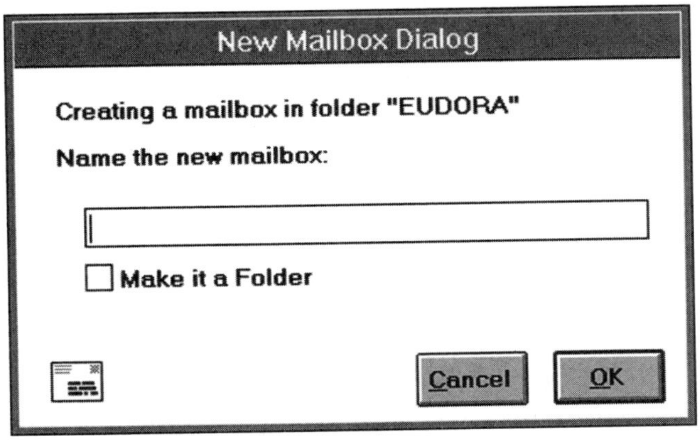

Figure 7.27 The New Mailbox dialog box; enter the name of the mailbox or folder you want to create.

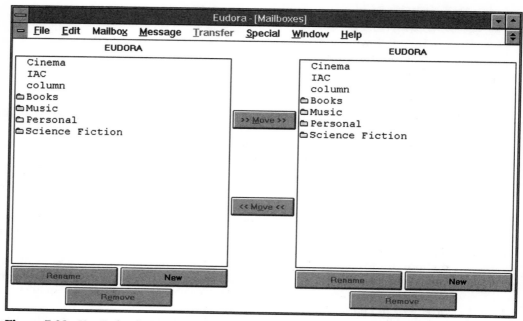

Figure 7.28   Use Eudora's Mailboxes window to manipulate your mailboxes and folders.

1. As you read a message (or with the message highlighted from the summary screen), pull down the Transfer menu.
2. Select New.
3. Enter the name of the new mailbox or folder.
3. Click on OK.

Your new mailbox will now appear when you pull down the Mailboxes menu. If you've created a folder, you'll now be prompted for a mailbox name to place within that folder. When you supply that information, the message you have just sent to it will be found in the newly created mailbox. In general, broad areas of information are chosen for folders, broken down by individual, more specific mailbox titles within them. If you have a particular topic about which you receive mail and there are no others related to it, an individual mailbox may be used instead of a folder. Whatever your choice, I think you'll find that setting up folders and mailboxes this way will keep your organization more responsive to the kind of work you do daily.

Using Nicknames

Internet addresses can be complicated, depending on the site. In fact, it's probably just as hard to remember a sequence like crosby@road.singapore.com as it is to recall a complete telephone number plus area code, or a postal address, especially if the computer names begin to get arcane. One of my favorite correspondents has this unlikely-sounding address: nacspns@ncsuadm.acs.ncsu.edu. How am I supposed to remember that?

Eudora provides a nickname feature that gets around this problem for your regular contacts. It allows you to use nicknames instead of the full address; in place of nacspns@ncsuadm.acs.ncsu.edu, I can send mail to lisa. Nicknames can be used not only in the To: field, but also in the Cc: or Bcc: fields of an outgoing message. Setting up such a nickname involves choosing the Nicknames item from the Window menu. When you do, the box shown in Figure 7.29 will appear.

In the Nicknames box, you can see that Eudora has provided a section for the nicknames you create, as well as a box for the addresses they refer to, along with a Notes field in which you can jot down any extraneous information you need about those names.

To create a nickname, follow these steps:

1. Click on the New button below the Nicknames box.
2. In the New Nickname dialog box that appears, enter the nickname you want to use.
3. In the Address(es) field, enter the complete e-mail address of the person referred to by the nickname.
4. Close the Nicknames box by double-clicking on the close box in the top left corner. You will be prompted to save any changes you have made while using the box.
5. Click on Save.

Eudora also offers you the ability to place the nickname on a so-called Quick Recipient list; if you do so, the Nickname will appear on the Message menu for even quicker reference.

Having set up a nickname, you'll find it easy to use. When you create a new message, all you have to enter in the To: field is the nickname. Eudora will supply the rest of the information when it sends your mail. Don't be confused when you try this; Eudora doesn't show you the complete address when you insert the nickname into your new mail message, but it does insert it when the mail is sent. If you have added your recipi-

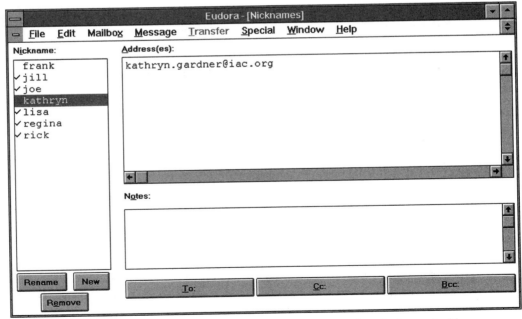

Figure 7.29 The Nicknames window lets you assign short names to lengthy Internet addresses.

ent to the Quick Recipient list, the person's nickname will appear on the Message menu, and will be visible when you choose the New Message To item. Simply click on the nickname to insert it.

Making nicknames isn't difficult, but it's often desirable to make them while you're actually reading mail. To do this, you must have the message in question open on the screen, or else selected as the current message from the mailbox window. Then follow these steps:

1. From the Special menu, choose the Make Nickname item.
2. Insert the new nickname in the dialog box that appears.
3. Click OK.

Nicknames are an interesting feature, as they save time; you can consider Eudora's nickname capability as being similar to pine's address book in making it easier for you to send mail. But you can also put the nickname feature to good advantage when sending mail to more than one person. This is because more than a single e-mail address can be referred to by one nickname. Suppose I want to send mail that I think would be of interest to an entire group of people that I regularly talk to about wine. I could create a nickname—perhaps I'd call it vino—and in the address field I would place each address I want my message to reach, separating them by using the **RETURN** key. Take a look at Figure 7.30 for an example of this process in action.

I can even use one nickname to point to another nickname. Having done this, I have created a mini-mailing list. It's not as complex as a LISTSERV, but it handles quick distribution of multiple messages.

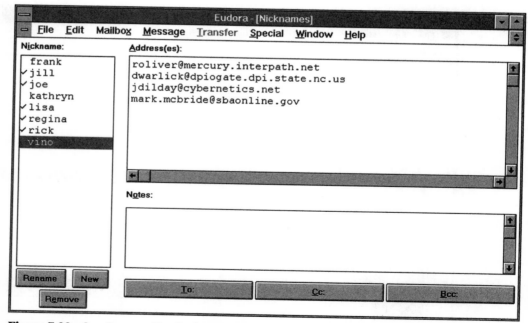

Figure 7.30 Creating a mailing list by using Eudora's nickname feature.

Searching Your Mail

How many times have you received mail about a subject and been unable to locate the message, even though you know you've saved it? Eudora's search function can help to find such messages; it examines the full text of the messages in your mailboxes and can pull references out even when all you remember is a single keyword. You can use the Find function within a single message as long as that message is open. But it is even more useful that you can search among multiple messages and across your entire range of mailboxes if necessary. Here's how to use this function:

1. Open the mailbox you want to search.
2. Choose Find from the Edit menu and Find from the submenu.
3. In the dialog box that appears, enter the text you want to find.
4. Click the Find button to start the search.

You can see the Find box in Figure 7.31. The buttons in the Find box work as follows:

Next	Continues to search within a single selected message or among all the messages in the current mailbox.
Next Message	Begins searching in the message after the current one. Continues to search even if it means opening up a new mailbox to do so.
Next Mailbox	Begins the search in the mailbox following the current one. Continues to search any subsequent mailboxes.

Notice that you have the further option of matching case, if you want to make the distinction between upper- and lowercase. You can also choose to search message summaries only by clicking on the appropriate box. In the latter case, Eudora will search only among the Sender and Subject fields of the message summaries in individual mailboxes. This option, as you would guess, makes for a faster search.

Getting the Most Out of Mail

I haven't explored all of Eudora's options, but good software is like that—it's so loaded with features that we tend to use the ones that fit our own needs first, and discover the hidden gold later. If you download and use the freeware version of Eudora, you will find tools aplenty for your mail work, and will probably be tempted to look into the added functionality of the commercial version. But whatever your decision on that score, remember that electronic mail is perhaps your most important Internet resource. As such, it demands the best mail reader you can find, and I'm sure Eudora won't disappoint you.

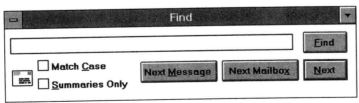

Figure 7.31 Eudora's Find box; enter a keyword to search for text.

In moving through the world of Internet mail, I've gone from the Unix mail program through pine to Eudora, at each step moving toward greater functionality and ease of use. The goal, as suggested by the title of this section on Eudora, has been mail management—you will reap much greater rewards from a program that can arrange and organize your work than from one that merely lets you send and answer mail. The Unix mail program's capabilities in this regard are minimal, although it does allow you to set up folders of mail, and use Unix tools on them. The pine program makes mail more intuitive by introducing an interface laden with on-screen help and a basic point-and-click interface. But it is with Eudora that we move into a true graphical mail program wherein search functions are readily integrated into the mix, and mailbox creation and management are central. Eudora is a major inducement to anyone straddling the fence between a shell account and the benefits of SLIP/PPP.

Electronic Mail Manners

The Internet may have an interesting effect upon literacy. With electronic mail, the written word is the medium—we're forced to use the alphabet and our wits to communicate. Thus people who wouldn't sit down to answer a written letter, preferring the telephone instead, find themselves in front of keyboards rocketing electronic messages off to friends and contacts around the globe. But letter writing itself is something of a lost art (when's the last time the average person wrote a longhand letter of more than the thank you note variety)? So we leave ourselves open for misunderstandings, gaffes, unintentional insults and a variety of other *faux pas*.

Little can be done about overt attempts to offend; thankfully, they're not all that common. But precisely because so many of the misunderstandings commonly found in electronic mail are inadvertent, it's useful to bear a set of rules in mind as you master this medium. Before long, the niceties of network behavior will be obvious from experience, but until then, adhering to these simple guidelines will ensure you get off to the right start.

Use Humor with Caution. Don't be misled—humor is more than welcome on the Internet, as a glance through the USENET newsgroups alt.best.of.internet or rec.humor.funny will quickly confirm. Judicious use of humor can brighten anyone's day, particularly those of us who spend the majority of our time in front of computer screens.

But be careful. The recipient of your message may not appreciate the sly dig which you, innocently enough, intended as a cheery *double entendre*. Sure, you just finished reading a Henry James novel, and your prose is honed to an incisive clarity that's the envy of your peers. But maybe your recipient prefers *TV Guide*, is in a bad mood this morning, and wouldn't recognize irony if it hit him or her broadside. How well do you know this person, anyway?

Because innocent epistles can so readily create discord, many people on the Internet, along with the various commercial networks, fall back on a set of pointers to make it clear when they're trying to be funny. The list of these *emoticons* or *smileys* is huge, but the one that's well-nigh universal is some type of smiling face. An imaginative use of the ASCII character set creates it:

:-)

Read it sideways and you've got the picture. Or maybe you'd want to suggest a fine-tuned *bon mot* followed by a wink. A simple character change handles it:

```
;-)
```

Try this sentence, with and without an emoticon:

```
Your reference wasn't exactly up-to-date.
```

versus

```
Your reference wasn't exactly up-to-date :-)
```

Or how about this:

```
I doubt Fred was aware of our conversation
```

which suggests a simple fact, versus

```
I doubt Fred was aware of our conversation ;-)
```

which suggests a nod and a conspiratorial wink. And then there's:

```
I doubt Fred was aware of our conversation :-(
```

a way of indicating our disappointment. We can even draw a crude portrait of ourselves as an emoticon:

```
Here's how I might look if wearing glasses and a goatee 8->
```

The set of emoticons has grown to gigantic proportions, a collection of electronic happy and sad faces too long to recount here. Read a little mail, browse through some USENET newsgroups, and you'll soon get up to speed with emoticons in all their variety. Then ponder whether you want to use them.

What's wrong with emoticons? Those who love language may find them disturbing. They suggest that their users don't know how to express themselves without the most obvious gesticulating, like the guy who accents every point he makes by waving his arms and making faces. The flip side is that emoticons can take the sting off what might seem a pointed remark. And because, as we use the Internet, we are typing out more messages at greater speed than ever before, it makes sense to take what measures we can to avoid conflict. It's your call.

Be Concise.   When you write an electronic message to someone, you're asking for a piece of that person's time. Remember what your English teacher told you—say what you have to say with a minimum of verbiage. This doesn't mean you can't enjoy conversations with friends on the topic of your choice, but if you're writing someone you don't already know, remember that your message may be one of hundreds that go through that person's mailbox every day. Most people move from initial wonderment at the capabilities of electronic mail to a sense of being bombarded on days when there are just too many messages to handle in too little time. A short, tight message is more likely to get results.

Make Your References Clear.   There's nothing quite so frustrating as receiving a message that says something like "Thanks for the information, but can you clarify what you mean in the third paragraph?" You can't remember who this person is, what information you sent, or what you may or may not have said in the third paragraph. Loose references like these may work if you're only talking to one or two on-line acquaintances, but they quickly become impractical when your list of contacts grows.

Most e-mail software makes provisions for quoting a message so you can avoid this confusion. mail, pine and Eudora let you incorporate a previous message in the current one, and other programs offer a variety of similar options. Often, the inserted text will be enclosed in brackets, telling you it's your original comment; the text is then followed by whatever thoughts your correspondent has on the subject.

Consider the following message.

```
It's the 23rd. Same place as usual—Fred.
```

This may mean nothing whatsoever to you. However, the following message has meaning.

```
<<I wonder if you know the date of the meteorology seminar? I've lost my invitation.>>
It's the 23rd. Same place as usual—Fred.
```

The latter is clear, quoting the original question and providing the answer. The key is to avoid ambiguity, to handle the communication in one pass, rather than forcing one party to send yet another message asking to be reminded of the original question.

Don't Waste Bandwidth.   Inserting text from a previous message, as in the previous example, can make things clearer. But anyone who has been on the networks for a time has received messages where lengthy e-mail was quoted in its entirety, and for absolutely no reason. The point about quoting is that it pinpoints the area in question. Why enclose an entire message if that message only contains one question needing an answer in the first place?

So be sparing with your quotes. If the message was a long one and you want to pare it down, you have no choice but to edit it. Some mail packages make this easier than others, which is why the search for the perfect mail program is an ongoing one.

Be Discreet.   There are any number of ways other people might see what you have entered in your message, so be cautious. If you're pondering saying something you consider absolutely private, talk yourself out of it. Handle that kind of communication in person. Chances are that 99 percent of your electronic mail will reach its destination in utter privacy, but who knows?

Electronic mail and fax machines have this in common: They're both more public than many people realize. The explosion of technology has given us tremendous new tools, but the price of their newfound power is our inability to properly secure them from prying eyes. How often has a critical business proposition been discussed through a fax machine? And how often is the fax left sitting in a place where any number of inquisitive office workers might read incoming material before it gets to the actual recipient? How many electronic mail messages have been read by the wrong person because somewhere along the line a computer routing the message wasn't sufficiently secure?

Don't Get Too Elaborate. Some people have an irresistible urge to pull out all the stops when writing electronic mail or posting messages to USENET. They'll shift back and forth from all caps to all lowercase and any mixture in between. They'll draw odd ASCII pictures that may or may not be decipherable. They'll have so much fun composing the message that they forget the person at the receiving end may want to get on with the day's work and is in no mood for buffoonery.

Know your audience. Special effects can have results different than those desired. Using all capital letters can suggest aggression, as in a shouting match. MAYBE YOU DON'T THINK SO, BUT I DO! In any case, getting the message across with clarity is the fundamental precept of electronic mail.

Choose Your Subjects Wisely. Being as clear and concise as possible in the subject field of your message means the person who receives it can readily decide what to do with the message. Put yourself in that person's shoes. With little time to spare and numerous messages waiting in the mailbox, the recipient wants to know which messages really need attention and which can be deleted quickly. A carefully chosen subject will help the recipient keep a tidy mailbox, and you'll also appreciate the effort when you look through your own mail and know exactly what you have waiting.

8

Electronic Mail as a Gateway to the Internet

The Internet has evolved in relatively haphazard fashion, with one set of users equipped with the latest tools while others worked a generation or two behind. It was natural, then, that a set of ingenious workarounds would arise for those people who had access to the Net through electronic mail alone. Most dial-up users fit into this category until recently, for the big commercial services like CompuServe and America Online, when they did make the move to connect to the Internet, first did it through e-mail. You wouldn't think you could do much with electronic mail other than exchange messages, but as we'll see, the range of capabilities is quite wide. You can use e-mail to retrieve files, run Gopher searches, consult a WAIS database, and even work, in rudimentary fashion, with the World Wide Web.

That such tools are available at all is a tribute to the ingenuity of their creators, who recognized a problem and set out to solve it, thus benefiting the legions of mail-only users at no profit to themselves other than the gratification of having helped the network community. And as is so often the case with the Internet, their tools are themselves rapidly moving toward obsolesence. The problem isn't so much that e-mail-only accounts can't be productive on their own; it's that the number of such accounts is dwindling. All the major commercial services are now moving toward fuller connectivity, so that the CompuServe user who once retrieved files through the mail-only workaround called ftp-mail can now do the same through a straight FTP connection, using CompuServe's WinCIM software. The same story is being told across the board as smart system managers realize the scope of the demand for Internet connectivity.

But let's not forget that the blessings of this kind of connectivity don't extend everywhere. Around the world, millions of people are about to be exposed to networking, and in most cases, that initial exposure will be on a very rudimentary level. The fact that people in the United States, western Europe, and parts of Asia enjoy full Internet services does not mean that the network can't be used by people in Africa, South America, and India, and to good advantage. These people may be working with a command line interface and a straight shell account, or perhaps a basic menu system, and they may be limited to nothing more than electronic mail through a local provider, but they can run most, if not all, of the major Internet functions by learning the workarounds presented here. When full connectivity comes, they'll be ready to enjoy its benefits.

And let's face it, there is a large user segment of bulletin board users who prefer to work through a local system at minimal to no cost to themselves, and whose exposure to the Internet is likewise limited to electronic mail. Many BBSs are experimenting with this kind of connection, and their users want to explore the network tools they've heard about, but perhaps they're not ready or able yet to make the jump to a full connection. Whether they're located in a technologically rich country or an area that's just beginning to acquire network tools, they can begin their experiments with the methods presented in this chapter. Above all, the message is this—get on the network, whether it's through e-mail, a shell account, SLIP/PPP, or a full network connection at your workplace. The idea is to get familiar with the tools.

Retrieving Files by Mail

You can take several different approaches to using the Internet by mail. It's possible to run a complete FTP routine, sending commands to a remote computer and having it process the request. It's also possible to tap the resources of a specialized mail server, whose job it is to maintain repositories of information, most of it textual in nature, and send requested documents to electronic mail addresses. You can even run Gopher and WAIS sessions by mail.

Specialized Mail Servers

For a look at mail servers, let's go to the InterNIC Directory and Database Services site, maintained by AT&T as a Directory of Directories about Internet information. The address is mailserv@ds.internic.net. Retrieving files from this site is simple; you use the **file** command in the body of your message. You follow this with the pathname for each desired file.

But first, we need to do some background work. When using any mail server, you should always make it a priority to get a help file, which lists the basic commands available. To do this at the InterNIC's mail server, send the single message **help** to the preceding address; leave the Subject: field blank. You will receive an extensive file with complete instructions on how to use the mail server.

Next, we need to know what directories and files are available at this site. To learn, we can send for a file that is the result of giving a recursive directory command to the mail server. We will send a message containing only the statement **file /ls-lR.** In sending this, we are asking the InterNIC for a listing of all files in all directories. Our message looks like the following:

```
% mail mailserv@ds.internic.net
Subject:
file /ls-1R
.
```

We will receive shortly a text file giving us this information, as shown in Figure 8.1, which shows the text as read through the pine mail reader. As you can see, the file we've retrieved has broken the information available at the InterNIC into separate directories. This is quite a long file, indicating the wealth of information stored at the InterNIC;

we're only examining a fraction of it in this figure. In fact, the file is so long that it arrives in parts, each of them 64 K long. Within each directory, files are listed. We can use this information to retrieve the file of our choice. To do so, we will send a message with the command **file** *filename* in it. The filename must include the complete path statement along with the name of the file.

For example, let's assume we want to retrieve the file guest.tutorial, which is listed in Figure 8.1 in the *internic.info* directory. We would send this command to the InterNIC mail server:

```
file /internic.info/guest.tutorial
```

The file will soon appear in our mailbox; it is a handy compendium of information about the InterNIC.

Notice the method I'm using here. To show you the commands needed to interact with the InterNIC's mail server, I am demonstrating a mail session using a Unix-based service provider. But if you are using an account with a local BBS or any other provider, you would send the same message through that system's mail gateway to the Internet. I use the Unix option here because demonstrating the same session for all the different bulletin board systems, commercial service providers, and other Internet access services would be impractical. Each system sports a different mail interface; I can't cover them all in the space allotted here.

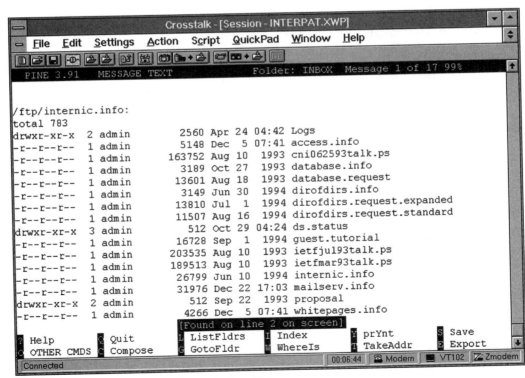

Figure 8.1 A partial listing of files at the InterNIC.

The important thing is that you master your provider's mail system. You should read hard-copy and on-line documentation for whichever provider you are using if you have any questions about sending such a message. Usually, the process involves specifying the Internet mail address with appropriate coding, after which you can proceed with the message itself. We discuss proper addressing for the commercial services at the end of this chapter.

You can see how mail servers work to bring you files in response to commands you send through e-mail. It would be useful to have access to a list of mail servers. Two documents can help us do this. Scott Yanoff's *Special Internet Connections*, discussed and retrieved in Chapter 5, provides regularly updated mail server information. There is also a document, available by e-mail or anonymous FTP, which provides further information.

What You Need: A List of Mail Servers

The Document: How to Find Sources, by Kent Landfield

How to Get It: You can retrieve the file by sending an e-mail message to the following address:

send-finding-sources-faq@sparky.sterling.com

Or you can retrieve it through FTP to this URL:

ftp://rtfm.mit.edu/pub/usenet/news.answers/finding-sources

Although this file targets people who are looking for source code (programs written in a particular programming language and available for study), it also contains a valuable section on mail servers.

Mail Server Commands

There are certain mail server conventions that you must follow when using the InterNIC's mail server. A message, for example, is limited to 15 queries or file requests, and the information returned by this method is limited to 500 K. If the size limit is exceeded, you will receive whatever portion of the material has been returned to that point. Although commands are not sensitive to case, parameters are; in other words, you should type your **ls-lR** command exactly as shown. Each command must be entered on a separate line to function properly.

Here are the basic mail server commands available, as listed by the InterNIC. The / symbol indicates a synonym. In item 4, for example, you could send either **ls** or **dir**.

```
help
person name, organization[, country]
institution name, country[, keyword, ...]
ls/dir path[, path, ...]
file path[, path, ...]
document-by-name/send name[, name ...]
document-by-keyword keyword[, keyword, ...]
```

```
resource-by-name name[, name, ...]
resource-by-keyword keyword [, keyword, ...]
whois name
limit value-of-max-msg-unit-size
encoding type(default, mime, uuencode or btoa)[, mandatory]
return-to/path return-address-or-route
begin
end/exit
```

InterNIC Mail Services

Let's now take a closer look at several of these commands. As you can see, there is quite a wide range to choose from. Remember to leave the Subject: field in your message blank when you use one of these commands.

WHITE PAGES QUERIES

White pages are directories, some of which are built using a standard for directory services called X.500 that is used to find people on the Internet. You can use these services to search for a person or an institution.

To find a person, use the **person** command, followed by the name of the person you're looking for. Thus:

```
person john smith, ATT, us
```

Note that the **person** command requires the person's name as well as an organization he or she is associated with. Usage of the country name is optional; the default is U.S.

To find an institution, use the **institution** command:

```
institution ATT, us
```

Note that this requires the institution name and country. Figure 8.2 shows the result of this search.

DOCUMENT QUERIES

You can request a specific document from the InterNIC if you know its name. This is particularly useful if you're looking for one of the Request for Comments documents, which the InterNIC maintains in their entirety. To do this for RFC-822, for example, you enter the command **document-by-name** followed by the document name. Thus:

```
document-by-name rfc822
```

You may also search for documents by keyword, through the **document-by-keyword** command. At least one keyword is required; more can be entered if necessary. Thus, I can look for documents on the subject of mail standards by sending a statement as follows:

```
document-by-keyword mail
```

This generates a list of the relevant files available at the site.

```
= INSTITUTION:  name = ATT  country = US
= White Pages Query Results:
= ATT                                                    +1 212-387-5400
=     aka: AT&T
=     aka: American Telephone
=
= ATT
=   32 Avenue of the Americas
=   New York
=   New York 10013
=   US
=
= Comments about the ATT Directory should be sent to sri@qsun.att.com
=
= Locality:    New York, New York
=
= Name:       ATT, US
= Modified: Wed Jun 16 19:09:32 1993
=       by: manager, att, US
```

Figure 8.2   A search for AT&T at the InterNIC.

FILE LENGTH LIMITS

Some commercial on-line services place limits on the length of incoming messages from the Internet. Because of this, you should know that you can limit the size of files you've specified for delivery from the InterNIC. The command is **limit.** Assume, for example, that your on-line service doesn't let messages longer than 50 K come into its system. You could issue the following command to limit the size of InterNIC materials; files longer than the limit would then be broken into parts. The default length is 64 K before this happens. You can change it as follows:

```
limit 50k
```

or whatever limit your system places upon you.

Mail Server Precautions

Be careful when sending messages to the InterNIC if you are accessing the Internet from a commercial provider like CompuServe. The reason: You want to be sure your commercial service handles the return mail properly so it's routed to you. To be absolutely sure you'll get what you request, you can add a path statement to your information request. Here's what it might look like when sent from CompuServe:

```
Mail! compose
Enter message. (/EXIT when done)
path 73537.656@compuserve.com
document-by-name rfc822
exit
/exit
```

What you see in this message is, first, a path statement, giving my CompuServe address for the return reply. After that is the request for a specific document. The request is followed by the **exit** command, which tells the InterNIC server to stop processing the message at this point and to ignore any following lines that might be interjected by the system I'm using. The final **/exit** command is the normal CompuServe end-of-message statement.

Finding and Using Other Mail Servers

The InterNIC is just one site with an active mail server. You will encounter more in your explorations of the Internet. For example, there is a series of mail servers that offer news about computers in agricultural science, along with newsletters and USDA market news. The Amateur Radio Relay League makes ASCII documents about ham radio available through a mail server. You can play the game of Diplomacy by mail or access complex biological data. Chapter 16 provides a listing of a number of interesting mail servers that you may want to explore.

The OSS-IS (Office Support System—Information Server) mail server makes government documents and selected network information available by mail, and is fairly typical of mail server operations. As with any mail server, the procedure is always two-part: First, send for any help or index document that will clarify what the mail server offers; second, request the actual document. To determine how to obtain a help file, consult a directory like the one in Chapter 16, or the Yanoff list mentioned earlier. Each mail server will have its own procedure. In the case of the OSS-IS server, the procedure is to send mail to the mail server with the message **send index**; the address is info@soaf1.ssa.gov.

Sending this message, I receive the document shown in Figure 8.3. This figure shows a segment of the file listing for the mail server. To retrieve a document, send e-mail to info@ssa.gov. Leaving the Subject: field blank, enter the command **send *document*.** For example, to retrieve the access_txt document, you would send the command **send access_txt.** The document will soon appear in your mailbox.

Using ftpmail

What happens if you need a file that's not located at one of the network information centers or other similar sites? The answer is, you can still retrieve the file using ftpmail, a program developed by Paul Vixie at the Digital Western Research Laboratory and the Digital Network Systems Laboratory from 1989 to 1993. To do this, you send an e-mail request. In the United States, send to one of these servers:

ftpmail@decwrl.dec.com

bitftp.pucc.princeton.edu

ftpmail@census.gov

ftpmail@sunsite.unc.edu

From other countries, send to one of the following:

ftpmail@grasp.insa-lyon.fr	France
ftpmail@doc.ic.ac.uk	United Kingdom
ftpmail@ftp.uni-stuttgart.de	Germany
bitftp@vm.gmd.de	Germany

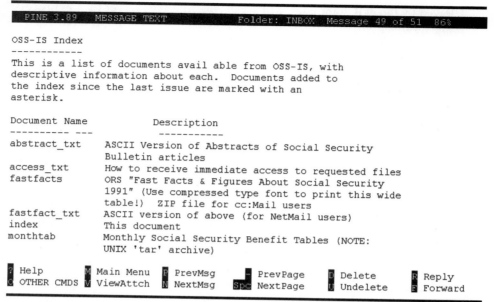

Figure 8.3   Response to a request to a mailserver.

ftpmail@cs.uow.edu.au   Australia
ftpmail@ftp.luth.se   Sweden

You can leave the subject field blank or not as you choose. The body of your message will contain the file information needed by the remote computer to process your request. The format is simple, and is best illustrated through an example. I want to retrieve the file internet.basics, which I know from my reading of the **00-README. FIRST** file is located at SURAnet. I also know from the directory that it's in the subdirectory called *pub/nic/internet.literature*. Here's how I can get it.

```
% mail ftpmail@decwrl.dec.com
Subject: internet.basics
connect ftp.sura.net
chdir pub/nic/internet.literature
get internet.basics
quit
```

This is a transcript of what I type using the Unix mail program from the system prompt. Notice what's happening in this mail request. I have used the title of the document I'm after as the subject line. Following this, I'm actually sending a series of commands to the remote computer. Each proceeds with an FTP session; the address specifies which machine to connect to, while the **chdir** command provides the proper path to the file I need, which is listed last. I close this with the command to end the connection; the final period is the command to the mail program to send my message.

Obviously, if you are using a different mail program, you would use whatever command that system required to send your message. You'll soon receive a return message acknowledging your request. And in a day or two, the file will arrive in your mailbox. Along with it will be a separate message showing the actual transaction as it occurred between ftpmail and the remote computer. You can see an example in Figure 8.4.

As you see, ftpmail handles the complete transaction, with no help required from your end. This method works well for regular text files, opening up any site that handles anonymous FTP for you to use through your mail gateway to the Internet. But be advised that due to the enormous increase in network traffic that has occurred over the past two years, ftpmail occasionally slows to a crawl, and sometimes fails altogether. Don't expect this service to be airtight.

Given the complexity of ftpmail procedures, it would be useful to have a background document explaining them in greater detail.

What You Need: A Primer on ftpmail Procedure

How to Get It: In the United States, use one of the following addresses:

ftpmail@decwrl.dec.com

bitftp@pucc.princeton.edu

Send mail with a blank Subject: field and a one-word message: **help**

From Europe, use this address:

ftpmail@grasp.insa-lyon.fr

Retrieving Binary Files by Mail

When you retrieve a file by ftpmail, you'll notice a critical fact: The file is sent to you in straight ASCII format. Why? Because it must adhere to the standards laid out in RFC-822, which govern how electronic mail is handled on the Internet. This is not a problem when you're receiving text. But for binary files, RFC-822 specifies that they must be converted to 7-bit ASCII characters, because the message header and body can only consist of such ASCII characters.

That means the file must first be converted into ASCII, received by you, and then converted back into a binary file before it can be used. Moreover, if the file is longer than the 64 thousand characters that can be sent in a single message, it will be broken into several messages and sent to you in pieces. Some on-line services place limits on the length of messages you can receive as well, so you must have some way to limit the size of a message you'll get in your mailbox.

Fortunately, ftpmail provides for such eventualities. Let's request a file from a Unix system. We'll ask ftpmail for a binary file—the GEOCLOCK program discussed in Chapter 5. If you look back at our search there, you'll find that GEOCLOCK is available, among other sites, at ftp.cso.uiuc.edu, in the directory */pc/exec-pc*. The filename is geoclock.zip. We can thus formulate the mail message to retrieve this file. Note that we're asking it to be sent in binary form (the FTP site will send the file via conventional FTP to the ftpmail server. The latter computer will then turn it into ASCII format and send it, by mail, to our computer):

```
Connecting to ftp.cso.uiuc.edu
220 ux3 FTP server (Version wu-2.4(5) Thu Aug 25 21:01:37 CDT 1994) ready.
--- logging in as user=anonymous password=-ftpmail/gilster@mercury.interpath.net account=...
---> USER anonymous
331 Guest login ok, send your complete e-mail address as password.
---> PASS <somestring>
230 Guest login ok, access restrictions apply.
---> TYPE A
200 Type set to A.
--- changing working directory to pc/exec-pc...
---> CWD pc/exec-pc
250 CWD command successful.
=== getting 'geoclock.zip'...
---> TYPE I
200 Type set to I.
---> PORT 16,1,0,6,6,153
200 PORT command successful.
---> RETR geoclock.zip
150 Opening BINARY mode data connection for geoclock.zip (106067 bytes).
226 Transfer complete.
--- mailing...
gilster@mercury.interpath.net... Connecting to mercury.interpath.net (tcp)...
gilster@mercury.interpath.net... Sent
gilster@mercury.interpath.net... Connecting to mercury.interpath.net (tcp)...
gilster@mercury.interpath.net... Sent
gilster@mercury.interpath.net... Connecting to mercury.interpath.net (tcp)...
gilster@mercury.interpath.net... Sent
geoclock.zip (pc/exec-pc@ftp.cso.uiuc.edu) (3 parts, 146164 bytes) sent to
gilster@mercury.interpath.net
---> (end of ftpmail session)
```

Figure 8.4   Transaction of the ftpmail request.

```
% mail ftpmail@decwrl.dec.com
Subject: geoclock.zip
connect ftp.cso.uiuc.edu
binary
uuencode
chdir pc/exec-pc
get geoclock.zip
quit
```

Let's go through these commands one by one to make sure they're clear. First, we've told ftpmail which computer we want to connect to. ftp.cso.uiuc.edu. With the next line, we've told it we are going to transfer a binary file.

The next line tells ftpmail to encode this file according to a utility called uuencode. In doing so, we are turning a binary file into ASCII characters. We use uuencode because there are software tools available for the standalone PC that can decode such files. That means we can bring the file onto our own hard disk and then uudecode it there (more about this later). Incidentally, if you don't specify that uuencode be used, the default encoding is btoa, which stands for Binary to ASCII. We'll request uuencode because we will soon have the software to decode it.

Don't be surprised if the encoded file is larger than the binary file size listed. The encoding process actually adds about 35 percent to the size of the files it translates; the file you receive is, of course, returned to its normal size when restored to binary form.

Finishing the mail commands, we've then told ftpmail to change to the *pc/exec-pc* subdirectory at the FTP site, and to get the file geoclock.zip.

When the file arrives, things get interesting. Remember, this is a binary file in ASCII format, so it's going to look funny. Figure 8.5 shows part of the first of the three messages received containing geoclock.zip. The program was broken into parts because each message defaults to a length of 64,000 bits.

If you were doing this through a Unix account, you could save the files on-line and decode them there before downloading them to your system. But for now I'm assuming you're using one of the non-Unix commercial providers by way of a mail gateway. That being the case, you need to save each of these files to your hard disk rather than reading them as mail. Give each of them a separate name. I could, for example, call the three parts of the file in question something like geo1.uue, geo2.uue, and geo3.uue, showing that they're related but separate parts of the same file.

You're doubtless wondering why I added a .uue extension to those files. The answer: The uudecode program we're going to use to decode them requires that extension to work. Note that all three files get the same extension.

```
Date: Sun, 30 Apr 95 01:26:41 -0700
From: "ftpmail service on ftp-gw-1.pa.dec.com" <nobody@pa.dec.com>
To: gilster@mercury.interpath.net
Subject: part 001 of geoclock.zip (pc/exec-pc@ftp.cso.uiuc.edu) [geoclock.zip]
(binary uncompressed uuencode)
X-Complaints-To: ftpmail-admin@ftp-gw-1.pa.dec.com
X-Service-Address: ftpmail@ftp-gw-1.pa.dec.com
X-Job-Number: 798731956.11248
Precedence: bulk
Reply-To: <nobody@ftp-gw-1.pa.dec.com>
X-UIDL: 799332223.024

begin 444 ftpmail
M4$L#! H    !   2\,A N0J-+@P$$  !D"    '     4D5!1"Y-12 ""AQ(4&"4
M.FG&K %!)OV<.0T41!28Y4T=$#&/"N %!)P^<,B!!$0!$!!XDX:.F@XH@'9)@P<
M$$&&\VH@0Y9XR<,,F_$!!2C$$$B$.D@+@%E$$+=E++D"LEH,'@>$L_  ]QEI1&=$
M&$$4B",)#!UD0W/F2$2N&E$#1#@H$@41&%1Z,,,1,U702&*&E1.+N-$/Y!.+R$L:XZCC&$$+
MKK#3:!OR#C )H#DLJ&OOooooo"MR[?\@oooolll   !DMUE84Z#R-$-oooolll    
```

Figure 8.5 A binary file rendered into ASCII.

Finding PC Unix Utilities to Convert Binary Files

Once these files are on your hard disk, you'll have to process them to turn them into the program or graphics file you were expecting. Yes, this is kludgy, but it works—remember that a full Internet account with a commercial provider will save you these additional steps, because you can simply use FTP to go to the site and retrieve the file without the added conversion routines here. Nonetheless, once you've run through this procedure a few times, it won't seem quite so off-putting.

To make our new file work, we need a utility program that converts encoded ASCII files back into their functional equivalents. As you saw, the program that encoded the files in the first place was called uuencode; its opposite is uudecode. There are programs for personal computers that convert a uuencoded file on your hard disk. If you were on-line with a Unix account, you could also do this using the system utilities there. Your system will probably offer the uudecode program (type **uudecode** to find out if it does). If so, you can actually perform the decoding process on your service provider's computer, downloading only the finished, decoded file.

Where do you get the decoding program? This is the tricky part, since you wouldn't be using FTP through mail like this unless you had no other access to FTP files, and without that access, you can't use FTP to find the unencoded utility program. Fortunately, this program, along with other Unix utilities for personal computers, can be retrieved on-line. You'll need to dig around in the file libraries at whichever commercial service you're using to find it. Look for any Special Interest Groups or Forums (or your commercial service's equivalent) dealing with telecommunications issues or with Unix.

On CompuServe, for example, you can use the IBM File Finder (IBMFF) or Macintosh File Finder functions. I searched IBMFF for the uudecode program and came up with numerous possibilities, as shown in Figure 8.6.

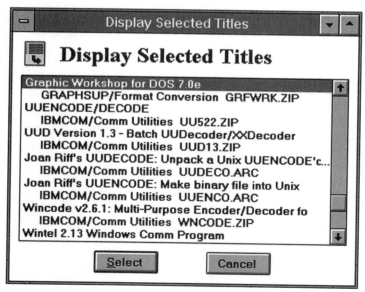

Figure 8.6 A few of the many uudecode programs available on CompuServe.

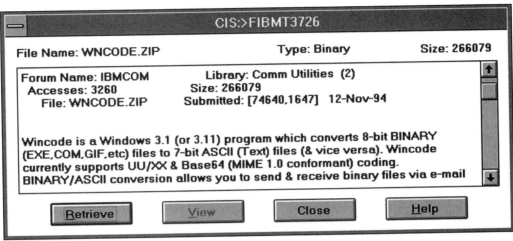

Figure 8.7   A CompuServe file description of the uudecode and uuencode utilities.

We can take a closer look at one of these files to make sure it's what we're after, as in Figure 8.7. And indeed, it is. You can download any of these files and unzip them on your computer with PKUNZIP (in this case, the file is stored on CompuServe in "zipped" format, as shown by the .zip file suffix in the preceding figure). So you're using PKUN-ZIP, a PC-based file decompression utility, to unpack a set of tools that will allow you to decode uuencoded files from the Internet.

If you're not on CompuServe but a different commercial service or BBS, browse through the file libraries to find the version of the Unix utilities that work on your kind of computer. They will form a critical part of your arsenal if you plan to use the Internet by mail alone. Here, for example, are the relevant utilities as adapted for the Macintosh. I found them by searching the Macintosh file libraries on America Online.

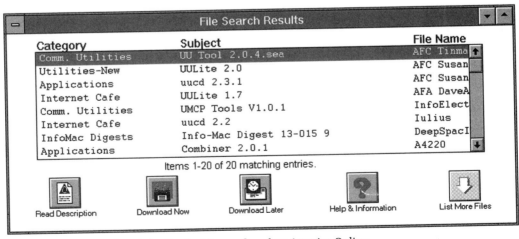

Figure 8.8   uudecode utilities for the Mac, as found on America Online.

Using the Unix Utilities to Convert Your Files

When you unpack the uudecode package, you'll find two programs, one for performing the decoding routine, the other for encoding files. We'll just work with uudecode, since all we want to do is get our files into working order. After all, we want a program we can run, rather than a document of cryptic-looking ASCII!

Here's how to decode our GEOCLOCK file:

```
uudecode geo1.uue
```

Note that, although you created several files with the .uue extension when you downloaded GEOCLOCK, you don't have to specify any but the first; uudecode will hop from one file to another to perform its routine. When you're through, you'll have a composite file called FTPMAIL.UU. This is the standard name assigned by ftpmail to the re-created binary file. Once we rename it geoclock.zip, we can take the final step. The .zip extension tells us the file has been compressed using PKZIP, a file compression routine available on all on-line services. We can use its counterpart PKUNZIP to restore it to full size. This will produce a package of files. Figure 8.9 shows what the uudecode process looks like from the DOS prompt. Now we can rename the file and unzip it as shown in Figure 8.10.

It's possible uudecode will stumble over something in the header information, not knowing how to bypass it, and thus stalling. For example, take a look at the ASCII readout of the first lines of our file, geo2.uue, shown in Figure 8.11.

You can see that the actual uuencoded file begins after the message header information is over. If uudecode stalls, you can edit the files yourself to remove the headers. Remove the header information from the second and third messages, so the uuencoded text is not broken by any header information between the three files. Then try uudecode again, and it should work. After all three files are trimmed this way, they're ready to be processed by uudecode. The syntax is **uudecode *filename1*.** In this case, then, I'll enter **uudecode clock1.uue.**

```
C:\uudecode geoclk1

UU-DECODE 4.21 FOR PC.  by Richard Marks

Destination is FTPMAIL.UU
Decoding GEOCLK1.UUE
...
End File encountered in file: GEOCLK1.UUE

Decoding GEOCLK2.UUE
....
End File encountered in file: GEOCLK2.UUE

Decoding GEOCLK3.UUE
...
Completed decode of file FTPMAIL.UU
```

Figure 8.9   Using uudecode to repackage geoclock.zip.

```
C:\ren ftpmail.uu geoclock.zip

C:\pkunzip geoclock.zip

PKUNZIP (R)     FAST!     Extract Utility     Version
1.1     03-15-90
Copr. 1989-1990 PKWARE Inc. All Rights Reserved.
PKUNZIP/h for help
PKUNZIP Reg. U.S. Pat. and Tm. Off.

Searching ZIP: GEOCLOCK.ZIP -


UnShrinking: READ.ME
  Expanding: MAP2.EGA
  Expanding: MAP1.EGA
  Expanding: GEOEGA.EXE
  Expanding: GEOCLOCK.DOC
UnShrinking: GEOCLOCK.DAT
  Expanding: GEO7EGA.EXE
```

Figure 8.10   Renaming and unzipping the program file.

Wincode—A Windows-Based Alternative

The previous procedure took you through the entire uudecoding process, helping you to arrive at a complete binary file. Now that you've seen it in action, you may choose to simplify the procedure by using a Windows-based program called Wincode. Written by George H. Silva, Wincode is a Windows 3.1 program that can handle both uuencode and uudecode functions. The program is freeware, feature-rich, and easy to install. Here's how to get it:

```
Date: Sun, 30 Apr 95 01:26:41 -0700
From: "ftpmail service on ftp-gw-1.pa.dec.com" <nobody@pa.dec.com>
To: gilster@mercury.interpath.net
Subject: part 001 of geoclock.zip (pc/exec-pc@ftp.cso.uiuc.edu) [geoclock.zip]
(binary uncompressed uuencode)
X-Complaints-To: ftpmail-admin@ftp-gw-1.pa.dec.com
X-Service-Address: ftpmail@ftp-gw-1.pa.dec.com
X-Job-Number: 798731956.11248
Precedence: bulk
Reply-To: <nobody@ftp-gw-1.pa.dec.com>
X-UIDL: 799332223.024

M1;^;(H ^@3,)\&7#'X!\@"]HOZV_41[/3SV_K\__#@ZP9;,Q%#/<%@2CD-90
M_!\"BL!= * ;2O'G*?V^OO\SL 9#!(/JA]&!I ]"S!?]/ZF4G:%6#A#A^_7\
MCP$P$P6)< B@I0G$$$JJE$S VO'KCC_J:-OH'++_$<X:3:W -Y>F )!E/Py^RB,#9\Q!1
MHP__^Y#_+RW_RW__(CP!3PO@@/. [$[P$*[F?_[3_E99,_^^RX**!*#,#*!2<$/\%^X9B+QW^
MS0]X.+\_Z=.8#@=P??O^?/]_/[/\Z!!C@/02`_=_,__*/.+F`#+T"_#]"+J.++_@"[&$<"X&#N%B
MD /, 6+NO-$$E77_/Y(,+[`+[`+P&<%[\_CC[&-_$_..$C[&CM `P<+6!!. /
```

Figure 8.11   The encoded file with message header.

What You Need: A Windows-Based uudecoding Program

The Program: Wincode

How to Get It: By anonymous FTP. The program is widely distributed on the Internet, as an archie search will reveal. Among the many possibilities, try the following URL:

ftp://mrcnext.cso.uiuc.edu/pub/win3/util/wincode.zip

Wincode makes encoding and decoding operations a snap. You can highlight the files you would like to decode and simply drag them to the Wincode icon. Encoding files is equally simple, a matter of drag and drop. The latter feature may turn out to be one of the most useful Internet tools in your arsenal. As you move deeper into the world of the Net, you will find that occasions often arise when you have a binary file you would like to send to a single recipient, or post on USENET for others to use. Wincode makes the complicated workings behind the scenes invisible, and quickly presents you with a finished file.

Downloading the Compression Utilities

Now that we have the principle down, we need another file, one called comp430d.zip, which is found at numerous sites around the Internet. For our purposes we'll retrieve it from oak.oakland.edu, which is one of several sites housing the huge Simtel20 software collection. comp430d.zip contains another useful utility, adapted for MS-DOS, called compress; the same program allows you to decompress files (but be sure to read the documentation that comes with the program to learn how!). You'll remember from Chapter 5 that some files are compressed to save space when they're saved; these files contain the .Z suffix to their filenames; such as worldmap.ps.Z, intro.doc.Z, and so on. People who use Unix-based service providers have no problem with compressed files, because they can decompress .Z files on their provider's machine. They do so by using the uncompress command; thus, uncompress powerbook.doc.z will uncompress the file on-line, leaving powerbook.doc, the original document, on disk.

But if you are going to unpack these files on your own machine, you need a utility program like the one we'll find inside comp430d.zip. I won't walk you through the entire process again, but here's the relevant request to send to ftpmail@decwrl.dec.com.

```
connect oak.oakland.edu
binary
chdir /SimTel/msdos/compress
uuencode
get comp430d.zip
quit
```

Remember: This is the basic request. You would alter it as necessary if you were receiving this file by ftpmail through a commercial on-line service. If necessary, you would add chunksize (see list of commands) information and a reply line, as shown previously. Always check with your commercial service with regard to any restrictions on the size of incoming messages.

Macintosh users also need a way to deal with Unix .Z files. The file is called Mac-Compress; at the time of this writing, it was in version 3.04. You will find it at many of the Macintosh sites, such as mac.archive.umich.edu as well as wuarchive.wustl.edu. For our purposes, I've listed it as found at oak.oakland.edu.

What You Need: A Compress/Decompress Program for the Mac

The Program: MacCompress

How to Get It: By anonymous FTP. Try any of the major Macintosh sites, like sumex-aim.stanford.edu or mac.archive.umich.edu. If these are too busy, try the following URL:

ftp://gatekeeper.dec.com/.8/text/TeX.new/tools/compress/mac/maccompress-32.hqx

You can use the procedures you've learned to acquire this file; send the appropriate commands to ftpmail@decwrl.dec.com or to one of the other ftpmail sites.

Basic ftpmail Commands

Following are the basic commands you can use when requesting a file through ftpmail.

connect	Tells ftpmail the site you wish to connect to. As you saw in the preceding examples, the syntax is simply **connect** *sitename,* as in **connect wuarchive.wustl.edu**. The default host, incidentally, is gatekeeper.dec.com.
ascii	Tells ftpmail the files you want are regular ASCII text files.
binary	A critical command. Use it when the files to be retrieved are compressed or binary files. If you fail to give this command for such a file, ftpmail will be unable to send you the program.
chdir	Allows you to change directories. Note that you are allowed only one **chdir** command per ftpmail session.
chunksize	Splits files into chunks according to the size you specify.
compress	Tells ftpmail to compress a binary file.
get	Retrieves the file you request. Thus **get geoclock.zip** gets that file according to the commands given previously.
uuencode	Tells ftpmail to send you the binary file in uuencode format. Don't forget to send this command, or your uudecode program won't be able to salvage the file.

Finding Files to Retrieve—archie through Electronic Mail

As you saw in Chapter 5, the archie program can be a useful way to locate files. The good news about using electronic mail as an Internet gateway continues, for archie is itself available through e-mail. The idea is to send an e-mail message to an archie server, which will conduct the search and send the results back to you. I might, for example, want to contact the SURAnet archie server, the same one I consulted in Chapter 5. To do so by mail, I would send mail to archie@archie.sura.net. Commands to the server must begin in the first column of the message to be effective.

In most cases, we use electronic mail to handle Internet chores only when other forms of access aren't available. But archie is different. A typical archie search, because of congestion at the site, can take quite a while, even with a direct network connection. So it often makes sense to send your request by mail and then proceed to your other work. Later in the day, you can check your mailbox to retrieve the results of your search.

The archie servers mentioned earlier make their services available through electronic mail. To refresh your memory, Figure 8.12 shows the list again.

The message containing your search commands should be sent to **archie@**_server_. Thus, to contact the archie server at Rutgers, you'd send mail to **archie@archie.rutgers.edu.**

Server Address	Location	Country
archie.internic.net	AT&T InterNIC Directory and Database Services, South Plainfield, NJ	USA
archie.sura.net	SURAnet, Baltimore, MD	USA
archie.unl.edu	University of Nebraska, Lincoln	USA
archie.rutgers.edu	Rutgers University, NJ,	USA
archie.ans.net	Advanced Network & Services, Inc., Elmsford, NY	USA
archie.au	University of Melbourne	Australia
archie.univie.ac.at	University of Vienna	Austria
archie.uqam.ca	University of Quebec	Canada
archie.doc.ic.ac.uk	Imperial College, London	United Kingdom
archie.funet.fi	Finnish University and Research Network	Finland
archie.th-darmstadt.de	Technische Hochschule, Darmstadt	Germany
archie.ac.il	Hebrew University of Jerusalem,	Israel
archie.unipi.it		Italy
archie.wide.ad.jp	WIDE Project, Tokyo	Japan
archie.sogang.ac.kr	Sogang University	Korea
archie.rediris.es	RedIRIS, Madrid	Spain
archie.luth.se	University of Lulea	Sweden
archie.switch.ch	SWITCH, Zurich	Switzerland
archie.ncu.edu.tw	National Central University, Chung-li	Taiwan

Figure 8.12 A list of public access archie servers.

Tracking Down Sherlock Holmes

An example will make this clearer. As a Sherlock Holmes fan, I might want to look for text files of Arthur Conan Doyle's novels, such as those being compiled by Project Gutenberg and the Online Text Initiative (more about this in Chapter 10). Let's ask archie for files containing the name Doyle by sending a message to the preceding address (leave the subject field blank). Starting at the first column, type **find doyle** and send the message:

```
: mail archie@archie.sura.net
Subject:
find doyle
```

By return mail, we get a list of sites. I show only the relevant ones in Figure 8.13.

The following are the major commands for using archie through electronic mail, along with comments.

compress   This command compresses and uuencodes the material sent to you. Upon receiving the material, you must remove everything before the "begin" line and run it through the uudecode program. The result, a .Z file, must then be uncompressed to get the final results. The compress command makes sense if you are working with large files, although you won't always know that when you send a request.

```
To: Paul A Gilster -- Computer Focus gilster@interpath.net
Subject: archie reply: prog doyle
Status: R


Sorting by hostname


Search request for 'doyle'


    Location: /pub/data/etext
       DIRECTORY rwxrwxr-x      1536  Dec 28 10:31    doyle
    Location: /usr/almanac/lib
       FILE        rw-rw-r--    5255  Apr 24  1992
etext-doyle.tab

Host src.doc.ic.ac.uk   (146.169.2.1)
Last updated 05:03  4 Jan 1993

    Location: /literary/published/usenix/faces/dg-rtp.dg.com
       FILE        r--r--r--    13231  Mar 23  1989   doyle.Z
    Location: /published/usenix/faces/dg-rtp.dg.com
       FILE        r--r--r--    13231  Mar 23  1989   doyle.Z
```

Figure 8.13   Results of a search for Arthur Conan Doyle materials.

help   Can get you out of trouble. If you send a command that archie can't understand, you'll receive a help message whether you asked for one or not.

set mailto   Normally, archie will return e-mail to the address it extracts from the header of your message. If you find a server unresponsive, adding a path command to the message can help to get things moving. Because a number of different commands can appear in the same message, you can insert this command after your search command. Remember when using more than one command, though, that all commands must begin in column one of the line. Using the **set mailto** command to specify my address, for example, I'd enter: **set mailto gilster@interpath.net**. The e-mail we just sent to archie.sura.net, then, would be:

```
% mail archie@archie.sura.net
Subject:
find doyle
set mailto gilster@interpath.net
```

find   This is the search command we encountered in Chapter 5. It looks through the archie database to locate any matches to your search term. Note: With an interactive Telnet session, you have the ability to set search terms, as you've just seen. Using mail, the system will default to the Unix regular expression search type, called regex. But you can change the search type with a **set search sub** command. The basic archie by Telnet commands, as discussed in Chapter 5, are available here. Just insert them into your message to the server.

quit   Tells archie not to interpret anything past the point where **quit** is inserted. Use it if you have an automatically inserted signature file that might contain a term that resembles a command. Notice we also used **quit** when sending commands to ftpmail, and for the same reason.

servers   Returns a list of all known archie servers.

whatis   Allows you to search the software description database for a given substring. The command ignores case.

Using archie by Mail through CompuServe

Just as we used a commercial on-line service to retrieve files, we can also use one to search for files with archie. Just remember to check out your system's local conventions for addressing. We've already seen how to address mail to the Internet from CompuServe. So to search an archie server from CompuServe—say, the one at Rutgers—we would send to this address:

```
>INTERNET:archie@archie.rutgers.edu
```

In a useful file archive called ftpnet.zip, located in CompuServe's TapCis Forum libraries, CompuServe whiz Dick Kahane points out an obvious fact: CompuServe users, no matter where they call in from, are connecting to computers in Columbus, Ohio. So, no matter your location, to minimize Net traffic and use the resource closest to you,

CompuServe users should tap one of three archie servers, as shown in the following CompuServe-style Internet addresses:

```
INTERNET:archie@archie.unl.edu
INTERNET:archie@archie.rutgers.edu
INTERNET:archie@archie.sura.net
```

The first of these is in Lincoln, Nebraska, the second in New Jersey, while SURAnet is based in Maryland. Using geographically nearby sites helps to avoid network congestion.

We've seen how to search for filenames that interest us. Let's now search for files indexed under a particular keyword. I'm going to use CompuServe to request an archie mail server to locate files indexed under the term *laser*. Figure 8.14 shows how the message will be structured in CompuServe's WinCIM software.

I've added a path statement for the return message just as a precaution. The next command is the **whatis** statement, which allows you to search the software description database for a particular word. We follow with the **quit** command.

WAIS by Electronic Mail

Another exciting development in resource discovery, WAIS, or Wide Area Information Servers, is also available by electronic mail. This system, discussed at length in Chapter 13, allows you to search for information using keywords. We'll use WAIS in Chapter 13 to run sample searches. But if you're a mail-only user, you can still use a mail server put together by Jonny Goldman at Thinking Machines Corp. (where the WAIS system was first developed). Anyone who wants to try WAIS by mail should first read through Chapter 13 to master the basics of WAIS searching.

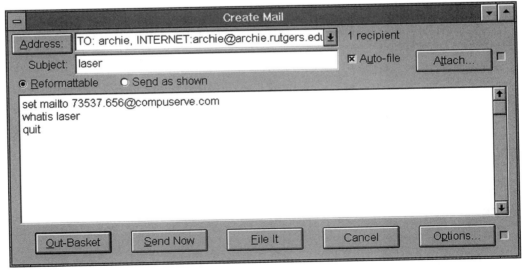

Figure 8.14   A CompuServe archie request.

The mail procedure is simple enough. You send a message to waismail@quake. think.com. The message should be formatted as follows:

```
search <source-name> keywords
```

source-name stands for the name found in the directory of servers without the .src suffix that characterizes them. Selected servers are listed in Chapter 16. And the WAIS discussion in Chapter 13 will show how you can search a general database of WAIS servers. A wealth of information is available through them.

You'll receive mail containing the results of the WAIS search. You can then request documents in the form:

```
retrieve docid
```

where **docid** is a WAIS document identifier. These document identifiers can be gigantic, and they have to be accurately transcribed or the command won't work. Be very careful when you enter a document ID into a message.

A sample search will make this clearer. Here's how I ran a WAIS search through e-mail for information. I'm querying the source nsf-pubs.src to find anything published by the National Science Foundation on the Internet. Note that I leave the .src off the end of the source statement.

```
% mail waismail@quake.think.com
Subject: WAIS Request
search nsf-pubs internet
```

A list of WAIS hits will be returned by electronic mail. Part of the list is shown in Figure 8.15.

From this list, we can choose a document we think most useful and retrieve it this way:

```
% mail waismail@quake.think.com
Subject: WAIS Request
DocID: 0 4830 /home/ftp/NSF/genpubs/nsf9110:/home/wais/wais-sources/nsf-
pubs@stis.nsf.gov:210%TEXT
```

I've pasted the document identification directly into my communications program and sent the message on its way. I'll soon receive the needed file in my mailbox.

For now, just note that WAIS searching by mail is workable, although it isn't exactly elegant. You'll learn much more about WAIS, which is one of the most exciting developments on the Internet, in Chapter 13. For now, I recommend that you retrieve a complete guide to the use of WAIS by mail.

What You Need: A User Guide to WAIS by Mail

How to Get It: Send e-mail to the following address:

waismail@sunsite.unc.edu

Leave the Subject: field blank and include the word **help** in the body of your message.

```
Searching: nsf-pubs
Keywords: internet


Result # 1 Score:1000 lines:  0 bytes:  59527 Date:     0  Type: TEXT
Headline: Title  : NSF9119 - STIS User's Guide
DocID: 0 59527 /home/ftp/NSF/genpubs/nsf9119:/home/wais/wais-sources/nsf-
pubs@stis.nsf.gov:210%TEXT


Result # 2 Score: 645 lines:  0 bytes:  29491 Date:     0  Type: TEXT
Headline: Title       : NSF9224--Network Information Services Manager(s) for
DocID: 0 29491 /home/ftp/CISE/program/nsf9224:/home/wais/wais-sources/nsf-
pubs@stis.nsf.gov:210%TEXT


Result # 3 Score: 516 lines:  0 bytes: 103293 Date:     0  Type: TEXT
Headline: Title  : NSF9130 - Undergraduate Level Math Sciences Education
Programs
DocID: 0 103293 /home/ftp/EHR/program/nsf9130:/home/wais/wais-sources/nsf-
pubs@stis.nsf.gov:210%TEXT


Result # 4 Score: 484 lines:  0 bytes:  19403 Date:     0  Type: TEXT
Headline: Title  : NSF Electronic Proposal Submission Project (EPS)
Information
DocID: 0 19403 /home/ftp/NSF/eps/epsinfo:/home/wais/wais-sources/nsf-
pubs@stis.nsf.gov:210%TEXT


Result # 5 Score: 484 lines:  0 bytes:  17909 Date:     0  Type: TEXT
Headline: Title  : CISE Newsletter, September 1992
DocID: 0 17909 /home/ftp/CISE/letters/lcise921:/home/wais/wais-sources/nsf-
pubs@stis.nsf.gov:210%TEXT


Result # 6 Score: 452 lines:  0 bytes:   4830 Date:     0  Type: TEXT
Headline: Title  : NSF 91-10 STIS Brochure
DocID: 0 4830 /home/ftp/NSF/genpubs/nsf9110:/home/wais/wais-sources/nsf-
pubs@stis.nsf.gov:210%TEXT
```

Figure 8.15 A mail request for a WAIS document.

Gopher by Electronic Mail

Gopher is a wonderful, menu-based interface to Internet resources; we will examine it closely in Chapter 12. Perhaps no better illustration of the ingenuity of electronic mail users exists than the e-mail implementation of Gopher. After all, the tool was designed to be used interactively. A system administrator puts up a menu of resources, and the user moves an on-screen marker to select an item of interest, pressing a **RETURN** to see it.

How can you translate these actions into electronic mail requests? Three e-mail gurus by the names of Fred Bremmer, Nick Hengeveld, and Matt Ranney figured out a way. The system works like this: You send mail to one of the following addresses; your message should contain no text and nothing in the Subject: field. The addresses are:

gophermail@calvin.edu   USA

gopher@earn.net   France

gopher@dsv.su.se   Sweden

gomail@ncc.go.jp   Japan

By return mail, you will receive a Gopher menu, as shown in Figure 8.16.

When using Gopher normally, which means interactively, you would select one of these on-screen items and press a **RETURN** to see it, or to see a submenu with further choices. Using Gophermail, you have a different methodology to work with. Place an **X** before the item you want to see, and send the document back to the Gophermail server. The item will be sent to you. The **X** should appear at the beginning of the line in your message. You do not need to edit out the rest of the message, as Gophermail ignores items without an **X**.

One of the joys of Gopher is that a Gopher server normally handles local material, such as the information about Calvin College at the top of the menu here, as well as national and international resources. Let's take a look, for example, at item 7 on the menu, which is called *Worldwide Resources/*. Any Gopher menu item with a slash after it

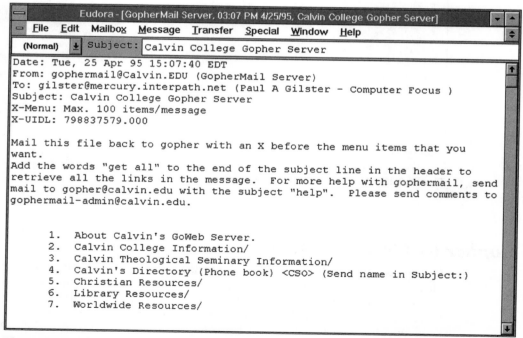

Figure 8.16   The introductory message from Gophermail as viewed in Eudora.

points to a submenu. We will place an **X** by this item and send the message back to the Gophermail server to see this submenu. Soon a response arrives, as shown in Figure 8.17.

At first glance, this appears to be the same message; it shows us a Gopher menu and instructs us to place an **X** beside the items we want. But note that now the menu has changed to reflect the submenu we have accessed. Our list of resources now includes other Gopher servers around the world, Internet phone and address directories, and resources on every continent. Each of these items in turn shows a submenu that we can access by, once again, placing an **X** beside the item we want and then mailing the menu back.

And here's a tip: If you know which Gopher site you want to access, you can retrieve its top-level menu by specifying its address on the Subject: line of your message to the Gophermail site. Thus I might send mail with the subject field showing this statement: english-server.hss.cmu.edu, to retrieve the main menu at one of the most comprehensive Gopher sites on the Net. I can then use the methods just described to explore the site.

Interactively, a Gopher session is simple and does not take up a great deal of time. Clearly, dealing with an extended set of menus through Gophermail can take up an afternoon, so the solution is, if ingenious, hardly ideal. But for those without Gopher access who yearn to use a resource available at a particular Gopher server, Gophermail at least offers the electronic mail alternative. Be sure to study the entire document Gophermail

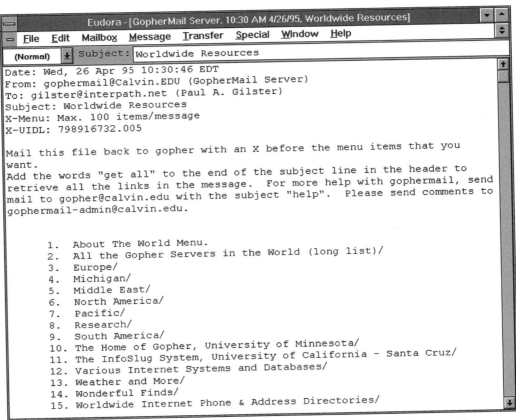

Figure 8.17 The submenu showing Gopher options worldwide, as returned by Gophermail.

returns to you each time; in addition to the actual Gopher menus, it contains information about how to customize Gophermail operations.

The World Wide Web by E-Mail

Multimedia by mail? Yes, it can be done, although without, let us say, most of the graphic and audio punch provided by the full-blown World Wide Web as seen through a good browser program. What we can do with mail is to retrieve a particular page from the Web in textual form, with the various links shown. To pull off this magic, we will contact a computer in Switzerland by mail and specify the URL of the World Wide Web page we want to see. Here's the address:

```
agora@mail.w3.org
```

To see a Web page, I would send the following message:

send *World_Wide_Web_URL*

where ***World_Wide_Web_URL*** is the URL of the site I want to see.

Web URLs begin with the http: prefix, and they're lengthy. For example, if I want to see a Web site offering Internet resources by topic, I could ask to see this URL:

```
http://www.clark.net/pub/journalism/awesome.html
```

To see this particular page, I would send this message:

send http://www.clark.net/pub/journalism/awesome.html

Soon the Web page would appear in my mailbox, as shown in Figure 8.18:

By using the **deep** command, you can retrieve not only the page in question, but the documents that are linked to it by hypertext. The command would be:

deep *World_Wide_Web_URL*

Depending on the page you're accessing and how many links it shows, this could result in quite a lot of information.

USENET by Electronic Mail

USENET really requires an interactive account for full participation. But there may be times when you, as a mail-only user to the Internet, would like to at least post a message, perhaps requesting responses to be sent to your mailbox. To do so, send your message to one of the following addresses:

newsgroup@charm.magnus.acs.ohio-state.edu	USA
newsgroup@cs.utexas.edu	USA
newsgroup@news.demon.co.uk	United Kingdom
newsgroup@nic.funet.fi	Finland
newsgroup@undergrad.math.uwaterloo.ca	Canada

where *newsgroup* is whatever newsgroup you would like the message to appear in.

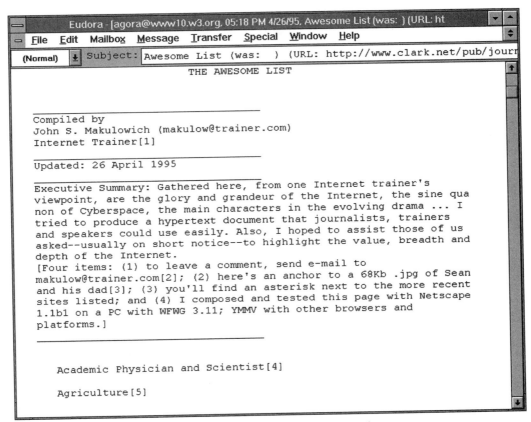

Figure 8.18   A World Wide Web page as transferred by electronic mail.

And note: When posting to USENET in this way, you must replace the periods in the newsgroup name with hyphens. For example, if I wanted to post a message to the alt.internet.services newsgroup, I would address it this way:

```
alt-internet-services@cs.utexas.edu
```

Is there any way to *read* USENET by electronic mail? The only solution I'm aware of is to go through Gophermail. A Gopher at Michigan State University is set up to handle USENET news, as is a counterpart Gopher in the United Kingdom. If you have absolutely no other recourse, you can, using the methods listed previously, send mail to one of the GopherMail servers and work your way, menu by menu, to the following sites:

```
gopher://gopher.msu.edu
```

Here, look under the News & Weather menu to locate USENET News.
In Europe, try:

```
gopher://gopher.bham.ac.uk
```

At this Gopher, choose the item *Usenet News Reader.*

Sending a Fax Using the Internet

Several services, some free and some commercial, allow you to send a fax using electronic mail. Let's examine the options.

InterFax

InterFax is a fee-based service (the current charge is $5 per month, which includes the first five fax pages; subsequent pages are .50 each) that allows you to send faxes to any destination. There is a one-time $25 sign-up charge. You can reach InterFax at this address:

> **INTERFAX**
> P.O. Box 162
> Skippack, PA 19474
> Voice:215-584-0300
> Fax:215-584-1038
> mailto:faxmaster@pan.com

FAXiNET

FAXiNET is a service that provides an interesting twist. It allows you not only to send faxes to machines in over 50 countries, but also to receive faxes, which are subsequently delivered to you as e-mail.

Two payment plans are available: for lower volume users, there is a one-time activation fee of $20 and a charge of .65 per faxed page. Rates go up if you plan to fax internationally. Contact:

> **ANYWARE ASSOCIATES**
> FAXiNET
> 32 Woodland Rd.
> Boston, MA 02130
> Voice: 617-522-8102
> mailto:info@awa.com
> http://www.awa.com/faxinet/

Interpage Fax Gateway

Interpage is a service designed to let you forward your e-mail to yourself as a fax message. When you set up an account with the company, you are charged for any faxes you receive. The service costs $5 per month plus .20 per minute for faxes, with rates going higher when your faxes leave U.S. borders. There is a $10 sign-up fee. For more information:

> **INTERPAGE**
> 203-499-5221
> http://interpage.net
> mailto:info@interpage.net

Remote Printing

Carl Malamud and Marshall Rose are conducting an experiment in remote printing. The idea is to explore how institutions can cooperate to provide a useful service to the network. In this case, companies and other organizations involved in the project have agreed to send faxes to certain areas, usually within local calling distance from their locations. When an Internet user sends an e-mail fax message, a computer examines the recipient's telephone number to see if any of the organizations involved in the project cover that destination. If they do, the message is delivered; if not, the user is notified by e-mail that the fax couldn't be delivered. The service is free.

For more information, you can send for the Frequently Asked Questions list about the service. Send mail to:

`tpc-faq@town.hall.org`

with the subject and message left blank.

And if you would like to see a current list of areas you can reach with this service, send mail to:

`tpc-coverage@town.hall.org`

with the subject and message blank.

To keep up with fax options over the Internet, you should be aware of Kevin Savetz' useful document on the subject.

What You Need: A Background Document on Internet Faxing

The Document: FAQ: How Can I Send a Fax from the Internet?

How to Get It: The document is posted regularly on the USENET newsgroups alt.internet.services, alt.online-service, alt.bbs.internet, alt.answers, and news.answers. You can also receive new editions automatically by sending mail to this address: savetz@rahul.net, asking to be added to the distribution list.

Finger by Mail

finger is a program we discuss in Chapter 14; it allows you to retrieve information about users and, in some cases, about a wide variety of information such as earthquake updates or popular music. Normally, finger is run as a program on your Unix service provider's computer. However, you can also use electronic mail to send and retrieve the results of finger queries. To do so, send e-mail to:

`infobot@infomania.com`

In the Subject: field, put this command: **finger** *user@site* where *user@site* is the address you want to reach. You will find a list of potential finger sites in Chapter 15's directory.

Suppose, for example, that you want to retrieve NASA headline news. The address is nasanews@space.mit.edu. Your e-mail request would then read:

`finger nasanews@space.mit.edu`

placed in the Subject: field of the message. Sending this, you will shortly receive an update on NASA press releases.

Sending Electronic Mail to Other Networks

If you have any doubts that Internet electronic mail opens out to networks across the world, consider the evidence of John J. Chew's *The Inter-Network Mail Guide*, available on the Internet both as a posting in various USENET newsgroups and also by download with anonymous FTP. Chew tracks the ways in which the various commercial providers maintain links to and from the Internet, and his list is growing with each new posting. A glance through it reveals linkages to such varied providers as Geonet Mailbox Systems, BIX, GreenNet, KeyLink, PeaceNet, SprintMail, and AppleLink, to name literally but a few. Chew's list will come in handy, and I advise you to get a copy.

What You Need: A List of Network Interconnections

The Document: Inter-Network Mail Guide, by John Chew

How to Get It: Through anonymous FTP. Try the following URL:

ftp://rtfm.mit.edu/pub/usenet/news.answers/inter-network-guide

You can also keep up with changes to this document by monitoring the USENET newsgroups comp.mail.misc and news.newusers.questions.

America Online

To send mail from the Internet to America Online, the syntax is *username@aol.com.* The user name should be all lowercase, with spaces removed.

Outgoing messages cannot be any longer than 32 K. On the PC version of America Online, incoming mail cannot be any longer than 8 K, which effectively prevents your using this service for ftpmail file transfers. On the Mac version of America Online, as well as the Apple II version and PC-Link, incoming mail cannot be any longer than 27 K. All characters except newline and printable ASCII characters are mapped to spaces. Users are limited to 75 pieces of Internet mail in their mailbox at a time.

To send mail from America Online to the Internet, simply enter the Internet address and write your message. Figure 8.19 shows the process in action.

BIX

To send mail from the Internet to BIX, the syntax is *username@bix.com.* To send mail from BIX to the Internet, enter the Internet address preceded by **to** at the Mail; prompt. The following is an example of a message being sent from BIX to the Internet:

```
Mail:to gilster@interpath.net
Enter subject: Mailing from BIX
Enter text. End with '. <CL>

This message is to test BIX's connections to Internet e-mail.

.
send/action:send
Sending..Memo 76679 sent
```

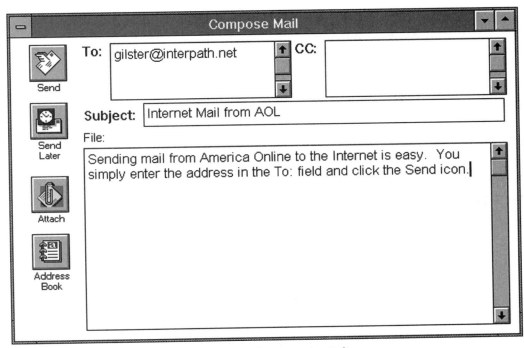

Figure 8.19   Sending a message to the Internet from America Online.

There is no monthly or per-message fee for Internet mail. You can move up to 10 MB per calendar month (in both directions, to and from the Internet), without any additional charges. Beyond that, the charge is $1 per 100 K transferred. Messages can be up to 0.5 MB in length in either direction; longer messages may be truncated.

CompuServe

To send mail from the Internet to CompuServe, the syntax is ***usernumber*@compuserve.com.** CompuServe user numbers contain commas, which must be changed to periods when you send from the Internet. Thus 12345,6789 becomes 12345.6789. To send me a CompuServe message, for example, you'd send to **73537.656@compuserve.com.**

To send mail from CompuServe to the Internet, as just shown, lead off the address with **INTERNET:** Sending a message to ftpmail, then, requires the address:

```
INTERNET:ftpmail@decwrl.dec.com
```

DELPHI

To send mail from the Internet to DELPHI, the syntax is: ***username*@delphi.com.** To send mail from DELPHI to the Internet, use the word **internet** followed by the recipient's name (with no spaces in between) enclosed in quotes. On DELPHI, to send a message to ftpmail, for example, you would address it to **internet"ftpmail@decwrl.dec.com".** The following is a sample message from Delphi to the Internet:

```
MAIL send
To:        internet"gilster@interpath.net"
Subj:      Test Message
Enter your message below. Press CTRL/Z when complete, or CTRL/C to quit:
Checking the DELPHI connection to the Internet.
^Z
```

GEnie

To send mail from the Internet to GEnie, the syntax is ***username@genie.geis.com.*** To send mail from GEnie to the Internet: After entering the Internet address, you are prompted for additional GEnie addresses, copies, and a subject line. You can then enter your text.

MCI Mail

To send mail from the Internet to MCI Mail, the syntax is: ***username@mcimail.com.*** MCI user names should have spaces replaced by an underscore. Thus, **Sam Spade** becomes **Sam_Spade@mcimail.com.** Conversely, it's possible to use an MCI user number. If Sam's number is 123-4567, simply remove the dash. Thus, **1234567 @mcimail.com.** If there happens to be more than one Sam Spade in the MCI directory, you can reach the desired party by sending to:

```
Sam_Spade/1234567@mcimail.com
```

To send mail from MCI Mail to the Internet, use the EMS option. Here's how to do it:

1. At the TO prompt, type recipient's name and the word EMS in parentheses.
2. At the EMS prompt, type **INTERNET.**
3. At the MBX prompt, type the recipient's Internet address. Note: If the Internet address exceeds 80 characters in length, you must split the address into multiple MBX lines. The split should occur at one of the following characters: @ ! %.
4. Only one Internet mailbox may be used with an individual TO or CC recipient.
5. Complete the mailing procedure as usual.

Figure 8.20 shows an example of sending a message to an Internet address from MCI Mail.

Prodigy

Prodigy is the huge commercial service created by IBM and Sears. To send mail from Prodigy to the Internet, you will need a program called Mail Manager. Jump to *About Mail Manager* while on-line to learn how to download it.

To send mail from the Internet to Prodigy, use the Prodigy user ID followed by the domain name. Thus, to send mail to klbc98x, you should address the message to **klbc98x@prodigy.com.**

Mailing Lists and Electronic Journals

A huge variety of mailing lists is available to people with electronic mail access to the Internet. So much is available here that it would make little sense to try to compress it

```
EMS:       INTERNET
      EMS    376-5414 INTERNET              NRI            Reston

Enter recipient's mailbox information.

MBX:       mike_banks@bix.com

If additional mailbox lines are not needed press RETURN.

MBX:

TO:        Mike Banks
           EMS: INTERNET / MCI ID: 376-5414
           MBX: mike_banks@bix.com

Is this address correct (Yes or No)? y

CC:

Subject: MCI Mail Check

Text: (Enter text or transmit file. Type / on a line by itself to end.)

Mike:

Please let me know if this message gets through OK.  It's routed to
your BIX account via MCI Mail.

Thanks!

Paul
```

Figure 8.20 Sending a message to the Internet from MCI Mail.

into a single chapter, much less the tail end of one. The next chapter, therefore, will explain how you can follow discussions on everything from nuclear physics to medieval archaeology by using your Internet mailbox.

Mailing lists moving across the Internet are available, as are academic discussions routed through gateways with BITNET. A final bonus: A large and growing number of electronic journals can be delivered to your mailbox, often as pointer messages with instructions on how to retrieve the entire issue. These, too, will be explained in the chapters that follow.

A Final Caution

While electronic mail offers rich resources from the Internet, you should be careful about incurring unnecessary expenses. As the next chapter demonstrates, mailing lists can tempt you with a dizzying number of subjects, but their daily message count can be high. If you use a commercial on-line service, you should carefully examine the provisions of your account to see what kind of charges may be involved. Some services carry charges to receive Internet mail, and some may limit the size of files you can store.

CompuServe's mail options are a case in point. The service offers two levels of access. One, a pay-as-you-go plan, simply charges you for the on-line time you spend as you retrieve your messages, whether they're from the Internet or somewhere else. The other, the standard plan, charges a flat rate of $9.95 for a range of basic services. One of these is mail.

Now it gets tricky. Although you aren't charged for connect time while using mail under this plan, you are charged by the message for Internet messages. There is a .15 minimum charge for receiving an Internet message of up to 7,500 characters, with an additional .05 per 2,500 characters. The plan does provide a monthly mail allowance of $9, so the cost of Internet messages could be absorbed up to that amount; you wouldn't, in other words, begin to pay until charges exceed $9.

However, as you learn your way around the Internet, you'll realize that bringing in big text files and binary files for decoding can quickly push you past the limit. Other services may not charge for receiving Internet messages, but may include a storage charge. DELPHI, for example, offers its Internet service for $3 a month in addition to its regular pricing plans; the Internet option includes a transfer allocation of 10 MB. This refers to the total volume of incoming and outgoing mail messages and FTP files. (Remember that DELPHI has full Internet access and hence provides FTP and Telnet services.) But the service also charges for storage—the first 25,600 characters are free, while each additional 1,024 characters are billed at .16 per month.

The point is, each commercial on-line system has its own billing mechanisms, and considering the volume of traffic the Internet can generate, you should check carefully to be sure you know what your system's requirements are. If you plan to pursue multiple mailing lists, for example, you may well decide you'll save money by opting for a full-service Internet provider offering extensive disk storage and, perhaps, a flat rate for access. You'll also, of course, enjoy the benefits of full Internet access, including Telnet and FTP.

9

The Art of the List

Mailing lists are a natural in the networked electronic environment. A user posts a message that is sent to a central computer; from there, the message is sent out to like-minded people who have subscribed to the mailing list in question. Gather people together under the umbrella of a shared interest and pretty soon the discussion gets lively as new ideas are explored and old notions challenged. Extend the concept into the universities, then into companies and homes, and you have a worldwide discussion of virtually any subject you choose to name. Think of mailing lists as extended user groups, or scholarly conferences by computer, or fan clubs with a daily presence. Whatever the metaphor, lists keep people talking to each other, and offer remarkable opportunities for education.

My mailbox says it all. An average morning takes me traveling through a wide realm of ideas, one I've tailored expressly to match my interests. A discussion of Anglo-Saxon England—was the burial site at Sutton Hoo a later artifact than is commonly thought? Can contemporary blood types be used to analyze settlement patterns in medieval Iceland? A look at computer networking—what on-line journals are about to be published, and what implications does the field of on-line publishing hold for research in a variety of disciplines? A debate on multicultural ethics—what preconceptions do Americans take with them when they visit Japan? What do the Japanese themselves think of foreign visitors? A question on CD-ROMs—which of the available CD-ROM players is the most reliable?

Messages on all these topics and more flow to me through mailing lists, a seemingly inexhaustible source of information and inspiration. Yet I've noticed that many network users don't take advantage of their power, preferring forums like USENET instead. Perhaps that's because of the more closed nature of a mailing list—only those who take the trouble to subscribe will receive the daily postings, thus limiting the audience to a group of people who may be more focused on the topic at hand. But I think it's also because of the origins of the mailing list in the academic community through a network called BITNET. Compared to commercial on-line services like CompuServe and America Online, BITNET was harder to use and intimidating, at least at first glance. Shouldn't a network linking major universities, a tool for discussion between academic specialists, be off-limits for the rest of us? Meeker souls may assume so, and so too may some academic users, a few of whom would prefer to keep their discussions entirely to themselves. Human nature is immutable, it seems; once we've found a place we like, it's tempting to close the doors to everyone else.

And then there's the need to master new procedures. The way we sign on for discussions, because it is often (but not always) automated, is itself off-putting. How do we sign on, and what happens if we make a mistake in what we tell the remote computer? For that matter, what happens when we decide to log off; how do we proceed? It's because of questions like these that many Internet users don't take full advantage of mailing list resources, (or consider them only as an afterthought.)

But you needn't feel overwhelmed. For one thing, BITNET is only one vehicle for the dissemination of mailing lists, and despite their intensive use in our universities, these lists are now found on all kinds of subjects, populated by a spectrum of users as wide as any found on USENET or CompuServe or anywhere else in the on-line world. For another, BITNET itself is growing closer to the Internet, its older protocols giving way to transmission by TCP/IP. Whereas, some years ago, we could draw clear lines of distinction between BITNET and the Internet—and among their users—it's no longer possible to do so. We don't have to worry about the differences—basic sign-up procedures get us on board, and the rules of participation are the same no matter what kind of mailing list we're using.

Exploration requires a certain single-mindedness—you don't go into a wilderness thinking you'll only explore those areas that make you the most comfortable. And as you're about to see when we learn to tap the Internet's mailing lists and, later, their file archives, these tools can be a challenge to use. The advantage you'll gain, though, is immense, as you realize what an excellent resource they are for those hoping to expand an education or explore an idea. We will begin our journey with a look at BITNET itself, the fulcrum of mailing list development in the 1980s. We will then proceed into a discussion of other forms of mailing lists. Thousands exist, making this unusually fertile ground for the intellectually adventuresome. The notion that such riches would be available to interested parties worldwide would have struck all previous generations of scholars as fanciful nonsense.

What You Need: Help documents for LISTSERV, ListProcessor, and Majordomo

How to Get Them: Send an e-mail message containing the word **help** to any site that runs one of these programs. To get the help document from BITNIC, send your message to:

   listserv@bitnic.bitnet

For ListProcessor, send to:

   listproc@listproc.net

For Majordomo, try:

   majordomo@csn.org

As you use a mailing list, you will often need to check out the commands available to the list management software it uses. At any time, sending a help message to the administrative address of the mailing list itself will result in the needed document.

Many mailing lists are, in the BITNET model, distributed by automated procedures that take advantage of list management software. We will focus in this chapter on LIST-SERV, created by Eric Thomas to handle the distribution of messages through BITNET. Another popular list program is called ListProcessor (often shortened to ListProc); it is the work of Anastasios Kotsikonas, and runs under Unix. I note that the Corporation for Research and Educational Networking, the power behind BITNET, has acquired rights to ListProcessor and intends to develop the software as part of its move into the Internet environment. A third tool is Majordomo, a program created by Brent Chapman.

If you intend to use mailing lists to best advantage, it would be a good idea to pick up help documents for each. You can then save these in your file library for later use as the need arises.

BITNET's Background

Created in 1981, BITNET was envisaged as a way of keeping faculty members at our universities in communication with their fellow institutions. For the concept, we thank Ira H. Fuchs, then Vice Chancellor for university systems at the City University of New York (CUNY), and Greydon Freeman, director of the Yale Computing Center at Yale University. Fuchs had IBM's example to look at: He knew that the giant corporation's VNET network connected its programmers, researchers, and managers worldwide, using IBM software and leased telephone lines. As VNET developed, each link added to the chain was responsible for its own connection to the network. VNET became a paradigm for what Fuchs and Freeman foresaw as a communications link for higher education.

CUNY was in some respects the ideal proving ground for such an experiment. Both CUNY and Yale had some experience using network software to connect their own computers; CUNY, in fact, connected 19 colleges across New York's five boroughs, and the linkage to Yale simply extended its reach. Fuchs and Freeman studied computing facilities at various institutions, concluding that an IBM-based communications protocol would make sense, given the number of users supported by Big Blue's machines. Folding into the concept the notion that computers could be used just as readily for textual data as computer programs, not to mention electronic mail, they began sending letters to schools with major IBM installations, encouraging them to participate in the new network. Despite its reliance on the IBM protocol, the computers on the Net range from IBM systems to VAX machines, Unix workstations, and a number of other computer types, all communicating using the same protocol. Once again, computer networking defeats the parochial limitations of operating systems and hardware.

The philosophy was straightforward: Each school was to pay for its own communications link to the network, and each would make it possible for at least one new member to connect to BITNET. And as the network grew, each member agreed to move traffic bound for other members with no charge. BITNET's computers use a *store and forward* method based on an IBM NJE (Network Job Entry) communications protocol—this means that a file goes from one site to another by passing through a series of intermediate nodes.

Moving over 9600-bps leased lines, each file must be sent in its entirety from one node to the next before continuing down the chain. If a connection between two nodes is severed, the file is simply stored until the connection is reestablished. In the absence of alternate routing strategies, a site can therefore be cut off, as can any site relying on mail passing through its computers. Imagine the early network as a tree, with its trunk at CUNY. Traffic to each host had only one path to follow, with the limitations that implies.

The system worked, but problems arose due to the nature of traffic flow in this kind of network topology. Slow network connections and a lack of redundancy hampered communications. The solution was to move BITNET traffic using the Internet's protocols, adding the routing redundancy and higher-speed connections offered by the TCP/IP network. In 1989, under the name BITNET II, BITNET was reorganized into regions, setting up computers in each as root nodes for that area. These nodes, in turn, were connected by high-speed data lines, forming in essence a high-speed backbone network for BITNET traffic.

The term BITNET stands for Because It's Time Network, a moniker that quickly began to prove itself accurate. After 18 months, the fledgling network had reached into 20 universities, one of them—the University of California at Berkeley—providing connections throughout the West Coast. By 1984, 100 organizations were included, over 500 by 1989. BITNET's corporate name changed to CREN (Corporation for Research and Educational Networking) when it merged with the Computer Science Network, or CSNET (originally funded by the National Science Foundation) in 1989. CSNET was discontinued in 1991, but CREN continues its robust work, organizing BITNET's far-reaching activities in support of education and research in a noncommercial environment.

IBM was more than an inspiration for BITNET; the company also provided initial funding for centralized network services with a 1984 grant. This led to the establishment of BITNIC, BITNET's Network Information Center, and the grant included an IBM mainframe computer which would serve as the central information site for the network. When the grant expired in 1987, BITNET's funding came solely from membership dues. Today, CREN counts 530 members in the United States and Mexico, including universities, colleges, research laboratories, primary and secondary schools, and government agencies.

But BITNET reaches beyond the United States and Mexico into more than 1,300 research sites around the world. Among the most significant BITNET international connections are those to NetNorth in Canada and TERENA in Europe. Both are loosely considered to be part of BITNET, though in fact each network is maintained individually. NetNorth began as an agreement between eight Canadian universities in 1983, linking IBM mainframe computers. EARN now connects over 750 computers in 24 countries, extending from Europe into Africa and the Middle East. BITNET also links to networks like GulfNet in the Persian Gulf area, RUNCOL in Colombia, ANSP in Brazil and CAREN in Asia.

The list of member institutions included in BITNET, EARN, and NetNorth is an impressive one indeed, from the Universidad Nacional de Cordoba in Argentina to the University of Bahrain, from the Pedagogical Institute of Cyprus to the University of Helsinki. There are links to Egypt, Hong Kong, Ireland, Hungary, Iceland, Peru, and India. Never have scholars been provided as useful a communications tool for keeping research up to date and colleagues informed of developments wherever they occur.

BITNET today is moving into new terrain, and of necessity. By 1993, the number of academic organizations connecting to the Internet outnumbered those with active BITNET links, and it was obvious that the future lay with Internet connectivity. The key was to make its 3 thousand discussion groups available through the Internet protocols. To this end, CREN and other organizations that have supported BITNET are turning toward the Internet with a variety of projects, including new list management software that will run on Unix machines and be optimized to work with TCP/IP. In addition, CREN is developing software clients for its members to ease the transition into the Internet, and its BITNET III project is designed to create a cooperative arrangement for dial-up access to Internet resources.

To keep up with BITNET's evolution, it would be helpful to have a central source. You can see the site I use in Figure 9.1, where I'm examining it through the Netscape Navigator program.

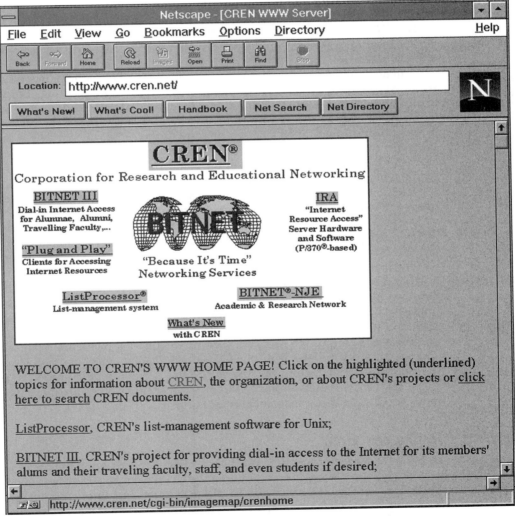

Figure 9.1   The CREN page is the place to keep up with the BITNET III project.

What You Need: A Way to Keep Up with BITNET News

The Site: The World Wide Web page maintained by CREN

Its Address: http://www.cren.net/

BITNET's Legacy

Before I explain the concept behind mailing lists, a few thoughts on what BITNET has meant to scholarship. In the early Middle Ages, Europe's schools were structured around a body of common knowledge which the scholar was expected to master. Unlike today's higher education, with its few requirements and curricula targeted toward career goals, early education was based on the premise that students should master knowledge across a broad spectrum.

Their studies were not confined to a specialty like mathematics or grammar, but included rhetoric, the art of speaking well, and communicating. Students were to acquire knowledge of geometry and astronomy, of dialectics and music. These seven liberal arts, known as the Trivium and Quadrivium, encouraged the dissemination of a broad cultural inheritance, and led directly to the scholasticism whose legacy was the great European universities at Paris, Oxford, Bologna, and Salerno. No student, whether studying law, medicine, or philosophy, could proceed without this rich grounding in truths then considered universal.

These notions, alien today, would come to fruition in the Renaissance, perhaps the last era in which people believed it was possible to master all human knowledge. Distant as it seems, the medieval system has much to teach us. Its scope was daring, its aim audacious, and today's intellectual accomplishments, from the equations that took Voyager to Neptune to the communications protocols that drive the Internet, descend directly from it.

Today we think in terms of specialties, and indeed, knowledge seems inescapably bounded by the limits of what a single individual can master in a lifetime. But we've become a culture of specialists to our loss, for the cross-linking of knowledge, the fertilization of ideas from a wide range of disciplines, is at the core of human inquiry. There are times as I go through my mail, reading mailing list messages from scholars worldwide on subjects ranging from the *Canterbury Tales* to particle physics research, that I suspect Roger Bacon, Duns Scotus, or Thomas Aquinas would have been right at home with network communications. In this as in other things, they are more modern than we imagine. Our challenge is to equal their curiosity.

When Analogies Fail

E-mail is remarkably versatile, yet it places few demands upon the imagination. We can relate it to its "real-world" counterpart—the U.S. Postal Service. The analogy is clear and workable. The Postal Service takes a physical letter, examines the address, and delivers it to the person listed at that address. The electronic mail system takes an electronic letter, uses the routing information in its header to track down the recipient, and delivers it to his or her mailbox. True, electronic mail is astonishingly fast, and its improvement over regular postal delivery is obvious. But the basic concept—one-to-one communication through a central delivery mechanism—is one we're all familiar with.

Where e-mail strains the limits of the analogy, though, is when we extend it into new terrain. If one-to-one delivery is what we think of when we speak of electronic mail, then how do we regard the one-to-many communication provided by a mailing list? Here, we are gathering mail at a central site and then distributing it to a group of interested people, who have specifically requested to receive mail in this way. What the group has in common is a shared interest, and any members of the group may participate in the resulting discussion. This is no longer a one-to-one but a one-to-many form of communication.

The two forms of mail have an evasive boundary, it's true. I can send a message to a colleague across the country and include a list of other recipients by using the mail program's carbon copy capabilities or those of pine or Eudora. I can set up things so my recipients know who else is receiving the message, or I can shield that information by using blind carbon copies, as we saw in Chapter 7. But even so, while I have enabled a one-to-many link, I haven't given it the institutional life or structure provided by a mailing list. What I've done informally as a one-time occurrence, mailing lists implement as a regular way of disseminating information, with their own set of protocols and responsibilities.

Bringing Order to the Chaos

Back in the 1960s, I discovered the joys of correspondence. In those pre-desktop computer days, a typewriter was the tool of choice, and I used my Smith-Corona, a beautiful old model passed along in the family since the 1920s, to write letters to fellow science fiction enthusiasts around the world. Each day, the trip to the mailbox was an adventure, because I never knew how many letters might be waiting. I was seldom disappointed, and never happier than when a particularly fat envelope arrived from one of my correspondents, carrying a round robin letter.

These letters weren't one-to-one communications either. You signed on to participate in a group discussion, whose topic could range far and wide. When you joined, it was customary to send a photograph and a brief biography so other people involved in the letter would know who you were. Then the letter would circulate. Each month or so, you received an envelope with letters from seven or eight other people. You read all of them and added your own comments to each. The discussion was public and you received responses from everyone involved.

Take the round-robin-letter concept and extend it into the world of electronic communications. Those same seven or eight people would find it easy to move messages over a network, but the situation could quickly get out of hand. Given that correspondents could reply to everyone and deliver the results the same day, the letter would circulate from person to person as if around the rim of a wheel, with no central source of organization. Instead of one person having the cumulative letter at a time, everyone would have a more or less up-to-date version of it. Anarchy would quickly reign as each correspondent added comments and differing versions shot across cyberspace.

Mailing lists counter such chaos, and they function remarkably well. A centralized structure is imposed over the circulating material, usually with a single person supervising the entire operation. Instead of bouncing and multiplying across the network, messages flow to the person in charge, who then sees that the discussion is moderated, or at least that each person's contributions become available for all to read. Best of all, this material is then delivered to your electronic mailbox, in the form of a series of messages that keep coming in until you resign from the group in question.

The Mailing List Community

Given BITNET's academic background, it's no surprise that many of the mailing lists you will likely encounter are research-oriented. You'll find lists populated with scientists, teachers, university librarians, and policy analysts. And given the diversity of their studies, the huge range of available topics ensures there will never be a shortage of reading material for the enterprising network participant. These lists proceed without fuss or fanfare. They're a quiet and continuing dialogue between some of the best minds in our culture, one of the academy's best kept secrets.

How do you know what's available? The answer is found in a document maintained by the BITNET Network Information Center, otherwise known as BITNIC, in Washington, DC. This organization maintains a list of BITNET discussion groups which can be had for the asking. The resultant document is large and contains the complete directory of what's current on the mailing list scene. It's a critical document for your network library.

What You Need: A Directory of All BITNET Mailing Lists

The Document: List of All LISTSERV Lists

How to Get It: By electronic mail. Send a message to listserv@bitnic.bitnet. Leave the subject field blank; in the message itself, enter only **list global.** The document will be sent to your mailbox. There, you can save it to a file for subsequent reference, printing out, or downloading.

If you need further information, contact:

BITNET Network Information Center
1112 Sixteenth St., NW, Suite 600
Washington, DC, 20036
202-872-4200

Incidentally, another useful way to search for LISTSERV lists is to use a WAIS server. WAIS, which we'll examine in Chapter 13, allows you to interactively search the List of Lists. More on using WAIS for this and other search tasks in that chapter.

Figure 9.2 shows a small sample of what you'll see when you receive this list. The section in question, drawn from the P section of the list, covers everything from public television stations to Canadian engineering, from packaging research to the Pacific Ocean. The name of each list is on the left, followed by the letter L. The network address and description follows on the right.

```
P-ONS          P-ONS@UHUPVM1.UH.EDU
               Traffic Departments of Public Television Stations

P-PALS         P-PALS@UHUPVM1.UH.EDU
               Ptv Programmer Assessing Loose Scenarios

P-TRACK        P-TRACK@UHUPVM1.UH.EDU
               Protrack Database Discussion List

PA_NET         PA_NET@LISTSERV.SYR.EDU
               Public Administration Network

PACE-L         PACE-L@GSUVM1.BITNET
               PACE-L -- PACE degree audit system discussion list

PACES-L        PACES-L@UNBVM1.BITNET
               Publications Assoc. of Canadian Engineering students

PACIE-L        PACIE-L@VILLVM.BITNET
               Forum for the Discussion for Pa. Council for Int'l Education

PACIFIC        PACIFIC@BRUFPB.BITNET
               FORUM FOR AND ABOUT PACIFIC OCEAN AND ISLANDS

PACKRND        PACKRND@NDSUVM1.BITNET
               Packaging Research and Development

PACRAO-L       PACRAO-L@ASUACAD.BITNET
               PACRAO-L/Discussion of PACRAO topics among PACRAO members

PACS-L         PACS-L@UHUPVM1.UH.EDU
               Public-Access Computer Systems Forum

PACS-P         PACS-P@UHUPVM1.UH.EDU
               Public-Access Computer Systems Publications
```

Figure 9.2 A sampling of the master list of BITNET mailing lists maintained by BITNIC.

BITNET lists range widely in subject and structure. Some are general, covering broad topics like philosophy or the outdoors. Others focus with laserlike precision: early English drama, Macintosh terminal emulation, Turkish studies. Some disseminate official information, like severe weather outlooks for various parts of the country. Others are loose discussions where anyone weighs in with an opinion and open debate reigns. Needless to say, the topic has much to do with the level of activity on the mailing list. A controversial subject may generate heated discussions and land 50 messages a day in your mailbox. A quieter list may chug along virtually unnoticed until a flurry of new messages arrive to remind you of its existence.

If you prefer not to scan through the entire global list of BITNET possibilities, there's a shortcut available. Rather than sending the **list global** command to the BITNIC LISTSERV, try **list global /topics.** If you were interested, for example, in physics, you might send **list global /physics.** Use the same BITNIC address as given. Later, we'll use this searching shortcut to target mailing lists for research purposes. But you really should keep a copy of the global list in your filing cabinet for reference.

Once you've established a presence on the World Wide Web with a browser program (and we'll discuss how to do this in Chapter 14), you can also search for mailing lists there. In Figure 9.3, you see the results of a search I ran from a site that offers a keyword search of Internet resources. I used the keyword *science* and proceeded to search; the server produced the hits shown in the figure in hypertext format. When I click on any of these items, I am presented a set of information about the group in question. To access this site, use the following URL:

```
http://www.austin.unimelb.edu.au:800/7m/acad/lists/acad
```

using a Web browser like Netscape or Mosaic.

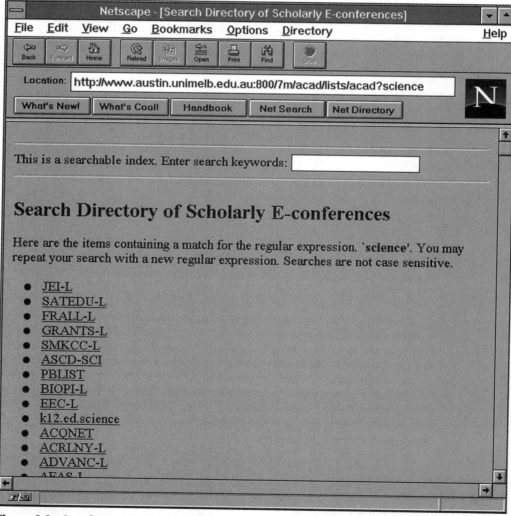

Figure 9.3   Searching a World Wide Web site to track down a mailing list.

The Niceties of Mailing List Participation

The original BITNET mailing lists weren't normal computer bulletin boards, nor are their descendants. In the case of academically oriented lists, they provide an opportunity to bridge the seemingly insuperable gap between universities too often isolated from society and a community of interested lay people who can benefit from exposure to their ideas. A mailing list is a tremendous vehicle for continuing education, for following up on interests you thought you left behind when you left school. It can be a medium for exploring ideas and keeping up with breakthroughs in both the humanities and the sciences.

For scholars, mailing lists have become a platform for collaborative work. Imagine talking to valued colleagues daily, whereas before your conversations were limited to occasional academic conferences. BITNET did exactly what Ira Fuchs and Greydon Freeman intended: It promoted contact with distant colleagues and distributed news throughout the research community. The ability for an outside observer to sit in on such a medium is one of the more remarkable features of your access to the Internet. And as new mailing lists spring up outside the academic model, we're seeing business and home users participating in discussions of a steadily growing range of topics, often using them for research and even marketing.

To use a mailing list properly, you should plan on listening and absorbing what you read before you leave any messages. In most of the mailing lists I subscribe to, I'm purely a listener, taking the opportunity to learn from the ongoing discussion. There's no point in jumping in unless you have something genuinely useful to add to the proceedings.

As you examine a new mailing list, then, the idea is to find out what the tenor of the discussion is, follow its byways, and benefit from the expertise you find there. Each mailing list has its own feel, and certain conventions may have emerged to guide its activities. Lists can be surprisingly informal, but the usual caveats about avoiding sarcasm and easily misunderstood comments apply.

Another caveat, and this is a big one: Be careful how you reply to a mailing list. Remember the number of subscribers out there. If you choose to send a message to a particular poster, you should ensure that you respond to his or her address only. Mailing lists can become hopelessly clogged with inconsequential messages meant for one pair of eyes only, but accidentally distributed to the entire subscription list by a careless use of the reply function.

This can be more or less of a problem depending upon your relationship to the people subscribing to the mailing list in question. But a sarcastic remark about someone's latest comment which you meant to pass along to a personal friend on the list might have implications for your on-line popularity if it were distributed to everyone. Be cautious, and keep in mind that a mailing list is a public forum, designed for an audience of interested if diverse peers. All will benefit when everyone plays by these simple rules.

Puzzling Out a BITNET Address

Armed with your master list of lists, you're in position to sign on and begin reading. But first let's examine a mailing list address. I'll choose the following entry:

```
TWAIN-L    TWAIN-L@YORKVM1.BITNET
           Mark Twain Forum
```

To sign up for this list, I'll need to send mail to the address specified. But first, let's examine that address more closely.

The conventional BITNET address would have been TWAIN-L@YORKVM1—that is, a mailing list (L) called TWAIN at YORKVM1. The latter follows BITNET user name and host name conventions. Such addresses were always limited to eight uppercase numbers and letters; I mention this because you may still see addresses like this, without periods in the address, as is standard with the Domain Name System. As BITNET evolved, an address like TWAIN-L@YORKVM1 would have been sufficient to deliver your message, but now that BITNET is flowing largely over the Internet itself, we need something else to make the address work.

Thus the updated address—TWAIN-L@YORKVM1.BITNET—which can also be written in lowercase, as twain-l@yorkvm1.bitnet. In other words, when you run into an older-style BITNET address, all you need to do to reach it is to add the .bitnet suffix; this allows the Internet to route your traffic as desired.

This method will probably work, and you should give it a try, but there are cases where mail addressed using this method will bounce. Some computers understand this shorthand routing, while others don't. Here's the alternative: Change the .bitnet address

```
twain-l@yorkvm1.bitnet
```

to this one:

```
twain-l%yorkvm1.bitnet@cunyvm.cuny.edu
```

When you do this, you are directing your traffic to a known BITNET gateway into the Internet; in this case, it is the node at CUNY, the Ur of BITNET sites). In more generic form, here is the format:

```
name%node.bitnet@gateway.address
```

This procedure of sending BITNET mail through an established gateway is commonly known as the *percent hack*, because of the percentage sign (%) that appears in its address. The Internet will only handle messages with a single @ symbol in them, which explains the need for the percent sign. Another gateway besides the one just used, incidentally, can be tried. You might, for example, route mail through mitvma.mit.edu, or pucc.princeton.edu. Thus, if you were attempting to send mail to TWAIN-L by this route, you could send it to twain-l%yorkvm1.bitnet@mitvma.mit.edu. It's a long address, but it will work if the standard .bitnet suffix fails.

LISTSERV Addresses

There are two addresses to work with when you are dealing with a mailing list. One is the site to which messages are routed; the other is the LISTSERV address, which is the place where administrative messages should go. Thus you handle your subscription and any other details regarding your receiving the list at this address: listserv@yorkvm1.bitnet. But all other messages go to the main address at twain-l@yorkvm1.bitnet.

Memorize that principle. The LISTSERV address is where you send routine administrative requests, including your initial sign-on. The mailing list address is where you send messages once you are already on the list, and this is the address from which you will receive the messages of other subscribers.

Recite the principle again, because it's important for the use of LISTSERVs and all other forms of mailing lists. The importance of this distinction will become clear in what follows.

LISTSERV and the Pleasures of Automation

Before sending our sign-up message to the Twain list, a bit of background. A particular protocol must be followed when you subscribe to these lists, not out of some longstanding computer tradition, but because of the necessities of handling automated traffic. For LISTSERVs are indeed automatic. The administrative to and fro involved with signing people up, removing them from lists, and what not, is handled by computerized list functions managed by a server. Remember, a server is simply a program running on a network machine; it has its own user identification and can often accept commands sent by electronic mail.

Most servers you'll deal with run the LISTSERV program written by Eric Thomas, which means the commands are common to all machines running LISTSERV throughout the system. LISTSERV began as a mailing list program created by Ira Fuchs and Daniel J. Oberst, but its quick growth and popularity created problems. The people in charge of the various lists were responsible for signing up new subscribers and deleting those who wanted to leave. For these volunteers, the workload soon became too heavy to handle.

Revised LISTSERV, which Thomas wrote in 1986, overcame the restrictions of the earlier version by providing new functions. The server could now maintain a list by handling subscription requests automatically, and data files could be maintained as list archives. BITNIC maintains a number of useful files which we'll use to build up our own BITNET library. With both files and electronic mail, our gateway access into BITNET precludes interactive usage of its facilities, so the process requires you to ask the server for specific data through a precise protocol.

The method is simple enough: You send mail to the server in question and the text of your message is interpreted as a command by that machine. Your entry to a LISTSERV is handled, then, by sending a properly formatted message to the correct address.

Let's use this method now to retrieve a core document called BITNET USERHELP. To get it, contact the BITNET Network Information Center by sending mail to **listserv@bitnic.bitnet.** Here's how the message will look as sent through the mail program:

```
% mail listserv@bitnic.bitnet
Subject:
get bitnet intro
```

Note that I left the Subject: field blank. The command takes up the first line of the message. Sending it, I receive in return a useful document containing material on BITNET's structure, the capabilities of its mailing lists, its links with other networks and more; there's even a suggested reading list.

Here's another document to add to the library.

What You Need: BITNET Background Information

The Documents: USING BITNET: AN INTRODUCTION

How to Get It: By sending mail to listserv@bitnic.bitnet. Send a message with no subject line. The message should read **get bitnet intro.**

Signing On to a List

To subscribe to the Twain list, I need only put the same principles to work. I send a message to listserv@yorkvm1.bitnet containing the following request: **subscribe twain-l Paul Gilster.**

Follow the format exactly, by placing the subscription statement before your name. Note, too, that the name I've entered is my actual name, not my electronic mail address. The LISTSERV is able to pull the information it needs out of the header of the message. Again, you can leave the Subject: field of your message blank, as the LISTSERV needs no information there. Send this message—and be sure you're sending to the LISTSERV administrative address rather than the regular mailing list address! You should quickly receive a message back letting you know what happened when you attempted to sign up. After sending the preceding mail to listserv@yorkvm1.bitnet, I received the message shown in Figure 9.4 (minus extraneous header information).

From this point on, I can expect my mailbox to swell with messages about the sage of Hannibal. Remember, from here on, messages you want to send to the list should be addressed to the list address, not the LISTSERV address. Similarly, administrative matters like signing off the list or suspending new messages while you're on vacation should all be handled through the LISTSERV address. What you don't want to do is to send an administrative request to the mailing list at large, which would cause it to circulate through all the subscribers' mailboxes. This would be embarrassing for you and aggravating for them, because it is a relatively common occurrence.

Here we must pause, because misusing a LISTSERV address is a fundamental network mistake. Every mailing list witnesses the annoying phenomenon of someone sending LISTSERV commands that are mailed out to all subscribers. Considering the volume of e-mail you're likely to encounter when you begin signing up for mailing lists, you won't appreciate such junk mail, and you won't want to be responsible for any yourself. So remember the principles:

- LISTSERV addresses are for administrative business, such as signing up to mailing lists, resigning from them, and so on. Again, the Twain list maintains its LISTSERV address as listserv@yorkvm1.bitnet.
- The list address is for sending messages to the entire mailing list. These are messages to the entire mailing list, messages that you want everyone to read. The Twain list uses twain-l@yorkvm1.bitnet for this purpose. Remember that the list address will generally have the -l suffix as part of its address, and you will be all right.

```
Dear networker,

   Your subscription to list TWAIN-L (Mark Twain Forum) has been accepted.

   Note: your distribution  options have been defaulted as per  the "SET TWAIN-L

REPRO" command.

   You may leave the list at any  time by sending a "SIGNOFF TWAIN-L" command to
LISTSERV@YORKVM1.BITNET  (or  LISTSERV@VM1.YORKU.CA).  Please  note  that  this
command  must NOT  be sent  to the  list address  (TWAIN-L@YORKVM1) but  to the
LISTSERV address (LISTSERV@YORKVM1).

   The  amount of  acknowledgement you  wish to  receive  from  this  list  upon
completion of  a mailing operation  can be changed by  means of a  "SET TWAIN-L
option" command,  where "option"  may be  either "ACK"  (mail acknowledgement),
"MSGACK" (interactive messages only) or "NOACK".

   Contributions sent to this list are  automatically archived. You can obtain a
list of  the available archive files  by sending an "INDEX  TWAIN-L" command to
LISTSERV@YORKVM1.BITNET  (or LISTSERV@VM1.YORKU.CA).  These files  can then  be
retrieved by means  of a "GET TWAIN-L filetype" command,  or using the database
search  facilities of LISTSERV. Send  an "INFO DATABASE" command  for  more
information on the latter.

   Please note that  it is presently possible for anybody  to determine that you
are  signed up  to the  list through  the use  of the  "REVIEW" command,  which
returns the network address and name of all the subscribers. If you do not wish
your name to be available to others  in this fashion, just issue a "SET TWAIN-L
CONCEAL" command.

   More information on LISTSERV commands can  be found in the LISTSERV reference
card,  which you  can  retrieve by  sending an  "INFO REFCARD"  command  to
LISTSERV@YORKVM1.BITNET (or LISTSERV@VM1.YORKU.CA).

Virtually,

   The LISTSERV management
```

Figure 9.4   A sample sign-up message for a BITNET mailing list.

Be sure you understand these fundamental principles before you become active on any mailing list. Using a LISTSERV will be a happier and more productive experience.

A general principle of computing applies here as well as elsewhere on the network— it's as important to know how to get out of something as it is to get into it. Many new-comers, excited by the wealth of knowledge and subject matter represented in the various kinds of mailing lists, subscribe to so many that their mailboxes contain hundreds of messages a day. Soon the traffic becomes overwhelming. To remove yourself from a mailing list, send mail to the LISTSERV address as before, but include the statement: **signoff** *listname.* To sign off the Twain list, for example, I would send the message **signoff twain-l** to the LISTSERV that maintains it. As you see, this information is included in the message from the Twain LISTSERV. This, incidentally, is why it's always a good idea to save the introductory message you receive from any mailing list. It will contain the basic instructions you need to handle such chores.

An alternative to resigning, of course, is to become such a whiz at mailbox manipulation that you sift through hundreds of messages a day and find the ones you want to read. I choose the latter course, because try as I may, I can't bring myself to leave many of the good lists. I often skim the message headers of a given list for a month or two without reading anything, but invariably something tweaks my interest and I'm back in.

It's common practice, incidentally, no matter how high your level of interest, to turn off the message flow if you plan to be out of town or otherwise away from your computer connection for any length of time. This prevents you from returning to a mountain of mail. To do so, send a **nomail** command to the relevant LISTSERV. For example, to suspend mail delivery from the TWAIN-L list, I would send:

```
set twain-l nomail
```

To reactivate the list, the command's opposite number is:

```
set twain-l mail
```

Another tool can be helpful when you're contemplating signing on to a mailing list. By sending a command to the relevant LISTSERV, you can receive information about the intended use of a given mailing list and the subscribers who currently use it (be advised—not all lists support this command). The form to follow is:

```
review listname
```

Use the LISTSERV address listed for the group you're interested in. To learn more about the Public-Access Computer Systems Forum, I could send the following command to pacs-l@uhupvm1.uh.edu:

```
review pacs-l
```

Soon I would receive a review message, as seen in Figure 9.5. The message will also include a list of subscribers, not shown.

LISTSERV Archives—Where the Treasure Is

But wait, we're not through with that Twain message. Take another look at it. Contributions to the list, it seems, are archived automatically. An index of the archived files can

```
*    Public-Access Computer Systems Forum
*
*    Review=         Public        Notebook=   Yes,N,Weekly,Public
*    Send=           Editor        Reply-tp=   List,Respect
*    Subscription=   Open          Stats=      Extended,Public
*    Formcheck=      No            Files=      Yes
*    Validate=       Store only    Mail-via=   Dist2
*    Errors-To=      Owner         Editor=     LIBPACS@UHUPVM1.UH.EDU
*
*    Owner= LIBPACS@UHUPVM1.UH.EDU
```

Figure 9.5 A review message provides background information about a mailing list.

be obtained by sending this command to the LISTSERV address: **index twain-l.** The files can be retrieved by using yet another command. Now we get an even broader glimpse of the powers of the LISTSERV system. Multiply the hundreds of lists you find in the document you retrieved from BITNIC and then consider the possibilities for archival storage of messages and other information inside those lists. Far from being a passive message-bouncing system, mailing lists emerge as a powerful research tool, provided you learn how to use it.

Let's get the index. After sending the **index twain-l** command to listserv@yorkvm1. bitnet, I receive the index partially shown in Figure 9.6. Interesting. I've compressed the figure to show you examples of the different kinds of information available here. Toward the top of the figure are such things as a user's manual and a book of quotations from Twain. I note that I can retrieve any of these through the **get twain-l *filename*** command. To understand what this means, note how the index is structured. The filename and filetype are separated. In the case of, let's say, the user's manual, the filename is survival, while the filetype is guide. And if you look further down in the figure, you'll see that we can also retrieve electronic texts of Twain's works in the same way. Each has a filename and filetype specified—the item called *A Ghost Story* is listed with a filename of ghost, and a filetype of text. And if you read across the figure, you'll see that access to these items is open to all. So, too, is access to the items at the bottom of the figure, where we see a list of logs from the mailing list. The list's activity from each month is evidently catalogued here.

Let's retrieve *A Ghost Story*. To do so, I send the command **get twain-l ghost** to the now familiar LISTSERV address, listserv@yorkvm1.bitnet. In return, I receive the story, which I can now read or search on my own computer. I can retrieve one of the logs the same way. If I want to see the log from April 1995, I can request **get twain-l log9504** from the same address. In return, I receive a list of all messages that moved across the mailing list during this period. Using archival files like these is an excellent way to catch up with a mailing list. If you want to know what the major issues are and how current messages fit in with the previous flow, retrieve a few earlier files and study them. No comment made in the list is lost.

It is helpful to know that back records of a mailing list are available, but studying each of them could become quite a chore if I were after, say, comments on a particular title. Let's say I want to find what people are saying about *Huckleberry Finn* in these parlous, multicultural times. Is there any way to home in on those messages just about Huck? Fortunately, the answer is yes.

LISTSERV's Database Capabilities

Look back at the original sign-up message from the Twain list, where you'll see that not only can we retrieve files, we can search for them using the LISTSERV database function. Remember, we can't use BITNET interactively because of the limitations of the gateway connections between it and the Internet. But the LISTSERV system includes database capabilities that can be used in so-called batch mode, meaning we can construct a complete search, submit it to a LISTSERV, and let the computer at the other end run its procedures, sending us the results. In this way, we can extract what we need from a given list's archives without having to go through the entire index.

To activate the procedure, we must use the LISTSERV Command Job Language Interpreter (CJLI), a set of conventions that the LISTSERV can work with. The follow-

```
*   TWAIN-L FILELIST for LISTSERV@YORKVM1.
*   TWAIN-L FILELIST for LISTSERV@YORKVM1.
*
*
**********************************************************************
*
*                          rec              last - change
*   filename filetype  GET PUT -fm lrecl nrecs  date     time    File description
*   -------- --------  --- --- --- ----- -----  --------  -------- ----------------
*
*   :::::::::::::::::::::::::::::::::::::::::::::::::::::::::::::::::::::
*
*   Miscellaneous files
*
*   :::::::::::::::::::::::::::::::::::::::::::::::::::::::::::::::::::::
*
*     The GET/PUT authorization codes shown with each file entry describe
*     who is authorized to GET or PUT the file:
*
*       ALL = Everybody
*       OWN = List owners
*
*   :::::::::::::::::::::::::::::::::::::::::::::::::::::::::::::::::::::
      SURVIVAL GUIDE     ALL OWN V     72    829 95/03/28 22:23:06 User's manual
      MT       QUOTES    ALL OWN V     65    118 92/12/19 17:09:46 Quotes by MT
      TWAIN    RESOURCE  ALL OWN V     72    161 94/01/02 15:12:10 Organizations
      TWAIN-L  OLDLOG    ALL OWN V     76    243 92/07/08 11:58:43 11 Mar 92 ff.
      MTP      INFO      ALL OWN V     75    363 92/07/16 20:35:11 MT Project
      TWAIN    SEX       ALL OWN V     67    453 93/11/02 14:17:03 Was Twain gay?
      TWAIN    OED       ALL OWN V     72   5697 93/11/28 00:17:14 Cites in OED

---- skipped material ----

* Electronic texts of works by Mark Twain
*
      TSA      TEXT      ALL OWN V     62   4406 93/05/30 18:21:16 TS Abroad
      TSD      TEXT      ALL OWN V     59   3085 93/05/30 18:21:25 TS, Det.
      ADAM     TEXT      ALL OWN V     57    512 93/07/29 00:43:54 Adam's Diary
      CRIME    TEXT      ALL OWN V     60    210 93/11/01 11:17:44 A New Crime
      ECONOMY  TEXT      ALL OWN V     60    299 93/07/29 00:44:11 Political Econ
      GHOST    TEXT      ALL OWN V     60    323 93/07/29 00:44:21 A Ghost Story
      JIMMY    TEXT      ALL OWN V     72    152 93/10/31 19:09:12 Sociable Jimmy
      NIAGARA  TEXT      ALL OWN V     60    361 93/07/29 00:44:31 Niagara

----skipped material ----

TWAIN-L  LOG9204     ALL OWN V     74     14 92/04/27 11:06:34 Started on Mon,
27 Apr 1992 08:03:48 -0700
   TWAIN-L  LOG9204D    ALL OWN V     73    146 92/04/24 16:59:28 Started on Fri,
24 Apr 1992 16:56:19 EDT
   TWAIN-L  LOG9205     ALL OWN V     80    262 92/05/31 20:30:51 Started on Wed,
27 May 1992 09:23:36 CDT
   TWAIN-L  LOG9206     ALL OWN V     80   1273 92/06/26 14:42:49 Started on Mon,
1 Jun 1992 08:35:00 LCL
   TWAIN-L  LOG9207     ALL OWN V     80   1424 92/07/30 14:10:15 Started on Wed,
1 Jul 1992 01:13:04 EDT

----etc.---
```

Figure 9.6 The index to the TWAIN-L mailing list.

ing is a sample search I constructed to look for messages containing the word *Huck* in the Twain archives:

```
//
Database Search DD=Rules
//Rules DD *
Search Huck in TWAIN-L
Index
/*
```

Examine this search routine for a moment. It's not necessary to master all the intricacies of the LISTSERV CJLI to put it to work. The basic template follows:

```
//
Database Search DD=Rules
//Rules DD *
command 1
command 2...
/*
```

We'll use this template as our search mechanism; LISTSERV understands what it means. I'll focus on the lines marked command. As you can see from the preceding sample search, the first command is clear-cut—search for any messages that include the word *Huck*. I've also asked that the results include an index telling us which messages meet the search criteria. We run the search by sending it directly to listserv@yorkvm1.bitnet. We get back the list shown in Figure 9.7.

As you can see, we found 287 messages meeting the search criteria, of which I've shown only a few. Of those listed, item number 82 seems germane; it, at least, has the title of the book listed as its subject. Let's also ask for messages 53 and 55, to find out what Huck has been up to in Hollywood and, to wrap it up for now, item 117. To retrieve these messages, we need to send another message to the LISTSERV. Use the same template, only with a different command inserted:

```
//
Database Search DD=Rules
//Rules DD *
Search Huck in TWAIN-L
Print all of 27 53 55 82 117
/*
```

As before, we'll receive a message about the status of our request and a file including the information we specified. In this case, we get our five messages, which turn out to be about cinematic treatments of Huck Finn, including one four-hour version shown on Public Television.

There's plenty of material here, but remember, TWAIN-L is but one of the numerous mailing lists available through our Internet gateway into BITNET. Browsing through the master list of mailing lists, another possibility emerges for Twain discussions. Because you don't have to be a member of the mailing list to get into its archives, you can explore freely through the wide range of possibilities. Here's the entry for a list specializing in American literature:

```
AMLIT-L    AMLIT-L@MIZZOU1.BITNET
     American Literature Discussion Group
```

```
Search Huck in TWAIN-L
--> Database TWAIN-L, 287 hits.

> Index
Item #   Date     Time   Recs   Subject
------   ----     ----   ----   -------
000011 92/05/31 13:15    26    Re: Hannibal, MO
000012 92/05/31 19:40    43    Hannibal
000014 92/06/01 10:07    39    RE: Hannibal
000027 92/06/05 13:09    37    RE: The Adventures of Mark Twain
000051 92/06/19 17:39    24    Re: stirring conversation up again -Reply
000053 92/06/22 08:03    37    Mark Twain in the movies
000055 92/06/22 09:42    20    Re: Mark Twain in the movies
000082 92/07/07 13:32    33    Huck Finn
000084 92/07/08 12:13    24    Old TWAIN-L log file
000086 92/07/12 13:38    24    MT books in machine-readable form?
000087 92/07/13 08:46    20    Re: MT books in machine-readable form?
000088 92/07/14 09:01   428    RE: Information on the Mark Twain Project and Its +
000091 92/07/21 00:04    17    Claymation _Adventures of MT_
000092 92/07/22 02:32    55    HF ms. reunited (UPI fwd)
000096 92/07/28 23:32    41    Was Huck Black?
000097 92/07/29 14:05   102    Howe's Fishkin's Twain's Huck
000098 92/07/29 15:53    44    FISHKIN BOOK
000099 92/07/30 14:06    14    re. Afro-American Huck
000113 92/09/08 22:51    18    Re: mt quote
000115 92/09/09 15:11    71    slc quote about Canadian book
000117 92/09/15 15:17    15    Rationales for banning _Huck Finn_?
```

Figure 9.7 Search results from a search of the TWAIN-L database, looking for information on Huckleberry Finn.

Surely there will be more Twain material here. Let's find out. The address is handled just as before. We need to contact not the distribution site, but the LISTSERV; we know, therefore, to mail to **listserv@mizzou1.bitnet.** First we'll ask for an index of files in the archive. The command, if previous experience is our guide, should be **index amlit-l,** providing AMLIT-L maintains an archive. Bingo. After sending that command to the LISTSERV, we receive back the index shown in Figure 9.8.

Now we know there's an archive there. Let's try something different; we will ask for any messages referring to *A Connecticut Yankee in King Arthur's Court.* Here's the basic search strategy:

```
//
Database Search DD=Rules
//Rules DD *
Search Connecticut Yankee AND Twain in AMLIT-L
Index
/*
```

Note that rather than searching under one word only, I asked to see the terms *Connecticut Yankee* (this should save us from people who are merely writing in from Connecticut—their address line might trigger our search) and I added *Twain* into the mix. I capitalize AND because it's, strictly speaking, a *Boolean operator,* otherwise known as a *logical operator.* Named after nineteenth century British mathematician George Boole,

```
   AMLIT-L FILELIST for LISTSERV@MIZZOU1.
*
*  Archives for list AMLIT-L (American Literature Discussion Group)
*
*  :::::::::::::::::::::::::::::::::::::::::::::::::::::::::::::::::::::
*
*  The GET/PUT authorization codes shown with each file entry describe
*  who is authorized to GET or PUT the file:
*
*      ALL = Everybody
*      OWN = List owners
*
*  :::::::::::::::::::::::::::::::::::::::::::::::::::::::::::::::::::::
*
*
*  NOTEBOOK archives for the list
*  (Monthly notebook)
*                                rec              last - change
* filename filetype   GET PUT -fm lrecl nrecs   date      time     Remarks
* -------- --------   --- --- --- ----- -----  --------  --------  ----------------
  ---------------
  AMLIT-L  LOG9404    ALL OWN V     87 12514 94/04/30 17:48:24 Started on Fri,
  1 Apr 1994 02:08:20 -0400
  AMLIT-L  LOG9405    ALL OWN V     82 11394 94/05/31 23:19:54 Started on Sun,
  1 May 1994 12:52:34 -0700
  AMLIT-L  LOG9406    ALL OWN V     80  6742 94/06/30 21:55:17 Started on Wed,
  1 Jun 1994 07:37:43 -0500
  AMLIT-L  LOG9407    ALL OWN V     80  5154 94/07/27 20:11:44 Started on Fri,
  1 Jul 1994 05:40:09 -0500
  AMLIT-L  LOG9408    ALL OWN V     87 17099 94/08/31 23:41:42 Started on Tue,
  2 Aug 1994 16:53:02 -0400
  AMLIT-L  LOG9409    ALL OWN V     90 15426 94/09/29 18:01:43 Started on Thu,
  1 Sep 1994 09:50:27 -0500
  AMLIT-L  LOG9410    ALL OWN V     80  9205 94/10/31 19:48:06 Started on Fri,
  30 Sep 1994 23:37:00 UTC
  AMLIT-L  LOG9411    ALL OWN V     80 10297 94/11/30 23:56:48 Started on Tue,
  1 Nov 1994 11:16:55 EST
  AMLIT-L  LOG9412    ALL OWN V     80 10775 94/12/31 04:35:26 Started on Thu,
  1 Dec 1994 00:11:04 -0600
```

Figure 9.8 A portion of the index to the AMLIT-L mailing list.

Boolean operators are used to specify the logical relationship between two concepts. In this case, the relationship is obvious—I want to see files containing both terms.

Figure 9.9 shows what happens when I send this search routine. Hmmm. Only four hits. Let's retrieve one of them.

```
//
Database Search DD=Rules
//Rules DD *
Search Connecticut Yankee AND Twain in AMLIT-L
Print all of 168
/*
```

And we retrieve a message discussing Twain's views of science in the novel.

```
> Search Connecticut Yankee AND Twain in AMLIT-L
--> Database AMLIT-L, 4 hits.

> Index
Item #    Date    Time   Recs    Subject
------    ----    ----   ----    -------
000578  94/05/04 23:26    13     Re: Demi-Hawthorne
000580  94/05/05 14:35    21     Re: Demi-Hawthorne
003071  94/11/21 14:08    41     Hello
006111  95/04/15 11:00    16     Connecticut Yankee
```

Figure 9.9 A search of AMLIT-L for *A Connecticut Yankee in King Arthur's Court.*

Delving Deeper into the Database

Using these LISTSERV database functions isn't elegant. But despite their clunky construction, these search statements can be useful tools for hunting information, and it behooves people seriously interested in using the networks as research tools to master their command structure. Before proceeding with a more refined search, then, let's consider how to get a complete set of database commands targeted especially to people with little knowledge of database systems. As always, the network helps us build up our online library.

What You Need: A Primer on LISTSERV Databases

The Document: Revised LISTSERV Database Functions

How to Get It: Through BITNET Network Information Center.

Send command **info database to listserv@bitnic.bitnet.**

You'll receive a lengthy document recounting basic LISTSERV database procedures, including search strategies that allow you to home in on precise information. BITNET's interface may be ragged, but the quality of the searches you can construct is limited only by your willingness to master its command structure. It would be nice to have interactive access to these databases; we wouldn't have to send multiple jobs to the LISTSERV, searching for information first, then asking for a specific retrieval. You can see why the move toward folding BITNET's formerly separate mailing procedures into the broader Internet is gaining such momentum. The quality of its discussions and archived information makes us hope for a time when it is easier to use by a broader audience.

Tapping LISTSERVs as a Reference Source

With the basic search strategy in mind, then, and with knowledge that a huge group of LISTSERV mailing lists exists, let's consider how we can use them as a reference source. We'll choose a subject and send a message to the LISTSERV at the BITNET Information

Center, asking it which lists apply most closely to our topic. Then we'll go into the archives and see if we can pull up anything of interest. You never know what might appear; this is like searching a huge library which only yields up its card catalog piece by piece as you move along your research path. Some searches yield more than you'd expect; others come up disappointingly short. The only way to know is to try.

For purposes of the hunt, assume we're interested in learning more about what's going on with the Hubble Space Telescope. The controversial orbiting observatory has been dogged by problems, yet it seems to be producing some interesting results despite them. What do experts in the field think about Hubble, and what are the chances it will still become the breakthrough telescope of the 1990s, as we had all along assumed it would be?

The first step in the search is to query BITNIC for which lists might apply. To do this, the routine is as follows. We'll send a command to listserv@bitnic.bitnet:

```
list global / space
```

The topic is intentionally broad; perhaps there's a list specifically devoted to the Hubble project, but by casting a wide net, we can look through the results and decide which list best meets our criteria. Don't be put off if your initial query yields few or no results. I searched the list first under the term *astronomy* and found nothing. But I knew there had to be an active set of discussions on these topics—too many researchers are on-line for there not to be. The choice of *space* as an alternate search term bore fruit, as the results in Figure 9.10 indicate.

The trick now is to decide which of these lists is the most likely to pay off. The News about Space from SEDS looks promising. We'll send a **review sedsnews** command to listserv@bitnic.bitnet. Figure 9.11 shows the relevant part of the reply. This looks like interesting material. Now we want to retrieve an index of available files. The Twain list has shown us how. We'll send the command **index sedsnews** to listserv@tamvm1. tamu.edu to see if there's an archive there. And yes, a message returns, listing what seem to be extensive logs from 1989 to present. So let's query that database as in the following:

```
//
Database Search DD=Rules
//Rules DD *
Search Hubble in SEDSNEWS
Index
/*
```

Back comes a remarkable list, some 750 citations on Hubble in this area. Clearly, we've stumbled upon a repository of space information. Figure 9.12 presents just a glimpse of this bounty.

As before, it's easy to pull one of these documents in. Let's get 9665, which talks about Hubble monitoring weather on other planets. We'll do it this way:

```
//
Database Search DD=Rules
//Rules DD *
Search Hubble in SEDSNEWS
Print all of 9665
/*
```

```
Excerpt from the LISTSERV lists known to LISTSERV@BITNIC on 27 Apr 1995 14:48
Search string: SPACE

************************************************************************
* To subscribe, send mail to LISTSERV@LISTSERV.NET with the following *
* command in the text (not the subject) of your message:              *
*                                                                      *
*                    SUBSCRIBE listname                                *
*                                                                      *
* Replace 'listname' with the name in the first column of the table.  *
************************************************************************

Network-wide ID  Full address and list description
---------------  ---------------------------------
AEROSP-L         AEROSP-L@SIVM.BITNET
                 Aeronautics & Aerospace History

CANSPACE         CANSPACE@UNBVM1.BITNET
                 Canadian Space Geodesy Forum

ISSS             ISSS@JHUVM.BITNET
                 International Student Space Simulations

NASMNEWS         NASMNEWS@SIVM.BITNET
                 National Air & Space Museum (NASM) Events at the Smithsonian

NETSPACE-STATS   NETSPACE-STATS@NETSPACE.ORG
                 Statistics about NetSpace

PASGC-L          PASGC-L@PSUVM.BITNET
                 Pennsylvania Space Grant Consortium

SEDSNEWS         SEDSNEWS@TAMVM1.TAMU.EDU
                 News about Space from SEDS

SNYSPACE         SNYSPACE@SNYCENVM.BITNET
                 SUNY Facilities Coordinators List

SPACE            SPACE@UBVM.BITNET (Peered)
                 SPACE Digest
                 SPACE@UGA.BITNET (Peered)
                 sci.space.tech Digest

SPACE-L          SPACE-L@WVNVM.BITNET
                 SPACESTAT User's Group

SPACE-SH         SPACE-SH@UGA.BITNET
                 sci.space.shuttle Digest

SPACENWS         SPACENWS@UGA.BITNET
                 sci.space.news digest

SPACEPOL         SPACEPOL@GWUVM.BITNET
                 Seminar Class:  IAFF 290 - Issues in Space Policy
                 SPACEPOL@UGA.BITNET
                 sci.space.policy digest

SPACESCI         SPACESCI@UGA.BITNET
                 sci.space.science digest
```

Figure 9.10 A search of BITNIC for space-related mailing lists.

```
    News about Space from SEDS
*
*   SEDSNEWS is an open list for distribution of informational postings
*   from several space research facilities. VERY ACTIVE. Be sure your mailer
*   can handle lots of traffic.
*   This list enhances the SEDS-L list which is an open discussion list.
*
*   REVIEW=         PUBLIC          NOTIFY=    YES
*   Send=           Public          Reply-to=  List,Respect
*   Subscription=   Open            Stats=     Normal,Public
*   X-Tags=         No              Files=     No
*   Ack=            No              Mail-via=  Distribute
*   LOOPCHECK=      NOTOCOUNT       NOTEBOOK=  YES,H,WEEKLY,PUBLIC
*   Errors-to=      OWNERS          Filter=    Only,POSTMASTER@*
*   Newsgroups=     bit.listserv.sedsnews
*   Safe=           Yes
*
*   Local=TAM*,*.TAMU.EDU
*
*   OWNER= FHD@TAMVM1.TAMU.EDU              (H. Alan Montgomery)
```

Figure 9.11   A description of the **SEDSNEWS** database.

```
009546 95/02/25 18:47   253   Space Calendar - 02/25/95
009555 95/03/01 16:03    17   XAFS
009579 95/03/04 19:24    67   ESA astronauts assigned to Tethered Satellite Syst+
009591 95/03/04 22:36  2215   STS-67 Press Kit (Forwarded)
009595 95/03/04 23:21   144   New ways to set the cosmic clock
009635 95/03/11 20:27    29   New Hubble Images of Comet Shoemaker-Levy Impacts
009653 95/03/17 15:28    53   Next Hubble Briefing Looks at Weather on Mars and +
009665 95/03/21 13:23    93   Hubble Monitors Weather on Neighboring Planets
009680 95/04/05 11:47    63   space news from Jan 2 AW&ST
009681 95/04/05 11:46    87   space news from Dec 12/19 AW&ST
009684 95/04/06 14:16    61   Hubble Images Distant Galaxies Through Cosmic "Zoo+
009694 95/04/07 14:08    59   Hubble Sees Oxygen-Rich Supernova Debris in Nearby+
009695 95/04/08 13:03    49   space news from Jan 9 AW&ST
009701 95/04/13 14:25    59   Hubble Views Neptune and Vesta
009705 95/04/19 11:36    94   Hubble Discovers New Dark Spot on Neptune
009706 95/04/19 11:40    94   Hubble Maps Surface of Vesta
009707 95/04/19 11:45    93   Vesta: Science Background
009708 95/04/19 14:02    18   Re: Hubble Maps Surface of Vesta
009710 95/04/20 21:12     9   Re: Hubble Discovers New Dark Spot on Neptune
009712 95/04/21 11:58    55   Top Ten Hubble 5th Anniversary Images Available
009717 95/04/24 14:16   346   Fifth Anniversary of Hubble Launch
009728 95/04/28 06:55   103   space news from Jan 16 AW&ST
```

Figure 9.12   Results of a search of **SEDSNEWS** for information on the Hubble space telescope.

Now we receive our first document from SEDS, which turns out to be a lengthy discussion about the early formation of galactic clusters which was originally issued as a NASA press release. We're in business. So far we've just asked this database for information about Hubble, and we got back far too many hits to read through them all. We must find a way to confine our search to a specific set of statements, homing in on what we want.

Narrowing Down the Search

We might, for example, become interested in Hubble's problems with its mirror. What exactly was wrong with it, and how adequate was its repair by the space shuttle? To run this search, we need to combine search statements as follows: **Search (hubble AND mirror) AND shuttle in SEDSNEWs.** Here, we've nested our search terms. The computer at the other end will search for every item mentioning both Hubble and the word *mirror;* it will then narrow the field by culling only the hits that also include the word *shuttle.* Let's see what happens.

```
//
Database Search DD=Rules
//Rules DD *
Search (hubble AND mirror) AND shuttle in SEDSNEWS
Index
/*
```

Figure 9.13 shows the response. Let's get several: 7196 looks useful, as it concerns Hubble testing. We'll also look at 7276, which discusses extravehicular missions in the rescue attempt, and 7535, which deals with servicing the telescope. We'll now change the search strategy to reflect what we need, though again embedding it in the standard search template.

```
//
Database Search DD=Rules
//Rules DD *
Search (Hubble AND Mirror) AND shuttle in SEDSNEWS
Print all of 7196 7276 7535
/*
```

By return mail, we receive the desired messages. We receive NASA updates, and a note about the servicing mission flown by the shuttle to correct the problems on the Hubble platform. What's happened to Hubble? An "aspherical aberration" in its primary mirror, for one thing. SEDSNEWS is filled with more details, if you're interested.

Using Logical Operators

Notice in the preceding search strategy how we *nested* terms; that is, we've included one set of terms inside another. The command we sent the LISTSERV was **Search (hubble AND mirror) AND shuttle.** The database looked for any documents containing both the terms *hubble* and *mirror.* It then checked for documents meeting that criteria that also contained the term *shuttle.* All of which produced a number of documents that helped us home in on our data.

```
> Search (hubble AND mirror) AND shuttle in SEDSNEWS
--> Database SEDSNEWS, 47 hits.

> Index
Item #   Date     Time   Recs    Subject
------   ----     ----   ----    -------
000157  90/03/28  12:04  149   Nasa News, 3/28/90
000329  90/07/05  18:14   92   NASA Headline News, 7/05/90
000375  90/07/28  19:19   90   NASA Headline News, 7/27/90
000385  90/08/08  15:33   74   THE HUBBLE SPACE TELESCOPE WILL MAKE IMPORTANT DIS+
000397  90/08/14  20:34  115   NASA Headline News, 8/14/90
000797  90/12/28  17:47  132   NASA Headline News, 12/27/90
001120  91/04/28  11:12   75   HUBBLE SPACE TELESCOPE COMPLETES FIRST YEAR
001966  91/10/17  17:58  138   NASA Headline News 10/17/91
002735  92/02/10  22:19  509   List of Large Astronomical Projects
002751  92/02/12  03:37  136   space news from Oct 28 AW&ST
002798  92/02/20  05:06   78   space news from Nov 11 AW&ST
002810  92/02/21  07:05  156   space news from Jan 20 AW&ST
003154  92/04/04  01:02  547   Large Astronomical Project Listing (long)
003722  92/06/25  21:58 2479   STS-46 Press Kit (Forwarded)
003815  92/07/06  21:32 1570   SpaceViews - July Boston NSS newsletter
003889  92/07/13  21:17 2680   STS-46 Press Kit [Updated version] (Forwarded)
004592  92/10/06  23:27  129   NASA Daily News for 10/06/92 (Forwarded)
004609  92/10/07  20:24  155   NASA Daily News for 10/07/92 (Forwarded)
004618  92/10/08  21:31  125   NASA Daily News for 10/08/92 (Forwarded)
004983  92/11/21  00:53  138   NASA Daily News for 11/20/92 (Forwarded)
005076  92/12/08  19:25  134   NASA Daily News for 12/02/92 (Forwarded)
005402  93/01/20  01:46  255   1992 - A Year To Remember
005724  93/03/08  23:24  289   JPL fact sheet
005760  93/03/12  16:12  119   Building WF/PC-2
006401  93/06/02  17:37   77   WFPC-2 Shipped
006497  93/06/15  21:11 2019   NASA media guide and public affairs contacts April+
006635  93/07/05  23:11 2791   STS-51 Press Kit (Forwarded)
006746  93/07/19  02:24  156   space news from May 24 AW&ST
006748  93/07/19  20:17  145   space news from May 31 AW&ST
006850  93/08/05  18:04  132   WFPC-2 Installation into HST
007196  93/09/30  01:01   95   Hubble instrument may receive further testing [Rel+
007275  93/10/13  20:03  202   Europe and the Space Telescope
007276  93/10/13  20:03  214   Five EVA sessions: The most complex Shuttle missio+
007277  93/10/13  19:54  251   The Space Telescope's three-year harvest
007278  93/10/13  20:05  215   The Hubble Space Telescope: Report on plans for th+
007302  93/10/21  21:24 1482   ACTS Acronyms
007367  93/10/31  07:23   80   NASA Daily News for 10/26/93 (Forwarded)
007404  93/11/12  03:15  478   JPL/Wide Field and Planetary Camera-II fact sheet +
007419  93/11/12  16:26 1927   STS-61 Press Kit (Forwarded)
007443  93/11/17  21:37   43   HQN93-66/STS-61 LAUNCH DATE SET
007454  93/11/19  08:10  160   * SpaceNews 22-Nov-93 *
007489  93/11/30  18:09  315   Claude Nicollier: The European astronaut bound for+
007535  93/12/05  06:27  272   Space Telescope servicing -- detailed mission prog+
007553  93/12/07  06:35   61   MCC Status Report 10
007557  93/12/07  15:47   72   MCC Status Report 11
007559  93/12/08  02:43   72   MCC Status Report 12
007561  93/12/08  15:17   84   MCC Status Report 13
```

Figure 9.13 A more complex search for information on Hubble's mirror, relating it to a shuttle repair mission.

But if you examine the list of hits from that search, you'll notice some of them are from 1990. Because we want to be as up-to-date as possible, we want to confine our searches to more recent postings. We can do it by including a data range in our search statement. Suppose I've chosen to look for any documents after January 1, 1995. I'd frame the statement:

```
//
Database Search DD=Rules
//Rules DD *
Search Hubble in SEDSNEWS since 95/1/1
Index
/*
```

In this case we have limited the search to all articles published after a certain date. You might not be as concerned about date limitations in certain fields; searching the TWAIN-L list for messages about Huck Finn, for example, probably wouldn't require you to limit the date so severely. But highly technical subjects that change quickly demand a date strategy.

Maybe you'd like to confine the search within a certain range of dates. Perhaps you read a message you want to recover. You know it appeared some time in January or February 1995, but can't recall the exact day. To set up this kind of search, the following strategy will work:

```
//
Database Search DD=Rules
//Rules DD *
Search hubble in SEDSNEWS from 95/1/1 to 95/3/1
Index
/*
```

Still not sure if you can find the desired message? You can use an asterisk to create an index of all messages in a given period. The following strategy will create such an index for November 1994, returning all messages from the month.

```
//
Database Search DD=Rules
//Rules DD *
Search * in SEDSNEWS from 94/11/1 to 94/12/1
Index
/*
```

The Revised LISTSERV Database Functions document we retrieved earlier provides a thorough grounding in search strategies. You should print it out now and examine its examples to learn the byways of using logical operators, especially if the strategy you need is complicated. Here are two other ways to use Boolean operators to set up a search strategy:

The OR operator: **Search mirror OR shuttle in SEDSNEWS**

Here we've told the LISTSERV to pull any document mentioning the word *mirror* or the word *shuttle;* the two terms don't have to be in the same document for the search to record a hit.

The NOT operator: **Search hubble NOT mirror in SEDSNEWS**

Here we've told the LISTSERV we're interested in a different kind of filtering process. We want messages mentioning Hubble, but are not particularly interested in those discussing its mirror problems. The search strategy above will pull only those Hubble messages without the word *mirror*.

Strategies can be thorny indeed, as a glance through some of the five- and six-line examples in Revised LISTSERV Database Functions will quickly establish. This is, of course, a major reason why these archival resources aren't used more frequently. But the the material is out there for those willing to make the effort.

Adding to the Library

Let's take a breather and generate some more reading material. Standard documents, like the Twain sign-on message we received, often point in the direction of new files that can help. They're like footprints in the sand; follow them and you'll often uncover unsuspected resources. I keep three-ring binders for printouts of such files, and they get heavy use as I work through the various BITNET commands. Try out your LISTSERV expertise now by retrieving these files:

What You Need: A BITNET Background Document and a Guide to BITNET On-Line Etiquette

The Documents: BITNET Userhelp, Mail Manners

How to Get Them: Through the BITNET Network Information Center. Send messages to this address:

listserv@bitnic.bitnet.

One message should read:

get bitnet userhelp.

This will get the background document. The other message should read:

get mail manners.

This will retrieve the etiquette document.

The BITNET Userhelp document is useful, approaching BITNET basics from the standpoint of the new user. But because we're drawing on BITNET information from an account on the Internet, not all the commands and user tips listed in the document are applicable to us. Remember, our only real link between the Internet and BITNET is our ability to move electronic mail between the two networks; direct file transfer between the two is not possible, nor do BITNET's protocols make interactive access feasible. But read through the document anyway; it's still a gold mine of background information. BITNET is a powerful resource despite its built-in limitations.

The BITNET Network Information Center, it's becoming clear, is a major stop on our quest for information on this network. It makes sense, then, to see what else is available in its archives. Print out the list and keep it with your other BITNET materials. The answers to most BITNET questions can be found in these files.

What You Need: An Index of Files at BITNIC

The Document: LISTSERV Filelist

How to Get It: Through the BITNET Network Information Center. Send a message to this address:

listserv@bitnic.bitnet

The message should read:

get netinfo index

The BITNET Network Information Center, incidentally, offers several interesting services you may want to consider. The free EDUPAGE electronic newsletter keeps you abreast of breaking stories in the information technology field. And consider some of the other EDUCOM possibilities listed here:

What You Need: An Electronic Newsletter on Networking Developments

How to Get It: Send e-mail to:

listproc@educom.edu

The body of the message should read:

sub edupage *your name*

In addition to English, the newsletter is available in Portuguese and Spanish. For more information, write to:

edunews@nc-rj.rnp.br

You may also be interested in another electronic service, a biweekly summary of EDUCOM news. To subscribe, send mail to:

listproc@educom.edu

with the message:

sub update *your name*

And you may want to check out the Electronic Newsstand for information from *EDUCOM REVIEW*, a hard-copy magazine focusing on learning, communications, and information technology. You can reach the Electronic Newsstand via Gopher at gopher.internet.com.

BITNET via USENET

Proving once again that the Internet loops around and through itself (a bit like the worm ourobouros, the legendary critter that eats its own tail), it's possible to pull in certain

BITNET mailing lists without any direct access to BITNET at all. Certain USENET newsgroups are a redistribution of some of the more popular BITNET lists. The Electronic Music Discussion Group, which the List of All LISTSERV Lists defines as EMUSIC-L@AUVM, shows up through USENET as bit.list-serv.emusic-l. The BITNET list on WordPerfect for Windows listed as WPWIN-L@UBVM makes a USENET appearance as bit.listserv.wpwin-l. And so on.

The difference? For one thing, only selected BITNET lists are distributed this way. And as opposed to regular BITNET lists, which allow you to receive the periodical postings in your mailbox, USENET access means you must go into the relevant newsgroup and activate a News Reader program like trn or WinVN to read postings. If you read a lot of newsgroups anyway, this may be the preferred method.

To find out which mailing lists are maintained on USENET, you need an updatable information posting.

What You Need: An Updated List of BITNET Lists on the Internet

The Document: Bit/Bitlist

How to Get It: Through the USENET newsgroup news.answers, where it's posted periodically.

Finding the Right Mailing List

With BITNET traffic increasingly routed through the Internet, several types of LISTSERVs now in use, and still more mailing lists managed directly by their moderators, we run into an unusual problem. As opposed to the USENET newsgroups, which are highly visible and updated on a regular basis when you log on to your service provider's computer, mailing lists can be hard to find. The new user may not know they exist, much less how to find a particular list that suits his or her interests. As always, the decentralized nature of the Internet ensures that, while the information is readily available on-line, the only people who will be able to find it readily are the people who already know where to look.

Fortunately, there are several ways to track down this information. Stephanie da Silva maintains an ongoing list of what's currently available. This is no small feat, since mailing lists are in a state of constant flux, with new ones being added as interests coalesce and old ones sometimes dying of attrition. Da Silva is representative of the people who perform yeoman work for the Internet community by bringing order to the chaos of the networks; the Internet, it is no exaggeration to say, could hardly proceed without them.

To receive da Silva's list, you have several options, perhaps the easiest of which is to subscribe to one of the several possible USENET newsgroups—news.lists, news.announce.newusers, or news.answers—where the list is posted as it undergoes regular revisions. I recommend news.answers, because it's a newsgroup where Frequently Asked Questions documents are posted, providing a window onto the information riches of USENET; we'll discuss how to use USENET newsgroups in Chapter 11. But there's also a quick FTP alternative, which I'll explain in a moment. I also list the massive List of Interest Groups compiled and maintained (currently) at SRI International Network

Information Systems Center in Menlo Park, California, which is available by FTP and several other sources:

- For the da Silva list, called Publicly Accessible Mailing Lists, try anonymous FTP to the following URL:

```
ftp://rtfm.mit.edu/pub/usenet/news.answers/mailing-lists/
```

The files are listed as part1, part2, and so on. You can use the FTP **mget** command to download multiple files in sequence.

- For the SRI List of Interest Groups, try this URL:

```
ftp://sri.com/netinfo/interest-groups.Z
```

This is a big file, so you may want to get it once for reference, and then rely on the USENET newsgroups to keep you up to date thereafter.

- A useful document called Some Lists of Lists, compiled by Marty Hoag, is likewise available, and can help you in your search for a particular topic. To obtain it, send mail to listserv@vm1.nodak.edu. Your message should read:

```
get list of lists
```

The Subject: field may be left blank.

- A useful, searchable resource is found on the World Wide Web, where you can contact the Directory of Scholarly E-conferences, a page that includes mailing lists as well as newsgroups. This list has been maintained for years by Diane Kovacs, of Kent State University Libraries, and made available first through FTP, then through the medium of the Web. You can see its Web site in Figure 9.14. Here, I have entered a request for mailing lists on biology; the server has produced the results shown. Each of them is a hyperlink, so that I can click on any of the entries to receive further information about the list. To use the keyword search of Kovacs' list, access the following URL:

```
http://www.austin.unimelb.edu.au:800/1s/acad
```

Or, if you prefer to dig into these files by FTP, you can try the following URL:

```
ftp://ksuvxa.kent.edu/library/acadlist.index
```

And if you want to receive the file by mail, send a message to listserv@kentvm.kent.edu; the message should read:

```
get acadlist index
```

Non-Automated Mailing Lists

A look through any of the preceding resources will demonstrate once again how many subjects can be discussed in the mailing list format. Figure 9.15 describes a mailing list called alife, which, according to da Silva's list, is maintained at a computer at UCLA in California.

Remember the mailing list principle: Addresses for routine maintenance and actual list participation are different. The centralized hub of the alife list is at UCLA. Electronic mail sent to this specific address will be redistributed to a list of people who have requested that they be added. What you see in Figure 9.15 is an address, alife-request@cognet.ucla.edu, which is actually one of two mailing list addresses that apply. Note the word -request in the middle of the address. It tells you that this is the address used to request entry onto the mailing list.

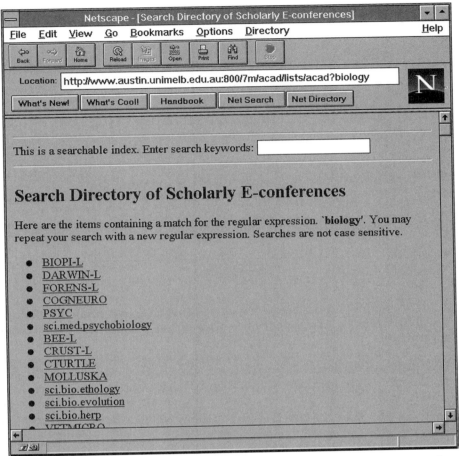

Figure 9.14 The directory of scholarly E-conferences includes mailing lists as well as newsgroups.

Now here is an important point. Lists whose addresses contain the word -request, unlike those run by a LISTSERV, are not automated. To join one, you would write to the address and simply ask permission to be included, and you should include your mailing list in the body of the message, as not all mail headers arrive intact. The need for exacting syntax disappears; you're now dealing with a person who's reading your message.

Suppose I want to sign up to the Animators List shown in Figure 9.16. The address is analogue-request@magnus.acs.ohio-state.edu. My mail session might look something like the following:

```
% mail analogue-request@magnus.acs.ohio-state.edu
Subject: Subscription
Could you please add me to the mailing list? My address is
gilster@interpath.net.
Thanks!
Paul Gilster
```

```
alife
      Contact: alife-request@cognet.ucla.edu

      Purpose: The alife mailing list is for communications regarding artificial
      life, a formative interdisciplinary field involving computer science, the
      natural sciences, mathematics, medicine and others.  The recent book
      _Artificial Life_, Christopher Langton, ed., Addison Wesley, 1989 introduces
      the scope of artificial life as a field of study.  Alife was chartered in
      February 1990 at the Second Artificial Life Workshop, held in Santa Fe &
      organized by the Center for Nonlinear Studies at the Los Alamos National
      Laboratory and the Santa Fe Institute.  The list is intended primarily for
      low-volume, high-content scientific correspondence and as a publically
      accessible forum for the interested members of the public.  Membership as
      of July 1990 includes archives/repository of past traffic, software and
      papers.  The list is maintained by the Artificial Life Research Group,
      Computer Science Department, Lindley Hall 101, Indiana University
      Bloomington, IN 47405. There are conditions on redistribution of the list
      in order to minimize any misunderstanding or exaggeration concerning this
      new area of study.
```

Figure 9.15 . Description of a typical mailing list.

And it shouldn't be long before a message appears, confirming my entry onto the list. I will also receive a document or two about the list containing guidelines and other information.

The -request part of the address, then, tells you that this is where administrative details for this mailing list are performed. It plays the same role as a LISTSERV address does, but you are speaking to a human being instead of a computer. And like LIST-SERVs, mailing lists like these maintain a separate address for their message traffic. This is where comments from list members are sent; once there, they are circulated to all other members of the list. The correct address for such mailings will be sent to you when you subscribe to the list.

So use the -request address for administrative functions only, and be sure to use it when you ask to be added to or deleted from the list. As soon as you begin to read mailing lists you'll realize that a key to keeping them functioning smoothly is this division of tasks. People who send administrative requests to the entire group of subscribers are doing nothing but taking up space in other people's mailboxes. Expect a few sarcastic comments if you make this elementary *faux pas*.

This situation most often arises when people want to resign from a mailing list. They send a message requesting their removal, often via the regular address rather than through the proper -request address. And when the administrator doesn't respond immediately—as is often the case, considering that people have other things to do than maintain mailing lists—a series of increasingly hostile messages follows, each of them going out to the entire list. Not only do the messages serve no purpose (the administrator will certainly honor such a request once he or she encounters it!), they break the continuity of any ongoing discussions and lower the tone of debate for everyone.

Thus, use caution when dealing with a mailing list, whether sending administrative messages or posting to the entire group. Many postings are limited in nature; you might, for example, want to send e-mail directly to someone who left a message for the group, informing that person of a particular thought he or she should have considered, or

```
Analogue Heaven
     Contact: analogue-request@magnus.acs.ohio-state.edu (Todd Sines)

     Purpose: The Analogue Heaven mailing list, founded in late 1992, is an unmoderated
     mailing list catering to the needs of those interested in vintage analogue electronic
     music equipment. Frequent for-sale items, repair tips, equipment modifications, ASCII &
     GIF schematics, and general contemporary & historical discussion of new and old analogue
     synthesizers, sequencers, drum machines, and effects units are common topics of the
     mailing list.  There is an FTP/Gopher site located at cs.uwp.edu with past discussions on
     various machines, a definitive guide to Roland synths, patch editors, modification
     schematics, GIFs/JPEGs of vintage synths, as well a few sound samples of some of the gear
     itself.


Animators List
     Contact: animate-request@xmission.com

     Description: This mailing list discusses aspects of creating animation, ranging from
     hand-drawn films to computer animated pieces. Artistic, technical and consumer concerns
     are addressed. Participants share information about equipment, programs and techniques.

     For animators or people interested in becoming animators. This is not just for fans of
     animation.

     Web Site: http://www.xmission.com/~grue/animate

     Last change: Mar 95


exotic-cars
     Contact: exotic-cars-request@sol.asl.hitachi.com (Joe Augenbraun)

     Purpose: The exotic-cars mailing list is a discussion group where owners and admirers of
     exotic cars can talk about all aspects of  them: buying, selling, maintaining, driving,
     styling, outlandish stories about Enzo, etc.

     An exotic car is a performance-oriented production car that was built in limited numbers.
     Ferraris, Lamborghinis, Maseratis, and Aston Martins all are exotics, Camaros aren't.
     There's a lot of grey area in between there, and discussion has ranged through some of
     the grey area.  Most of the discussion, though, has been about cars that fit well within
     the exotic definition given above.

     To subscribe, send a message saying that you wish to subscribe to
          exotic-cars-request@asl.hitachi.com

     Last change: Mar 95


ht_lit
     Contact: kmennie@chat.carleton.ca (K.M. Mennie)

     Purpose: ht_lit is a list for the discussion of hypertext fiction, hypertext theory, &
     hypertext and literary studies. More information is on the web:
     <a href = http://chat.carleton.ca/~kmennie/ht_lit.html>here</a>

     To subscribe, send a message to
          subscribe@journal.biology.carleton.ca
     with
          subscribe ht_lit
     in the body of the message.

     Last change: Feb 95
```

Figure 9.16 Sample descriptions of mailing lists.

```
orienteering
     Contact: orienteering-request@graphics.cornell.edu (Mitch Collinsworth)

     Purpose: Discussion of the sports of orienteering and rogaineing. Orienteering is the
     sport of navigating through unknown terrain with the use of map and compass.  It is
     commonly conducted either running or cross-country skiing depending on the season.
     Rogaineing is a similar sport with the main differences being that it is done over long
     distances and in teams rather than individually.

     Available in both digest and mailing list formats.  Please specify which you prefer when
     subscribing.  This list is gatewayed to the Usenet group rec.sport.orienteering.

     Last change: Mar 95
```

Figure 9.16   (*Continued*)

expressing your unhappiness with one of the other posters on the list. It's easy (too easy, some would say) to use your mail program's reply function to do this, with the result that what you have to say goes not only to your intended recipient, but to the entire list.

There is an axiom among those who fly for a living, which says that there are two kinds of pilots: those who have landed with the landing gear up, and those who will. Similarly, there are two kinds of mailing list participants: those who have embarrassed themselves with the public promulgation of a private message, and those who will. If you can learn from your mistakes, you will do this only once.

Figure 9.16 shows some examples, drawn more or less at random, of the kind of mailing lists you'll encounter when browsing the da Silva list (I have weighted the figure toward -request lists, but the da Silva list also contains the entire range of LISTSERVs; it's quite comprehensive).

As we found with LISTSERV lists, these -request lists also maintain archives; at least, many of them do. For example, the list called Analogue Heaven makes files available at an FTP site, while the Animators List also maintains a World Wide Web server, as does the list called ht_lit (the latter, which specializes in hypertextual fiction, is also managed by an individual; note that you write to a specific person's e-mail address to subscribe). An FTP site means the material in the list is being stored on a computer at the site listed; you can download it at your discretion, but you don't have to use the clumsy command language and mail your requests, as you have to do with BITNET. A Web page gives the list even greater flexibility in displaying past documents and archiving files.

Tapping a List Site

Let's go into the Animator's List archives and see what we can find. The URL:

```
http://www.xmission.com/~grue/animate
```

We'll examine how to contact these World Wide Web URLs in Chapter 14; for now, simply note the kind of information available. You can see the result in Figure 9.17. Notice how the Web has provided expanded access to the mailing list's resources. The intent of the list manager is to include on this page animations created by list members, as well as papers written by them, and job openings in the industry. If we were to scroll down through this page, we would also find complete information about the Animators List,

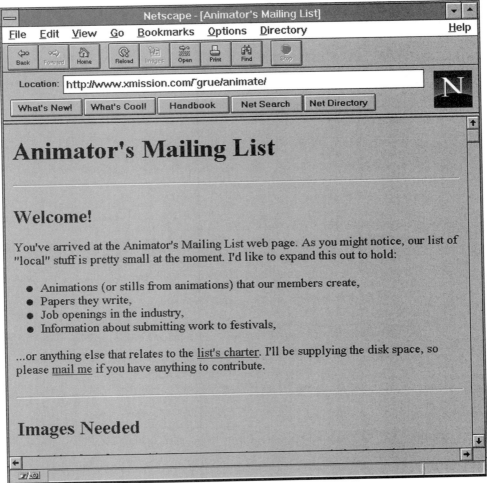

Figure 9.17 A mailing list archive as viewed through the World Wide Web.

links to other animation resources on the Internet, and a list of books on the subject. As the Web expands, such list-related sites will supplement and enhance the e-mail based activity of the subscribers. Always check to see whether a mailing list you are involved with maintains an FTP site or World Wide Web page.

Keeping Up with Mailing Lists

One of the keys to using the Internet effectively is to keep up with new areas of interest as they arise. A basic subscription, therefore, should be to a list called newlists. It's designed to tell you about each new list as it appears. Using newlists, you'll get in on the ground floor of groups that particularly interest you. Figure 9.18 shows an example of the kind of message (minus the usual header information) you'll receive when the newlists mailing list is feeding your mailbox regularly.

```
MILHST-L on LISTSERV@UKANVM.BITNET          Military History
       or LISTSERV@UKANVM.CC.UKANS.EDU

   MILHST-L is an unmoderated list provided as a forum for discussion by
   scholars and students of Military History.  It is intended to serve
   Service historians, academic historians, and those for whom military
   history is a non-professional but abiding interest.

   Comments and discussions of the military affairs of any period or
   place are welcome, and social, economic, and political factors are
   considered an integral part of the subject.

   Given the wide scope of the subject, subscribers should take
   particular care to make their subject lines clear and descriptive.

   MILHST-L is an international list and will have no "official"
   language.  Contributors may choose the idion in which they feel most
   comfortable and which they believe will be best suited for
   communicating their thought to the list membership.

   To subscribe, send by e-mail to LISTSERV@UKANVM or
   LISTSERV@UKANVM.CC.UKANS.EDU with the following message in the BODY:

      SUB MILHST-L yourfirstname yourlastname

   Postings should be sent to MILHST-L@UKANVM on BITNET or to
   MILHST-L@UKANVM.CC.UKANS.EDU on the Internet.  and problems should be
   reported to the owners.

   Owners:  Patrick Hughes   JPHUGHES@UKANVM.BITNET
                        or   JPHUGHES@UKANVM.CC.UKANS.EDU
            Lynn Nelson      LHNELSON@UKANVM.BITNET
                        or   LHNELSON@UKANVM.CC.UKANS.EDU
```

Figure 9.18   An example of a message from the newlists mailing list.

What You Need: Announcements of New Mailing Lists

How to Get Them: By subscribing to the newlists list. Contact the list at this address:

listserv@vm1.nodak.edu

Your message should read

subscribe new-list *your_name*

If you decide to subscribe to a list, be advised: There is no guarantee you can get in. Although I've yet to be refused entry to any list (and subscribe to quite a few), there is no automatic right of entry into any of them. For one thing, the moderator and readers of the list are in charge; how they choose to restrict access is up to them. For another, restricted access may imply not so much a desire to keep people off the list, as a need to conserve system resources. After all, maintaining a mailing list takes time and effort, as well as storage space on the moderator's computers. If such resources are limited, the number of subscribers may need to be capped.

The Future of BITNET

For some time now, the need for BITNET to upgrade its services has been obvious. The network had hitherto been limited to a maximum transmission speed of 9600 bits per second, whereas other networks are moving toward information exchange in the range of millions of bits per second. The failure of a single BITNET node could block a file from going through to its destination, while Internet mail can find an alternate route when a particular link fails. And BITNET was never interactive for outside users; your Internet connection wouldn't allow you to do anything more than send the kind of automated requests we've worked with in the last few pages. That's quite a contrast to interactive Telnet and FTP, not to mention WAIS, and what's happening with the World Wide Web.

The BITNET II project, begun in 1989, was an attempt to improve on these limitations by allowing BITNET traffic to move over the high-speed TCP/IP links that drive the Internet. These changes added dynamic routing capabilities and reduced the cost of leased lines, while converting to TCP/IP also meant that a LISTSERV could use an Internet-style address, with the Domain Name System employed instead of the eight-character names common to BITNET. The result: a gradual merging of the networks in terms of what the user sees. You no longer have to work so hard to interpret a BITNET address, for example, as it's usually listed in Internet format. BITNET III is further proof that CREN intends to continue the revitalization of these valuable mailing lists and let them grow with the worldwide Internet.

At present, we see a mixture of the old and the new. Many BITNET sites retain their identity, but numerous others have simply closed their nodes and now operate solely through the Internet. Again, this does not mean that the mailing lists that have proven so valuable to scholars and researchers have disappeared from the scene; far from it. But they're now using the Unix listserv software, or one of the other software tools dedicated to distributing mailing lists. We'll examine these mailing lists in the next chapter, explaining how to use them.

On the level of the individual computer user, the role of electronic text continues to be intriguing. I've always had a weakness for magazines, for example. New subscription offers tempt me on a regular basis, and my mailbox is generally stuffed with everything from computer journals to newsletters on cooking techniques and magazines about music and science. But somewhere along the line, as you get involved with networked mailing lists, you begin to realize that your time isn't infinite. I can read only so much in a given day, and I get so much out of my network participation through mailing lists that I'm reluctant to exit from any of them.

We've yet to move to a paperless office, despite decades of promises and the bright prospect of high-end scanners and optical character recognition (OCR) software. So I assume there will always be a place for *The Financial Times, Bon Appetit,* and *BBC Clas-*

sical Music Magazine at my house. But the interactive nature of on-line mailing lists, and the certain promise of refined user interfaces in the future, makes them a tough act to top. The growing presence of on-line journals means that more and more of my reading will take place on a computer screen, or through the auspices of my laser printer.

These new forms of communication are clearly here to stay, with implications we're only beginning to understand. In the next chapter, we'll look at some different permutations of electronically delivered text. Next stop: a host of on-line journals, and several projects that make the dissemination of formerly print-limited words their *raison d'etre*.

Electronic Magazines, Newspapers, and Project Gutenberg

Although the Internet has a bright future in the realms of digitized audio and video, it continues to carry huge amounts of information in purely textual form. ASCII text is far from dead, notwithstanding a torrent of interest in multimedia. In fact, if we step back from the technological edge to consider how to distribute information widely, we invariably fall back on ASCII. You must have a properly equipped workstation to view Internet video (discussed in Chapter 17), but even an antiquated 8088 computer can display straight ASCII. And anyone talking seriously about developing a digital library out of today's networks must consider how to make that library's information accessible.

In his superb book *Silicon Dreams: Information, Man, and Machine*, Robert W. Lucky ponders the relationship between pictures and text. The eleventh edition of the *Encyclopedia Britannica*, published in 1911 and said to be the last attempt to distill the entire range of human knowledge, contained approximately one picture for every four pages of text. The 1985 edition of the same encyclopedia contains two pictures per page, most of which are color photographs. Digitize the latter and you would find that most of the bits that resulted would be devoted to pictures, because pictures demand massive amounts of storage space as compared to text.

As Lucky notes, without the pictures, the digitized *Britannica* loses almost none of its information content. Without the text, the encyclopedia becomes useless. The row of video tapes in which I archive my old movie collection contains more bits than all the books that line my library shelves. But no one would compare the quality of information provided by my collection of Bogart movies to what's available in my set of G. K. Chesterton's works, or, for that matter, my battered collection of P. G. Wodehouse.

What's going on here? As our culture continues to replace textual information with pictures, we must ask whether the content of our information is not spiraling downward. True, we continue to widen the data pipeline, making it relatively simple to transmit pictures to remote destinations. But is a picture really worth a thousand words? Or is the truth that a word is worth a thousand pictures? I suspect the second statement is closer to being correct, because words involve the human imagination in ways that pictures can't. As Lucky puts it, ". . . pictures are the fast food, the junk food, of the information age."[1]

None of which is to deny the exciting possibilities of real-time video and audio. But our fascination with the image can obscure the fact that literature has existed for millenia without such graphic niceties. The human imagination is the beneficiary of today's networking technology; it would be a shame to focus so tightly on digitizing CNN news or an NCAA basketball game that we neglect to mine our culture's wealth of textual data. As we will see in this chapter, a series of on-line text projects are now working hard to prevent that outcome.

Growing directly out of the wide circulation of ideas through text, electronic journals are also coming into vogue, providing unprecedented delivery mechanisms to those interested in a host of topics. As these on-line publications attest, the Internet holds the potential for supplementing traditional publishing techniques and, in many cases, improving on them. From the standpoint of the social welfare—disseminating as much of our cultural inheritance as possible through the most accessible means—nothing beats Project Gutenberg, an attempt to spread billions of copies of electronic texts worldwide within the next 10 years. Add the Online Book Initiative and you have a concerted effort to change the way we view the written word.

We must also factor in what appears to be an exponential increase in the number of newspapers that are about to take the plunge into the Internet. Early electronic editions, like the *San Jose Mercury News*, appeared through commercial services like America Online or CompuServe, but cost considerations as well as an interest in broadening their audience have led editors to embrace the Internet. They've seen that the trend toward graphical browsing tools and the World Wide Web is evidently unstoppable, and want to combine their content—complete text, in many cases, with accompanying photographs, maps, and diagrams—with the hypertextual ease of access the Web handles so well. Maybe we won't all read our morning paper in front of a computer screen, but electronic editions allow editors to present their content in efficient new ways; you can search back issues, for example, or target precisely the kind of story you want to see.

Ambitious? Sure, but these and other on-line text projects are thriving. Along with their growth comes a continuing dialogue about the potential for the electronic medium to create a massive repository of cultural information—you can sit in on these deliberations through the contacts this chapter provides. In other words, don't be seduced by sight and sound. The real work of the Internet proceeds through the explosion of ideas, mediated by a delivery system as old as Sumeria—the written alphabet and its digital representation as text.

The Electronic Publishing Edge

People have been saying for a long time now that electronic communications would eventually replace paper. In fact, one vision of the early desktop computer days was that computers had rendered paper obsolete. The "paperless office" was a utopian notion; we would all work in offices without filing cabinets, transacting our business on computer terminals, handling all incoming correspondence as electronic mail. Those retrograde souls who persisted in sending us paper mail wouldn't constitute a problem; we'd simply feed their letters into our scanners and work with the digital representations of their work.

The paperless office may yet appear, but not any time soon. Despite advances in scanning technology and optical character recognition, paper is still being generated, aided and abetted by the ease that modern printer technology brings to the process of printing. Nor, despite a drumbeat of theorizing, have electronic news vendors knocked our traditional newspapers out of the running. There's reason for thinking they never will; despite our environmental concerns, it's far more satisfying to have a second cup of coffee over a morning newspaper than while reading a morning computer screen full of news.

But don't count electronic publishing out. The benefits of this medium are so striking that it's certain to grow in importance as the network resources available to it make delivery ever easier. And while we'll leave news gathering and dissemination to a later chapter, our discussion of proliferating text is the ideal place to consider the growth and implications of on-line journals. Those who minimize the importance of mailing lists, for example, don't realize how much exciting publishing is going on within them, nor do they take advantage of the wealth of research material these ventures are generating every day.

Perhaps the best way to view electronic publishing is as an adjunct to the traditional publishing industry. The early implementers in this field tended to be journals that were relatively specialized in nature; Oxford University Press, for example, which we consider momentarily, has shown interest in publishing scholarly journals over the Internet, where their quick dissemination allows for scholars to stay updated on work in their fields. This shouldn't surprise us. When editors can be reasonably sure that their magazines' audience will have network connections because of academic affiliations or because of the nature of the topic, the benefits of the medium begin to emerge: easy-to-access archives of past issues; searchable indices; sharply reduced costs, due to unnecessary postal and production expenses.

The broadening of the arena to include newspapers and magazines like *TIME* and *WiReD*, to name but two prominent examples, comes about because of the changes in the Internet's audience that have occurred within the past several years. This worldwide network is no longer in the hands of specialists, and it was only a matter of time before the huge changes in network demographics would be noticed by smart editors who were looking for new ways to reach their subscribers, and to entice new ones. While the mass circulation magazines and newspapers are engaged in exciting network forays now, we can expect the next few years to be laden with new ventures and the on-line appearance of old ones.

We are, in short, on the verge of an explosion in publishing, the likes of which haven't been seen since the surge in popular literature that came about in the Depression years in the United States. Newsstands then were jammed with reading material; new titles proliferated, many of them dropping by the wayside after short runs, some going on to become standards in the marketplace. There will surely be numerous false starts in the electronic publishing field, but so, too, will there be unexpected successes, as the details of fomat and an evolving consensus on design begin to emerge. A key issue: The appearance of reliable billing mechanisms, which will take the Internet publishing industry out of the realm of experiment and into the commercial world for good.

Scholarly Journals Go Electronic

If you're at all familiar with Oxford University Press, it won't surprise you to learn that the prestigious publishing house publishes a journal called *Postmodern Culture*. After all, the publication sounds like Oxford's cup of tea. It's a peer-reviewed journal of criticism on contemporary literature, aesthetic theory and culture, with an interdisciplinary twist. And while the journal has been published at North Carolina State University since September 1990, it's never had the kind of clout behind it that Oxford can provide.

So what's the news? What intrigued the editors of *The News & Observer*, Raleigh's hometown paper, enough to give the story prominent placement and a color photo of the journal's editors was this: *Postmodern Culture* is entirely electronic. Its distribution, handled through Internet connections worldwide, began through a mailing list and continues in vibrant form on the World Wide Web.

Reaching *Postmodern Culture* is as simple as going to the right address on the World Wide Web (we'll examine how to do this in Chapter 14). For now, note the URL:

```
http://jefferson.village.virginia.edu/pmc/contents.all.html
```

This is a computer at the University of Virginia, which joins North Carolina State University and Oxford in this publishing venture. When you view this site with a graphical browser, you see an attractively formatted Web page that allows you to examine the current issue or to see archived past issues. Figure 10.1 shows the table of contents of one recent issue.

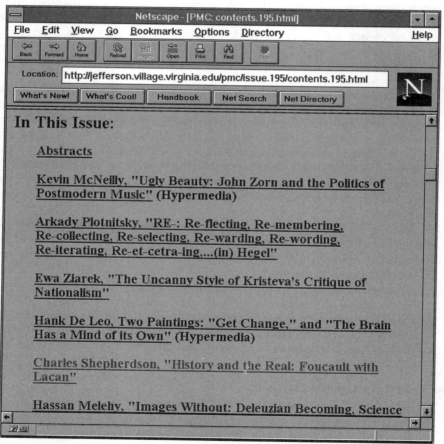

Figure 10.1 *Postmodern Culture's* presence on the World Wide Web.

Note that all of these feature articles are hypertextual in nature; click on one of them to call it up to the screen. You have at your disposal the complete text of the journal, along with reviews of recent books and other commentary. What's more, *Postmodern Culture* is taking advantage of this new medium in an extraordinary way. The publication offers an interactive site, shown in Figure 10.2, in which scholars can engage in on-line conversations about topics of the moment. These discussions are then archived and made available for future reference.

You reach this page by following a hyperlink from the main *Postmodern Culture* page. Based upon the number of archived discussions, the site has seen plenty of traffic.

Postmodern Culture is not Oxford's first venture into the realm of electronic publishing. Indeed, the press set up an electronic publishing research unit in late 1985 and began releasing products into the electronic markets in 1988. According to another on-line publication, *Public-Access Computer Systems News,* Oxford currently produces over 50 electronic packages ranging from general reference materials to science, medicine,

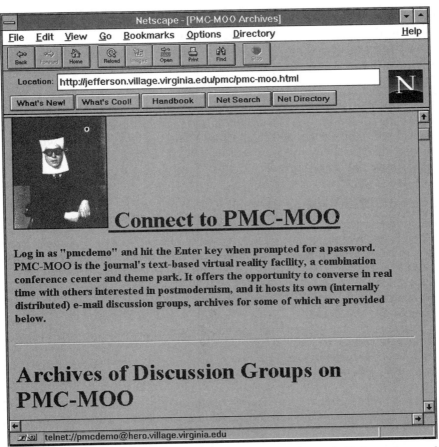

Figure 10.2 An interactive site allows the journal's readers to hold discussions and maintain them in archives.

the humanities, and social sciences. But *Postmodern Culture* is Oxford's first *networked* electronic publication.

Why would a conservative publishing house like Oxford become so involved in on-line communications? Why, for that matter, would the editors of an academic journal decide networked distribution was the optimum way to reach their readers? If you consider the disadvantages of traditional print media, the answers begin to emerge. A printed and bound journal can take months, even years, to produce, whereas electronic publication is much quicker. Particularly in the fields of science and technology, reducing the lag time before getting material into print can be significant.

On the other hand, the electronic publishing frontier raises questions. *Postmodern Culture*, for example, can also be retrieved article by article through electronic mail, a useful way to access it for those without the benefits of graphical Web browsers. If the printed version of a journal, or its Web equivalent, presents articles in a single issue for review, should an electronic journal always do the same? Or does it make more sense to distribute articles singly, as they arrive, thus keeping a constantly updating database of features available for readers? For that matter, for those without Web access, is it better to receive a journal in the form of abstracts sent to your mailbox, along with further information about how to access the full article? These questions and more continue to define the debate about the electronic journal.

Our most glittering breakthroughs often have retrograde implications; that is, they call up echoes of a past we thought long abandoned. Think of Charles Dickens, whose novels, giant tomes like *Bleak House* and *David Copperfield*, once appeared in the form of serial publications, a chapter at a time. Electronic publishing lets you release a journal an article at a time, building up a comprehensive collection of material at a central archive site, if that is your chosen method. The technique seems workable, and as we're about to see, has proven itself worthwhile; you get your material while it's "hot off the presses." The real issue for publishers now will be to define their medium, particularly as they move out onto the Web.

PACS-L: Electronic Publishing by Mail

One on-line journal I have found useful I discovered by browsing through the network, where I found a mailing list called PACS-L, the Public-Access Computer Systems Forum. The remarks I read implied it was filled with discussions of network issues; in particular, PACS-L seemed to be concerned with the electronic dissemination of documents and the significance of the medium. These issues already intrigued me. In fact, I was just then beginning to track Project Gutenberg, a remarkable attempt to create an on-line library of literary works.

The List of Lists we retrieved earlier showed this entry for PACS-L:

```
PACS-L        PACS-L@UHUPVM1.UH.EDU
              Public-Access Computer Systems Forum
```

Using the address listed, I sent a subscription request: **subscribe pacs-l Paul Gilster.** In PACS-L, I learned about the Public-Access Computer Systems News, an electronic newsletter. Subscribing to the newsletter was equally simple. I sent a message to the same address, with the message **subscribe pacs-p Paul Gilster.** PACS-P was also listed in the master list:

```
PACS-P        PACS-P@UHUPVM1.UH.EDU
              Public-Access Computer Systems Publications
```

A subscription to PACS-P brought *Public-Access Computer Systems News* and another publication called *Public-Access Computer Systems Review*. The first of these, according to the information accompanying it, is published irregularly at the University of Houston, and contains news of happenings in the world of electronic publishing. Among the news items in my first issue was the story on Oxford University Press announcing its plans for *Postmodern Culture*.

The concept seemed simple enough: publish a battery of articles on the topic in question and distribute the articles through the network to subscribers rather than by traditional postal methods. The benefits in terms of cost savings and reduced time to destination were clear. After looking through *Public-Access Computer Systems Review*, I began to understand the potential of the medium. Traditional journals include references to articles used in research, but to track them down you have to go to the library. An electronic journal can rely on a text archive, so references are easy to check by calling up the article itself over the network.

Electronic text also speeds retrieval of back issues. Traditional journals stack up in a library or, worse still, in your closet at home. Finding an article in a two-year-old issue of a particular journal is a hassle, involving checking dates and page numbers before finding the article. Electronically archived back issues can be made available on-line. A quick scan through the *Public-Access Computer Systems Review* materials made it clear they are doing just that. As with the Mark Twain list, the PACS publications contained numerous index files. Back issues were available by sending to the LISTSERV the command:

```
/INDEX PACS-L
```

The system works like a charm. For my purposes, finding information on the current state of electronic journals, it would be hard to overstate how useful these electronic archives turned out to be. The *PACS Review* contains numerous articles available on-line. I found Edward M. Jennings' "EJournal: An Account of the First Two Years," Ann Okerson's "The Electronic Journal: What, Whence and When?" and a helpful piece called "Online Journals: Disciplinary Designs for Electronic Scholarship," by Teresa M. Harrison, Timothy Stephen, and James Winter.

Figure 10.3 contains a sample of the cumulative index I retrieved from the PACS-L server.

The index went on for several pages, with articles on electronic publishing, information policy at universities, managing a LISTSERV discussion group, document retrieval systems, and CD-ROM technology. In addition to the feature articles, there were regular columns and reviews of various books, as well as editorials. All in all, it would be hard to locate a better repository of information on this new medium. On-line dissemination leaves traditional modes of publishing in the dust—try going to your local library and tracking down up-to-the-minute data on electronic journals. What a contrast!

To retrieve the files I was interested in, I sent an e-mail message to listserv@uhupvm1.uh.edu, the address listed on the PACS cumulative index file. (As we've seen, I could also have used listserv@uhupvm1.bitnet; either would have gotten through.) I sent the command **get bailey1 prv2n2 f=mail** to retrieve a very challenging symposium on

```
SCHLABAC  PRV5N1      ALL OWN V      65     624 94/03/15 10:31:48
CAPLAN    PRV5N1      ALL OWN V      65     206 94/03/15 10:32:02
CONTENTS  PRV5N2      ALL OWN V      65     137 94/04/25 14:10:29
BAILEY    PRV5N2      ALL OWN V      65     472 94/04/25 14:10:43
CONTENTS  PRV5N3      ALL OWN V      65     140 94/06/21 15:11:26
PRICEWIL  PRV5N3      ALL OWN V      65     755 94/06/21 15:11:42
CONTENTS  PRV5N4      ALL OWN V      65     144 94/07/26 15:47:34
WIELHORS  PRV5N4      ALL OWN V      65     743 94/07/26 15:48:07
CRAWFORD  PRV5N4      ALL OWN V      65     138 94/07/26 15:48:21
CONTENTS  PRV5N5      ALL OWN V      65     153 94/08/24 13:35:16
BARRY     PRV5N5      ALL OWN V      65    2659 94/09/19 16:36:42
CRAWFORD  PRV5N5      ALL OWN V      65     151 94/08/24 13:36:03
CONTENTS  PRV5N6      ALL OWN V      65     158 94/09/19 14:59:52
MORGAN    PRV5N6      ALL OWN V      65     984 94/09/19 15:00:08
CRAWFORD  PRV5N6      ALL OWN V      65     149 94/09/19 15:00:26
CONTENTS  PRV5N7      ALL OWN V      65     160 94/11/22 15:42:27
PRICEWIL  PRV5N7      ALL OWN V      65    1020 94/11/22 15:42:51
CAPLAN    PRV5N7      ALL OWN V      65     251 94/11/22 15:43:18
CONTENTS  PRV6N1      ALL OWN V      65     159 95/03/21 17:05:46
BAILEY    PRV6N1      ALL OWN V      65     779 95/03/21 10:34:40
INDEX     PR          ALL OWN V      65     480 95/03/21 10:57:35
```

Figure 10.3 A portion of the index from the PACS server.

the uses of the new medium. As you can see from the excerpted index, each file contains a precise accession statement. The **f=mail** comment tells the server to send the article through the mail system.

When the article arrived, I saved it as a file using pine's export command. I then downloaded the file from the host computer. Alternatively, I could have used the Unix more command to page through it a screen at a time to make sure it was something I could really use before downloading it. And needless to say, this archived material is a powerful repository of information when you add LISTSERV database search capabilities into the mix.

Journey to the Newsstand

While publications can be made available in a variety of formats, there is no question that the World Wide Web is becoming the publishing mechanism of choice. Current as well as back issues are made available by hypertext link, while the Web's way with graphics ensures that illustrations and covers from these issues can be presented along with the text. You can see a typical magazine site in Figure 10.4.

The magazine, *Sunset,* is a prominent regional magazine available on newsstands all over the United States. If you will examine the figure, you'll see that covers from its back issues are presented below the introductory text. Each of these covers is set up as a hyperlink; click on any of them to go to that issue. Figure 10.5 shows the May 1995 issue.

You'll notice that the scroll bar to the right of the Netscape browser screen indicates that more of the page is available. If we were to scroll down this page, we would find hyperlinks to any article that had been published in that issue. Usefully, there is also a search capability on this page, letting you enter a keyword and examine the issue for what you need.

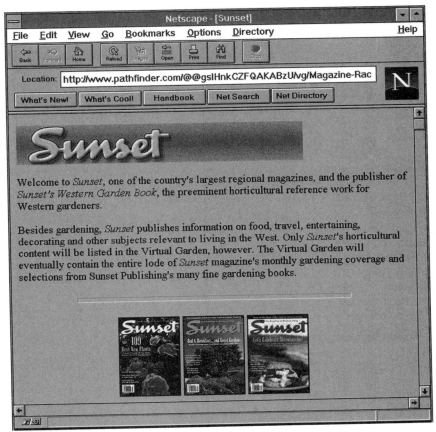

Figure 10.4 *Sunset Magazine* takes a position on the Internet.

Figure 10.6 shows you a specific article; this one is about growing basil in your garden. The full text is presented along with accompanying illustration of a dwarf dark opal basil plant.

The main *Sunset* Web page also provides you with the ability to send a letter to the editor, as well as a link to *Sunset*'s Virtual Garden, an on-line resource for the home gardener.

Interested in learning more about on-line magazines? One site that will definitely be worth your time is this one:

```
http://www.pathfinder.com/
```

Pathfinder is a Web site created by TIME Inc., publishers of *Sports Illustrated, Fortune, People, Southern Living, Money, Sunset,* and, of course, *TIME Magazine* itself. The company is adding to its content on the Web on a daily basis, with the kind of display and searching capabilities that make its offering truly useful. Figure 10.7, for example, shows you the current selection for *Money Magazine*'s Personal Finance Center. Notice that search capabilities are built in. Each of these entries is a hyperlink, so you can thread your way through the current issue with ease.

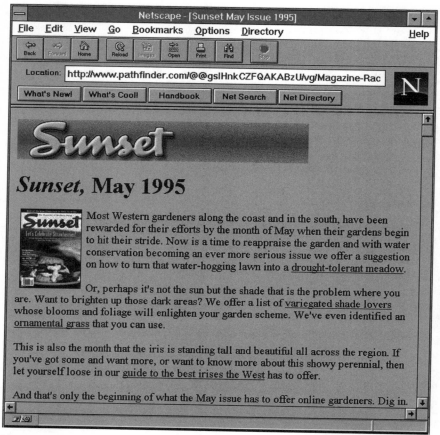

Figure 10.5 Examining an issue of *Sunset Magazine* on-line.

As is usual with Internet resources, I found myself pausing in my research as I ran across still further links to information I hadn't realized was available. *Money Magazine* provided an article on emerging markets investing that absorbed me for a time; I then ran into its Investor Databank, which contains a database of company profiles from The Reference Press. As the number of on-line magazines continues to grow, we'll find more and more information that can be searched using rapidly evolving Web searching engines like those described in Chapter 14.

No newsstand worth its salt doesn't contain a wide selection of newspapers, so let me clue you in on another priceless site. The address is:

```
http://marketplace.com/e-papers.list.www/e-papers.home.page.html
```

This is a World Wide Web page containing several hundred newspaper projects; it's continually updated, so if you're looking for a particular newspaper, this is the place to start.

Both large dailies and small town and regional weeklies appear on this list. Take a look at the Casper Wyoming *Star-Tribune*, which has established a particularly full-featured Web site at its URL, as shown in Figure 10.8.

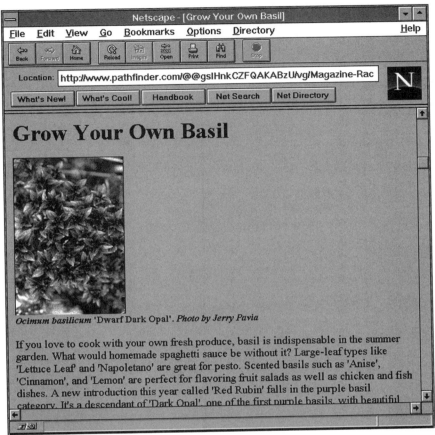

Figure 10.6 The full text of an article is supplemented by graphics, making for an attractive screen presentation.

`http://www.trib.com/news/wyoming/docs/wyonews.html`

Here, I'm examining the local news, and have the capability of searching past issues as well. The Trib also offers a searchable Associated Press service, an on-line comics page, video clips from CNN, and national and international news.

    Many newspapers are taking advantage of the hypertextual nature of the Web to offer links to other news sources. In Figure 10.9, you can see the *San Jose Mercury News* page. It contains an emphasis on business uses of the Internet, with clickable links to the major commercial sites and directories. The news is then presented with hyperlinks to related stories and columns. Such information sources are an indication that newspaper editors are moving in haste to discover what advantages the Internet can hold for their publications. Expect this trend to intensify in the coming five years.

Magazines by FTP and Gopher

    The World Wide Web is an ideal medium for magazines, since it lets them exploit page formatting, illustrations, and all the touches that give a printed journal its visual appeal.

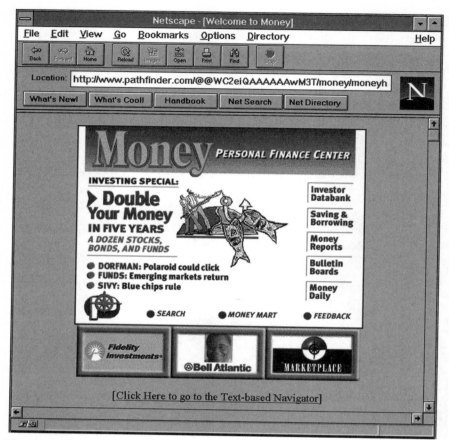

Figure 10.7 *Money Magazine's* Personal Finance Center shows how hyperlinked information can change the experience of reading a magazine.

But if you lack a SLIP/PPP connection and thus lack graphical capabilities, don't despair. Many magazines are available through FTP and Gopher, providing access to the full text of past issues. For example, you can download back issues of *PC Magazine* using anonymous FTP to the following URL:

```
ftp://ftp.cco.caltech.edu/pub/ibmpc/pcmag/
```

When you check into this site, you'll find yourself in an archival directory, as shown in Figure 10.10. Each of the issues available has been compressed for storage purposes, as you can tell from the .zip suffix on the filenames.

Gopher is also a useful way to view magazines on-line. We'll examine Gopher in detail in Chapter 12; for now, it's sufficient to note that this network tool provides a menu structure for networked information. We can use Gopher, for example, to reach the Electronic Newsstand service run by The Internet Company in Cambridge, Massachusetts. The company specializes in making products available over the Internet.

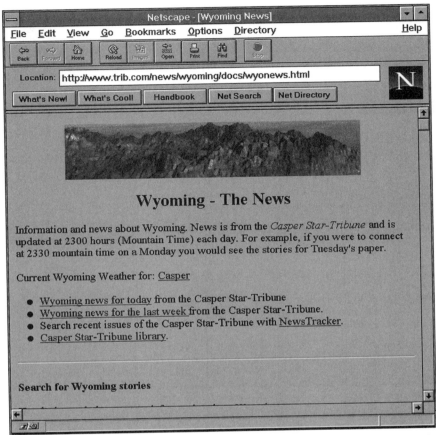

Figure 10.8 The Casper, Wyoming *Star-Tribune,* a model for what newspapers can do on the Internet.

To reach the Electronic Newsstand, we can use a Gopher client to the address gopher.internet.com. The command is **gopher gopher.internet.com,** given at your service provider's command prompt. (If this doesn't work, there are other options, as explained in Chapter 12.) Here we find a wide variety of magazines and other resources. Among information providers available through the Internet Company are Counterpoint Publishing (federal databases), the Electronic Newsstand itself (based in Washington, DC), and Daniel Dern's Internet Info, which contains network material collected by the popular Internet author.

We focus here on the Electronic Newsstand, which appears as item 9 on the main Gopher menu at the Internet Company. Choosing this item, we move to the screen shown in Figure 10.11.

A wide variety of magazines is accessible by descending through the menu structure here, pressing a **RETURN** after moving the marker to the appropriate item. Special subscription offers are made available, and often the selected contents of a recent or current issue. Figure 10.12, for example, shows an excerpt from an article running in *The New Yorker.*

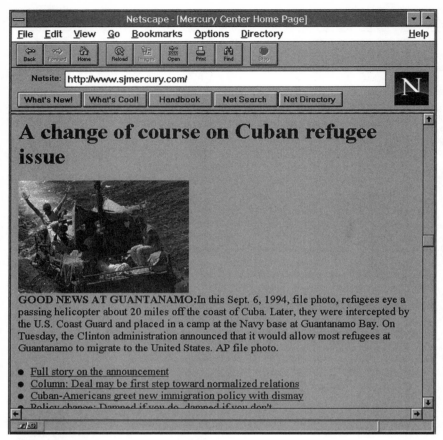

Figure 10.9 The *San Jose Mercury News* on-line.

```
-rw-r--r--   1 pcpublic guest     70229 Jun  5  1990 vol9n02.arc
-rw-r--r--   1 pcpublic guest    192905 Jun  5  1990 vol9n03.arc
-rw-r--r--   1 pcpublic guest    235858 Jun  5  1990 vol9n04.arc
-rw-r--r--   1 pcpublic guest     29789 Jun  5  1990 vol9n05.arc
-rw-r--r--   1 pcpublic guest     91475 Jun  5  1990 vol9n06.arc
-rw-r--r--   1 pcpublic guest     64167 Aug  1  1990 vol9n07.zip
-rw-r--r--   1 pcpublic guest     36231 Jun  7  1990 vol9n08.zip
-rw-r--r--   1 pcpublic guest     53726 Jun  7  1990 vol9n09.zip
-rw-r--r--   1 pcpublic guest     89487 Aug  1  1990 vol9n10.zip
-rw-r--r--   1 pcpublic guest     27047 Aug  1  1990 vol9n11.zip
-rw-r--r--   1 pcpublic guest     66115 Aug  1  1990 vol9n12.zip
-rw-r--r--   1 pcpublic guest     58049 Aug  1  1990 vol9n13.zip
-rw-r--r--   1 pcpublic guest     57532 Oct 26  1990 vol9n14.zip
-rw-r--r--   1 pcpublic guest     32587 Oct 26  1990 vol9n15.zip
-rw-r--r--   1 pcpublic guest    100043 Oct 26  1990 vol9n16.zip
-rw-r--r--   1 pcpublic guest     49013 Oct  1  1991 vol9n17.zip
-rw-r--r--   1 pcpublic guest     60398 Oct  1  1991 vol9n18.zip
-rw-r--r--   1 pcpublic guest     40589 Oct  1  1991 vol9n19.zip
-rw-r--r--   1 pcpublic guest     61733 Oct  1  1991 vol9n20.zip
-rw-r--r--   1 pcpublic guest    238611 Oct  1  1991 vol9n21.zip
-rw-r--r--   1 pcpublic guest     43873 Oct  1  1991 vol9n22.zip
226 Transfer complete.
6643 bytes received in 1 seconds (6.5 Kbytes/s)
ftp> _
```

Figure 10.10 Examining magazine holdings at an FTP site.

```
┌──────────────────────────────────────────────────────────────┐
│        Internet Gopher Information Client v2.0.16              │
│                                                                │
│              The Electronic Newsstand(tm)                      │
│                                                                │
│  -->  1.  Visit our WWW site: http://www.enews.com/            │
│       2.  Introduction to The Electronic Newsstand/            │
│       3.  Notice of Copyright and General Disclaimer -- Please Read │
│       4.  Magazines, Periodicals, and Journals (all titles)/   │
│       5.  Electronic Bookstore/                                │
│       6.  Electronic Car Showroom(tm) (Toyota U.S.A. and more!)/ │
│       7.  Business and Finance Center/                         │
│       8.  Computer and Technology Resources/                   │
│       9.  Entertainment Area/                                  │
│      10.  Health and Medical Center/                           │
│      11.  The Renaissance Room/                                │
│      12.  Sports, Recreation and Leisure Center/               │
│      13.  Travel Resources/                                    │
│      14.  News Services/                                       │
│      15.  Search All Electronic Newsstand Articles by Keyword / │
│                                                                │
│                                                                │
│  Press ? for Help, q to Quit, u to go up a menu    Page: 1/1   │
└──────────────────────────────────────────────────────────────┘
```

Figure 10.11   The Electronic Newsstand.

```
┌──────────────────────────────────────────────────────────────────────┐
│ April 24, 1995 -- The Last Battle, Report From Vietnam (3k)      22%   │
│ +------------------------------------------------------------------+   │
│ Magazine: The New Yorker                                               │
│ Issue: April 24, 1995                                                  │
│ Title: The Last Battle, Report From Vietnam                            │
│ Author: Neil Sheehan                                                   │
│                                                                        │
│ What follows is an excerpt from "The Last Battle," by Neil             │
│ Sheehan. It appears in the April 24, 1995 issue of The                 │
│ New Yorker. Copyright 1995 All Rights Reserved.                        │
│                                                                        │
│                                                                        │
│ The old Mi-8 betrayed its age by shuddering in protest as              │
│ it hovered to land at Cat Bi, the airport for Haiphong,                │
│                                                                        │
│ where a covey of Mitsubishis was waiting to take us to                 │
│ our next stop--Kien An, a village fifteen kilometres                   │
│ southwest of the port. Captain John Collie, an intense,                │
│ highly organized man with close-cropped, graying hair                  │
│ and bright-blue eyes, had hired a hundred and ten                      │
│ Vietnamese--about eighty per cent of the available labor               │
│ in the village--to excavate a fishpond. He was preventing              │
│ +------------------------------------------------------------------+   │
│ [Help: ?]   [Exit: u]   [PageDown: Space]                              │
└──────────────────────────────────────────────────────────────────────┘
```

Figure 10.12   An excerpt from *The New Yorker*.

Titles include popular magazines in everything from sports to travel, literature, and music.

Finally, you won't want to miss *WiReD Magazine*'s presence on the Net, which includes articles about networking and its social implications from this remarkable magazine. You can reach *WiReD* through Gopher at this URL:

```
gopher://gopher.wired.com
```

The magazine's address on the Web is:

```
http://www.wired.com/
```

It will be interesting to observe whether on-line availability turns into a successful tool for expanding subscription lists. Exactly how publishers work out the confluence between free information and their subscription base will be fodder for marketing seminars for years to come.

Given the fast rate of change in the on-line magazine world, it would be helpful to have a renewable source of information.

What You Need: News about On-line Publishing

The Source: The Online-News Mailing List

How to Get It: Send electronic mail to the following address:

majordomo@marketplace.com

Your message should read:

subscribe online-news

Into the Realm of the Outrageous

A healthy tension exists between the scholarly uses to which the Internet has always been home and the frenetic activity occurring along its margins. As a communications medium, the network reflects its occupants, whose interests are diverse, and whose new capabilities in the field of self-publishing have proven irresistible. How else to explain the growth in another type of on-line journal, the so-called *e-zine?* We now leave the realm of the mainstream press and move directly into the counterculture. If it can be expressed digitally, there's probably someone out there who plans to publish it.

E-zine stands for electronic *zine*, which is usually the work of a single person expressing a particular point of view. Controversy abounds—put an electronic printing press in the hands of virtually anyone and you're sure to hear viewpoints beyond the norm. And as you would suspect, the quality of the enterprise varies dramatically from zine to zine. Let's examine what's available in this energizing format, and explain how you can best access the zine of your choice. Who knows, you may eventually decide to publish a zine of your own.

The first step is to procure a listing of electronic magazines available over the Internet. Its compiler is John Labovitz, johnl@netcom.com.

What You Need: An Electronic Listing of Zines

How to Get It: By anonymous FTP to the following URL:

ftp://ftp.netcom.com/pub/johnl/zines/e-zine-list

You can also get the list on USENET, where it is regularly updated and posted on the following newsgroups: alt.zines, alt.etext, misc.writing, alt.internet.services, and news.answers.

Some of the zines compiled by Labovitz are quite good. *The Amateur Computerist* is a personal favorite; under the guidance of editor Ronda Hauben, it is documenting the development of USENET and other network resources. *InterText* is a journal specializing in various genres of fiction, from science fiction to mainstream literature. Jason Snell edits the bimonthly magazine, which is available through FTP, World Wide Web, Gopher and other sources. And here's a dandy, available through a LISTSERV-mediated mailing list: *The Mini-Journal of Irreproducible Results* produces reports from the fringe of research, including, as stated in the description on the Labovitz list, "haphazardly selected superficial (but advanced!) extracts of research news and satire from the *Journal of Irreproducible Results.*"

Figure 10.13 shows an example of a journal called *Voices from the Net.* Like many zines, it is available through FTP as well as Gopher.

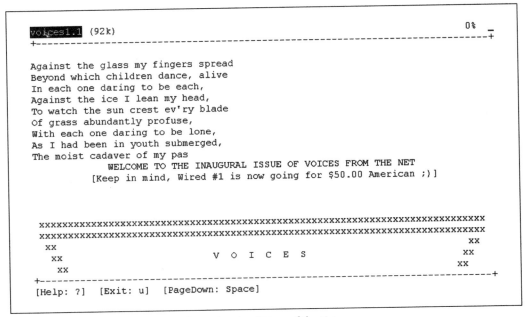

Figure 10.13 A table of contents from the zine *Voices of the Net.*

Finding Other Journals

A subscription to PACS-L and its on-line publications is one way to keep up with the world of electronic publishing, and the Labovitz list is likewise essential. But journal titles aren't always easy to come by, and new ones are being created all the time. Although, as with most Internet information gathering, you must hustle to accumulate the right information, the project is do-able, if complicated.

One file maintained in the BITNET Network Information Center contains information about electronic journals. Though not as timely as it might be, it's a good place to begin. Figure 10.14 shows descriptions of some electronic journals, as culled from the BITNIC list.

What You Need: A Core List of Electronic Journals

The Document: BITNET Servers

How to Get It: Send a **get bitnet servers** command to listserv@bitnic.bitnet.

This document, incidentally, is a list of network services not limited to electronic journals. It's a useful addition to your file library for BITNET materials.

Perhaps the best way to keep up with electronic journals is through the Directory of Electronic Journals and Newsletters, compiled by Michael Strangelove at the University of Ottawa. The huge directory includes background information on starting an electronic journal or newsletter, and lists almost 100 journals in its latest issue. It also includes extensive listings for HyperCard stacks, digest-style newsletters, a bibliography for further reading, and much more. Lengthy descriptions of each publication are particularly valuable, and full instructions are given on how to subscribe.

What You Need: A Resource Guide for Electronic Journals and Related Resources

The Document: The Directory of Electronic Journals and Newsletters

How to Get It: Send the following commands to listserv@uottowa.bitnet.

get ejournl1 directry
get ejournl2 directry

Note the spelling; it's important.

Looking through this list, I found one item, shown in Figure 10.15, of particular interest to anyone planning to get seriously involved with electronic journals. It is the List Review Service.

Athene

    Athene is a free network "magazine" devoted to amateur fiction written by the members of the online community. Athene does not limit itself to any specific genre, but will publish quality short stories dealing with just about any interesting topic, including:

                science fiction   fantasy
                religion   mystery
                computers   humor
                psychology   sports
                politics   business

    To subscribe, mail a request to Jim McCabe, MCCABE@MTUS5. Be sure to mention if you want it in ASCII or Postscript.

BioSphere Newsletter

    BioSphere newsletter may be of interest for those of you concerned about the problems facing our environment. To get a subscription, send this command to LISTSERV@UBVM: SUB BIOSPH-L your_full_name.

|EJournal
|
| EJournal is an all-electronic, Bitnet/Internet distributed, peer-reviewed,
| academic periodical, concerning the theory and praxis surrounding the creation,
| transmission, storage, interpretation, alteration and replication of electronic
| text. It also covers the broader social, psychological, literary, economic and
| pedagogical implications of computer-mediated networks. Please send subscription
| requests to EJOURNAL@ALBNYVMS via mail.

Mednews

    Mednews is a weekly electronic newsletter. Regular columns consist of medical news summary from USA Today, Center For Disease Control MMWR, weekly AIDS Statistics from the CDC, plus other interesting medical news items. To subscribe, send the following command to LISTSERV@ASUACAD via mail or message: SUB MEDNEWS Your_Full_Name.

Psychnet

    Psychnet is a weekly newsletter keeping the psychology community informed and in contact. To subscribe, send mail to Robert C. Morecock, EPSYNET@UHUPVM1.

|USSR-D
|
| USSR-D (USSR news and information digest) is a regular digest of traffic culled
| from USSR-L (USSR news & information list), a public discussion and distribution
| list dedicated to the dissemination and analysis of nonclassified news and
| information regarding the Union of Soviet Socialist Republics and its past and
| present (if not future) constituent Soviet Socialist Republics. To subscribe
| send the command Sub USSR-D
|
| Your_full_name to LISTSERV@INDYCMS.

Figure 10.14 Descriptions of on-line journals from the BITNIC list.

```
> List Review Service <

The LIST REVIEW SERVICE quantitatively and qualitatively explores e-mail
distribution lists (primarily BITNET LISTSERV Lists). The cataract of
information available to those with network access make all but the most
cursory examinations of lists possible.  Akin to book and restaurant reviews,
each issue begins with a narrative description of usually one week's worth of
monitoring, then presents simple statistical data such as the number of
messages and lines, number of queries and non-queries, number of subscribers
and countries represented, list owner, location, and how to subscribe.

The editor sees the publication as a means to cross-fertilize user
perceptions of network resources (i.e., active proselytization for
cyberspace). The service attempts to explore as wide a range of lists as
possible, from the hard sciences to the fuzziest of the humanities.

ISSN: 1060-8192

Posted bi-weekly on LIBREF-L. To subscribe to LIBREF-L, send a single line
message with no subject to Bitnet address LISTSERV@KENTVM or Internet address
LISTSERV@KENTVM.KENT.EDU consisting of: SUBSCRIBE LIBREF-L your_name

Submissions:

No

Related List:

LIBREF-L

Back Issues:

Available by searching the LIBREF-L archives by ISSN (1060-8192), or by
request from the editor of the LIST REVIEW SERVICE.

Contact:

Raleigh C. Muns, Editor, Reference Librarian
SRCMUNS@UMSLVMA.BITNET
Thomas Jefferson Library
University of Missouri-St. Louis
8001 Natural Bridge Rd.
St. Louis, MO 63121
ph: (314) 553-5059
```

Figure 10.15   A description of the List Review Service.

A subscription here can be useful indeed, giving you an overview that can tell you when a list is promising, and when you'd just as soon skip it. We could use more review services like this on a wide range of Internet resources.

Another good reference source is a World Wide Web page originally made available through CERN, the Swiss laboratory that was the birthplace of the Web. Here you will find links to numerous magazines; click on the journal and you're taken there. The Virtual Library page is shown in Figure 10.16.

What You Need: A Reference Guide to On-Line Publications

The Source: A World Wide Web page at CERN

How to Get It: Access the following URL:

http://www.edoc.com/ejournal

Finally, Princeton University makes available a listing of journals by title that can help you move quickly to what you need, or scan the listings to see what's new.

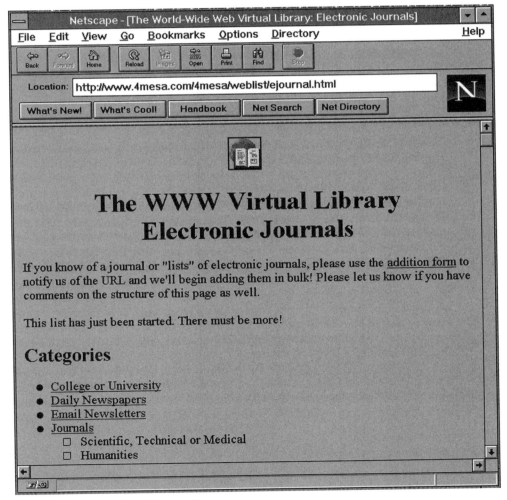

Figure 10.16 The Virtual Library Page

What You Need: A Listing of Journals by Title

The Source: Princeton University's World Wide Web page

How to Get It: Access the following URL:

http://aaup.pupress.princeton.edu:70/1/journals/titles/

You should also be aware of a wonderful collection of electronic journals at the following URL:

ftp://ftp.cic.net/pub/e-serials/

Here you have the ability to browse through CICnet's Electronic Journal Project, containing helpful on-line material and the latest news on electronic publishing. You can also use Gopher to this site:

gopher://gopher.cic.net/

Descriptions are provided for each journal listed.

Project Gutenberg and the Next Publishing Revolution

Johann Gutenberg, a fifteenth century German printer, is widely credited with being the first European to print with movable type, in the process changing the way books were produced, and leading, ultimately, to the enfranchisement of a population of readers—most of whom would not have been able to afford expensive hand-copied books and wouldn't, in many cases, have known how to read them.[2] Ironically, little of Gutenberg himself is known; the man who helped disseminate knowledge like no other left no genuine portrait behind him, and details of his life are scant.

Michael Hart was once obscure himself, but now that he's been written up in the *Wall Street Journal* and other prestigious venues, that is changing. His labors on behalf of the on-line dissemination of knowledge are well-known within the Internet community, and if you mention Project Gutenberg even to non-network people, many will acknowledge having heard the name. Hart's work taps Gutenberg for its inspiration in a pointed way. Like the German printer, Hart is fiddling with technology to improve the way books are produced. If Gutenberg had lived to use the Internet, he'd be more than a little interested in what Hart is doing through Project Gutenberg.

To understand the concept, think about what Gutenberg did. Before his invention, books were rarities, each laboriously copied by hand. To make a second copy of a particular book involved going through the entire process again. Medieval manuscripts are lovely creations, often laid out with an exquisite calligraphy. But their scarcity meant few people owned a book. The invention of movable type allowed books to reach a wider and wider audience, until we reach the late twentieth century when paperback books are accessible to virtually anyone.

Hart has similar designs on the written word in our day. His goal is to give away a trillion books by 2001 or, to put it more succinctly, to copy the text of some 10 thousand books into digital form and distribute them at no cost to an ever broadening base of readers. His vision is of a society where the great works of literature are available at nominal cost to all.

Hart has been at this for 22 years, and he currently presides over an army of several hundred volunteers with teams now working in all major languages. They have what some might think the most tedious job in the world: entering whole novels and other works into formats Project Gutenberg can use. (I'm a volunteer, and I'll be working for a while. My book is Boswell's mammoth *Life of Johnson.*)

What happens, meanwhile, to libraries and the people who use them? Hart believes that the libraries of the future will bear the same relation to today's libraries that the best libraries of our culture bear to medieval book collections, where books were chained to the shelves. "It costs me .39 cents to buy a 1.44 MB floppy," he says. "That means if I put *Alice in Wonderland* on there 10 times, it costs me .04 per copy. If I compress it, it costs me less than .02 per copy. You're getting close to a penny a book, a virtually free book." This price reduction, Hart noted in an on-line posting, is on the same order of magnitude as the price reductions books experienced after the invention of movable type, with equally dramatic implications for the spread of the electronic word.

Hart explained these notions in a guest editorial in *Database Magazine* in 1990.[3] The library of the future would be searchable by computer, its collections capable of being "transmitted via disks, phone lines, or other media at a fraction of the cost in money, time, and paper as with present day paper media. These electronic books will not have to be reserved and restricted to use by one patron at a time. All materials will be available to all patrons from all locations at all times." Hart's vision is a far cry from today's libraries, where books are all too often missing from the shelves, information resources bottlenecked at terminals, and media readers ringed by lines of waiting people.

Hart's work flows into the Internet through computers at the University of Illinois campus in Champaign-Urbana, where he has been given computer time despite having no official connection with the school. He's an adjunct professor at Illinois Benedictine College in Lisle, where creating electronic libraries is his sole occupation. Although Hart has released a few copyrighted books, copyright restrictions keep him working largely within the public domain, but the copyright issue is continuing to evolve. Will copyright law have to change due to the potential for unauthorized redistribution of electronic documents? Whatever happens, Project Gutenberg must choose its material with care. An international copyright lawyer is now working with the project to help clarify these issues.

To learn more about the rapidly expanding world of on-line libraries and how Project Gutenberg is contributing to their evolution, you can tap USENET.

What You Need: A Source of Information on Project Gutenberg

The Source: A USENET Newsgroup called bit.listserv.gutnberg

How to Get It: Subscribe to the list using a USENET News Reader. We'll discuss these procedures in the next chapter. You can also access Project Gutenberg through its World Wide Web page. The URL:

http://jg.cso.uiuc.edu/pg_home.html

Whether or not you read this newsgroup, you can always use FTP to tap the archives, where you can download useful information, such as an index of books currently available (updated regularly through the newsletter) and a file specifically written for new users. Archives of past newsletters, as you would suspect, are also available on-line.

What You Need: An Index and New User File for Project Gutenberg

How to Get Them: Use anonymous FTP to the following URL:

ftp://mrcnext.cso.uiuc.edu/etext/articles/

For the index, look for the file 01INDEX.GUT. The general user file is NEWUSER.GUT. This directory contains much additional information about the Project.

Project Gutenberg's actual holdings are, of course, available here as well. The directory /etext/etext95 holds books added in that year, just as /etext/etext94 holds the 1994 additions, and so on. Looking through the currently available titles, I found a wide range of familiar authors. Here is Lewis Carroll's *Alice in Wonderland*, Melville's *Moby Dick*, and Hawthorne's *The Scarlet Letter*. Not all entries are prose—Milton's *Paradise Lost* weighs in, about as nonprosaic an entry as you can get. Not all works are literary, either, as *Roget's Thesaurus* and the *CIA World Factbook* attest. There is even a collection of census data and several useful books on the Internet itself, including the first edition of Brendan Kehoe's *Zen and the Art of the Internet*, which made an on-line appearance before becoming a printed book.

Let's look at one of the available texts, H. G. Wells' *The War of the Worlds*, which can be accessed in the /etext/etext92 directory under two filenames: WARW10.TXT for the straight ASCII version, and WARW10.ZIP for the compressed version. (You'll need PKUNZIP to extract the file, which is compressed to roughly half its former size by the software.) After several pages of information on Project Gutenberg and a series of legal disclaimers and notes on how to distribute the material, we get to the text itself, as shown in Figure 10.17.

It's quite a story and, as a long-time Wells enthusiast, I heartily recommend another Project Gutenberg holding, *The Time Machine*, which is available in the same directory. I already own copies of both in traditional paper format, of course, so of what use are their digital counterparts? If I were a student, I could use such a text for a wide range of analysis. Even a basic word processor gives me the capability to search for text, so checking on key ideas or concepts by way of performing various kinds of literary study should be a snap. More significantly, for those without access to the paper copies, having the text available in this form, readily distributable, is far better than no text at all.

It's a big project, but Project Gutenberg aims high, dominated by a long-term vision. "Somewhere between the present and Star Trek, all that stuff gets into the computer," says Hart. "Nobody ever questions that all the books ever written are in the Enterprise's computer. But nobody ever asks how they got there. We're the ones putting them in."

```
The War of the Worlds, by H(erbert) G(eorge) Wells [1898]

    But who shall dwell in these worlds if they be
    inhabited?  .   .   .   Are we or they Lords of the
    World?  .   .   .   And how are all things made for man?--
        KEPLER (quoted in The Anatomy of Melancholy)


                        BOOK ONE

                 THE COMING OF THE MARTIANS


                       CHAPTER ONE

                    THE EVE OF THE WAR


    No one would have believed in the last years of the nineteenth century that
this world was being watched keenly and closely by intelligence greater than
man's and yet as mortal as his own; that as men busied themselves about their
various concerns they were scrutinised and studied, perhaps almost as narrowly as
a man with a microscope might scrutinise the transient creatures that swarm and
multiply in a drop of water.  With infinite complacency men went to and fro over
this globe about their little affairs, serene in their assurance of their empire
over matter.  It is possible that the infusoria under the microscope do the same.
No one gave a thought to the older worlds of space as sources of human danger, or
thought of them only to dismiss the idea of life upon them as impossible or
improbable.  It is curious to recall some of the mental habits of those departed
days.  At most terrestrial men fancied there might be other men upon Mars, per-
haps inferior to themselves and ready to welcome a missionary enterprise.  Yet
across the gulf of space, minds that are to our minds as ours are to those of the
beasts that perish, intellects vast and cool and unsympathetic, regarded this
earth with envious eyes, and slowly and surely drew their plans against us.  And
early in the twentieth century came the great disillusionment.

    The planet Mars, I scarcely need remind the reader, revolves about the sun at
a mean distance of 140,000,000 miles, and the light and heat it receives from the
sun is barely half of that received by this world.  It must be, if the nebular
hypothesis has any truth, older than our world; and long before this earth ceased
to be molten, life upon its surface must have begun its course.  The fact that it
is scarcely one seventh of the volume of the earth must have accelerated its
cooling to the temperature at which life could begin.  It has air and water and
all that is necessary for the support of animated existence.

    Yet so vain is man, and so blinded by his vanity, that no writer, up to the
very end of the nineteenth century, expressed any idea that intelligent life
might have developed there far, or indeed at all, beyond its earthly level.
Nor was it generally understood that since Mars is older than our earth, with
scarcely a quarter of the superficial area and remoter from the sun, it necessar-
ily follows that it is not only more distant from time's beginning but nearer
its end.
```

Figure 10.17 The beginning of H.G. Wells' *The War of the Worlds* from Project Gutenberg.

ASCII Text and the Vernacular

A battle is developing in Internet circles concerning ASCII, the American Standard Code for Information Interchange. An ASCII file is one that contains characters drawn from the ASCII character set, which contained 128 characters in its original form, and twice that in the so-called *extended character set* used in IBM-compatible computing. (The additional characters provide technical, graphics, and foreign language capabilities.) The rising controversy involves ASCII as a format for on-line text.

Ponder the issues here. ASCII offers the solution to a problem: how to move textual material between different kinds of computers. After all, from the first days of computing we have lived with incompatible filetypes, operating systems, and software applications. Think of ASCII as a format for exchanging information. You run a DOS machine, and your associate down the hall likes a Mac. But an ASCII file is readable on both. And it's readable on the Unix box at the end of the corridor.

The problem: ASCII, plain and unadorned, can't do some things. I can't underline text in vanilla ASCII, nor can I send italic characters in an e-mail message in ASCII. An electronic text thus misses out on much of the formatting that could make its appearance more elegant and informative. The answer, say some, is to adopt formats like PostScript, a page description language developed by Adobe Systems, Inc. PostScript allows you to print a page including text and graphics, embedding information about each in the document itself. The page is formatted precisely as you'd like it, and you can print out a PostScript document on any printer with a PostScript interpreter. No wonder a segment of the on-line community favors using PostScript or other formatting tools to make electronic text more useful.

But a problem arises immediately. What about people without access to PostScript printers? What happens to the idea of universal text access if you spread around documents so laden with formatting codes that users spend most of their time stripping out irrelevant information rather than using the text? For that matter, what if you compress files in such a way that some users can't figure out how to unpack them?

The problem is not easily managed, and remains the subject of intense on-line debate. As in virtually all aspects of computing, the search for standards defines the limits of the possible.

Dante, Still Divine, and a Host of Other Projects

If Dante Alighieri wasn't a genius, then the word has no meaning. There are those who think the medieval Florentine poet ranks with Homer and Shakespeare in the triad of poetry's greatest luminaries. And certainly, *The Divine Comedy*, a magnificent poem celebrating his love for a woman named Beatrice and illuminating the medieval outlook on life, shows no signs of losing its power despite its age. The tale of the poet's journey through Hell, Purgatory, and Heaven, guided first by the Latin poet Vergil and then by the spirit of his beloved Beatrice, inspired generations of writers with its seemingly effortless *terza rima* verse. And at Dartmouth College, Dante's work has taken on new form.

Dartmouth is home to the Dante Project, an attempt to let scholars and other interested parties examine the poet in new ways. The project has created a searchable database of commentaries on *The Divine Comedy* ranging over six centuries. Scholars who tap the action here can use a variety of search techniques to gather data, saving what could frequently amount to hundreds of hours of manual research. The full text of *The*

Divine Comedy is likewise available, and can be queried by a given search term or by line number. Working with Princeton University and the Dante Society of America, Dartmouth is using technology to make the ancient come alive in new and unexpected ways.

The Dante Project is a sterling example of where we're headed. It's esoteric for many of us, but it's an indication of how library resources are being shaped by networked technology to give us insights into textual materials. You can look at the Dartmouth contribution by using Telnet to library.dartmouth.edu. At the prompt, enter **connect dante** and you'll be presented with several introductory screens listing the materials available for searching, and then a basic search interface. The system is easy to use but you'd better know your Italian!

Two other Dartmouth resources should hold your attention if on-line literature is your interest. The college keeps Shakespeare's plays and sonnets available through its Online Library Catalog, with simple search commands for finding that key phrase you're trying to relocate. Telnet to lib.dartmouth.edu. At the prompt, enter **select file shakespeare plays** or **select file shakespeare sonnets** depending on your destination. The King James Version of the Bible is also available at the same address. Enter **select file bible** to get there.

I dived into the sonnets database to track down a favorite poem. I couldn't remember the number, but the phrase "bare ruin'd choirs" had potent associations. Figure 10.18 shows what happens when you search this repository. Full instructions for managing the search strategy are provided on-line. They're clunky but usable.

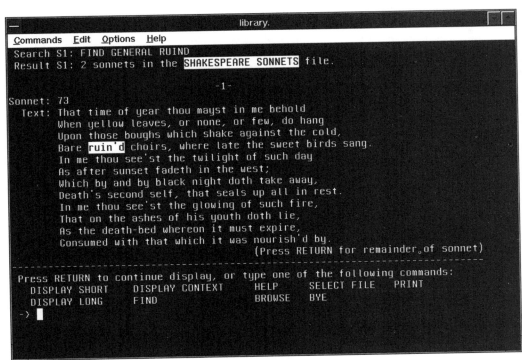

Figure 10.18   Recovering a misplaced sonnet from Dartmouth's database.

Another text project, the Online Book Initiative, began as an informal discussion group, and has evolved into a major attempt to turn literary works and other materials into electronic text. The OBI is run by Software Tool & Die in Brookline, Massachusetts (the address is obi@world.std.com). The project maintains two mailing lists devoted to the issues surrounding its venture, one for discussion of electronic text and other topics, the other for announcements only. Those interested in the growth of this medium may want to explore one or both. You can use anonymous FTP to look at what's available; many of these texts don't duplicate what's on Project Gutenberg.

What You Need: Access to the Online Book Initiative Archives.

How to Get It: Use anonymous FTP to the following URL:

ftp://ftp.std.com/obi/

You will find the various works listed here, accessible for download.

A look through the directory listings gives you a feel for the breadth of the interests of OBI's contributors. Figure 10.19 shows a brief section of the obi directory. Note that each of these entries is itself a directory branching out from the obi root. The Online Book Initiative is also available through the Gopher at The World, a major Internet service provider. The URL is gopher://world.std.com; your command would be **gopher world.std.com**; or you could use Telnet, as we'll discuss in Chapter 12. Figure 10.20 shows one of the more interesting OBI items, the great Anglo-Saxon poem *Beowulf*, as read through The World's Gopher.

```
drwxrwxr-x   2 obi        512 Sep 19  1991 ECPA
drwxrwxr-x   3 obi        512 Jul  6 18:11 EFF
drwxr-xr-x  13 102        512 Aug 22 04:12 Economics
drwxrwxr-x   2 obi        512 Sep 19  1991 Edwin.Abbott
drwxrwxr-x   2 obi        512 Sep 19  1991 Emily.Bronte
drwxrwxr-x   2 obi        512 Sep 19  1991 Ethnologue
drwxrwxr-x   2 obi        512 Sep 19  1991 Ezra.Pound
drwxrwxr-x   2 obi        512 Sep 19  1991 FIPS
drwxrwxr-x   3 obi        512 Sep 19  1991 FSF
drwxrwxr-x   4 obi        512 Oct 14 00:10 Fairy.Tales
drwxrwxr-x   3 obi        512 Dec  6  1991 FoundingFathers
drwxrwxr-x   2 obi        512 Sep 19  1991 GIFNews
drwxr-xr-x   3 102        512 Mar 12  1992 GNU
drwxrwxr-x   2 obi        512 Sep 30 16:27 George.Bush
drwxrwxr-x   2 obi        512 Sep 19  1991 Grimm
drwxrwxr-x   4 obi        512 Oct  4 23:21 HM.recipes
drwxrwxr-x   2 obi        512 Sep 19  1991 Haring
drwxr-xr-x   2 obi        512 Feb 12  1992 Harkin
drwxrwxr-x   2 obi        512 Sep 19  1991 Henry.David.Thoreau
```

Figure 10.19 Some holdings at the Online Book Initiative.

You'll note from examining Figure 10.19 that the OBI includes more than classic works of literature. True, it contains works by Emily Bronte and Henry David Thoreau, but George Bush? The OBI's charter is clearly stated in an article project director Barry Shein wrote for the *GNUS Bulletin*.

> There exists huge collections of books, conference proceedings, reference materials, catalogues, etc., which can be freely shared. Some of it is in machine-readable form, much of it isn't. The purpose of the Online Book Initiative is to create a publicly accessible repository for this information, a networker's library.

The OBI has set up two mailing lists, one for general discussion about the issues involved, another for announcements only. To subscribe to either of these lists, send a message to Software Tool & Die as follows.

What You Need: A Mailing List for the Online Book Initiative

How to Get It: Send e-mail to obi@world.std.com, asking for entry into either of the lists.

The Internet Wiretap, meanwhile, located in Cupertino, California, has assembled an intriguing collection of information that it makes available through its Gopher. The URL is:

```
gopher://wiretap.spies.com/
```

```
The Internet Wiretap edition of

BEOWULF

From The Harvard Classics, Volume 49.
Copyright, 1910 by P.F. Collier & Son.

This text is in the public domain, released July 1993.

Prepared by Robin Katsuya-Corbet <corbet@astro.psu.edu>
from scanner output provided by Internet Wiretap.


        B E O W U L F

Translated by Francis B. Gummere

PRELUDE OF THE FOUNDER OF THE DANISH HOUSE

LO, praise of the prowess of people-kings
of spear-armed Danes, in days long sped,
we have heard, and what honor the athelings
--More--[0%]
```

Figure 10.20 *Beowulf* on the net.

Here you can find White House press releases, the Wiretap Online Library, an archive of electronic texts, government and civics information, and a master index of the full-length electronic books found at the Wiretap. Anyone interested in the dissemination of literature on-line will want to examine this site.

Living on the Textual Frontier

Electronic text is growing fast, its spread unchecked by any centralized organization. With no single gateway to these materials, users must search widely to find what's being placed on-line. Along with the proliferation of documents are the inevitable hardware concerns that rise with their availability. Even if text is circulating freely, is it as usable as it could be? Display quality is a key factor. The ergonomics don't always encourage reading a document for hours at a time on a screen where glare and less-than-ideal resolution are problems.

We're still on the frontier of electronic text, with the inevitable squabbles about territorial rights and differing ideologies sometimes encouraging the notion that promoting this medium is more like a range war than a reasoned move into a new form of access. But the technology is changing so fast that circulating texts on the network is becoming easier and easier. High-density storage vehicles, including huge hard disks and optical cartridges, will soon make concerns about the viability of massive text storage seem naive. Enhance these text warehouses with improved search software and you create benefits impossible to have been imagined by readers scant years ago.

Despite the heated debates these issues often generate, something less than anarchy is going on as we try to determine what standards will govern electronic books. Meanwhile, the journals created on-line seem to be reaching critical mass, with the benefits of archival availability becoming obvious to their readers. These matters are being debated on the Internet's mailing lists and their BITNET-born cousins, making it possible for any of us to take part in the continuing evolution of the printed word.

Keep your eye on developments in the World Wide Web as we move ever deeper into the electronic word era. What we miss when reading standard electronic text is the formatting that the printed word can bring in book or magazine fashion. Font changes please the eye (when they're not overdone), while photographs and graphics can add visual interest to printed materials. With the Web, we have a tool that allows us to ship both text and graphics, including photos, over the Internet.

Figure 10.21 is an example of what a Web page can be. This is a section of the C. S. Lewis home page; on it, you can see hyperlinks to a wealth of Lewis-related resources, including his literary works in on-line versions, a biography, photographs, and other memorabilia. To examine the C. S. Lewis page, try this URL:

```
http://sleepy.usu.edu/~slq9v/cslewis/index.html
```

This hypertextual linking between the various resources related to our topic is what makes the Web so special; keeping one page as our central site, we can readily move out to similar materials.

Figure 10.22 shows another specialized literary site, this one devoted to the works of Edgar Allen Poe. The same advantages of quick access and linked information apply here. You can reach the Poe site at this URL:

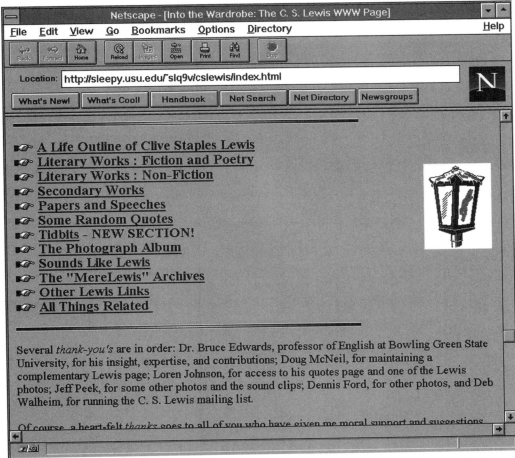

Figure 10.21 The C. S. Lewis home page, with links to writings by and about the great scholar and Christian apologist.

```
http://infoweb.magi.com/~forrest/index.html
```

Finally, you'll find an exceptional resource that lists on-line publications of all kinds at this URL:

```
http://www.etext.org/
```

In many respects, the large number of resources you will find in such sites is an indication of how quickly the Internet is maturing into a diverse and rich source of information. Its former emphasis upon technology and research is being added to by educators, editors, and those with a passion for language. While the future of electronic text is not entirely clear—how many people will read a work on a computer screen, for example?—its quick spread tells us that, in some fashion, the printed word and its digital representation are inextricably linked.

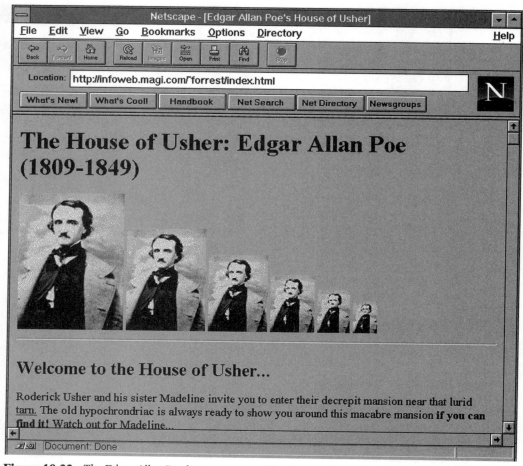

Figure 10.22   The Edgar Allen Poe home page provides plenty of reading and information for students of the macabre.

Chapter 10 Notes

1. Lucky, Robert W. *Silicon Dreams: Information, Man, and Machine.* New York: St. Martin's Press, 1989. p. 290.
2. The cost of books in the Middle Ages was remarkable by today's standards. According to Michael Hart in a telephone conversation with the author (January 7, 1993), book prices dropped by a factor of 400 as a result of Gutenberg's work. Intriguingly, this is roughly the difference between the cost of today's conventional, paper-bound book and the cost of putting the same book on a 1.44 MB floppy disk.
3. *Database*, December 1, 1991.

11

USENET: Keeping Up with the News

I'm not sure where I'd be without comp.risks, a moderated on-line discussion about the hazards associated with computers and high technology. Enthralled with networks, we sometimes forget that computing takes place within a context of social responsibility, and the comp.risks newsgroup is a valuable check on unbridled technophilia. On one day, for example, a quick check of postings revealed stories on computer glitches in a recent space shuttle launch attempt, safety-critical software, the security questions surrounding electronic mail, and more. Moderated by Peter G. Neumann, the Forum on Risks to the Public in Computers and Related Systems is sponsored by the ACM Committee on Computers and Public Policy. For those interested, it's also available as a mailing list. Send to risks-request@csl.sri.com to join, or keep reading to learn how to keep up with its discussions through USENET.

comp.risks is but one of a profusion of newsgroups carried on USENET and dedicated to every conceivable subject. In this chapter, we'll look at the variety available to you, and explain how you can sign up for newsgroups, or more precisely, how you can winnow out the newsgroups you'd prefer not to read. A number of different programs allow you to manage newsgroup activities, and we'll look at two of them. The first, WinVN, is a graphical newsreader that functions in the SLIP/PPP environment. The second, trn, is a Unix newsreader available at most service provider sites for those with shell access to the Internet. Both programs will be related to the broader issue of USENET itself, and how its newsgroups can help you to stay abreast of new developments on the Internet.

What Is USENET?

USENET is itself a network, but it isn't the Internet. Its traffic moves over the Internet, but it also moves over other networks. USENET began as an implementation of the Unix-to-Unix Copy Protocol or UUCP, but today, non-Unix machines commonly participate in USENET, and UUCP is only one of the mechanisms carrying its traffic. You can get to USENET and take part in its discussions because network interconnections make it possible.

USENET seems to mean User's Network, although the term is questionable, since USENET's originators created the word from a contraction of USENIX Network (USENIX being the largest user group for Unix). It was created in my part of the country by two graduate students at Duke University, Jim Ellis and Tom Truscott, in 1979. The first two hosts were, reasonably enough, called duke and unc, and the initial software to carry the news traffic was written by Steve Bellovin, a graduate student at the University of North Carolina at Chapel Hill. The USENET notion began to spread when its founders distributed the early news software through USENIX.

Today, the network has grown to enormous size with virtually no organizational structure. The key to USENET participation is that anyone, or any organization, can join; the only thing required is another machine with which to communicate. Lacking a central authority, the network likewise lacks any centralized funding. Each host on the network pays for its own transmission costs and allows traffic from other sites to flow. USENET is thus a self-policing network, discouraging commercial use and enforcing certain standards of network etiquette solely by the power of peer pressure. The lack of centralized enforcement can sometimes be exasperating, as heated discussions called *flame wars* spiral out of control and the ratio of noise to signal increases alarmingly on certain newsgroups. For all that, though, USENET provides a vital and compelling destination for network users.

USENET Newsgroups

For the modem user, USENET newsgroups will seem in many ways familiar. They're simply discussion areas where ideas can be exchanged. CompuServe users will think in terms of *Forums*, DELPHI users in terms of *Special Interest Groups* or *SIGs*, GEnie users in terms of *RoundTables*, and so on. But the concept is the same. You can post a message on-line and read the responses to it that build up over time. Because numerous people are reading the same material, a collection of such responses begins to accumulate. All the messages written on the same topic are considered to form a *thread;* that is, although they may be posted at different times and interspersed with other messages, they maintain a consistent subject matter.

You can subscribe to a particular newsgroup, page through it using a software reader, organize the messages according to threads so you can follow discussions better, add messages commenting on what people have said, and ask questions. Often one thread will branch into another, as subjects begin to diverge and suggest new areas of investigation. A good newsgroup can be a lively place, with well-defined personalities emerging amid an atmosphere of inquiry and excitement. In any case, it's safe to say you won't be bored. The number of newsgroups is increasing constantly (I found over 10 thousand the last time I ran a check), and it's likely that even the most abstruse topic will find representation somewhere on USENET.

USENET Topics

But there are differences between USENET and commercial on-line services. Perhaps the most obvious is that commercial services keep tighter control over their topics. You might be interested in investing, for example, and become involved in CompuServe's

Investor's Forum. If your particular interest was futures trading, you'd find a special message section devoted to the topic; if you chose, you could participate in that section alone. The same forum would have sections for stock traders, the bond market, options, mutual funds, and a host of other investment topics. All of this is inside a single forum, although, to be sure, there are other financial sources on CompuServe.

USENET, on the other hand, boasts a huge variety of newsgroups organized by a very broad hierarchical structure. They break down into the following major categories.

comp   Topics for computer professionals and amateur computerists alike. Here you'll find information on hardware systems, software, computer science, and various computer-related subjects. Some examples will illustrate the diversity of the category:

comp.ai	Artificial intelligence discussions.
comp.archives	Descriptions of public access archives.
comp.compression	Data compression algorithms and theory.
comp.dcom.fax	Fax hardware, software, and protocols.
comp.graphics.animation	Technical aspects of computer animation.
comp.lang.c++	The object-oriented C++ language.

sci   Research in the sciences is the organizing theme here. These newsgroups are highly specialized and usually followed by professionals in their fields. Some examples:

sci.bio	Biology and related sciences.
sci.engr.biomed	The field of biomedical engineering.
sci.materials	All aspects of materials engineering.
sci.physics.fusion	Fusion, especially "cold" fusion.
sci.virtual-worlds	Modelling the universe.

soc   Social issues and world cultures make up the discussions in the soc classification. This can be one of the most intriguing areas of USENET, as the international topics draw comment from all over the world. They're especially useful if you try to keep up with the news in a particular country. Alternatively, if you have a sociological bent, you'll find material about cultural trends. You can see from the following newsgroups how diverse the soc groups can be:

soc.couples	Discussions for couples.
soc.culture.bangladesh	News and comments about Bangladesh.
soc.culture.celtic	Irish, Scottish, Breton, Cornish, Manx, and Welsh issues discussed.
soc.roots	Family history research and other genealogical matters.
soc.veterans	Social issues relating to military veterans.

talk   There's no shortage of talk on USENET or, for that matter, on any other computer network. The ability to put views into widespread circulation holds a certain compulsive charm to many people, even those who normally keep their thoughts to themselves when not on-line. The result is debates, sometimes tendentious, often interesting, on topics without obvious resolution. Care to sound off about gun control? Abortion? Health care? You've found the place. Here are some recent topics:

talk.bizarre	The unusual, bizarre, curious.
talk.philosophy.misc	Philosophical musings on all topics.
talk.politics.mideast	Debate over Middle Eastern events.
talk.religion.misc	Religious and ethical issues.

Remember to bring your sense of humor when you get into these newsgroups.

news   A critical area, news is the section of USENET that focuses on happenings around the Internet. You'll find announcements of new newsgroups, changes in software, postings of background files, called FAQs (Frequently Asked Questions lists) for particular newsgroups, and the answers to common questions. Some examples:

news.admin.policy	Policy issues about USENET.
news.announce.important	General announcements of interest to all.
news.future	The future of network news systems.
news.newusers.questions	Questions and answers for users new to USENET.

rec   These are the hobbyist groups, such as:

rec.aquaria	Keeping fish and aquaria as a hobby.
rec.arts.drwho	Discussion about the TV character Dr. Who.
rec.arts.movies	Discussions of movies and moviemaking.
rec.arts.wobegon	Focus on the "Prairie Home Companion" radio show.
rec.aviation.ifr	Flying under Instrument Flight Rules.

misc   This category comprises anything that doesn't fit comfortably within the other categories. Predictably, its interests are wide and often have nothing whatsoever to do with computers. Witness the following examples:

misc.consumers.house	Owning and maintaining a house.
misc.jobs.offered	Announcements of positions available.
misc.rural	Issues concerning rural living.
misc.kids	Children, their behavior, and activities.

Think of these newsgroup categories as the core of USENET; they're circulated worldwide, although they do not make it into every network with USENET access. Any site can decide not to carry one or more of the groups, so the distribution varies. Remember, USENET lacks a central organization, which means there is no control over who gets a particular news feed or how individual articles are sent out through the net. There are, in fact, a set of alternative hierarchies for newsgroups that have also gained some currency. They're not carried everywhere either, often because they may interest only a limited audience, or because they may be quite lengthy and/or controversial.

alt   The alt category is broad. Some of these newsgroups are excellent discussion areas; others are trivial. But the idea is to let people say what they want, and you can tune out any newsgroup that doesn't suit your tastes. And be advised: There is some excellent material within the alt hierarchy. Some sample groups:

alt.aeffle.und.pferdle	German TV cartoon characters.
alt.alien.visitors	UFO sightings and more.
alt.books.reviews	Book discussions.

alt.gourmand	Recipes and cooking.
alt.radio.scanner	Radio scanners.
alt.internet.services	Questions and news about what's available on the Internet.

Whatever your interest, there's likely to be somebody discussing it in one of the alt newsgroups.

bionet   High-level, professional discussions among biologists.

bit   A useful grouping, bit is the hierarchy where the more popular BITNET mailing lists can be found on USENET. You might want to get involved with these if you'd prefer not to receive BITNET lists in your mailbox.

biz   These are groups with a business tilt. As you'd expect, the focus tends to be on computer products and services, but broader items of interest to the business community are also discussed. This is the place to be if you seek news about a new product or an enhancement to an old one. Some examples:

biz.comp.telebit	Support of the Te'lebit modem.
biz.sco.announce	SCO and related product announcements.
biz.dec	Digital equipment and software.
biz.jobs.offered	Position announcements.

clari   ClariNet is an electronic publishing service providing a live feed from the Associated Press wire service. The news is collected and converted into USENET format before being posted. It's a subscription service, so not all servers will offer ClariNet. For those that do, here's an example of the kind of material you'll find in this grouping:

clari.biz.economy.world	Reports on international economic issues.
clari.biz.market.dow	Tracks market activity.
clari.canada.briefs.west	Regional news from Canada.
clari.feature.mike_royko	The popular Mike Royko column.
clari.news.europe	European events.

gnu   This group is set up for discussions by and about the Free Software Foundation (FSF). The FSF was established with the charter to remove restrictions on copying, redistributing, and modifying software, meaning anyone could copy and distribute a program without worrying about constraints such as licensing agreements. The Foundation's take on all this is to produce free software replacements for some proprietary software. This project has focused on GNU, an operating system that provides compatibility with Unix. GNU, another acronym (and a recursive one at that), stands for GNU's Not Unix.

gnu.announce	Status and announcements from the project.
gnu.emacs.vm.bug	Bug reports on the Emacs VM mail package.
gnu.misc.discuss	Discussion about GNU and free software.

k12   Discussions of interest to teachers and students from kindergarten through high school. Thus:

k12.chat.elementary	Informal discussion among elementary students, grades K–5.

| k12.chat.junior | Informal discussion among students in grades 6–8. |
| k12.chat.senior | Informal discussion among high school students. |

msen   Offers articles from the Reuters news service in a variety of newsgroups.

vmsnet   For users of Digital Equipment Corporation's VMS operating system and participants on DECnet, the worldwide network using the DECnet protocols. DECnet is sometimes called the DECnet Internet.

Be advised, too, that local hierarchies exist; interpath.info and interpath.helpdesk, for example, are available at Interpath, my service provider here in Raleigh. The first handles basic newsgroup information about the services Interpath provides to its customers. The second fields questions related to the network's operations. You subscribe to and read these groups the same way you do any newsgroups, but their distribution is limited, and postings on them are of regional or local interest.

Useful USENET Lists

Since there are thousands of newsgroups, how do you know what's out there and, better still, how do you subscribe? The first question is answered by noting there are places on USENET where information about such matters is routinely posted, thanks to the good offices of a battery of volunteers. Somehow these individuals find time in their schedules to produce helpful indices, commentaries, and background information that anyone on the network can use. You will learn how to sign up for USENET newsgroups shortly, but for now, note two sources you'll want to keep in your permanent file. After you have gone through sign-up procedures, you can get them on USENET itself.

What You Need: A Listing of Active USENET Newsgroups

The Documents: List of Active Newsgroups and Alternative Newsgroup Hierarchies. Gene Spafford developed these lists, at no small cost of time and effort; they're now in the hands of David Lawrence and Mark Moraes.

Where to Get Them: Both lists are regularly posted in a variety of USENET newsgroups: news.lists, news.groups, news.announce.newusers, news.announce.newgroups, news.answers. As part of maintaining an active USENET presence, you should plan on subscribing to several. For now, I recommend news.announce.newusers. How to subscribe and keep up with such newsgroups forms the subject of the remainder of this chapter.

Reading the News

To access USENET newsgroups, you'll need a newsreader program. This can be handled in two ways. Using a shell account, you can use the newsreader program at your service provider's site. Just as it was necessary, for example, to use the FTP client located on the service provider's computer to manage a file transfer, a newsreader program running under Unix can be tapped to read newsgroups, resign from them, save messages as files for later downloading, respond to posted messages, and, in general, tailor the news environment to meet your own needs.

If you're a SLIP/PPP user, you will also use a newsreader program, but because you have a true connection to the Internet, you can use any of the client programs available. In both cases, you participate by telling the system to go to the particular newsgroup in which you are interested. You read the messages by using the appropriate commands. You page through the messages, usually viewing them in threads, so that you see everything that has been posted on a particular topic before moving on to the next one. This isn't terribly different from what you may already have experienced with a commercial on-line service like CompuServe, except that now you have different options to work with. Various programs can be used; if you dislike one, you can choose a different newsreader.

Unix newsreaders have typically cryptic names; they're called rn, or nn, or trn, or tin. Graphical newsreaders likewise come in a variety of shapes. There's Trumpet for Windows, and Newswatcher (for the Macintosh). WinVN is popular with Windows users, and News Express is gaining adherents, while Nuntius remains one of the most popular Macintosh newsreaders. For the purposes of our discussion, I'll walk you through, first, WinVN, a fine newsreader that makes managing newsgroups a logical and enjoyable process. I'll then examine trn, to show how efficiently a Unix-based newsreader can function with a shell account. As opposed to rn, the warhorse of Unix newsreaders and the most ubiquitous of them all, trn provides a crucial advantage: it's a threaded newsreader, allowing you to keep your information categorized by subject as you read.

WinVN—Reading the News Graphically

You should evaluate client software from the standpoint of how easily it allows you to do your work. On that score, WinVN is a champ. Its pull-down menus and readily configurable interface give you maximum control over your newsreading activities. But remember this: No matter which newsreader you choose, the basic issues underlying the interface remain the same. A newsreader has to create a list of newsgroups, based upon the groups offered by your service provider. It has to enable you to log on to your service provider's system to download information about the newsgroups to which you have subscribed, while letting you ignore the others. It must provide you with an ability to keep up with new newsgroups, and must make it easy for you to compose replies to postings.

ESTABLISHING YOUR NEWSGROUPS

WinVN does all this and more. As with any newsreader, the first thing you need to do is to subscribe to the newsgroups you want to see. And before your newsreader can do that, it must download a complete list of the newsgroups made available by your provider. When you first load WinVN, you will be asked whether you would like to download such a list. When you proceed to do so, you'll wind up with a dialog box like the one shown in Figure 11.1.

The list breaks down the newsgroups by hierarchy (on the top left), while below, it shows the newsgroups in that hierarchy. You can subscribe to a group by double-clicking on it. In the example, I have double-clicked on the news.answers newsgroup, which should be one of your primary subscriptions. It is in this newsgroup that Fre-

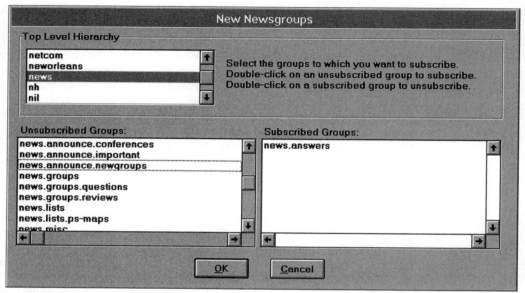

Figure 11.1   The newsgroup dialog box in WinVN.

quently Asked Questions documents from the various newsgroups are assembled; there is a wealth of information in such listings. As you can see, the news.answers group appears in the list of subscribed groups on the right.

Figure 11.2 shows the entire list of newsgroups in the form of a scrollable box. As you can see from the top of the figure, my provider currently offers a whopping 10,038 newsgroups, a figure that is growing daily as new groups are created. The groups I have subscribed to are shown at the top of the screen, while the rest of the newsgroups follow below. I can use the scroll bar to the right of the window to move through the list.

Here's how easy it is to subscribe to a new group:

1. From the Group menu, choose the Find command.
2. Enter the name of the group you want to subscribe to.
3. With that group's name highlighted, choose Subscribe Selected Groups from the Group menu.

The group will now appear at the top of the screen, along with your other subscribed newsgroups.

Rather than assuming when you first log on that you are subscribed to all the newsgroups, WinVN simply provides you with the opportunity to subscribe to those groups you would like to see. With over 10,000 newsgroups available from my provider, I know how difficult it can be to make the decision as to which groups to get involved with. But you should certainly consider using WinVN itself to help you out. By using the Find command from the Group menu, you can search for newsgroups that fit your needs. If you're interested in aviation, for example, you could enter that as your keyword, and WinVN would go to any groups with that keyword in their names. You could then make a decision as to whether to subscribe to that group.

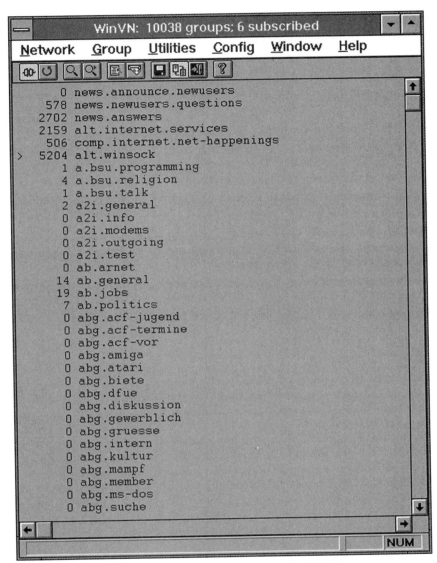

Figure 11.2   The list of available newsgroups as seen by WinVN.

The Find Next command can then be used to take you through the entire list. In using both commands, I found the following aviation-related newsgroups: alt.disasters. aviation, aus.aviation, clari.biz.industry.aviation (the latter is a news service with updates about the industry), eunet.aviation, fido.ger.aviation, francom.aviation, rec.aviation, rec.aviation.announce, rec.aviation.answers. . . . Get the idea? In fact, the rec.aviation newsgroups comprised some 15 sources of information on everything from soaring to ultralight aircraft. The point is, if you're interested in something, you're bound to find a newsgroup populated by people with similar interests.

THE CORE NEWSGROUPS

In some ways, the heading of this section is a misnomer. These newsgroups aren't necessarily core groups in the sense that everyone is expected to read them. But some newsgroups can make the life of the new USENET participant a great deal easier. The following lists some I think you'll find rewarding, and I recommend you sign up for them in your first go-around.

comp.internet.net-happenings   Regularly updated news about new sites and interesting destinations.

news.announce.important   A moderated conference with general announcements of interest to the entire USENET community.

news.announce.newsgroups   Announcements of the formation of new newsgroups.

news.announce.newusers   Explanations of basic USENET conventions for new users.

news.answers   Periodic USENET postings giving background information about the topics covered in many newsgroups.

news.newusers.questions   Your chance to ask questions. You should avail yourself of this opportunity, as you have USENET experts worldwide standing by to help you.

alt.internet.services   Useful discussions of Internet issues. You can learn a great deal by following this group.

READING A NEWSGROUP

By clicking on any newsgroup, I can receive a list of postings in that newsgroups. In Figure 11.3, I have clicked on the news.answers newsgroup and asked to see the most recent 250 articles. The list is shown in a scrollable box of its own; I use the scroll bar to move through the posted articles.

To the far left is the number of the posting, followed by the date, the poster's name, the length of the document, and, finally, the title. You can scroll through the list looking for items of interest; a good newsreader is built so that you don't have to read through everything. And when you find something you do want to read, the model remains as before—use the mouse:

1. Find a posting you want to read.
2. Double-click on it to call it to the screen.

Figure 11.4 shows the result of clicking on one of the documents in the news.answers newsgroup. The document appears in its own window.

The Windows-based model of WinVN keeps operations constant no matter what you are trying to do. In each case, you are dealing with scrollable information and use mouse clicks to achieve results. Notice, also, that as you read this text, you have pull-down menus available that allow you to search within the document, to view the next article in sequence, or to respond to the posting. You can also save the file on your computer, or print it out for future reference. SLIP/PPP means that you are working with the file on your own machine, without the need to first save it to your provider's computer and then download it.

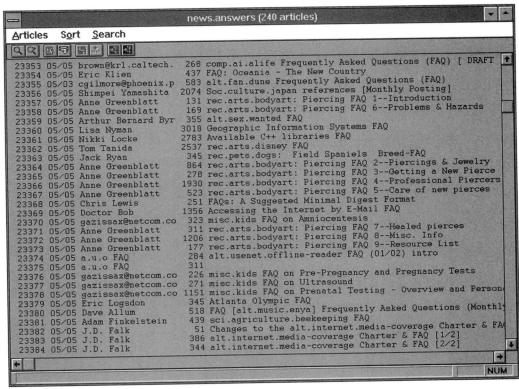

Figure 11.3   Recent postings in the news.answers newsgroup.

WinVN's viewing options make reading a newsgroup simple. You invoke them from the View menu. Using them, you can do the following:

- View the next article in the thread.
- View the next article in sequence.
- View the next article with the same subject.
- View the previous article.
- View an article that has been scrambled using rot13.

The latter deserves a brief mention. Some newsgroups contain postings that may be considered offensive to some readers. To avoid exposing them to traffic they don't want to see, posters use rot13, which is a simple coding device that makes the text look scrambled. By clicking on the rot13 option when you encounter such an article, you can unscramble it if you choose. In this way, you know that the only people who will see the article are those who have chosen to decode it.

RESPONDING TO ARTICLES

Newsgroups like news.answers are meant for back and forth messaging; they exist to post documents considered valuable by the USENET community, and are read-only. But

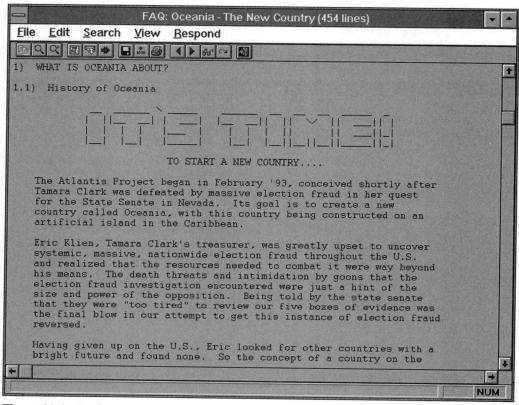

Figure 11.4   Reading a posting in news.answers with WinVN.

most newsgroups exist to facilitate communications, giving you the chance to add your own thoughts to what is going on. So let's look at another newsgroup, one called news.newusers.questions. Anyone just getting involved with the Internet will find this a useful newsgroup to maintain a subscription with. Numerous answers are provided here to the kind of questions that baffle the novice.

WinVN's Respond menu provides you with the ability to do three things:

- You can post a public message in response to a message you've just read. To do this, pull down the Respond menu and use the Followup Article command.
- You can post a follow-up message that will be delivered by electronic mail. You would do this in those cases where a reply by mail makes more sense because the topic is likely to be of interest to a limited number of people. Some posters explicitly ask that replies be sent to their mailbox. To respond by mail, pull down the Respond menu and use the Followup Mail command.
- You can forward the message to another address. To do this, pull down the Respond menu and use the Forward Article command.

Responding to a message produces the screen shown in Figure 11.5. Notice how WinVN has simplified the process by anticipating your needs. The text of the original message is reproduced inside your reply. But it is also shown with brackets to the left of the text, indicating that it is being inserted into a reply message. Quoting from a previous message is always a good idea, in order to make sure that people reading subsequent messages can understand what the discussion is all about. But it's also a good idea to edit such quotations, keeping the quoted text as short and to the point as possible. There is no point in using up bandwidth unnecessarily. You can edit the quotation and then include your own text following it.

CREATING A NEW POSTING

When you want to start a new thread of your own in a newsgroup, the method is straightforward:

1. Pull down the Articles menu from the newsgroup window.
2. Choose the New Article command.

When you do so, you will see the screen shown in Figure 11.6. Here you have the opportunity to create your own message.

SAVING MESSAGES TO YOUR DISK

Cruising through the USENET newsgroups can be an exhilarating experience as you locate information about hobbies, possible clients, or reference sources for future use.

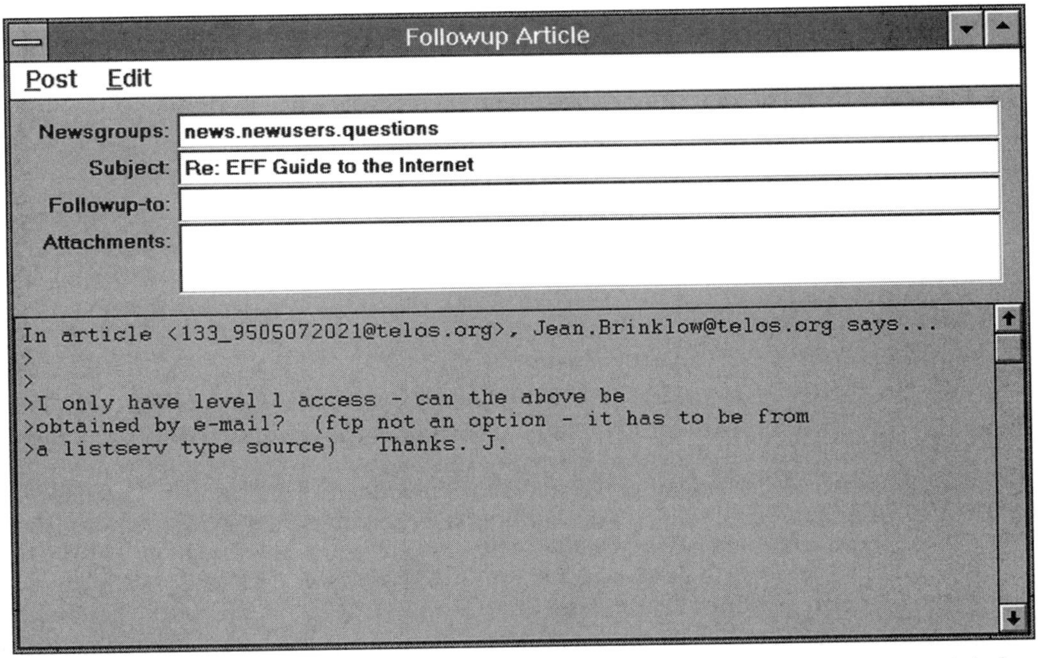

Figure 11.5 WinVN inserts the original message inside your reply, so that you can quote it before adding your own response.

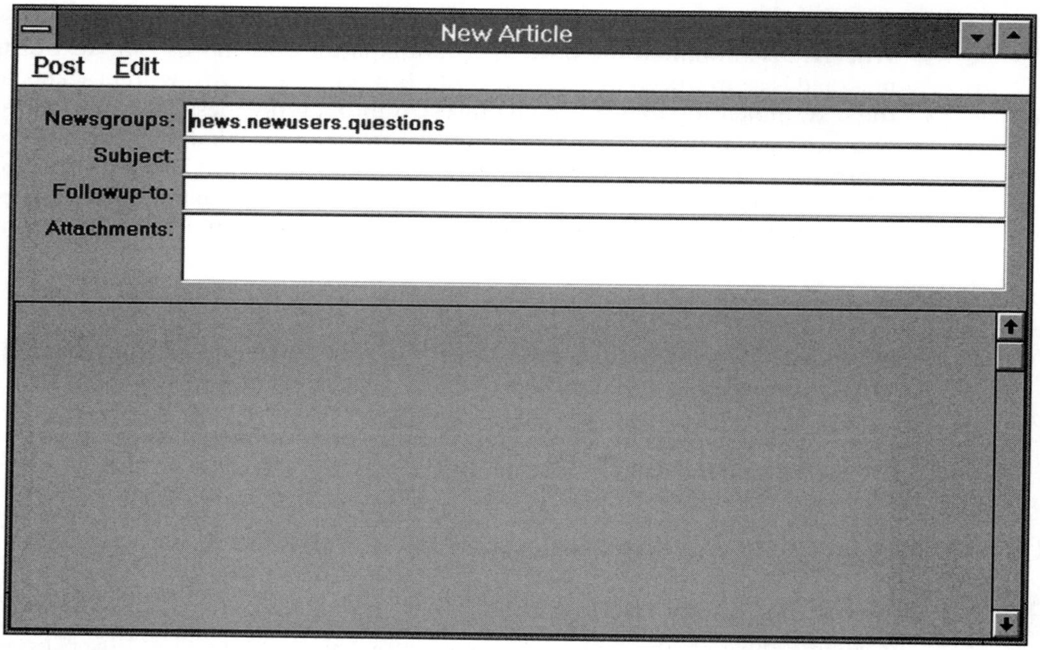

Figure 11.6   The screen within which you enter a new message.

To save such materials to your disk is a simple matter:

1. Pull down the File menu.
2. Choose the Save command.
3. Enter a filename for the saved article.

You can choose to append to this file or not, but doing so gives you the ability to add other articles that follow the same subject to the original posting. In this way, you can build up an archive of the newsgroup in question, saving those postings of particular interest.

DECODING NEWSGROUP POSTINGS

USENET news travels in ASCII format, as is standard on the Internet. This means that a posted message, if it is a binary file, like a photograph, a drawing, or a software program, must be translated from that format into ASCII, using the uuencode methods we discussed in Chapter 8. When you've downloaded the file, you then need to decode it using uudecode; and as we saw in the aforementioned chapter, a variety of software programs exist that allow you to do this.

A good newsreader will simplify this process by allowing you to download and decode such files at the same time. Using WinVN, for example, I can look through the postings on a given newsgroup, select those I want to see by using a Ctrl-click combination, and then tell the program to download the decode each of these files. The program allows me to choose a destination directory for the files and then goes to work.

An example of the kind of newsgroup where binaries are frequent is comp. binaries.ms-windows. Here you will find software written for the Microsoft Windows environment. Similar newsgroups exist for other platforms: comp.binaries.mac, comp.binaries.amiga, comp.binaries.ibm.pc, and so on. Another place to look is in the alt.binaries hierarchy. Let's examine a group called alt.binaries.clip-art, where you can find interesting postings for insertion into documents. I can either subscribe to the group or can simply examine it by double-clicking on its listing in the master list of newsgroups. The group is shown in Figure 11.7. Notice that regular postings coexist with binaries here, as users discuss clip art and also contribute their own to the Net.

Let's get the file called badcigar.gif. The .gif extension tells us that this is a binary file in Graphics Interchange Format, a format common to image files. The following procedure will procure the file:

1. Highlight the file by clicking on it once.
2. Pull down the Articles menu and choose the Decode Selected Articles command. You will see the dialog box shown in Figure 11.8. The most important thing to do here is to enter the pathname for the directory in which you want to save the decoded file. You can accept the default settings for now otherwise; they'll result in the article appearing on your disk in the directory specified.
3. Click on OK to start the decoding process.

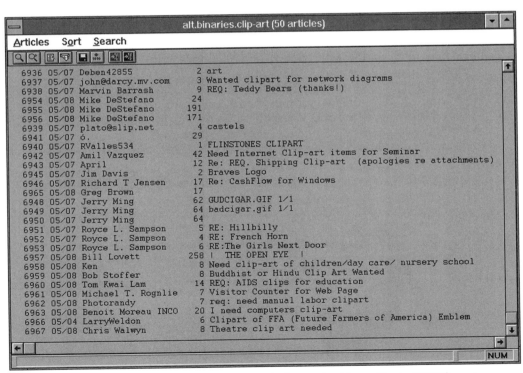

Figure 11.7   The newsgroup alt.binaries.clip-art, which contains binary files in ASCII format.

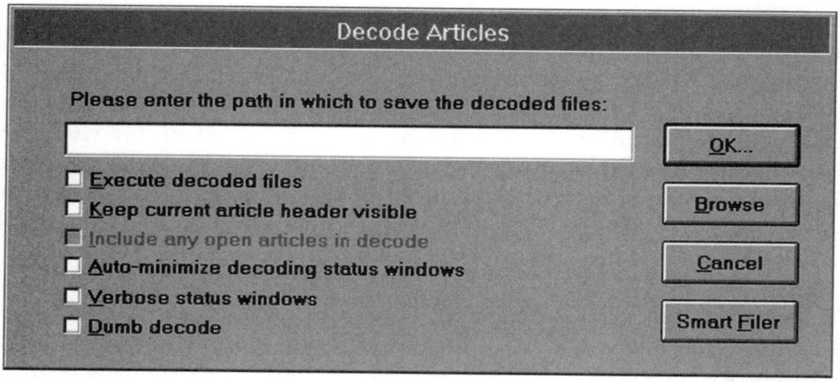

Decode Articles

Please enter the path in which to save the decoded files:

OK...

☐ Execute decoded files
☐ Keep current article header visible
☐ Include any open articles in decode
☐ Auto-minimize decoding status windows
☐ Verbose status windows
☐ Dumb decode

Browse

Cancel

Smart Filer

Figure 11.8   This dialog box prompts you for a pathname for the decoded file.

You will see a progress window as WinVN decodes the file and a message when the decoding process is complete. Figure 11.9 shows the finished clip art, decoded and viewed on my machine.

A shell program like trn can't handle such seamless decoding of binary files, but it's still possible to download them and decode them a step at a time, as described later in this chapter.

CATCHING UP WITH THE NEWS AND EXITING WINVN

In most newsgroups, you won't read every posting; the sheer number of messages makes that all but impossible. Newsgroup reading is more a matter of hunting through the list of message subjects, looking for those that interest you, and then reading the messages on that subject in threaded fashion. When you've finished, you've pulled what you wanted out of the newsgroups, but the other articles are still unread. You don't want to see them again the next time you ask to see this particular newsgroup, so the thing to do is to tell the software to mark the entire newsgroup, with all messages in it, as read. That way, only unread messages will be marked as such the next time you log on.

Figure 11.9   A successfully decoded image from the alt.binaries.clip-art newsgroup.

To "catch up" your newsgroup in WinVN, do the following:

1. Pull down the Articles menu from the newsgroup postings window.
2. Click on Catch-Up and Exit.

You can see this process in action in Figure 11.10. All messages in the newsgroup will now be marked as read. You will now be taken back to the list of newsgroups, from which you can read another group or exit, as you choose.

To exit WinVN, do the following:

1. Pull down the Network menu from the newsgroups screen
2. Click on Exit.

Exploring Graphical newsreaders

If you're interested in exploring WinVN, you can download it from the following URL:

```
ftp://ftp.ksc.nasa.gov/pub/win3/winvn/wv16_99_.zip
```

WinVN is an example of what can be done in a graphical, windows-based environment to facilitate reading USENET. But don't pick up one or another newsreader and stop there. A host of possibilities exist, all of which contain their strong points. One of the most interesting developments in the newsreader field of late has been the emergence of Netscape. Designed as a browser for the World Wide Web (and discussed at length in

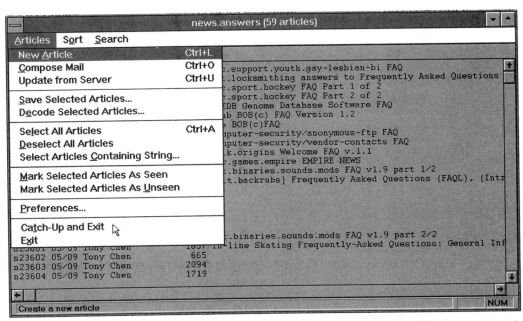

Figure 11.10 Catching up to the news in WinVN; all articles in the newsgroup will be marked as read.

Chapter 14), Netscape brings graphics, audio and moving video into your Internet experience by tapping a system of hypertextually linked information. And among its other talents, it is a superb newsreader.

You can see an example of Netscape at work in Figure 11.11. The figure shows the newsgroup comp.internet.net-happenings, one of the basic newsgroups I use to keep up with Internet events. Each of the postings is shown as a hyperlink; the underlining on each tell me that all I need do to see the post is to click on it. Notice that I have a toolbar across the top of the window that lets me move to a screen for posting new articles, or catch up entirely with the newsgroup now visible. I can also unsubscribe, or move to my list of subscribed newsgroups, with a click of the mouse.

It's a useful environment for newsreading, but Netscape has another trick up its sleeve. In Figure 11.12, you can see what I mean. Here, we are looking at a posting from

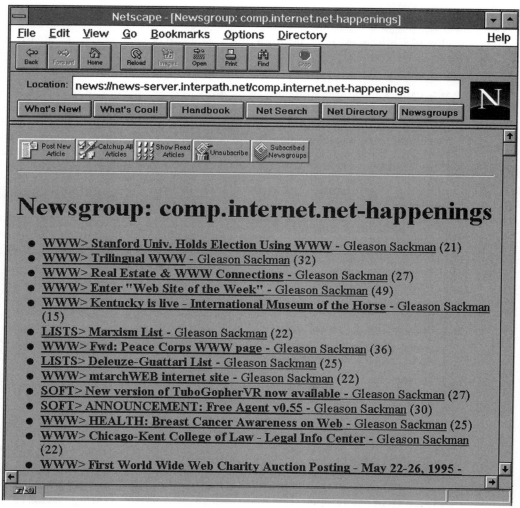

Figure 11.11 Reading a USENET newsgroup with the Netscape browser.

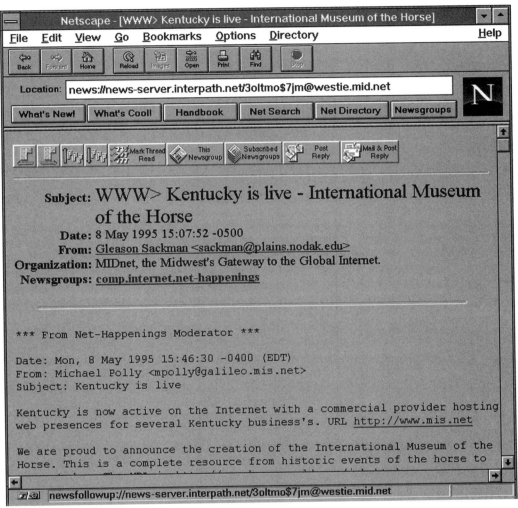

Figure 11.12   Netscape allows you to travel via hyperlink to sites mentioned in USENET postings.

the list shown in the previous figure. The posting tells us about a new World Wide Web site having to do with something called the International Museum of the Horse. But notice that the Web site itself is underlined. This means that we can click on the reference to go directly to the site. We can explore this World Wide Web page at our leisure; when we're ready to return, another mouse click takes us straight back to our newsgroup.

This is heady stuff. If we were to read of an interesting site in another newsreader, we'd have to jot down the address, then go to our Web browser and enter the address to see it. Netscape pulls these functions into a single package, making the news reading experience that much more useful, and saving us time. It will be interesting to see how other Web browsers handle newsgroups. The whole category of browsing tools is undergoing profound change as developers compete to produce an all-purpose interface to the

Internet. And we can expect the dedicated newsreader programs to begin to implement such hypertextual links as well. On the Net, no software program stays the same for long.

Reading the News with trn

Shell account users now know the routine: to make a program work, you type its name at the command prompt. We start pine by typing **pine,** followed by a **RETURN.** And we start trn, the best of the Unix newsreaders, by typing **trn,** followed by a **RETURN.** But first, a historical note. It used to be that first-time users were automatically subscribed to all the newsgroups at their site. Unsubscribing was easy enough; you just typed a **u** at a newsgroup prompt, and you were out of there. But then you realized you were at the top of a very long list, being led through it in prompted fashion one newsgroup at a time. Newsgroup after newsgroup would come up. Did you have to unsubscribe to each one individually?

My first entry into USENET, through The WELL in San Francisco, was an eye-opener. I knew I wanted to read several newsgroups having to do with computer security issues, but I didn't know how to find them. And before I could read anything, I had to page through hundreds upon hundreds of newsgroups, telling each whether I wanted to subscribe to it. I did what most novices do in such a situation: I worked through the entire list, the whole time thinking there was probably some easy-to-use mechanism that would allow me to handle the problem in a few minutes, if only I could discover it.

Later, I learned I was right and that I wasn't alone. Every day on newsgroups like news.newusers.questions, someone asked how to avoid going through the entire list of newsgroups, unsubscribing to each. The answer was to open up a special file and make some relatively simple changes to it. But this seemed like brain surgery to most modem users, who were more comfortable with a menu structure and a more intuitive command system that let them sign up for what they wanted. Fortunately, new software has solved that problem, but there is still the issue of determining which newsgroups you want to subscribe to in the first place, without having to go through each and read it long enough to make that decision. If it strikes you that USENET and the Unix tools available weren't designed with user-friendliness in mind, you're absolutely right.

Creating .newsrc

Nonetheless, the rewards of USENET are worth the effort. Let's plunge ahead by invoking trn. Call your service provider and enter **trn** at the command prompt.

```
% trn
```

What you'll see next should look something like Figure 11.13. You can use the **SPACEBAR** to move to the first prompt. trn will examine the latest newsgroups added at your site and prompt you as to whether you want to subscribe. You'll see the groups listed one at a time, along with a prompt, as in the following:

```
Newsgroup rec.arts.marching.band.college not in .newsrc -- subscribe? [ynYN]
```

Enter an **N** at this prompt; this will tell trn to move through the entire list of new newsgroups, leaving them all unsubscribed. When trn reaches the end of the list, it will present you with a prompt like this:

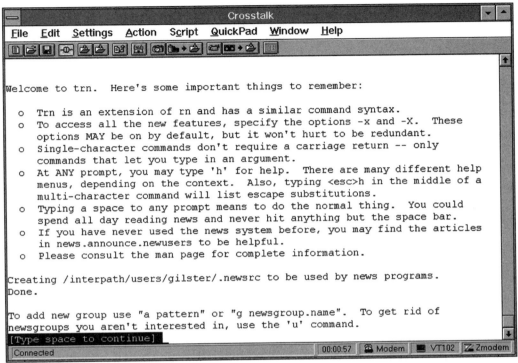

Figure 11.13 Invoking trn for the first time, as viewed in Crosstalk for Windows.

```
****** End of newsgroups -- what next? [qnp]
```

Although it may not seem like it, we've already done something important. As shown in Figure 11.13, trn was trying to set up a file called .newsrc. This is going to be a core file for our USENET participation, because it's responsible for telling the newsreader which newsgroups we plan to follow. When you run trn for the first time, the program looks for this file; if trn doesn't find .newsrc, it will create it. Contained within the .newsrc file is the list of newsgroups available through the server at your site. At present, because you're not subscribed to any newsgroups; this file is empty.

    The job now is to make some additions to trn, to tell it what we want to read. Let's sign up for the alt.internet.services newsgroup, since it's such an important stopping-off point for novices. Many of the basic questions you'll have as you wade into USENET will come up again and again here, along with with answers.

    To add this newsgroup, tell trn to go to that group by using the g command:

```
****** End of newsgroups -- what next? [qnp] g news.announce.newusers
```

You'll get this response:

```
Newsgroup alt.internet.services not in .newsrc -- subscribe? [ynYN]
```

The answer is obvious. Choose y for yes. You'll see this prompt:

```
Put newsgroup where? [$^.Lq]
```

Since we're just adding our first newsgroup, there's no need to worry about its placement. Just hit a **RETURN** to accept the default. You'll now see the newsgroup itself:

```
====== 30645 unread articles in alt.internet.services -- read now? [+ynq]
```

There aren't actually 30,645 postings waiting for us to read; many of them will have been taken off-line by the system administrator to save disk space. But my recommendation would be to reply with a **c** command. This tells trn to consider all these messages read; the next time you sign on, you will start with messages that have accrued since you gave this command.

Our goal is to set up trn for future use. Your first priority should be to get the relevant groups on your subscription list and then proceed to learn the basics of reading them. Type a **c** at the prompt, then, and you'll see this:

```
Do you really want to mark everything as read? [yn]
```

Choose the y again, and you'll see:

```
Marking alt.internet.services as all read.
****** End of newsgroups -- what next? [qnp]
```

Using the above principles, you can start signing up for any groups you want to see; I recommend joining, in the beginning, the list of core newsgroups described earlier in this chapter. Use the **g** command followed by the name of the newsgroup to which you want to subscribe. Some of the groups will prove interesting beyond your expectations; you'll be delighted you subscribed to them. Others will be unexpectedly quiet, with only a message or two a week; some won't have any traffic for long periods. And some will be so busy that you'll finally decide you don't have time to spend on them, and you'll unsubscribe. But these are decisions that can only be made with experience, and as you work through your first week or two of USENET activity, you'll begin to see how newsgroups fit into your routine. The beauty of the process is that you can tailor it explicitly to your own interests.

Using trn to Read Your Newsgroups

One advantage of trn is that it's a simple program to use, although it offers options that can make it both more complex and more powerful. As we've seen, you start it by entering **trn** at the system prompt. This time you should be shown a prompt asking you whether you want to read the material in your various newsgroups. It will look like this, depending on which newsgroups you've chosen:

```
Unread news in news.answers                30 articles
Unread news in news.newusers.questions     12 articles
Unread news in news.software.readers        5 articles
Unread news in comp.mail.misc               6 articles
etc.

******** 1 unread article in news.answers--read now? [+ynq]
```

As noted before, the suggested commands inside the bracketed box aren't the only possibilities, but they do represent the ones you'll probably use. A **y** will cause the first article to appear. An **n** will skip this newsgroup and take you to the next one. A **q** will quit trn altogether.

Choose a **y** now to display the first article. You'll see a screen like the one in Figure 11.14. This is a USENET message, or part of one; it's also called a posting. We're in the newsgroup news.answers, as can be seen from the top of the message header. Notice that this is a moderated newsgroup, meaning messages don't just accumulate here at random, but are sorted and presented through the intervention of a USENET volunteer, who is acting as the publisher of this collected material. Moderated newsgroups, you'll find, often provide more valuable information in less space than their unmoderated cousins, because a good moderator will make sure the material stays on track. In this case, news.answers is designed as a repository of periodic postings, usually known as FAQs (for Frequently Asked Questions); these are lists of the most common queries in each newsgroup, assembled so the group doesn't spend its time answering the same questions over and over.

Newsgroup Header Information

Look more closely at the header and you'll see information not too dissimilar from what appears on a mail message. The message number is followed by a note in brackets telling

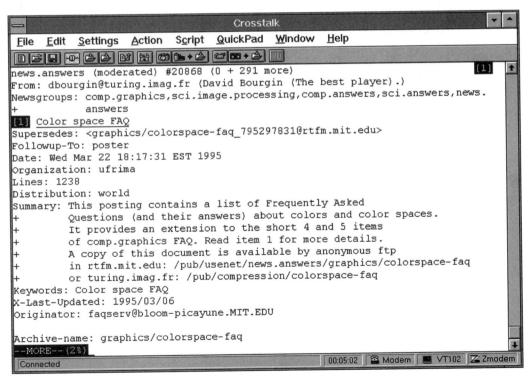

Figure 11.14 A typical USENET message.

you how many more unread messages there are in this newsgroup. The header marked **Newsgroups:** tells you that this posting went to other groups besides news.answers.

It was also sent to comp.graphics, sci.image.processing, comp.answers, and sci. answers. These groups make sense; we can see that the message is a list of frequently asked questions about graphics, color and space.

The heading Followup-To: poster tells you who to contact about this list of questions; in this case, it's the person who posted the article. The organization name, presumably a business name, is ufrima; its address is shown after the From: header at the top of the message. The date of the posting is listed, along with the total number of lines. Just below this is a statement of when the file was last modified. This is included because a FAQ is frequently updated, and you want to keep track of which version you should keep and which might be obsolete. Finally, an archive name, graphics/colorspace-faq, tells us you can also find the FAQ at an archive site.

Paging through a Posting

This FAQ is a long posting. Note at the bottom of the screen the statement of where you are in the message:

```
--MORE--(2%)
```

This tells you there's more to come, and that at present you've read only 2 percent of the entire message. To proceed, press the **SPACEBAR,** *not* the **RETURN** key. (If you use **RETURN,** you advance one line at a time, which, on a message this size, will quickly cause you to wish you had never heard of USENET!) Each subsequent pressing of the **SPACEBAR** takes you down one more page on the screen.

Now, using the **SPACEBAR** and reading as you go, you could work your way through the entire FAQ. On the other hand, maybe you're not that interested in graphics. To proceed immediately to the next message, you can press the **n** key. Pressing it at any —MORE— prompt will take you to the next message. Figure 11.15 shows another message from news.answers.

Many of the fields are the same, although we do note some changes. The FollowUp-To: field, rather than suggesting a reply to the poster of the message, asks that you send any responses directly to the newsgroup comp.infosystems.www.misc. We're also given information about the posting's relationship to previous FAQs. This document has a Supercedes: field, meaning the document replaces one called www/faq/part1_ 795297831@rtfm.mit.edu (the latter address at MIT is an archival site for newsgroup FAQs). The originator of this posting is listed as faqserv@bloom-picayune.mit.edu., and the archival name is www/faq/part1. Finally, we see that the FAQ was last modified on January 26, 1995.

Working through the Topics

We can see from the bottom of the screen that this is another long document; we've only reached the 2 percent mark in our reading of it so far, and again, we can use the **SPACE-BAR** to page through the text, or the **n** command to move to the next document. Reading a USENET newsgroup this way is interesting as you begin to learn how the groups are constructed; it shows you what kinds of information are available on them. However, the charm is likely to wear off quickly as you realize how many messages remain in this

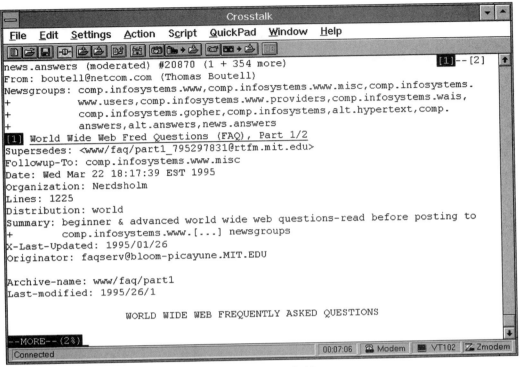

Figure 11.15 Another USENET message with different fields.

particular group. And if you look back at the list of groups we encountered when we first started up trn, you'll see how much reading is ahead if you continue this way. So let's consider another alternative. Let's press an **n** to abort our reading of this FAQ and move immediately to the next message. Then we'll try something new. With a new message on the screen, enter a plus sign: **+**. It will cause the screen display to change completely. Figure 11.16 shows what you'll see.

Examine the new screen closely. We have a listing of the messages in the news.answers newsgroup. Each message is labeled with a single letter at the left margin, along with the name of the poster and, most useful of all, the title of the message. This is helpful indeed. Not only does the listing give us an overview of message traffic on the newsgroup, it also allows us to pick and choose among the messages we'd like to work with. At the bottom of the screen is further information. The Select threads statement tells us that the messages we're looking at here are threaded; that is, they are put together in terms of their content, so we read them in logical order. This saves you from reading part one of a two-part posting, reading several messages in between, and only then getting to part two.

The statement Top 5% means you are looking at 5 percent of the message traffic available in this newsgroup. The bracketed Z, or [>Z], means you can read all the messages if you choose. The system is also telling you that this is the default; do nothing more than press the **RETURN** key or the **SPACEBAR** here and you'll be taken to

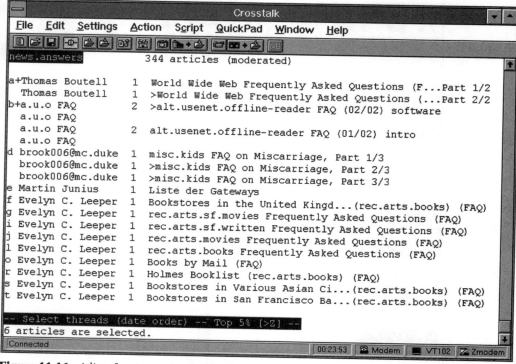

Figure 11.16   A list of messages invoked by the plus (+) key.

the first message, as though you had marked every message for reading. But before we do that, we will look at the message threads on this page and examine how to read them.

trn is easy to work because message selection is simple. To mark a particular message or thread for reading, simply enter the letter next to it. If I want to read the FAQ Bookstores in the United Kingdom, I note its letter, an f. If I enter an **f,** the display changes to show this message has been chosen. A plus sign (+) will appear next to it.

```
f+Evelyn C. Leeper 1 Bookstores in the United Kingd...(rec.arts.books) (FAQ)
```

To read the message, I press a capital **D.** This marks the unselected articles on the current page as already read. It then displays the articles that were selected. Doing this now, I'll see the first of the selected messages, as shown in Figure 11.17. If I choose not to read this message, pressing an **n** will take me to the next message I have selected.

Pressing an **n** after the last marked message takes you back to the message selection screen. You can keep paging through it with repeated **D** commands, reading as you go. When you have worked through all the available messages, you will be taken to the prompt for the next newsgroup. If you're ready to exit at this point, a **q** will take you back to your service provider's command prompt.

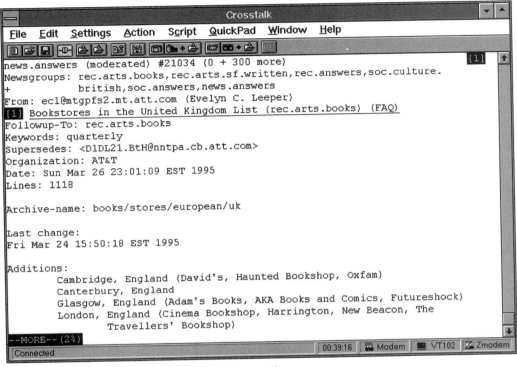

Figure 11.17 A message generated with **D** command.

Responding to a Posting by Mail

As you read the newsgroups, you'll soon become familiar with their conventions and begin to follow ongoing discussions. At some point, you may want to add your own thoughts to what someone else has said. You have two options for doing so. You can respond by sending an electronic mail message to the sender, or you can respond within the newsgroup itself by posting a follow-up message.

Replying by electronic mail is easy. After you finish reading the message you want to respond to, you'll be given a prompt that looks like:

```
End of article 30651 (of 30663) -- what next? [npq]
```

Enter an **r** here. This should result in a response like the one in Figure 11.18.

trn is asking whether I want to include an already prepared file in my answer. The word none in brackets means the default is not to include any file; pressing a **RETURN** here will cause the system to assume I don't wish to include one. Now I am prompted about which editor I will use:

```
Editor [/usr/ucb/vi]:
```

```
To: pangloss@swift.com
Subject: Re: C news on ultrix 4.3
Newsgroups: triangle.wizards
In-Reply-To: â@swift.com
Organization: CONCERT-CONNECT -- Public Access UNIX
Cc:
Bcc:


(Above lines saved in file /home/gilster/.rnhead)

(leaving cbreak mode; cwd=/home/gilster)
Invoking command: Rnmail -h /home/gilster/.rnhead


Prepared file to include [none]:
```

Figure 11.18 Mailing a response to a USENET message.

The default at Interpath (and at many system provider sites running Unix) is vi. Again, I can choose this default by pressing the **RETURN** key. At that point, I'll be put into the vi editor and can compose my reply. When finished with the message, I will press the **ESC** key to into vi's command mode; after that, a **wq** followed by a **RETURN** will take me out of vi and give me the option of sending, editing, or aborting my message.

I could, of course, avoid vi altogether when prompted for a choice of editor. Instead of entering **vi**, I could enter **pico**, followed by a **RETURN.** The choice of editors is yours, and will be determined by your own taste.

Note that by pressing the **r** key, I told trn to send a message to the originator of the posting. If I had chosen to include the original posting for reference, I could have done that by following the same procedure, but using the command **R.**

Responding and Posting in Newsgroups

If you prefer submitting a follow-up article to the newsgroup rather than responding by electronic mail, that's easily done as well. Use the **f** command at the end of the posting or, if you choose to include the original message, the **F** command. You'll be prompted as follows:

```
End of article 41 (of 41)--what next? [npq] f
```

Here's what you'll see:

```
Are you starting an unrelated topic? [yn] n
```

I've entered an **n** at this prompt, to indicate we are staying within the same topic as we write our message; if you want to start a new topic, you'd choose the **y,** in which case you'd be prompted for the topic. Now we see this:

```
(leaving cbreak mode; cwd=/home/gilster)
Invoking command: Pnews -h /home/gilster/.rnhead

This program posts news to many machines throughout the city.
Are you absolutely sure that you want to do this? [ny]
```

The message asks if we're sure we want to post our message. The newsgroup in question is city-wide, so we're reminded that our posting will go throughout the coverage area—Raleigh, Durham, and Chapel Hill. The message is a reminder that frivolous postings take up bandwidth and should therefore be avoided. Assume we think our posting important enough to merit inclusion in the newsgroup. We choose a **y.**

```
Prepared file to include [none]:
```

As before, we're prompted for a prepared file. We press the **RETURN** key to indicate no file inclusion will be necessary.

```
Editor [/usr/ucb/vi]:
```

And again, we're asked for an editor. Choosing vi simply by entering a **RETURN,** we're taken back to the vi screen, where we can compose and send our message.

As with responding through electronic mail, we have options for including the original message in our response. To do this, use an **F** instead of an **f** as the follow-up posting command. Figure 11.19 shows what an inserted message looks like.

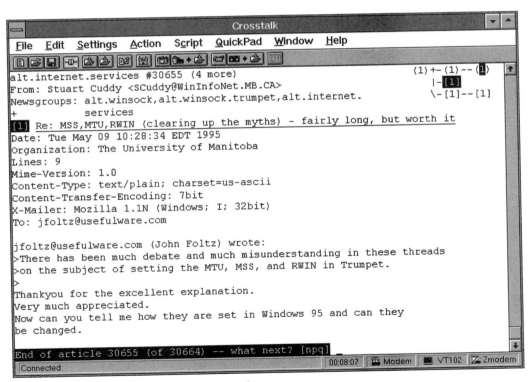

Figure 11.19 A message inserted inside a reply.

As you see, the original message is followed by the comment. The reason for doing this is that people sign up for many newsgroups, and it's easy to forget exactly which message a particular posting refers to. Quoting the message ensures that everyone's memory is refreshed.

If you'd like to try posting without going "live," so to speak, consider a post to the misc.test group. It was established for test postings, making it a good place to aim for when you first try out these commands. The recipients are guaranteed to be patient people.

When New Newsgroups Are Created

Newsgroups are being created all the time. Indeed, one of the great pleasures of USENET is the vitality of such entries, as like minds find each other and begin to share common interests. trn will notify you when new newsgroups have become available from your server. When this happens, the message differs from the usual one when you first invoke the program. It will look like this:

```
Checking for new newsgroups...

Newsgroup rec.arts.tv.tiny-toon not in .newsrc--subscribe? [ynYN]
Newsgroup k12.news not in .newsrc--subscribe? [ynYN]
```

You now have several options.

Y   Adds all the new newsgroups, putting them at the end of the .newsrc file and marking them as groups you want to read.

y   Adds only the newsgroup you've been asked about.

N   Adds all new groups to the end of your .newsrc file, marking them as unsubscribed.

n   Forgets about the newsgroups entirely.

Once you have answered the question of whether you want to subscribe, you'll also have a range of options about where to put each newsgroup. The following prompt will appear:

```
Put newsgroup where? [$^.L]
```

The options are as follows:

^	Puts the newsgroup first among groups you read.
$	Puts the newsgroup last among your groups.
.	Puts the newsgroup before the current newsgroup.
-newsgroup name	Puts the newsgroup before the newsgroup you name.
+newsgroup name	Puts the newsgroup after the newsgroup you name.
L	Lists newsgroups and their positions.

Growing an Article Tree

Note, incidentally, the small diagram in the top right corner of Figure 11.19. This is the article "tree" for that message; it shows you how the article fits in with other messages of its thread (you won't see this if the article isn't threaded). All replies branch off from the original messages; in trn terminology, "child" articles branch off from "parent" articles.

The numbers in the tree are all the same: ones. This means the subject of the thread hasn't changed during its existence. Read the tree from left to right. The original message is at the left. Replies branch off from it. Unread articles are always enclosed in brackets; articles you've read are in parentheses. The article currently being displayed is always highlighted, including its brackets.

When a thread grows lengthy, the article tree can become unwieldy, but it gives you a good sense of where the message you're reading stands in relation to what has gone before. For further information on trn's article trees, you can look in the manual for trn by giving the command **man trn** at your system provider's command prompt.

Posting a New Message on a Different Topic

Suppose now that you choose to post a new message; your topic will be different than anything now under discussion. We can do this with trn's **f** command as well. As you're reading a newsgroup, use the **$** command to position yourself past the last message in the current group. You should see something like this:

```
End of article 21415 (of 21474)--what next? [npq])
```

Enter a **$** command and you'll receive this prompt:

```
What next? [npq]
```

At this prompt, use the **f** command to begin a message. You'll be prompted for Subject: and Distribution: You will see on-screen:

```
Subject:
```

Enter whatever subject is appropriate. The next prompt will ask how widely this message should be distributed:

```
Distribution:
```

A **RETURN** enters the default distribution for the newsgroup in question. Remember, the network is worldwide, and the last thing you want is to distribute your posting beyond the boundaries of its applicability. Distribution lists depend on the server you're using, but some common terms follow.

world	Worldwide distribution.
na	Distribution limited to North America.
usa	Distribution limited to the United States.

nc	Distribution limited to North Carolina, or whatever state is indicated.
city	Limited to a particular community.
organization	A particular group of local users, and so on.

Assume world is the default. Should you decide to post to a group with world-wide coverage, but limit your posting to a particular area, you must enter one of these terms in the Distribution: field.

Now you'll be asked whether you know what you're doing:

```
This program posts news to thousands of machines throughout the entire civilized
world. Your message will cost the net hundreds if not thousands of dollars to
send everywhere. Please be sure you know what you are doing. Are you absolutely
sure that you want to do this? [ny] y

Prepared file to include [none]:

Editor [/usr/ucb/vi]:
```

After answering a **y** to continue, you're subsequently prompted as to whether you want to include a prepared file. You could do this if you had a file you wanted to fold into the message, but for now, assume you don't. Answer with a **RETURN,** which triggers the default command of **none.** Next you're asked which editor you want to use; the answer again is **RETURN** for the default editor on your system. It's most likely to be vi.

Figure 11.20 shows what you see next, a vi screen with a series of possible fields to fill out before you begin your message. As you can see, the Newsgroups: and Subject: fields have already been filled in by the software. The next fields are:

Summary	Here you can enter a summary of the article you're about to write. Make sure you're precise about this, so people who only read headers will know what they're getting into if they call up your message.
Expires	If you enter a date here, your article will be deleted after this date. Your request may be ignored depending on the site. Can be left blank.
Sender	No need to put anything here unless you're sending the article for someone else. If you are, put your own name in.
Followup-To	This field is where follow-up messages related to your message will be sent. You could put a single newsgroup name here, or else use the word poster. That indicates you are collecting comments and will summarize them later. You can leave this blank if you choose.
Distribution	For determining how far the article will travel. You've already answered this, so you can leave it blank.
Keywords	This field might or might not be useful. Some mail readers can use keyword entries entered here. Filling it in is optional.

Having filled out these fields or not as you choose, you can now enter your message. When you're through, you'll be prompted like this:

```
Send, abort, edit, or list?
```

Choose an **S** to send your message, an **a** to abort it.

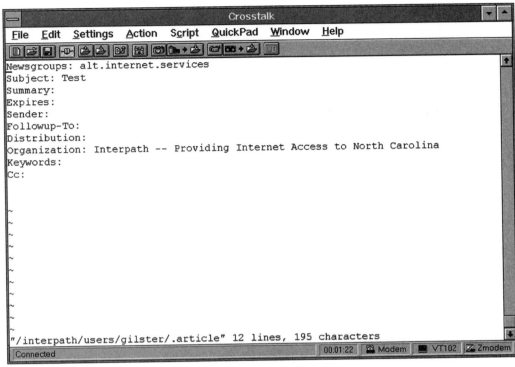

Figure 11.20 The vi screen as you post a new message.

Saving the News

Read USENET for even a few days and you're bound to begin accumulating interesting material you'd like to save. But remember that when you want to save a message that SLIP/PPP and shell accounts work differently. With WinVN, you could simply save a displayed article to your hard disk; it was already located on the disk as you read it. With a shell account, you have to save the article to your service provider's disk; you can then download it at a later time to your own. The **s** command handles the save process. At the end of the article you're reading, or the end of one screen of the article, type an **s**. Figure 11.21 shows a message I've decided to save, the FAQ for a newsgroup on cryptography. I can give the **s** command at the first prompt at the bottom of the screen, followed by the filename of my choice.

Now the system will note such a file doesn't yet exist. The prompt is:

```
File /interpath/users/gilster/News/crypto doesn't exist--
       use mailbox format? [ynq]
```

I'm being asked what format to put the file in. If I choose mailbox format by typing a **y,** the file is saved in a way that my mail reader can understand. I could call it up with the **mail -f** *filename* command to read it. I would see the following prompt:

```
Saved to mailbox /interpath/users/gilster/News/crypto
```

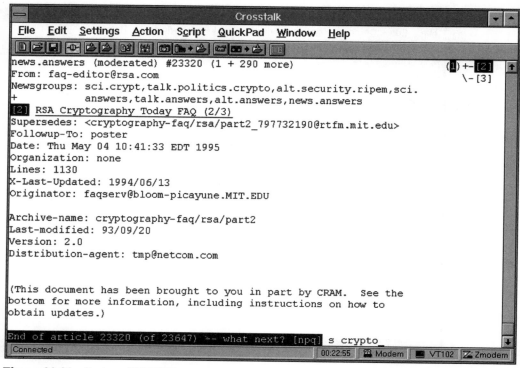

Figure 11.21   Saving a USENET message.

If I choose no, or **n**, the file is saved just as it looks on the screen, as a file in the corresponding directory:

```
Saved to file /interpath/users/gilster/News/crypto
```

Using a Saved File

trn has now saved the file under the name you specified. You must switch to the directory where it's kept to use it. As you can see from the preceding, in my system, the directory is *interpath/users/gilster/News*. Using the **cd News** command, I can switch to that directory and then determine the directory's contents using the **ls** command. I'll see something like the following:

```
comp/          crypto          news/          triangle/
```

Note that three of these items are directories, as shown by the slash after their names. The other is the file I have just saved. I can now download it to my own system for saving on disk, printing, or whatever.

Getting Out of a Newsgroup

Maybe you'd prefer to move out of this newsgroup and on to another before you've finished reading your articles. A **q** will cause trn to leave its article selection mode and take you to the next available newsgroup, where you can make a newsgroup selection command. To remind you, this is the newsgroup selection command prompt:

```
******** 14 unread articles in news.newusers.questions--read now? [+ynq]
```

No matter what newsgroups you're working with, the prompt is always [+ynq].

If you want to move to a different newsgroup, you can do so with the **g** command at this prompt; **g news.answers** will take me directly there. If I'm not already a subscriber, I'll be asked if I want to become one.

Using a Kill File

Given the huge amount of information flowing through the various newsgroups, we could profit from some kind of filter, a custom-designed way to block out messages we don't want to see. No newsreader is very good at this yet, but trn does allow you to set up a so-called *kill file*. This is simply a file in which you can enter words or names you would like to exclude from your reading. When you set up a kill file, articles containing the term you put in the file do not appear on the thread selection menu, reducing your workload.

To set up a kill file for a particular newsgroup, use the **Ctrl-K** command, either at the thread selection level or the article-reading level. The kill file is immediately created and is placed inside the vi text editor. You now enter the words you want the kill file to search for; you can also edit the file to remove previous terms you have entered.

Perhaps you are reading a newsgroup on modern art and a lengthy discussion has emerged about architecture. Uninterested in the subject, you want to block such messages from your reading list. To do so, you would press **Ctrl-K** and enter the following into your kill file:

```
/architecture/j
```

The term in question, as you can see, is surrounded by slashes, and is case-insensitive (although the **j** modifier must be in lowercase as shown). If you choose to tell trn to block any articles containing the term *architecture* anywhere in their headers, you would use this command:

```
/architecture/h:j
```

And you can even search the entire text of articles by using this command:

```
/architecture/a:j
```

When you next read the newsgroup in question, trn will search for articles containing the terms you have entered in the kill file. When it finds one, it will give you the article number and a statement about how it has disposed of it:

```
2418    Junked
```

From this point on, you can go to the thread selection menu to read articles as usual.

Reading articles in a newsgroup may also clue you in to the fact that certain posters are not providing information that you can use. Perhaps a particularly garrulous person is annoying you with lengthy messages. To remove this person from your reading, you can put his or her address in your kill file along with the **h** modifier. Here is an example:

```
/gbshaw@fabian\.com/h:j
```

Here we have put gbshaw@fabian.com on our blacklist. The backslash in the statement is there for a reason. The period (.) character must be preceded by a \ because otherwise it may be misinterpreted by Unix as part of a regular expression, which is used for complicated search operations.

A kill file can be useful in particular situations, but don't forget that you've created one. After all, the subject that you don't want to read about in a newsgroup today may later pique your interest. Because it is simple to edit a kill file to make necessary changes, think of the file as a temporary expedient to handle certain newsgroup scenarios, rather than as a set of parameters to be left in place from now on. Active use of your kill file can make your USENET reading more focused and more enjoyable.

Exiting trn

A **q** entered while you're reading messages will quit the selection process and take you back to the newsgroup selection command for the *current* newsgroup. At the newsgroup selection prompt, you can enter another **q** to quit trn altogether.

Four Levels of trn Commands

By now, the command structure of trn may be evident. There are several command levels.

1. The first level is the set of commands you can use *at the newsgroup selection prompt,* which is what you see when you enter trn, and where you emerge when you finish reading one newsgroup and are on your way to another.
2. The second command set occurs *at the thread level,* where you have a variety of options to manipulate threads.
3. The third set is at the level of *the individual article,* comprising those commands you can use to work with an individual posting, including making a reply to it.
4. The fourth set is the commands available *as you're paging through a multipage article.* On this level, trn is similar to the more program, and we need not delve deeply into its command structure. But the other three levels do need our attention.

trn Newsgroup Selection Commands

You've just entered trn and encountered a prompt, asking you what you want to do about a particular newsgroup. The prompt looks like this:

```
******** 16 unread articles in alt.fan.wodehouse--read now? [+ynq]
```

The following commands will show you what you can do at the *newsgroup selection prompt.* Some of these commands are basic; you'll use them every time you put trn to work. Others are obscure, and may never draw your attention, but you may be surprised how useful they can be.

y	Read this newsgroup consecutively.
+	Display a thread selector screen.
=	List the subjects of the articles in this newsgroup. Unlike the + command, an = will not provide threading. It will simply list the number of each article along with its title. To read a thread, you would have to note the numbers of each article in that thread, then enter each number as you go.
u	Unsubscribe from this newsgroup.
c	Catch up with all the messages in this newsgroup. This means trn will mark all the messages in the group as read.
A	Abandon any changes regarding the read or unread status of this newsgroup since you started trn. You might use this, for example, if you decide not to read a set of articles and then change your mind.
n	Go to the next newsgroup containing unread messages.
N	Go to the next newsgroup, whether it contains unread messages or not.
p	Return to the previous newsgroup with unread news.
P	Go to the previous newsgroup, whether it contains unread news or not.
-	Go to the previously displayed newsgroup.
1	Go to the first newsgroup.
^	Go to the first newsgroup with unread news.
$	Go to the last newsgroup.
g *name*	Go to the newsgroup matching the name you enter. You can subscribe to new newsgroups by going to them, as we saw earlier.
/*pattern*	Search for a newsgroup matching the pattern you've entered. For example, if I enter **/comp.** at the prompt, I'll see something like this:

```
Searching...

[0 unread in comp.ai.digest--skipping]
[0 unread in comp.archives--skipping]
[0 unread in comp.binaries.hypercard--skipping]
[0 unread in comp.binaries.ibm.pc--skipping]
[0 unread in comp.dcom.telecom.digest--skipping]
[0 unread in comp.mail--skipping]
[0 unread in comp.mail.mhs--skipping]
[0 unread in comp.mail.mhs.arpa--skipping]
******** 8 unread articles in comp.mail.misc--read now? [+ynq]
```

	trn has skipped those .comp groups having no unread messages, flagging the first newsgroup in the .comp category where I do have unread messages.
?*pattern*	Search backward for newsgroup matching the pattern you enter. Appending an **r** to either of these searches will cause trn to stop at each newsgroup to prompt you whether you want to read it, even if it includes no new messages.
l *pattern*	This is a handy command. It searches a list of unsubscribed newsgroups for a particular pattern. Use it, for example, if you're doing research and

want to know whether there's a USENET group involved in your topic. Suppose I was preparing a study of Groucho Marx. I might search the USENET groups for **l humor.** Here's what I'd get:

```
Unsubscribed but mentioned in /home/gilster/.newsrc:

alt.humor.oracle
rec.humor
rec.humor.d
rec.humor.flame
rec.humor.funny
rec.humor.oracle
rec.humor.oracle.d
```

m *name* This command is useful if you want to change the order in which your newsgroups are presented. If you simply type an **m** with no name, followed by a **RETURN,** you'll be prompted to move the newsgroup to a new location. Here are the choices:

^	Puts the newsgroup first.
$	Puts the newsgroup last.
.	Puts it before the current newsgroup.
−*newsgroup name*	Puts it before that newsgroup.
+*newsgroup name*	Puts it after that newsgroup.
L	Lists newsgroups and their positions.

o *pattern* Display only those newsgroups matching the pattern you list.

a *pattern* Display newsgroups matching your pattern, including unsubscribed newsgroups.

L List contents of current .newsrc.

q Quit trn.

x Quit, restoring .newsrc to the way it was before you started trn.

trn Thread Selection Commands

This section describes the commands you can use at the *thread level.* They're available to you when you're looking at a screen with the thread titles listed, as follows:

```
a Tod Hagan 2   internetMCI & Linux
  Robert Brown
b Peter Conway      1   Nationwide UUCP Access!
d GENE EHRICH       1   Request for Quotation
e Celestin Company  1   Providers of Commercial Internet Ac...(POCIA) Directory
f adesai@cyberenet  1   >WWW Space Wanted
g sales@tiac.net    2   The Internet Access Company (TIAC) serves ...Area Codes
  RayG
i CDHRiehle 1  >ISP Watch - Buyers Be Aware!!
  Daniel P Dern     1   >Ethics and courtesy
j jarrow    1   interaccess vs netcom

-- Select threads (date order) -- Top 20% [>Z] --
```

At this prompt, you have the following choices:

a-z, 0-9	Select or deselect the thread by its letter or number.
RETURN	Start reading the newsgroup. If no threads are selected, start at the beginning of the group.
z	Same as **RETURN.** Start reading the newsgroup.
y	This is a toggle switch. If you choose a thread for reading and then change your mind, you can deselect it with a second **y** command.
k	Mark the current thread as killed.
m	Unmark the current thread.
—	Allows you to create a range of numbers, upon which the last marking action takes effect. Thus I could use **m** to unmark a thread, and then enter **a-c** to unmark those numbered postings. This is relatively clumsy to use, but it works when you want to unmark a large range of threads.
@	Toggle all thread selections. In other words, if you've marked the first four threads for reading and then enter the **@,** you'll unmark the first four and mark all the rest.
n or **]**	Move to the next thread.
p or **[**	Move to the previous thread.
<	Move to the previous page.
>	Move to the next page.
^	Move to the first page.
$	Move to the last page.
X	Mark any unselected articles as read, and start reading the articles you have selected.
D	Mark unselected articles as read, and begin reading the articles you have selected. If no articles are marked, a **D** command causes trn to proceed to the next page.
J	Mark all articles you have selected as read. Use this command if you change your mind after marking a large number of articles.
/pattern	Search all articles for the pattern you have chosen. Entering **/compuserve,** for example, allows you to search for messages containing the word compuserve. If trn finds any, it will print the number of the articles, as follows:

```
/compuserve
6952
6953
Done
Selected 2 threads.
```

Pattern searching like this can save you time if you're browsing through a newsgroup for particular information. You can also enter a series of modifiers in the form ***/pattern/modifiers*** to limit your search. For example:

/compuserve/h	Scans headers only for *compuserve*.
/compuserve/a	Scans entire articles for *compuserve*.
/compuserve/r	Scans previously read articles for *compuserve*.
N	Leave this newsgroup without changing it and proceed to the next newsgroup.
U	A handy command, **U** switches between read and unread articles. This allows you to toggle back and forth; if you remember seeing an interesting article yesterday that you read but neglected to save, you could use **U** to call up a list of read articles, find your article, and read it again.
L	Change the trn display. Use it as a toggle switch, to move back and forth between terse mode (no authors shown for the articles), and verbose mode (authors shown).
^k	Edit kill file.
q	Quit selection mode.
Q	Quit and return to newsgroup selection prompt for this newsgroup.

trn Article Selection Commands

This section describes the commands you can use *while a particular article is on-screen.* You have moved past the thread selection commands by choosing an article to read. At the end of the article, you'll see this prompt:

```
End of article 2400 (of 2402)--what next? [npq]
```

At this prompt, you have the following choices:

n or **<spacebar>**	Move to next unread article. If you're reading a threaded discussion, this moves to the next posting in the discussion on that topic.
N	Move to next article.
Ctrl-N	Scan for next unread article with same subject.
p	Move to previously read article.
P	Move to previous article.
Ctrl-P	Move to previous unread article with same subject.
>	Read the next selected thread.
<	Read the previously selected thread.
t	Display a diagram of the article in relation to other articles in the thread. This information is normally shown at the top right of a message's first screen.
number	Go to specified article. **9368** takes you to the article with that number in the newsgroup.

/pattern/modifiers	Scan forward for an article matching the pattern you've indicated in the subject line. ***?pattern?*** scans backward. With both of these commands, you can use modifiers:

r	Scan articles you've already read.
h	Scan headers.
a	Scan entire articles.
c	Make case-sensitive.

Examples: **/maps/h** searches forward, examining the headers of messages for the word maps. **?maps?r** searches backward, examining the subject line of articles you've already read for the word maps.

f	Submit a follow-up article to the newsgroup. Can also be used to post a new article if you follow the prompts and insert a new topic.
F	Submit a follow-up article that includes the article you're responding to.
r	Reply to the sender of the article by mail.
R	Reply to the sender by mail and include the article.
s	Save to a file. Follow this with a filename. Thus **s library** saves the article to a file called library.
w	Save to a file, but without the header.
c	Catch up. Marks all articles in the newsgroup as read.
b	Back up one page.
^	Go to first unread article.
$	Go to end of newsgroup.
m	Mark article as unread.
M	Mark an article as still unread even after you've exited the newsgroup.
,	Mark the current article as read, along with its replies.
J	Mark the entire thread as read.
^k	Edit kill file.
=	List the subjects of unread articles.
+	Enter thread selection mode.
U	Unread articles. When you give this command, you'll receive a prompt for what you want to mark as unread. The possibilities are:

+	Go back to select thread mode, with all articles marked as unread.
t	Mark this thread's articles as unread.
s	Mark the current article and its descendant articles as unread.
a	Mark all articles in the newsgroup as unread.

n	Use this if you change your mind. It leaves everything as it was.
u	Unsubscribe from the current newsgroup.
q	Quit the current newsgroup.
Q	Quit the current newsgroup but remain at the newsgroup selection prompt for that group.

Moving Photographs over the Network

You wouldn't know it to look at them on-line, but some of the postings that move over USENET are actually photographs and graphics. A number of newsgroups handle such traffic, from alt.binaries.pictures to alt.fractals.pictures. Looking through a file list from alt.binaries.pictures, I find such scenes as a sunset, a satellite view of the western United States, a shot of Bruce Lee, and a bit of Chinese art, most of it available in GIF format. GIF stands for Graphics Interchange Format, which has become a standard for storing pictures. Another format you'll see on occasion is JPEG, a storage format with built-in compression to save disk space. Often a graphics file will be zipped; it will sport a .zip file suffix, as in sunset.zip, and will need to be unpacked before it can be viewed.

We know that a graphical newsreader like WinVN makes it possible to select and decode binary photographs automatically. This is helpful indeed, for the appearance of a USENET message containing a photograph is intimidating. You can see an example of one in Figure 11.22. And while a Unix shell account doesn't automate the process, we can still download and use photographic items.

Working with uudecode

To do this, we'll first need to save and download a graphics file. I can use the **s** command as I'm reading the file to save it to the disk on my service provider's computer. Notice that our file contains two parts; many graphics files contain more than this. You must save each part as a separate file. I usually give each saved file an identifiable name. In this case, since we're dealing with a picture of a bridge, I'll call the first file bridge1.uue and the second bridge2.uue. Why the .uue suffix? If you read the chapter on using the Internet by mail, you'll recall that the suffix is necessary because we're going to use a program, uudecode, that requires that suffix on the files it manipulates.

Once I've saved both files and exited trn, I can download the files with the command **sx-b bridge1.uue bridge2.uue.** Once I have both files on my own hard disk, I'm ready to go to work. I'll first need to get uudecode, the software program that can turn this ASCII soup into something a graphics viewer can understand. In Chapter 8, we found it on CompuServe. You can also get it through anonymous FTP from a number of sites. The box on the next page shows how.

Untangling an Image on Your Computer

Once you have a copy of uudecode, as well as the image files, on your own computer, you can go off-line and decode them. If you're a **DOS** user, for example, you would enter the command **uudecode bridge1.** (At this point, you don't need to mention the .uue extension, because uudecode will look for and find it. It will also move on immediately to the second of the two files, decoding it and combining it with the first.) You will then have a workable graphics file that can be called up inside an appropriate graphics viewer.

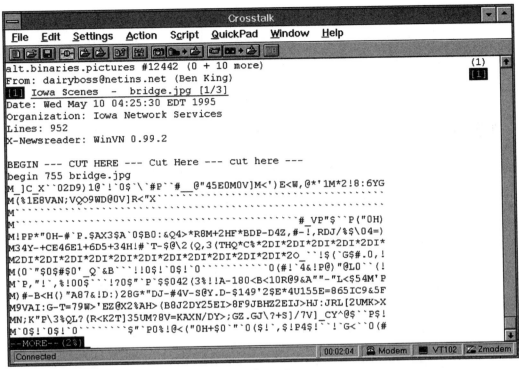

```
                              Crosstalk                           ▼  ▲
  File  Edit  Settings  Action  Script  QuickPad  Window  Help
  ▣▣▣◫▣▣▣▣▣▣◦▸▣ ▣◦▸▣ ▣
  alt.binaries.pictures #12442 (0 + 10 more)                   (1) ▲
  From: dairyboss@netins.net (Ben King)                        [1]
  [1] Iowa Scenes  -  bridge.jpg [1/3]
  Date: Wed May 10 04:25:30 EDT 1995
  Organization: Iowa Network Services
  Lines: 952
  X-Newsreader: WinVN 0.99.2

  BEGIN --- CUT HERE --- Cut Here --- cut here ---
  begin 755 bridge.jpg
  M_]C_X``02D9)1@`!`0```0````#_VP!#``(!`0$!`0(!`0$"`@("`@0#`@("`@4$
  M(%E8VAN;'!_``$!@`0(`@0(`@0(`@0``````````````#_VP!#`0(""`@("
  M```````````````````````````````````````````````# _VP"__O)(""
  M`````````````````````````````````````````## _VP"_$`"("``````
  M!PP`"``H0`P`!`@$`$`#`$`@$`$`#!!A$0`!Q`E!)RBw$B$0`#`N0;
  M34Y-+CCE!1E+6D41H!N`A!`ahu`'UDYlmhnp`L@D$%%V9F:IqrS4W6Q8iJusK*0
  M2DI.kCp-sLm6ucrK2xscXJzdHV2d3h5eoOEhYaHiIovKKmrrK2uGBucnK0*
  Mt+Tk9vf4-b(0`"$0$#$0`_Q`_&B`@`$!0!!!!!0`!A`!1`4`$&!`&!Y`#`.(
  M`P`,!0-`P0$&`$!`<$$-_qQ%B0US/%1J`(hO.QQR-``C:0_2_Z_`_0`0`Q`P
  M)#4S-oD3&Xb<VW/\_8$E/*__aA"Y`hAX(f"A`!`Qp&@1`!"!+(_7(5$O965E/F@
  M9VdoaWpTH9_`H`mAgvLhw@Ck/YY9Y6]0H6b9pj@'s@!j&&@U>`q'xZ`ac9eX>X
  Mn8;K"P\3%QL?(R<K2T)35UM?8V=KAXN/D)7V[_CY_^P!`@A@#P$`AP#`#+X
  M`O-$!OP!0`````$$/@$#$`B$A`A#$S3&"#A.'`Q`!!#;((`$$`'`QP"@>("(!`(#`
  --MORE-- (2%)
  Connected                        00:02:04  🖳 Modem  ▣ VT102  ▨ Zmodem
```

Figure 11.22   The ASCII representation of a bridge in Iowa.

Tracking Down a File Viewer

Which graphics viewer? Fortunately, numerous viewers are available over the Internet. As we did with uudecode, we can use archie to find one. Because VPIC is a popular program, we will look for it. At your system's command prompt, then, enter **archie -m 25 vpic** (the **-m 25** statement reduces the number of hits you'll get to 25). This, of course, assumes you have an archie client available through your service provider. If you don't, you can run an archie search. When I did this recently to find VPIC, I tracked down numerous sites, such as ftp://oak.oakland.edu. The complete URL there was:

What You Need: A Program for uudecoding

The Programs: For MS-DOS machines, use uudecode. For Windows machines, use Wincode.

How to Get Them: These programs are available at numerous sites. For now, try to retrieve uudecode for MS-DOS at the following URL:

ftp://oak.oakland.edu/SimTel/msdos/decode/uuexe532.zip

Wincode for Microsoft Windows can be found at this URL:

ftp://mrcnext.cso.uiuc.edu/pub/win3/util/wincode.zip

```
ftp://oak.oakland.edu/SimTel/msdos/gif/vpic60e.zip
```

You'll need to unzip this file and read through its documentation before using it, but when you do, you'll find that the incomprehensible ASCII text we downloaded from USENET has now turned into a lovely photograph of an Iowa scene, as shown in Figure 11.23. Don't forget, too, that Windows versions of display programs are abundant; you might run an archie search for a program called Lview, which is excellent.

FAQs and How to Find Them

Frequently Asked Questions are those questions that you don't want to tie up bandwidth by asking. They're such common queries that everyone is tired of answering them, and although USENET etiquette implies a forgiving attitude towards novices (indeed, it's part of the credo that experienced users should help newcomers wherever they can), in most cases such help will come in the form of a pointer to the relevant FAQ. After obtaining and reading this document, you may well find your question answered. If, on the other hand, it doesn't appear in the FAQ, then by all means float it past the newsgroup's membership.

Where do you find FAQs? One certain method is to follow the newsgroup in question, where the FAQ will be reposted sooner or later. Another method is to keep an eye out in news.answers, where FAQs are also posted as they arrive.

On the other hand, you may not want to wait for the latest FAQ if you have a question that needs answering now. Fortunately, many newsgroups maintain archives where

Figure 11.23 The photograph decoded; a bridge in Iowa.

their FAQs are stored. comp.ai.news.answers, for example, offers an archive where you can find its document Frequently Asked Questions About AI. It's archived as ai-faq/ part1. news.announce.newusers offers a FAQ called Answers to Frequently Asked Questions about USENET. It's available in an archive under the name usenet-faq/part1.

What You Need: An archive for USENET FAQs

Where to Find It: Go to the following URL:

ftp://rtfm.mit.edu/pub/usenet/news.answers/

A very useful periodic posting that can keep you up to speed about which news-groups offer which FAQs is Jonathan I. Kamens' List of Periodic Informational Postings. Kamens is one of those USENET volunteers who keep the whole show rolling; we heavy USENET users owe him and his like a considerable debt of gratitude.

What You Need: A Way to Keep Up with USENET FAQs

The Document: List of Periodic Informational Postings, by Jonathan Kamens

How to Get It: It's available when updated on the newsgroup news.answers. You can also retrieve it through this URL:

ftp://rtfm.mit.edu/pub/usenet/news.answers/periodic-postings/

The filenames are part1, part2 and so on.

USENET Rules of the Road

Like any other communications medium, from CB radio to smoke signals, USENET has developed its own set of rules and regulations. True, no central organization exists to enforce them, but a broad consensus has emerged regarding the proper way to behave. You'll want to be sensitive to the nuances of the on-line world, not only to avoid poten-tial embarrassment, but to contribute to USENET's growth as a powerful tool for learn-ing, one that works only when everyone concerned makes the necessary effort.

Do You Really Need to Post?

This may seem an odd question; putting your thoughts on-line for other people to read is what USENET news is all about, but within limits. Think of your local movie theater. You've settled in to enjoy the show, but right behind you is a family who seem to think they're watching the movie in their living room. They comment on every action and carry on a conversation about what happened at work that day. It doesn't take long before your enjoyment of the film is spoiled. It's time to look for a new seat.

A newsgroup can fall prey to the same problems. Some participants jump into con-versations without getting a good feel for what's going on, and include messages that may be off the subject not only of the thread, but of the entire newsgroup. In addition to needlessly congesting the network with this traffic, they've broken the continuity of ongoing discussions. So post carefully, and give some thought to what you have to say. The very power of USENET, its international reach to a vast audience, can become a liability if network users don't play by the rules.

Use E-Mail Where You Can

Frequently, the best way to send a message is through e-mail. Maybe you'd like to thank someone for his or her help in answering a question you posted last week. Why waste network bandwidth on it, when a simple e-mail note would suffice? The most common example of this kind of thing is the "me too" posting. Someone asks whether anyone reading the newsgroup knows a good source for popcorn poppers. Immediately, three other people leave a message saying, in essence, "I want to know the same thing." These messages are superfluous and, if sent at all, should be directed by e-mail to the person posting the original message.

Know Your Destination

Having decided your contribution is worth the bandwidth, think carefully about where you want it to go. The major newsgroups we've examined are posted all over the world, while other groups are regional or local in nature, like the mcnc and triangle groups I subscribe to. It's one thing to post a favorite recipe on an international cooking newsgroup; it's quite another to post a review of your favorite restaurant on that same group, considering your message will be read by thousands of people who could care less if the Crab Rangoon at Joe's Place in Spokane, Washington, is particularly good on Tuesdays.

Use Descriptive Titles for Your Postings

Most of us sign up for more newsgroups than we can possibly read all the way through; that's one advantage of using software that's lets us identify articles by title. But the advantage amounts to little when the titles we are presented with are vague or incomprehensible. Then we must call up the article anyway to see what it is or, more likely, simply ignore it altogether. Make your titles count.

Avoid Advertising

USENET grew up in a noncommercial environment with an emphasis upon communications rather than proprietary rights. This noncommercial bias remains today, although there are certain hierarchies, notably the biz groups, that challenge the old orthodoxy. You can post a product announcement, for example, as long as you're posting in an appropriate group, like comp.newprod. And when making such an announcement, you should stick to the facts rather than hyping the product. A low-key approach designed to inform readers of particular newsgroups about products of interest to them is acceptable. Hawking your company's wares by posting in multiple newsgroups and engaging in blatant advertising is not.

Avoid Flame Wars

Flames are messages stuffed with opinion and argument; flame wars are the verbal equivalent of a catfight. There are places, like the talk newsgroups, where debate can lead to such wars, and they're fine in their place. But tying up the network with a barrage of personal invective is a sure way to lose the attention of anyone serious about the topic.

Keep Your Signature Short

Signature files are those standard inserts we looked at in Chapter 7, on electronic mail. They usually contain your name, address, and any other pertinent information. Long signatures tie up bandwidth and become exasperating when the same individual uses them over and over in a discussion. In particular, you should avoid wasting everybody's time with crude ASCII drawings or other forms of digital preening.

Exercise Care in Quoting

It's often helpful to quote a message you're responding to, to remind everyone of the context of your posting. But do you really need to quote all three pages of a message, with your comments interspersed between the lines? Choose only the part of the message that is germane to the conversation, adding your comments after it.

News Isn't Always News

In an era of CNN and satellite communications, we don't need to use USENET to find out what's happening in the way of breaking events. So if the urge strikes you to fire off a message to your favorite newsgroup announcing the latest sports scores or the defeat of an incumbent senator, remind yourself that most of your audience will consider this old news by the time they read it.

Clarity Is All

Because USENET is a nonverbal medium, we lose all the signals normally available to us in conversation. As with electronic mail, remember that a wide audience might not understand messages of exceeding subtlety, and that sarcasm might easily be inferred from a message someone else took as merely humorous. If you're in doubt how something you write might be interpreted, do one of two things:

- Consider whether your comment should be sent in the first place. (Is there a good reason why you're uneasy?)
- Consider flagging it with a smiley face like :-) to indicate humor.

If you still like the message but detest smiley faces (good for you!), consider rewriting to avoid unnecessary confusion.

Summarize the Good Stuff

One of the prime directives of USENET computing is to help other people, especially new users. As part of that effort, it's considered good form to create summaries of useful information you've received. If you ask, for example, for help in understanding how a particular issue is being considered by Congress and receive a host of replies, write a summary of the responses and post it on the network for others to see.

Such a summary should be carefully done, however; you don't want to tie up bandwidth by pasting all these messages into one slapdash file and shipping it out. Instead, cut out extraneous information, including headers, and compile the responses into a single file. Write a summary that meaningfully pulls together the information, and remember to give credit to the people who helped.

Network etiquette seems like a trivial subject at the beginning, but after you've accumulated some experience with USENET, you'll understand that this cooperative enterprise only works when these basic rules are followed. If you have further questions about how to use the network, you should tap two useful documents which, between them, can solve most on-line questions about manners.

What You Need: A Primer on USENET Etiquette

The Documents: Rules for Posting to USENET, by Mark Horton, and A Primer on How to Work with the USENET Community, by Chuq Von Rospach.

How to Get Them: Both are posted regularly to news.announce.newusers and news.answers.

And if you've mastered these rules, another document, written by Brad Templeton, will ensure you never forget them. It's a wickedly funny recitation of the major USENET rules as told through a question and answer session with an on-line etiquette maven. "This is intended to be satirical," says the note at the beginning of the piece. "If you do not recognize it as such, consult a doctor or professional comedian." I doubt, though, that you'll have much difficulty making the distinction.

What You Need: A USENET Etiquette Primer for Laughs

The Document: Dear Emily Postnews

How to Get It: It's regularly posted on news.newusers.questions.

A USENET Bibliography

Detailed explanations for new users about how USENET works are provided in the news.announce.newusers group, through a number of documents which are regularly posted on-line. We've already discussed some of them here. But if you want to acquire the complete list of reading for new users, here is what is recommended in the Frequently Asked Questions document for another key group, news.newusers.questions:

A Primer on How to Work with the Usenet Community

Answers to Frequently Asked Questions about Usenet

Emily Postnews Answers Your Questions on Netiquette

Hints on Writing Style for Usenet

Rules for Posting to Usenet

What is Usenet?

Also provided in the news.announce.newusers newsgroup are a host of reference documents that you may want to make use of as you expand your USENET presence. These are:

A Guide to Social Newsgroups and Mailing Lists
Alternative Newsgroup Hierarchies, Part I
Alternative Newsgroup Hierarchies, Part II
How to Create a New Usenet Newsgroup
How to Get Information about Networks
Introduction to news.announce
Introduction to the news.answers newsgroup
List of Active Newsgroups, Part I
List of Active Newsgroups, Part II
List of Moderators for Usenet
List of Periodic Informational Postings, Part 1/7
List of Periodic Informational Postings, Part 2/7
List of Periodic Informational Postings, Part 3/7
List of Periodic Informational Postings, Part 4/7
List of Periodic Informational Postings, Part 5/7
List of Periodic Informational Postings, Part 6/7
List of Periodic Informational Postings, Part 7/7
Publicly Accessible Mailing Lists, Part 1/8
Publicly Accessible Mailing Lists, Part 2/8
Publicly Accessible Mailing Lists, Part 3/8
Publicly Accessible Mailing Lists, Part 4/8
Publicly Accessible Mailing Lists, Part 5/8
Publicly Accessible Mailing Lists, Part 6/8
Publicly Accessible Mailing Lists, Part 7/8
Publicly Accessible Mailing Lists, Part 8/8
USENET Software: History and Sources

If you choose not to retrieve these documents in the news.announce.newusers newsgroup itself, you can use the archive site at rtfm.mit.edu. The URL is: ftp://rtfm.mit.edu/pub/usenet/new.answers/

12

Gopher: Information by Menu

It was an inevitable problem, but its dimensions still stagger the imagination. Put information on a hard disk and you can find it using basic retrieval software, some of whose tools are built into the various computer operating systems themselves. Put information on an office network and you can still track it down; there just aren't that many machines to be concerned about. But start widening the network, making it into a company-wide net linking offices in different geographical sites, or spreading it across the ocean to hook up with foreign subsidiaries, and you've made information retrieval a much more dicey proposition.

Then look at information retrieval from the standpoint of the Internet. We learned in Chapter 2 that the Internet isn't a single network; it's a metanetwork, a network of networks, subsuming under its spacious mantle a wide variety of hardware and software links through thousands of separate networks, all of which can talk to each other and exchange text and other data. How can you search through this material? There are no central providers, no archives applicable to all these resources. Information can be hiding across town or around the world, and despite your best efforts, you may not be able to locate it.

That's where search techniques come in, and a new generation of tools designed to work with, not be defeated by, the chaos of widespread network communications. In this and the next two chapters, we'll look at them in their profusion: archie, Gopher, WAIS, WWW, Veronica, and more. No one of them can be said to have solved this dilemma, but together, they offer a measure of control over network resources that was unheard of just a few years ago. The fast spread of these tools, the World Wide Web in particular, suggests the demand will drive further growth in this arena.

Gopher Tracks Resources

Which is easier to use, a menu or a blinking prompt? Would you rather work with a list of choices or have to type in a command? There are plenty of people out there, old hands in the computer business, who'd prefer to work with a naked prompt. Give them a C> or a % to play with and they're happy. But move beyond this core group of Unix wizards and hard-core MS-DOS types, and you'll find a wider audience with no interest in mastering cryptic command structures. Sure, they'll use them when they have to but they'd prefer something more intuitive. This is especially true of the large modem-using community now learning about and beginning to utilize the Internet.

To such people, using the Internet seems like a hit or miss proposition, one based on luck more than skill. There's a grain of truth in this assessment, too. Even old hands will tell you how they "stumbled" upon a great new database, how they "wandered into" a useful FTP site, how they "saw a reference to" a new mailing list. There's no way to quantify this, of course, but looking through my various sources, subscriptions, address books, and whatnot, I'd be surprised if I found more than 30 percent of them in any organized fashion. An old professor of mine used to extol the virtues of spending time in the library, whether you need a new book or not. He'd say, "If you just browse the shelves, you'll find things that will jog your thinking, books that will surprise you." He was right, as I long ago confirmed, and what he says applies to the Internet.

Gopher Burrows In

Browsing has its drawbacks. It may be fun, but you're probably not getting paid to spend all day prowling around cyberspace. That's where Gopher comes in. Created at the University of Minnesota, developed by project leader Mark P. McCahill and a team of programmers, Gopher gives you an interface you can work with, one that can organize and arrange this vast wealth of information into some kind of order. You can look at a Gopher menu and see at a glance what resources are available to you. You can page through it, going deeper and deeper into its submenus, to explore more specific options. You can then move directly to those resources while staying inside the Gopher system. Library catalogs, USENET newsgroups, databases on scores of topics—you name it and you can tap into it through Gopher.

The fun part of all this is that Gopher shields you from the action. Contrast it to using a straight Telnet session to gain access to a particular service. With Telnet, I need to enter a command, say, **telnet bbs.oit.unc.edu.** In doing so, I invoke the Telnet program and tell it a specific address to which it needs to connect. Naturally, I am constrained by the need to know the address, as well as any necessary log-on information. This is a highly specific, targeted operation. Each new Telnet address requires me to repeat a specific command sequence.

Gopher does all this behind the scenes, by letting you make a menu selection. In the case of Telnet connections, Gopher presents you with a menu of choices, usually arranged by subject or in some other fashion that seemed reasonable to the system operator who created the Gopher you're using. You move an on-screen marker to the Telnet site you'd like to visit and press the **RETURN** key. Gopher then goes out and sets up the Telnet session for you, often supplying you with the necessary log-in information. True, once you have connected to the remote computer, you still must operate within its command structure, but the connection itself is painless, a matter of point and click.

Nor is Telnet the only resource to which Gopher can connect. You can read text files on-line easily, paging through them, mailing them to other addresses, or saving them to your workspace at your service provider's site. You can tap WAIS to search a remote database, running your search through the Gopher interface, a process that can take some of the mystery out of WAIS, even if it doesn't let you get at the complete range of

WAIS tools. You can also look at CSSO servers, which allow you to query directories at various universities to find electronic mail addresses and more.

The important thing to remember is that Gopher allows a server to point to another server where a particular resource exists. That means Gopher can include services not just on the local computer, but all over the Internet. Ideally, a Gopher is a combination of useful local features specific to that site and connections to a wide range of services, including other Gophers, around the network. For the novice, Gopher thus means the chance to range freely over the globe within an interface that is nonintimidating.

Mark McCahill sees this as one of Gopher's greatest strengths.

> When we designed the user interface, we based it on the fact that the people who work on this project aren't full-time programmers. They spend part of their time programming and part of their time answering questions from users at our campus help facility. So the last thing we wanted to do was to create something that creates more questions for us. When you get 25 percent of all programmers' time spent on answering user questions, you get a good feel for what you can get away with. We did a fair amount of user testing to make sure we weren't confusing people. The strength of Gopher is that it's simple and painless to use, and that's why it has grown.

As we will soon see, Gopher's interface also poses several challenges, some of which are solved by programs like Veronica and Jughead. These tools allow us to use Gopher in more specific ways, searching for menu items on Gophers throughout the Internet or at specific Gopher sites. But there is no question that as one of the Internet's first user-friendly search tools, Gopher should be an early stop for any network newcomer.

A Choice of Clients

It doesn't matter much which client you use to access Gopher. The basic menu structure remains the same no matter what your program, and this is true whether you're using a shell account or a SLIP/PPP connection. In Figure 12.1, you can see Gopher as presented by IBM's Internet Connection for Windows software. As you can see, the program appears with the usual Window-based features, like pull-down menus.

For my money, this is one of the best Gopher clients on the market; notice the use of the toolbar across the top of the screen, with the major functions made readily accessible. To move to a particular menu item, I simply point the mouse at it and double-click.

Figure 12.2 shows you the same Gopher site as viewed through Netscape. Although Netscape is designed as a World Wide Web browser, it can perform numerous chores, including handling FTP sessions and working with Gophers. In this environment, each menu item is set up as a hyperlink; again, I point the mouse to what I want to see and double-click to move to that item. Like the IBM Gopher client, Netscape provides me with easy-to-use buttons and pull-down menus. Any other Web browser can handle the same functions, as we'll see in Chapter 14. The important thing to note is that the client software is simplifying our task of access.

Now examine Figure 12.3. Here you see the basic Unix Gopher client, as viewed through a shell account. Again, you are viewing the same Gopher site, only this time, because you're using the client running on a service provider's machine, you lack the pull-down menus and mouse support. But if you examine the figure, you'll notice that the basic interface remains easy to use. To see something, I move the on-screen pointer to that item by using the Arrow keys, up or down; a press of the **RETURN** key then calls

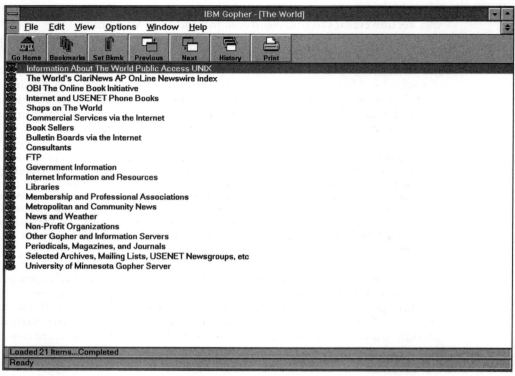

Figure 12.1   Gopher as viewed through IBM's Gopher client.

that item to the screen. A variety of other commands are available; they can be discovered by using the ? key to generate a list. But the interface is undemanding—95 percent of my work can be done simply by moving the pointer and hitting the **RETURN** key.

Because it's easy to use and ubiquitous, I'll use the Unix Gopher client to illustrate this chapter. Translating between it and the other client programs is simply a matter of comparing pull-down menu items with the commands used with the Unix program. Whichever client you choose, Gopher will prove a helpful way to work your way into large information collections.

A Dynamic Menu Structure

Realize that Gopher is far from a static thing. Although a menu looks fixed, a declaration of resources from which you must choose, Gopher's menus are actually dynamic. The first menu you see is based on what the server you've contacted shows you. From that point on, the menu structure depends upon the resources Gopher is contacting. So while you're looking at a static screen, you're actually seeing the results of Gopher's linkages across the Internet. And by making all of these resources available through a single interface, Gopher greatly simplifies the retrieval process.

No wonder Gopher took the Internet by storm, especially early on. We can track the action through statistics maintained by the former NSFnet, bearing in mind that they

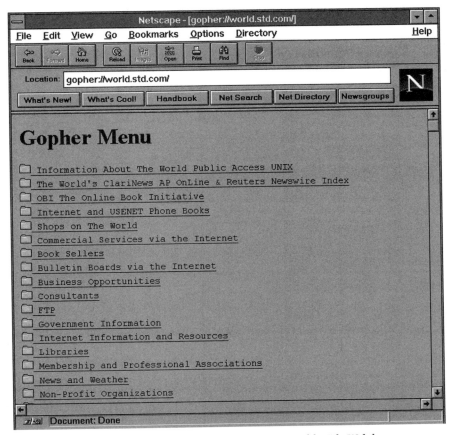

Figure 12.2 Gopher as viewed through the Netscape World Wide Web browser.

reflect only a portion of total Internet traffic. As of November 1992, Gopher had become the sixteenth most popular protocol in use on the Net, rising from two-hundredth only a year before. The increase in Gopher traffic volume in that period was 4,400 times. By May 1993, it had reached the twelfth spot on the list; by February 1994, it had risen to sixth. But 1994 was also the year when the World Wide Web began its massive growth, noticeably slowing the appearance of new Gophers as many information providers moved to the Web protocols. Today, Gopher remains a widespread and useful tool, though one that is probably just as often accessed by people with Web browsers as through client programs specifically created for Gopher use.

Gopher by Telnet

The Internet always provides a variety of ways to access a service. You can reach Gopher, as we've seen, through client programs running on your own computer or by using the Unix client running at your service provider's site. As we saw in Chapter 8, you can even use Gopher through e-mail, if that's your only entryway. You can also use Telnet. Access-

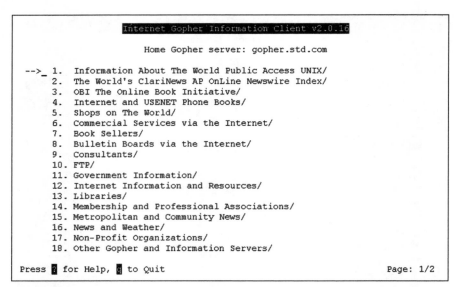

Figure 12.3   The Unix Gopher client.

ing an Internet tool through a local client is always the preferable choice, as it places less of a workload upon an already overcrowded network. But there are times when Telnet is the only possibility. Table 12.1 is provided to show you the Telnet-accessible Gopher sites available as of this writing.

To make a Telnet connection to one of these sites, simply enter the Telnet command followed by one of the above addresses. Thus, **telnet consultant.micro.umn.edu;** the login is gopher. Your Telnet connection should be to a site near you rather than halfway around the world; again, the idea is to minimize workload on the system. Bear in mind that Gophers usually provide connections to other Gophers; in other words, once you've entered the Gopher system, the resources of all the other Gophers out there are available.

But before you set up that Telnet connection, find out whether you can take the client route. If you're using a shell account, you will probably find a Gopher client already installed on your system. You can check this by typing the command **gopher** at your service provider's prompt. If Gopher isn't available, you will see a message like this:

```
gopher: Command not found.
```

This tells you that Telnet is the only option for Gopher access (other than e-mail). If, on the other hand, a Gopher client is available, you will see a screen like the one in Figure 12.3 (although the contents of the Gopher you see will depend upon what your local system administrators have chosen to make available).

Both Telnet and the Unix client will show you the same screen (and a SLIP/PPP client will be similar), so from this point on, we will examine Gopher without regard to how you've reached it. Just remember to use a client program if you can, a Telnet session if you must.

Table 12.1   Gopher Sites Available through Telnet

Address	Location	Login
ux1.cso.uiuc.edu	University of Illinois at Urbana-Champaign	gopher
panda.uiowa.edu	University of Iowa	—
gopher.msu.edu	Michigan State University	gopher
consultant.micro.umn.edu	University of Minnesota	gopher
gopher.ohiolink.edu	Ohio Library and Information Network	gopher
ecosys.drdr.virginia.edu	University of Virginia	gopher
gopher.virginia.edu	University of Virginia	gwis
info.anu.edu.au	Australian National University	info
gopher.puc.cl	Pontificia Universidad Catolica de Chile	gopher
gopher.denet.dk	DENet (Danish research and academic network)	gopher
ecnet.ec	EcuaNet;Corporacion Equatoriana de Informacion (Ecuador)	gopher
gopher.brad.ac.uk	University of Bradford (United Kingdom)	info
gopher.th-darmstadt.de	Technische Hochschule Darmstadt (Germany)	gopher
gopher.ncc.go.jp	National Cancer Center, Tokyo	gopher
gopher.uv.es	Universidad de Valencia (Spain)	gopher

The Gopher Screen

Let's now examine Gopher's screen. In Figure 12.3, we are looking at the Gopher maintained by The World. Because the server we are accessing is located at The World's offices in Brookline, Massachusetts, we receive information about that service, along with useful tips, such as background data on the local Gopher itself and material designed for new users of this service provider's system. The address here is gopher.std.com. Expressed as a URL, it would be listed this way:

```
gopher://gopher.std.com/
```

This URL tells us we will use Gopher to contact the Gopher at gopher.std.com. Shell users would get to the address using this command at their provider's prompt:

```
gopher gopher.std.com
```

This activates the Gopher client on the service provider's machine and then gives it an address to contact.

Gophers frequently provide local content. For example, if you contact a Gopher at the University of Illinois, you would see screens with information about campus events, regional information in and around Champaign-Urbana, and the like. The URL for the Illinois site is:

```
gopher://gopher.uiuc.edu
```

Similarly, the University of Iowa makes information available about Iowa City, news of the university, and so on.

But Gopher is also the key to much wider forms of access. As you can see from The World menu, there are entries for an AP newswire index from ClariNet, Internet and USENET directories, local information about The World, bulletin board systems available through the Internet, booksellers, FTP sites, government information, and more. Clearly, The World's Gopher is a rich source of information. Note that all of the entries in Figure 12.3 end with a slash, as in *18. Other Gopher and Information Servers/*. The slash is significant; it tells us that if we choose this item, we will receive another menu with further options on it. If we choose item 18, the screen changes to show a choice of magazines for our perusal, as in Figure 12.4.

The actions we take to use this Gopher are simple. The arrow that we see pointing to the first item in both figures can be moved by using the **Up** or **Down Arrow** keys. We could also move it by entering the number of the item we would like to move to and pressing a **RETURN.** In either case, the arrow will move to reflect our choice.

As you can see, using Gopher isn't taxing. The relevant actions are laid out for you at the bottom of the screen. At the Other Gopher and Information Servers menu, for example, entering a **u** will back you up one screen. A **q** exits the program, and a **?** calls up a help screen showing you the basic Gopher commands.

All of the menu items except two contain submenus; this is indicated by the slash following them. One of them is a searchable index, which is shown by the question mark:

```
2. Search All the Gopher Servers in the World<?>
```

And item 15 contains a form, which is indicated by the double question mark following its entry:

```
15. Gopher Server Registration<??>
```

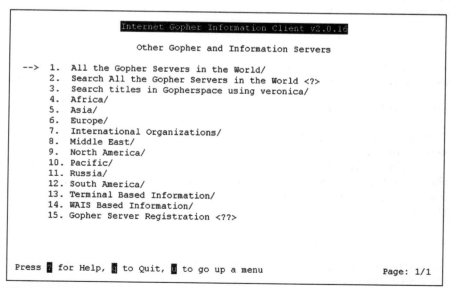

Figure 12.4 The submenu for Gopher services around the world.

Notice that all the other entries have to do with Gophers around the world, allowing us to choose a Gopher by continent or geographical area. And one item promises to let us search what we find on those Gophers:

```
3. Search titles in Gopherspace using veronica/
```

We'll examine this last option closely a little later in this chapter.

The basic Gopher principle remains intact. We move the arrow key to reach the item we want to see, following it with a **RETURN.** We will then be presented with a submenu to examine. Thus, the Gopher methodology: move deeper into the menu items of our choice, picking documents to read, sites to access or creating a search. Move back up the menu tree to follow other menu branches back down into their own lower layers. Our Gopher work is a series of descents and ascents through rich mines of information.

Mailing and Saving Gopher Files

In the menu we just discussed, we were working with a series of choices, most of which were followed by the slash that betokens another menu beneath. Select a menu item without a slash, on the other hand, and you're asking to see a document. If I were to choose item 1, *Information About The World Public Access UNIX/* from the top menu in Figure 12.3, I would find menu items that ended in a period (.) rather than a slash. Pressing the **RETURN** at one of them would yield a text file. Figure 12.5, for example, shows an introductory document that explains The World's services.

Home in on the bottom line for a moment. It tells us that we can use the SPACEBAR to page through the document:

```
[Help: ?] [Exit: u] [PageDown: Space]
```

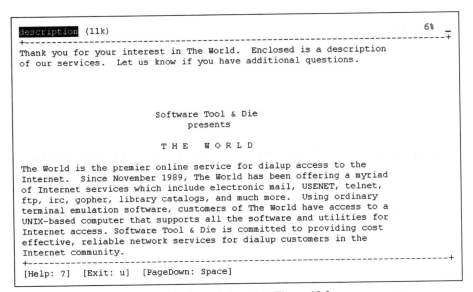

Figure 12.5   A text file available through item 1 in Figure 12.3.

When we do so, we eventually reach the end, where we will be presented with another series of options:

```
[Help: ?] [Exit: u] [PageUp: b]
```

Thus the basic Gopher reading commands. The **SPACEBAR** takes us deeper into the document; the **b** key moves us back up one page at a time. Notice that Gopher simplifies the process by giving us these commands on the screen, rather than assuming we know them in advance.

Documents are useful when read on-screen, but it would be more helpful still if we could mail them to other people, or mail them to our own mailbox. For that matter, it would be useful to be able to save them to disk. Here's how to mail this file to yourself:

1. Press the **m** key.
2. Enter your address in the field that appears.
3. Press **RETURN** to send the document as a message.

You can see the address field that appears when you press the **m** key in Figure 12.6. The file will soon appear in your electronic mailbox.

You can also save this file. A graphical client program makes this easy; you pull down the File menu and choose the **Save** command. Using the Unix client, however, is not difficult either. The **s** command saves the file on your service provider's computer; you can then download it when you're through with Gopher for the day. Here's how:

1. Press the **s** key.
2. Enter a filename into the field that appears.
3. Press a **RETURN** to save the file.

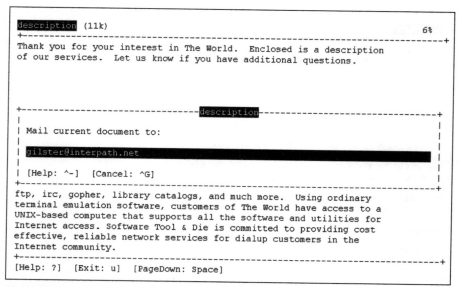

```
description (11k)                                                          6%
+------------------------------------------------------------------------+
Thank you for your interest in The World.  Enclosed is a description
of our services.  Let us know if you have additional questions.



    +----------------------------description----------------------------+
    |                                                                    |
    | Mail current document to:                                          |
    |                                                                    |
    | gilster@interpath.net                                              |
    |                                                                    |
    | [Help: ^-]  [Cancel: ^G]                                           |
    +--------------------------------------------------------------------+
ftp, irc, gopher, library catalogs, and much more.  Using ordinary
terminal emulation software, customers of The World have access to a
UNIX-based computer that supports all the software and utilities for
Internet access. Software Tool & Die is committed to providing cost
effective, reliable network services for dialup customers in the
Internet community.
+------------------------------------------------------------------------+
[Help: ?]  [Exit: u]  [PageDown: Space]
```

Figure 12.6 Gopher prompts for a mail address.

You can see the filename field in Figure 12.7. Notice that the client has prompted me for a filename, and suggests Description because that was the name of the item on the Gopher menu. Alternately, I can type in any filename I choose. Usually I'll pick something a bit more descriptive, so I'll remember what this file is all about. And, since I'm normally downloading to an **MS-DOS** based computer, I'll have to keep that filename consistent with DOS-based file structures (I don't have to do this when I'm downloading on my Power Mac, needless to say).

What happens if you're using Telnet to connect to Gopher? Because you don't have an account on the machine you're accessing, you won't be able to save a file there, but mail is still an option. You'd use the **m** command as before, entering your e-mail address, and before long the file would appear.

Finding Files with Gopher

Let's look at how Gopher can help us with an FTP search by choosing menu item 10 from the top menu on The World's Gopher. Now, as shown in Figure 12.8, we're prompted for the type of search we'd like to run. Notice that we can use archie to run a search for particular files, or we can tap The World's own FTP archive. We can also move to several other FTP sites, or follow the menu to a whole listing of popular sites by choosing item 4.

When I choose item 2 to run an archie search, I will be given two more choices:

```
1. Exact search of archive sites on the internet <?>
2. Substring search of archive sites on the internet <?>
```

Notice that both of these items end with a question mark; this tells us that there is a search field beneath this menu entry. An exact search, as we saw in Chapter 5, lets us look for a specific filename; a substring search lets us search for a keyword even if it's embedded inside another word.

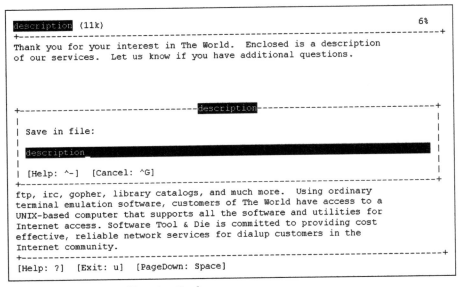

Figure 12.7   Saving a file using Gopher.

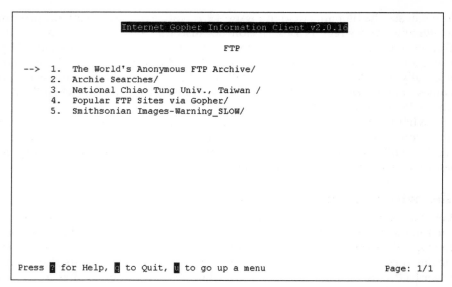

Figure 12.8   Beginning a search with Gopher.

My godson has taken a lively interest in astronomy, and I know there are some interesting software packages that simulate the solar system and the night sky. Let's see if we can find one by asking for an exact search, using the term *astronomy*. Choose 1, then, and you'll be prompted to enter a search term, as appears in Figure 12.9. As you can see, I've entered the search term in the blank. And Figure 12.10 shows what the system calls up.

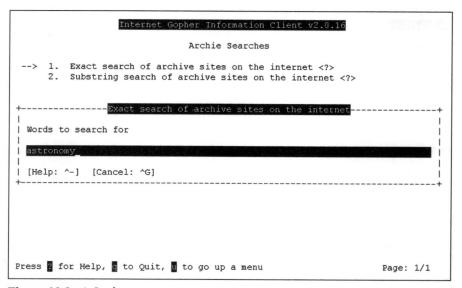

Figure 12.9   A Gopher query screen.

```
┌──────────────────────────────────────────────────────────────────────┐
│              Internet Gopher Information Client v2.0.16                 │
│                                                                         │
│        Substring search of archive sites on the internet: astronomy    │
│                                                                         │
│  -->_    Searching Archie server at archie.sura.net                     │
│      2.  ftp.sunet.se:/pub/usenet/alt.answers/astronomy//               │
│      3.  ftp.sunet.se:/pub/mac/umich/misc/astronomy//                   │
│      4.  nic.switch.ch:/mirror/umich-mac/misc/astronomy//               │
│      5.  plaza.aarnet.edu.au:/micros/pc/garbo/pc/astronomy//            │
│      6.  extro.ucc.su.oz.au:/pub/usenet/news.answers/astronomy//        │
│      7.  ftp.sunet.se:/pub/usenet/news.answers/astronomy//              │
│      8.  plaza.aarnet.edu.au:/usenet/FAQs/alt.answers/astronomy//       │
│      9.  plaza.aarnet.edu.au:/usenet/FAQs/news.answers/astronomy//      │
│     10.  ftp.std.com:/pub/astronomy//                                   │
│     11.  ftp.lth.se:/pub/netnews/news.answers/astronomy//               │
│     12.  plaza.aarnet.edu.au:/micros/pc/garbo/windows/astronomy//       │
│     13.  ftp.bhp.com.au:/mac/mirrors/umich/misc/astronomy//             │
│     14.  ftp.bhp.com.au:/pc/garbo/pc/astronomy//                        │
│     15.  ftp.bhp.com.au:/pc/garbo/windows/astronomy//                   │
│     16.  ftp.luth.se:/pub/mac/.2/mirror.umich/misc/astronomy//          │
│     17.  plaza.aarnet.edu.au:/micros/mac/umich/misc/astronomy//         │
│     18.  ftp.bhp.com.au:/internet/FAQs/news.answers/astronomy//         │
│                                                                         │
│  Press ? for Help, q to Quit, u to go up a menu       Page: 1/3         │
└──────────────────────────────────────────────────────────────────────┘
```

Figure 12.10   Results of the *astronomy* search.

Gopher has located sites containing astronomy programs and data. You can pick one of the selections by moving to it with the arrow keys, and pressing the **RETURN** key to call up the item you choose.

Looking at this list, I'm interested in the twelfth item, because it's in a subdirectory that looks germane: */micros/pc/garbo/windows/astronomy//*. This is how a Gopher search for an FTP site has to proceed; Gopher isn't perfect, and it can't tell you which of these directories is necessarily the best one for the job. Much of our information gathering, in fact, has to involve trying out likely looking candidates and seeing if they pay off, much as you would browse through books in a bookstore looking for just the title you need. Let's try item 12, then, and see what we can find. The results are shown in Figure 12.11.

Now we're in luck. Here's a file called skymap22.zip, that sounds like some kind of planetarium program. To retrieve it is again a simple matter of putting the arrow to the right of item 3 and pressing another **RETURN.** Now a screen opens and prompts us for information on where to put the file. I've told the system to save the file as skymap22.zip, as shown in Figure 12.12.

Gopher now will retrieve the file for me. No need to go out and perform FTP procedures, switching directories, and wandering through the file holdings looking for what I need. Gopher has managed the entire operation, while keeping the action transparent to me. If I didn't know what was happening, I'd think I had stayed at The World.

You'll notice in the preceding search that Gopher, when it had found files meeting my search criteria, also gave me further information. skymap22.zip is tagged as a binary file in the menu presentation. Here and there in your Gopher searches, you'll run into the problem of finding a type of file your Gopher client won't be able to work with. The Gopher+ protocol is the solution to that problem. The protocol allows client and server to negotiate the types of data the client can handle.

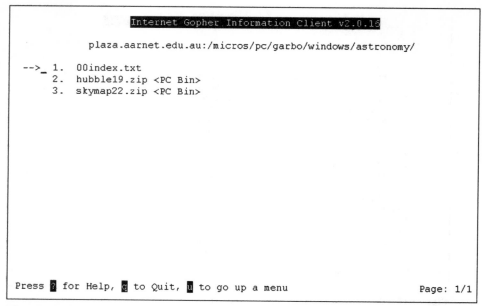

Figure 12.11 A set of astronomy files found by Gopher.

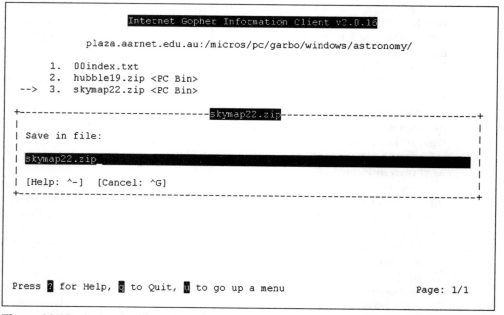

Figure 12.12 Saving the file with Gopher.

If the preceding search sounded familiar, it's because our quest for an FTP archive site worked with archie. You probably caught on to that when we were prompted for either an exact search match for our search term or a substring search. You'll also run into Gopher sites where you're simply presented with an alphabetical list of FTP servers. In that case, it's a matter of paging through the list to find a particular source of interest to you. Obviously, a link with archie allows Gopher to be powerfully useful in finding information or programs when you don't know initially where to look.

And because archie is the underlying program, you shouldn't be surprised if you run into delays. The archie system worldwide is heavily taxed as more and more users learn their way around the Internet. If Gopher seems to be taking a long time to service your request, it's probably because the archie server the Gopher is contacting is busy at the moment. Sometimes you'll just have to wait for a more opportune time and try again.

The Gopher Command Structure

In keeping with the theory that good software should be simple to operate, the Gopher client I've been using boasts relatively few commands; a view of its help message will summon up a scant two screens worth of information. Let's run through the basic functions now, before moving on to see Gopher in action with other kinds of data search.

To Move the Cursor

Up Arrow	Moves you to the previous line.
Down Arrow	Moves you to the next line.
Right Arrow	Displays the current item. Pressing the **RETURN** key will have the same effect.
Left Arrow	Moves up one level. You can also use the **u** command.
Space	Displays the next page. The PageDown key has the same effect.
b	Displays the previous page. You can also use the PageUp key.
0–9	Goes to the item specified.
m	Returns to the main menu.

To Work with Bookmarks

Bookmarks are a key feature in Gopher; using them, you can mark where you are in a particular search and return to that location easily. You might not think you need a bookmark, but they're handy for more than jogging your memory. Backing up and down through a sequence of menus is fascinating at first, as you learn what resources are available. After the fifth or tenth time, though, you'd like to find a quicker way to get where you're going. Think of bookmarks as *hot keys* you can use to set a marker and then return directly to that page without all the intervening menus. Here are the bookmark commands:

a	Adds an item to your bookmark list.
A	Adds the current directory/search to the bookmark list.

The difference between the two add commands is this: A lowercase **a** command will note a specific item, such as one line from a menu, and will return you immediately to that item upon your request. An uppercase **A** command will return you to an entire screen of information, such as a page from the menu; there, you can make further choices before proceeding.

v   Views the current list of bookmarks.

d   Deletes a bookmark.

Once you start experimenting with bookmarks, I doubt you'll want to give them up. Everyone finds particular Gopher items to which they return again and again. You might, for example, find that you use a particular Telnet site frequently, and prefer to do so through Gopher rather than by making the connection through Telnet yourself. You could set up this site on your bookmark page; any time you want to return to it, press a **v** and you'll be whisked directly to that item, rather than having to move through the menus to reach it.

Your Gopher bookmark page will look like any other Gopher menu. The items you add are "live"; they can be accessed by moving the arrow to them and pressing a **RETURN.**

And, once you've begun to move around the Gophers out there, you will find numerous sites with intriguing resources. Remember, your bookmark page does not limit you to the current site. You can take a Gopher menu item to another Gopher, move through its menus, and set up one of its items on your bookmark page. In this way, you build a customized menu that reflects your interests. It might contain resources at 10 different sites, including Telnet connections and WAIS databases ready for searching.

Other Gopher Commands

s   Saves the current item to a file.

S   Saves the current menu listing to a file.

q   Exits Gopher, prompting you to be sure that's what you want to do.

Q   Exits Gopher, with no prompt.

D   Allows you to download a file.

=   Displays technical information about the item currently being displayed.

^   Displays technical information about the directory currently being displayed.

o   Allows you to open a new Gopher server.

O   Allows you to change the options Gopher is working with.

/   Allows you to search for a particular item in the menu. This command will pop up a dialog box asking you to enter the search term. It will then search for that term for you, a useful feature on very large menus.

n   Finds the next occurrence of the search term you've specified.

Gopher and Telnet

Gopher can sift through a wide range of resources. In Figure 12.13, I have continued prowling through the Gopher at The World, looking into the menu entry called *Commercial Services via the Internet.* Here I find a screen listing not only a series of inter-

```
              Internet Gopher Information Client v2.0.16

                     Commercial Services via the Internet
    -->  1.  Information about the Commerical Services menu
         2.  BRS (Bibliographic Retrieval Service) [McLean, VA] <TEL>
         3.  BioTechNet - +1 508 655 8282 <TEL>
         4.  Compuserve--Type 'CIS' at 'HOST NAME' <TEL>
         5.  Datapac information +1-800-267-6574 // via hermes <TEL>
         6.  Datastar <TEL>
         7.  Delphi <TEL>
         8.  Dialog [Palo Alto, CA] <TEL>
         9.  Dow Jones News/Retrieval [Princeton, NJ] <TEL>
        10.  EBSCONET <TEL>
        11.  LEXIS/NEXIS (Mead Data Central) [Dayton, OH] <TEL>
        12.  Legi-Slate Info Service <TEL>
        13.  Med Help International <TEL>
        14.  Newsnet // via hermes <TEL>
        15.  OCLC <TEL>
        16.  Research Library Information Network (RLIN) [Stanford, CA] <TEL>
        17.  WLN - Western Libraries Network (free til 1 Oct 1992) <TEL>


    Press ? for Help, q to Quit, u to go up a menu          Page: 1/1
```

Figure 12.13   Sources of commercial information on Gopher.

esting destinations, but also one that illustrates the various ways Gopher goes about getting its information.

Noteworthy here are the terms in brackets at the end of each entry. It's useful to know, for example, that we can get into CompuServe with a simple Gopher choice. How? Through Telnet, coded here as <TEL>. Here too are such interesting items as a link to BRS, the Bibliographic Retrieval Service, and one to DIALOG, as well as Dow Jones News/Retrieval. It's also useful to know when we're trying to log on to a commercial on-line service that item 7 is out there, a link to DELPHI. Let's try it and see how Gopher handles a Telnet session. We'll move the pointer to item 7 and press the **RETURN** key. And an interesting thing happens, shown in Figure 12.14.

This message gets our attention. It's nothing to worry about. Gopher is telling us that by setting up a Telnet session, it's losing control over what happens next. There is an escape mechanism available, as shown in the warning message: You can enter a **Ctrl-]** to return to the Telnet prompt. This, followed by a **quit** command, should get you back home to Gopher, as much as the concept of "home" has meaning in networked cyberspace.

Press **RETURN** to proceed. The following should occur:

```
Trying 192.80.63.3 ...
Connected to delphi.com.
Escape character is '^]'.

Username:
```

We must supply a password and username, for this is a commercial system.

In general, using Telnet through a Gopher can save you some aggravation, since Gopher's menu structure presents you with a range of possible destinations, and will also guide you through login information at sites that are available to the general public

```
 ┌──────────────────────────────────────────────────────────┐
 │            [Internet Gopher Information Client v2.0.16]     │
 │                                                            │
 │                Commercial Services via the Internet         │
 │                                                            │
 │     1.  Information about the Commerical Services menu      │
 │     2.  BR+----------------------[Delphi]----------------+  │
 │     3.  Bi|                                             |  │
 │     4.  Co|  Warning!!!!!, you are about to leave the Internet |
 │     5.  Da|  Gopher program and connect to another host. If  |
 │     6.  Da|  you get stuck press the control key and the     |
 │ --> 7.  De|  ] key, and then type quit                 |  │
 │     8.  Di|                                             |  │
 │     9.  Do|  Connecting to delphi.com, port 23 using telnet. |
 │    10.  EB|                                             |  │
 │    11.  LE|                                             |  │
 │    12.  Le|                                             |  │
 │    13.  Me|                        [Cancel: ^G] [OK: Enter]_ |
 │    14.  Ne+----------------------------------------------+  │
 │    15.  OCLC <TEL>                                          │
 │    16.  Research Library Information Network (RLIN) [Stanford, CA] <TEL> │
 │    17.  WLN - Western Libraries Network (free til 1 Oct 1992) <TEL>      │
 │                                                            │
 │  Press ? for Help, q to Quit, u to go up a menu    Page: 1/1 │
 └──────────────────────────────────────────────────────────┘
```

Figure 12.14 Gopher's Telnet reminder.

(the DELPHI site lacked such a login because it is a subscription service, for paying members only). Remember that when you use Telenet through Gopher, you're in the hands of the remote system as long as your session with that system is in progress. Use its commands to log off. But if you get stuck, it's always possible to return to the Gopher menu by using the Ctrl-] command that exits a Telnet session.

Gopher and the Public Library

The intriguing thing about using Gopher is that you're never quite sure what will turn up. The resources available are so vast and, in many cases, so surprising, that exploring them can be a full-time occupation. It's useful, for example, to know that Gopher is one way you can explore the library systems at various universities. More and more libraries are coming on-line all the time, often accessible through Telnet procedures. We've already seen how Gopher can simplify Telnet; now let's look at some other ways it can help us manage information. In Figure 12.15, I'm explaining a Gopher menu that provides access to libraries.

We have an interesting list, offering library catalogs around the world as well as in the United States. But pay particular attention to item 1, listed as *American English Dictionary,* and followed by a <?>. The question mark alerts us to the fact that we're dealing not with a subdirectory but an index. This can be a handy way to search for information indeed. Figure 12.16 shows what we see when we press a **RETURN** at item 1.

Interesting indeed, for now we can enter a search term to track down a specific word. President Clinton has been described by one columnist as "peripatetic." What does the word mean? We can enter it in the search field and press a **RETURN** to find out. The results are shown in Figure 12.17.

Gopher has built another menu, based on the results of the search. In this case, the word we're after and a series of closely related terms (from the phonetic standpoint, any-

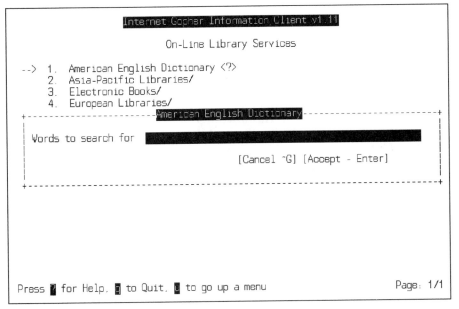

Figure 12.15   A library services menu.

Figure 12.16.   A dictionary search screen.

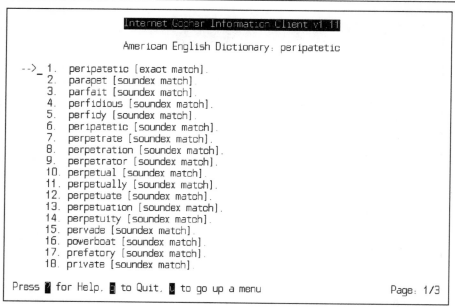

```
┌─────────────────────────────────────────────────────────────────────┐
│              │Internet Gopher Information Client v1.11│               │
│                                                                       │
│                American English Dictionary: peripatetic               │
│                                                                       │
│   -->_ 1.  peripatetic [exact match].                                 │
│        2.  parapet [soundex match].                                   │
│        3.  parfait [soundex match].                                   │
│        4.  perfidious [soundex match].                                │
│        5.  perfidy [soundex match].                                   │
│        6.  peripatetic [soundex match].                               │
│        7.  perpetrate [soundex match].                                │
│        8.  perpetration [soundex match].                              │
│        9.  perpetrator [soundex match].                               │
│       10.  perpetual [soundex match].                                 │
│       11.  perpetually [soundex match].                               │
│       12.  perpetuate [soundex match].                                │
│       13.  perpetuation [soundex match].                              │
│       14.  perpetuity [soundex match].                                │
│       15.  pervade [soundex match].                                   │
│       16.  powerboat [soundex match].                                 │
│       17.  prefatory [soundex match].                                 │
│       18.  private [soundex match].                                   │
│                                                                       │
│  Press ▓ for Help, ▓ to Quit, ▓ to go up a menu       Page: 1/3       │
└─────────────────────────────────────────────────────────────────────┘
```

Figure 12.17   Results of a dictionary search.

way) are provided. Nothing drives home the point more forcefully that Gopher's menus are dynamic, changing with new circumstances according to the queries put to it. Choose the first item on the list to get our definition:

```
per.i.pa.tet.ic \.per-*-p*-'tet-ik \adj : performed or performing
    while moving about : ITINERANT
```

And now we see the justice of the comment, used to describe a president whose jogging is widely observed.

On to the libraries. I'm curious about whether or not P. G. Wodehouse has made much of an impact in the Far East. After all, much of this area was once occupied by British colonial administrators, for whom Wodehouse's Bertie and Jeeves were inspired choices as reading material. Has anything of this fondness for daffy Edwardian behavior remained? We can check out the holdings of libraries in the Far East by using Gopher. I'll find out by returning to the menu of *On-Line Library Services/*, where I can choose item 2, *Asia-Pacific Libraries/*. I'm prompted with a submenu of library choices, as shown in Figure 12.18.

Let's examine item 8, Hong Kong University of Science and Technology, accessible through Gopher's Telnet connection. Again, we're prompted that we're about to leave the Gopher system, and then, after a **RETURN,** delivered to Hong Kong, as shown in Figure 12.19.

The library search is relatively straightforward, and techniques for browsing vary depending on the library you've contacted. For now, I'll just mention that I located such immortal works as *Aunts Aren't Gentlemen, Cat-nappers, Leave it to Psmith,* and *The Pothunters and Other School Stories,* among others, in Hong Kong, so the works of the master continue to flourish far from his home.

```
Internet Gopher Information Client v1.11

                    Asia-Pacific Libraries

 -->_ 1. Australian Bibliographic Network <TEL>
     _2. Australian Defence Force Academy <TEL>
      3. Australian National University <TEL>
      4. Curtin University of Technology - Australia <TEL>
      5. Deakin University - Australia <TEL>
      6. Edith Cowan University - Australia <TEL>
      7. Griffith University - Australia <TEL>
      8. Hong Kong University of Science and Technology <TEL>
      9. James Cook University - Australia <TEL>
     10. La Trobe University - Australia <TEL>
     11. Monash University - Australia <TEL>
     12. Murdoch University - Australia <TEL>
     13. Northern Territory University - Australia <TEL>
     14. Royal Melbourne Institute of Technology - Australia <TEL>
     15. University of Adelaide - Australia <TEL>
     16. University of Canberra - Australia <TEL>
     17. University of Melbourne - Australia <TEL>
     18. University of New England - Australia <TEL>

Press ? for Help. q to Quit. u to go up a menu        Page: 1/2
```

Figure 12.18   Library sources in Asia and the Pacific.

```
          Hong Kong University of Science & Technology      HKUST
                     Library Online Catalog




              A > AUTHOR
              T > TITLE
              S > SUBJECT
              W > keyWORDS
              C > CALL NO

              R > RESERVE Lists
              I > Library INFORMATION

              X > Change language to Chinese
              V > VIEW your circulation record
              D > DISCONNECT
          Choose one (A.T.S.W.C.R.I.X.V.D) _

   Students who are graduating this year, and wish to have borrowing privileges
   after graduation can apply for a Library Card at the Circulation Counter.
   ***   The card is free to HKUST graduates, and is renewable annually.   ***
```

Figure 12.19   Hong Kong University of Science and Technology Library catalog opening screen.

Keeping Pace with Gopher

Given how handy Gopher is at these and other search tasks, it would be useful to have a way to keep up with developments in what some developers call "the meta-burrow."

What You Need: A Way to Track Gopher Developments

The Source: The USENET Newsgroup comp.infosystems.gopher

Look especially for the Gopher FAQ—Common Questions and Answers About the Internet Gopher. You can retrieve this FAQ from the newsgroup itself, or from the following URL:

ftp://rtfm.mit.edu/pub/usenet/news.answers/gopher-faq

Moving between Gophers

Considering the diversity available in the Gopher universe, we need an easier way to move from one Gopher to another than working our way through menu trees. One way, as we've already seen, is to use bookmarks, which can set up frequently visited sites as Gopher menu items. But perhaps we simply want to go to a new site without necessarily saving it as a bookmark. This is where the **o** command comes in.

Suppose I am working my way through Gopher menus at a particular site and decide I want to move to another Gopher. When I press the **o** command, I will see the screen shown in Figure 12.20. Notice that a box has opened within which I have already

Figure 12.20   Switching to a new Gopher site; I have already entered the address of the site I'm trying to reach.

entered the address of the Gopher I want to reach. When I press the **RETURN** key, Gopher will switch to the new site. This is a useful command to know about, because it saves you from having to exit Gopher, type in the **gopher** command with the new address specified, and return to the system. You'll find yourself using it often as you move between new sites.

Gophers Galore

Another nice thing about Gophers is that there are so many of them. If I follow the menu structure at The World and go to the *Other Gopher and Information Servers/* screen, I'll be presented with an extensive list. I can look for North Carolina sites, or I can extend my reach to the entire United States, to South America, to Asia and the Pacific, Europe, and the Middle East.

There's a Gopher, for example, at National Chung Cheng University, Chia-Yi, Taiwan, R.O.C., and another at TECHNET in Singapore. The University of Western Australia is represented, as is Keio University in Japan. Ten Israeli Gophers are readily accessible, while the Universidad de Santiago in Chile and the University de Campinas in Sao Paolo, Brazil are part of the South American contingent. In Europe, the choice is wide, from the DENnet Danish Academic Network to the Department of Physics in Pisa, Italy. Oxford University is here, and so is Stockholm.

The screens I'm given at The World are not indexed; you have to page through them to see what's there. Figure 12.21 shows an example from the South American list.

These are abundant materials for the searching, but wading through screen after screen to find what you're after can be time consuming indeed. Surely there's a better way.

```
┌─────────────────────────────────────────────────────────────┐
│         Internet Gopher Information Client v2.0.16            │
│                                                               │
│                            All                                │
│                                                               │
│  -->  1.  Antonio Narino University/                          │
│       2.  Argentina's top-level domain/                       │
│       3.  BBRC - Brazilian Bioinformatics Resource Center/    │
│       4.  Base de Dados Tropical (Tropical Data Base), Campinas, Brasil/ │
│       5.  CHILE - Red Universitaria Nacional (REUNA)/         │
│       6.  COLOMBIA - Universidad de los Andes/                │
│       7.  CONICYT - CHILE/                                    │
│       8.  Centro de Informacion y Documentacion (FUNDACID)/   │
│       9.  Comision Nacional de Actividades Espaciales (CONAE) -- Argentina/ │
│      10.  Cuyonet Gopher Server/                              │
│      11.  ECUADOR - EcuaNet/                                  │
│      12.  ESPOL - Escuela Politecnica del Litoral, Guayaquil - Ecuador/ │
│      13.  Ecuador Gophers/                                    │
│      14.  Ecuador Ministerio de Relaciones Exteriores/        │
│      15.  Escuela Politecnica Nacional (Ecuador-South America)/ │
│      16.  Facultad de Ciencias Astronomicas y Geofisicas/     │
│      17.  Gopher CONICIT - VENEZUELA/                         │
│      18.  Gopher REACCIUN/                                    │
│                                                               │
│  Press ? for Help, q to Quit, u to go up a menu    Page: 1/4  │
└─────────────────────────────────────────────────────────────┘
```

Figure 12.21 A partial list of South American gophers.

Veronica Saves the Day

And indeed, there is. Its name is Veronica. We've already looked at archie, the useful tool that helps us determine where a given file or computer program can be found among the various FTP sites. Veronica takes the archie concept and applies it to Gophers. Whereas archie lets you do a keyword search to track down a given file, Veronica provides keyword searches of the titles of Gopher items. Given the proliferation of Gophers and their continuing growth, Veronica is essential.

An aside: how these tools get named is always interesting. I'm reminded of a conversation with a contact in Washington, DC. She had inquired about my e-mail address, and when I gave it to her, asked the significance of rock as the machine name (this was before the demise of the CONCERT-CONNECT service I once used; there, my address had been gilster@rock.concert.net. "Well," I replied, "it's CONCERT-CONNECT, so I guess musical names are appropriate here. There's another machine named banjo." She laughed, and said she knew what I was talking about, adding "all our computers are named after tropical fruits." I mention this so you won't be surprised at the diversity of machine and program names you're likely to run into on the Internet. As with most matters computational, whimsy plays its role.

Maybe Veronica is named after Veronica Lake, one of my favorite actresses from Hollywood's golden era. Alas, no. According to its originators, Fred Barrie and Steve Foster at the University of Nevada, Veronica actually stands for Very Easy Rodent-Oriented Net-wide Index to Computerized Archives. Of all things, another computer acronym! (And if Veronica also reminds you of a character from the comic strip Archie, you're not alone).

What Veronica Does

If Veronica is like archie in some ways, it differs significantly in others. archie can tell you that the file earlgrey.zip is a compressed archive containing tips on how to make good tea; it can tell you exactly where to find it, too. At that point, you have to set up an FTP session to actually retrieve the file. You and archie have parted company. Veronica has no such restraints; she'll go out and get the material directly from the data source. And because you're using a Gopher client to do all this, the search is simple to manage and as powerful as Gopher itself.

There are no Veronica clients; at least, not yet. You get to Veronica by going through a normal Gopher client; the two are tightly integrated. You may well find that the Gopher server accessed by your service provider already has a link to Veronica, in which case getting a look at the system is easy. But if it doesn't, you can still reach Veronica in two ways:

- Try the Gopher at the following URL:

  `gopher://gopher.micro.umn.edu`

  This is the Gopher at the University of Minnesota. The menu you'll see will present you with a choice that points to other Gopher and information servers. Take it, and from the submenu, choose the item *Search titles in Gopherspace using veronica/.* But explore your local Gopher first. More and more Gophers now provide Veronica on their menus.

• If you're without a Gopher client, you can use Telnet to reach one of the Gopher sites listed earlier in this chapter. As always, use the site nearest to you to cut down on network lag and reduce system congestion.

What you'll see after taking either of these choices will correspond to what follows.

Veronica Goes to Iowa

Let's look at how to put Veronica to work. Using the Gopher at the University of Minnesota, I generate the Veronica menu in Figure 12.22. Note the question marks at the end of the last eight menu items. These indicate we have a searchable index to work with if we choose that menu item. Items 10 and 11 are documents providing useful information about Veronica itself. You should read both to keep up with Veronica.

Notice, too, that some of these items search Gopher directories, while others search throughout Gopherspace. Actually, a Veronica search can be restricted to a number of different data types, or combinations of them. You might, for example, search for any mentions of the word *history* that include links to Gopher directories or Telnet links. For the purposes of this book, I'll show you the simplest Veronica search method first, which is run by entering a single keyword. Then we'll consider how to tighten up the search.

Let's give Veronica a spin now by taking choice 15, which allows us to search through what Veronica calls "Gopherspace"—the cybernetic connections between the Gophers around the globe. Choosing menu item 15, then, we see the screen in Figure 12.23.

Before entering a keyword, ponder for a moment what we're dealing with here. Gopher taps resources throughout the Internet worldwide. Why, then, use Veronica when Gopher seems to offer all we need? The answer is as close as the opening screen of whatever Gopher server you access. At that site, there is usually a mixture of local and more broadly based information. At The World, as we saw in the beginning, data about

```
        Internet Gopher Information Client v2.0.16

            Search titles in Gopherspace using veronica

   -->

       3.  Find GOPHER DIRECTORIES by Title word(s) (via NYSERNet) <?>
       4.  Find GOPHER DIRECTORIES by Title word(s) (via PSINet) <?>
       5.  Find GOPHER DIRECTORIES by Title word(s) (via SUNET) <?>
       6.  Find GOPHER DIRECTORIES by Title word(s) (via U. of Manitoba) <?>
       7.  Find GOPHER DIRECTORIES by Title word(s) (via UNINETT..of Bergen) <?>
       8.  Find GOPHER DIRECTORIES by Title word(s) (via University of Koe.. <?>
       9.  Find GOPHER DIRECTORIES by Title word(s) (via University of Pis.. <?>
      10.  Frequently-Asked Questions (FAQ) about veronica - January 13, 1995
      11.  How to Compose veronica Queries - June 23, 1994
      12.  More veronica: Software, Index-Control Protocol, HTML Pages/
      13.  Search GopherSpace by Title word(s) (via NYSERNet) <?>
      14.  Search GopherSpace by Title word(s) (via PSINet) <?>
      15.  Search GopherSpace by Title word(s) (via SUNET) <?>
      16.  Search GopherSpace by Title word(s) (via U. of Manitoba) <?>
      17.  Search GopherSpace by Title word(s) (via UNINETT/U. of Bergen) <?>
      18.  Search GopherSpace by Title word(s) (via University of Koeln) <?>

   Press ? for Help, q to Quit, u to go up a menu        Page: 1/2
```

Figure 12.22 The opening Veronica menu.

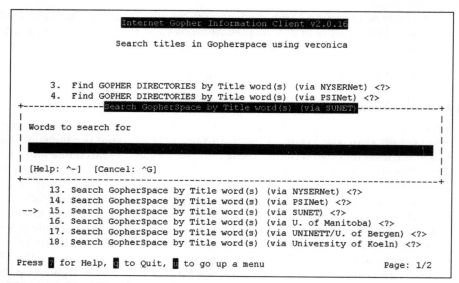

Figure 12.23 A Veronica search screen.

the service provider and its capabilities is provided on the Gopher menu. We'd like to rummage through Gopherspace for this kind of material, locally available but often interesting beyond the audience it was originally intended for.

I went to college in Iowa, for example, so maybe I'd like to check in with what's happening in the land of tall corn. One possibility would be to take the *Other Gophers/* menu item and look through all the Gopher servers until I found one or more that sported Iowa connections. With Veronica, all I need to do is ask the question by entering *iowa* as the keyword. Let's try that now, and see the results, as in Figure 12.24.

We see a customized menu generated expressly as the result of our search strategy. The menu format is familiar enough—it's just Gopher, the interface we've already become familiar with. But look at the menu items—we're a long way from North Carolina, Toto, even though these menu selections are all immediately accessible, just as if they were found on the local Gopher server.

The breadth of information is noteworthy. We've retrieved selections at the University of Iowa and Iowa State University, as well as Central College of Iowa. We have a link to the University of Iowa's Student Computer Association BBS, as well as an article on grants in the state, and a menu item offering links to library catalogs there, and an update on free speech issues that is apparently linked to a local news story. If you didn't catch it, note particularly the bottom right of the screen, where you'll see that this is, in fact, only page (1) out of 12 possibilities. Clearly, we've struck paydirt in our search for Iowa information. I can almost see the wind rippling through the cornstalks now.

The sharp-eyed will have noticed that I switched Veronica servers to run the actual search on our keyword. The reason is that the Veronica system has become so overloaded that it's frequently impossible to connect to the first server you request; instead, you receive a reply like this one when you attempt to make the connection:

```
         Internet Gopher Information Client v2.0.16

    Search GopherSpace by Title word(s) (via University of Koeln): iowa

-->_ 1.  09/08/94 Free Speech at Iowa Update
     2.   RINGROSE@IASTATE.EDU          ! Ringrose, Sharon; Chem, Iowa State..
     3.  CLINTON U-S POL  (L) By MERIDETH BUEL/DES MOINES, IOWA
     4.  univ.of.iowa.cost.report
     5.  Iowa              (IA)
     6.   Iowa Public Interest Research Group (IPIRG)/
     7.  University of Iowa, Student Computer Association BBS
     8.  Central College of Iowa
     9.  1994-06-15-President-in-Photo-Op-with-Bonnie-Campbell-of-Iowa
    10.  HISTORY OF TEACHER EDUCATION AT IOWA STATE UNIVERSITY
    11.  iowa.v0-0.ps
    12.  Iowa Grant Collaboration
    13.  University of Iowa, Student Computer Association BBS/
    14.  University of Northern Iowa
    15.  1994-06-15-President-in-Photo-Op-with-Bonnie-Campbell-of-Iowa
    16.  Re: Bridges in Iowa
    17.  University of Iowa Libraries/
    18.  VALIDATION OF THE RAND SELECTIVE INCAPACITATION SURVEY AND  THE  IO..

Press ? for Help, q to Quit, u to go up a menu          Page: 1/12
```

Figure 12.24   Results of a Veronica search under the term *iowa*.

```
Search GopherSpace by Title word(s) (via SUNET): iowa
--> 1. *** Too many connections - Try again soon. ***
```

When this happens, you'll want to work through the list of Veronica servers. Your Gopher client will save the basic search term for you, so that all you have to do is move the marker down to the next server on the Veronica list and press the **RETURN** key twice to run your search. Eventually, you'll find a server that's available and can process your request. You might also want to run the request at a different time of day, when the traffic load might be lighter. But the real solution to this problem lies in the creation of more Veronica servers to better distribute the immense load.

It's interesting to realize one ramification of Veronica: As we look at the list generated here, we're probably dealing with a variety of Gopher servers, but we don't have to know which is which. A specific item, such as *The Timber Industry of Iowa*, could be coming out of a server in Iowa City, or Ames, or Cedar Rapids, for all we know. And because we're using Gopher as the client, we can save menu items that seem interesting in our bookmark list, so we can return to them without going through the entire menu tree.

On the other hand, maybe you'd like to know where your information is coming from. We can generate such information with an equal sign command. Entering = with the arrow placed to the left of the item in question will tell us what we need. Putting the arrow on item 1 and pressing =, this is what I see:

```
Link Info (0k)      100%
+--------------------------------------------------------------------------+
#
Type=0
Name=09/08/94 Free Speech at Iowa Update
Path=\mailboxes\comgrads\09084102.009
```

```
Host=cios.11c.rpi.edu
Port=70
URL: gopher://cios.11c.rpi.edu:70/0%5cmailboxes%5ccomgrads%5c09084102.009
```

Now we know the host name for this information: cios.11c.rpi.edu; we also have the complete URL to the item.

Retrieving text or any of the menu items works the same as the Gopher procedures we've already talked about. Figure 12.25, for example, is the result of placing the arrow on item 8. What we receive in return is a screenful of information about how to contact Central College of Iowa's on-line library catalog.

Finding Something to Read

I find Veronica extremely useful in tracking down things I've heard about while eavesdropping on the networks. Spending a lot of time monitoring USENET newsgroups, for example, I often run into references to interesting new offerings. *Fineart Forum* is one of them. All I knew about it was that it was available as an on-line journal, but I didn't know where or what kind of material it published. Veronica seemed a natural at trying to locate the journal. I searched by Gopher directories this time to see if I could find any that branched off to further information about this journal. Entering *fineart* as my search term, I retrieved the information shown in Figure 12.26. This looks promising. I'll choose the entry marked *Fineart Forum/*.

We can see by the slash that there's another menu behind this level. Working through these menus, we can actually gain access to the journal as shown in Figure 12.27.

Finding these resources available through a comparatively simple Veronica search means we can do something about cleaning up our mailbox. Mine, for example, is stuffed every morning with all the journals I subscribe to. When I discovered the Veron-

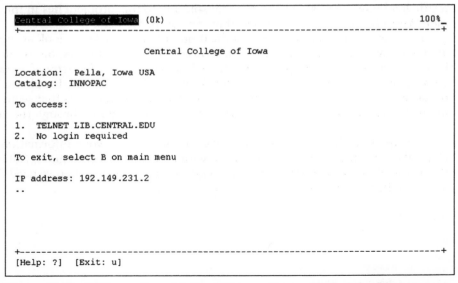

Figure 12.25 Pulling up Central College's library address, with the help of Veronica.

```
        Internet Gopher Information Client v2.0.16

    Find GOPHER DIRECTORIES by Title word(s) (via University of Koeln): fineart

-->_  1.  Fineart Forum/
      2.  FINEART (pilotObject)/
      3.  FINEART/
      4.  FineArt Forum/
      5.  FINEART/
      6.  FINEART/
      7.  701.101 FineArt Forum Online/
      8.  fineart.forum.vol5/
      9.  FINEART/
     10.  FineArt Forum/
     11.  fineart.forum.vol6/
     12.  FineArt Forum/
     13.  fineart-forum/
     14.  FineArt Forum/
     15.  FINEART/
     16.  FINEART/
     17.  FINEART/
     18.  17 out of 76 (get info here)./

Press ? for Help, q to Quit, u to go up a menu          Page: 1/1
```

Figure 12.26   Results of a search under the term *fineart*.

ica option, I realized I didn't need all those subscriptions. When I want to read something, all I have to do is query the database and track down the relevant journal. Some subscriptions, of course, are necessary; the journals you're most interested in should stay in your mailbox, because you'll be notified every time a new issue comes out. But if your interest is marginal, a Veronica search is perhaps the best way to go.

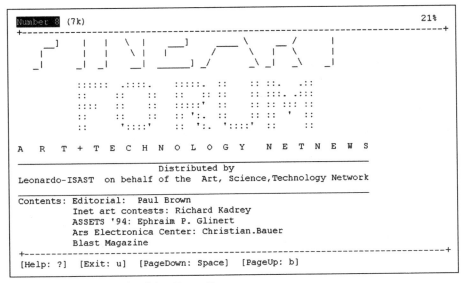

Figure 12.27   A sample of the *Fineart Forum*.

Tightening Up a Veronica Search

Veronica offers you the ability to tighten up your search by adding the –t suffix, followed by a particular data type. For example, suppose you want to search for Gopher menu items that contain the term *botany*. But you are looking specifically for Telnet sites, places where you might find a database on the subject. Rather than searching for the term *botany* by itself, you could use the term *botany* –*t8*. This will search for Telnet connections, as marked by the <TEL> suffix on Gopher menus, which also include *botany* in their menu description.

The –t option is dependent on the data types that Gopher uses. These are listed here. You can learn more about how to search using these data types in my book *Finding It on the Internet* (John Wiley & Sons, 1994), which goes into detail about Veronica search strategies.

0	A file
1	A directory
2	A CSO server
3	ERROR
4	A Macintosh file in BinHex format
5	A DOS binary archive
6	A uuencoded file
7	A searchable index
8	A Telnet connection
9	A binary file

And here are the experimental types:

s	A sound file
g	A GIF image file
M	A file containing MIME data, which is an evolving method of multimedia mail communications
h	An HTML file (see Chapter 6 for more information on HTML)
I	An image file
i	An inline text file used by panda (an Internet front-end based on Gopher)
T	A Telnet 3270 session

Combining Search Terms

You can also combine search terms when you run a Veronica search. Veronica assumes you have supplied an AND connector whenever you list more than one word. Thus, searching for *gin rummy* would turn up any menu items containing the term *gin* and the term *rummy;* they would not necessarily appear in sequence. If you typed the search terms as *gin and rummy,* you would get the same result.

The OR statement tells Veronica to look for Gopher menu items that contain one or the other of the words you've specified. Your search for *Clinton* or *Yeltsin*, then, will flag menu items containing either name.

Veronica also enables you to use parenthetical expressions. We could set up a search under the terms *cocktail (highball or martini)*, which would break down this way: Veronica would look for any menu item containing the term *cocktail*, and also containing either the term *highball* or *martini*. Remember, the AND connector is assumed; thus, we don't have to enter it (although we can if we choose) in our search term: *cocktail (highball or martini)* is the same statement as *cocktail and (highball or martini)*.

The NOT qualifier is occasionally useful as well. Using it, we can expressly rule out certain terms; *microsoft not gates* searches for any menu items containing the term *microsoft*, but excludes those using the term *gates*. This can be a handy way to reduce the number of hits, especially when terms are often found together. Thus *clinton not hillary* would focus in on the President, while excluding the First Lady.

You should be aware of the useful wild card function performed by the asterisk (*). Veronica will interpret an asterisk as representing any possible extensions to the search term. Thus, the term *comput** would find entries under *computer, computing, computational*, and so on.

Finding a Graphical Gopher

Interested in moving into a graphical Gopher environment? If you're a SLIP/PPP user, you can extend Gopher's already easy-to-use interface into a still more intuitive realm by tapping WSGopher. This excellent program, created by Dave Brooks, is available over the Net.

Figure 12.28 shows WSGopher at work. In the figure, I have moved to the home Gopher at the University of Illinois that is established as the program's default. You can easily change the home Gopher to one closer to your site by pulling down the Configure menu and choosing the Home Gopher Server item. Notice the use of the Windows environment; each new item accessed by WSGopher appears in its own window. Saving materials to your hard disk is a matter of pulling down the File menu and choosing the **Save** command.

One of the benefits of a well-designed program like WSGopher is that it makes the bookmark process easy to manage. In Figure 12.29, you can see some of the numerous bookmarks that the program contains. Notice that these are broken out by category, to

What You Need: A Graphical Gopher Client

The Program: WSGopher

Where to Get It: Try the following URL:

ftp://dewey.tis.inel.gov/pub/wsgopher/

As of this writing, the filename was wsg-12.exe. This is a self-extracting file. Execute the file in the DOS environment and it will unpack the various files.

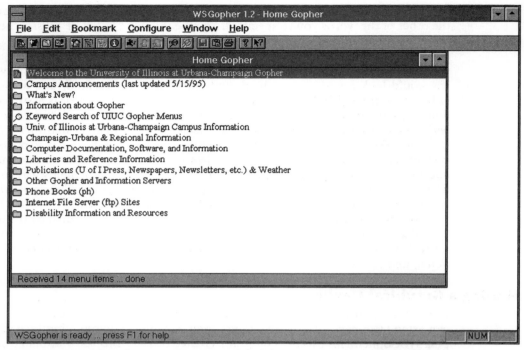

Figure 12.28   WSGopher at work, using its default home page at the University of Illinois.

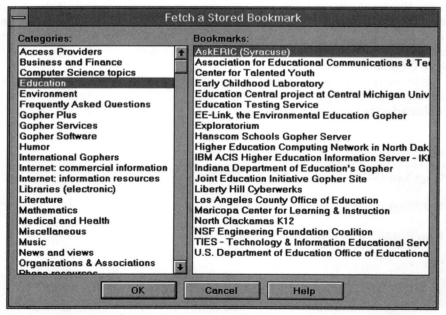

Figure 12.29   One of WSGopher's most useful features is its fully catalogued list of bookmarks.

What You Need: A Gopher Client for the Macintosh

The Program: TurboGopher

Where to Get It: Use anonymous FTP to this site:

ftp://boombox.micro.umn.edu/pub/gopher/Macintosh-TurboGopher/

Look for a file called TurboGopher2.0.sea.hqx.

make finding what you need a simple process. Adding bookmarks of your own is easily managed by pulling down the Bookmark menu from the main WSGopher screen.

Macintosh users will find many of the same useful features in the program I recommend for their machine. It's called TurboGopher, and it's available from the same site that created the Gopher system at the University of Minnesota.

Jughead—Cutting Gopher Down to Size

The biggest problem with the Gopher/Veronica combination is that it ranges so widely. Ask Veronica to find Gopher menu items containing the word *wine*, and it will hunt throughout the world for hits. This is terrific if you want to run a comprehensive search and have the time and patience to go through all the screens of results. On the other hand, there are situations when you want to search a restricted area. A full-featured Gopher may be stuffed with good material, which you want to search without going beyond the local site. Veronica can't do that for you.

Enter Jughead. Obviously, Jughead is a compatriot of archie and Veronica, at least in terms of its comic book affiliations. Created by Rhett Jones at the University of Utah Computing Center, Jughead was designed to make restricted searches of gopherspace possible. The system administrator at a university can set up a Jughead server to allow users to search only the Gopher at that university. Indeed, this is where we find most of the Jughead servers, at academic institutions. They appear as regular, searchable items on Gopher menus.

The University of Buffalo, for example, sets up Jughead on its Gopher this way:

```
Index to UB gopher space (jughead).

-->1. About.jughead.
    2. Search UB CIT Menus using jughead <?>
```

while the University of Texas at Austin presents the same sort of menu item this way:

```
Jughead: Search gopher menus at UT Austin

-->1. About Jughead.
    2. Jughead: Search menus in UT Austin gopherspace <?>
```

You can see that we are dealing with searchable indices, as marked by the <?> suffix. As with Veronica, when you press a **RETURN** with the arrow marker opposite Jughead, you wind up with a search screen. There, you enter your search term and again press a **RETURN.** The results appear as a regular Gopher menu.

If you would like to get some practice using Jughead, run a Veronica search using the search term *jughead -t7.* This will call up screens worth of searchable indices containing the term *jughead.* Move the marker as necessary and press a **RETURN** to search any one of them.

HYTELNET Power

HYTELNET is a useful catalog of Internet-accessible libraries, Free-Nets, and a wide variety of other information sources. The free program is available through anonymous FTP; if you're using either an IBM-compatible computer or a Macintosh to access the Internet, you should download and examine this program. Unix and VMS versions are also available. As a resident program, HYTELNET can be popped up at a moment's notice to solve the thorniest of navigational problems. We owe Peter Scott, of the University of Saskatchewan Libraries in Saskatoon, a debt of gratitude for this fine tool. Earl Fogel, also at Saskatchewan, created the Unix and VMS versions.

Figure 12.30 shows the opening screen of HYTELNET's on-line version, which gives you a feel for the system. In this figure, I am examining the program through the text-based World Wide Web browser called lynx. If you want to evaluate HYTELNET or use it on-line on a regular basis, you can point your browser to the following URL:

```
http://www.usask.ca/cgi-bin/hytelnet/
```

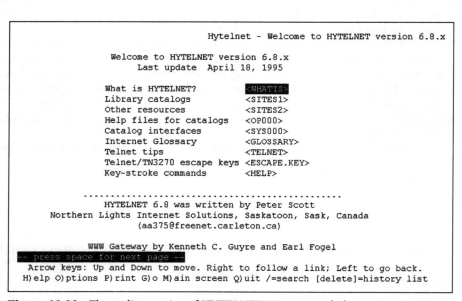

Figure 12.30   The on-line version of HYTELNET. You can work deeper into its menu structure by pressing the **RETURN** key.

What You Need: A Program with Information about Internet Resources

The Program: HYTELNET

Where to Get It: Through anonymous FTP. Go to the following URL:

ftp://ftp.usask.ca/pub/hytelnet/

As of this writing, the filename for the PC version is hyteln68.zip. The Macintosh version is hytelnet68.sit.bin. Both are located in directories branching off from the URL given.

In Figure 12.31, I have moved deeper into HYTELNET and am examining a list of sites, available by Telnet, on specified topics. Notice the range of possibilities here. I can examine databases, Free-Nets, bulletin board systems, archie servers and more.

Moving through these resources is managed by putting the on-screen highlight on the item in question and pressing the **RETURN** key. I'll put the highlight on *Electronic books* and press **RETURN,** calling up the screen shown in Figure 12.32. Here you see a list of books available by Telnet access. HYTELNET shows us where we have to go; the URL is:

```
telnet://consultant.micro.umn.edu
```

We log on as **gopher** and follow the directions HYTELNET provides.

Of course, you don't have to use Telnet to reach this Gopher site if you have a Gopher client available; you can even use Veronica to track down the book of your choice at other sites if you choose. The benefit of HYTELNET is that you can run this

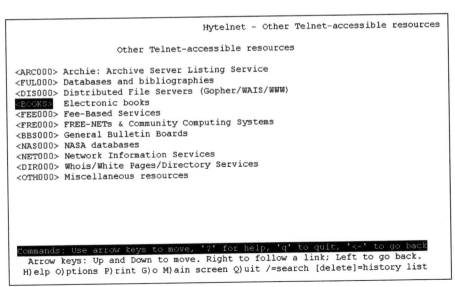

Figure 12.31 Examining a list of Telnet sites by topic with HYTELNET.

```
                                          Hytelnet - Electronic Books (p1 of 5)

                            Electronic Books

TELNET CONSULTANT.MICRO.UMN.EDU or 134.84.132.4
login: gopher
Select Libraries
Select Electronic Books

1990 USA Census Information
Aesop's Fables
Aladdin and the Wonderful Lamp
Alice's Adventures in Wonderland (Carroll)
CIA World Factbook 1991
Clinton's Inaugural Address
Complete Works of Shakespeare
Far From the Madding Crowd (Hardy)
Federalist Papers
Gift of the Magi (O. Henry)
Herland (Gilman)
Hunting of the Snark (Carroll)
-- press space for next page --
  Arrow keys: Up and Down to move. Right to follow a link; Left to go back.
 H)elp O)ptions P)rint G)o M)ain screen Q)uit /=search [delete]=history list  _
```

Figure 12.32 Electronic books and the site at which to access them.

search quickly through the offices of a resident program, or tap it on-line, to find what you need fast.

The information necessary for loading HYTELNET on your computer comes with the compressed package you'll download. Once installed, the program is called up by pressing the **Ctrl-BACKSPACE** key combination. The **ESC** key then returns the program to background operations, allowing you to proceed with your other work. Alternatively, it's possible to enter **Alt-T** to remove HYTELNET from memory.

Keeping up with Internet resources isn't easy, which means that HYTELNET itself must constantly change to reflect new developments. Here's a way to keep up:

What You Need: A Source of HYTELNET News

The Source: The mailing list HYTEL-L at the University of Saskatchewan. You can also read new messages in the USENET newsgroup bit.list-serv.hytel-1

How to Get It: Send mail to listserv@kentvm.bitnet. The message should read **sub hytel-1 your name.**

13

WAIS: Tracking Down Information

"A cookbook approach just won't work," said Jane Smith, assistant director of the Clearinghouse for Networked Information Discovery and Retrieval. "These tools are changing so fast that as soon as you explain how to use one of them, the information will be obsolete."[1] We were discussing resource finders, tools like WAIS and World Wide Web, which are the subject of this chapter, in the lobby of MCNC's Center for Communications. The Clearinghouse supports and promotes the use of network tools like these. It's even testing a new generation of systems that add features to the WAIS engine, developed by Thinking Machines Corporation, which we'll discuss shortly. And Smith was right.

That was in 1993, and the picture has only gotten more complex. Today, resource discovery is one of the Internet's fastest moving targets. Breakthroughs are occurring in a host of areas, perhaps most significantly on the World Wide Web, and useful client software is proliferating to take advantage of the ever deepening information pool. At the same time, battles rage over which tool is the right one for the job. The Web may be the engine pulling the Internet train at the moment; can we figure out an effective way to search it? Gopher remains a powerful alternative for text-based systems; can we cut across its menu structure to locate data? And WAIS remains viable for large database searching; can we engineer a front end for the system to make it accessible to the novice? All these questions cluster around our common need, to locate resources on the Net.

And the questions don't end there. Which models do we use for information discovery? Should directories of information about the Internet be maintained at some central site, or widely dispersed to allow for maximum accuracy and updating? Is anyone truly in charge of the information retrieval process, and is there any way to determine which standards will come out on top? The answers, as we'll see in this chapter, don't come easy.

In the meantime, you and I have some work to do. Faced with the challenge of the skeet shooter, trying to hit a rapidly moving target with some fast moves and a weapon that sprays shot over a wide area, I'll try to show you how WAIS works; we'll move on to the World Wide Web in the next chapter. We'll take a brief look at a WAIS server that's accessible through Telnet, but I plan to stop there only briefly. In the world of WAIS, the text-based clients I've worked with have proven unsatisfactory; they're awkward and difficult to use. I'll turn instead to a graphical WAIS client to illustrate how the system works. No matter what client you use, the basic principles you'll see illustrated here will apply to any WAIS search.

Wide Area Information Servers

On-line text, as we saw in earlier chapters, is proliferating. But text, for all its utility, presents formidable retrieval problems. WAIS, the Wide Area Information Servers system, was developed to address such searching. The idea is to let the user search for a combination of keywords by sending search strings to the appropriate WAIS server machines. Each of these servers offers one or more collections of documents available for the search routine. Documents that contain the specified keywords are flagged, and the information is returned in hierarchical order based on the frequency of each keyword and the distance between keywords in the document. The documents your search flags can then be requested from the server and displayed on-screen.

The client/server model is the key. The client is the program you deal with as you enter your queries and refine them; it's what you see as you work with WAIS. The server is where the data you're after is stored. You're using the client to connect with one or more servers each time you run a WAIS search.

The benefit of the WAIS protocol, which handles the byplay between client and server, is that it allows the client to work with simple English search terms. The client will convert these into the protocol, which transmits them over the network to the server. On the server end, the results of the search are processed and retransmitted back to the client via the same protocol.

WAIS and the Luck of the Irish

You'll understand WAIS better if you ponder the alternative to using it. There are hundreds of WAIS servers, for example, containing material accessible through other means. A database of recipes can be found through the WAIS database called usenet-cookbook.src (the .src suffix means you're dealing with WAIS; it stands for source). These recipes are largely those that have appeared in the USENET newsgroup rec.food.cooking. They're also available at an anonymous FTP site, gatekeeper.dec.com.

If all you knew was that a recipe for Irish stew existed somewhere on the Internet, you could go after it in two ways. Through anonymous FTP, you'd go to the site. Once on-line there, you could change to the *pub/recipes* directory and look for what you need. Note how directed a process this is. You have to know where the site is, and which directory at that site to examine for what file. You have to find the specific file and retrieve it.

Here's the WAIS alternative: By querying the WAIS source usenet-cookbook.src, you could tell your client program to search for the term *irish stew*. The software would handle the protocol conversion and query the server, whereupon a series of articles might be obtained that mention Irish stew. The benefit for you, the end user, is in search time; the WAIS software does the work for you, leaving you with the relatively trivial task of searching through the results to find which of the retrieved titles most closely resembles what you want. Having made that decision, you could then have the full text sent to your mailbox.

Looking for something like Irish stew in a recipe database, you'll likely find that one WAIS search does the trick. Broader search concepts, however, can call for a different technique. Using *relevance feedback,* you can progressively refine your search to track down just the information you need. This allows you to select particular results of the search and mark them as relevant. You can then run the search a second time. The server takes into account the documents you've marked and looks for others that bear similarities to them. This generally means those documents that share a large number of common words.

A New Paradigm for Searching

If you've ever used Dow Jones News/Retrieval, you've experienced something similar in the company's DOWQUEST service, which was the first commercial system to put relevance feedback to work. DOWQUEST brought a new paradigm to the search process. In the past, the Dow Jones text databases of newspaper and magazines articles had always used standard Boolean search techniques; indeed, these methods are still available today. Users have to specify exact search words and connect them with Boolean terms like AND or NOT to show the desired linkage between the items.

DOWQUEST threw away the Boolean connectors. The precise syntax of searching gave way to something more akin to brainstorming. You list words that play a major role in your subject and turn DOWQUEST loose. Looking for material on scheduling software, for example, you might enter the terms *calendar scheduler personal information manager.* No connecting terms are required, and the order of the words is immaterial. DOWQUEST goes out and retrieves a list of hits that contain these terms. You can then flag the best examples from this list of documents and ask the service to run the search again, this time finding more documents that are similar to the ones you liked.

Relevance feedback is a powerful search technique; in the hands of skilled searchers, it offers broad retrieval capabilities. But what's even more encouraging is that the method holds out the promise of effective searching for those without the inclination to master conventional Boolean models. The relevance feedback capabilities we will examine here through the WAIS access program called swais are not well developed; they're difficult to use and not always effective. But the WAIS engine that works behind them is continually being refined. When we turn to a graphical WAIS client, you will see how searching can become an increasingly natural process, as the software takes some of the load off the searcher. In this way, WAIS points in the same direction that the Internet at large is taking, toward wider access and a set of intuitive, rather than exclusive, search tools.

We have researchers at Thinking Machines Corporation, a producer of massively parallel computers and information retrieval engines, to thank for the initial work on the concept; the company's Brewster Kahle conceived WAIS, and it was developed jointly by Thinking Machines, Apple Computer, KPMG Peat Marwick, and Dow Jones and Company. Thinking Machines has made a public-domain version available that will run on many systems; the company also markets a commercial implementation. Kahle, who remains an important figure in WAIS' development, now runs his own company, WAIS Inc. For him, the definition of his product is a simple one. "WAIS is an infrastructure," Kahle says, "helping people ask novice questions of large collections of information around the world."[2]

A Multitude of Data Sources

The other powerful component of WAIS is its combination of data sources. Putting together a wide variety of databases is useful, but the sheer proliferation of data presents search problems. You might spend your time retrieving what you need from one database, only to realize that two others also contain relevant information. I run into this problem all the time. An on-line search through CompuServe's Magazine Index Plus database finds an article I need. But I know DIALOG contains databases covering different journal sources; I'll have to try there, too. But DIALOG and CompuServe use different interfaces, and their billing structures vary widely. Both, in turn, are different from Dow Jones News/Retrieval. Because of this, tracking down articles on a particular concept can take all afternoon, and burn up plenty of money.

Using WAIS, on the other hand, you have the ability to specify multiple databases to be searched sequentially, the results appearing in a list, ranked according to those items that most closely meet your criteria. The end user can thus tap a variety of databases through a single user interface and with one search. It's as if I could tell all the information services that I needed to search under a specified set of terms. By running one search, I could query across the board, and would have only one list of results to work with.

WAIS can be powerful indeed, but the very proliferation of data sources creates a problem. Useful as WAIS servers are, how do you know how to find them? There are hundreds of WAIS databases available on servers throughout the world. Fortunately, there are some ways around the problem. Thinking Machines maintains a Directory of Servers. The Directory can be queried like any other WAIS database, returning information on the servers most likely to be useful in finding a given topic.

The WAIS Protocol

Why does WAIS seem to be taking off? A major reason, surely, is the fact that the protocol driving it is open. (The protocol is known as Z39.50 by the National Information Standards Organization; it has been supplemented to meet the needs of full-text information retrieval.) The idea is that WAIS can't work unless there are enough databases out there running the protocol to make this search tool viable. When it published the specifications for the protocol, Thinking Machines spurred development of a wider market. The result: a growing number of information providers who have reason to support the WAIS project and to develop servers that will function under the protocol. Another key is the active work of CNIDR, the Clearinghouse for Networked Information Discovery and Retrieval. A specific goal of CNIDR is to develop a public-domain WAIS implementation, testing WAIS systems with improved features.

Fortunately, the protocol is hardware independent as well, eliminating the problem of developing a solution under one hardware system and being unable to apply it to others. Since the WAIS software can manage data negotiations with a variety of hardware and software platforms, providers are not constrained by their existing equipment and can develop WAIS servers confidently. Although the original client software was developed, for example, on the Apple Macintosh, programs now exist for a wide variety of operating systems. We should expect this development to continue as WAIS gains in popularity and utility.

The WAIS Support Consortium exists to address questions relating to the spread of WAIS and its future direction. There will be much to consider. Intriguingly, although the basic Z39.50 protocol was developed to manage bibliographical retrieval tasks, it was extended to handle more than text. Internet users will also be able to use WAIS to retrieve video and audio materials.

A Basic WAIS Search

Let's examine text-based WAIS by going to the University of North Carolina, which maintains a number of WAIS servers at its site. Connecting there will require us to Telnet to the following URL:

```
telnet://sunsite.unc.edu/
```

The variant of WAIS we'll be using here is actually called swais, for "screen WAIS." This is a character-oriented interface, WAIS in its baldest form. The login at UNC is shown here:

```
% telnet sunsite.unc.edu
Trying 198.86.40.81 ...
Connected to sunsite.unc.edu.
Escape character is '^]'.
***************** Welcome to SunSITE.unc.edu *****************
SunSITE offers several public services via login. These include:

NO MORE PUBLIC gopher login!
Use lynx the simple WWW client to access gopher and Web areas
For a simple WAIS client (over 500 databases), login as swais
For WAIS search of political databases, login as politics
For WAIS search of LINUX databases, login as linux

For a FTP session, ftp to sunsite.unc.edu. Then login as anonymous

For more information about SunSITE, send mail to info@sunsite.unc.edu

Unix(r) System V Release 4.0 (calypso-2.oit.unc.edu)
login:
```

Notice the options available here. To log in and search using the text-based WAIS client, use **swais** as your login. But notice that UNC also makes more targeted searching possible. You can log in with the word **politics** and be taken to a WAIS database that focuses on political issues. Another, with the login **linux,** houses information about the Linux operating system, a variant of Unix that runs on IBM-compatible equipment.

If you choose **swais** as your login, you will be taken to a screen like the one in Figure 13.1.

Browsing WAIS for Sources

What's available through WAIS? After signing on at UNC, we see a list of WAIS databases. The list can be paged through by using the **Down** and **Up Arrow** keys. You can also move up and down by using the following command keys:

J   Causes swais to move to the next page of sources.

K   Causes swais to move to the previous page of sources.

```
SWAIS                           Source Selection               Sources: 593
   #            Server                        Source                 Cost
001:   [          archie.au]   aarnet-resource-guide              Free
002:   [ndadsb.gsfc.nasa.gov]  AAS_jobs                           Free
003:   [ndadsb.gsfc.nasa.gov]  AAS_meeting                        Free
004:   [       munin.ub2.lu.se] academic_email_conf               Free
005:   [          sv3.cnusc.fr] acubase                           Free
006:   [      archive.orst.edu] aeronautics                       Free
007:   [bruno.cs.colorado.ed]  aftp-cs-colorado-edu               Free
008:   [nostromo.oes.orst.ed]  agricultural-market-news           Free
009:   [       sunsite.unc.edu] alt-sys-sun                       Free
010:   [      archive.orst.edu] alt.drugs                         Free
011:   [     wais.oit.unc.edu]  alt.gopher                        Free
012:   [       sunsite.unc.edu] alt.sys.sun                       Free
013:   [     wais.oit.unc.edu]  alt.wais                          Free
014:   [                     ]  American-Music-Resource            Free
015:   [       munin.ub2.lu.se] amiga_fish_contents               Free
016:   [   coombs.anu.edu.au]   ANU-Aboriginal-EconPolicies   $0.00/minute
017:   [   coombs.anu.edu.au]   ANU-Aboriginal-Studies        $0.00/minute
018:   [         150.203.76.2]  ANU-ACT-Stat-L                $0.00/minute

Keywords:

<space> selects, w for keywords, arrows move, <return> searches, q quits, or ?
```

Figure 13.1   A list of WAIS sources at sunsite.unc.edu.

Note the range of possibilities available. On the screen in Figure 13.1 there are databases on music, aeronautics, a WAIS newsgroup, and an agricultural market resource. And we're still in the A listings.

The swais Commands

swais uses a text editor called ex, which, in keeping with Unix programs like mail and vi, offers an inscrutable command structure. It's possible to play around with swais without knowing anything about ex, but to avoid frustration, it's a good idea to generate a list of basic swais commands. This is done by typing a question mark (**?**) at the prompt. What we get in return is a list of the commands in question. They are:

j	Move to the next WAIS database. You can also use the **Down Arrow** or **Ctrl-N.**
k	Move to the next WAIS source. You can also use the **Up Arrow** or **Ctrl-P.**
J	Move to the next screen. Or use **Ctrl-V.**
K	Move back one screen. Or use **ESC.**
###	Move to the database corresponding to the number you type.
/keyword	Search for a database containing your search term.
SPACEBAR	Select the currently highlighted database for searching.
=	Remove any previous selected database from your list of search databases.
v	View information about the current database.

RETURN	Run a search.
s	Select new databases.
w	Select new keywords.
o	Set and show the options in use by swais.
?	Show a display of swais commands.
H	Display a history of swais.
q	Leave swais

Running a Sample Search at SunSITE

Let's run a basic search using the WAIS system at UNC. To begin, use Telnet to the previously mentioned site: sunsite.unc.edu. At the prompt, enter **swais** as your login. Be careful here; when you are prompted for a terminal type, the default is "unknown"—don't, in other words, enter a **RETURN,** or the system won't know the kind of terminal you are using. Be sure to type **vt100** when asked for terminal type, as shown here:

```
TERM = (unknown) vt100
```

The WAIS database listings will now be loaded, as we saw in Figure 13.1. You will want to practice moving the cursor, using the commands just given, to get a feel for the system. Remember that by pressing the **SPACEBAR** with the highlight on a particular database, you are selecting that database for a search.

WAIS can help us home in directly on what we need. Suppose I'd like to learn more about how the educational system is making out in terms of federal funding. To learn, I move through the list of WAIS databases until I find one called US-Budget-1995. By pressing the **SPACEBAR,** I can select this database for searching. I will see the following:

```
072: * [     calypso-2] US-Budget-1995          Free
```

Notice the asterisk near the left-hand side of the line. This tells us that the database has been selected and is now available for the search.

We search a WAIS database by choosing appropriate keywords and submitting them to the search engine. Since I'm interested in education, I will use that as my keyword. To begin the search, it's necessary to use the **w** command. This places the keyword in the search field. In Figure 13.2, I have entered the keyword and am about to run my search.

Pressing the **RETURN** key begins the search, which causes the client to translate the search term through the WAIS protocol and send it to the appropriate server. We wind up with the result shown in Figure 13.3, a list of files WAIS found that contained the desired search term.

Give this list some scrutiny. The first item contains what appears to be an overview of the budgetary process as it relates to education—it's called *Investing for Productivity.* There is also a list of Federal programs by agency, which would tell us which agency was funding what programs involving education. There is even a table of budget authority by function, and various specialized documents on such topics as bilingual education, nutrition, and educational costs.

But before we examine any of these documents, let's take a closer look at the search results screen and see what it's telling us. Note the two columns on the far left. One gives

```
SWAIS                       Source Selection                  Sources: 76
  #          Server                          Source                   Cost
055:    [                 ]  sustainable-agriculture                  Free
056:    [                 ]  Tantric-News                             Free
057:    [                 ]  Tar-Heel-index                           Free
058:    [                 ]  UNC-Davis-CDs                            Free
059:    [                 ]  UNC-Davis-GovDocs                        Free
060:    [                 ]  UNC-Davis-State-Documents                Free
061:    [                 ]  UNC-Davis-Talking_Books                  Free
062:    [                 ]  UNC-mail-ids                             Free
063:    [                 ]  UNC-Periodicals-index                    Free
064:    [  sunsite.unc.edu]  UNC-SILS-Masters-Papers                  Free
065:    [                 ]  UNC-UL-AudioCDs                          Free
066:    [                 ]  UNC-UL-Talking_Books                     Free
067:    [                 ]  UNC-video-holdings-index                 Free
068:    [                 ]  UNC-Wilson-manuscripts                   Free
069:    [          calypso]  unchtml                                  Free
070:    [        calypso-2]  uncroothtml                              Free
071:    [        calypso-2]  US-Budget-1993                           Free
072: *  [        calypso-2]  US-Budget-1995                           Free


Keywords: education_

Enter keywords with spaces between them; <return> to search; ^C to cancel
```

Figure 13.2   The swais screen, showing the keyword selection at the bottom left.

us an ascending list of numbers, the other a score. WAIS is looking for the most likely candidates for our search results. From the information we've given the system, those results with a perfect 1,000 score (there is only one of them in this case) are the closest to what we're looking for, at least, as far as WAIS knows. We can browse down through the list by pressing the **SPACEBAR** after positioning the highlight on any document we want. Don't assume that because some documents got high scores the others are not worth your

```
SWAIS                         Search Results                    Items: 40
  #     Score    Source                   Title                        Lines
001:   [1000]  ( US-Budget-1995)  Chapter 3B: Inversting for Productivity   4701
002:   [ 850]  ( US-Budget-1995)  Full List of Federal Programs by Agency  18940
003:   [ 570]  ( US-Budget-1995)  Table 8.1--Outlays by Budget Enforcement  1780
004:   [ 441]  ( US-Budget-1995)  Table 3.1--Outlays by Superfunction and   2109
005:   [ 301]  ( US-Budget-1995)  Introduction                             1555
006:   [ 301]  ( US-Budget-1995)  Table 5.1--Budget Authority by Function   1009
007:   [ 279]  ( US-Budget-1995)  Office of Postsecondary Education          129
008:   [ 215]  ( US-Budget-1995)  Office of Special Education and Rehabili    64
009:   [ 193]  ( US-Budget-1995)  Nutrition Research and Education Service     29
010:   [ 193]  ( US-Budget-1995)  Office of Bilingual Education and Minori     27
011:   [ 193]  ( US-Budget-1995)  Office of Vocational and Adult Education     24
012:   [ 193]  ( US-Budget-1995)  National Commission on Responsibilities      32
013:   [ 182]  ( US-Budget-1995)  Chapter 7: Summary Tables                 1614
014:   [ 182]  ( US-Budget-1995)  Education Benefits                           34
015:   [ 172]  ( US-Budget-1995)  Barry Goldwater Scholarship and Excellen     17
016:   [ 161]  ( US-Budget-1995)  National Commission on Cost of Higher Ed     17
017:   [ 161]  ( US-Budget-1995)  National Commission on Independent Highe      17
018:   [ 161]  ( US-Budget-1995)  National Commission on Migrant Education      16


<space> selects, arrows move, w for keywords, s for sources, ? for help_
```

Figure 13.3   A list of hits found by swais under the keyword *education*.

attention. Although WAIS attempts to classify its findings, you will often see useful documents with low scores, which is simply an indication that the software isn't perfect.

Figure 13.4 shows you the result of choosing the first document. As you can see, the document focuses on the administration's plans for education under the current budget, and offers broad information that later entries in our list will describe in detail. Some time spent paging through our hits will be well spent, uncovering how the budget addresses educational issues.

To leave the search, we can press an **s,** which takes us out of the individual document and back to the list of sources. To deselect the US-Budget-1995 database, we press the **SPACEBAR** again, and the asterisk will disappear. We can now run another search if we choose, perhaps running it against multiple databases instead of just one. To exit swais, we press a **q**. Notice that the basic commands are presented at the bottom of the screen.

Summarizing a swais Search

For clarity, here are the major components of the swais search we just ran:

1. Choose one or more WAIS databases by placing the highlight bar over the database in question and pressing the **SPACEBAR.**
2. Use the **w** command to move to the keyword field.
3. Enter your keyword(s).
4. Press a **RETURN** to run the search.
5. Choose a document from your search results by placing the highlight over it.
6. Press the **SPACEBAR** to view the document.
7. Use the **s** command to move back to your list of hits. Here, you can view as many of them as you wish by using the **SPACEBAR.**
8. Exit swais by using the **q** command.

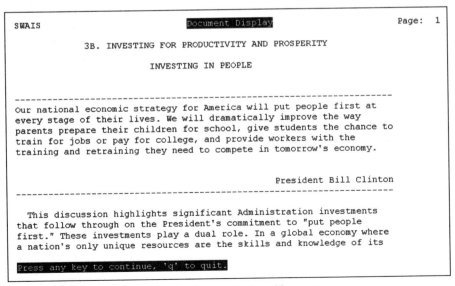

Figure 13.4 Examining one of the documents found by swais.

A Wide Range of Servers

WAIS databases come in all manner of subjects. Some hold materials gathered from USENET newsgroups; mailing lists are archived in the same way. This is a useful adjunct to the newsgroups and mailing lists themselves. The WAIS procedure is much quicker than going through LISTSERV search protocols, and provides a higher likelihood that you'll find the information you need. In addition, swais remembers search strategies. You can run a search in multiple databases at once, significantly cutting down your search time, and can flag multiple hits to be sent in batch mode to your mailbox.

Other WAIS databases contain bibliographies, or reports, abstracts, and papers under various subjects, many of them technical in nature. It's natural enough to find a heavy concentration of computer materials here, but there are also resources like book reviews, materials on a variety of world religions, useful archives of zip codes, weather information, documents from such groups as the Electronic Frontier Foundation, Project Gutenberg and more. You'll find the working documents from the Internet Engineering Task Force here, along with discussions related to the commercialization and privatization of the Internet. More databases are being added all the time.

A Graphical WAIS Search

You've just seen the most elementary form of WAIS search. I used the character-based swais interface, which is available to anyone with a shell account on the Internet, and searched a single database to pull up information. But WAIS is capable of considerably more complexity. It's possible, for example, to select multiple databases against which to run our search, and to use relevance feedback techniques that let us progressively refine our list of results. As mentioned earlier, it's also useful to examine WAIS in a graphical environment, where the demands of command entry are eased by pull-down menus.

But first, there's an issue that needs addressing. There are hundreds of WAIS databases scattered on servers throughout the world. The perfect database for our purposes might be out there, but how would we know how to find it? When we used the computer at the University of North Carolina, we were merely paging through a list of WAIS servers looking for something interesting. It would be much more helpful if directories of WAIS servers existed that could help us find what we need. Fortunately, they do, and we can search them just as we search any other WAIS database. Using keywords, we can determine which WAIS server is the most likely to house our information.

Let's try out all the options by running a more complicated WAIS search, one that uses a directory of servers first, and then moves on to search the databases it recommends. I could run this search with swais, but since I've already shown you how the character-based interface works, I'll now move to a graphical program called WinWAIS. This program, created by Microelectronics and Computer Technology Corporation, was originally made available on the Internet as shareware, but is now freeware. You can retrieve it at the following URL:

```
ftp://ftp.einet.net/einet/pc/
```

At the time of this writing, the filename was ewais204.zip. Anyone with a SLIP/PPP connection to the Internet would be well advised to download this program, since of all Internet chores, WAIS tends to be the most complicated to use in the shell environment. As you'll see, WinWAIS helps enormously.

Here's the game plan: I would like to extract some potentially useful investing information from the WAIS system. In particular, I've heard that Latin America may be an emerging area for economic growth in the early part of the twenty-first century. If I wanted to learn more about these economies and how to invest in them, how would I use WAIS?

Figure 13.5 shows the primary WinWAIS screen. You can see that the interface is lean but readily understandable. The keyword field is found at the top of the screen, and submitting the keyword to the WAIS system is done by clicking on the large Ask button to the right. To use the system, we must first tell it which WAIS server to consult. This is done in the following way:

1. Pull down the Edit menu.
2. Choose the Select Sources option.

When you do this, a list of sources will appear, as shown in Figure 13.6.

At present, there is only one source available, the Directory of Servers at Thinking Machines Corp., where so much of the early work on WAIS was done. We can add to this list as we go, using methods I'll show you in a moment. But for now, the important thing is to select the Directory of Servers by highlighting it and choosing the Select button. This moves the Directory into the list of selected sources, as shown in the figure. Clicking on the OK button then takes us back to the search screen with the Directory of Servers as our primary WAIS database.

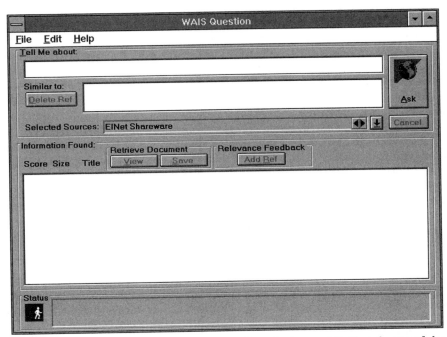

Figure 13.5 The primary WinWAIS screen. Note the keyword field at the top of the screen.

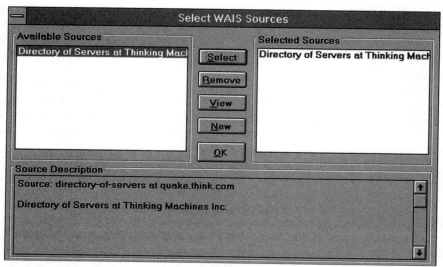

Figure 13.6 Setting up a database for searching with WinWAIS.

I'll query the directory by asking to see any databases that contain keywords relating to the Latin American economies; I enter these in the top field on the main WinWAIS screen. The search begins with these keywords:

```
latin america economy stock market
```

Figure 13.7 shows the results of this search:

If you'll examine these results with care, you'll notice a number of items that clearly don't apply to our interests, and some we're just not sure of. Here's one called agricultural-market-news, which may or may not be useful (does it involves commodities in South America, such as coffee?). Here's another called ANU-Endangered-Languages, which doesn't seem to have much to do with South America. And what about document_center_catalog? Let's find out more about these sources.

To do so, we can make a request of WinWAIS. We simply highlight the database about which we need information and then press the View button. Figure 13.8 shows the result of doing this for the agricultural-market-news database.

By examining the textual description of this WAIS source, we see that it does indeed take itself out of contention. Its coverage of agricultural news seems limited to the United States alone. A similar inspection of the other databases reveals that ANU-Endangered-Languages is an archive of a mailing list devoted to such languages, which was created at Australian National University, while document_center_catalog is a service dedicated to government and industry specifications and standards. Has WAIS gone berserk?

Not berserk, perhaps, but running up against its own nature. WAIS is looking for databases that meet our search terms. But we've given it terms that can be interpreted in various ways. When we tell the Directory of Servers that we want servers dealing with the stock market, it will look just as diligently for the term *stock* as it will for *stock market*. The result is a hit on an entry like the document_center_catalog, which mentions

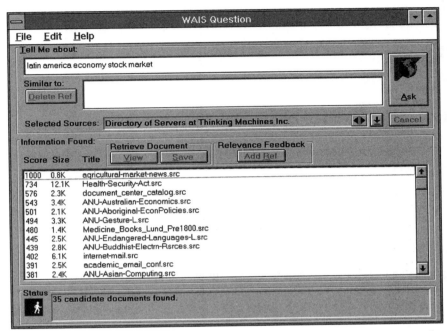

Figure 13.7 Results of the search for information about Latin American economies and stock markets.

one of our keywords in its entry, but in no way fits into our search needs. The same thing has happened with ANU-Endangered-Languages—one of our keywords has triggered it as a hit, but we immediately see that it can be discarded. If you look at the numerical rankings for these sources to the left of the list, you'll see that only one receives a score of 1,000. WAIS is telling us that none of these are close matches.

Widening the Search

Maybe we should work on our search terms. We're looking for information about Latin America and its various economies. But we've been too specific thus far in our search. There may well be large amounts of WAIS information out there in servers whose charter is to cover broader themes. So, rather than searching under *stock market*, let's broaden the search to terms like *economy* and *finance*, leaving *latin america* in the search. We'll go back to the main WinWAIS screen and modify our keywords accordingly to run another search. The results are shown in Figure 13.9.

This list, however, remains unpromising. What we're running into is that economic and financial information remains relatively untapped by WAIS servers. We've also seen a limitation of WAIS—it pulls up hits with no connection whatsoever with the topic in hand, because of the way it searches for the words we give it to look for. In this case, we're faced with having to look through these sources to see if any of them apply. We can work through the entries to examine whichever seem promising by using the same methods shown previously. And indeed, the one called academic_email_conf may have some interest. It's a database of information about newsgroups and electronic confer-

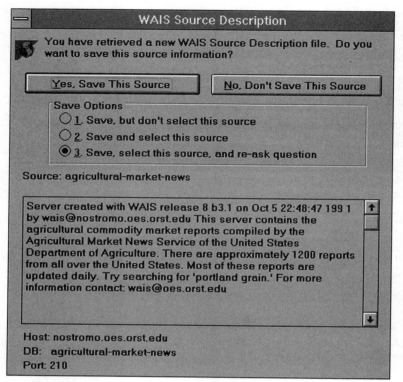

Figure 13.8   Examining the specifics of a WAIS database.

ences. Although South and Central America do not yet maintain a strong presence on the Internet, let's see if some of these discussion groups have something to show us.

To do so, we'll search the academic_email_conf database. To choose it as a source, we need only press the appropriate button on the screen description of the database. If you will look back at Figure 13.8, you'll see that each database description contains two buttons, one that allows you to select that database as a source for your next search, and another that allows you to pass it by. We'll select the button that allows us to save the source. Notice that there are three subsequent buttons that can modify what we do with the source:

- Save, but don't select this source: This button allows us to save the description of the database for possible use in future searches, but it doesn't select it for the current search.
- Save, and select this source: This button saves and selects the source for use in the current search.
- Save, select this source, and re-ask question: This button saves and selects the source, and allows us to move immediately to submit the same keywords to the new source.

By choosing the third button, we can proceed with our search of the new database. The keywords remain in the search field on the main WinWAIS screen, so all we need to do is

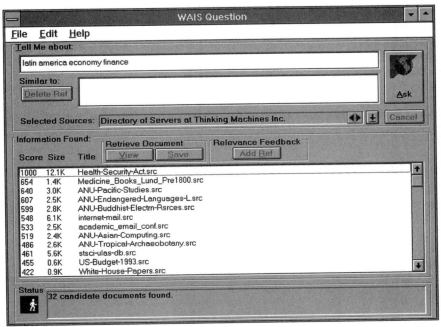

Figure 13.9　Results of a modified keyword search in WinWAIS.

to press the Ask button to submit the search. This time it will not go to the Directory of Servers but to the academic_email_conf database. The results are shown in Figure 13.10.

Using these methods, we have completed a search of a single WAIS database. To see an entry, it's only necessary to highlight it and click on the View button (or double-click the entry itself). Here, for example, is the entry for the soc.culture.latin-america newsgroup; I've called it up by clicking on the second entry in Figure 13.10.

```
LN: soc.culture.latin-america
TI: Topics about Latin-America.
SU: (U) soc.culture.latin-america
ED: No
AR:
MO:
SA: Local Usenet Newsreader
KE: Latin America
```

This particular WAIS database merely holds contact information about newsgroups and mailing lists, so the document is nothing more than a pointer. Other WAIS databases, of course, hold documents of greater length; for that matter, WAIS can be used to index virtually any kind of digital resources, including images, sound, and moving video. All that's needed is a set of keywords with which the item can be indexed.

Relevance Feedback Techniques

Let's now give relevance feedback a try. Doing this with swais can be a chore, since it involves a series of commands and very little visual feedback when you're setting them

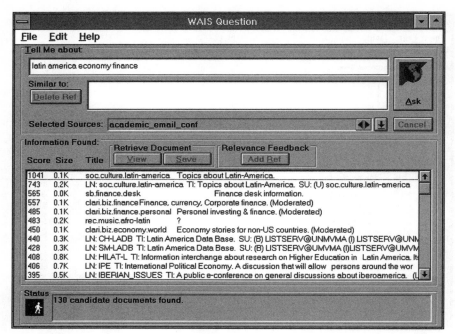

Figure 13.10   Results of a search through the academic_email_conf database.

up. But WinWAIS makes relevance feedback relatively simple. Remember the principle here: relevance feedback lets you mark certain items as being close to what you want to see. When you rerun the search, the WAIS system will try to bear your selections in mind as it creates a new hit list, one that should, theoretically, be closer to what you're trying to find.

Here's the method:

1. Highlight an item you'd like to mark as being relevant to your search.
2. Click the Add Ref button. This will cause the item to appear in the Similar to: window.
3. Work through the list of hits and highlight any other items that seem particularly useful, and thus a model for what you want to see.
4. Click the Add Ref button for each.
5. Run the search again by clicking on the Ask button.

In Figure 13.11, you can see that I have set up several items in the Similar to: window using these methods. I have then run a new search, which calls up a different list of hits than what we saw previously or, at least, ranks them in a different order, based upon their relevance. From this search, I've found a number of conferences that can be used to monitor events in Latin and South America, as well as newsgroups about the area. It would be possible for me to sign on to any of these by using the methods discussed in Chapter 9.

Searching Multiple Databases

We've seen how to search a single database. But often, we'd like to search more than one site with a single search. Suppose I'd like to pull up information about science fiction. I can go to the directory of servers and run my search using that term as my keyword. When I do, the screen of hits shown in Figure 13.12 appears.

Now we know not to be surprised by the eclectic nature of some of these hits, since WAIS is searching for any database containing the term science or fiction, as well as any where the terms appear side by side. The top two entries seem to be the most germane to our search, so let's select both databases to be used in it. The method remains the same as it did when we selected the academic_email_conf database earlier:

1. Highlight the database you want to add to your list.
2. Click on the View button to see its description.
3. Click on the Yes button to save this database as a source for the search.

Having highlighted the first two databases, Science-Fiction-Series-Guide and sf-reviews, I can enter my search term. I'll see if WAIS has anything to say about the popular television series "The Outer Limits," which I used to watch as a kid. At this point, the screen will look as it does in Figure 13.13. You can see the search term at the top of the screen. The two databases chosen for this search don't appear in the Selected Sources window, but that window does tell us that we have chosen two databases for the search, and we could use the pull-down arrow to see the list. Running the search has generated

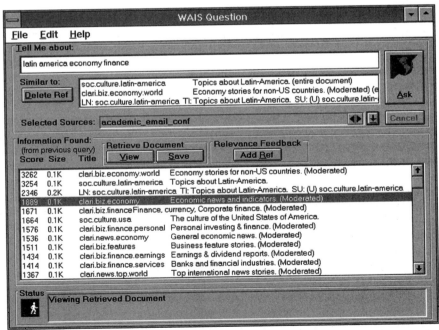

Figure 13.11 Using relevance feedback to augment the WinWAIS search. Note the articles selected as relevant in the middle window.

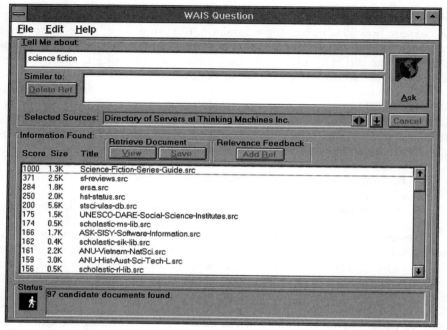

Figure 13.12   Running a search for science fiction–related databases in the directory of servers.

a list of hits that draws on what is found in both databases. Figure 13.14 shows one of the results. The document refers to "The Outer Limits" as part of a review.

WAIS by Gopher

As mentioned earlier, it's possible to access WAIS resources through a Gopher server. Let's build a hypothetical search. Assume we're in the market for information about music. How do we know what early music sounded like? What about *really* early music, such as what would have been performed in ancient Athens? As in the previous case, I'm constructing the question as I go; my goal is to show you what WAIS is really like, rather than to manufacture searches that have a predesigned outcome. Let's slip into Gopher and see what we find, using its interface to run our search.

Many Gophers provide links to WAIS information. For the purposes of this search, I enter a Gopher at the University of Illinois; there, I find a menu item called *Other Gopher and Information Servers*. You'll find an item like it at most Gopher sites, since Gopherspace is a virtually seamless, connected medium. And from the list of resources on this Gopher, I pick an item called *WAIS Based Information*. You can see the list of WAIS databases generated by this choice in Figure 13.15.

We can query a directory of servers through Gopher just as we did with the Win-WAIS client program. So let's see if we can find out some information about music. Which WAIS servers are likely to help us out? Figure 13.16 shows the search screen as Gopher presents it. We can enter *music* as our search term and we're off. Another **RETURN** key application produces a list, shown in Figure 13.17, of possible WAIS sites for data on what we're looking for.

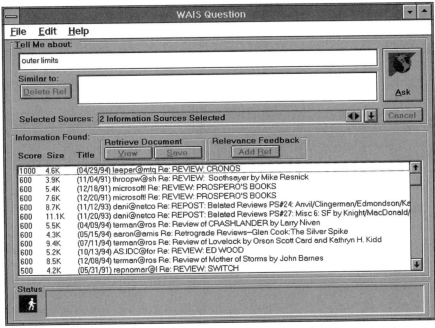

Figure 13.13 Searching multiple science fiction databases for information about the television series "The Outer Limits."

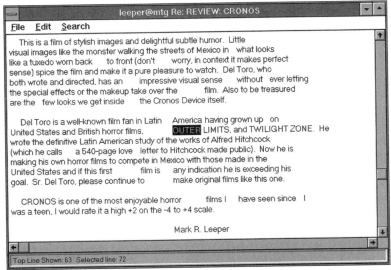

Figure 13.14 An article called up by our search for "The Outer Limits." Note that the search terms are highlighted.

Let's take item 2, rec.music.early.src, to see if we can learn anything about music in the ancient world. We will launch another search by pressing the **RETURN** key to select that database. At that point, we'll use *greek* as our search term and send it to the database. The results, shown in Figure 13.18, are encouraging, listing quite a few hits that might work out.

At this point, you should note the differences on-screen between Gopher and other clients. If we generated this same list using a swais or a WinWAIS search, we'd see a numbered list of hits, the possibilities with the highest relevance labeled 1,000. Here we have no such gradation. If we page through this list (we can do so using the **SPACEBAR,** or alternatively, using the + and − keys), we'll see there are a number of potentially useful entries scattered throughout the list. It's not possible to pull off the top three or four and declare them the best candidates.

What's happening? Well, using WAIS resources, Gopher has produced a list of useful information, ranking the items according to what it thinks we're after. At this point with WinWAIS, we would use relevance feedback to home in on items we need. But we have no way to introduce relevance feedback into the equation with Gopher. The first list we get is the one we're stuck with, which means we'll need to go over that search list from top to bottom.

Gopher is easy to use. We can query the directory of servers within it, then use the **RETURN** key to query the databases we need. But, unlike WinWAIS, we cannot use multiple servers at once for our search. That means a WAIS search using Gopher can be a more time-consuming process, depending on what you need.

Items 11, 17, and 18 catch my eye immediately; they seem to be discussing the question precisely. At this point, I don't have to have memorized the Gopher commands. With any Gopher, I can enter a question mark (**?**) to find out what the command possi-

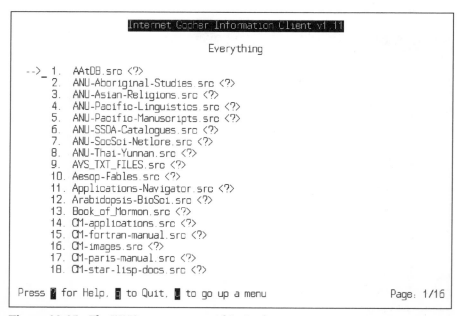

Figure 13.15   The WAIS menu screen within Gopher.

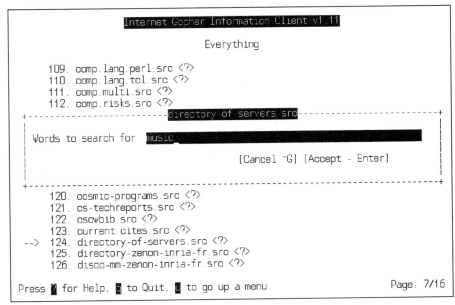

Figure 13.16   Searching for *music* using WAIS within Gopher.

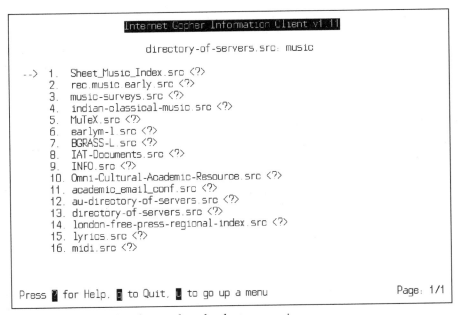

Figure 13.17   Results of a search under the term *music*.

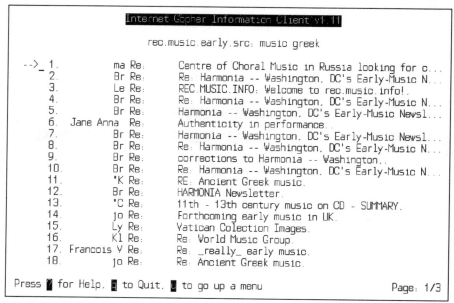

Figure 13.18   Results of refining the *music* search with the term *greek*.

bilities are. We did this when we were examining Gopher in Chapter 12. Figure 13.19 shows a partial list of the relevant commands.

The **a** command is promising. It lets us add the current item to a bookmark list. We can use an **a** at each of the first three lines, placing the highlight over each by moving the bar down with the arrow key. Now we've created a separate screen (accessible by a **v** command) of the items we consider the most interesting. An **s** command will then save whichever files we want to keep.

Did the search produce useful results? Definitely. I found a helpful message from the EARLYM-L mailing list on ancient music. Here were summarized the major sources on the subject, giving me enough information to explore as deeply into the material as I might wish.

WAIS through the World Wide Web

We've seen that it's possible to search a directory of servers to find which WAIS databases are the most appropriate for our needs. But my own experience with WAIS is that such a search sometimes fails to turn up all the possibilities. It's a good idea, then, to go through a list of WAIS databases on occasion to familiarize yourself with them and to note any that appear to have long-term interest for your work. One way to do this is to use a WAIS site on the World Wide Web. I'll save the bulk of our Web discussion for the next chapter, but I do want to give you an important address for WAIS work:

```
http://www.wais.com/newhomepages/surf.html
```

By putting this address into a World Wide Web browser, we can access the site at WAIS Inc., a company specializing in the WAIS search engine and its commercial applications. Figure 13.20 shows the home page at WAIS Inc.

```
Bookmarks
---------
a : Add current item to the bookmark list.
A : Add current directory/search to bookmark list.
v : View bookmark list.
d : Delete a bookmark/directory entry.

Other commands
--------------
s : Save current item to a file.
D : Download a file.
q : Quit with prompt.
Q : Quit unconditionally.
= : Display Technical information about current item.
O : change options
/ : Search for an item in the menu.
n : Find next search item.

The Gopher development team hopes that you find this software useful.
If you find what you think is a bug, please report it to us by sending
e-mail to "gopher@boombox.micro.umn.edu".


Press <RETURN> to continue, <m> to mail, <s> to save, or <p> to print:_
```

Figure 13.19 The basic Gopher commands for WAIS, listed by entering a **?** command.

The WAIS Inc. site is of interest for several reasons, not the least of which is that it too contains a directory of servers in easily viewable format. Part of this list is shown in Figure 13.21. As you can see, each of these items is set up as a hyperlink, meaning that to obtain information about the item, we simply click on that item after positioning our mouse cursor on it.

Suppose, for example, that I want to search the database macintosh-tidbits.htm. Tidbits is a well-regarded electronic magazine specializing in Macintosh issues and the broader question of Internet connectivity. I recall reading an article in it that dealt with the recent purchase of ANS by America Online. This was a significant move, because ANS for years ran the network backbone called NSFNET for the National Science Foundation. By purchasing ANS, America Online indicated its intention to expand its offerings in terms of the Internet.

When I double-click on the Tidbits database entry, the screen shown in Figure 13.22 appears. Notice that we have a full description of the database itself (a useful thing, since many WAIS databases sport cryptic names, making it hard to discover what's in them until you check out the site description). And we can enter a keyword in the search field. I could use *america online* or *ans*, or both. But since I recall the term *nsfnet* in the article, I'll use it.

Soon I receive a list of hits, as shown in Figure 13.23. Here again, the hypertext model means that we can click on any of these items to call it up to the screen. Figure 13.24 shows the result of doing so on the most recent article. If I used the scroll bar to the right of the screen, I could readily move through the document. Note that my search term, *nsfnet*, appears in bold, to make it easy to find the exact reference I need.

The method WAIS uses in conjunction with the World Wide Web is called WAISGATE, for Web to WAIS Gateway. It's a handy system to know about in these days of

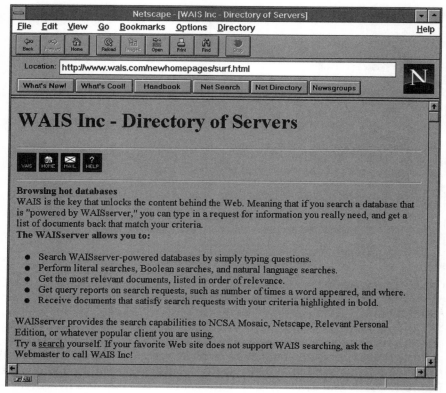

Figure 13.20 Examining the home page at WAIS Inc., which presents a way to search WAIS databases through the World Wide Web.

increasing interest in the World Wide Web, because it means you can run a WAIS search without leaving the confines of the World Wide Web browser itself. But enough of this teaser about the World Wide Web. We're almost ready to examine the Internet's hottest tool by itself. But first, a few WAIS tips.

Searches That Puzzle: Use Your Head

The best advice I can give you about WAIS is to keep your expectations under control and use your head. WAIS is a powerful search system, a tool that will begin to gather the vast textual resources of the Internet into a logically driven, readily searchable whole. But the process is a lengthy one, not likely to be accomplished any time soon. More servers have to come on-line, quite a few more, and the client and server software to manage them will be undergoing a gradual evolution in the direction of ease of use and more intuitive interfaces.

Until the bright future arrives when WAIS searches, no matter which client you use, are as simple as querying your computerized rolodex for the number of a friend, here are some thoughts on how you should use WAIS.

Think in reductionist terms. Since your first queries are likely going to be directed at a master directory of servers, try to remember the basic principles that drive your

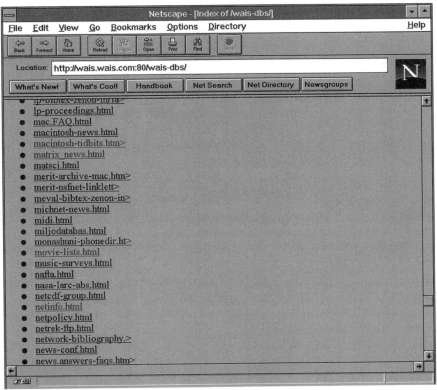

Figure 13.21 A list of publicly accessible WAIS servers; each is set up as a hyperlink.

search. If you're looking for images of Mars taken by the Viking lander, it may make more sense to query this database of databases under terms like *astronomy* and *space* rather than *mars* and *viking*. The broader context of the search is what you're after, because you're asking the server to provide you with information about which databases specialize in what *category* of knowledge.

Be flexible. I can almost guarantee that the great majority of search strategies anyone runs with WAIS will need to be adjusted before completion. Accordingly, you have to maintain a flexible frame of mind when working with WAIS, as you do with any other form of on-line searching. Prepare to modify your search terms when you retrieve drastically different series of hits than you had expected. Plan to feed WAIS a variety of strategies, examining the results until you think your hit list is close enough for you to begin narrowing it down with relevance feedback techniques. If you're lucky, you may get to this point relatively early in the search process. If you're unlucky, you won't get to it at all, because the information you're after isn't yet available through a server.

Avoid Unrealistic Expectations. Hype tends to be the name of the game, in the computer business more than in most industries. And while the future of WAIS seems unlimited, the present forces us to deal with a gradually growing infrastructure that can't yet meet a wide variety of our research needs. Sometimes you'll be able to home in on what you need with laser-like precision, but many other searches will bring you more ambiguous results, similar to what we found while searching for information on the

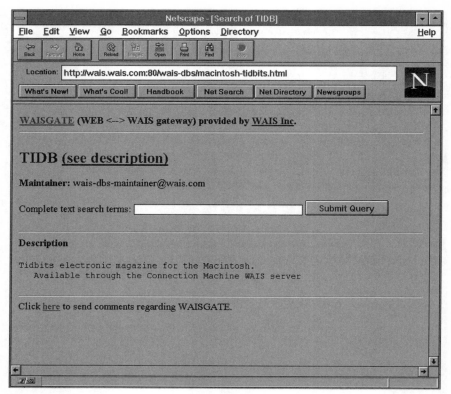

Figure 13.22   Examining a particular WAIS database; note the data entry field.

Latin American economies. We found some good sources which could help us build up background data, but we didn't find any databases specifically targeting our search terms.

All that will change as more and more WAIS servers come on-line, and we'll be seeing a growing presence from commercial providers as well. In fact, the real excitement in coming years is going to come from watching the WAIS server list grow larger and larger. For that reason, keep using WAIS. The more skilled you become around its quirks, the more likely you'll be able to draw full power out of it. And as more servers come on-line, the more effective your searching will become.

Learn as you go. Keyword hunting is something of an art; after a while, you get the feel for it, but struggling through those early searches can be a frustrating experience. One way to learn is to look at a document or two containing material you find appropriate to your search. Page through it with an eye toward finding words that appear frequently. These may well be the best keywords to run on your next search. Remember, searching is highly targeted. What you're after may be obvious to you, but not to a computer at the other end of the line. Browsing through a few documents can often supply terms you simply hadn't thought of in your planning.

Stay relevant. Relevance feedback is the most exciting and useful area of WAIS development. As the system now stands, WAIS pulls keywords from your queries and uses them to run its search routines. The problem, as we've seen, can be retrieving small

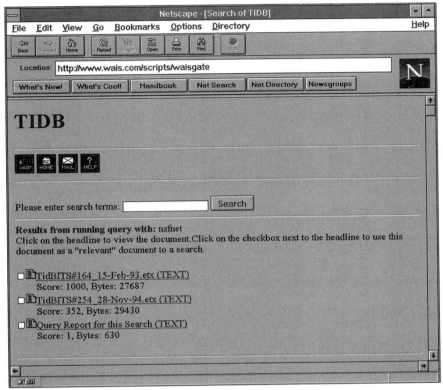

Figure 13.23   A list of hits from our search on the keyword *nsfnet*.

numbers of hits, or at the opposite end, large lists of seemingly irrelevant information. What's needed are refinements in the model used for making the initial query, along with effective means of limiting and specifying categories of information. We'd like, for example, to be able to tell WAIS, "Show me every document with a date later than July 1, 1995 that contained the words *nuclear* and *reactor* but did not contain the word *weapon*."

WAIS and Its Limitations

If WAIS strikes you as less than perfect, you're right. While you can search under multiple terms, you can't yet limit your search by date, and standard Boolean search procedures aren't necessarily available. But it's clear the trend of WAIS development is in the direction of greater power. WAIS is but a glimpse of the kind of search tools we're moving to on the Internet; its swift acceptance demonstrates how widespread is the need for such tools, and how successfully WAIS has stepped in to address it.

Keeping Up with WAIS

This is exciting stuff, on the very edge of development in the Internet community. If you'd like to keep up with what's happening, there are mailing lists that can do the trick.

Brewster Kahle speaks of a future where WAIS has created a new kind of publishing. "WAIS is an infrastructure for helping people not only use remote sources, but help-

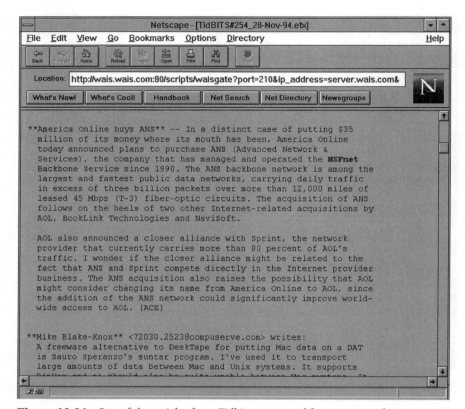

Figure 13.24   One of the articles from Tidbits uncovered from our search.

What You Need: A Way to Keep Up with WAIS

How to Do It: The wais-discussion list is a lively place to maintain a subscription. Send requests to join to wais-discussion-request@think.com. And you may want to look into the newsgroup comp.infosystems.wais; all discussions on the wais-discussion mailing list go to comp.infosystems.wais as well. And check the WAIS documents at Thinking Machines Corp.; here is the URL:

ftp://quake.think.com/pub/wais-doc/

Also check the directory pub/wais-inc-doc, which contains subdirectories containing numerous WAIS documents. You can connect directly to WAIS Inc. at this URL:

ftp://ftp.wais.com/pub/wais-inc-doc/

And don't forget the World Wide Web site for updates:

http://www.wais.com/newhomepages/surf.html

ing people make information available," Kahle said. "Everybody has something to say; everybody has a newsletter, a piece of expertise, a favorite recipe. They might be an expert on car types or IBM clones. If we can make a system that helps people share that expertise, we as a societal organism become richer."[3] Kahle's new company, WAIS Inc., recently acquired by America Online, should be in the forefront of such developments.

Chapter 13 Notes

1. When I spoke to Jane Smith originally in January of 1993, search tools were only beginning to proliferate. Today we must also reckon in the enormous changes wrought by the World Wide Web, with its whole new set of search engines.
2. From a telephone interview with Brewster Kahle January 24, 1993. As president of WAIS Inc., Kahle remains in the the thick of the information discovery adventure.
3. *Ibid.*

14

The World Wide Web

The story of the Internet is increasingly the story of the World Wide Web. This once obscure method of linking resources has moved to the top of the network's most accessed features list, with the growth in new World Wide Web sites reaching an astounding 20 percent per month. The reason? More than any other Internet resource, the World Wide Web allows users to use the network in an intuitive, logical environment. Moreover, the interface that makes that access possible provides not only textual data, but full-motion video, audio, crisp graphics and photographs, and on-screen formatting. It's the difference between a typewritten document and a printed magazine. Both convey content; one is visually striking and approachable.

For the World Wide Web to take off as it has, two things were necessary. First, there had to be an easily accessible client program that made using the Web possible for the average person. And second, the type of Internet connection available to such people had to allow the full exploitation of the software. Both requirements were met by the end of 1993, as the National Center for Supercomputing Applications made its Mosaic program available for Internet users, while the needed SLIP/PPP connections fell dramatically in price. As we moved into 1994, it became clear that the World Wide Web, as viewed through a *browser* program like Mosaic, would increasingly define how the Net's new citizens found their way around cyberspace.

But, of course, there is a third requirement. Not even the best access tool can succeed unless there is content on the Internet to be accessed. By mid-1995, that problem was clearly being solved. When business discovered the Internet, World Wide Web sites began to spring up with abandon, joining the already existing academic and research-oriented sites. Web designers speak in terms of *home pages*—these are simply entryways into a particular collection of information at a given site—and it would not be long before such pages proliferated. Bookstores went on-line, as did flower shops, even pizza sellers. Governments took to the Web to produce colorful travel and commerce-related descriptions of their countries, while service providers began to realize that a World Wide Web page could be a starting point for anyone wanting to learn more about their offerings. On-line libraries weighed in, and magazines, both commercial and amateur, fought for the attention of the reader.

Must you have a SLIP or PPP connection to take advantage of the World Wide Web? If you hope to experience all that the Web has to offer, the answer is yes, because the combination of text, graphics, and other forms of media is what has made the Web the hottest Internet protocol. But character-based interfaces like those available through the average shell account can also check into the Web, although only to view the text available on each home page. An excellent client program called lynx makes this possible. Chances are you'll eventually move into the SLIP/PPP environment in any case, but if you're currently limited to a text-based interface, learn as much as you can now with lynx and plan for an upgrade to a fully graphical client.

In this chapter, I'll show you how to get up and running with lynx before proceeding into the graphical realm. Although I'll be using the Netscape browsing program to illustrate how the Web functions, bear in mind that any Web browser can access the sites we'll visit here. Thus, whether you're using Mosaic, or Cello, or lynx itself, you can take a look at the same sites, even if you'll see a different interface with each program. As with other Internet resources, the idea isn't to become hung up on the choice of tool, but rather, to understand the underlying system and the way it helps you to access network information.

The Concept of Hypermedia

Hypertext was invented in the mid-1960s by Douglas Engelbert at SRI. The new form of nonsequential text display received a powerful boost when Apple Computer introduced Hypercard, a hypertext program that brought the concept to the attention of anyone with a Macintosh. The promise of hypertext was in its ability to link information. You could set up links between core concepts in a text, so that if you needed more information about a certain item, you could click on it to call up background material on the screen. On the other hand, if you already knew the background of the idea, you could move directly to the next concept, thus streamlining the process of reading and research.

The notion of hypertext is closely tied to the name of Ted Nelson, who was for years the guiding force behind a system called Xanadu, an attempt to create a universal library of knowledge implemented through this model. Today's fast-growing library of CD-ROMs demonstrates that hypertext is only part of the issue of linking information. We speak now of hypermedia, the linking of any form of digital information using the same model. A CD-ROM encyclopedia, for example, could include links to stored audio or video; click on the right place in an entry on Richard Nixon and you might hear his resignation speech, or see him boarding the helicopter for his final presidential ride. Multimedia CD-ROM implementations of this technology provide a glimpse of what the Internet is rapidly becoming, a Web of hypermedia resources splashed with sound, color, and learning.

Initially developed at the European Laboratory for Particle Physics by Tim Berners-Lee, the World Wide Web is powerful and, like other forms of hypermedia, it's immense fun to work with. Not only that—it's audacious. Imagine the metaphor; just as you can link concepts in a hypertext document, you can travel through the Internet's cyberspace using World Wide Web links. And since any digital resource can be linked to a Web page, you can see that a given Web "document" might itself be composed of links to computers in various countries around the globe. If I were setting up a page devoted to great works of art, for example, I might include several images and text files on my own computer, but it would also make sense to include a link to the wonderful art collection made available from the Louvre. Although I didn't create that collection, it can form an integral part of the Web page I develop to showcase art and technology.

Delving into the Web with lynx

The first step in accessing the World Wide Web is to activate your Web browser. If you're a shell account user, you can check to see if lynx is available by typing its name at the user prompt:

```
% lynx
```

In Figure 14.1, you can see lynx at work.

The program, when first called, logs on to a Web page. The one in the figure is at the University of Kansas, where lynx was developed. We will then be able to go out from this site to examine other Web pages by entering a simple set of commands. What we want to do is to move to a particular Web page. Its address is as follows:

```
http://www.yahoo.com/
```

The http statement tells us that this is a World Wide Web page; more about what the initials mean in a moment. The key now is to get there. From the main lynx screen, enter this command:

```
g http://www.yahoo.com/
```

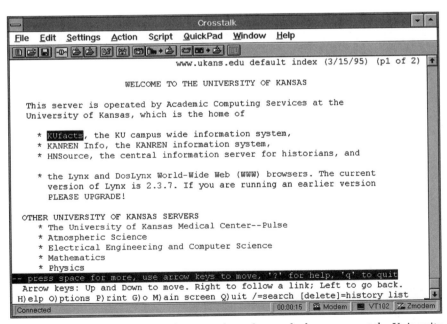

Figure 14.1   The lynx browser, here seen logged on to the home page at the University of Kansas, where the program was developed.

You should see the screen shown in Figure 14.2, which is the introductory screen at the site. Yes, the URL gives you a lengthy statement to type, and many Web sites sport even longer ones, but as you become familiar with the system, such issues won't trouble you. Good browser programs let you create bookmarks for sites you access frequently, so in many cases you'll only enter such addresses once.

To explore the subjects here, we simply move the highlight to whichever of the underlined terms we want to see, using the arrow keys. You can see the major commands listed at the bottom of the screen. Of most importance to us is that the **Down Arrow** key takes us, one link at a time, through the items on the screen. When we reach the item we want to see, the **Right Arrow** key allows us to take that choice and call up the item. In lynx, hyperlinks are shown either as underlined, or displayed in a different color than the rest of the text. Figure 14.3 shows the result of moving to the Entertainment link and choosing it, moving into the subsequent Automobiles category and displaying the results found there.

Yahoo is a topic-oriented catalog of Internet sites. At each level, we move deeper into the subject tree. We finally reach the point where we are choosing between individual home pages. Figure 14.4 shows you one such home page, this one focusing on British cars.

On the level of the individual home page, the method for access is exactly the same. We move the on-screen highlight to the place we want to examine and then press the **Right Arrow** key to see it. In this way, lynx provides those without graphical display capabilities the chance to use the World Wide Web, although we can already see one drawback—it would be much quicker to be able to position a mouse on the link we want to see, without having to move through all the options by using the arrow keys. And, of course, we would get a more eye-catching display.

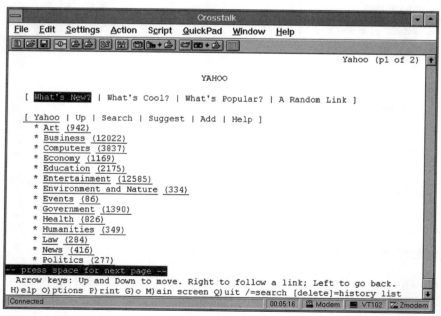

Figure 14.2   The home page at Yahoo, a category-based list of Web sites.

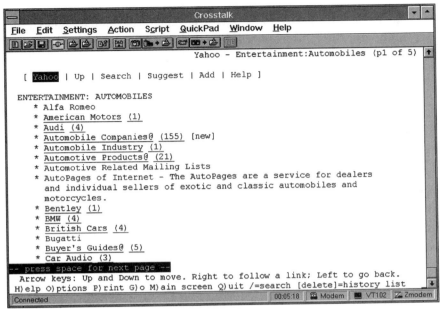

Figure 14.3   Moving deeper into the Yahoo database; here, we are examining a set of Web pages specializing in cars.

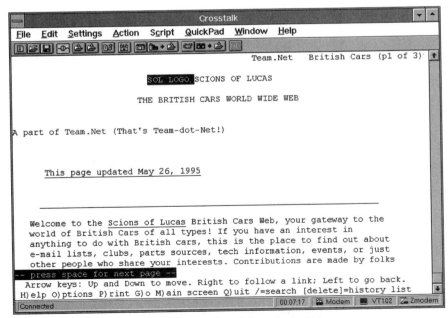

Figure 14.4   An individual home page found through the Yahoo system.

By now, the nature of the Yahoo page is becoming clear. Yahoo is a collection of World Wide Web resources categorized by topic. This remarkable site is the work of Jerry Yang and David Filo, two electrical engineering students at Stanford University. You use Yahoo by choosing the general topic you want, and then move deeper into the category until you finally access World Wide Web pages that suit your interest. Many people find the Yahoo site an indispensable catalog of Internet resources. Other sites like Yahoo are beginning to appear to address the problem of finding information.

The lynx Commands

Let's examine the lynx commands in greater detail. As we've seen, the basic movement commands are shown at the bottom of the screen:

Down Arrow	Moves you to the next hyperlink.
Up Arrow	Moves you to the previous hyperlink.
Right Arrow	Follows a link (that is, opens the underlying document).
Left Arrow	Goes back to the previous link.
SPACEBAR	Moves you to the next page of the document.
-	Moves you to the previous page.

And here are the rest of the commands you may find helpful with lynx:

a	Adds the current link to your bookmark file. As we'll see shortly, book-marks let you keep track of the many World Wide Web sites you visit, just as Gopher bookmarks allow you to categorize your Gopher sites.
c	Lets you send a comment to the document owner.
d	Lets you download the current link. In the case, for example, of an image file, you could download the image for subsequent viewing on your own machine.
g	Lets you go to a specified URL. You'll use this command to enter URLs that you read about and want to try for yourself.
h	Calls up a help screen.
m	Returns you quickly to the main screen.
o	Lets you set lynx options.
p	Lets you print to a file or send a page via mail.
q	Quits lynx. Use **Q** to exit without prompts.
r	Removes a bookmark.
/	Lets you search for a string within the current document. This is especially handy when you're dealing with a long document and want to move quickly to your information.
v	Lets you view your bookmark file.
z	Cancels the transfer in progress.
BACKSPACE	Goes to the history page, which shows the URLs you have examined during the current session.

=	Shows file and link information.
!	Allows you to move to your default Unix shell.
Ctrl-R	Reloads the current file and refreshes the screen.
Ctrl-W	Refreshes the screen.
Ctrl-G	Cancels the document transfer.

In Figure 14.5, you see the result of creating a bookmark. While browsing through the Yahoo system under the category of *Architecture,* I came across the AEC InfoCenter Building Project Library and decided it would be helpful to save it as a bookmark. I did so using the **a** command, as shown in the preceding command list. When I subsequently press the **v** key, I am presented with a list of my bookmarks. In this case, there is only one, since I have just begun compiling this list.

Bookmarks are stored as URLs; all I need to do to move back to this page is to press the **Right Arrow** key, and I am taken to the site. Note also that it is easy enough to remove any bookmark by using the **r** command. lynx provides helpful summaries of its command structure in the form of an on-line manual, so it's easy enough to call up any commands that escape your memory.

Using a Graphical Web Browser

Using the Web with a graphical browser is handled in much the same way. The SLIP/PPP user activates the browser program and watches as it logs on to whatever home page has been set up in the software. In many cases, the home page will be determined by the ser-

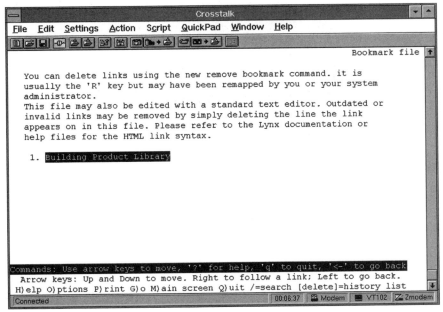

Figure 14.5 A bookmark created with lynx appears as a hyperlink; click on it to go directly to the site.

vice provider, who will offer a central site for Web access. In other cases, the browser will log on to the place where the software was developed. Mosaic, for example, is set up to initially log on at the NCSA, the site of its creation, while Netscape logs on at Netscape Communications Corporation, where support and services are provided. In each case, the home page can be changed at the discretion of the user. Figure 14.6 shows you the home page at Netscape.

Moving to a new address with Netscape is likewise done by entering the address. Only now we're in a graphical environment. To change addresses, do the following:

1. Pull down the File menu.
2. Choose the Open Location item.
3. Enter the address at Yahoo (as shown) in the field that appears.
4. Click on **OK.**

Figure 14.7 shows the result of these actions. We have now logged on to the Yahoo page at Stanford.

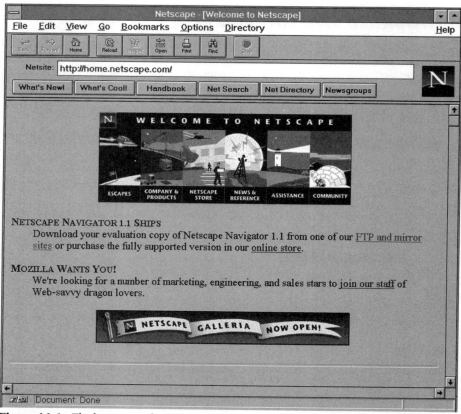

Figure 14.6   The home page for Netscape appears by default when you first use the browser to log on to the Web.

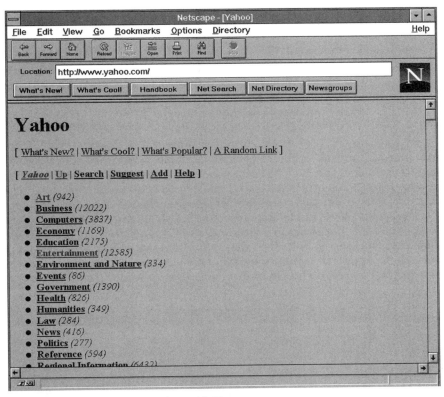

Figure 14.7 Logging on to Yahoo with Netscape.

How the Web Works

The Netscape browser handles its information in the same way that lynx does, although the display is much different. Each hyperlink is underlined. To get to one, we simply move the mouse cursor to that item and click on it. Notice, too, that we have a toolbar across the top of the screen that allows us to accomplish the major movement commands. For example, if I move to a particular page and decide to move back to the previous one, I could simply click on the **Back** arrow in the toolbar. Notice that a series of other buttons is available. These allow me to accomplish such tasks as reloading the current Web page, printing the page, or searching for information within it. I can do these chores with lynx as well, but without the helpful graphical interface Netscape provides. Here are the basic Netscape movement commands as displayed on the toolbar:

Back   Allows you to move to the previously selected document.

Forward   Allows you to move forward to display again a document you have already seen. If you haven't yet gone back to retrieve a previous document, the **Forward** button will be dimmed and unusable. It becomes active once you move to a prior document.

Home   Takes you to the home page established in Netscape. When you first use the program, this home page will be found at Netscape Communications

Corp. It provides a wealth of background material about the program and
the Internet.

Reload   Loads the current page again.

Stop   Discontinues the current download. You can use this button if you change
                  your mind about seeing a site; it may happen, for example, that as a
                  lengthy page is being downloaded, you realize it will not be of interest. The
                  Stop button lets you move on.

   By following Yahoo's links through a topic, I can move to World Wide Web pages
that suit my interests. In Figure 14.8, for example, I have moved to the *San Jose Mercury
News* for a look at the day's headlines. Notice that the newspaper has set up a hyperlink
to a story from each of its major sections, from international news to national, local and
state; it also contains links to editorials, sports, even the comic section.
   Navigation is as simple as point-and-click. In Figure 14.9, I have moved to a story
about Microsoft Corporation. What you should notice here is the clever use of hyperlinks. In each case, the link offers the chance to move deeper into the story. Other hyperlinks, shown along the top of the page, take us to other sections of the newspaper that
may interest anyone who finds this page useful. And, of course, note the graphical

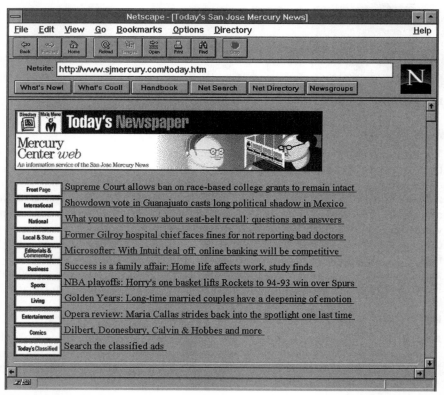

Figure 14.8 The *San Jose Mercury News* is a pioneer in the effort to move newspapers
on-line.

touch—a photograph of Microsoft founder Bill Gates. The lynx user could read through this material and use the hyperlinks, but the graphical formatting and typeset quality of the page would not be available. You can see, I think, why so many newspapers have begun to explore the World Wide Web as a medium for displaying the news. The Web allows readers to home in on exactly what they're looking for, not to mention the fact that it saves on the cost of paper.

The basic premise of hypermedia is that it allows the reader to control the flow of information. Think of it this way: when you read a bound book, you move through it from one page to another, reading sequentially. It may be that you encounter passages containing information that you already know. Nonetheless, other than skimming ahead as best you can, you must move through this material to get to the new items you're looking for. Hypermedia allows you to choose your own route through the information field, while supplementing it with sound and image. It makes us explorers of information and, theoretically, allows us to target what we need, thus saving time and allowing us to be more productive. Of course, it also makes us browse through links to see what's on the other side, so it may be that some of the productivity gain is mitigated by the natural curiosity factor. The Web is as fascinating as an old curiosity shop stuffed with relics, one of those places where everything you encounter leads you to something else.

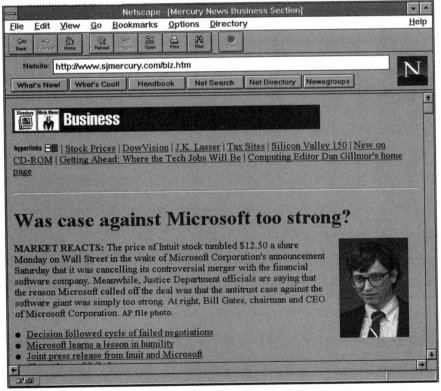

Figure 14.9 Reading an individual newspaper story on-line.

Hypertext Transport Protocol

Having come this far, we now need to examine the basic terms you're likely to encounter as you explore the Web. We've already run into HTTP, which is used to alert us to the fact that the URL we are talking about is a World Wide Web page. Now let's explore how the system is put together through a series of protocols that were developed at CERN by Tim Berners-Lee, the man who made this whole phenomenon possible. It was Berners-Lee who developed HTTP, or HyperText Transport Protocol. This is the basic protocol that the Web uses to move its information.

We just moved through the World Wide Web to access information at several different sites. Remarkably, the process was seamless; we didn't need to know where the computers were located that supplied our data, because the transaction was hidden from us by the browser we were using. This process works because HTTP allows the browser to make the necessary information request of the server. Every time we click on a hyperlink, in other words, the client uses the information in the URL being clicked on and connects to the appropriate server. It then requests that the server send the specified document, embedding links to whatever graphics, audio, and text are involved in that particular page. It receives the information from the server and, following this, closes the operation. When we click on another hyperlink, the same process starts again.

This is an important concept, for novices assume, reasonably enough, that after their browser has accessed a World Wide Web page, the connection to the site involved remains in effect. Actually, what has happened is that the document has been downloaded to the computer's memory; it could be saved to disk or printed, as necessary. It is only when another hyperlink is clicked that the browser makes a new information request of a server, thus initiating a new connection.

What happens if the site you're hoping to see is no longer connected, or has changed its address since you saw reference to it? Frustratingly, the browser you're using will seem to hang up as it awaits a signal that the remote site is not available. This is why the Netscape toolbar includes a stop sign icon. If you click on this icon when the browser seems to be frozen, Netscape will stop trying to make the connection and will return to normal operations. Mosaic users can do the same thing by clicking on the Mosaic icon to the top right of the main screen.

The tools we have examined, like WAIS, Gopher, and FTP, are all examples of protocols that work in the client/server environment. But beyond the capabilities of these protocols, HTTP includes the ability to extract information from the client program and distribute it to other programs on the server. The way the server deals with these so-called gateway programs is managed by the CGI, or Common Gateway Interface, specifications. And because HTTP also includes the ability to return information produced by programs running on the server, the protocol becomes a flexible tool for the delivery of hypertextual documents.

Think of the WAIS databases we examined in the previous chapter. There, you saw an example of how WAIS Inc. makes available a World Wide Web page with every WAIS database it knows of on the page. To search, you click on the database name and then enter a search term in the appropriate field. What is going on behind the scenes is that the gateway program is making available the underlying database, and providing the kind of interactive search, through an on-screen form, that turns the Web into a dynamic search mechanism. We will see more uses of CGI as the Web develops, because commercial operations need to use forms to process orders and to make information available to a controlled list of subscribers. Expect important advances in scripting tools, and the CGI standard itself, as we proceed.

Hypertext Markup Language

The display you see through your client program is determined by two factors: the client program itself, and the underlying formatting applied to the Web document being accessed. All clients will reproduce the basic information sent to them, but the screen display will differ according to the client's interface. But behind any Web document, we need to have a standard way of describing a document. This is where another acronym—HTML—comes in. HTML stands for HyperText Markup Language. If you get into the business of creating a Web page of your own, you'll need to master HTML, but fortunately, HTML isn't terribly difficult to learn. Unlike most programming languages, its list of functions isn't extensive but the effects you can achieve with just a few statements are remarkable.

Take a look, for example, at Figure 14.10, which is a World Wide Web page that focuses on the country of Peru. It has been created by the Internet Network of Peru to offer the Web a selection of Peruvian images, music, and travel information. The figure shows how the page combines imagery—as in the top design containing a ceremonial

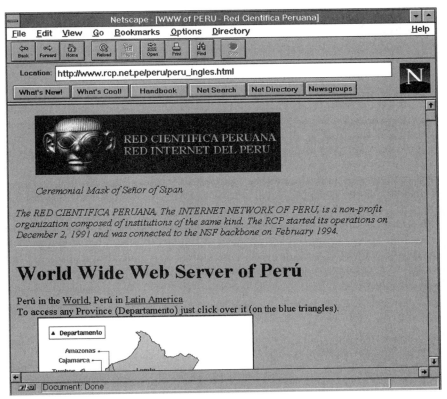

Figure 14.10   A World Wide Web page focusing on Peru.

mask, and in the interactive map that begins to appear at the bottom—with text in several different fonts. Hyperlinks, as we're now used to seeing, appear in underlined form. A color figure would also show that they appear in blue, while the rest of the text is black.

The mystery behind the creation of such a page can be revealed with the right browser. Using Netscape, for example, we can pull down the View menu and choose the Source item to see the actual HTML coding that underlies this page. You can see the result in Figure 14.11.

What Netscape has done is to present the HTML text in a scrollable window, so that we can work through it on-screen or, if we choose, print it out. And if you take a look at the coding, you'll see that it's nothing but straight ASCII text. The trick is to learn the various statements that place items on the page and call upon stored digital resources to display them.

Examine Figure 14.11 carefully, and you'll begin to see the relationship between it and the World Wide Web page it represents. Notice, for example, this statement:

```
World Wide Web Server of Peru&uacute;
```

You begin to realize that the h1 statement appears as a header on the actual page, while the final, cryptic comment:

```
&uacute;
```

seems to apply to the accented u character at the end of the word Peru. We then see another instance of the h1 statement, only this time it's preceded by a slash that tells us that it represents the end of the header statement.

In such ways are World Wide Web pages built. Note, too, at the top of the figure how the graphic item is inserted. You can see that figures are actually .GIF files that have been called upon by the HTML coding. When the HTML page is represented on-screen, it is the result of the client calling up from the server the information, including the stored .GIF file, that is stored there. And you can see that an HTML file can be constructed to call upon any digital resources that might be available at the site; thus the possibility of setting up audio (the Peru site contains some marvelous Andean music), or moving video, or, as in the case of this page, an interactive country map.

HTML, it turns out, is a variant of SGML, or Standard Generalized Markup Language, a widely used tool for describing documents in terms that computers can understand. One of the most important of the HTML coding features is the one that allows hyperlinks to be created. If we go back to Figure 14.8, you can see that at the bottom of the figure several hyperlinks exist, as shown by their underlining. It is possible, for example, to call up a map of Peru in relation to the rest of the world by clicking on the hyperlink marked World. In HTML form, this hyperlink is represented this way:

```
<a href=/gif/peru_mundo.gif">World</a>
```

Here again, it is the coding of the HTML file that allows the client program, in this case Netscape, to present the information on-screen and make it accessible as a hyperlink.

It is not necessary to learn the vagaries of HTML to use the World Wide Web; far from it. The Web itself was created with an eye toward burying these complexities behind an easy-to-use interface. All the user needs to do is to be able to point the mouse to the appropriate hyperlink and click. But if you do get interested in HTML, a number of sites on the Internet have opened up that specialize in its creation. You might, for example, want to consult some of the following possibilities:

http://www.ucc.ie/info/net/htmldoc.html

http://melmac.harris_atd.com/about_html.html

http://www.utirc.utoronto.ca/HTMLdocs/NewHTML/intro.html

Another excellent source is Ian S. Graham's *The HTML Sourcebook* (John Wiley and Sons, Inc., 1995), which covers the language in great detail. And if you're getting serious about HTML design, you'll be glad to know that a number of good programs exist to help in editing these documents. They include HTML Writer, HoTMetal for Windows, HTML Assistant, HyperEdit, and HTML for Word 2.0, all for the Microsoft Windows environment; and HTML SuperText Editor, HTML.Edit and HTML Editor, for the Macintosh. The following URLs point to resource lists for such editors:

http://www.utirc.utoronto.ca/HTMLdocs/pc_tools.html

http://www.utirc.utoronto.ca/HTMLdocs/mac_tools.html

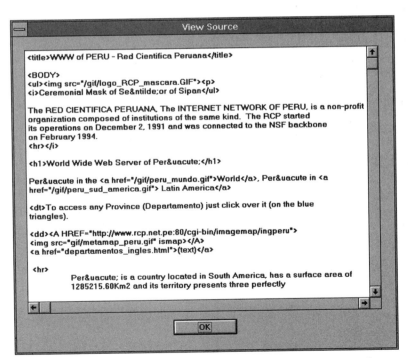

Figure 14.11   Examining the HTML code that underlies the Peruvian home page.

Uniform Resource Locators

By now the significance of URLs—Uniform Resource Locators—should be clear. I've been using them throughout this book to point to resources because they offer an economical way to specify where something is on the Internet in a single statement. The HTTP protocol defines the format for URLs, and because our Web browser can access not only hypertextual and hypermedia sites, but also FTP, Gopher, and even USENET information, it makes sense to learn the URL format for each. The basic URL statements were discussed in Chapter 1; for now, simply remember that the type of resource to be accessed is specified at the beginning of the URL statement. This is why hypermedia links are always referenced with http, as in the preceding examples. The http statement tells us that this is a resource to be accessed through the HTTP protocol.

As we saw, when your browser has completed a connection to a remote site, the request for information it sends is in the form of a URL. The information request can also include further details, such as the URL of the document from which you have made your request. And when you follow through with more complex interactions, such as posting a message to a USENET newsgroup, you will be sending still more information along with the URL. Nonetheless, the URL itself is the core concept for the average user; it specifies the location, in precise terms, of the resource he or she is trying to access.

Tuning Up Your Browser

No one set of commands works for all browsers; after all, these are individual programs, constructed to perform according to interface requirements determined by their developers. But because the underlying protocols remain the same, all browsers share a basic set of features. Learn what these are with Mosaic and you can move quickly to Netscape, or Cello, or any of the other browsers now coming to market. Indeed, we can expect a surge in the number of browsers now that interest in the Web seems to be peaking. Look for a variety of interface possibilities, and new concepts from companies like Sun Microsystems (with a browser called HotJava) and Silicon Graphics. But expect the essentials of Web exploration and use to provide common ground for using the software.

That being said, let's take another look at Netscape, my pick of the current browsers. If you haven't seen it, you can retrieve this fine program from a number of sites. The primary site at Netscape Communications Corp., as you might expect, has been flooded with activity due to the success of the program; this means that you may attempt to log on there but be unsuccessful. But as we saw in Chapter 5, mirror sites are created for just such an eventuality. So here are several options. At Netscape itself, try these URLs:

ftp://ftp.netscape.com/netscape1.1/

ftp://ftp2.netscape.com/netscape1.1/

And try the following mirror sites from various places around the world.
From North America:

ftp://wuarchive.wust1.edu/packages/www/Netscape/netscape1.1/
ftp://ftp.cps.cmich.edu/pub/netscape/
ftp://ftp.utdallas.edu/pub/netscape/netscape1.1/

ftp://ftp.micro.caltech.edu/pub/netscape/
ftp://unicron.unomaha.edu/pub/netscape/netscape1.1/
ftp://server.berkeley.edu/pub/netscape/
ftp://SunSITE.unc.edu/pub/packages/infosystems/WWW/clients/Netscape/
ftp://magic.umeche.maine.edu/pub/Mirrors/nscape/

From South America:

ftp://sunsite.dcc.uchile.cl/pub/WWW/netscape/netscape/

From Europe:

ftp://sunsite.doc.ic.ac.uk/computing/information-systems/www/Netscapes/
ftp://ftp.sunet.se/pub/www/Netscape/netscape1.1/
ftp://ftp.luth.se/pub/infosystems/www/netscape/netscape/

From Africa:

ftp://ftp.sun.ac.za/pub/archiving/www/mcom/netscape/

From Asia:

ftp://sunsite.ust.hk/pub/WWW/netscape/
ftp://SunSITE.sut.ac.jp/pub/archives/WWW/netscape/
ftp://bash.cc.keio.ac.jp/pub/inet/netscape/
ftp://ftp.glocom.ac.jp/pub/net/netscape/
ftp://ftp.pu-toyama.ac.jp/pub/net/WWW/netscape/
ftp://ftp.cs.titech.ac.jp/pub/net/WWW/netscape/netscape1.1/
ftp://ftp.nc.nihon-u.ac.jp/pub/network/WWW/client/netscape/
ftp://ftp.elcom.nitech.ac.jp/pub/netscape/
ftp://ftp.leo.chubu.ac.jp/pub/WWW/netscape/netscape1.1

The Netscape Screen

A graphical browser makes the Web an exciting place to be because it lets you focus on what you came for—content. In Figure 14.12, you see a typical Web page as displayed by Netscape, along with a description of the major features of the browser. This, by the way, is a wonderful page for Hitchcock buffs. It contains biographical material, a complete filmography, information on the director's famous cameo appearances in his films, backgrounds on the actors who worked with him, and clips from some of his most masterful screen moments. It's a wonderful illustration of the power of the World Wide Web.

From top to bottom, here are the main features of this page:

Title Bar	The title of the document currently being viewed.
Menu Bar	The pull-down menus containing basic browser commands.

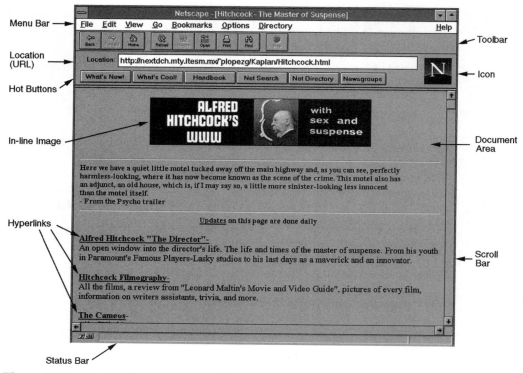

Menu Bar →

Location
(URL) →

Hot Buttons

In-line Image →

Hyperlinks

→ Toolbar

← Icon

Document
Area

Scroll
Bar

Status Bar

Figure 14.12   A typical home page as displayed by Netscape.

Toolbar	Contains icons that you can click on to perform Web tasks, thus creating shortcuts to using the menu bar.
Location	The URL of the Web page currently being displayed.
Hot Buttons	Netscape provides a second toolbar, which works much like the first. The difference is that these links are established to Web pages that are of interest to Netscape users. The first, for example, provides examples of newsworthy Internet features, while the second takes you to a list of the latest Web sites that have caught the attention of Netscape's developers.
Netscape Icon	This icon is useful because it becomes animated when Netscape is actively downloading a document. You can stop such a download by clicking on the **Stop** button on the toolbar.
Document Area	This is the space where the document is displayed. Notice that a scroll bar appears to the right of the image. You can move through the page to display the complete document.
Hyperlinks	Within the document, you can see hyperlinks in one of three ways. They can be underlined, as they appear in Figure 14.10. They will also appear in blue (although this doesn't show up in the figure). Finally, a hyperlink causes the Netscape cursor to change to a

pointing figure of a hand (this is how you will determine whether an image on-screen may itself be a hyperlink to another document). Clicking on such a hyperlink takes you to it.

Status Bar   When you place the cursor on a hyperlink, its URL will appear in the status bar at the bottom of the screen. This can be a handy feature, since it tells you whether the information you are thinking about accessing is available on the same computer, or is a link to a file at a distant site.

In-line Image   An in-line image is one that can be displayed directly by your browser on the screen. Larger images must often take advantage of an external viewer program (depending upon which browser you use). Many pages are constructed so that you can click on an in-line image to download a larger and more detailed version of the same image.

While your choice of browsers will determine exactly how the screen is presented, the similarity between Mosaic and Netscape in terms of functionality is marked. Each may have its own way of doing things, or may refer to functions with slightly different terms, but the tasks it must perform are identical. It's also true that a good browser is customizable, so that you can turn on and off certain features of the screen display. As you work with your browser, you'll do well to examine its configuration options to tune up the display so that it suits your taste.

Using a History List

Earlier in this chapter, we looked at how you can move around in a document being displayed by Netscape, or change between documents by using the toolbar. There come times, however, when the simple forward and back commands don't suffice. After all, the World Wide Web encourages you to explore by following hyperlinks. Perhaps you follow a series of links to see where it will take you and ultimately decide you want to return to the page where you started from. You could click on the toolbar icon that takes you to the previous document, but you'd have to click it over and over again to find the original page. This is where a history list can help.

Browsers keep such lists to record every place you've been during the current on-line session. You can call the list up, select the site to which you want to return, and click on it, thus avoiding the repetitive clicking that would otherwise be necessary. To see the Netscape history list, for example, you simply pull down the Go menu and choose the **View History** command. The history box will look like Figure 14.13.

The most recently visited site is at the top of the list, with the rest presented in reverse order according to the sequence of access. To move to any of these URLs, you simply highlight the site and click on the appropriate button; alternatively, double-click directly on the URL to achieve the same effect.

Browsers are able to work efficiently with history lists because they store some documents in memory. This memory *cache* allows the browser to call up some documents almost instantly; rather than returning to the Web to retrieve the page all over again, the browser simply calls it from the cache. Whether your browser will be able to call a particular page from the cache depends upon the order in which you accessed it. Browsers

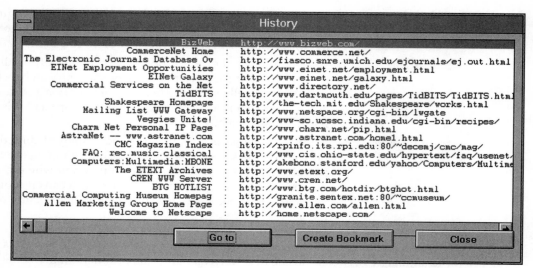

History	
BizWeb	http://www.bizweb.com/
CommerceNet Home	:	http://www.commerce.net/
The Electronic Journals Database Ov	:	http://fiasco.snre.umich.edu/ejournals/ej.out.html
EINet Employment Opportunities	:	http://www.einet.net/employment.html
EINet Galaxy	:	http://www.einet.net/galaxy.html
Commercial Services on the Net	:	http://www.directory.net/
TidBITS	:	http://www.dartmouth.edu/pages/TidBITS/TidBITS.html
Shakespeare Homepage	:	http://the-tech.mit.edu/Shakespeare/works.html
Mailing List WWW Gateway	:	http://www.netspace.org/cgi-bin/lwgate
Veggies Unite!	:	http://www-sc.ucssc.indiana.edu/cgi-bin/recipes/
Charm Net Personal IP Page	:	http://www.charm.net/pip.html
AstraNet -- www.astranet.com	:	http://www.astranet.com/home1.html
CMC Magazine Index	:	http://rpinfo.its.rpi.edu:80/~decemj/cmc/mag/
FAQ: rec.music.classical	:	http://www.cis.ohio-state.edu/hypertext/faq/usenet.
Computers:Multimedia:MBONE	:	http://akebono.stanford.edu/yahoo/Computers/Multim
The ETEXT Archives	:	http://www.etext.org/
CREN WWW Server	:	http://www.cren.net/
BTG HOTLIST	:	http://www.btg.com/hotdir/btghot.html
Commercial Computing Museum Homepag	:	http://granite.sentex.net:80/~ccmuseum/
Allen Marketing Group Home Page	:	http://www.allen.com/allen.html
Welcome to Netscape	:	http://home.netscape.com/

Go to   Create Bookmark   Close

Figure 14.13   Netscape's History list lets you move back to sites you've already examined in the current session.

can only store so many documents in the cache; if you try to retrieve a document that is no longer available there, it will be obvious because the page will reload much more slowly than the recently cached documents.

Using a Bookmark List

Browsers are getting more sophisticated all the time. Indeed, the release of Netscape was a marked improvement over the original Mosaic model. While it was developed by many of the people who had worked on Mosaic at the National Center for Supercomputing Applications, Netscape moved well beyond the model to produce a browser optimized for communications in the new Internet environment, where the average user gains access with a modem and runs a SLIP/PPP account to handle the data transactions. Netscape improved upon many features of Mosaic and introduced new ones, such as an ability to display text even while in-line images were continuing to load. But both Netscape and subsequent versions of Mosaic offered a key feature that is common to all good browsers—the ability to maintain a bookmark list.

We looked at bookmarks when we examined Gopher in Chapter 12. The problem with gigabytes of networked information is that there is no overall structure that can be imposed upon the system. Bookmarks let us mark items we find of particular interest and build a list of those items. The better the browser, the better the bookmark feature, since what we are after is the ability to manage our information. Netscape, for example, allows us not only to list those sites we find interesting, but to edit our listing so that we can categorize our sites into topics. That way, when we return to our bookmark list, we can see immediately which sites fit into what subjects. Believe me, after you've worked with your browser for a while, you'll appreciate these abilities to catalog information. A bookmark list can be utterly unmanageable without them.

Let's say I've been exploring the Web and have found a place that intrigues me. To turn the current page into a bookmark, all I need to do is pull down the Bookmarks

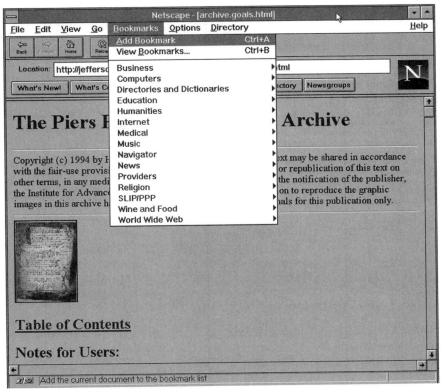

Figure 14.14 A bookmark menu, divided into categories for easy reference.

menu. In Figure 14.14, you see the result of doing so. Notice two things. First, at the top of the pull-down menu, there appears an **Add Bookmark** command which I can click on to add this site to my list. Also notice that, extending down from this point, a series of topics is presented. I have set each of these up as part of my Internet work. You will see that each contains a marker that tells us we could move to it and a submenu would appear. This is how I have categorized the Web pages I most often use, each of them nested inside a larger topic.

Browsers allow you to create such categories in various ways. Netscape makes it relatively simple; you take the View Bookmarks option and are presented with an editing screen. You can see this screen in Figure 14.15. Within this screen, you can decide which topics you want to use for your bookmarks, and you can move current bookmarks so that they fit inside those topics. Notice the Up and Down buttons; these allow you to place the bookmark within your list of categories. You can also perform useful functions such as importing a bookmark file; in this way, a friend could provide you with a list of bookmarks on a particular topic, or you could export your own list of bookmarks to someone else. And you have the ability to create new headers and separators as you choose; this keeps your list readable and organized in tight fashion.

Whichever browser you are using, be sure to examine how its bookmark feature works. A little time spent now learning how to categorize your bookmarks will be repaid

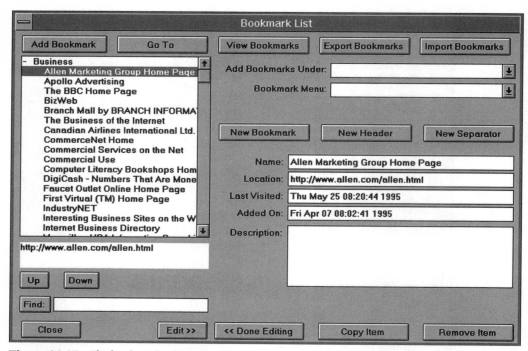

Figure 14.15 The bookmark editing screen gives you complete control over setting up new categories and moving bookmarks within those categories.

handsomely at a later date, when you won't have to work through long lists of unorganized bookmarks to find the one you want. I expect that bookmark organization will be an area in which major developments are made in the coming generation of browsers.

Exploring the Web with Search Tools

In the early days of Web exploration, the medium was balky and difficult to use. It wasn't that the hyperlink concept was deficient or that HTTP didn't do its job. It was that, to find a resource, you had to keep moving through hyperlinks, without any central organization to lead you to where you wanted to go. Thus the challenge of hypermedia. After all, a printed book superimposes a structure upon the material it presents. We may skim through certain chapters to get to items of particular interest, but the structure remains to keep us oriented. Hypermedia offers no such structure; instead, we the readers (or listeners, or viewers, as the case may be) impose our own definitions and concepts upon the material we want to see.

Recognizing the limitations of this principle, a number of developers have moved to create searchable Web indices or, in some cases, search engines that can pull up lists of sites for you to examine. These tools vary in terms of how easy they are to use and how efficiently they search. They also vary in terms of access. As you might imagine, a Web search engine is an extremely popular device; anyone with a yen for exploring will want to use it. This means that you may attempt to access the site only to find that it is simply too busy at the moment. Until we gain much broader bandwidth throughout the Internet, problems like these will recur. The only solution is to keep trying when this happens, because the rewards are great.

One search engine that I like to use is called the Web Crawler. You can access the Web Crawler database at the following URL:

```
http://webcrawler.cs.washington.edu/WebCrawler/WebQuery.html
```

This site, at the University of Washington, maintains a database of Web information that is updated regularly to keep up with the explosive growth of the medium. And, like a good search engine, it's easy to use. You simply enter the keyword on which you want to search and submit the query to Web Crawler. Soon a list of results will appear, each a hyperlink to the site.

In Figure 14.16, you see the Web Crawler search screen. You insert your keyword in the search field that appears immediately above the Search button (it's necessary to place the cursor inside that field and then click on it before you can actually enter the keyword). Notice the field that appears just below and to the right of that button. This lets you determine how many hits you want to see on your keyword list. Normally, I recommend leaving this number where it is, at 25, so that the system doesn't get swamped

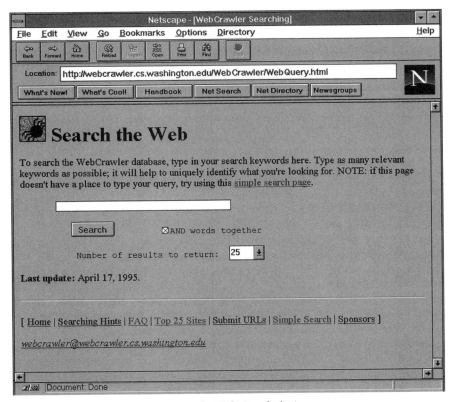

Figure 14.16   The search screen at the Web Crawler's site.

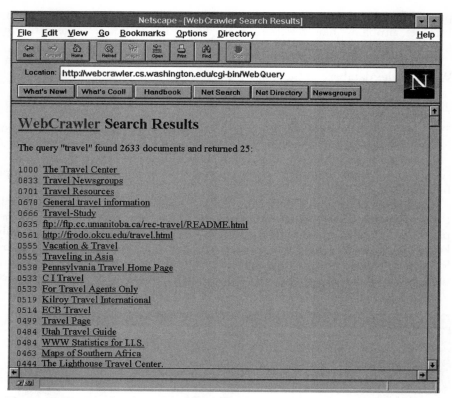

Figure 14.17   Results of a Web Crawler search under the keyword *travel*.

with the response. But if your search returns 25 items that aren't useful, you may want to broaden your search to include 50 items to see if that helps. It may also be necessary to change your keyword.

Let's run a simple Web Crawler search. Let's say I'd like to learn whether there are any World Wide Web sites that specialize in travel-related topics. I can use *travel* as my keyword, entering it in the search field and clicking on the Search button to launch the search. The results are shown in Figure 14.17.

Notice that we have a whopping 2,633 documents that the database identified in some way with the keyword *travel*. Of these, according to my instructions, 25 were shown. Each is underlined, indicating that it is a hyperlink. By clicking on the item called Maps of Southern Africa, I move to the page shown in Figure 14.18. Not bad, eh? I have entered a keyword and have been given a choice of documents which, if I so chose, could expand through changes to the keyword, or by asking for a longer list of results.

You can now see that a search engine like Web Crawler will let us obtain some degree of control over the unorganized mass of information that comprises the World Wide Web. Coupling a search engine with your browser's bookmark function allows you to build up a list of favorite sites which, in turn, will often lead you to other sites of interest. Be sure to learn as much as you can about the search engine you use, since a properly constructed search is the one most likely to yield results. Web Crawler, for example, works best when you keep the And box checked, allowing you to enter keywords that will

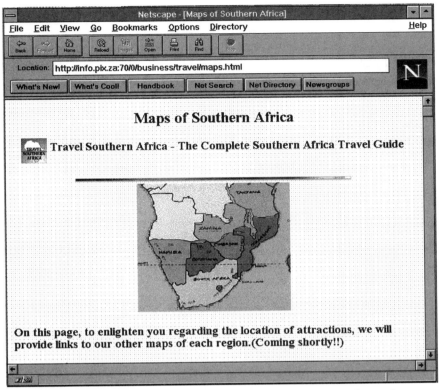

Figure 14.18 A page about travel in southern Africa, as found by Web Crawler.

be separated with an AND statement. Although each search engine will have its quirks, practice will make you more comfortable with them. Be on the lookout for new entries in this field as well.

Here are some other search engines I recommend you examine:

The World Wide Web Worm
http://www.cs.colorado.edu/home/mcbryan/WWWW.html

Carnegie Mellon Lycos
http://lycos.cs.cmu.edu/

JumpStation
http://js.stir.ac.uk/jsbin/jsii

You'll also want to check an interesting home page that focuses on Web search engines. You will learn about ongoing research in this area and new search engines as well. The URL is:

http://web.nexor.co.uk/mak/doc/robots/active.html

Browsers As All-Purpose Internet Interfaces

One of the major problems that browsing programs solve for us is the Internet's cryptic interface, which, in a shell account, is usually reduced to a single prompt. But beyond their graphical features, browsers also provide an interesting new take on Internet information gathering. They allow us to perform many of the basic Internet chores under the same basic interface, so that we don't, for example, have to go shifting from one client to run a Gopher search to another to run a Web session and a third to examine an FTP site. Any good browser will let you access all these resources and more, so that the Internet really does begin to take on a seamless appearance. This is quite an advance from the network world of even a few years ago, when it seemed that every task had its own tool.

Getting your browser to go to different kinds of resources is not difficult. It's all done through the familiar URL concept. Suppose, for example, that I want to see a particular Gopher. The URL is as follows:

```
gopher://wiretap.spies.com/
```

To reach the site, I simply pull down Netscape's File menu and choose the Open Location option, just as if I were going to another World Wide Web page. Placing the URL in

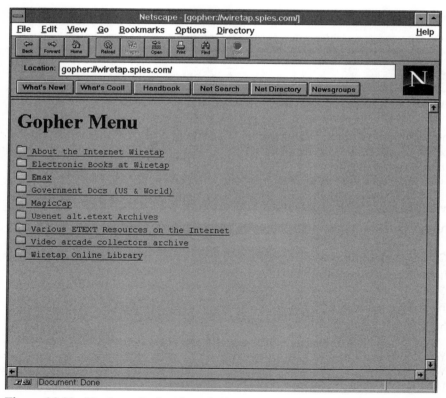

Figure 14.19 Viewing a Gopher through Netscape; note the use of icons.

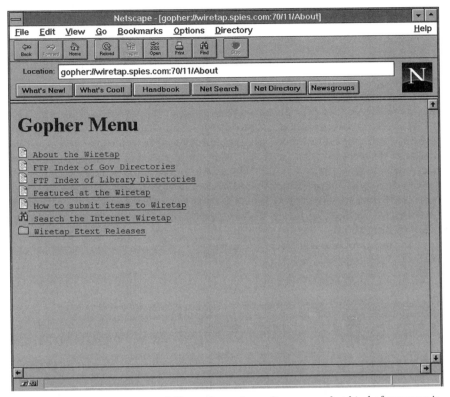

Figure 14.20 Netscape uses different icons depending upon what kind of resource is available for access.

the field that appears, I can click on **OK** to go to the site. The display is shown in Figure 14.19.

Here, the display is familiar. Each Gopher menu item is shown as a hyperlink. To move to it, all you need do is position the mouse accordingly and click it. Notice the folder icons to the left of each item, indicating that a submenu lies beneath them. Netscape is clever in its use of icons to show you what kind of information you are dealing with. Figure 14.20 gives you an example of how the browser deals with both text files and searchable information. As you can see, the document icon is a miniature of a typewritten or typeset page; the search icon is a pair of binoculars.

The browser is equally adept at moving to FTP sites. The method is identical:

1. Pull down the File menu.
2. Choose the Open Location item.
3. Fill in the URL in the field that appears.
4. Click on **OK**.

In Figure 14.21, you see the result of my going to an FTP site. The URL is:

```
ftp://mrcnext.cso.uiuc.edu/pub/
```

Again, note the use of icons. And notice that, as opposed to providing commands at a prompt to change directories, we are now in an environment where the basic movements are made by clicking on the appropriate command; thus we have a hyperlink that takes us to the next higher directory. Using a good browser to conduct FTP work is a joy. You can find what you need more quickly than through conventional character-based methods, and you can display small graphics and text files on-screen as you examine a particular directory (although larger files should always be downloaded, so you don't tie up the site unnecessarily when other people may be trying to access it).

File downloads are likewise rendered easy. If you find a binary file that you'd like to download, clicking on it calls up the screen shown in Figure 14.22. Here, you are given the choice of saving the file to disk or configuring a viewer with which to examine the file. By telling the browser to save the file, you are setting up a download, and you will be given the chance to tell Netscape into which directory on your hard disk you want the file to be downloaded.

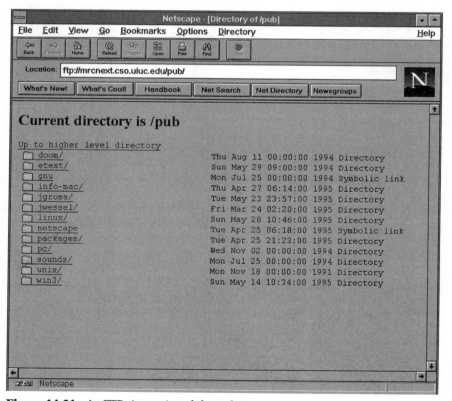

Figure 14.21 An FTP site as viewed through Netscape.

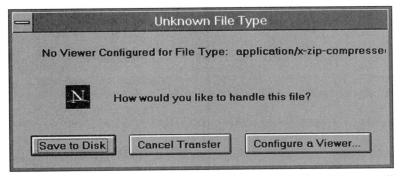

Figure 14.22 When you download a file from an FTP site, Netscape will produce a box like this one, giving you options for handling the file.

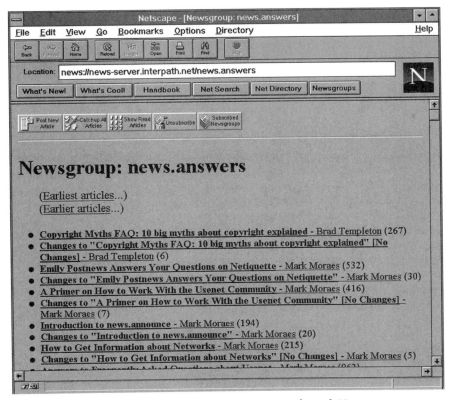

Figure 14.23 Looking at the newsgroup news.answers through Netscape.

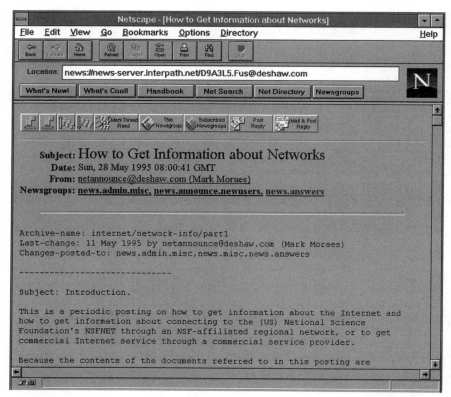

Figure 14.24   Examining an individual newsgroup document through Netscape.

Even USENET can be read with a browser. In fact, Netscape's newsgroup features are so advanced that it competes directly with more specialized browsers like WinVN and Newswatcher. The newsgroups are accessed in the following way:

1. Pull down the Directory menu.
2. Choose the Go to Newsgroups option.

Once you access a newsgroup, you will see a screen like the one in Figure 14.23. This happens to be the newsgroup news.answers, one of my primary newsgroups, since it is the place where Frequently Asked Questions documents from many newsgroups are posted. As you can see, all the news items are shown as hyperlinks, so that I can click on whichever item I want to read and go straight to it. In Figure 14.24, I have chosen a document to read.

Again, you can see that the browser has introduced icons that make our navigation chores easy. We can click on a button to mark the thread as read, or we can click on another button to move back to the newsgroup and its listing of articles. The newsgroup screen also provides icons that allow us to perform the major tasks, such as catching up with all the articles.

Browsers vary in how they handle these display chores, but the principle remains the same. A good graphical browser lets you complete the necessary tasks at a variety of sites, within a framework of pull-down menus and point-and-click commands. It also provides an icon-based view of the resources available at that site, making for easy navigation. Finally, it allows for the display of files in cases where you may not be sure that you want to download a given item, or when you want to view a small text file onscreen to learn, for example, about other files at the same site that may be of interest. All of these are reasons why you will want to choose your browser with care.

Keeping Up with the Web

You may remember that I've used a particular newsgroup as a way of keeping up with Internet news. This newsgroup, comp.internet.net-happenings, provides frequent postings that inform you about new Web sites, along with other kinds of Internet resources. By examining the newsgroup through Netscape, you can see another benefit of a good Web browser. Remember: Each newsgroup document is presented as a hyperlink, which means you can click on the item to go to it. Beyond this, each time a URL is provided within the text of a newsgroup posting, Netscape makes it into a hyperlink itself. Thus, if you're reading about a site that intrigues you, you don't have to jot down its URL. You can click on it to go right to it.

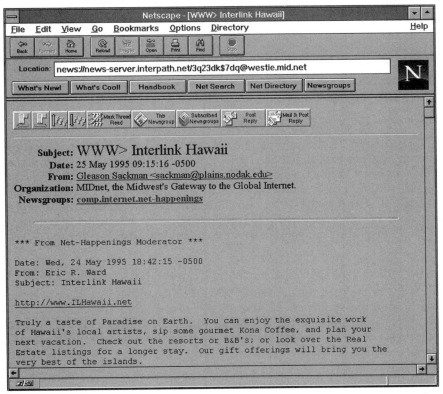

Figure 14.25 An item from the newsgroup comp.internet.net-happenings; notice the URL of the site described here, which is shown as a hyperlink.

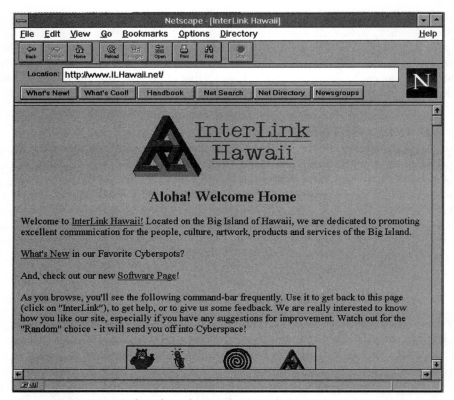

Figure 14.26   Moving directly to the site shown in the newsgroup.

In Figure 14.25, for example, I have called up a particular story that caught my eye in comp.internet.net-happenings. This is a Web page that has just gone on-line; it specializes in items about Hawaii. Notice that the URL shown for the site is itself a hyperlink. When I click on it, I move directly to the site, as shown in Figure 14.26. And when I'm ready to return to the newsgroup, I simply click on the Back button to do so. In such ways does a good browser help to integrate the diverse Internet functions we use daily.

You'll also want to be aware of an excellent Web site:

http://www.w3.org/

This is the home page for the World Wide Web Consortium, which was created to work toward common standards for the growth of the Web. The Consortium is run by the Laboratory for Computer Science at the Massachusetts Institute of Technology, and its home page contains links to a wealth of Web information, everything from HTML background documents to the latest news about the Web and the protocols that make it function. Be sure to check this page regularly if you want to keep up with the latest Web information.

Finally, the following newsgroups will keep you current:

comp.infosystems.announce

comp.infosystems.www.users

comp.infosystems.www.providers

comp.infosystems.www.misc

alt.hypertext

And, for news about browsers:

`alt.winsock`

As always, staying current with Internet news means invoking a number of different resources. And with the ongoing expansion of the World Wide Web, there's no shortage of material.

15

An Internet Toolbox

To call the Internet a maze of contradictions is to state the obvious. Even as excitement builds and new participants sign on to the networks, there comes a realization that Internet tools are still in their infancy. Because of its history as a gradually interconnecting network of networks, the Internet can't boast any unified command structure. Improvements come from below, through the efforts of creative talents like Brewster Kahle, Mark McCahill, Tim Berners-Lee, and the team that developed the World Wide Web. They and their numerous counterparts are helping us to find new ways to pull information out of cyberspace.

In this chapter, we examine a number of other tools that make it easier to get around this uncharted domain. While each is capable of being used on its own, tools like netfind or WHOIS point in a common direction. Think of the phone book analogy, as do most people who work with these applications; the common nickname for this category, in fact, is *white pages*. They're under development to help us track down people on the network.

We have a long way to go. A common question from new users is, where do I go to search a directory of Internet addresses? Most people take it for granted that there is an obvious answer. After all, commercial on-line services offer member directories, and in our noncomputerized lives, looking up a person or a business telephone number by name is trivial, even if we can't in most cases do it on a computer. But finding people on the Internet is a conundrum. Some are easy to track down; others are as difficult to find as Livingston was for Stanley.

Why is this so? Perhaps the dimensions of the problem will become clear if you realize that there are indeed directories of the Internet. Not just one or two, but hundreds. Using a variety of technologies, organizations have established listings of key personnel, many of them set up with the WHOIS program we'll examine shortly. That means that large corporations may well be searchable, as well as universities, most of whose faculty now have some kind of network address. Libraries are coming on-line, as well as the research centers and laboratories that have always been core players in the Internet.

Trying to find the present address of an old friend thus poses a challenge. Are you sure he or she uses the Internet? Do you already know where he or she works? And is the organization large enough that it's reasonable to expect Internet connectivity and a directory there? In that case, you can search for your friend, but only after you determine what the address of his or her organization's directory is. Bear in mind that, for a variety of reasons, even if you track down the correct company and address for its directory, your friend still may not appear in it. But then again, maybe so.

You could try the InterNIC—surely a "directory of directories" will list your friend? But the InterNIC's offerings possess the same limitations. Out of a universe of perhaps 30 million users, the number of people included under the umbrella of any given directory tool is vanishingly small. Your friend could be a mailing list regular or USENET junkie whose name is commonplace to readers of particular newsgroups around the world, yet he or she still might not appear in the InterNIC's listings.

No one directory, in other words, and no one tool, will unfailingly come up with the address you need. To approach the Internet for such information, then, requires a battery of tools. We examine them here, noting that the area of directory development is one of the most pressing issues confronting the network. The huge influx of new users places an unexpected strain upon a system that already worked poorly at locating people. Developing solutions to this problem, which means finding ways to collate widely distributed information, keep it updated, and make it readily searchable, is not going to be easy.

Using WHOIS

Originally set up as a database of registered information running at a single ARPANET Network Information Center, WHOIS is now spread over the Internet; hundreds of sites make this information available through servers. Each WHOIS record contains a unique identifier, a name, and other fields depending on the type of information it contains. What's in a WHOIS database? Anything from domains, hosts, and networks, to the people on them.

The original WHOIS database was maintained at the Defense Data Network Information Center by Government Systems, Inc., of Chantilly, Virginia. With the arrival of the new InterNIC services in 1993, however, this site was no longer used for civilian registrations.

Today, the InterNIC host for WHOIS searches is whois.internic.net. We can access the site through Telnet, as in Figure 15.1. As you can see, we have a range of options. Entering **whois,** we get the following screen:

```
[vt100] InterNIC > whois
Connecting to the rs Database . . . . . .
Connected to the rs Database
InterNIC WHOIS Version: 1.0 Tue, 30 May 95 08:12:35

Whois: cerf, vinton
```

Now we can ask for a particular person. I've queried this database about Vinton Cerf (note the syntax: last name first, with the two names separated by a comma). Quickly I have a response:

```
Whois: cerf, vinton
Cerf, Vinton G. (VGC) CERF@NRI.RESTON.VA.US
```

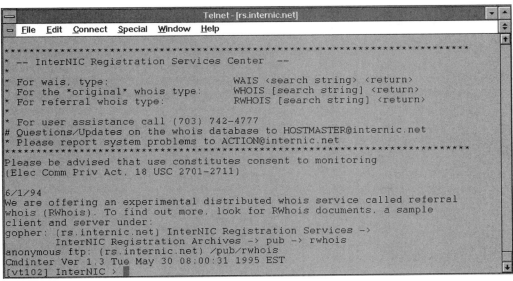

Figure 15.1   Logging on for a WHOIS search at the InterNIC.

```
Corporation for National Research Initiatives
1895 Preston White Drive, Suite 100
Reston, VA 22091
(703) 620-8990
```

```
Record last updated on 08-Apr-94.
Whois:
```

If you're not sure of a person's full name, you can enter a last name, and WHOIS will produce a list of possibilities, from which you can choose the person you're after.

It's likely that your service provider offers a WHOIS client program. If so, the usage is as follows:

`whois [-h` *host*`]` *name*

Examine this command for a moment. The **whois** command is followed by a host name, which tells the system which WHOIS database you want to search. This, in turn, is followed by the keyword you want to use. A search for Dr. Cerf through the InterNIC using a WHOIS client would appear this way:

`whois -h whois.internic.net cerf`

Notice that the-h remains, to be followed by the address of the database you are searching. A client program makes it possible for you to contact a wide variety of WHOIS databases easily, whereas using Telnet to a particular site requires you to log on at that site and then run a search of a single database.

One caution: Using the **whois** command by itself will likely search the database at nic.ddn.mil. Due to changes involved in the creation of the InterNIC, this database will be up to date for MILNET addresses only. Use whois.internic.net as the site name to query the InterNIC. Here, you see the result of running the previous search using a WHOIS client at my service provider's site:

```
% whois -h whois.internic.net cerf
Cerf, Vinton G. (VGC) CERF@NRI.RESTON.VA.US
   Corporation for National Research Initiatives
   1895 Preston White Drive, Suite 100
   Reston, VA 22091
   (703) 620-8990

   Record last updated on 08-Apr-94.

The InterNIC Registration Services Host contains ONLY Internet Information
(Networks, ASN's, Domains, and POC's).
Please use the whois server at nic.ddn.mil for MILNET Information.
```

Note the warning about the MILNET server in the last line (and note how long it has been since this record was updated—Cerf is now at MCI!).

With a large number of WHOIS databases out there, it would be helpful to acquire a list.

What You Need: A List of WHOIS Servers

The Document: The List of Internet WHOIS Servers

How to Get It: Through anonymous FTP. Use the following URL:

ftp://sipb.mit.edu/pub/whois/whois-servers.list

Here's a small portion of the list:

```
Preferred server name            Associated institution
----------------------------------------------------------------
camb.com                         Cambridge Computer Associates C=US
gte.com                          GTE Laboratories C=US
whois.pacbell.com                Pacific Bell C=US
wp.psi.com                       Performance Systems International C=US
whois.sunquest.com               Sunquest Information Syst

teetot.acusd.edu                 University of San Diego C=US
zippy.telcom.arizona.edu         University of Arizona C=US
ducserv.duc.auburn.edu           Auburn University C=US
whois.bates.edu                  Bates College C=US
```

The complete list is an extensive one. If you are looking for someone at a particular institution, you will want to check this list to determine whether that organization makes a WHOIS directory available. You can then specify that directory as the one you'll search with a WHOIS client. If I wanted to search the Pacific Bell WHOIS server for someone named Smith, for example, I would use the following command:

```
whois -h whois.pacbell.com smith
```

There are, as you might imagine, quite a few of them.

WHOIS is not an intuitive system; you are, after all, dealing with a command line interface. But if you get stuck, a help system is always available on-line; simply enter the command **help** at the prompt, as shown here:

```
Whois: help
Select the sub-topic you wish help on. Type '?' for a list of options;
hit RETURN to return to WHOIS.

A HELP command, one of the following:
EXIT     FILE     GOTO     HELP     QUIT     TOPIC
or Choose a topic, one of the following:
Handles                              KEYWORD overview
Mailboxes                            Names
Output keywords                      OVERVIEW
Record types                         Subdisplays
Updates, suggestions, bug reports    WHOIS help
Choose a subtopic (? for help):
```

We're beginning to see WHOIS databases appearing on the World Wide Web as well. In Figure 15.2, you can see how the Web can be used to set up a search form for WHOIS. Of course, we're still faced with the central problem of WHOIS directories; you have to

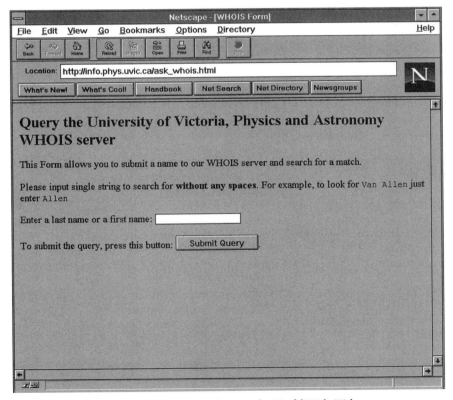

Figure 15.2 Setting up a WHOIS search using the World Wide Web.

search them one at a time. Fortunately, work is ongoing to develop improved user inter-faces, which may eventually make it possible to use the entire range of databases through graphical client software.

One note of caution: It is not considered good form or, indeed, acceptable behavior on the Internet to make long series of requests, in an attempt to download an entire directory. These databases are proprietary; at least, most sites consider them so. Were they to be used for commercial or marketing purposes, it is more than likely that system administrators would begin closing them to access from outsiders. This is not an out-come that will benefit anyone on the Internet. Instead, WHOIS databases should be used for the purposes they were designed to serve: targeted searches for individuals.

NETFIND

Another useful network tool is netfind, which offers searching for individuals by name and domain. To try netfind, Telnet to **ds.internic.net.** Log on as **netfind** with no pass-word. There are also a number of alternative servers available; using the one closest to you makes sense and conserves network resources. The list of alternative servers follows in Table 15.1. Figure 15.3 shows what you see when you log on at redmont.cis.uab.edu, at the University of Alabama at Birmingham.

Table 15.1   netfind servers

Server Address	Location	Country
archie.au	AARNet, Melbourne	Australia
bruno.cs.colorado.edu	University of Boulder, CO	USA
dino.conicit.ve	Consejo National de Investigaciones Cientificas y Technologicas, Caracas	Venezuela
ds.internic.net	InterNIC Directory & Database Services, South Plainfield, NJ	USA
eis.calstate.edu	California State University, Fullerton, CA	USA
krnic.net	Korea Network Information Center	South Korea
lincoln.technet.sg	Technet Unit, Singapore	Singapore
malloco.ing.puc.cl	Catholic University of Chile, Santiago	Chile
monolith.cc.ic.ac.uk	Imperial College, London	United Kingdom
mudhoney.micro.umn.edu	University of Minnesota, Minneapolis	USA
netfind.ee.mcgill.ca	McGill University, Montreal, Quebec	Canada
netfind.elte.hu	Eotvos Lorand University, Budapest	Hungary
netfind.fnet.fr	Association FNET, Le Kremlin-Bicetre	France
netfind.icm.edu.pl	Warsaw University, Warsaw	Poland
netfind.if.usp.br	University of Sao Paulo, Sao Paulo	Brazil
netfind.mgt.ncu.edu.tw	National Central University	Taiwan
netfind.sjsu.edu	San Jose State University, San Jose, CA	USA
netfind.uni-essen.de	University of Essen	Germany
netfind.vslib.cz	Liberec University of Technology	Czech Republic
nic.uakom.sk	Academy of Sciences, Banska Bystrica	Slovakia

```
% telnet bruno.cs.colorado.edu
Trying 128.138.243.150 ...
Connected to bruno.cs.colorado.edu.
Escape character is '^]'.

SunOS UNIX (bruno)

Login as `netfind' to access netfind server

login: netfind

=======================================================
Welcome to the University of Colorado Netfind server.
=======================================================

Alternate Netfind servers:
        archie.au (AARNet, Melbourne, Australia)
        bruno.cs.colorado.edu (University of Colorado, Boulder, USA)
        dino.conicit.ve (Nat. Council for Techn. & Scien. Research, Venezuela)
        ds.internic.net (InterNIC Dir & DB Services, S. Plainfield, NJ, USA)
        eis.calstate.edu (California State University, Fullerton, CA, USA)
        krnic.net (Korea Network Information Center, Taejon, Korea)
        lincoln.technet.sg (Technet Unit, Singapore)
        malloco.i
        monolith.cc.ic.ac.uk (Imperial College, London, England)
        mudhoney.micro.umn.edu (University of Minnesota, Minneapolis, USA)
        netfind.ee.mcgill.ca (McGill University, Montreal, Quebec, Canada)
        netfind.elte.hu (Eotvos Lorand University, Budapest, Hungary)
        netfind.fnet.fr (Association FNET, Le Kremlin-Bicetre, France)
        netfind.icm.edu.pl (Warsaw University, Warsaw, Poland)
        netfind.if.usp.br (University of Sao Paulo, Sao Paulo, Brazil)
        netfind.mgt.ncu.edu.tw (National Central University, Taiwan)
        netfind.sjsu.edu (San Jose State University, San Jose, CA, USA)
        netfind.uni-essen.de (University of Essen, Germany)
        netfind.vslib.cz (Liberec University of Technology, Czech Republic)
        nic.uakom.sk (Academy of Sciences, Banska Bystrica, Slovakia)


I think that your terminal can display 24 lines.  If this is wrong,
please enter the "Options" menu and set the correct number of lines.

Top level choices:
        1. Help
        2. Search
        3. Seed database lookup
        4. Options
        5. Quit (exit server)
-->
```

Figure 15.3   Logging in to a netfind server.

Using netfind is simple; you enter keywords about the person in question. The trick is knowing which keywords to enter. Watch what happens now as I try two different searches. First, let's suppose you want to look me up in the netfind system. You already know my name and the fact that I log on in North Carolina through a system called Interpath. If you can be this precise, your search will proceed swiftly. Take a look at the results of entering **gilster interpath north carolina** in the search field, as shown in Figure 15.4 (note that the search terms are separated by spaces; no periods are involved).

If you examine this figure, you will see the key to netfind's operations in the following statements:

```
( 1) SMTP_Finger_Search: checking domain interpath.com
The domain 'interpath.com' does not run its own name servers,
        and there is no aliased domain IP address/CNAME/MX record for
        this domain -> Skipping domain search phase for this domain.
( 2) got nameserver dns2.interpath.net
( 2) got nameserver dns1.interpath.net
( 2) SMTP_Finger_Search: checking domain interpath.net
```

The program is looking for finger information about the person in question—in this case, me. We will examine the finger program later in this chapter; basically, it allows you to track down information about people at a given site (along with a variety of other options). By being as precise as we were, we allowed netfind to go directly to Interpath and pull up finger information about me there. What you see displayed is the same information you would see if you had entered the command **finger gilster@interpath.net.** netfind reports I am currently logged on at this site, which, of course, I am because I am going out from the site to search netfind.

The entire process may go on for screen after screen in some cases. netfind will check domains and then hosts. In the domain part of the search, it is looking for mail-forwarding information, while in the host part, it is performing finger searches into the hosts. The information produced by the search includes any problems netfind ran into while running its search, information about the most promising e-mail address for the person in question, and a statement of when and where the person most recently logged on, as shown in Figure 15.4.

Let's examine keyword strategy for a moment, now that we've found our target. netfind is structured so that the first thing you enter should be a name. It can be a first or a last name; it can be a log-in name, for that matter, but you can only specify one name at a time. The name should be followed by a set of keywords describing where the person works—this can be organizational or geographical information. You also can enter the name of an institution or a city, a state, a country. You can't, however, enter the host part of a domain name. If you were searching for a person who worked at a machine named ricks, the name ricks would not help you find your man, but the rest of the information would. Thus, you could search under the keywords *henreid casablanca*, and so on to track down henreid@ricks.casablanca.com (not a real address, alas).

Note, too, that we can't search domains per se. You couldn't find Mr. Henreid by searching under casablanca.com, but you could search using the keywords *casablanca com* (note the separation between keywords and the lack of a period).

Think back to our first search. You wouldn't need to use a directory to find people if you knew a great deal about them; most of the time you have only a name and, perhaps, an organization name or even a geographical area. Now suppose you wanted to find me with just this information: *gilster raleigh north carolina.* In Figure 15.5, I have tried these keywords. Take a look at the results.

I have truncated the list considerably; at the time of this writing, netfind located over 150 domains to search in Raleigh. These were followed by this statement:

```
Enter selection (e.g., 2 0 1) -->
```

```
Enter person and keys (blank to exit) --> gilster interpath north carolina
Please select at most 3 of the following domains to search:
        0. interpath.com (interpath, a division of capitol information
           systems,)
        1. interpath.net (interpath, raleigh, north carolina)
        2. pdial.interpath.net (interpath, raleigh, north carolina)
Enter selection (e.g., 2 0 1) --> 0 1


( 1) SMTP_Finger_Search: checking domain interpath.com
The domain 'interpath.com' does not run its own name servers,
        and there is no aliased domain IP address/CNAME/MX record for
        this domain -> Skipping domain search phase for this domain.
( 2) got nameserver dns2.interpath.net
( 2) got nameserver dns1.interpath.net
( 2) SMTP_Finger_Search: checking domain interpath.net
( 2) do_connect: Finger service not available on host interpath.net ->
    cannot dp
------
Domain search completed.  Proceeding to host search.
------
( 2) SMTP_Finger_Search: checking host www.interpath.net
( 3) SMTP_Finger_Search: checking host mercury.interpath.net
( 4) SMTP_Finger_Search: checking host mail-hub.interpath.net
( 5) SMTP_Finger_Search: checking host www2.interpath.net
( 1) SMTP_Finger_Search: checking host ftp.interpath.net
SYSTEM: mercury.interpath.net
        Login name: gilster                In real life: Paul A Gilster - s
        Directory: /interpath/users/gilster    Shell: /bin/csh
        On since May 30 08:52:23 on ttyub from stargazer.interp
        1 minute 3 seconds Idle Time
        Mail last read Mon May 29 14:36:24 1995
        No Plan.


 SYSTEM: www.interpath.net
        Login name: gilster                In real life: Paul A Gilster - s
        Directory: /interpath/users/gilster    Shell: /bin/csh
        On since May 30 08:52:23 on ttyub from stargazer.interp
        1 minute 3 seconds Idle Time
        Mail last read Mon May 29 14:36:24 1995
        No Plan.



 FINGER SUMMARY:
 - Found no address records for the domain 'interpath.com',
   indicating it is probably not directly connected to the Internet.
   Netfind can only locate users at directly connected sites, or sites
   that set up Internet-reachable white pages servers.
 - The most promising email address for "gilster"
   based on the above finger search is
   gilster@mercury.interpath.net.


 Continue the search ([n]/y) ? -->
```

Figure 15.4 A precise search yields quick results.

```
Enter person and keys (blank to exit) --> gilster raleigh north carolina
Netfind: your search covers more than 150 domains
Partial list of domains that matched your search:
        acs.ncsu.edu (academic computing services, north carolina state univers)
        adm.ncsu.edu (administration office, north carolina state university, r)
        aemp.ncsu.edu (north carolina state university, raleigh)
        aif.ncsu.edu (north carolina state university, raleigh)
        aisg.com (accura innovative services group, raleigh, north carolina)
        allen.com (allen marketing, raleigh, north carolina)
        alphanum.com (alphanumeric systems, inc, raleigh, north carolina)
        ambra.com (ambra computer corporation, raleigh, north carolina)
        ara.com (applied research associates, inc, raleigh, north carolina)
        aren.org (animal rights electronic network, raleigh, north carolina)
        arrc.ncsu.edu (north carolina state university, raleigh)
        asci.ncsu.edu (north carolina state university, raleigh)
        asiral.com (alpha-numeric systems, raleigh, north carolina)
        bae.ncsu.edu (north carolina state university, raleigh)
        bas.ncsu.edu (north carolina state university, raleigh)
        bayleaf.com (bayleaf software, raleigh, nc, raleigh, north carolina)
```

Figure 15.5   Searching netfind using geographical terms.

We can look through the list and pick the right domain, if we know what it is. At that point, we can proceed with the netfind search.

Or we can get still more creative with keywords. Suppose, for example, that you remembered my address, including the term *net*. You weren't, perhaps, sure of which network I was connected to, but you remembered the word *net* somewhere in the name. In that case, you could try adding *net* to the search statement. Here, I've tried entering **gilster net north carolina.** Now netfind has more to work with; as compared with the over 150 domains it found on our last search, it now narrows to 28, as shown in Figure 15.6.

This may be enough to joggle your memory; you see number 14 on this list and decide it is the correct network. Entering a **14** at the prompt, followed by a **RETURN,** you will soon see netfind lock onto the Interpath server.

```
( 1) got nameserver dns.interpath.net
```

And soon the search will run at Interpath and reveal the correct finger information, containing my address.

You can see how elastic a process the netfind search is. Sometimes, though, you will retrieve too many hits for netfind to work. For example, while it is a good idea to include geographic terms in your search, you want to make them as precise as possible. Had you entered **gilster north carolina** as your only search terms, you would have retrieved a huge list of North Carolina possibilities, along with a final message from netfind:

```
Please form a more specific query.
Enter person and keys (blank to exit) -->
```

In this case, the only thing to do is take the program's lead and make your search terms more precise.

The primary limitation of netfind, as has become obvious, is that you won't find the person in question unless you already have a pretty good idea where he or she is. Think of this program as a tool that helps you zero in on a target you already have in your

```
Enter person and keys (blank to exit) --> gilster net north carolina
Please select at most 3 of the following domains to search:
        0. astral.net (oblique enterprises, greensboro, north carolina)
        1. charweb.org (charlotte's web free-net, charlotte, north carolina)
        2. code.net (collaborated development network, charlotte, north carolin)
        3. concert.net (communications for north carolina education, research, )
        4. core.net (core network, charlotte, north carolina)
        5. cybernetics.net (creative cy
        6. cybernetx.net (cybernetx, inc, charlotte, north carolina)
        7. cybertech.net (cybernet technologies, durham, north carolina)
        8. dcm.net (data center management, charlotte, north carolina)
        9. dialin.net (indial network, charlotte, north carolina)
       10. dialout.net (outdial network, charlotte, north carolina)
       11. fx.net (fxnet, charlotte, north carolina)
       12. fxnet.net (fxnet, charlotte, north carolina)
       13. infosys.net (piedmont infosys, greensboro, north carolina)
       14. interpath.net (interpath, raleigh, north carolina)
       15. nando.net (the news and observer publishing corporation, raleigh, n)
       16. nc.net (internet america north carolina operations, alpharetta, geo)
       17. ncih.net (state telecommunications services, raleigh, north carolin)
       18. ncmicro.net (ncmicro online information systems, winston-salem, nor)
       19. ncren.net (north carolina research and education network, research )
       20. netpage.net (netpage, charlotte, north carolina)
       21. ols.net (online south, inc, tobaccoville, north carolina)
       22. opti.net (pujan corporation, inc, raleigh, north carolina)
       23. outdial.net (outdial network, charlotte, north carolina)
       24. pager.net (netpage, charlotte, north carolina)
       25. thought.net (thoughtnet, greensboro, north carolina)
       26. vnet.net (vnet internet access, charlotte, north carolina)
       27. net.uncwil.edu (university of north carolina, wilmington)
       28. pdial.interpath.net (interpath, raleigh, north carolina)
Enter selection (e.g., 2 0 1) -->
```

Figure 15.6 Result of a more specific search using netfind; note that the number of domains located by this search is significantly smaller than before.

sights, rather than one that lets you shoot haphazardly, hoping to hit something along the way. The other netfind limitation is also significant: Some sites disable finger, so that netfind can't track down anything to work with.

It would be useful to be able to keep up with netfind news.

What You Need: A Source for News about netfind

Where to Get It: Use anonymous FTP to the following URL:

ftp://ftp.cs.colorado.edu/pub/cs/distribs/netfind/

This directory contains several files of interest, and is the place to look to see what netfind creator Michael Schwartz is up to now. And if you really want to delve into the specifics of how netfind works, consult the following file:

ftp://ftp.cs.colorado.edu/pub/cs/techreports/schwartz/PostScript/Netfind.Gathering.ps.Z

X.500 and the Conquest of Paradise

Given the chaos of Internet directory services, it was natural enough that various attempts at standardizing them would appear. Developed by the CCITT (Consultative Committee for International Telegraph and Telephone) and the ISO (International Standards Organization), X.500 was designed as such a distributed directory standard. The system makes it possible to refer to people by a "distinguished name," which can be retrieved from an X.500 directory and mapped onto the appropriate mailbox address. While we are seeing some deployment of X.500, it has hardly become the ubiquitous standard its proponents initially hoped for, even if sites are available for searching. What X.500 will need is enough sites to begin using the system so that the amount of data available with it becomes genuinely useful.

One system you may want to examine to get the flavor of X.500 is called PARADISE. This is an experimental X.500 service; it can be accessed at the following URL:

```
telnet://paradise.ulcc.ac.uk
```

Log on as **de.** Once on-line, you can search for information about people and organizations, retrieving electronic mail addresses, telephone and fax numbers, and more.

Your job is to provide name information and the location of the person. The directory service will run a search to find information that matches your search commands. Naturally, the directory service won't do you any good if the people you're looking for don't work for organizations that are taking part in the project. Figure 15.7 shows what you'll see when you Telnet to the PARADISE server.

Two types of search are available. A simple search is used when you're looking for a specific person, department, or organization, and the prompts mentioned help you home in. A more powerful search method for multiple organizations lets you search when you know the name of the person and his or her country, but don't know the name of his or her organization. In this case, the program searches widely through organizations to match the string you've entered; if you omit the organization name entirely, it will search through the entire list of organizations in that country.

Begin by typing in the name of the person you're looking for, either as a full name or just a last name. You move through several fields in such a search, and you are prompted for department, organization, and country. Here's what a simple search screen looks like, as shown in Figure 15.8. You answer at the prompt with a name; you're then prompted for the remaining fields.

For more information about PARADISE, contact the following address:

PARADISE Project
University College London, Computer Science
Gower Street, London WCIE 6BT,UK
E-mail:info-server@paradise.ulcc.ac.uk

Knowbots and the Intelligent Directory

The problem that even the best Internet directory tools cannot address is the diversity of their interfaces. If you become accomplished at using WHOIS, for example, you will need to learn a completely new set of keyword skills with netfind, and the same is true of PAR-

ADISE or any other X.500 project. What we would like to see is a program that is smart enough to understand how such diverse directory engines work, and easy enough to use that it can walk us through our searches. There is, in fact, no program that can do all of this, but Knowbot Information Service's Knowbot is an interesting take on the idea.

The Knowbot can pull data from WHOIS servers and a variety of campus directory systems. It can look into X.500 databases, can use finger as a search tool, and can even delve into the MCI Mail database. In a way, WAIS offers a concept similar to that of the Knowbot. In providing a consistent interface to a range of different databases, WAIS makes our searching easier, and cuts down on the amount of time and frustration we would otherwise experience looking up commands. The beauty of a true Knowbot is that

```
% telnet paradise.ulcc.ac.uk
Trying 128.86.8.56 ...
Connected to paradise.ulcc.ac.uk.
Escape character is '^]'.


To use the Directory Service, login as dua

SunOS UNIX (fortnum.nameflow.dante.net)

login: de
                Welcome to the NameFLOW-Paradise Directory Service

Connecting to the Directory - wait just a moment please ...
You can use this directory service to look up telephone numbers and electronic
mail addresses of peop
NameFLOW-Paradise Directory Service.

Select the mode you would like:

S Simple queries - if you know the name of the organisation you want to search
  (this is how the interface always used to behave)

P Power Search - to search many organisations simultaneously

B  Browser - best suited for exploring the Directory

Y Yellow Pages - power searching but allows user to search for an entry
  based on criteria other than the entry name

U Enter search string in form of User-Friendly Name - e.g,
    p barker, ucl, uk

I Brief instructions explaining the program modes and how to use the program

? The help facility - usage and topics

Q To quit the program

Enter option:
```

Figure 15.7   The entry screen at the PARADISE server.

```
You will be prompted to type in:

:- the NAME of the person for whom you are seeking information
:- their DEPARTMENT (optional),
:- the ORGANISATION they work for (optional if power searching), and
:- the COUNTRY in which the person or organisation is based.

On-line HELP is available to explain in more detail how to use the
Directory Service.  Please type ?INTRO (or ?intro) if you are not familiar
with the Directory Service.

?            for HELP with the current question you are being asked
??           for HELP on HELP
q            to quit the Directory Service (confirmation asked unless at the
             request for a person's name)
Control-C  abandon current query or entry of current query

Simple query mode selected
Person's name, q to quit, * to browse, ? for help
:-
```

Figure 15.8   A sample search in PARADISE.

it would be easier to use than WAIS. Once armed with the information we were after, it would find it without any subsequent user intervention. Several companies are exploring this idea; in addition to Knowbot information service project in Reston, Virginia, SandPoint Corporation of Cambridge, Massachusetts and Advanced Research Technology of Rosemout, Pennsylvania are at work.

You can try out Knowbot Information Service's netaddress program by using Telnet to the following URL:

```
telnet://info.cnri.reston.va.us:185
```

Figure 15.9 shows you what you will see as you connect to this address. You can use a single query to set off a search through a variety of information services, with the results presented in a uniform format. The search syntax is simple. At the > prompt, you enter a name, preceded by the word **query.** In other words, to search for Vinton Cerf using the Knowbot, we enter the command **query vinton cerf.** The Knowbot will then begin its search, as shown in Figure 15.10.

You can also use a Knowbot to narrow in on a person when you know something more than the person's name. If, for example, the target of your search is a user of MCI Mail, you could tell Knowbot to search that database using the **service** *directory* command—**service mcimail** does the trick. You can then run the address search knowing the results will be constrained to include only those people in the MCI Mail database.

The following describes the basic Knowbot commands:

service   Adds a given directory service to the list of services searched by the Knowbot. If you don't specify a particular service, netaddress will use a default list of services.

```
% telnet info.cnri.reston.va.us 185
Trying 132.151.1.15 ...
Connected to info.cnri.reston.va.us.
Escape character is '^]'.

                    Knowbot Information Service
KIS Client (V2.0).    Copyright CNRI 1990.    All Rights Reserved.


KIS searches various Internet directory services
to find someone's street address, email address and phone number.

Type 'man' at the prompt for a complete reference with examples.
Type 'help' for a quick reference to commands.
Type 'news' for information about recent changes.

Backspace characters are '^H' or DEL

Please enter your email address in our guest book...
(Your email address?) > gilster@interpath.net


>
```

Figure 15.9   Logging on to the Knowbot.

```
> query vinton cerf
Trying whois at ds.internic.net...

The ds.internic.net whois server is being queried:

No match for "CERF and VINTON"

The rs.internic.net whois server is being queried:

Cerf, Vinton G. (VGC)               CERF@NRI.RESTON.VA.US
    Corporation for National Research Initiatives
    1895 Preston White Drive, Suite 100
    Reston, VA 22091
    (703) 620-8990

The nic.ddn.mil whois server is being queried:

No match for name "CERF,VINTON".
Trying mcimail at cnri.reston.va.us...
Name:        Vinton G. Cerf
Organization: MCI Data Svc
City:        Reston
State:       VA
(Press RETURN to continue)
```

Figure 15.10   The Knowbot proceeds to search through different databases, sparing you the trouble.

services	Lists the services available through the Knowbot.
org	You can search using organization as a qualifier; **org digital equipment,** for example, calls up only those people who list that company as their organization.
country	Lets you pull up everyone on a specific directory from a given country.
ident	Allows you to search for a service-specific identifier instead of a user name. I might want to search for a user named Charles Johnson under his user name **cjohn,** for example.
query	Entering **query** *username* is the same as simply entering the user name at the >prompt. It simply tells the Knowbot this is the name to search for.
quit	Quits the Knowbot.

The results of a Knowbot search are also available by mail. You can send a message to either of the following addresses:

```
kis@cnri.reston.va.us
netaddress@sol.bucknell.edu
```

The body of the message is processed as command input to the Knowbot, and the results are then mailed back to you.

Users are encouraged to make comments about the Knowbot. The address is:

```
kis-support@cnri.reston.va.us
```

And if you become intrigued with the concept, there is a mailing list you can join by sending mail to this address:

```
kis-users@cnri.reston.va.us
```

Finding People with CCSOs

We have learned that Gopher can be a helpful navigational tool, presenting data to us in the form of menus. On many Gopher screens, you will find a directory tool called a CCSO. The term stands for Computing and Communications Services Office, a reference to the department at the University of Illinois at Urbana-Champaign where this tool was developed. The nomenclature can be a bit confusing, because sometimes you'll see these items labelled CSO (with a single 'C'); this stands for the original Computing Services Office (before a name change), and for a long while these directories were simply called CSOs. But whether the site you're using calls them CCSOs or CSOs, what they are is a handy way to find people quickly. Many large organizations maintain these directories at their sites.

Of course, the same proviso applies to CCSO servers that characterizes the rest of these tools (except the Knowbot)—CCSOs are directories of particular organizations. To search for people at multiple sites, you will have to move from one CCSO server to another, and there is no guarantee that any particular organization will maintain one. However, if you are looking for someone on a university campus, the chances increase that there will be a CCSO available. To find one, examine a nearby Gopher for items marked *Phone Books/* or something similar. In Figure 15.11, I have presented a screen from the Gopher at The World; there, the relevant main menu item is *Internet and USENET Phone Books/*. Selecting that item and moving to the next level item *Phone books at other institutions/*, I press a **RETURN** again to arrive at the screen shown in Figure 15.11. I can choose item 8, *North America/*, to call up the screen shown in Figure 15.12.

Notice that there are 14 screens of directories available (as shown by the 1/14 notation at the bottom right of the figure). Entries marked with a <?> are indices, searchable through keywords. Entries marked <CCSO> are the servers we'll focus on. The son of a

```
             Internet Gopher Information Client v2.0.12

                   Phone books at other institutions

   -->   1.  About Phone Books. . .
         2.  Search All the Directory Servers. . . <?>
         3.  All the directory servers in the world/
         4.  Africa/
         5.  Asia Pacific/
         6.  Europe/
         7.  Middle East/
         8.  North America/
         9.  South America/
        10.  International Organizations/
        11.  X.500 Gateway (experimental)/
        12.  whois information and server list




Press ? for Help, q to Quit, u to go up a menu          Page: 1/1
```

Figure 15.11 Looking for CSO sites with Gopher.

```
             Internet Gopher Information Client v2.0.12

                          North America

   -->   1.  Albert Einstein College of Medicine <CSO>
         2.  American Mathematical Society Combined Membership List <?>
         3.  Arizona State University <?>
         4.  Auburn University <?>
         5.  Bates College <CSO>
         6.  Baylor College of Medicine <CSO>
         7.  Board of Governors Universities (Illinois) <CSO>
         8.  Boston University <CSO>
         9.  Bradley University <CSO>
        10.  Brigham Young University <CSO>
        11.  Brown University <CSO>
        12.  Bucknell University <CSO>
        13.  Bull HN Information Systems <?>
        14.  California Institute of Technology <?>
        15.  California State University - Fresno <?>
        16.  California State University - Hayward <?>
        17.  California State University - Sacramento <?>
        18.  Calvin College <CSO>

Press ? for Help, q to Quit, u to go up a menu          Page: 1/14
```

Figure 15.12 A partial listing of North American phone book entries.

friend of mine attends Cornell University in Ithaca, New York. Let's see if we can find him using a CCSO. We'll choose item 29, *Cornell University* <CCSO>. The interesting screen shown in Figure 15.13 appears.

This is a form we can fill in to find the person we need. I'll enter my friend's son's name thus: **christopher allen** followed by a **RETURN.** I enter the name this way because I know he goes by Chris, but I'm not sure whether that or his full name would be listed in the index. If he's entered as Christopher, I'll be okay, and indeed, his name appears.

```
          name: Christopher John Allen
 send_email_to: cjal@cornell.edu
      nickname: callen
campus_address: 521 Sheldon Ct.
             : Ithaca, NY 14850
  campus_phone: 3-7901
       project: try and make it to the summer
```

These CCSO searches can also use wild cards. If I had chosen to, I could have tried **ch* allen** to see what the system would come up with. I could have used **chris*allen,** for that matter, since the first five letters of Christopher and Chris are identical. A wild-card asterisk simply indicates that the system should try to find anything that matches the letters I've typed, along with any other letters that might follow them. I might thus have encountered a Charles Allen using my **c* allen** search strategy. The ? wild card, incidentally, does not work with CCSO name servers.

Note in the example that you aren't restricted to searching by name. If I had remembered that my friend's son had an electronic mail address of cjal@cornell.edu, I could have entered that in the relevant field and pulled up the same information. The fields available for searching are name, phone number, and e-mail address; not all items in the

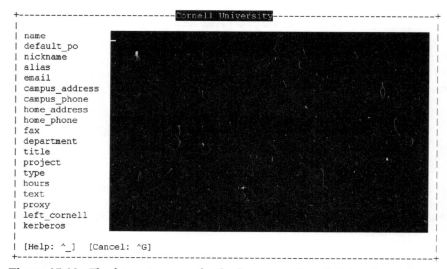

Figure 15.13   The data entry screen for the directory at Cornell University.

previous entry are indexed, but being able to search in these fields should retrieve the information you need in most cases. Because they're popular at universities, CCSO servers can be a fast and easy way to track people down, especially when used through the kind offices of Gopher.

Campus Wide Information Systems

Another alternative if you're looking for someone at a college or university is to find out whether that institution maintains an on-line information service. Campus Wide Information Systems (CWIS) are becoming more prevalent all the time, and many of them are excellent. I frequently use Gopher to look through these systems. Many Gophers contain CWIS information (you can search using Veronica to track these down). In addition, there is a WAIS server, cwis_list.src, containing a searchable list of CWIS servers prepared by Judy Hallman at the University of North Carolina at Chapel Hill. You can search it by using Telnet to the following URL:

```
telnet://sunsite.unc.edu
```

If the campus you're interested in offers a CWIS, you'll find it on this list. Another good source for CWIS information is Peter Scott's HYTELNET program, discussed in Chapter 12.

Judy Hallman's list of CWIS servers is also available through anonymous FTP, and it's a handy thing to have if you think you'll be trying to track down campus addresses.

What You Need: A List of CWIS Servers

The Document: CWIS-L

How to Get It: Through anonymous FTP to the following URL:

ftp://ftp.oit.unc.edu/pub/docs/about-the-net/cwis/cwis-1

A CWIS is a repository of campus information that can be reached by any workstation at the university that has communications capability. These services vary from school to school, not only in terms of content but also in terms of the software that drives them. But you can expect to find menu-driven systems allowing you to choose information on campus events and services, lists of job openings and housing possibilities, class schedules, directories of faculty and students, grant opportunities, and more. Frequently, the system will be set up to enable electronic mail or discussion groups, though such services are generally only available to registered users. You may also find library search capabilities open to the public.

It would be unthinkable to discuss CWIS systems without making mention of Cornell University, whose CUINFO has been on-line for over a decade thanks to the dedicated work of Steven L. Worona. While earlier systems had become available, including services at the University of Illinois at Champaign-Urbana and Stanford University, Cornell's may have been the first real bridge to the nonmainframe community. It is an exem-

```
                                                    Rutgers INFO (p1 of 4)
            INFO: THE RUTGERS CAMPUS-WIDE INFORMATION SYSTEM


    If you need help, hit the carriage return key -- except for Mosaic or
    other mouse-based software, click your mouse on "About INFO".

      * [1]About INFO: how to use it, sending suggestions/evaluations
      * [2]Important daily messages (Updated Jun 22.)
      * [3]Please fill out this survey concerning Rutgers Info

    ABOUT RUTGERS AND THE COMMUNITY
      * [4]General University Info., Maps, Holidays, Regulations, Ask
        Questions
      * [5]Academics: Courses/Sched, Acad/Res depts, Sch. Info, Chronicle
      * [6]Research: Research and Sponsored Programs, Corporate Liaison,
        Grants
      * [7]Computing Facilities, Services and Network information
      * [8]Library: Services, Online Databases, IRIS.
    -- Press space for more, u to return to previous, '?' for help, 'q' to quit
      Arrow keys: Up and Down to move. Right to follow a link; Left to go back.
      H)elp O)ptions P)rint G)o M)ain screen Q)uit /=search [delete]=history list
```

Figure 15.14   The main menu at Rutgers University's CWIS.

plar of what a well-designed campus system can achieve. Unfortunately, it is no longer accessible by Telnet.

In Figure 15.14, the introductory screen from INFO, the CWIS at Rutgers University, is presented. This screen should give you a feel for the wide variety of information available here. Each of these menu items contains submenus. Figure 15.15 shows the menu for Rutgers University's calendar and other information.

```
                     General Information about the University (p1 of 2)
              GENERAL INFORMATION ABOUT THE UNIVERSITY

        TXT [1]About the University
        TXT [2]Academic calendar and staff holidays 1994-1996
        TXT [3]University Regulations and Procedures Manual
        TXT [4]BUILDING ON EXCELLENCE Strategic Plan for Rutgers - New
        Brunswick
        TXT [5]The Committee on Computing & Information Planning Report

        DIR [6]Quality and Communication Improvement Programs (QCI)
        DIR [7]University's Code of Student Conduct as of January 1995
        DIR [8]Maps of and Directions to the various campuses of
        Rutgers University.
        TXT [9]Rutgers presence at Recruitment Events (graduate
        programs only)
        TXT [10]Send a question to Colonel Henry (non-computer-related
        questions, please.)
        TXT [11]Read answers from Colonel Henry to questions posed
        TXT [12]Send a question to "ask HAL" (computer-related
    -- Press space for more, u to return to previous, '?' for help, 'q' to quit
      Arrow keys: Up and Down to move. Right to follow a link; Left to go back.
      H)elp O)ptions P)rint G)o M)ain screen Q)uit /=search [delete]=history list
```

Figure 15.15   Examining upcoming events at Rutgers University.

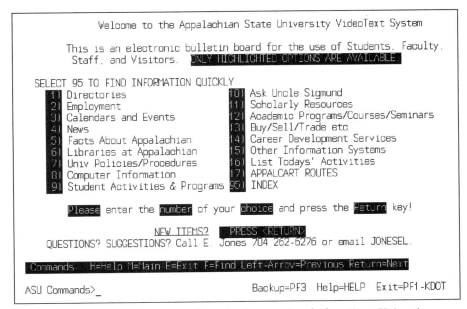

Figure 15.16 Introductory screen from the CWIS at Appalachian State University.

There is no standard for Campus Wide Information Systems as yet; the variety of user interfaces is wide. Figure 15.16, for example, is the opening screen from the CWIS at Appalachian State University in Boone, North Carolina.

Here again, we have an easy-to-use menu system with choices leading to submenus and eventually to text. No matter which software implementation you run into, CWIS systems are a great way to find people, and their growth into broader forms of information implies an interesting convergence with the Free-Net systems we discussed in Chapter 3.

Because CWIS systems are an exciting area of Internet development, it would be useful to find a way to keep up with the field. Fortunately, that's easy.

What You Need: A Mailing List for CWIS Systems

The List: CWIS-L

How to Get It: Send e-mail to the following address:

listserv@wuvmd.bitnet

Your message should contain the following statement:

subscribe cwis-1 *your_name*

Leave the Subject: field blank.

Finger Finds People and Information

You can find out who else is logged in to the system you're using by entering finger at the system prompt. You'll get a list of active users, like the following:

```
Login      Name                    TTY    Idle   When         Where
dwight     Dwight Eisenhower --     p0            Mon 08:20    nb1.concert.net
nocs       Network Operations C     p1     58     Mon 08:27    elvis.concert.ne
gkc        G K Chesterton -- Pe    *p2            Mon 08:53    nb1.concert.net
bogart     Humphrey Bogart -- Y     p3     4      Mon 08:28    nb-clt.concert.n
pablo      Paul A Gilster -- Co     p6            Mon 09:25    nb1.concert.net
walt       Walter Johnson -- Wa     p7     1      Mon 09:19    nb2.concert.net
manny      Emmanuel Kant -- Cr      p8     9      Mon 08:38    boogie.concert.n
jackson    Jack Benny -- cbs ra     p9     4d     Wed 14:07    mayur.mc.duke.ed
```

finger can also reach out into the network if you use it in conjunction with a user name. Here's what I get when I finger my account at The World:

```
% finger pag@world.std.com
[world.std.com]
world -- IP19 IRIX release 5.3 version 11091811

pag . Paul A Gilster Login Tue 30-May-95 5:07PM from gilster.pdiat
   [4597,4597] </home/ie/pag>; Group: pag
   Groups: pag

  pag has no new mail, last read Tue 30-May-95 5:08PM
```

What you get from a finger search varies depending on how much information is available at the site. finger may list the log-in name, full name, office location, and phone number, log-in time, idle time, the time mail was last read, and the contents of the .plan and .project files from the home directory of current users. The latter are files that you can create, listing information about your current activities, office hours, inclinations, philosophical musings, or most anything else you would care to insert. Someone using finger would then be able to read this material about you.

What one site does, however, does not necessarily parallel the practices of another. finger may be disabled at some locations for security reasons, while another system administrator may use it to supply information freely. The best way to find out is to try finger and see what you get. In many cases, you can use the program to generate information about not just one but all the users at a particular remote site. To do so, use the command **finger@***sitename.* Thus, **finger@med.unc.edu** produces a list similar to the one you could run at your own site with a straight **finger** command, but now the results are a listing of the people logged on at UNC's Medical School.

What happens if you don't know the log-in name for a particular user? No problem. You can type in part of the person's name and finger will produce a list of possible hits. Entering **finger g** at Interpath, for example, produces a list of everyone with a G as their middle initial. Entering **finger wilson** gives me a list of everyone with the name Wilson who's currently logged on, even if their log-in names are trw and gwilson. Again, it's necessary to point out that finger searches like this may or may not work depending on the site. This makes finger an imperfect tool, if a frequently useful one.

But finger has other tricks to work with. It can be used to tap into a wide range of information. Try the following command: **finger quake@geophys.washington.edu.** Instead of being sent information about a particular user at the site, you'll get an update on recent earthquake activity, as shown in Figure 15.17.

There aren't many finger sites that provide this kind of information, but those that are currently accessible are interesting. You'll find NASA's Headline News at this site:

nasanews@space.mit.edu

```
% finger quake@geophys.washington.edu
[geophys.washington.edu]
Login name: quake                     In real life: Earthquake Information
Directory: /u0/quake                  Shell: /u0/quake/run_quake
Last login Thu Jun  1 01:26 on ttyp2 from linet01.li.net
Mail last read Tue Apr 25 03:34:56 1995
Plan:
The following catalog is is for earthquakes (M>2) in Washington and Oregon
produced by the Pacific Northwest Seismograph Network, a member of the
Council of the National Seismic System.  Catalogs for various regions of the
country can be obtained by using the UNIX program `finger quake@machine'
where
the following are machines for different regions.

gldfs.cr.usgs.gov   (USGS NEIC/NEIS world-wide), andreas.wr.usgs.gov (North-
ern
Cal.), scec.gps.caltech.edu (Southern Cal.), fm.gi.alaska.edu (Alaska),
seismo.unr.edu (N
eqinfo.seis.utah.edu (Utah), sisyphus.idbsu.edu (Idaho)
slueas.slu.edu (Central US), tako.wr.usgs.gov (Hawaii),

Additional catalogs and information for the PNSN (as well as other networks)
are available using the World-Wide-Web (mosaic) system at URL:
 `http://www.geophys.washington.edu/'
DATE-TIME is in Universal Time (UTC) which is PST + 8 hours. Magnitudes are
reported as local magnitude (Ml).  QUAL is location quality A-good, D-poor,
Z-from automatic system and may be in error.
  DATE-(UTC)-TIME    LAT(N) LON(W)   DEP  MAG QUAL COMMENTS
  yy/mm/dd hh:mm:ss   deg.   deg.    km   Ml
  95/04/28 18:34:12  46.45N 121.86W   9.6 2.5  B    31.3 km  NE of Spirit Lake
  95/05/02 17:37:45  47.40N 124.78W  34.9 2.1  B    67.5 km SSW of Forks
  95/05/04 22:22:43  48.58N 122.08W   3.3 2.0  C    15.0 km  NE of Sedro Wool-
ley
  95/05/05 21:52:43  47.75N 122.40W  19.9 2.3  A    17.1 km WNW of Kirkland, Wa
  95/05/06 06:01:06  46.71N 120.83W   6.6 2.2  B    28.7 km WNW of Yakima
  95/05/14 09:12:47  47.76N 122.05W   1.4 2.4  B     6.9 km WNW of Duvall
  95/05/18 15:53:33  46.71N 120.55W   7.9 2.4  B    14.9 km NNW of Yakima
  95/05/18 16:00:23  47.93N 121.88W  13.9 2.0  B    11.1 km  NE of Monroe
  95/05/19 17:21:15  45.86N 120.38W  15.8 2.0  B    60.6 km  SW of Prosser, Wa
  95/05/20 12:48:48  46.86N 121.93W  13.4 4.1  A FELT  14.1 km WNW of Mount
Raini
  95/05/24 17:00:50  46.40N 123.83W   8.1 2.5  C    24.8 km   N of Astoria,OR
```

Figure 15.17   Results of a **finger** command to quake@geophys.washington.edu.

(thus your command is **finger nasanews@space.mit.edu**). There's a forecast of auroral activity at this site:

```
aurora@xi.uleth.ca
```

And be sure to try the following address:

```
coke@cs.cmu.edu
```

This one is an Internet-accessible Coke machine; check it out to see how the Net can monitor, with a fair amount of whimsy, our most pedestrian activities.

On the face of things, finger doesn't seem like the kind of tool that would make an appearance on the World Wide Web, but events have proven otherwise. What makes the Web capable of carrying finger information is its ability to work with forms. In Figure 15.18, you can see one such form. This is a finger gateway available at the following site:

```
http://www.globalc.com/cgi-bin/finger
```

As you can see, I have already entered information in the dialog box, and am about to press the **RETURN** key to call up the information. A number of such finger gateways now exist; you can find them by running a Web Crawler search on the World Wide Web

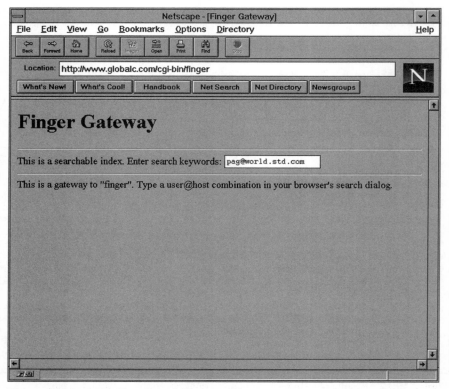

Figure 15.18   A World Wide Web browser offering a gateway to finger services.

under the keyword *finger* (or use one of the other search tools mentioned in Chapter 14). In fact, we're beginning to see not just finger but X.500 capabilities made accessible through the Web, as witness Figure 15.19, in which we have a dual-purpose gateway.

Expect the number of such gateways to grow as the Web becomes yet more pervasive, and as the capabilities of its browsers continue to develop.

To keep up with new finger sites, you can check the work of the indefatigable Scott Yanoff. Take a look at the following URL:

```
http://sundae.triumf.ca/fingerinfo.html
```

As you can see in Figure 15.20, Yanoff has set up a home page with links to all the interesting finger sites he's aware of, broken into categories. It's a page you may want to add to your list of World Wide Web bookmarks.

Digging Out a Name from USENET

Perhaps you've been reading USENET newsgroups for a while now and would like to contact someone whose name you ran across in one of them. But you don't know the person's e-mail address. Fortunately, all is not lost. An address database tapping USENET newsgroups can be found at rtfm.mit.edu. This database is easy to use and can be queried by e-mail, making it ideal for those without full Internet access.

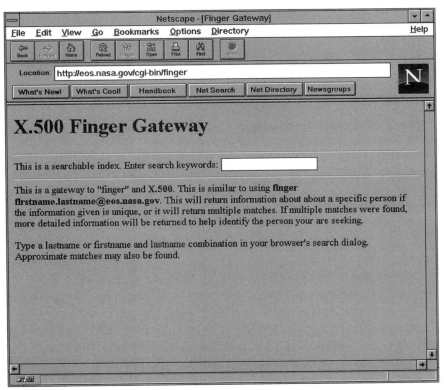

Figure 15.19 The Web can also be used to check for information in X.500 directories.

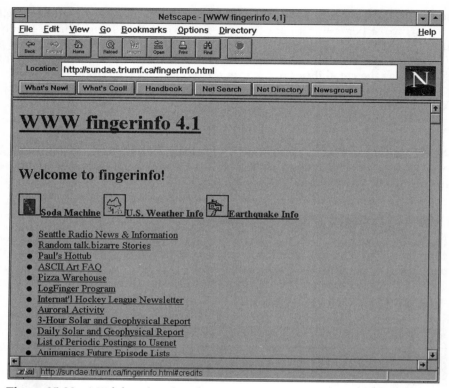

Figure 15.20 A Web-based guide to finger sites.

Here's the procedure. Send mail to the following address:

```
mail-server@rtfm.mit.edu
```

In the body of the message, enter this:

send usenet-addresses/*name*

where *name* is either a first or last name of the person you're looking for. I might send, for example, a message like this one:

send usenet-addresses/gilmore

to track down a USENET poster with that last name. One caveat: Characters like apostrophes have to be replaced with a period for the search to work. O'Toole becomes **o.toole** in the search command.

Need more than one person's address? You can send multiple requests by putting them on separate lines in the same message, but each will be answered in a separate reply. You can also tap into this database with a WAIS search. There is a WAIS database with the name usenet-addresses, which can be searched using standard WAIS methods.

BITNET Names

Tracking down someone on BITNET can get interesting. Fortunately, many BITNET sites have nameservers that you can query. You'll want to get a list of these sites.

What You Need: A List of BITNET Nameservers

The Document: BITNET Servers

How to Get It: Send e-mail to the following address:

listserv@bitnic.bitnet

In the body of your message, give this command:

send bitnet servers

To find someone on BITNET, you can send e-mail to the relevant server. Leave the subject field blank and make your request the first line of the message. To find John Smith at American University, for example, I would send a message to listserv@auvm.bitnet, an address I've taken from the BITNET Servers file.

```
% mail listserv@auvm.bitnet
Subject:
whois smith, john
```

Using the NetMail Database

The Merit Network NetMail database provides information for a university or other organization's mail site names, covering BITNET, UUCP, and the Internet. Ask it, for example, for a list of mail sites at unc.edu, the University of North Carolina at Chapel Hill academic computing center, and it produces this:

```
There are 5 sites found for UNC.EDU

Internet Sites:
   CS.UNC.EDU
   DOPEY.CS.UNC.EDU
   SAMBA.ACS.UNC.EDU
   THORIN.CS.UNC.EDU
   UNCLEV.UNCH.UNC.EDU
```

To use the Merit database, try the following URL:

```
telnet://hermes.merit.edu/
```

At the Which Host? prompt, type the following:

netmailsites

You'll be given the opportunity to search three times on any single connection.

You can use this database in several ways. If you already know the e-mail address, you can enter the address (using the part after the @) to see if it is a known site name. Alternatively, you can enter a location. The database searches for exact words, but you can add a **?** to the end of an entry to make it look for any words matching a wider description. An entry like **richmond,** for example, is very specific. The entry **rich?** will search for any word beginning with rich, but having any other possible endings. Thus you might find Richmond, Richland, Richebourg, and so on.

Entering **north carolina** as my search term, I receive a list of 39 sites, from the North Carolina State University Department of Nuclear Engineering to a UUCP connection at the Sun Microsystems North Carolina sales office. Entering **univ? Missouri** as my search terms, I receive a list of 24 sites in the University of Missouri system, as shown here:

```
UMRVMB              University of Missouri Rolla Campus
UMRVMC              University of Missouri Rolla Campus
UMRVMD              University of Missouri Rolla Campus
UMSLVAXA            University of Missouri St Louis Campus
UMSLVMA             University of Missouri St Louis Campus
UMSLVMB             University of Missouri St Louis Campus
UMVMA               University of Missouri Central Facility
```

This information is shown in the default terse mode, giving the site name and name of the institution. A **set verbose** command provides full information on each site. Having set that, for example, I see a fuller listing for one of the computers at the University of Missouri's St. Louis campus:

```
UMSLVMB
    Alternate Name(s):
    CPU: IBM 4381
    OS: VM/SP
    University of Missouri St Louis Campus
       Office of Computing and Telecommunications;St. Louis, MO
       63121-4499 US
```

NSLOOKUP

Although not available at all sites, nslookup can provide information on Internet domain nameservers. Ever wondered, for example, what the government calls its computers? We can find out by using nslookup. If it's available from your service provider, you will be able to access this program by typing **nslookup** at the command prompt. You should then see the program's own prompt, a simple >. I'll tell nslookup I want to examine the domain house.gov by using the server there.

```
> server house.gov
Default Server: house.gov
Address: 137.18.128.6
```

I can use the **ls** command to get further information. By entering **ls house.gov,** I get a list of the host computers used there. It's a huge list; here's just a bit of it:

```
quorum_router          137.18.24.31
carbon                 137.18.128.7
CS/1IPSN               137.18.24.16
GejdensonFP            137.18.90.1
GejdensonFP            137.18.240.48
mac_pacic              137.18.240.74
RoseSvr                137.18.240.89
ts2652-1               137.18.24.19
ts2652-2               137.18.24.22
ts2652-3               137.18.24.23
ts2652-4               137.18.24.24
WIND                   137.18.240.218
```

nslookup is no problem to use. The following describes the basic commands.

root   Sets the default server to the root. The root server has the top-level domain information.

server *name*   Sets the default server.

ls *name*   Lists the names of host computers that are servers for that domain. You can set this up as a file by using the command **ls** *name* >*filename.* In the previous example, using this command would have prevented most of the output from running off the screen. Instead, we would have a file that could then be read with the next command.

view *file*   Sorts the output from the **ls** command and lets us view it with the more program.

finger *name*   fingers the host you specify. This command, of course, is how nslookup ties into our search for users. Having identified the hosts at a particular domain, you can then find out who is using a host, or ask whether a specific user is doing so, using the finger commands.

exit   Leaves nslookup.

The Mother of All Directories

In January 1993, AT&T announced it had signed a cooperative agreement with the National Science Foundation to develop the next generation of directory for NSFNET. Just as the Internet is a network of networks, the new directory was seen as a directory of directories, pointing to the wealth of information sources on the network. Included are key data like FTP sites, lists of servers, lists of directories of various kinds, library catalogs, and other material. The notion is to make all of this easy to get to by creating simple user interfaces. In addition, AT&T plans to use the X.500 specification to create directory services listing users of the Internet and resources available on-line.

Is AT&T's approach the right one, and is a centralized directory structure the optimum way of organizing Internet information for the benefit of all? Many network tools, after all, like Gopher, netfind, or WAIS, work under the distributed model. Gopher doesn't function because it taps into a primary database; rather, it has been designed to work with information in a variety of formats clustered in sites around the world. Working from the top down may be a model that appeals to one set of planners, but going into uncharted waters and bringing the information back home is another way of approaching the task. The kinds of decisions that will be made over these issues will shape the Internet as it evolves into a broadly based communications tool for consumer and specialist alike.

You can reach the InterNIC Directory of Directories in various ways. Try Telnet to the following URL:

```
telnet://ds.internic.net
```

Or try the World Wide Web:

```
http://www.internic.net/ds/dsdirofdirs.html
```

Figure 15.21 shows you the home page at this site.

Real-Time Conversation

You're not limited to electronic mail when you want to contact someone on the Internet. A handy program called talk actually lets you go "live." You type on your keyboard; your friend types on his or hers, both of you sitting at your terminals at the same time. In this way, it's possible to maintain an active conversation, very similar to what happens on the

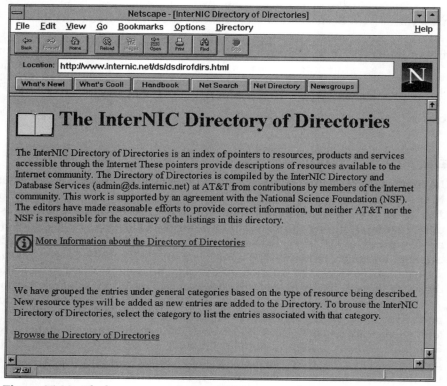

Figure 15.21   The home page at the InterNIC Directory of Directories.

commercial networks when people use the "chat" or "conferencing" capabilities. These services have become very popular on CompuServe and America Online.

To run talk, simply give the address of the person you want to talk to; **talk summers@alphabettica.com,** for example, displays a message on your friend's screen that you're available for a chat. By responding in like fashion, he or she can initiate a two-way discussion. Because incoming text can interrupt whatever you're trying to enter, the talk program gets around the problem by giving you a split screen to work with. You see what you enter at the top of the screen, while your friend's response appears on the bottom.

talk is enjoyable, if trivial, once you've worked out the kinks. It's difficult, for example, to handle pauses in a conversation. Without verbal cues or physical gestures, you don't really know whether you're supposed to say something or whether your correspondent is simply gathering his or her thoughts before continuing. Then, too, there's the question of productivity. You find after a while that simultaneous typing doesn't produce a very high information flow; you can ratchet up the content by 10 or so if you simply pick up the phone and call this person. Nonetheless, as a diversion from a long day at the office, talk has its charms.

One-to-one conferencing is the easiest way to start this kind of interactive discussion, but you can also get involved with multiple parties. If you have any CompuServe or America Online experience, you'll recall that users often gather in the various forums to hold regular conferences; the other commercial on-line services offer similar features. Here the strains of the on-line medium as applied to conversation really show. Because so many people have access to their keyboards at the same time, conventions are used to regulate the traffic. A formal conference, for example, might require each user to enter **ga** or "go ahead" after concluding his or her thoughts. Questions could be signaled by a **?,** which would indicate to the moderator that a particular person wanted to speak. The moderator's job is to monitor the flow of the conversation.

On the other hand, many such conferences are entirely free-form, with people chipping in where and when they please. This can lead to virtual anarchy on-screen, but there are those who thrive on it, forming on-line friendships and exploring ideas. The Internet, too, makes multiple party conferencing a reality; its implementation is known as Internet Relay Chat, or IRC.

IRC was written by Jarkko Oikarinen in 1988; since its origins in Finland, it has spread throughout the world. Using the system, people talk, either in groups or one to one, on specific "channels"—virtual meeting grounds where like-minded people can assemble. You may have first heard about IRC during the Persian Gulf war, when users kept abreast of news updates on a single IRC channel. You reach the world of IRC by using a client program, or you can go through a Telnet connection. The disadvantage of the latter is that public access sites frequently change, and may limit the hours that people can use their systems, as well as the number of users.

To try out IRC on a public client program with Telnet, try the following URLs:

telnet://ircd.demon.co.uk 6666

telnet://sci.dixie.edu 6677

telnet://irc.tuzvo.sk 6668

Use **irc** as your login.

You can keep up with public access IRC sites by consulting Scott Yanoff's *Special Internet Connections* document. We retrieved this text in Chapter 5, and it includes information on how to receive regular updates.

Many Unix-based systems will also offer you the option of calling IRC up from the command prompt. You can invoke it by entering **irc.** If you wish to use a nickname dissimilar from your log-in name, enter the command **irc *nickname*** instead. Figure 15.22 shows what you'll see in a typical IRC chat session, which I began by entering **irc** at the command prompt on my account at The World.

Look at the screen in Figure 15.22, which contains some interesting information. You'll see there were 3,394 users and 2,767 "invisible" users on 87 servers worldwide at the moment I initiated IRC. Invisible users, it turns out, are users who are on secret or hidden channels; their names do not turn up in a list of active users. More than three thousand users talking at once can make for overwhelming message traffic. This, of course, is why IRC divides its traffic into channels; 1,831 channels are currently operational, making room for plenty of conversations, and providing at least a vague semblance of ordering by topic.

We can generate a list of available channels by using the **/list** command. Doing this for the entire list creates many screens full of channels, of which I'll show you only a small percentage, in Figure 15.23.

You can join a channel with the **/join** command. This is where things get hard to follow. You have to develop a certain tolerance for nonsequential text. Figure 15.24 shows, for example, what I saw on-screen recently when I joined a channel called canada.

This probably gives you a bit of the flavor of IRC. The screen is split so that you can enter your own comments at the bottom, which will then be seen by everyone. There are

```
*** Connecting to port 6667 of server irc.std.com
*** Welcome to the Internet Relay Network pag (from world.std.com)
*** If you have not already done so, please read the new user information
with
+/HELP NEWUSER
*** Your host is world.std.com, running version 2.8.20
*** This server was created Sun Sep 4 1994 at 16: 48:11 EDT
*** umodes available oiws, channel modes available biklmnopstv
*** There are 3394 users and 2767 invisible on 87 servers
*** There are 78 operators online
*** 1831 channels have been formed
*** This server has 4 clients and 1 servers connected
*** - world.std.com Message of the Day -
*** - 6/12/1993 18:02
*** _
*** -                  Welcome to World's IRC server
*** _
*** -         For additional details on IRC, check 'help irc' on World.
*** -           Topics include a guide to basic commands and a schedule
*** -             of special IRC discussions for World customers.
*** _
*** _
*** Mode change "+i" for user pag by pag
[1] 09:46 pag (+i) * type /help for help
```

Figure 15.22   Beginning of an IRC session.

```
*** #TUEBINGEN 8        Haengen wir den Chauvi raus ...
*** #Konstanz   4
*** #report     1
*** #ccc        1        Chaos Computer Club - Ulm
*** #amigager   4
*** #OS/2       4
*** Prv         5
*** #linux      13       Free 386 Un*x/X11/tcp ++ (/msg linuxbot help)
*** #meditatio 4
*** #nippon     10       TGIF!!!  Let's party!
*** #malaysia   36       WOI..BALIK STUDY SEMUA!!!!
*** #Services   7
*** #Amiga      29       Cryo has an A1200 to add to his orphan collection
*** #eu-opers   15       European IRC operators' hangout
*** #AmigaSwe   2
*** #BTHS       1
*** #Kristanzo 2
*** #espanol    31       ALEJANDRO SANZ
*** #bondage    17       Hat to da Back
*** #Turks      6
*** #Twilight_  28        tzoper is a boojum snark!
[1] 14:58 pag (+i)* type /help for help
```

Figure 15.23   Partial list of available IRC channels.

also commands for a wide range of options including private conversations, generating help screens (use the **/help** command), finding out who is on-line, and more.

It would be useful to have access to further information about IRC.

What You Need: Documents about Internet Relay Chat

How to Get Them: The first, a Frequently Asked Questions document, is definitely the place to start. You can retrieve it from the following URL:

ftp://rtfm.mit.edu/pub/usenet/news.answers/irc-faq

But you should also take a look at some World Wide Web sites with IRC information. Check the following URLs:

http://www.kei.com/irc.html

http://alpha.acast.nova.edu/irc.html

http://urth.acsu.buffalo.edu/irc/WWW/ircdocs.html

The following describes some of the basic IRC commands. Preceding a command with a backslash ensures that it's treated as a command, and not as a message that will be sent to other participants.

```
<Kemal> bull: hirvonen@ucsvax.ucs.umass.edu    I am in Australia actually, we
+just talk a lot

<RingMan> kemal:do oyu like reading, sports?
<Aedes> hi euph
<Kemal> ringman: I read an awful lot
*** Fuzzie (EROBERTS@192.203.164.120) has joined
channel #canada
<Fuzzie> hi all :)<F0MU>
<Euphrasie> hello!!
<Renard> hiya fuzz
<Euphrasie> hi fuzzie!!
<RingMan> Kemal:can I suggest a good book?
<Cheaka> kemal-all i can say is,don't worry about it things will  work
+themselves out for you. sure life can be hard at times but they always work
+themselves out in the end
```

Figure 15.24   An example of an IRC session in progress.

/bye	Synonymous with **/quit,** this command allows you to leave any channel at any time.
/invite *nickname*	Sends a message to someone on a different IRC channel that you'd like them to meet you on your channel.
/join *#channel-name*	Lets you join the channel of your choice. All channel names include a # sign in front. Note: You can also create your own channel by the command **/join #channel-name** where you're entering the name of the channel you want to create.
/list	Lists all available channels for IRC.
/msg *nickname*	Allows you to send a private message to a person.
/summon *username*	Invites someone who is not using IRC to join you in chatting. Note: This requires the user name at the person's site, rather than an IRC nickname. Thus **/summon flr@samson.utn.edu** summons that person to a chat.
/who *#channel*	Tells you which users are participating in a given channel. The listing includes the person's nickname, along with an electronic mail address.
/whois *username*	Gives you the identity of anyone on the channel.

If all the commands just listed (and these are a fraction of what's available on IRC) have you wondering if you can ever learn how to use the system, be advised that there is a better way. With a SLIP/PPP connection, you can use a graphical client program that makes most of the IRC chores trivial. In Figure 15.25, you see one such program in action. This is WSIRC, a shareware program created by Caesar M Samsi. The program is logically designed and easy to use.

For example, when you give the **/list** command to see what channels are currently available, WSIRC will create a list to the right of the screen that contains a scrollable window listing all the channels. To join a channel, you need only double-click on it and

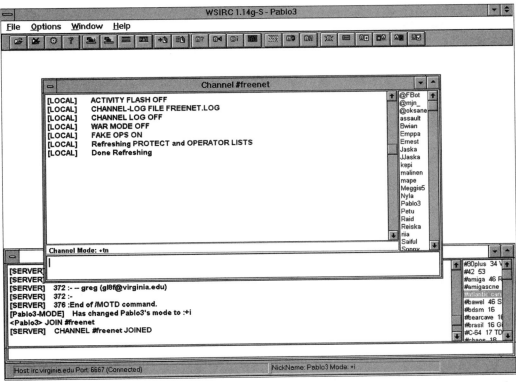

Figure 15.25 The shareware program WSIRC makes using IRC easier, letting you concentrate on the conversation.

you are there. In the centered window in Figure 15.25 is a channel called freenet; I have just joined it, and am waiting for the first messages to appear. To the right of the text area is a list of users currently on this channel. Behind it is a window with messages from the IRC server. WSIRC comes with a full listing of available servers. In general, the principle is to choose one close to you geographically, although you may have to experiment; many sites restrict who can connect to their services.

If you're interested in exploring this program, you can retrieve it from the following sites:

ftp://cs-ftp.bu.edu/irc/clients/pc/windows/wsirc14g.zip

ftp://winftp.cica.indiana.edu/pub/pc/win3/winsock/wsirc14g.zip

ftp://ftp.undernet.org/

And from Europe:

ftp://ftp.demon.co.uk/

ftp://ftp.funet.fi/pub/msdos/networks/irc/windows/wsirc14g.zip

Which IRC server to use? The IRC FAQ contains the following possibilities to get you started:

From the United States:

irc.bu.edu
irc.colorado.edu
mickey.cc.utexas.edu

From Canada:

irc.mcgill.ca

From Europe:

irc.funet.fi
cismhp.univ-lyon1.fr
irc.ethz.ch
irc.nada.kth.se
sokrates.informatik.uni-kl.de
bim.itc.univie.ac.at

From Australia:

jello.qabc.uq.oz.au

From Japan:

endo.wide.ad.jp

Well-Populated Dungeons

The Internet provides ample opportunities for recreation, including on-line versions of backgammon and chess, addresses for both of which can be found in Chapter 16. But one category of recreation deserves special mention here, since it ties in so closely with Internet Relay Chat (think of it as IRC with superimposed organization). The cryptic acronym MUD stands for Multiuser Dungeon, which in turn stands for role-playing games based on text. You might do most anything in such a game, from going off to an idyllic landscape to meditate, to slaying dragons and rescuing maidens. As you proceed by way of Telnet, you receive a series of choices about your next action, and you enter your reply. The system considers your reply and acts upon your command.

A wild variety of MUDs exist, springing from the original MUD created by Richard Bartle and Roy Trubshaw at the University of Essex in England. With new versions appearing frequently, it's helpful to keep up with the MUD community by tapping a USENET newsgroup devoted to such things.

What You Need: A Way to Keep Up with MUDs

Where to Find It: The USENET newsgroups are your best bet. Try any of the following, but pay special attention to rec.games.mud.announce:

> alt.mud
> rec.games.mud.admin
> rec.games.mud.announce
> rec.games.mud.diku
> rec.games.mud.lp
> rec.games.mud.misc
> rec.games.mud.tiny
> alt.mud.german
> de.alt.mud

And consider the FAQ at the following URL:

ftp://rtfm.mit.edu/pub/usenet/news.answers/games/mud-faq/

The files are part1.Z, part2.Z, and so on.

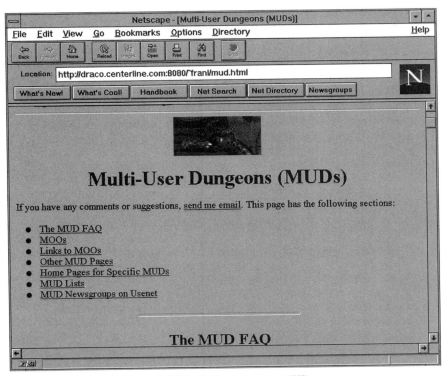

Figure 15.26   Using the World Wide Web to examine MUDs.

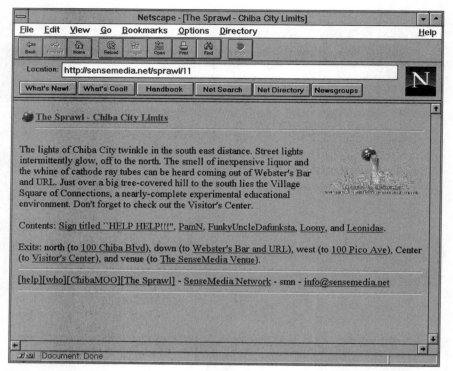

Figure 15.27 Entering a virtual city through a Web gateway.

MUDs have taken naturally to the World Wide Web. In Figure 15.26, you can see a home page that specializes in MUDs and their object-oriented cousins, MOOs (MUD Object Oriented). FAQs are available here about the various systems, as well as links to MUD and MOO sites. The URL is:

```
http://draco.centerline.com:8080/~franl/mud.html
```

We're beginning to see the adoption of MUDs into the HTTP environment through systems that incorporate hypertextual linkages into the virtual universes they create. Clearly, the future of MUDs is as much graphical as it is textual. Take a look at the ChibaMOO, home of The Sprawl. Here, you have a public access MOO site working through the World Wide Web. In Figure 15.27, I have moved into Chiba City; notice that I have a range of motion commands available, allowing me to begin my explorations. Each click leads me deeper into the virtual city.

If you're interested in exploring Chiba City, take a look at the following URL:

```
http://sensemedia.net/sprawl
```

16

A Directory of Internet Resources

It's interesting to speculate how big a volume it would take to create a truly complete Internet directory, listing every conceivable resource from FTP sites, WAIS servers, mail servers, Telnet destinations, and more. Whatever the answer, a single chapter like this one can only hope to suggest useful and interesting material for your browsing and reference. Inevitably, many of the sites here, especially the Web sites, reflect my own parochial interests, though I've attempted to broaden their scope by working in what seem to be popular destinations as reflected in some of the directory materials listed.

Archie Sites

Table 16.1 shows archie sites worldwide that are available through Telnet. You should use Telnet to connect to archie only if you do not have an archie client available. When using Telnet, choose the site nearest you to prevent network congestion. Log in as **archie.**

Mailing Lists

BITNET DOCUMENTS

Lists available files at BITNIC.
Access: Send electronic mail to BITNIC. The message should read **get netinfo filelist.**

If the address listserv@bitnic.bitnet fails, try using a BITNET gateway. For example:

```
listserv%bitnic.bitnet@cunyvm.vm.edu
```

or

```
listserv%bitnic.bitnet@mitvma.mit.edu
```

Table 16.1   archie Servers Worldwide

archie.au	University of Melbourne	Australia
archie.univie.ac.at	University of Vienna	Austria
archie.bunyip.com	Bunyip Information Systems, Inc.	Canada
archie.cs.mcgill.ca	McGill University	Canada
archie.uqam.ca	University of Quebec	Canada
archie.funet.fi	Finnish University and Research Network	Finland
archie.univ-rennes1.fr		France
archie.th-darmstadt.de	Technische Hochschule, Darmstadt	Germany
archie.ac.il	Hebrew University, Jerusalem	Israel
archie.unipi.it	University of Pisa	Italy
archie.wide.ad.jp	WIDE Project, Tokyo	Japan
archie.kornet.nm.kr	KORNET	Korea
archie.sogang.ac.kr	Sogang University	Korea
archie.uninett.no	Trondheim	Norway
archie.icm.edu.pl	Warsaw University	Poland
archie.rediris.es	RedIRIS, Madrid	Spain
archie.luth.se	University of Lulea	Sweden
archie.switch.ch	SWITCH, Zurich	Switzerland
archie.ncu.edu.tw	National Central University, Chung-li	Taiwan
archie.doc.ic.ac.uk	Imperial College, London	United Kingdom
archie.hensa.ac.uk	University of Kent at Canterbury	United Kingdom
archie.sura.net	BBN Planet Southeast	USA
archie.internic.net	AT&T InterNIC	USA
archie.rutgers.edu	Rutgers University, NJ	USA
archie.ans.net	Advanced Network & Services; Elmsford, NY	USA

BITNET HELP DOCUMENT

A list of the basic LISTSERV commands.
Access: Send electronic mail to listserv@bitnic.bitnet. Leave subject field blank. The body of the message should read **help.**

Also available through listserv@bitnic.bitnet.

BITNET MANUAL

This includes *The BITNET Guide for the Compleat Idiot,* a manual that will answer many basic questions.
Access: Send electronic mail to BITNIC. The message should read **get bitnet userhelp.**

BITNET USER GUIDE

An introduction to BITNET use.
Access: Send electronic mail to BITNIC. The message should read **get bitnet intro.** Consult the following directory files to help you find mailing lists matching your own interests.

DIRECTORY OF SCHOLARLY ELECTRONIC CONFERENCES

A comprehensive listing of academic conferences divided into categories, with the liberal arts section presented in subsections. Compiled by Diane K. Kovacs.
ftp://ksuvxa.kent.edu/library/acadlist/
Because the directory is maintained in parts, it's advisable to download and read the file ACADLIST README for further information about which parts you need and how to download them.
The extensive listing of mailing lists maintained at SRI International is quite a read, but going through it carefully can alert you to many interesting newsgroups you might not otherwise hear about. So make acquiring the List of Lists an early goal.

LIST OF INTEREST GROUPS

Mammoth listing of mailing lists on the Internet and BITNET. Maintained at SRI International NISC.
ftp://ftp.sri.com/netinfo/interest-groups

PUBLICLY AVAILABLE MAILING LISTS

Compiled by Stephanie da Silva, this useful publication catalogs mailing lists in eight parts. Posted on USENET newsgroups news.lists, news.announce.newusers.
ftp://rtfm.mit.edu/usenet/news.announce.newusers
Files: Publicly_Accessible_Mailing_Lists,_part1
Files: Publicly_Accessible_Mailing_Lists,_part2
etc.

LISTSERV LISTS

Collects all mailing lists available by way of BITNET.
mailto: listserv@bitnic.bitnet. Leave subject field blank. The body of the message should read **list global.**

Campus Wide Information Systems

Campus wide information systems (CWIS) are proliferating, with news of interest to the local university and college communities, and often, gateways into library systems and information attractive to a wider audience. The basic document on these systems is Judy Hallman's *Campus Wide Information Systems*. You can retrieve this list of campus systems and Free-Net bulletin boards worldwide, along with log-in instructions, through anonymous FTP as follows.
ftp://ftp.oit.unc.edu//pub/docs/about-the-net/cwis/cwis-1
Meanwhile, here are some sample CWIS to get you started:

ARIZONA STATE UNIVERSITY PEGASUS AND ASEDD

Contains a directory to university staff and the Arizona State Economic Development Database.
tn3270 asuvm.inre.asu.edu
Login: helloasu

DIXIE COLLEGE WORLDWIDE WEB SERVER

An exceptionally full-featured CWIS containing various information gateways as well as campus information.
http://www.dixie.edu/

HOLY CROSS

Contains campus catalog for Holy Cross, along with its student handbook, campus libraries, a course guide, news and entertainment, athletics, and various directories.
telnet://hcacad.holycross.edu
Login: view
Password: view

MOUNT HOLYOKE COLLEGE CAMPUS INFOSYSTEM

Links to introductory Internet services and directories for the campus.
http://www.mtholyoke.edu/

NORTH CAROLINA STATE UNIVERSITY HAPPENINGS!

Contains the University Infobook, with information broken down by schools and departments. Also faculty and student directories, computing center news, and NCSU library information, as well as a variety of newsletters.
telnet://ccvax1.cc.ncsu.edu
Login: info

OBERLIN ONLINE

A Web server for Oberlin College, with links to its library and campus wide news events. Text-based versions of all menus are also made available.
http://www.oberlin.edu/home.html

PENNSYLVANIA STATE UNIVERSITY

Local information and schedules. Weather forecasts, news of cultural events, campus directories, and student services.
tn3270 psuvm.psu.edu
Login: Enter **EBB** on the COMMAND line.

RADFORD UNIVERSITY WORLD WIDE WEB SERVER

Directories and calendars for campus events and the full course catalog, as well as pages for faculty and staff.
http://www.runet.edu/

RUTGERS UNIVERSITY

Course catalogs, university activities, computer services, on-line library catalog, weather, and news.
telnet//info,rutgers.edu

SUINFO: Syracuse University Campus Information System

A campus system providing catalogs and local news. Other offerings include Educational Resources Information Clearinghouse (ERIC database), as well as archived information from a number of BITNET discussion groups.
telnet://acsnet.syr.edu
Login: Tab to the command line (you'll tab right past the logon and password lines) and enter **suinfo.**

Tennessee Technological University

Campus announcements, registration information, and schedules, with links to the university's other Internet resources.
http://www.tntech.edu/

Tilburg University, Netherlands, Kubgids

On-line public access library catalog, along with a series of databases holding information on computer science, economics, and business.
telnet://kublib.kub.nl
Login: kubgids

University of Minnesota Twin Cities

A CWIS run through a Gopher at the University of Minnesota, with the usual Gopher benefits of access to services like FTP, archie and WAIS. This is where Gopher started. The campus information is available in this format, along with a wide variety of computer-related information.
telnet://consultant.micro.umn.edu
Login: Gopher

University of North Carolina at Chapel Hill, Office of Information Technology Information Center

Included in the campus news here are university newsletters, a campus directory, and material from UNC's Office of Public Information.
telnet://info.acs.unc.edu

University of Pennsylvania—Penninfo

Along with directories and campus calendars, this system contains an abundance of information on computing topics including Internet-related material. Access to library catalogs and articles from campus publications can be found here.
telnet://penninfo.upenn.edu

University of Texas—Houston Medical School

Contains a medical school shareware archive and links to medically related Internet sites.
http://www.med.uth.tmc.edu/

Directories and Guides

AARNET RESOURCE GUIDE

An Australian version of the Internet Resource Guide. Look in this directory for a variety of materials pertaining to the Guide. Available through anonymous FTP:
ftp://aarnet.edu.au/pub/resource-guide/

BIG DUMMY'S GUIDE TO THE INTERNET

A broad overview of Internet topics in HTML format, with access information and tips on the use of the basic services, as well as a useful directory of resources.
http://conx.bu.edu:80/CCS/bdgtti/

THE BTG HOT LIST

A useful breakdown of Internet tools, from search engines to government information and links to computer-related Web sites.
http://www.btg.com/hotdir/btghot.html

CMC STUDIES CENTER

John December has compiled this list of pointers to Internet information. Covers all aspects of computer-mediated communication.
http://www.rpi.edu/;tddecemj/cmc/resources.html

THE COMBINED AAUP JOURNALS CATALOG

Catalogs scholarly journals published by the Association of American University Presses. You can search journals by full text through a WAIS search, or search by title and keywords.
http://aaup.pupress.princeton.edu:70/1/journals/

COMMERCIAL SITES INDEX

A directory of commercial services, products, and information.
http://www.directory.net/

A CRUISE OF THE INTERNET

This is a software program written as a basic tutorial to Internet services.
ftp://nic.merit.edu/resources/cruise.dos/meritcrz.exe
For the Macintosh:
ftp://nic.merit.edu/resources/cruise.mac/merit.cruise2.mac.hqx
This file has information about how to download the complete package.

EFF'S GUIDE TO THE INTERNET

An Internet overview.
ftp://ftp.eff.org/pub/Net-info/EFF_Net_Guide/netguide.eff
Versions of the Guide for various word processors are available in the following directory:
ftp://ftp.eff.org/pub/Net-info/EFF_Net_Guide/Other_versions/

EINET GALAXY

A directory of resources that is categorized by topic and can be searched. Numerous links to sites make this a good place to browse for general information.
http://www.einet.net/galaxy.html

ELECTRIC MYSTIC'S GUIDE

An intriguing and exhaustive compendium of Internet sites with a religious theme. The material is presented in several different files that you can download using the **mget** command.
ftp://pandal.uottawa.ca/pub/religion/electric-mystics-guide*

ELECTRONIC JOURNALS DATABASE

Useful contact information and descriptions for Internet-accessible journals.
http://fiasco.snre.umich.edu/ejournals/ej.out.html

ELECTRONICALLY ACCESSIBLE ZINES

John Labovitz' guide to the active on-line publishing phenomenon known as the zine.
ftp://ftp.netcom.com/pub/john1/zines/e-zine-list

THE FREE ON-LINE DICTIONARY OF COMPUTING

A dictionary of computer and communications-related terms that's ideal for helping you out when all those acronyms begin to get you down.
http://wombat.doc.ic.ac.uk/

FTP SITE LISTINGS

A World Wide Web page with FTP FAQs and listings by site name; includes archie searching.
http://www.ripco.com:70/1s/ftp

A GUIDE TO INTERNET/BITNET

This is a three-part guide, compiled by Dana Noonan, containing listings of on-line library catalogs in the United States as well as abroad, with news about special collections and a tutorial on use.
ftp://vm1.nodak.edu/nnews/GUIDE1.NNEWS, and so on

GUIDE TO NETWORK RESOURCE TOOLS

Overview of the major Internet tools in hypertext format, with links to references for individual tools.
http://www.earn.net/gnrt/notice.html

HYTELNET

Peter Scott's hypertext program for locating Internet resources. Can run as a memory-resident program under MS-DOS; Macintosh and Amiga versions are also available. For the Macintosh version:
ftp://ftp.usask.ca/pub/hytelnet/mac/hytelnet.mac.sea.hqx

For MS-DOS:
ftp://ftp.usask.ca/pub/hytelnet/pc/hyteln65.zip
For the Amiga version:
ftp://ftp.usask.ca/pub/hytelnet/amiga/Ami-HyTelnet.lha
Note: File numbers change as new versions are released.

INFORMATION AVAILABLE ON THE INTERNET: A GUIDE TO SELECTED SOURCES

Compiled by the SURAnet Network Information Center. Lists information sources on the Internet.
ftp://ftp.sura.net/pub/nic/infoguide/chapter.1
This information is made available in the form of various files in this directory. Note: These numbers change as subsequent editions are released.

THE INTERNET COMPANION

Portions of Tracy LaQuey's introductory volume about the Internet are available here.
ftp://ftp.std.com/OBS/The.Internet.Companion/internet.companion

INTERNET RESOURCE GUIDE

A large and extremely quirky index to resources on the Internet, containing listings of a variety of computational resources, library catalogs, archive sites, on-line address books, and networks connecting to the Internet. Dial-up users will find it easiest to retrieve on-line as a single text file totaling almost 600 K.
ftp://ds.internic.net/resource-guide/wholeguide.txt
Be advised: This file contains control characters that make viewing parts of it with a text editor problematical.

THE INTERNET TOOLS SUMMARY

Lists tools available on the Internet that can be used for information gathering and research.
http://www.rpi.edu/Internet/Guides/decemj/itools/top.html

InterNIC DIRECTORY OF DIRECTORIES

A collection of ASCII files of Internet resources listed by topic. A major source for Internet file hunting.
http://ds.internic.net/cgi-bin/tochtml/0intro.dirofdirs/

THE MAASINFO DIRECTORIES

Compiled by Robert E. Maas, MaasInfo.TopIndex is an index to major Internet services (nicknamed the Index of Indexes), while MaasInfo.DocIndex is an index of Internet documents and tutorials. These are among the most helpful directory documents available on the Internet, although the formatting makes them hard to read.
ftp://nic.wisc.edu/userinfo/hints/maasinfo
Files: maasinfo.docindex and maasinfo.topindex

NETLINKS

Particularly useful for novices, this site offers help on network etiquette and resources on everything from mailing lists to USENET newsgroups, along with links to World Wide Web picks of the day.
http://www.interlog.com/;tdcsteele/netlinks.html

NixPub Long Listing Public/Open Access Unix Sites

An annotated list with descriptions and contact information. Posted to USENET groups comp.misc, alt.bbs, alt.bbs.lists.
ftp://pit-manager.mit.edu/pub/usenet/comp.misc./Nixpub_Posting_(Long)
There is also a shorter version in the same directory, with the filename Nixpub_Posting_(Short).

Public Dialup Internet Access List

The useful list of public access service providers maintained by Peter Kaminski. Note: This list contains only sites offering FTP or Telnet services; sites offering news and mail only can be found using the NixPub list posted previously.
ftp://ftp.netcom.com/pub/info-deli/public-access/pdial

Special Internet Connections

A frequently updated list of services available over the Internet. Compiled by Scott A. Yanoff and posted to the USENET newsgroups alt.internet.services, comp.misc, biz.comp.services, alt.bbs.internet, news.answers. Indispensable, especially in its hyper-linked World Wide Web version.
ftp://csd4.csd.uwm.edu/pub/inet.services.txt
http://slacvx.slac.stanford.edu:80/misc/internet-services.html

STING Computing Dictionary

A handy on-line dictionary of computing terms.
http://crl.nmsu.edu/dicts/STINGToc.html

Surfing the Internet: An Introduction

A useful and lighthearted tour of Internet resources. Highly recommended.
ftp://nysernet.org/pub/resources/guides/surfing.2.0.3.txt

Using Networked Information Sources: A Bibliography

Deirdre Stanton's bibliographical guide.
ftp://infolib.murdoch.edu.au/pub/bib/stanton.bib

WAIS Inc. Directory of Servers

WAIS is a powerful information retrieval engine, but you have to have a directory of servers to find the database you need. This site brings a complete directory to the World Wide Web.
http://www.wais.com/newhomepages/surf.html

WEB OF WONDER

Another site offering Internet information by topic; works well in conjunction with the Yahoo service mentioned later.
http://www.digimark.net/wow/

WHOLE INTERNET CATALOG

Based upon *The Whole Internet Catalog* by Ed Krol, this site offers a wide range of resources by topic.
http://gnn.com/gnn/wic/index.html

WORLD WIDE WEB CONSORTIUM

This site contains numerous resources about the Web itself, including a library of resources catalogued by topic.
http://www.w3.org/

YAHOO

An essential guide for using the World Wide Web. This site breaks down Web pages by topic, and is one of the most comprehensive directories on the Internet.
http://www.yahoo.com/

World Wide Web Search Engines

The World Wide Web poses major challenges for information seekers. While its hyper-media format makes moving between different sites a simple matter, it makes directed searching more difficult. Until recently, you couldn't enter a keyword and search Web pages for the term you needed. But that situation has begun to change, as new search engines appear. Using them, you can begin to isolate the particular Web pages that suit your requirements, even though without the precision that is available using pinpoint Boolean search techniques of the kind used in traditional database searching. With tens of thousands of Web pages now available and more coming on-line every day, you'll soon learn to use these search engines to begin your information retrieval process.

INFOSEEK

A powerful search engine that uses keywords or phrases as input. You can check out the following site for information and learn how to open an account; a variety of pricing options are available, and you can receive a free standard membership for the first month.
http://www.infoseek.com:80/Home

JUMPSTATION

Allows you to query a database of document information, with results returned as hyperlinks to the sites. You can search by title, header, and subject.
http://js.stir.ac.uk/jsbin/jsii

LYCOS—THE CATALOG OF THE INTERNET

Searches World Wide Web pages along with FTP and Gopherspace, with weekly updates. This is a superb search engine from Carnegie Mellon University, but it can be

difficult to use because of the demand upon its servers.
http://lycos.cs.cmu.edu/

WEB CRAWLER

Now in the hands of America Online, the Web Crawler allows you to search for Web pages by keyword, returning a number of hits which are user selectable.
http://webcrawler.cs.washington.edu/WebCrawler/WebQuery.html

THE WORLD WIDE WEB WORM

A full-featured search engine that provides keyword and Unix regular expression searches. Allows you to specify limits on the number of hits you want to see.
http://www.cs.colorado.edu/home/mcbryan/WWWWintro.html#instr

A Potpourri of World Wide Web Sites

Perhaps in an earlier edition of this book it would have been possible to provide a representative list of World Wide Web sites. But today, their numbers dwarf the imagination. I'm reduced to presenting a few sites that I've found to be of interest personally, in hopes that they will capture your interest as well. With the World Wide Web, the best initial approach is to examine some of the sites listed in the earlier part of this chapter, sites like Yahoo and Web of Wonder, which offer a breakdown of Web pages by topic. You can then turn your attention to the Web search engines in the previous section to search for specific information. Finally, you can browse among sites you've seen recommended, like those that follow. Perhaps the best way to really get the feel of the Web is to move between such sites when you have a few hours of free time on your hands. Hypermedia means never knowing for sure where you're going to wind up.

BBC HOME PAGE

The home of the world's most respected journalistic entity. Here you can browse through program schedules and pick up loads of information about BBC Television, Radio, and World Service.
http://www.bbcnc.org.uk/worldservice/index.html

BIG DUMMY'S GUIDE TO THE INTERNET

A hyperlinked resource offering an overview of the Internet.
http://conx.bu.edu:80/CCS/bdgtti/

BRANCH MALL

A good example of the shopping mall concept as adapted for cyberspace. Offers links to everything from flower shops to clothing stores.
http://branch.com:1080/

THE BUSINESS OF THE INTERNET

A well-constructed site that examines how business can use the Internet, with plenty of background information for beginners.
http://www.rtd.com/people/rawn/business.html

CHARM NET PERSONAL IP PAGE

A wonderful source of information for anyone interested in learning more about SLIP/PPP.
http://www.charm.net/pip.html

COMMERCIAL COMPUTING MUSEUM

An intriguing site specializing in computing history.
http://granite.sentex.net:80/;tdccmuseum/vwttp.html

COMMERCENET

The home page for one of the biggest experiments in bringing Internet business to the general public.
http://www.commerce.net/

COMPLETE WORKS OF SHAKESPEARE

The Bard's work available through hyperlinks, with useful glossaries and a search capability. An outstanding site.
http://the-tech.mit.edu/Shakespeare/works.html

COMPLETE WRITINGS AND PICTURES OF DANTE GABRIEL ROSETTI

A hypermedia archive that includes on-line text and a beautiful collection of Rosetti's artwork in digital form. If you have a taste for pre-Raphaelite art, this is the place.
http://jefferson.village.virginia.edu/rossetti/rossetti.html

COMPUTER LITERACY BOOKSHOPS HOME PAGE

A fine way to browse an on-line database of books by author and title; you can also look up book reviews.
http://www.clbooks.com/

COMPUTER-MEDIATED COMMUNICATION MAGAZINE

A superb on-line magazine in hypertext format. Explores Internet issues from the standpoint of their impact upon culture and society.
http://sunsite.unc.edu/cmc/mag/current/toc.html

THE CONSUMMATE WINSOCK APPS LIST

If you're a SLIP/PPP user, finding the best shareware and freeware applications can be time-consuming. This excellent page links you to sites from which you can download them.
http://wwwvms.utexas.edu/;tdNeuroses/cwsapps.html

ETEXT ARCHIVE

An archive of electronic texts, broken into categories including on-line magazines, electronic books, political archives and mailing lists.
http://www.etext.org/

GATEWAY TO WORLD HISTORY

Links to sites studying world history. Perhaps the best central site for the collection of historical information.
http://neal.ctstateu.edu/history/world_history/world_history.html

GROWTH OF THE WORLD WIDE WEB

Use this site to keep up with the fast growth of the Web.
http://www.netgen.com/info/growth.html

INTERESTING BUSINESS SITES ON THE WEB

A list of sites that covers business uses of the World Wide Web, broken into types of use.
http://www.rpi.edu/;tdokeefe/business.html

INTERNET GUIDE TO LIVE MUSIC

Concert venue listings, reviews, and tour itineraries for popular artists.
http://underground.net/Wilma/

LABYRINTH

A master collection of materials relating to the Middle Ages. This is an outstanding example of how the Internet can be used to pull together scholarly resources.
http://www.georgetown.edu/labyrinth/labyrinth-home.html

A NAPA VALLEY VIRTUAL VISIT

Exactly what it says it is, this page gives you the chance to tour Napa Valley wineries and take a look at the hotel and restaurant scene.
http://www.freerun.com/

ONLINE NEWSPAPER SERVICES RESOURCE DIRECTORY

A site listing links to newspaper publishers offering online services.
http://marketplace.com/e-papers.list.www/e-papers.home.page.html

PROVIDERS OF COMMERCIAL INTERNET ACCESS

A directory of access providers throughout the world.
http://www2.celestin.com/pocia/

REALAUDIO HOME PAGE

RealAudio is an application that lets you play audio clips without noticeable delay. It should help to spread audio resources, especially in the business context.
http://www.realaudio.com/

SILICON SURF

This page, from Silicon Graphics, features the company's products, including their innovative new Web browser, called WebSpace.
http://www.sgi.com/

Sun Microsystems Hot Java

Keep an eye on this page, which highlights the Sun Microsystems' Hot Java browser. Hot Java offers animation and a more flexible interface for Web pages.
http://java.sun.com/

The Tech Classics Archive

This page has 184 works by 17 classical authors in translation.
http://the-tech.mit.edu:80/Classics/index.html

TidBITS

An excellent on-line magazine of news for Macintosh users.
http://www.dartmouth.edu/pages/TidBITS/TidBITS.html

Time Magazine Home Page

Read the latest news on-line at this excellent site. A model for the distribution of magazine-based information.
http://www.pathfinder.com/time/timehomepage.html

Veggies Unite!

A searchable vegetarian cookbook, with recipes from people all over the Internet. You'll never lack for things to do with zucchini again.
http://www-sc.ucssc.indiana.edu/cgi-bin/recipes/

The Virtual Mirror

A wonderful place to keep up with new sites on the Internet. Includes useful Net news updated weekly, as well as a business directory.
http://mirror.wwa.com/mirror/

Web Museum

Links to outstanding museum exhibits on the Internet. Take a look at the works of Cezanne or roam the streets of Paris.
http://sunsite.unc.edu/louvre/

The Wine Page

Oenophiles will love this page, which contains a tour of Washington State wineries and links to the ever-increasing number of wineries on the Internet.
http://augustus.csscr.washington.edu/personal/bigstar-mosaic/wine.html

WWW Classical Music Resources

Links to all the major Web sites involved with classical music.
http://www.maths.ed.ac.uk/people/anich/music/

ZDNET

A wonderful resource, this site offers links to the range of Ziff-Davis publications, including *PC Week, PC Magazine, PC Computing,* and *MacWeek.*
http://www.ziff.com/

Finger Sites

CROSSWORD INFORMATION

Information about a daily Internet crossword puzzle.
Access: finger xword@acy.digex.net

DATABASES QUERIES

This finger server allows you to search databases. For more information, retrieve the help file as follows.
Access: finger help@dir.su.oz.au

EARTHQUAKE INFORMATION

Information about recent earthquake activity.
Access: finger quake@geophys.washington.edu

ENTERTAINMENT NEWS

An electronic update on show business happenings.
Access: finger adam@mtv.com

EVENTS IN HISTORY

Updates on historical events day by day.
Access: finger copi@oddjob.uchicago.edu

INTERNET DATA BY FINGER

A variety of Internet materials available through finger.
Access: finger help@dir.su.oz.au

MUSIC ON THE CHARTS

The top hits week by week.
Access: finger buckmr@rpi.edu

NASA HEADLINE NEWS

A summary of daily press releases from NASA.
Access: finger nasanews@space.mit.edu

STD HOURLY AURORAL ACTIVITY STATUS REPORT

This is a regular report on auroral activity; reports are made hourly, and watches and warnings are listed.
Access: finger aurora@xi.uleth.ca

SEASONAL HURRICANE FORECASTS

Hurricane data.
Access: finger forecast@typhoon.atmos.colostate.edu

SOFT DRINK UPDATES

An amusing finger application that tells you the status of a soft drink machine.
Access: finger info or graph@drink.csh.rit.edu

STAR TREK QUOTES

Pearls of wisdom from TV's hit science fiction show.
Access: finger franklin@ug.cs.dal.ca

TRIVIA AND MORE

Assorted oddball information.
Access: finger cyndiw@magnus1.com

TV RATINGS

The Nielsens provided through the Internet.
Access: finger normg@halcyon.halcyon.com

WWW FINGERINFO

A World Wide Web page with links to all of the major finger servers. Indispensable for exploring these sites.
http://sundae.triumf.ca/fingerinfo.html

FTP Sites

Here are a handful of interesting sites out of the thousands available on the Internet. Your own list of favorite destinations will grow as you try these and others.

APPLE COMPUTER

Documents and software including System 7.0.
ftp://ftp.apple.com/

CICNET ARCHIVES

Useful directory of electronic serials; also Internet Talk Radio shows.
ftp://ftp.cic.net/

DIGITAL EQUIPMENT CORPORATION

This site houses over 7 GB of programs and information about the Internet and DEC's equipment.
ftp://gatekeeper.dec.com/

ECIX ENERGY AND CLIMATE INFORMATION EXCHANGE

This is the FTP site for the Institute for Global Communications, which hosts EcoNet, PeaceNet, and ConflictNet. You can download files on efficient energy use and environmental issues, with policy statements, newsletters, and other materials on the environment.
ftp://igc.apc.org/

ELECTRONIC FRONTIER FOUNDATION

Useful for back issues of newsletters, articles, and other documents relating to issues of computer security, privacy, and freedom in the information age.
ftp://ftp.eff.org/

EUDORA

Perhaps the best program for accessing Internet e-mail for users with a SLIP/PPP account is available at this site.
ftp://ftp.qualcomm.com/

FREE-NETS

Providing abundant local information as well as links to the broader Internet, Free-Nets are multiplying rapidly. You can access the primary site for Free-Net information at the following URL.
ftp://nptn.org/

GENERAL ACCOUNTING OFFICE REPORTS ARCHIVE

Includes reports (full-text) from the U.S. General Accounting Office. This is a pilot project to determine whether there is sufficient interest to warrant making all GAO reports available over the Internet.
ftp://cu.nih.gov/

THE INTERNET EDGAR DISSEMINATION PROJECT

This new offering allows you to receive any 1995 filings to the Securities and Exchange Commission that are normally available to the public.
ftp://town.hall.org/edgar

THE INTERNET SOCIETY

A primary site for Internet information, including statistics and network maps.
ftp://ftp.isoc.org/

MUSIC ON THE NET: LYRIC AND DISCOGRAPHY ARCHIVE

A compendium of song lyrics and discographies collected at the University of Wisconsin Parkside. Over 225 discographies and 1 thousand songs.
ftp://vacs.uwp.edu/

NASA ARCHIVES

NASA press releases are available here, along with data files and images, plus indices to NASA information. This is a fine source of material about the space program; the collec-

tion of GIF images is remarkable, with images from missions from Voyager to the shuttle. Shuttle mission status reports plus material on Magellan, Galileo, and other projects.
ftp://explorer.arc.nasa.gov/

NATIONAL CENTER FOR SUPERCOMPUTING APPLICATIONS

The home of the NCSA Mosaic program.
ftp://ftp.ncsa.uiuc.edu/

NETSCAPE COMMUNICATIONS CORP.

Here you can find the Netscape browser, which has become a popular tool for accessing the World Wide Web.
ftp://ftp.mcom.com/
ftp://ftp2.mcom.com/

THE OAK REPOSITORY

A service of Oakland University, Rochester, Michigan, this is an Internet site with extensive holdings in PC and Unix software.
ftp://oak.oakland.edu/

OS/2 ARCHIVES

Users of OS/2 will want to know about this one, the largest FTP archive of OS/2 materials.
ftp://ftp-os2.cdrom.com/

OXFORD UNIVERSITY TEXT ARCHIVES

Those interested in electronic text will want to check out this site.
ftp://black.ox.ac.uk/

PROJECT HERMES: U.S. SUPREME COURT OPINIONS

Contains full text of U.S. Supreme Court opinions. Text is available in both ASCII format as well as ATEX, a document processing and typesetting format.
ftp://ftp.cwru.edu/hermes/

PROJECT GUTENBERG

The home site for Project Gutenberg is the place where you can find text files of classic works of literature.
ftp://mrcnext.cso.uiuc.edu/

RIPE NETWORK COORDINATION CENTER ARCHIVE

European users will find this site a major source of Internet information.
ftp://ftp.ripe.net/

STANFORD UNIVERSITY ARCHIVES

The largest collection of Macintosh software available on the Internet.
ftp://sumex-aim.stanford.edu/

SUNSITE

A popular site with abundant software holdings.
ftp://sunsite.unc.edu/

SURANET FTP SERVER

A useful compendium of basic Internet materials, with tutorial information on common procedures and more.
ftp://ftp.sura.net/

UNIVERSITY OF MICHIGAN SOFTWARE ARCHIVES

Collections of public domain, freeware, and shareware. Operating systems include Macintosh, IBM PC, Apple 2, Atari, and NeXT.
ftp://archive.umich.edu/

UNIVERSITY OF VAASA, FINLAND

PC and Macintosh software.
ftp://ftp.uwasa.fi/

USENET ARCHIVES

Whenever you need Frequently Asked Questions documents from one or more newsgroups, you can check out this site, which houses them in a valuable archive.
ftp://rtfm.mit.edu/pub/usenet/

UUNET

One of the major FTP sites for a wide variety of software.
ftp://ftp.uu.net/

WASHINGTON UNIVERSITY PUBLIC DOMAIN ARCHIVES

Huge collection of public domain and shareware software for PCs, Macintoshes, and a wide variety of other hardware. Contains mirrored archive of the SIMTEL20 holdings. A valuable source for software.
ftp://wuarchive.wustl.edu/

THE WORLD

Maintained by Software Tool and Die in Brookline, Massachusetts. Archives from the Online Book Initiative and a wealth of interesting publications.
ftp://ftp.std.com/

Gopher Sites Available Through Telnet

To log on at these Gopher sites, use **gopher** as your login name unless advised otherwise.

Address	Location	Login
ux1.cso.uiuc.edu	University of Illinois at Urbana-Champaign	gopher
panda.uiowa.edu	University of Iowa	
gopher.msu.edu	Michigan State University	gopher
consultant.micro.umn.edu	University of Minnesota	gopher
gopher.ohiolink.edu	Ohio Library and Information Network	gopher
ecosys.drdr.virginia.edu	University of Virginia	gopher
pubinfo.ais.umn.edu	University of Minnesota (Note: access this system with tn3270 rather than Telnet)	
gopher.virginia.edu	University of Virginia	gwis
info.anu.edu.au	Australian National University	info
gopher.puc.cl	Pontificia Universidad Catolica de Chile	gopher
gopher.denet.dk	DENet (Danish research and academic network)	gopher
ecnet.ec	EcuaNet; Corporacion Equatoriana de Informacion (Ecuador)	gopher
gopher.brad.ac.uk	University of Bradford (United Kingdom)	info
gopher.th-darmstadt.de	Technische Hochschule Darmstadt (Germany)	gopher
gopher.ncc.go.jp	National Cancer Center, Tokyo	gopher
gopher.uv.es	Universidad de Valencia (Spain)	gopher

Intriguing Gopher Sites

With the number of Gophers growing all the time, the Internet user is in the delightful position of blundering into new resources on a daily basis. Here are a few interesting sites to get you started. You can reach them by following Gopher menu links to other Gophers or by using a local client. To reach The WELL from a shell account, for example, your command would be **gopher gopher.well.sf.ca.us**.

AMERICAN MUSIC RESOURCE

Collection of bibliographies, lists, and text files about American music and related issues.
gopher://calypso-2.oit.unc.edu/

ASKERIC

Plentiful information from the Educational Resources Information Center, a federally funded information system that catalogs educationally related information.
gopher://ericir.syr.edu/

BBSs AVAILABLE BY TELNET

This is the site if you're trying to reach bulletin board systems available on the Internet.
gopher://gopher.tamu.edu/

CLASSICS FROM THE DURHAM INFORMATION SERVICE

A British Gopher focusing on classics, theology, and medieval history.
gopher://delphi.dur.ac.uk/

COALITION FOR NETWORKED INFORMATION

The Current Cites database along with a variety of other network materials including papers from EDUCOM.
gopher://gopher.cni.org/

DETROIT FREE PRESS

Extensive journalism information and articles on issues relating to newspapers and the electronic media.
gopher://gopher.det-freepress.com/

ELECTRONIC REFERENCE BOOKS

An excellent gathering place for the variety of reference books available on the Internet.
gopher://scilibx.ucsc.edu/

FSU COLLEGE OF BUSINESS GOPHER

Interesting links to business resources all over the Internet.
gopher://cob.fsu.edu/

GLOBAL DEMOCRACY NETWORK

Information on human rights issues and documents worldwide.
gopher://gopher.gdn.org/

GOPHER ON ECOLOGY

A University of Virginia project called EcoGopher, with interesting information on earth sciences and environmental issues.
gopher://ecosys.drdr.virginia.edu/

GOPHER JEWELS

A handy and growing list of interesting Gopher sites is found as part of this CWIS. Look under *Other Gophers and Information Resources/* for this item.
gopher://cwis.usc.edu/

HUMAN GENOME MAPPING PROJECT

Background information and databases related to the attempt to map the human genome. A major site for anyone interested in genetics.
gopher://gopher.hgmp.mrc.ac.uk/

THE INTERNET COMPANY

Text and subscription offers from a variety of magazines in its Internet Newsstand along with material from such resources as Counterpoint Publishing's material from the Federal Register, and Internet pointers collected by author Daniel Dern.
gopher://internet.com/

THE INTERNET WIRETAP

One of the best Gophers for collections of text, with plentiful resources from the classics to the modern age.
gopher://wiretap.spies.com/

LIBRARY RESOURCES ON THE INTERNET

Extensive information on how to search the wide variety of library cataloging systems available through Telnet.
gopher://gopher.uiuc.edu/

MARKET BASE

A catalog of on-line goods and services.
gopher://mb.com/

MATHNEWS

A newspaper related to developments in mathematics.
gopher://descartes.uwaterloo.ca/

USENET NEWS BY GOPHER

A variety of sites offer Gopher-based USENET access.
gopher://info.mcc.ac.uk:4320/
gopher://info-server.lanl.gov:4320/
gopher://aurora.latech.edu/
gopher://gopher.ru.ac.za:4324/
gopher://usage.csd.unsw.oz.au:4320/

U.S. GOVERNMENT GOPHERS

A large collection of links to government materials. This is the place to start if you want to use Gopher to access the federal government.
gopher://peg.cwis.uci.edu/

VOICE OF AMERICA GOPHER

News from the U.S. overseas broadcasting service.
gopher://gopher.voa.gov/

WEATHER INFORMATION

Among a variety of Gophers offering meteorological data, this one includes forecasts and GIF images.
gopher://wx.atmos.uiuc.edu/

WHOLE EARTH LECTRONIC LINK (THE WELL)

Rich collection of documents and links to other services, including articles from the *Whole Earth Review*.
gopher://gopher.well.sf.ca.us/

WiReD Magazine

Anyone following the fortunes of the network will want to check out this Gopher, which is maintained by *WiReD Magazine*. Look for articles from the magazine on-line.
gopher://wired.com/

The World

An on-line service provider whose Gopher contains everything from government information to the Online Book Initiative, with much material for the Internet newcomer.
gopher://world.std.com/

Internet Relay Chat and Other Interactive Sites

Chat: Conversational Hypertext Access Technology

This is a natural language information system using technology developed by Communications Canada. Information is available on AIDS, epilepsy, and the Canadian Department of Communications. There are also two intriguing natural language programs, one called Alice, the other Maur. In the first, you hold a simulated conversation with a student at a university; in the second, you converse with a dragon.
telnet://debra.dgbt.doc.ca:3000

Internet Relay Chat

Here are two IRC sites available by Telnet:
telnet://irc.tuzvo.sk:6668
telnet://ircd.demon.co.uk:6666
Login: irc

Monochrome

A multiuser messaging system. You can log on as a guest, or send an e-mail message to gain full access to the system.
telnet://proton.city.ac.uk
Login: guest

Olohof's BBS

telnet://morra.et.tudelft.nl 2993
Login: guest

Library Catalogs

Computerized library catalogs are becoming more common every day, in the form of On-Line Public Access Catalogs, or OPACs. These systems provide you with the chance to search a given library's holdings free of charge. They do not give access to the books or journals in the catalogs. Here are some directory materials to help you get a handle on on-line library catalogs.

INTERNET-ACCESSIBLE LIBRARY CATALOGS AND DATABASES

This list was compiled by Art St. George and Ron Larsen, and lists over 100 library catalogs available on the Internet. Also contains information on Campus Wide Information Systems and Free-Nets.
ftp://ariel.unm.edu/library/internet.library

UNIVERSITY OF NORTH TEXAS' ACCESSING ON-LINE BIBLIOGRAPHY DATABASES

This is Billy Barron's list of worldwide libraries with on-line access to their catalogs, including log-in instructions and a useful appendix on common library systems.
ftp://ftp.utdallas.edu/pub/staff/billy/libguide
Files: libraries.intro, libraries.africa, libraries.americas, libraries.asia, libraries.australia, libraries.europe, libraries.instructions
A sampling of Internet-accessible library catalogs follows.

BISON: SUNY BUFFALO ONLINE CATALOG

BISON stands for Buffalo Information System Online. The system contains information about holdings of the University Libraries of the University of Buffalo. Provides descriptions, call numbers, and availability.
telnet://bison.cc.buffalo.edu

CARL: COLORADO ALLIANCE OF RESEARCH LIBRARIES

Access to a wide variety of databases. You can search through academic and public library on-line catalogs, current article indices like UnCover and Magazine Index, the Academic American Encyclopedia, the Internet Resource Guide, and more. Gateways to other library systems as well. Access is limited for some items.
telnet://pac.carl.org

CUNYPLUS: CITY UNIVERSITY OF NEW YORK ONLINE CATALOG

An on-line catalog providing holdings of many City University of New York campus libraries. Like BISON, this is a NOTIS catalog, with a standard command set.
Access: tn3270 128.228.1.2
At the command line, enter **dial vtam**. From the VTAM menu, move to CUNYPLUS and press **RETURN**. Enter **lucu** to start CUNYPLUS.

ELIXIR: SUNY BINGHAMTON ONLINE CATALOG

Provides access to holdings of SUNY Binghamton. A NOTIS-based catalog with standard command structure. Access to some features is restricted to users with a valid SUNY Binghamton ID.
Access: tn3270 bingvmb.cc.binghamton.edu
Enter **dial vtam** at the command line, and **elixir** at the vtam menu.

LAUNCHPAD

UNC's on-line service with access to library systems around the world. Although it can be slow, Launchpad's interface is well worth a look.

telnet://launchpad.unc.edu
Login: launch

LAW LIBRARY ON-LINE

Here you can track down legislation from all 50 states, along with a variety of other legal information.
telnet://liberty.uc.wlu.edu or telnet
Login: lawlib

LIBRARY CATALOGS ON-LINE

Software Tool & Die in Brookline, Massachusetts makes available a list of public access library catalogs, along with other library-related information.
ftp://ftp.std.com/obi/Access

LIBRARY OF CONGRESS

The ultimate library database, containing millions of records for books and other publications.
telnet://locis.loc.gov
Note: You can also reach this system by Gopher:
gopher://marvel.loc.gov/

LIBCAT

A handy document summarizing library resources available on the Internet.
ftp://dla.ucop.edu/pub/internet/libcat-guide

MELVYL: CATALOG DIVISION OF LIBRARY AUTOMATION

This is a catalog of monographs and serials held by the nine University of California campuses and affiliated libraries. Represents nearly 11 million holdings in the university system, the California State Library, and the Center for Research Libraries. Also provides access to MEDLINE and Current Contents, and gateways to many other systems. Access to some databases is restricted.
telnet://melvyl.ucop.edu

NYPLNET: NEW YORK PUBLIC LIBRARY ONLINE CATALOG

Offers databases covering New York Public Library branch libraries catalog and metropolitan Inter-Library Cooperative System Regional Catalog, along with the library's Dance Collection Catalog.
telnet://nyplgate.nypl.org
Login: nypl
Password: nypl

OASIS: THE UNIVERSITY OF IOWA LIBRARIES

Contains more than 1 million bibliographic records. Includes all catalogued materials in the main library and 11 departmental libraries published since 1980. Includes Law Library and government materials.

telnet://oasis.uiowa.edu.
Enter **1** at the menu for OASIS access.

OCLC: World's Largest Bibliographic Database

Provides access to more than 22 million books and library materials on the OCLC union catalog, along with other databases, both commercial and noncommercial. Authorization and password are required to use this service.
telnet://epic.prod.oclc.org

Princeton University Online Manuscripts Catalog

More than 56 thousand records, ranging from individual letters of George Washington to collections of material, like the papers of publisher Charles Scribner's Sons.
telnet://pucc.princeton.edu
Login: Press **RETURN**, then enter **folio**.

Purdue University Thor

On-line database of material in the Purdue University Libraries. Contains all serials and books added to the libraries after June 1976.
Access: tn3270 lib.cc.purdue.edu

Victoria University of Wellington Library

Offers the catalog of the university library.
telnet://library.vuw.ac.nz
At the LOGON PLEASE: prompt, enter **OPAC**, followed by a **RETURN**.

Mail Resources

If you're planning to use electronic mail to retrieve files, you should download the following file first:

FTP Mail Servers

Among other things, this file contains a handy list of mail servers, from which you can retrieve files by mail if you lack access to FTP. Compiled by Jonathan Kamens.

```
ftp://rtfm.mit.edu/pub/usenet/news.answers/finding-sources
```

The following is a potpourri of Internet services available through electronic mail. The address given under access information is the address to which you should send the listed command by mail.

Almanac

This information server answers electronic mail requests. Includes USDA market news, reports, newsletters, journals, and articles on agricultural science.
Access: Send e-mail to one of the following addresses, including the message **send guide** in the body of the letter.

almanac@esusda.gov
almanac@oes.orst.edu
almanac@ecn.purdue.edu
almanac@silo.ucdavis.edu
almanac@ces.ncsu.edu

AMATEUR RADIO RELAY LEAGUE

You will be sent information on how to retrieve information on amateur radio operations, including how to get an amateur license, examinations and requirements, the nature of RF radiation, and data on other ham radio FTP sites.
mailto:info@arrl.org
Leave the Subject: field blank and enter **help** in the message field.

BIBLIOGRAPHIC MAILSERVER FOR ARTIFICIAL INTELLIGENCE LITERATURE

A service of the University of Saarbruecken, Germany, this mailserver allows users to retrieve bibliographical information about artificial intelligence publications. You can retrieve further information by sending e-mail to the following address:
mailto:lido@cs.uni-sb.de
Subject: lidosearch info english. Leave the body of the message blank.

CancerNET: THE NATIONAL CANCER INSTITUTE

This is a useful way to keep up with news about cancer using electronic mail. It uses the NCI's Physician Data Query system to make available updates in both English and Spanish. You can also obtain a list of patient publications available from the Office of Cancer Communications.
mailto:cancernet@icicb.nci.nih.gov
Leave the subject field blank. In the body of the message, enter **help** to receive current information. This will get you a CancerNet contents list, which you can use to request specific items of information. These include PDQ State-of-the-Art Treatment Statements (for Physicians), PDQ Patient Information Statements, PDQ Supportive Care Statements, and PDQ Cancer Screening Guidelines.

CAREER CENTERS ONLINE

A resume listing service and jobs database offering search by location and other features.
mailto:occ-info@mail.msen.com
Command: **help**

COMSERVE: THE HUMAN COMMUNICATIONS FORUM

An electronic information service focusing on communications studies. Announcements are periodically distributed in issues of its electronic news bulletin. Maintains indices of articles on communications studies, along with a directory service for users.
mailto: comserve@vm.ecs.rpi.edu
To obtain a description of Comserve commands, send mail with the following command in the message field: **send comserve helpfile**.

DIPLOMACY

A wide variety of Diplomacy games, including variants like Chaos (34 players), Britain (Britain starts with six armies), and Fleet_Rome (Rome begins with a fleet instead of an army), are available for playing through electronic mail. You can learn more about the process by sending e-mail with the single statement **help** in the body of the message to one of the Diplomacy sites.

mailto: judge@morrolan.eff.org

Other possibilities: judge@gu.uwa.edu.au, judge@shrike.und.ac.za, judge-@u.washington.edu.

FAXGATE

A subscription service allowing you to send faxes by computer. You can retrieve further information by electronic mail.

mailto: faxgate@elvis.sovusa.com

In body of message, enter **help**.

FTP BY MAIL

To retrieve files when you don't have FTP capability, use e-mail.

mailto: ftpmail@decwrl.dec.com

Leave the subject field blank. In the body of the letter, enter **help** on the first line, **quit** on the second. This will generate a file with instructions on using the system.

GENBANK

Information on genetics available through a comprehensive database. This service is available through three addresses:

mailto:gene-server@bchs.uh.edu

Other sites: retrieve@ncbi.nlm.nih.gov and blast@ncbi.nlm.nih.gov

Enter **help** in the Subject: field.

NETLIB

Mathematical and other scientific software is available through a gateway machine at Oak Ridge National Laboratory in Oak Ridge, Tennessee.

mailto:netlib@ornl.gov

Leave the subject field blank. In the body of the letter, write **send index**.

OSS-IS

Government documents, FTP lists, Frequently Asked Questions documents, and more.

mailto:info@soaf1.ssa.gov

Command: **send index**

REDUCE

The symbolic algebra system REDUCE is supported by an on-line software library.

mailto:reduce-netlib@rand.org

Leave subject field blank. In message, write **send index**.

STATLIB

This is a system for the distribution of statistical software by electronic mail. A wide variety of datasets and programs is available.
mailto:statlib@lib.stat.cmu.edu
Leave the subject field blank. In the message, write **send index**.

TUGLIB

Software from the TeX User Group. TeX is a powerful text formatter widely used in the computer science community.
mailto:tuglib@science.utah.edu
Leave subject field blank. In the message, write **send index**.

USENET ORACLE

The answer to all your questions is to be found here. By sending mail to the USENET oracle, you can quickly find out what this inscrutable being, distantly related to the oracle at Delphi, thinks about your problems.
mailto:oracle@cs.indiana.edu
Enter **oracle most wise, please tell me** in the subject field. The body of the message should contain only your question. You may be asked to answer a question yourself as a way of thanking the oracle for its help.

WORLD WIDE WEB BY MAIL

A mail service that allows you to receive ASCII text of World Wide Web pages.
mailto:listproc@www0.cern.ch
In the body of your message, put the word **help**.

On-Line Journals and Newsletters

On-line journalism is a rapidly growing field. The first stop in exploring it is to acquire the following directory.

DIRECTORY OF ELECTRONIC JOURNALS AND NEWSLETTERS

Directory containing scholarly lists and electronic newsletter titles. Compiled by Michael Strangelove.
mailto:listserv@acadvml.uottawa.ca

Leave subject field blank. In body of message, write

GET EJOURNL1 DIRECTRY
GET EJOURNL2 DIRECTRY

spelled exactly as shown.
Here are some interesting journals to begin your reading.

ALAWON

This is an on-line journal produced irregularly by the American Library Association. It is available without charge and only accessible in electronic form.
mailto:listserv@uicvm.uic.edu
In the message, enter **subscribe ala-wo *your_name***.

THE AMATEUR COMPUTERIST

A wonderful journal studying the growth of networking and pondering its implications.
ftp://wuarchive.wust1.edu/doc/misc/acn

BLINK MAGAZINE

On-line journals are moving to the Web in great numbers. This one includes both fiction and nonfiction about the on-line world.
http://www.acns.nwu.edu/blink/

COMPUTER-MEDIATED COMMUNICATION

Lengthy and excellent articles about using computers to communicate.
http://www.rpi.edu/;tddecemj/cmc/mag/current/toc.html

CURRENT CITES

Useful citations from various journals concerned with networks and information technology.
ftp://a.cni.org/pub/Current.Cites

DISTED: ONLINE JOURNAL OF DISTANCE EDUCATION

Distance education involves using radio, television, computers, and other techniques to reach wider geographical areas. Can involve anything from grade school classes to post-secondary education and adult education.
mailto:listserv@uwavm.bitnet
Your message should contain the command **sub disted *your name***.

FINEART FORUM

A lively electronic journal tracking the arts.
mailto:fast@garnet.berkeley.edu

INTERPERSONAL COMPUTING AND TECHNOLOGY

Studying the nature of the electronic journal.
mailto:listserv@guvm.bitnet
In the message, enter **subscribe ipct-1 *your_name***.

THE LYNX

Coverage of the Internet with emphasis upon Web issues.
http://www.cityscape.co.uk/lynx

MATRIX NEWS

Particularly strong at tracking network growth, this journal provides interesting reviews and commentary.
mailto:mids@tic.com

PHRACK

A journal specializing in topics of interest to hackers, containing both technical and legal information.
ftp://ftp.uu.net/doc/literary/obi/Phracks

POSTMODERN CULTURE

Literary and cultural studies, with an emphasis on an interdisciplinary approach to contemporary literature, theory, and culture.
http://jefferson.village.virginia.edu/pmc/contents.all.html
mailto:pmc@unity.ncsu.edu
In the message, type **sub pmc** *your_name*.
Or you can use FTP for back issues:
ftp://ftp.ncsu.edu/pub/ncsu/pmc/pmc-list

PSYCHE

A journal discussing the nature of human consciousness, with perspectives from cognitive science, philosophy, psychology, neuroscience, artificial intelligence, and anthropology.
mailto:listserv@nki.bitnet
In the message, enter **subscribe psyche-1** *your_name*.

QUANTA

A journal of fact and opinion, offering articles and fiction.
ftp://ftp.uu.net/doc/literary/obi/Quanta/

VOICES FROM THE NET

A useful and wide-ranging publication covering network developments and key figures.
ftp://ftp.spies.com/Library/Zines

Telnet Resources

The years have not been kind to Telnet. Going through the Telnet-accessible resources for this section, I noticed time and again that administrators were moving them into the World Wide Web environment. In many cases, the Telnet-accessible resource remains but is now in hyperlinked format, accessible through lynx via the Telnet connection. You'll still find interesting sites here, but their numbers are dwindling in favor of the rapidly expanding Web.

Agriculture

ATI-NET

This is the Advanced Technology Information Network, designed to provide information about markets in California. Data on agricultural markets, international exporting, and

the educational community is available here. Includes biotechnology information. Individual systems provide information for the agricultural market, international exporting, and the educational community.
telnet://caticsuf.csufresno.edu
Login: super

CLEMSON UNIVERSITY FORESTRY AND AGRICULTURAL NETWORK

A battery of information on everything from weather to economics, from plants and engineering to home, health, and family. Also includes a section on K-12 education.
telnet://eureka.clemson.edu
Login: PUBLIC

IOWA STATE UNIVERSITY SCHOLAR

Extensive database of documents on agriculture.
telnet://isn.iastate.edu
Login: scholar

Aviation

GTE CONTEL DUAT SYSTEM

Two systems, one for certified pilots, the other for nonpilots. This service gives you access to weather briefings, both local and along the route of flight. It also includes a comprehensive flight planning system that computes a flight log. The planner can produce a route automatically, or it can be given an origin, intermediate points, and destination, producing a shortest-path route. Uses the FAA database of airways, airports, and navigation aids for the continental United States.
telnet://duat.gtefsd.com (pilots only)
telnet://duats.gtefsd.com (nonpilots or pilots)

Business

ECHO

Business databases from the European Commission Host Organization.
telnet://echo.lu
Login: echo

GIGABUCKS

An electronic simulation of stock market activity.
telnet://castor.tat.physik.uni-tuebingen.de
Login: games

IOWA ELECTRONIC MARKET

Looking to learn more about the financial markets? The Iowa Electronic Market allows you to speculate safely. You can set up a trading account and trade a variety of contracts. The Iowa Earnings Market includes portfolios based on the quarterly earnings per share of specific companies. The Iowa Economic Indicators Market works with fluctuations between the Mexican peso and the U.S. dollar. Short sales and margin purchases are not allowed.
telnet://ipsm.biz.uiowa.edu

STOCK MARKET REPORT

a2i Communications offers a free market report in its guest menu; this is a public access Unix provider that also gives you full sign-up information and other particulars here. The stock market news is largely set up to track the communications and computer industries.
telnet://a2i.rahul.net
Login: guest

VIENNA STOCK EXCHANGE

Check the activity at a European exchange.
telnet://fiivs01.tu-graz.ac.at
Login: BOERSE

Communications

IGC: INSTITUTE FOR GLOBAL COMMUNICATIONS

The on-line home for the environmental and peace movements, providing communications services and access to a variety of networked information. IGC is the Institute for Global Communications. It includes PeaceNet, EcoNet, ConflictNet, and HomeoNet. A subscription to PeaceNet provides access to EcoNet and ConflictNet. This service charges a monthly subscription fee.
telnet://igc.org
Login: new. At the password prompt, press **RETURN** to begin the registration process.

WASHINGTON UNIVERSITY WORLD WINDOW

This broad-based site offers you a huge range of network services, from library catalogs, both foreign and domestic, to government libraries, publicly accessible databases, Campus Wide Information Systems, and more. It's a good place to become familiar with as you learn your way around the Internet, suggesting sites for future direct Telnet activity.
telnet://library.wustl.edu

Computer Information

HEWLETT-PACKARD CALCULATOR BBS

HP uses this system to support its calculator customers. A variety of conferences are available for customers, as is a download area.
telnet://hpcvbbs.cv.hp.com
Login: lynx

UNIVERSITY OF NORTH CAROLINA AT CHAPEL HILL BULLETIN BOARD SYSTEM

Electronic mail, software, access to USENET newsgroups, and library catalog searching. Of particular interest is LIBTEL, an information resource access system that allows you to search library catalogs worldwide using an intuitive user interface. The system also taps the Library of Congress catalogs maintained by Data Research Associates. Users likewise can Telnet into a variety of bulletin board systems, and use Gopher, World Wide Web, and HYTELNET.
telnet://bbs.oit.unc.edu
login: bbs

Education

DARTMOUTH DANTE PROJECT

As described in Chapter 10, the Dartmouth Dante Project is particularly exciting for Renaissance scholars. It's a full-text database containing not only Dante's *Divine Comedy* but also centuries worth of commentary. This database is a showcase for what can be done in a variety of disciplines with fast search software and wide access to core materials.
telnet://library.dartmouth.edu
This will take you into the Dartmouth College Library Online System.
At the prompt, enter **connect dante**.

HEALTH SCIENCES LIBRARIES CONSORTIUM

A useful software database containing programs for both PC and Macintosh platforms; specializes in health science issues.
telnet://shrsys.hslc.org
Login: cbl

HERO

The Higher Education Resources and Opportunities database tracks information from the world of higher education, including news of fellowships, grants, and other faculty developments.
telnet://fedix.fie.com
Login: new

NATIONAL DISTANCE LEARNING CENTER

Database specializing in distance learning issues.
telnet://ndlc.occ.uky.edu
Login: ndlc

NATIONAL EDUCATION BULLETIN BOARD SYSTEM

This system is operated by the National Education Supercomputer Program. It's a collection of conferences you can access, including forums on education and colleges, as well as telecommunications and other computing topics.
telnet://nebbs.nersc.gov
Login: new
You'll be prompted for additional information to set up a user identification and password.

NATIONAL REFERRAL CENTER MASTER FILE

A useful listing of sources on numerous technological and scientific topics, frequently updated.
telnet://locis.loc.gov
Password: organizations

Geography

GEOGRAPHY SERVER

Geographic information offered by city or area code. Data comes from the U.S. Geological Survey and the U.S. Postal Service. The database includes all U.S. cities, counties, and states, as well as some U.S. mountains, rivers, lakes, and national parks. Queries should generally look like the last line of a postal address, as in Dunn, NC 28334. This produces information including population, latitude/longitude, elevation, and more.
telnet://martini.eecs.umich.edu:3000

GLOBAL LAND INFORMATION SYSTEM (GLIS)

An interactive source of information useful for earth science and global change studies. Includes geographic coverage maps and other images.
telnet://glis.cr.usgs.gov
Login: guest

Government Information

CAPACCESS—THE NATIONAL CAPITAL AREA PUBLIC ACCESS NETWORK

Legislative, judicial, and executive branch information and forums for discussions about federal programs and services.
telnet://cap.gwu.edu
Login: guest
Password: visitor

FDA: THE FDA ELECTRONIC BULLETIN BOARD

This BBS, provided by the Food and Drug Administration, contains a large repository of information related to the agency's mission. It includes news releases, a drug and device product approvals list, current information on AIDS, an FDA consumer magazine index and selected articles, and an index of FDA news releases. Speeches given by the FDA commissioner and deputy are also available here, as is congressional testimony by FDA officials. An on-line manual for using the system is available.
telnet://fdabbs.fda.gov
Login: bbs
Password: bbs

FEDERAL INFORMATION EXCHANGE

Contains FEDIX, an information system linking federal government agency information with colleges and universities, and MOLIS, the Minority On-line Information Service, with current information about historically black colleges and universities. A wealth of information on federal education and research programs, scholarships, fellowships and grants, as well as news.
telnet://fedix.fie.com

FEDWORLD

A host of information from the federal government, provided through the National Technical Information Service.
telnet://fedworld.gov

IRIS—INTERNAL REVENUE INFORMATION SERVICES

IRS tax forms, instructions, and publications. Over 500 tax forms available for downloading, along with Frequently Asked Questions for both individuals and business.
telnet://fedworld.gov
Choose option 1, IRIS
Login: guest

THOMAS—LEGISLATIVE INFORMATION ON THE INTERNET

Use this Telnet connection to view THOMAS through the lynx browser. THOMAS provides the full text of bills before the U.S. Senate and House of Representatives.
telnet://thomas.loc.gov
Login: thomas

Legal Information

LAWNET: COLUMBIA LAW SCHOOL PUBLIC INFORMATION SERVICE

Provides legal information and access to catalogs. You can search the law school library system called PEGASUS. Other options include the main library catalog at Columbia, as well as textual data on law firms, U.S. courts, and other material.
telnet://lawnet.law.columbia.edu
Login: lawnet

Mathematics

NATIONAL INSTITUTE OF STANDARDS AND TECHNOLOGY COMPUTING AND APPLIED MATHEMATICS LABORATORY

A cross-index of mathematical software in use at this site.
telnet://gams.nist.gov

Medicine

HEALTH SCIENCES TECHNOLOGY ASSESSMENT

Clinical practice guidelines.
telnet://text.nlm.nih.gov
Login: hstat

MEDLINE

A database maintained by the University of Medicine and Dentistry of New Jersey.
telnet://library.umdnj.edu
Login: library

NATIONAL LIBRARY OF MEDICINE

This database service allows you to search the holdings at the NLM, including books and journals.
telnet://locator.nlm.nih.gov
Login: locator

Meteorology

NOAA EARTH SYSTEM DATA DIRECTORY

This is an information resource for identification, location, and overview descriptions of Earth Science Data Sets. Managed by the National Oceanic and Atmospheric Administration.
telnet://nodc.nodc.noaa.gov
Login: NOAADIR

UNIVERSITY OF MICHIGAN WEATHER UNDERGROUND

From the College of Engineering, University of Michigan, a wealth of data. U.S. forecasts and climate data, current weather observations and long-range forecasts, Canadian weather, earthquake reports, and severe weather outlooks, among much else. The system is easy to use and powerful.
telnet://downwind.sprl.umich.edu:3000

Recreation

BACKGAMMON PLAYING

The first Internet backgammon server is surely the harbinger of more interactive sports to come.
telnet://fragge165.mdstud.chalmers.se:4321
Login: guest

CHESS SERVER

This system lets you play chess through the Internet against real-time human opponents. You can maintain a clock, compute player ratings, watch games in progress, choose from a variety of display styles, and talk to other users of the system while you're on-line. A series of help files (enter **help**) walk you through the basic features.
telnet://iris4.metiu.ucsb.edu:5000
Login: *your_name*

Another chess site:
telnet://coot.lcs.mit.edu:5000
Login: *your_name*

GAMES GALORE

A variety of on-line games is available here. A good place to check for MUDs.
telnet://herx1.tat.physik.uni-tuebingen.de
Login: games

GO SERVER

The Oriental game of Go is considered by some to be more challenging than any other board game. Here you can play it interactively with a keyboard.
telnet://igs.nuri.net:6969

HAM RADIO CALLBOOKS

A database of ham radio call-signs established at the University of Buffalo by Devon Bowen, KA2NRC. Enter **help** for information. You can filter searches by call-sign, city, first name, last name, street address, and more.
telnet://callsign.cs.buffalo.edu:2000

Also try:
telnet://ns.risc.net
Login: hamradio

PROFESSIONAL SPORTS SCHEDULES

You can track the schedules of professional teams here, either for a single day or a season. Available sports and their addresses are shown here:

NBA schedules: telnet://culine.colorado.edu 859

NHL schedules: telnet://culine.colorado.edu 860

Baseball schedules: telnet://culine.colorado.edu 862

NFL schedules: telnet://culine.colorado.edu 863

SCRABBLE

Match your wits against other Scrabble enthusiasts.
Access: telnet://next7.cas.muohio.edu:8888

Science

ENVIRONET

Database materials on space-related environment issues.
telnet://envnet.gsfc.nasa.gov
Login: Envnet
Password: Henniker

NASA EXTRAGALACTIC DATABASE

Extensive bibliographies and database material on deep-space astronomy.
telnet://ned.ipac.caltech.edu

NNDC ONLINE DATA SERVICE

Managed by the National Nuclear Data Center at Brookhaven National Laboratory, the NNDC database contains information of interest to scientists involved in physics and related fields.
telnet://bnlnd2.dne.bnl.gov
Login: nndc

NODIS NATIONAL SPACE SCIENCE DATA CENTER

A wealth of space-related data.
telnet://nssdc.gsfc.nasa.gov
Login: nodis

STI INFO

A site that helps you track developments with the Hubble space telescope.
telnet://stinfo.hq.eso.org
Login: stinfo

STIS: SCIENCE AND TECHNOLOGY INFORMATION SYSTEM

Provides a way to search through publications of the National Science Foundation and materials related to its activities. Access to NSF's press releases is one good way to keep up with events of importance to the Internet at large. You'll also find reports from the National Science Board here, along with descriptions of research projects that the NSF is funding. Documents can be searched on-line, and materials can be retrieved either through anonymous FTP or delivered by electronic mail.
telnet://stis.nsf.gov
Login: public

Sociology

LOUIS HARRIS DATA CENTER: THE INSTITUTE FOR RESEARCH IN SOCIAL SCIENCE

A database containing data from the Harris Organization, along with other polling information. Over 750 Harris polls are located here, providing insights into American society. Users can search the text of all Harris Survey questions back to roughly 1960 looking for particular topics.
Access: tn3270 uncvm1.oit.unc.edu
Login: irss1 or irss2
Password: irss

Software

UNIVERSITY OF IOWA

The University of Iowa's FTP archives, accessible via a Telnet connection.
telnet://grind.isca.uiowa.edu

Usenet Resources

ALTERNATIVE NEWSGROUP HIERARCHIES

Descriptions of alternative newsgroup hierarchies, from alt and bionet to clarinet and gnu. Posted on USENET newsgroups news.lists, news.groups, news.announce.newusers. Also available as follows:
ftp://rtfm.mit.edu/pub/usenet/news.announce.newusers/Alternative_Newsgroup_Hierarchies

LIST OF ACTIVE NEWSGROUPS

A key directory of newsgroups maintained by David Lawrence and Mark Moraes; includes short descriptions of each group. Posted to USENET newsgroups news.lists, news.groups, news.announce.newusers.
ftp://rtfm.mit.edu/pub/usenet/news.announce.newusers/List_of_Active_Newsgroups

LIST OF PERIODIC INFORMATIONAL POSTINGS

This is a compilation of Frequently Asked Questions for the USENET newsgroups; it's maintained by Jonathan I. Kamens. The list reflects postings available at the FTP site.
ftp://rtfm.mit.edu/pub/usenet/news.answers/periodic-postings
Files: part1, part2, part3, part4, part5, and so on.

REGIONAL NEWSGROUP HIERARCHIES

Newsgroups that are restricted to local geographical areas. Posted to USENET newsgroups news.lists, news.groups, news.announce.newusers.
ftp://rtfm.mit.edu/pub/usenet/news.announce.newusers/Regional_Newsgroup_Hierarchies

WAIS Databases

The list of WAIS databases here is merely suggestive of the growing WAIS presence on the Internet. I've attempted to give you an idea of the range of material available.

ASTRONOMY

astro-images-gif.src
Sources of astronomical images in GIF format.

BIOLOGY

biology-journal-contents.src
Periodical references to journals on molecular biology.
bionic-databases-limb.src
A list of databases available to molecular biologists.

BUSINESS

agricultural-market-news.src
Agricultural commodity market reports from the U.S. Department of Agriculture.
usda-rrdb.src
U.S. Department of Agriculture economic research

COMPUTER HARDWARE

alt.sys.sun.src
Archived news articles from alt.sys.sun newsgroup.
archie.au-mac-readmes.src
Index of files for the Macintosh archive on archie.au.
archie.au-pc-readmes.src
Index of files for the Amiga archives on archie.au.
ibm.pc.FAQ.src
Information about IBM PC systems.
info-mac.src
An archive of the info.mac discussion forum.
macintosh-news.src

Publications of interest to Macintosh users.
NeXT.FAQ.src
Information about NeXT computer systems.

COMPUTER SCIENCE

cacm.src
Communications of the ACM.
comp.archives.src
An index of articles on software posted to comp.archives.
nren-bill.src
The High Performance Computing Act of 1991.
risks-digest.src
Collection of the RISKS digest, which discusses the risks involved with using computers.

EDUCATION

bit.listserv.cwis-l.src
An archive of Campus Wide Information Systems.
ERIC-archive.src
Material from the Educational Resources Information Center.
kidsnet.src
An archive on computer networking for children and their teachers.

GOPHER

alt.gopher.src
Archive of the alt.gopher newsgroup.

HUMANITIES

anu-socsci-netlore.src
Information about network resources of particular interest to academic researchers in the social sciences, arts, and humanities.
bryn-mawr-classical-review.src
Reviews of books on Latin and Greek classical literature.
humanist.src
Archive of the humanist discussion list maintained at Brown University.
journalism.periodicals.src
The Journalism Periodicals Index.
poetry.src
Complete poems of Shakespeare and Yeats.
proj-gutenberg.src
Documents produced by Project Gutenberg.
roget-thesaurus.src
Roget's Thesaurus, provided by Project Gutenberg.
sf-reviews.src
Science fiction reviews.

LAW

eff-documents.src
Documents from the Electronic Frontier Foundation.
supreme-court.src
U.S. Supreme Court decisions.

LIBRARIES

bit.listserv.pacs-1.src
The archives of the PACS-L list established by the University Libraries and the Information Technology Division of the University of Houston.
current.cites.src
Index of journals on electronic publishing, optical disk technologies, computer networking, and information transfer.
hytelnet.src
Information sources accessible by Telnet
online-libraries-st-george.src
The St. George's directory of libraries and CWIS.

METEOROLOGY

weather.src
Weather information, including surface analysis weather system maps.

MUSIC

lyrics.src
The lyrics for a selection of contemporary music.

NETWORKS

aarnet-resource-guide.src
A copy of the AARNet Resource Guide.
comp.archives.src
Archives of the comp.archives newsgroup.
comp.dcom.fax.src
Archive of comp.dcom.fax newsgroup.
cwis_list.src
Judy Hallman's list of Campus Wide Information Systems (CWIS).
com-priv.src
Discussions about issues related to the commercialization and privatization of the Internet.
comp.risks.src
Archives of the comp.risks newsgroup; useful discussions of computer security.
cs-journal-titles.src
Indexes article titles and authors from some 600 journals, books, and other publications relating to computing.
eff-documents.src
Documents from the Electronic Frontier Foundation.
file-archive-uunet.src
Directory listing of the archive on uunet.uu.net.

internet_info.src
Texts, guides, and information on Internet use and etiquette.
internet-resource guide.src
Guide to using the Internet.
internet-rfcs.src
Internet Request for Comments documents.
internet_services.src
Documents describing services available on the Internet.
internet-user-glossary.src
This server includes basic terms and acronyms you'll encounter around the network.
isoc.src
Documents from the Internet Society.
lists.src
Several master lists of newsgroups, mailing lists, electronic serials, and journals.
matrix_news.src
Material from Matrix News, a network newsletter.
netinfo-docs.src
Files on accessing the Internet and its resources.
news.answers-faqs.src
Contains all Frequently Asked Questions (FAQ) from the USENET newsgroup news. answers.
rfc-index.src
An index of the list of Internet RFCs.
uunet.src
UUNET directory listing of FAQ from all newsgroups.

POLITICS

us-congress-phone-fax.src
Telephone and fax numbers for members of the U.S. Senate and House of Representatives.
us-state-department-travel-advisories.src
The U.S. State Department Consular Information Sheets and Travel Warnings.
world.factbook93.src
The 1993 World Factbook produced by the CIA, with information on countries and cities.

RELIGION

bible.src
King James version of the Bible.
Quran.src
The Koran.

SOFTWARE

cica-win3.src
An index to the Microsoft Windows archive at the Center for Innovative Computing Applications (cica.cica.indiana.edu).
comp.binaries.src
An archive for the comp.binaries newsgroup.
jargon.src

Collection of computer terms.
unix.FAQ.src
Information about Unix.
unix-manual.src
Manual pages for Unix.
wuarchive.src
The directory listing of the software archive at wuarchive.wustl.edu.

WAIS

alt.wais.src
Articles from the alt.wais newsgroup.
cnidr-directory-of-servers.src
A directory of servers operated by CNIDR, The Clearinghouse for Networked Information Discovery and Retrieval.
directory-of-servers.src
Directory of servers at quake.think.com.
unc-directory-of-servers.src
University of North Carolina directory of WAIS servers.
wais-discussion-archives.src
An electronic discussion forum about WAIS.
wais-talk-archives.src
Informal discussions about WAIS.

White Pages Directories

White Pages are directories of users. They usually contain information on e-mail addresses and telephone numbers, as well as postal addresses, and they can be searched.

WHOIS Servers

The following are the basic White Pages options.

INTERNIC DIRECTORY AND DATABASE SERVICES

Directory services using X.500 technology provided through a variety of interfaces by AT&T.
mailto:mailserv@ds.internic.net
In body of message, enter command **help**. This will generate a list of mail server commands. Or, telnet ds.internic.net. This will take you to the InterNIC Directory and Database Services Main Menu. You will be prompted from there to conduct a search for persons or institutions.

Knowbot Information Service

A single query here can search through a variety of sources including the InterNIC database and MCI Mail.
Access: whois -h nri.reston.va.us
telnet://nri.reston.va.us:185

NASA Ames Research Center Electronic Phone Book

This is an electronic directory of NASA employees, searchable by using WHOIS.
Access: whois -h x500.arc.nasa.gov name

Netfind

Allows you to search for people by name and domain.
telnet://bruno.cs.colorado.edu
Log on as netfind.
Or go to one of the following sites:

Server address	Location	Country
archie.au	AARNet, Melbourne	Australia
bruno.cs.colorado.edu	University of Boulder, CO	USA
dino.conicit.ve	Consejo National de Investigaciones Cientificas y Technologicas, Caracas	Venezuela
ds.internic.net	InterNIC Directory and Database Services, South Plainfield, NJ	USA
eis.calstate.edu	California State University, Fullerton, CA	USA
krnic.net	Korea Network Information Center	South Korea
lincoln.technet.sg	Technet Unit, Singapore	Singapore
malloco.ing.puc.cl	Catholic University of Chile, Santiago	Chile
monolith.cc.ic.ac.uk	Imperial College, London	United Kingdom
mudhoney.micro.umn.edu	University of Minnesota, Minneapolis	USA
netfind.ee.mcgill.ca	McGill University, Montreal, Quebec	Canada
netfind.elte.hu	Eotvos Lorand University, Budapest	Hungary
netfind.fnet.fr	Association FNET, Le Kremlin-Bicetre	France
netfind.icm.edu.pl	Warsaw University, Warsaw	Poland
netfind.if.usp.br	University of Sao Paulo, Sao Paulo	Brazil
netfind.mgt.ncu.edu.tw	National Central University	Taiwan
netfind.sjsu.edu	San Jose State University, San Jose, CA	USA
netfind.uni-essen.de	University of Essen	Germany
netfind.vslib.cz	Liberec University of Technology	Czech Republic
nic.uakom.sk	Academy of Sciences, Banska Bystrica	Slovakia

NYSERNet/PSI Online X.500 Directory

A directory of personnel covering some 88 organizations in the United States. Includes name, electronic mail address, postal address, telephone number, and job title. Supports the OSI X.500 directory standard.
telnet://wp.psi.com
Login: fred

PARADISE—The Cosine Directory Service

An experimental X.500 service in the United Kingdom providing information about people and organizations.
telnet://paradise.ulcc.ac.uk
Login: de

WHOIS

Listing of WHOIS servers on the Internet; compiled by Matt Power. Appears on USENET newsgroup info.nets.
ftp://sipb.mit.edu/pub/whois/whois-servers.list

A large number of sites now run WHOIS servers, providing database services about people and associated information.

Access: whois -h site person

where site is the server site, and person is the name of the person you're searching for. You can use WHOIS to access the InterNIC with the **whois -h rs.internic.net** command.

To search for a MILNET address, use **whois -h nic.ddn.mil**.

17

The Future of the Internet

Anyone who has lived through the incredibly short evolution of the personal computer knows how hazardous it is to predict the future. Nonetheless, certain trends seem certain to gather momentum as the Internet grows. Experiments in audio and the transmission of video images point to a bright future for multimedia messaging and the delivery of a new category of product over a medium once relegated to text. The appearance of Internet Talk Radio was a confirmation of this movement, as listeners worldwide gained access to a half-hour show on the Internet delivered via binary data. More recently, we have seen client programs like CuSeeMe (video conferencing from the desktop) and Internet RealAudio (fast exchange of large audio materials) redefining how we will use the Internet. Clearly, tomorrow's network will encompass a much broader range of data types than could have been imagined even a few years ago.

Moving from technology to politics and economics, we're also witnessing the transformation of the Internet from a research-based, government-supported institution into a commercial medium. It is unclear whether the idea of the Internet itself has undergone a fundamental change, but the evidence mounts that as we build tomorrow's so-called information highway, we will be leaving behind the cooperative research model and moving toward something that resembles cable television as much as it does interactive computing. On that front, the ending of the NSFNET's role as primary Internet backbone in the United States places control over the network there, as much as can be determined, in the hands of the long-distance telephone carriers. All of which raises compelling questions about the role of government in the information age, its ability to regulate the new medium in the same way it once did the evolving telephone industry, and the question of who will have the opportunity to use the emerging new resources.

Part of the access question has already been answered. The surge in modem users has fundamentally changed the Internet's demographics. A few years ago, getting connected to the Net meant working for an organization whose own network was already connected. That usually meant a school, or a research laboratory, or a government organization, and it always meant one network tying into a larger network, which is, after all, where the word Internet comes from.

Today, we have moved into the era of the individual user. As we've seen, getting an individual account on the Internet is easier than it has ever been, because a new class of service provider has entered the market. This is a trend that continues to accelerate, and as it does, the Internet will become well-nigh ubiquitous. Network visionaries speak of Internet connections becoming as common as telephone jacks; buy a new home and your Internet hookup is already wired in. This seems fanciful at present, but the enfranchisement of the individual user is a step in this direction, and powerful demand may well validate the concept over the course of the coming decade.

How, then, do we avoid creating a kind of class war based upon information access? For if the wealthier segments of our society have access to an information highway whose use requires expensive equipment and sophisticated software, what of the poor? Can we ensure that the Internet is as widely distributed and as fairly administered as the telephone system? And should we insist that full Internet capabilities be provided by every public library, using the same model of information distribution that compels us to educate our citizens through tax-supported revenues? If so, where does the money come from?

You can see that we are on the edge of a great public debate, not only in the United States but worldwide, about not just the ability to reach the Internet, but about the intrinsic value of the Internet as well. The Net carries information in a free, almost anarchical way, a fact that is increasingly seen as a source of problems. Should it be as easy for our children to download pornographic photographs as it is to access the Oresteia? Do we want them to be reading Nazi propaganda with the same ease that they read the latest news from an on-line newspaper? And if government intervenes in the process, will the outcome be for the better or for the worse?

The Internet's technological evolution, then, has far outstripped the laws—and the values—that it challenges. We find ourselves in the uncomfortable position of examining a fait accompli, one with wonderful possibilities for education and research, and certainly with implications for how we conduct commerce, yet one that makes local communities suddenly global, with all the trauma that transformation suggests. The Internet goes right over the heads of any attempts to impose local censorship or regulation. The challenge of the coming years will be to determine whether it can continue to organize itself for the good, or whether it will fall prey to the worst instincts of the fast-buck artists, the fanatics, and the bureaucrats.

Internet Audio

Not that technology will stand still while political and economic realities sort themselves out. In fact, the Internet has always been characterized by a frenetic pace of change, its growth driven by hardware and software developments that pushed it into new terrain. Chief among these today are new capabilities in sight and sound that move us dramatically away from the old, text-dominated model of the network in the 1980s. We've already seen that the World Wide Web has caught this wave, employing graphics, audio and moving video to change the way we view information. A number of other projects are equally intriguing, even if they lack the Web's ubiquity.

Consider audio itself. If a "message" can contain nested audio and video submaterials, we are beginning to redefine what we mean by the term. A similar refocusing is changing our understanding of the term "publication." Traditionally, of course, publishing meant using a printing press to produce what we computer types call hard copy.

Electronic publishing changed the rules by making journals and other textual information available on demand through computer networking.

Now an exciting technology known as *multicasting* is bringing the potential for sight and sound to the average workstation. It was inevitable, then, that a consumer-oriented medium would develop, utilizing audio over the network; it stretches our definition of the term "radio." Internet Talk Radio was the first such service, an information provider in radio magazine format, sort of an "All Things Considered" for Internet consumption.

The brain child of author and Internet world traveler Carl Malamud[1], Internet Talk Radio's shows are distributed on the network itself in the form of massive audio files—roughly 30 MB per hour of programming—professionally produced and transported worldwide. The talk is technical, though Malamud aims to work on topics you won't find in the standard trade press. This is an insider's view of the Internet, one that includes such features as "Geek of the Week," in which prominent network figures are interviewed. Although saved in a Sun Microsystems audio format, the show can be translated by utility programs for listening on a Macintosh or a PC.

Internet Talk Radio is run from Malamud's Internet Multicasting Service in Washington, which also includes a second "channel" of broadcast information called Internet Town Hall. You can see the Internet Town Hall home page in Figure 17.1

Internet Town Hall is something of a public affairs outlet, with broadcasts from the National Press Club that have included a number of prominent speakers, including

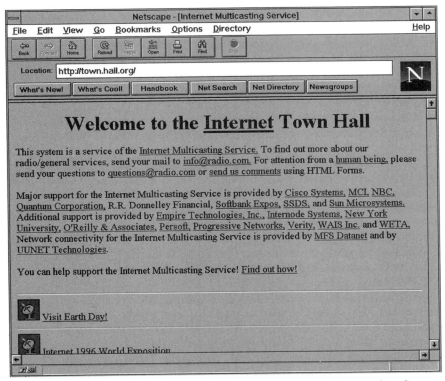

Figure 17.1   Internet Town Hall blends computer-driven interactivity with audio programming, in a fascinating experiment in crossing the lines of media.

What You Need: Background Materials on Internet Talk Radio

Where to Get Them: Through anonymous FTP. Try the following URL:

ftp://sunsite.unc.edu/pub/talk-radio/

You can also pick up the Internet Talk Radio FAQ at this site:

ftp://rtfm.mit.edu/pub/usenet/news.answers/internet-talk-radio/

Finally, you'll want to examine the Web page:

http://town.hall.org/

Vice President Al Gore. Internet Multicasting Service also rebroadcasts in digital format a number of radio shows and the audio portion of the television show "Computer Chronicles."

What else might you find on Internet Talk Radio? Malamud speaks of travel information and restaurant reviews as one possibility, with additional features on mailing lists and books, as well as coverage of key industry functions. Internet Talk Radio could develop into a useful and diverting information forum if its current plans to summarize technical topics go through. Beyond that, ITR offers the promise of a new medium, one that borrows the best of its chosen metaphor—radio—and brings to it the flexibility of computer processing and distribution. As the first attempt to bring regular organized news and information by means of audio into the computer information flow, Malamud's effort will be something to track carefully.

If Internet Talk Radio demonstrates that the Internet can carry sound as readily as text, so does the increasing inclusion of audio files on World Wide Web sites around the world.

The key issue is size, which raises a question unlikely to be resolved any time soon: Is the movement of massive audio files over the network a brainstorm or simply a colossal waste of bandwidth, considering that a text file of the half-hour show's proceedings could convey the same information in a package that seems, by comparison, minute? If you're intrigued by such issues, you may want to listen in to the discussion on alt.internet.talk-radio, a USENET newsgroup that has sprung up around the new offering.

The biggest problem about Internet audio is simply the amount of time it takes for audio to be downloaded to your computer; this is true whether you're running a SLIP/PPP connection or working through a shell account. Thus the announcement that Progressive Networks, a Seattle-based communications company, had produced a program called RealAudio caused considerable excitement on the Net. RealAudio allows large audio files to be played over the Internet without the lengthy time lags; the effect is similar to using a cassette recorder, although the equipment required is a desktop PC and a voice-grade telephone line. You can see the RealAudio home page in Figure 17.2. You can learn more about ReadAudio at this site:

http://www.prognet.com/

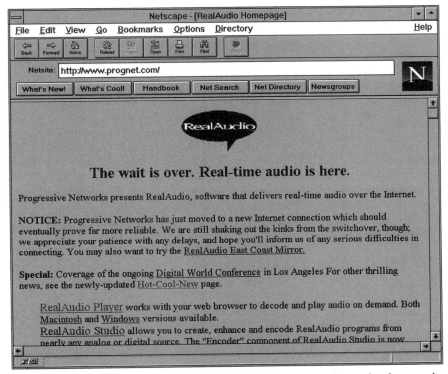

Figure 17.2 The RealAudio home page, featuring a product that makes large-scale audio possible over an Internet connection.

And while you're examining Internet audio, be sure to check out the Internet Phone program. This one is a different take on pumping sound over the Net; you can carry on two-way conversations with anyone likewise equipped with the Internet Phone software, provided you have a Windows-compatible audio board. The system voice uses compression to move your words with a minimum of delay over the network. The software can be evaluated for free; try this URL:

```
ftp://ftp.vocaltec.com
```

Enter **ftp** as your user name. You can find out more about VocalTec Inc. and its unique product at its Web site:

```
http://www.vocaltec.com/fdx.htm
```

IP Multicasting—The Internet by Sight and Sound

Attendees at the Internet Engineering Task Force's meeting in Boston in July 1992 weren't the only ones who could follow the proceedings. Ninety-five workstations in 10 countries, from Australia to Canada to Japan, the United Kingdom, and the United States, received live audio from the site, using built-in audio hardware and special software; an additional 75 workstations received slow-frame-rate video, which was displayed after decompression at each machine. IETF's November 1992 meeting in Washington, DC saw a similar demonstration of the Internet's ability to move real-time audio and video to a geographically dispersed audience.[2]

While it may raise eyebrows at first, the idea of transporting such signals over a network makes sense. If you can digitize a message or a still image, you can also digitize a voice or a video clip of someone delivering a speech. And while the participants in these IETF experiments share a common enthusiasm, they also agree that a significant number of resource management issues must be addressed before real-time Internet audio and video will become commonplace. Not all routers carrying Internet traffic, for example, can support audio and video multicasting, making it necessary for Steve Casner and Steve Deering—the Internet's audio/video team—to construct what Casner called "a virtual multicast network of tunnels layered on top of the physical backbone and regional networks."[3] Multicasting, then, has given rise to a new backbone—the MBONE, for Multicast Backbone—which will serve as a testbed for continued audio and video experimentation.

Because of the high bandwidth demands of these projects, the MBONE functions almost like an old-fashioned telephone tree.[4] Multicast technology configures network routers so they know about the special communications channels for this traffic. When someone on that communications channel sends a packet to a multicast address, the routers that are part of the multicast "tree" copy the packets to the appropriate routers further down the tree, or to the ultimate hosts as the case may be. Traffic is delivered only as necessary.

Why the term "multicast?" A *broadcast* is sent out to everyone; a *unicast* goes from one point to another. A multicast, by logical extension, is the movement of information from point to multipoint, traveling only to specified destinations on the Internet. Video thus far is slow, some two to six frames per second. "It's a bit like watching a movie from 1910," comments Vinton Cerf. "But that's partly a function of available bandwidth. There's a lot of compression going to get this to work."[5]

What's ahead for the Internet as the multicast idea begins to solidify? One obvious development, according to Cerf, is the likelihood of services charging fees depending on the type and quantity of their traffic. It's one thing to route text data in ASCII files across the Internet. But what happens when particular sites need to consume vastly higher

What You Need: The Technical Details on Multicasting

The Document: Frequently Asked Questions on the Multicast Backbone (MBONE)

How to Get It: You can retrieve the text file from this URL:

ftp://isi.edu/mbone/faq.txt

And an HTML version of the same file is available at the following site:

http://www.eit.com/techinfo/mbone/mbone.faq.html

amounts of bandwidth as part of their activities? Distinctions between the kind of data moved and the cost of moving it are bound to become sharper in coming years.

Right now you need a sophisticated workstation to receive these transmissions—Casner and company have been working with Sun SPARCstations and Silicon Graphics Indigo machines, and it's clear that these cutting edge technologies will remain experimental for some time to come. But if you're intrigued by the possibility of audio and video over a networked computer, you may want to read the technical details in a document Steve Casner has developed. It's available by anonymous FTP.

Nothing encapsulates the popular idea of future Internet use more than projects like this; we imagine sitting in front of our terminals engaging in effortless voice conferencing, or connecting to friends and relatives overseas. And there is no question that the convergence of telephony and digital communications of all kinds will make many of these applications easy to use. But work must be done between now and then to ensure broadened data paths that can carry the high volume of traffic thus generated. Internet technology and software development is forging well ahead of the current capabilities of the system, especially as it labors under the intense load created by millions of new users. Groundbreaking applications like IP multicasting point not only to future utilities, but also to the limitations of the system we currently work with.

Browsing in the Third Dimension

You can see that the trend captivating developers today is realism. We are moving away from the text-based model into a network world in which objects look like they do in real life, and the senses of sight and sound can be stimulated in a format that approximates what we see every day, rather than what we learned in a computer science course. If the World Wide Web has been a major part of this sea change, it is to the Web that canny developers look as they contemplate the next step in the logical progression toward on-line verisimilitude. It is the advent of the so-called three-dimensional browser, the network tool that lets you navigate through a custom-tailored world, working with the scenes that the home page designer has chosen.

In this view, even the relatively straightforward World Wide Web interface is restrictive. It forces us to look for underlined text that indicates the presence of hyperlinks. It sets up pages in static fashion, so that what we see is an endless round of magazine-style articles with clickable images and sounds. The new Web browsers are designed to bring virtual reality techniques to the desktop. Their producers, companies like Sun Microsystems and Silicon Graphics, are convinced that adding greater realism and graphic punch to the Internet will propel its use to still further heights. They will make the already interactive medium livelier, more colorful, and full of surprises.

Take Sun Microsystems' HotJava browser. The Java programming language allows developers to include small programs (Sun calls them "applets") in the graphics presented on a particular Web page. This means that, instead of downloading separate programs to run various functions, the user can take advantage of whatever effects are embedded in the Web page immediately. The result should be greater interactivity. By including applets intended to show off the particular page to the best effects, its designers will be able to rotate images in three dimensions, make calculations on the screen, manipulate data on the fly. Enthusiasts sketch a future in which Web pages can be used by companies to conduct one-on-one sales sessions; you log on to a site and interact with a virtual clerk to buy what you need, or make your way through a 3-D on-line catalog.

Some 20 companies are now working on browsers that, in one way or another, exploit the potential of virtual reality. Soon we may be using the Web to walk through virtual landscapes, manipulate artificial environments, and take journeys through imaginary worlds. All of which is exciting news, providing that equipment requirements don't bar a majority of users from taking advantages of these features. Full graphical access to the World Wide Web even as it is today is by no means a given; in many areas of the world, Internet access is through a shell account only. Such users will not be able to benefit from browsers that require full Internet packet exchange to function. Nor can we assume that every user will have the sophisticated workstation, or even the 486-class computer with large amounts of memory, needed to run the new-generation tools. Whether they become curiosities or breakthrough applications in tomorrow's network depends less, then, upon their capabilities than it does upon the status of the Internet at large. Bandwidth is a key, as is sheer processing power.

If you're interested in following the fortunes of the latest browsers, try these URLs:

http://www.hyperion.com/intervista/

http://www.sgi.com/

http://www.ub.com/

http://java.sun.com/

Commerce Takes to the Data Packets

All of this represents quite a change for the Internet. The image of a sober, almost staid research network buzzing with arcane discussions for a highly select audience is giving way. It began almost imperceptibly, with changes around the edge of things. The cartoon character Dilbert appeared one day being "sucked into cyberspace" in one of the newspaper strip's more colorful episodes. At the end of the cartoon, readers found a message from the artist: "Internet ID:scottadams@aol.com." Soon other media were sprouting Internet IDs. National Public Radio began advertising an Internet address, making it easy for listeners to comment on its programming. Newspaper ads from computer manufacturers listed Internet addresses for further information. And, in perhaps the defining move of the commercial revolution, business cards increasingly featured phone, fax, and Internet address. Of all things, the Net had begun to acquire a cachet—what serious businessperson could afford to be without a mailbox on the Net?

As early as 1993, the *Palo Alto Weekly* began carrying advertisements for the Alain Pinel Realty Company of Saratoga, California. The ads featured photographs of each of the 35 realtors who worked for the agency. Under each picture was an Internet address. Other companies quickly followed suit. After all, the great bulk of the Internet consists of local area networks (LANs) inside larger companies. The restriction on commercial traffic once embodied by the National Science Foundation's Acceptable Use Policy disappeared with the removal of the NSFNET's functions. Anyone hoping to move commercial materials over the Internet today can do so, although a sensible awareness and adherence to Internet traditions continues to be a prerequisite.

The Internet's demographics are relentlessly changing. While 50 percent of connected hosts are governmental or academic in nature, fully 9 out of 10 new connections go to commercial sites. Want to order a book on-line? You can do so on the Internet, through the Online Bookstore at Software Tool & Die. Want to cut publishing costs and make life easier on editors? Addison-Wesley already uses the Internet to receive book proposals and perform basic copy editing chores, while publishers like John Wiley & Sons have established presences on the World Wide Web, offering catalog browsing, excerpts from books, and background information on authors. A number of large corporations, including General Motors and General Electric Co., are using the Internet to aid in corporate research, not to mention benefiting from electronic mail communications. Apple Computer has even made its System 7 operating system available by anonymous FTP from apple.com.

"By June of 1991," says Vinton Cerf, a key figure in the development of the original TCP/IP protocols, "50 percent of all registered hosts on the system were commercial. That's an important metric; commercial use is the Internet's fastest growing component."[6]

But surely it is the World Wide Web that has proven the most congenial home for business. The combination of typeset quality formatting along with graphics and linkages to resources like sound and moving video has proven irresistible to marketers. We've begun to see small to medium-size business embracing the Internet, with operations as diverse as flower shops, pizza delivery services, and CD stores now going online. Also noteworthy is the appearance of the network shopping center, in which numerous stores take up on-line positions under the umbrella of a central provider. Take a look at Figure 17.3, where you can see how one such operation supports its vendors.

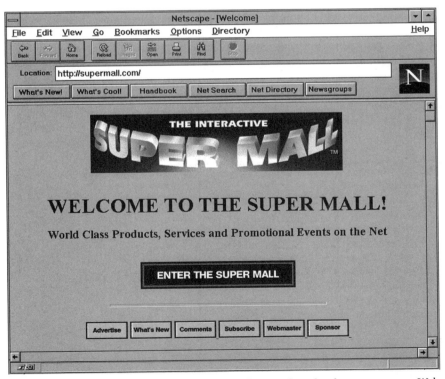

Figure 17.3 An interactive mall like this one offers vendors the chance to operate Web sites under the "roof" of a single provider.

The confluence between government and private industry will be interesting to watch as plans for furthering the Clinton administration's National Information Infrastructure continue to unfold. Consider what is happening in Silicon Valley a harbinger of things to come. Smart Valley Inc., a nonprofit consortium, and Enterprise Integration Technologies, a local consulting firm, have received a $4 million boost from the federal government, along with matching funds from the state of California. The aim: to build CommerceNet, a low-cost, high-speed Internet access provider.

With backing from Apple Computer, Hewlett-Packard, Lockheed Corp., Pacific Bell, National Semiconductor Corp., and Sun Microsystems, the project has clearly caught the attention of business. CommerceNet, like many other Internet newcomers, will likely serve as a testbed for advanced network concepts, including the introduction of multimedia into a variety of on-line offerings for both home and business. Just how we manage the necessary tweaking between government and industry is an issue that continues to preoccupy those concerned with the future of the network. But for now, CommerceNet is up and running. You can see its home page in Figure 17.4.

What the Internet has always lacked is security; in fact, the idea of sending mission-critical data through its matrix is one that still brings shudders to many system administrators. But there has been significant movement on this score. Faced with an expanding market, companies like Netscape Communications Corp. and Spyglass Inc. have developed secure servers to make it possible for consumers to transmit information

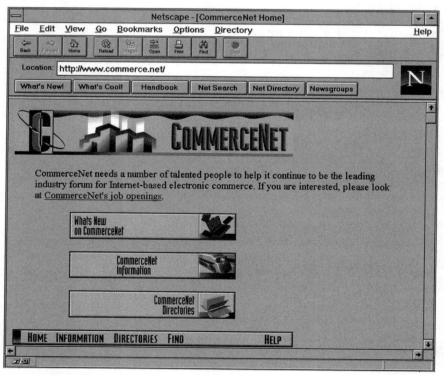

Figure 17.4 The home page for CommerceNet.

like credit card numbers over the network. We've also seen a number of transaction methods being explored by various firms anxious to take advantage of the Internet business rush. DigiCash is an Amsterdam-based company that uses encryption to verify the identity of a purchaser, with fund verification for every purchase. Other companies working in this field include Cybercash, First Virtual Holdings, NetCash, and OpenMarket. If you're interested in this area, you may want to check the following URLs:

http://digicash.support.nl/publish/digibro.html

http://www.openmarket.com/

http://www.fv.com/

Corporations large and small are experimenting with everything from electronic mail as a replacement to courier services to archival sites available through FTP for their remote offices. The Internet is being used by some as a wide area network, connecting corporate sites in various countries; for others, it becomes the enabling device for the establishment of the "virtual corporation"—the company that is basically a cluster of communicating, independent freelancers.

Here in North Carolina, three telephone companies—Southern Bell, GTE, and Carolina Telephone—are building the North Carolina Information Highway (NCIH). The first tenant of the NCIH will be the state, which has sunk some $4.4 million into the technology to network the first 104 sites statewide. Moving out of an initial grid of medical centers and schools, the state intends to reach some 3,300 locations by the end of the decade, linking government offices, the prison system, and more. And while government will be the anchor tenant of the NCIH, the telephone companies plan to tariff services for a wide variety of business users.

With video applications on demand and the capability of moving massive amounts of data over a newly installed fiber network, the NCIH attracts business interest because of its undeniable potential. Corporations can benefit through remote training, workgroup collaboration, data sharing, and a host of other capabilities whose impact won't be felt until they can be tested in the field. The Internet is not an information highway in this sense, but surely it is interest in exploring network possibilities that has driven so many firms into acquiring their own network addresses.

And it is likewise undeniable that today's services—electronic mail foremost among them—are in active use today. Consider Industry.Net. It's a network of over 100 thousand buyers and specifiers, working with 3 thousand manufacturers who are anxious to promote their products. By providing product information, e-mail to each participating company, access to publications, and news briefs to its members, Industry.Net gathers the resources many professionals need, and places them in a readily accessible on-line site (http://www.industry.net). Over 250 thousand product descriptions and photographs are available in its database, with downloadable software, catalogs, and brochures likewise offered on-line, and 30 thousand new files added each month. Sites like these reveal a business picture that includes widely dispersed productivity-enhancing tools and lower costs in terms of transportation and telephone bills.

Meanwhile, a new breed of entrepreneur has taken to the data paths. Joel Maloff runs The Maloff Company in Dexter, Michigan. Maloff, a former vice president at Advanced Network & Services, provides seminars nationwide at which interested businesspeople can learn more about the Internet (jmaloff@aol.com). He is joined by other active promoters of the network, including Rob Hertzberg, who edits the *Internet Business Report*, a monthly out of Manhasset, New York, which targets the intersection of networking and commerce (rob@ost.com). In Washington DC, Jayne Levin's *The Internet Letter* covers network developments with a keen eye on political and social implications (netweek@access.digex.net). And ponder the fortunes of *Internet World*, which has grown into a full-color glossy monthly out of its origins as a small, quietly circulated newsletter (meckler@jvnc.net).

Corporations Jockey for Position

Any sufficiently powerful technology will remap the business world, as companies move to exploit the possibilities of the new medium. Certainly the telecommunications arena has already witnessed a sea change, as we've broadened the connection between computers and telephones to include the transmission of all forms of digital data, and not just the human voice. The battles being fought today, as companies merge or attempt to merge (always with an eye toward the reaction of federal regulators) will certainly shape the data highway to come. It is likely that working out the ramifications of the Internet's networking technology may take a generation.

Telecommunications is a $1 trillion industry in today's terms, one that is growing so fast that projecting revenues even a decade away is all but impossible. The explosion of new businesses is being motivated by advances in fiber optics and wireless communications, all driven by the need to find better ways to move information into home and business. The players: the telephone companies, both the long-distance giants and the Baby Bells, as well as smaller local firms, the cable television companies, and, increasingly, the entertainment industry. Not content to be merely carriers of information, the new telecommunications model calls for the inclusion of content into the mix. We will all want something worthwhile to watch if we're to receive 500 television channels, and there had better be plenty of serious destinations for research and education if the information highway is to succeed.

The problem with the information highway as it is currently being sold is that many futurists fail to factor in basic truths about human nature. Given the interactive nature of the Internet and the capabilities of today's—not to mention tomorrow's—entertainment systems, we have to recognize that the television model is not sufficient to describe what we are building. Rather than being passive consumers of information, the digital citizen wants to be plugged into a responsive electronic world, one that can be used to perform everything from making selections about which movie to watch to participating in educational events for business and personal growth. The interactive medium is one in which the home and business user is empowered to make choices about generating such content. What a challenge this represents to content providers of all stripes, who have enough trouble filling the limited cable capacity of today's televisions with anything worth watching.

A sense of unease is settling in, as companies work to strengthen their hand in this new, high-stakes poker game, all the while wondering just how it will turn out. What are the names of the people who dominate the digital headlines? Ted Turner, the founder of CNN. Rupert Murdoch, chairman of The News Corporation, as well as owner of the Fox broadcasting network and Delphi Internet Services. Steven Spielberg, not because he has created compulsively watchable science fiction films, but because he and his company, DreamWorks, are making deals that affect the digital delivery of tomorrow's entertainment. Bill Gates, Microsoft's ubiquitous chairman, who is driving the industry toward integrated networking by incorporating Internet access into the Windows operating system.

Everywhere, the word is convergence. You find book publishers incorporating CD-ROMs as additions to their bound titles, and bringing out digital, multimedia versions of material that would previously have appeared solely in print. We've seen that newspapers have moved dramatically into the new medium, taking up positions on the World Wide Web even before it has become clear that such offerings will be profit-makers. Time Warner offers *Time Magazine* on-line in spectacular, searchable form. And deals galore have appeared, some that will disappear in the wake of federal intervention, or the threat of same. The $10 billion merger between Viacom and Paramount Communications was a pattern for the corporate mega-merger. Rupert Murdoch sold a major stake in his News Corporation to MCI Communications, yet another bridge between carrier and content, while the unconsummated affair between Bell Atlantic and Tele-Communications Inc. reminded us that we still have a Federal Communications Commission, and that its reach, like that of the rest of the federal government, can be a long one.

Meanwhile, the video-on-demand business is in field trial status, as cable and telephone companies explore the possibilities. This is happening even as Washington seems to be easing the regulatory barriers that have kept cable operators and telephone companies from competing with each other. The new environment thus generated will be one in which companies will slug it out over who gets content to its final destination the most efficiently. The name of this game is bandwidth. With coaxial connections already present in many homes via cable television, the possibility of using this data path for digital delivery is seemingly irresistible. The reverse scenario—allowing telephone companies to provide video-on-demand services over their lines—is likewise compelling. We can expect an era of increased experimentation and a multitude of false starts. But that is how any technology resolves its core issues.

Does the digital future mean an expanded and greatly more powerful television set for your home? Or do we funnel the incoming data to a new generation of PCs, now grown powerful enough to form the nucleus of the so-called home entertainment center? No one knows. Indeed, the question of just how the technology will be implemented is a defining one; more than a few fortunes will be lost, and won, on the outcome. But as the demise of NSFNET reminds us, the future of the Internet is now very much in the hands of commercial companies whose decisions will affect the entire economy. Key questions of access—how much does it cost to use the new services, and where are they available—will preoccupy us for years to come. There is no point in building a data highway if it is too expensive for any but the technological elite. For that matter, there is little point in building a data highway that is so heavily weighted toward entertainment that the possibilities of on-line education are lost beneath a new generation of digital sitcoms. Key to this debate will be the continuing controversy over the role of the federal government as an instrument of regulatory power in a time of frenetic business growth.

The Rise of the Telecommuter

But mega-mergers, while making for spectacular reading in the financial press, ultimately come down to their effect upon the individual. The digital future is one in which we will have the ability to lead our lives in new ways. Consider what is happening in a quiet village called Colletta di Castelbianco in the Italian coastal region of Liguria. The little town is providing a foretaste of what the commuter of tomorrow may do every day. Colletta di Castelbianco is a thirteenth century township finally abandoned because its steep slopes and difficult climate could not support agriculture. Today, its stone buildings have been bought up in their entirety by an Italian property company that has decided to make the site into Italy's first Internet village. The company, SIVM of Alessandria, Italy, is laying a fiber-optic ISDN network through the ancient stone structures, allowing users to enjoy the benefits of separate, high-speed channels for voice, data, and fax. Even the village's bar and restaurant will be linked to the Net.[7]

Thus the time-honored dream of the digital commuter: If you have a telephone connection, you can work anywhere. The Internet brings new credence to the notion. Hooked into a world of multimedia sight and sound, linked to your company by electronic mail, able to download current projects from a corporate server by FTP, or search the company database by Telnet, you are effectively freed from at least some of the constraints of the traditional 9 to 5. Whether human nature is quite so malleable is another issue. People vary in their ability to work alone; some enjoy it, others find it oppressive, and miss the familiar chatter around the water cooler. But there is no question that those with a yen for living in the wilds will increasingly have the option of doing so while maintaining an active presence at their place of employment. Assuming, of course, that they have their employer's blessing.

And did you note the fact that Colletta di Castelbianco is not just a series of connected residences but a wired village? When you can stop in at the local coffee house and order a cappucino, to be enjoyed while following World Wide Web links on terminals at your table, you are living in a truly cyberlinked environment. The small number of Internet cafes and bookstores—traditional businesses with links to the Net provided as a service to customers—have proven that the concept is a workable one, so we can expect to see innovations like this spread into other forms of activity. E-mail terminals at the baseball stadium? Web browsers on airline flights? The future probably holds these and more.

The Limits of Regulation

The future also holds misunderstandings. By providing access to a worldwide store of information, the Internet has effectively changed the way we view a local community. Can local laws, for example, regarding pornography be applied to material generated far beyond the confines of that community? If so, how do we do so in the digital era, when it's as easy for a user to tap into an FTP site in Finland as it is to run down the street to the local newsstand? Because these issues are not readily resolved, it's not surprising to see lawmakers questioning whether unlimited access to the Internet is indeed a good thing.

Thus a bill introduced before the United States Senate in 1995, one which could drastically curtail access to the Internet. The work of Senator James Exon (D.-Neb.), the bill would impose fines of up to $100 thousand and jail terms of up to two years upon those using telecommunications devices to send obscene, indecent, or harassing material over the network. While intended as a check upon digital pornography of the kind that freely flows through a number of USENET newsgroups, the Exon bill raises serious concerns about the effect of regulation upon freedom of speech and expression.

In a nutshell, S.314, called the Communications Decency Act of 1995, would amend the Communications Act of 1934 to replace the word "telephone" with the term "telecommunications equipment." The result would be to apply existing provisions against obscene or harassing phone calls to all forms of networked communication, which could mean anything from the Internet to commercial on-line services like CompuServe, and local bulletin boards systems. The bill was designed to target anyone who "... makes, transmits or otherwise makes available any comment, request, suggestion, proposal, image, or other communication which is obscene, lewd, lascivious, filthy or indecent."

And here we run into a conundrum, one caused by the advance of technology. Laws designed for telephones cannot be applied across the board to networked digital communications. In the simplest case, a person who receives obscene or threatening telephone calls is being harassed, and has every right to expect protection from the laws. By contrast, a person who seeks out sexually explicit material on the Internet is more participant than crime victim. Explicit photographs, for example, cannot be retrieved from the Internet without considerable effort, in which case the question becomes, who is the victim, and of what crime?

Moreover, restricting Internet content at any level raises the question of what is offensive. To one segment of the population, discussions of birth control or abortion may appear censurable; to others, they are topics in an ongoing debate about reproductive rights and government policy. To begin shutting down discussion on a worldwide network because a prosecutor in a particular state finds that debate obscene is to produce a chilling effect upon the expression of ideas at all levels. It would also demand of service providers that they examine every data packet that transits their network to ensure that it meets the necessary standards. Such a requirement would effectively close down the Internet access business as a commercial proposition.

There are no easy solutions to the problems raised by Internet pornography, but it is heartening to see that the Internet access business is taking its own steps to deal with the issue. Many providers offer parents provisions for blocking sexually explicit materials so that they will be effectively unavailable to their children. Others simply restrict the access of customers below 18 years of age. And we are beginning to see the introduction of new software programs to deal with this issue, allowing filtering of content by parents to ensure a measure of personal control over what their child sees. Issues of censorship will continue to dog the Internet, but it seems clear that imposing unenforceable local standards upon a global network is not only ill-advised but ultimately unworkable.

Of Highways and Realities

As new technologies enter adolescence and commercial activity increases, the Internet faces a bevy of issues. The termination of NSFNET's once central role as the Internet's backbone network in the United States leaves implications for both the academic community and the broader commercial base. Changes in subsidies for university networks place the burden upon regional service providers and the schools they have long maintained to find new ways to pay for their operations, distributing the costs as broadly as possible. The National Science Foundation, meanwhile, will put its money into a substantially reduced backbone network connecting supercomputer and other high-technology research sites. Toward this end, NSF is developing a network that will pump data at 155 Mgbits per second, a backbone that will no longer play a significant role in providing basic connectivity for institutions. The days of NSFNET as a backbone connecting regional networks are over.

Also ending, we may hope, is a classic misunderstanding about the nature of the Internet. Academic users, accustomed to a network that sent them no monthly bills, tend to assume that network access is free; indeed, postings on USENET often reflect this assumption. We know now that the Internet is free in the same way that interstate highways are free; that is, they, like the network, have grown up in an environment that nurtures them with the taxpayer's dollar. Moving into the commercial arena means we come closer to linking network usage with the cost of providing the service. What seems to some as crass commercialism is, then, only the obvious working of a market economy.

We must also raise a related issue. Is the future of the Internet inevitably tied to corporation-funded research, producing high-speed testbeds for new technology and, in the process, improving the corporations' competitive position? If so, how is a balance to be struck between business interests and the public welfare? These issues continue to be debated as the National Information Infrastructure, of which the current Internet is to be only a part, takes shape in the minds of its proponents.

Pumping Up the Data Flow

What kind of networking future does the U.S. government have in store? Vice President Al Gore speaks of an information highway that will link not only universities, research centers, and government agencies, but secondary and even elementary schools to digital resources.

In the 1980s, Gore, then a senator, was instrumental in lobbying for the fiber-optic links that would become the NSFNET backbone. It was in November 1987 that the Federal Coordinating Committee for Science Engineering and Technology proposed the NREN—the National Research and Education Network—in a report to Congress. The idea seemed simple: We already had a collection of computer networks, mostly academic and research-oriented, that moved data across a backbone of connections at some 56 thousand bits per second. The NREN proposal was to increase that speed up to as much as a billion bits per second by the mid-1990s. Once built, the network would be commercialized, allowing the federal government to turn over operations to private companies.

This would be a fast network indeed. One billion bits per second, or one gigabit, is a speed that would allow you to send 300 copies of *Moby Dick* over the network every second. No wonder the NREN's most fervent backers, including the vice president, saw the visionary network as a national data highway, and likened it to the interstate highway system in terms of its effect upon economic growth for all regions of the country. It was Gore who was responsible for getting the idea through Congress in the form of the High-Performance Computing and Communications Act of 1991, which provided $2.9 billion dollars over five years toward the NREN. The High Performance Computing and High Speed Networking Applications Act of 1993, sponsored by Rep. Richard Boucher (D.-W.Va.), expanded the Gore bill to include access to health-care facilities and schools at all levels.

Today, the vision the NREN embraced remains alive, but the reality of its implementation has shifted in favor of the Internet, whose growth is considered part of the development of the Clinton administration's National Information Infrastructure project. Consider the NREN as having consisted of enhancements to the federally funded portion of the Internet, with continuing development under the NSF in various high-speed test sites. The broader, public access network now appears almost certainly to be the result of the continuing evolution of today's Internet. And whatever terminology we use to describe it, the issues remain the same. All of them revolve around access.

For the Internet, despite being global, is far from ubiquitous, even today. Although major universities invariably have access, an Internet account is a luxury for students and faculty at many smaller colleges, and generally out of the question for high-school and grade-school teachers and students. An information superhighway is all about access, about bringing these resources to the researchers and educators who need them. Tomorrow's network would attempt to connect all academic and research organizations as well as all government agencies. And it would make access to those resources available throughout society.

A Vision of a New Network

Tomorrow's network will revolve around a series of computer capabilities, augmented by connections to powerful hardware resources. These features, all of them available in some form today, could be enhanced and distributed throughout society, reaching from laboratories and universities to two- and four-year colleges, to K-12 schools, and into the home. They include electronic mail, high-resolution graphics, full-motion video, and sound. They include computer libraries which could be tapped to provide information on almost any subject.

What could you do with such a network? As opposed to the exchange of electronic mail, tomorrow's network offers the possibility of *interactive* audio and video. Imagine researchers separated by geography using their computer screens to work on intricate specifications in real time, making dynamic changes to plans and working out new strategies based on visual data at each workstation. Such a network would also handle video telephone connections, so that each researcher could talk to his or her opposite number on-screen, and see that person responding (whether this is a genuine advantage is a matter for speculation).

Not just drawings could be examined in this way, of course, but also medical imagery including patient records and X rays, which could be analyzed by specialists no matter what their physical location. Now extend the idea into the realms of art, of literature, of entertainment. If video and voice can flow over the network, so can music, or plays, or poetry readings. Pipe such traffic into the home through fiber-optic links and you complete a transition, taking the Internet from a specialist's tool to the primary communications medium for a computerized society.

Powerful support has arisen in the networking community for applications like these. Putting such capabilities into primary and secondary schools could bring a wealth of library tools to students; corporations could readily tap available databases. The grandest vision incorporates a truly national network which would include community access at all levels of society. Indeed, the enthusiastic response to the Internet in the library and K-12 education communities bodes well for the development of multimedia and remote learning, using network tools that will take advantage of ever broadening bandwidth. Such tools might include knowledge robots—Knowbots, which would be sent through the network to obtain specific information for their users, as well as electronic directories with the addresses of users and services, along with user interfaces that don't restrict access to the technologically sophisticated.

It's a staggering vision—students routinely logging on to the Library of Congress, laboratory researchers exchanging high-resolution imagery in pursuit of medical breakthroughs—but there remain serious questions about how such a network is to be organized. We've seen that the present-day Internet, despite its explosive growth in recent months, remains difficult to use and, for a broad spectrum of non-networked individual users, challenging to access. Tapping it requires relatively arcane knowledge of commands and procedures which many service providers have difficulty explaining to the novice. Documentation can be technically intimidating, which is why books like this are necessary. The ever-changing dynamics of network tools ensures there will be no early end to such needs.

A Question of Access

The inevitable question, then, is who will use tomorrow's network? Raising the Internet's speed limit into the gigabit range is unquestionably important, but prudent policy also dictates we address some of the network's shortcomings, or the Net will emerge as the tool of a technological elite, effectively off-limits save for those savvy enough to capitalize on it. What we need, say some observers, more than network speed, is attention to user interface issues. Why build a network if the majority of potential users can't figure out how to use it? Why build it, for that matter, if access is in the hands of an entrenched elite whose self-interest dictates restricting it to like-minded specialists?

Tom Grundner, director of the National Public Telecomputing Network in Cleveland, recalls reading a string of messages about the proposed NREN from academics worried about the general public gaining access, one of which concluded, "Why should we let them use it at all?" It's not an attitude Grundner finds amusing. "Academic computing centers are designed to provide services to the people who work there and 35 of their buddies," Grundner said. "They don't care if anybody else on campus ever has access to this stuff, much less whether the public at large does. The worst nightmare of the academic computing people would be to have the Internet opened up to anyone who wanted to have access to it."[8] Yet as we have seen, that is precisely what is happening.

As for the vision of the information highway sketched out by Al Gore, Grundner opposes it, saying it lacks a coherent vision for the development of community computer systems. Instead, his energies are applied to the development of Free-Nets, those computer networks, examined in Chapter 3, that link the public to Internet resources while offering abundant community information and a user-friendly interface. Grundner is trying to put networking within reach of anyone with a modem. It will do us little good, he thinks, to train students to use a network if, as soon as they graduate, their access to its resources is cut off.

Who's Going to Build It?

An equally critical consideration is, who is going to build the data superhighway? Is tomorrow's network to be, like the interstate highway system, a structure built by the government but otherwise unregulated? Or is it to follow the model of the national power grid, and be a privately constructed network submitting to federal and state regulation so that affordable access is guaranteed? Already the two camps are taking the field, with Vice President Gore arguing that the private sector may not be willing to take on such a risky investment, and that if it did, the danger of the network's becoming restricted in its access is too great. Gore argues for a government-constructed public network regulated and managed for all Americans to use.

Building an information highway is no small undertaking. Moving data networks like this one into the home requires replacing the copper telephone wires that currently feed most homes with high-capacity fiber-optic cables. While most long-distance lines have already undergone such conversion, the so-called local loop between the home and the local telephone switch remains largely copper-based, and thus of insufficient bandwidth to carry the huge dataflow proposed for the future. Telephone equipment at both the long-distance and local levels would need upgrading as well to handle the required bandwidth and stand up to the anticipated traffic flow. Critical to the discussion is the meeting ground between private investment and universal access, a murky terrain whose cartography is under active investigation.

While some computer companies look forward to the possibility of increased equipment sales as the Internet grows, other firms are concerned about the federal government's role in developing the network. AT&T is but one company uneasy about the potential of the government creating a network that would operate in competition with the established telecommunications carriers. And at the Electronic Frontier Foundation, Lotus Development Corporation founder Mitchell D. Kapor has suggested the whole enterprise offers too grandiose a vision. Kapor insists that Integrated Services Digital Network technology, capable of being carried over standard copper wires, offers a quick way to make many of these services available to the widest possible audience. The ISDN choice would also offer significant cost savings over other forms of connection.

Whatever the merits of ISDN, the Electronic Frontier Foundation (EFF) is an organization worth your attention. Founded in 1990, EFF advocates freedom of expression in digital media and the application of constitutional principles to computer communications. While the EFF is perhaps best known for its role in the successful lawsuit of software game publisher Steve Jackson against the U.S. Secret Service, the organization is also active in shaping debate over such issues as commercialization of the Internet, privacy in computer communications, and the emergence of on-line "virtual" communities.

To learn more about the EFF, contact:

THE ELECTRONIC FRONTIER FOUNDATION
1667 K St. NW, Suite 801
Washington DC 20006–1605 USA
Voice: 202-861-7700
Fax: 202-861-1258
mailto:ask@eff.org
http://www.eff.org/

A Truly Global Network

We think of the Internet as a global network, and indeed it is; we can send and retrieve messages and files from just about anywhere with a network connection. But that's just the point. Is the Internet destined to be a tool of the economically advantaged, or will nations in the developing world gradually take their place among the network's citizenry?

No one can drive a network into an environment where computers are nonexistent, but it's clear from recent Internet meetings that drawing attention to the network's advantages can have a quickening effect on the state of the art wherever such meetings are held. Vinton Cerf points out that holding a meeting of the Internet Society in San Francisco offers few technological challenges, but that hosting one in Prague, where the 1994 meeting was held, made demands on the infrastructure of a recovering nation. "Our hope," says Cerf, "is that as we hold meetings like this, there will be some leave-behind effect, that investment will persist beyond the period of the meeting."

The Internet Society also sponsors a committee on technology in developing countries, part of whose objective is to supply educational materials to researchers and engineers in key locations worldwide. An annual workshop provides training in the installation and use of the network to participants from countries with scant Internet deployment. Clearly, the development of the Internet Society itself is a symptom of the network's coming of age, as it moves from the necessary management of engineering issues to the broader implications of technological change.

The goal of an emerging global network must be access to those places where information is least available. Just as no Internet vision without comprehensive access is compelling, no global communications strategy without an aggressive campaign of technological enfranchisement makes sense. We've seen how much we can do with a desktop personal computer and a modem connection to the Internet. Imagine these benefits translated to countries where libraries are scarce, books rare, researchers and scientists disconnected from the work of their peers. The Internet's future is bright, but no one committed to the social benefits of computer networking will deny there's plenty of work to be done.

Chapter 17 Notes

1. Malamud's *Exploring the Internet* is one of the most curious, and hugely enjoyable, books ever written about the Internet. Malamud physically travels to Internet sites worldwide, along the way talking to major network figures and sampling restaurants from every cuisine imaginable.
2. Ron Frederick's "IETF Audio & Videocast." *Internet Society News* Vol. 1, No. 4, 19 tells this story.
3. Casner, Steve. "Second IETF Internet Audiocast." *Internet Society News* Vol. 1, No. 3, 23.
4. This comparison, and much of the material in this paragraph, derive from a telephone interview with Internet Society president Vinton Cerf, April 22 and 23, 1993.
5. *Ibid.*
6. *Ibid.*
7. Marshall, Lee. "A Telecommuter's Rural Idyll." *Financial Times*, May 27, 1995.
8. Telephone interview with Tom Grundner, January 21, 1993. As you will see in the appendix, the worldwide network of community-based computer systems championed by Grundner has grown rapidly in the two years since.

APPENDIX

Dial-Up Internet Service Providers and Public Access Unix Sites

Contents

The following list of Internet service providers and public access Unix sites draws on several sources. Chief among them are Peter Kaminski's *Public Dialup Internet Access List* (PDIAL) and Phil Eschallier's *NixPub Long Listing of Public/Open Access Unix Sites*. In addition, the Internet Society maintains an excellent listing of access providers around the globe, one that I have consulted frequently in my work. This document, Barry Raveendran Greene's *Network Service Providers Around the World*, proved invaluable. The material on Free-Nets comes from the National Public Telecomputing Network.

My intent was to create a list of maximum utility to modem users interested in accessing the Internet. Accordingly, this appendix falls into four broad categories. The initial list covers Free-Net sites around the world; these are community-based bulletin board systems that provide varying kinds of Internet access. The second list covers U.S. service providers offering full Internet access; that is, not just electronic mail and USENET but also Telnet and FTP, among other services. The third part of the appendix, drawn from the NixPub list, covers public access Unix sites in the United States. These sites offer e-mail and USENET, but usually lack FTP and Telnet capabilities. The fourth and final part of the appendix is a directory of international service providers.

A Word on Sources

Peter Kaminski's PDIAL is widely distributed on the Internet, and is Copyright 1992–1993 by Peter Kaminski. Material drawn from it is used here with his permission.

PDIAL focuses on dial-up service providers that offer full Internet access, including FTP and Telnet capabilities as well as electronic mail. The NixPub list takes a different tack; as a listing of public access Unix sites, it includes full access Internet providers as well as Unix systems offering electronic mail and USENET newsgroups only. It also lists Unix systems with no Internet connectivity whatsoever.

Why list sites without any Internet connectivity here? Because Unix systems are those most likely to provide local access to electronic mail to the Internet, and perhaps other services, in the future. Any of the NixPub sites are therefore worth watching as possible future providers of some form of Internet connectivity.

Barry Raveendran Greene's *Network Service Providers Around the World* maintains a broader focus. Not every provider listed in Greene's work specializes in dial-up modem access, but I have decided to include many of these companies anyway, because so many firms are now moving to offer SLIP/PPP connectivity in addition to their other service possibilities. The Greene list provides more detailed information than I offer here, particularly with regard to coverage areas, and I recommend that you consult it along with this list as you choose a provider near you. *Network Service Providers Around the World* is Copyright 1994 by Barry Raveendran Greene and the Internet Society.

The National Public Telecomputing Network is actively building the worldwide network of Free-Net systems described in Chapter 3. The list of Free-Net sites provided here was made available by permission of the NPTN.

In the material that follows, I have broken down information by country. Information from the lists has been supplemented by direct contacts with service providers. It was possible to gather more information from some systems than others; in each case, I list as much as I know and use the latest possible version of all sources.

Inevitably, some of the material included here, especially in regards to access charges, will have changed by the time you read the document. We are witnessing a huge influx of new providers, with invariable effects upon pricing. Be sure to check with any prospective provider to get the latest pricing information, and to learn about new service areas.

Complete information about additional sources for international Internet access is provided in the fourth section of this appendix.

Obtaining Updated Lists

There are various ways to obtain the frequently updated PDIAL. The list is posted to the USENET newsgroups alt.internet.access.wanted, alt.bbs.lists, alt.online-service, ba.internet and news.answers.

Alternatively, you can retrieve it by sending e-mail to info-deli-server@pdial.com. Enter **send pdial** as the subject of your message. To receive future editions as they are published, send e-mail with the subject **subscribe pdial** to info-deli-server@pdial.com. To use the FTP archive, go to this URL:

```
ftp://ftp.best.com:/pub/kaminski/
```

And the World Wide Web page is:

```
http://www.pdial.com/
```

NixPub Long Listing, Phil Eschallier's list of Public/Open Access Unix Sites, is likewise available on-line. It is regularly posted to the USENET newsgroups comp.misc, comp.bbs.misc, and alt.bbs. To subscribe to the NIXPUB-LIST mailing list, send e-mail to mail-server@bts.com. Enter as your message **subscribe nixpub-list** *your name.*

The same address may be used to retrieve the current list. Send e-mail to mail-server@bts.com with the message **get pub nixpub.long** or **get pub nixpub.short,** depending on which version you want. Finally, the NixPub list is available by anonymous FTP from:

```
ftp://vfl.paramax.com/pub/pubnet/nixpub.long
```

The following notice appears on the NixPub list, and is repeated here at the request of Phil Eschallier: "The nixpub listings are (C) Copyright 1993–95, Bux Technical Services. This publication is released for unlimited redistribution over any electronic media providing it remains in its original form. Publishing, removing this copyright notice, or in any way revising this document's contents is forbidden without written consent from the owner."

The material drawn from the NixPub list is used here, with some deletions where redundancies occurred, with the permission of Phil Eschallier. I have chosen to maintain the formatting he uses in NixPub for these entries to differentiate between public access Unix sites and full access service providers.

For updated Free-Net information, check the following URL:

```
http://www.nptn.org:80/about.fn/By_State.txt.html
```

The list is conveniently searchable by state.

To access Barry Raveendran Greene's *Network Service Providers Around the World,* use this URL:

```
http://www.isoc.org/~bgreene/nsp-index.html
```

I have cited material from Greene's list with his permission. The following notice appears on his document: "Copyright 1994 by Barry Raveendran Greene and the Internet Society. Permission to use for non-commercial, personal, or educational purposes.

This copyright and permission notice must appear in all copies. Permission is also granted to mention, cite, refer to, or describe this document in books, products, or online services (but not to reproduce in whole or in part without permission.)"

Greene's fine overview of Internet-available provider information is offered at this URL:

```
http://www.isoc.org/~bgreene/nsp-c.html
```

And I cannot close this section without mentioning the following URL:

```
http://thelist.com/
```

Using this Web page, you have access to provider information presented by area code, to make it simple to home in quickly on what you need. This site, called The List, is provided by Colossus Inc., a World Wide Web company based in Chicago, Illinois, and is sponsored as well by Internet Direct and I-Site.

Free-Net Sites around the World

The following list of Free-Net sites comes from the National Public Telecomputing Network, and is used with that organization's permission. In the list, you will see references to *affiliates*, which are active Free-net sites organized according to the principles of the NPTN. You will also see mention of *metro* sites, which are Free-Nets in cities of over 50 thousand in population; *rural* sites, which include Free-Nets that cover a broader, and less populated, geographical area, and 'educational' sites, which focus on learning-related issues. Those sites marked as having *organizing committees* are in the preliminary stages of Free-Net development and have not yet gone on-line.

UNITED STATES

ALABAMA
Affiliates
  Metro
    Mobile Area Free-Net
    Geoff Peacock
    Voice: 205-344-7243
    E-mail: geoff@ns1.maf.mobile.al.us
    Modem: 334-405-4636
    Telnet: ns1.maf.mobile.al.us
Organizing Committees
  Metro
    Tennessee Valley Free-Net—Huntsville
    Billy Ray Wilson
    Voice: 205-544-3849
    E-mail:

    Tuscaloosa Free-Net—Tuscaloosa
    Dr. Ron Doctor
    Voice: 205-348-2398
    E-mail: rdoctor@ua1vm.ua.edu

ALASKA
Organizing Committees
  Metro

AnchorNet—Anchorage
Peg Thompson
Voice: 907-261-2891
E-mail: pegt@muskox.alaska.edu

FairNet—Fairbanks
Mark O. Badger
Voice: 907-474-5089
E-mail: ffmob@aurora.alaska.edu

ARIZONA
Affiliates
  Metro

AzTeC—Tempe
Joseph A. Askins
Voice: 602-965-5985
E-mail: joe.askins@asu.edu
Modem: 602-965-4151
Telnet: 129.219.13.60
Visitor login: guest (password: visitor)

ARKANSAS
Organizing Committees
  Metro

Greater Pulaski County Free-Net—Little Rock
John Eichler
Voice: 501-666-2222
E-mail: john.eichler@grapevine.lrk.ar.us

CALIFORNIA
Affiliates
  Metro

Los Angeles Free-Net—Los Angeles
Avrum Z. Bluming, M.D.
E-mail: aa101@lafn.org
Voice Info: 818-954-0080
Modem: 818-776-5000
Telnet: lafn.org
Visitor login: Select #2 at first menu

SLONET—San Luis Obispo
Phil Wagner
Voice: 805-544-7328
E-mail: pwagner@slonet.org
Modem: 805-781-3666
Telnet: 199.74.141.2
Visitor login: sloguest

Educational

CORE—Seal Beach
Keith Vogt
Voice: 1-800-272-8743
E-mail: kvogt@eis.calstate.edu
Modem: <service not available>
Telnet: eis.calstate.edu

Rural

Redwood Free-Net—Ukiah
Pat Hunt
Voice: 707-463-4154
E-mail: pat@pacific.net
Modem: <service not available>
Telnet: <service not available>

Organizing Committees

Metro

No. Calif. Regional Computing Network—Chico
Patrick Blythe
Voice: 916-891-1211
E-mail: pblythe@aol.com

Davis Community Network—Davis
Ann Mansker
Voice: 916-752-7764
E-mail: acmansker@ucdavis.edu

Orange County Free-Net—Orange County
Kent D. Palmer, Ph.D.
Voice: 714-762-8551
E-mail: palmer@world.std.com

Sacramento Free-Net—Sacramento
Cynthia Mulit
Voice: 916-484-6789
E-mail: sndview@netcom.com

San Diego County Free-Net—San Diego
Joyce Kennedy
Voice: 619-431-1660
E-mail: jlk@sunfeatures.com

Silicon Valley Public Access Link—San Jose
Marc Siegel
Voice: 415-968-2598
E-mail: msiegel@svpal.org

Santa Barbara RAIN—Santa Barbara
Timothy Tyndall
Voice: 805-967-7246
E-mail: rain@rain.org

COLORADO
Affiliates
  Metro
    Denver Free-Net—Denver
    Drew Mirque
    Voice: 303-270-4300
    E-mail: drew@freenet.hsc.colorado.edu
    Modem: 303-270-4865
    Telnet: freenet.hsc.colorado.edu
    Visitor login: guest

CONNECTICUT
Organizing Committees
  Metro
    Danbury Area Free-Net—Danbury
    Diane Greenwald
    Voice: 203-797-4512
    E-mail: waldgreen@bix.com

    CPBI Free-Net—Hartford
    Alfred Steel
    Voice: 203-278-5310, ext 1230
    E-mail: steela@csusys.ctstateu.edu

FLORIDA
Affiliates
  Metro
    SEFLIN Free-Net—Broward County
    Elizabeth Curry
    Voice: 305-357-7318
    E-mail: currye@mail.seflin.lib.fl.us
    Modem: 305-765-4332
    Telnet: bcfreenet.seflin.lib.fl.us
    Visitor login: visitor

    Alachua Free-Net—Gainesville
    Bruce Brashear
    Voice: 904-372-8401
    E-mail: bruce@freenet.ufl.edu
    Modem: 904-334-0200
    Telnet: freenet.ufl.edu
    Visitor login: visitor

    Tallahassee Free-Net—Tallahassee
    Hilbert Levitz
    Voice: 904-644-1796
    E-mail: levitz@cs.fsu.edu
    Modem: 904-488-5056
    Telnet: freenet.fsu.edu
    Visitor login: visitor

Suncoast Free-Net—Tampa Bay
Marilyn Mulla
Voice: 813-273-3714
E-mail: mullam@firnvx.firn.edu
Modem: <service not available>
Telnet: <service not available>

Organizing Committees
  Metro
Miami Free-Net—Miami
Elizabeth Curry
Voice: 305-357-7318
E-mail: currye@mail.seflin.lib.fl.us

Naples Free-Net—Naples
Dr. Melody Hainsworth
Voice: 1-800-466-8017
E-mail: hainswm@firnvx.firn.edu

Palm Beach Free-Net—Palm Beach
Elizabeth Curry
Voice: 305-357-7318
E-mail: currye@mail.seflin.lib.fl.us

Sarasota-Manatee Area Free-Net—Sarasota
Bill Touchstone
Voice: 813-371-0811, ext 5196
E-mail: billt@lds.loral.com

MCNet—Stuart
Gretchen Hammerstein
Voice: 407-221-1410
E-mail: ghammers@admin.co.martin.fl.us

GEORGIA
Affiliates
  Rural
Worth County-Sylvester Ga. Free-Net—Sylvester
Kent A. Guske
Voice: 912-776-8625
E-mail: Kent_Guske@peanut.org
Modem: 912-776-1255
Visitor login: guest

Organizing Committees
  Metro
404 Free-Net—Atlanta
Mike Bernath
Voice: 404-892-0943
E-mail: mike_bernath@solinet.net

HAWAII
Organizing Committees
  Metro
> **The Aloha Free-Net Project—Honolulu**
> Robert Mathews
> Voice: 808-533-3969
> E-mail: mathews@gold.chem.hawaii.edu
>
> **Maui Free-Net—Maui**
> Donald Regalmuto
> Voice: 808-572-0510
> E-mail: don.regal@tdp.org

IDAHO
Organizing Committees
  Metro
> **Panhandle Free-Net—Sandpoint**
> David Sawyer
> Voice: 208-265-2955
> E-mail: solutions@ins.infonet.net

ILLINOIS
Affiliates
  Metro
> **Prairienet—Champaign-Urbana**
> Ann P. Bishop
> Voice: 217-244-3299
> E-mail: abishop@uiuc.edu
> Modem: 217-255-9000
> Telnet: prairienet.org (192.17.3.3)
> Visitor login: visitor

Organizing Committees
  Metro
> **Shawnee Free-Net—Carbondale**
> Robert A. Pauls
> Voice: 618-549-1139
> E-mail: bob.pauls@shawnee.org
>
> **SWIF-NET—Edgemont**
> Gary A. Ulery
> Voice: 618-397-0968
> E-mail: gulery@minuet.siue.edu

INDIANA
Organizing Committees
  Metro
> **Michiana Free-Net Society—Granger**
> Donald McLaughlin

Voice: 219-282-1574
E-mail: dmclaugh@darwin.cc.nd.edu

IOWA
Organizing Committees
  Metro
    CedarNet—Cedar Falls
    Robert Muffoletto
    Voice: 319-273-6282
    E-mail: muffoletto@uni.edu

    Iowa Knowledge Exchange—Des Moines
    Gary Barrett
    Voice: 515-242-3556
    E-mail: garyb@ins.infonet.net

    Fairfield Free-Net—Fairfield
    Steve Terry
    Voice: 515-472-7494
    E-mail: sterry@ins.infonet.net

KENTUCKY
Organizing Committees
  Metro
    Pennyrile Area Free-Net—Hopkinsville
    Mark Roseberry
    Voice: 502-886-2913
    E-mail: mroseberry@delphi.com

    Owensboro Free-Net—Owensboro
    Donna Treubig
    Voice: 502-686-4530
    E-mail: donna@ndlc.occ.uky.edu

LOUISIANA
Affiliates
  Metro
    Greater New Orleans Free-Net—New Orleans
    Gordon H. Mueller
    Voice: 504-286-7187
    E-mail: nrrmc@uno.edu
Organizing Committees
  Metro
    BRAIN—Baton Rouge
    Ann McMahon
    Voice: 504-346-0707
    E-mail: anniemac@acm.org

    Acadiana Free-Net—Lafayette
    Bob Brantingham

Voice: 318-837-9374
E-mail: bobbrant@delphi.com

MARYLAND
Organizing Committees
 Metro
Free State Free-Net—Baltimore
Andree Duggan
Voice: 410-313-9259
E-mail: aduggan@well.sf.ca.us

Chesapeake Free-Net—Easton
David M. Boan, Ph.D.
Voice: 410-822-4132
E-mail: david_boan@mail.bluecrab.org

Garrett Communiversity Central—McHenry
Donald Storck
Voice: 301-387-3035
E-mail: 71072.2304@compuserve.com

MASSACHUSETTS
Affiliates
 Educational
UMASSK12—Amherst
Morton Sternheim
Voice: 413-545-1908
E-mail: mms@k12.oit.umass.edu
Modem: 413-572-5583 or 413-572-5268
Telnet: k12.oit.umass.edu
Visitor login: guest

MICHIGAN
Affiliates
 Metro
Greater Detroit Free-Net—Detroit
Paul Raine
Voice: 810-574-8549
E-mail: info@detroit.freenet.org
Telnet: detroit.freenet.org
Visitor login: visitor

Genesee Free-Net—Flint
Mike Mosher
Voice: 810-232-3667
E-mail: mmosher@gmi.edu
Modem: 810-232-9905
Telnet: genesee.freenet.org
Visitor login: guest

Educational

Education Central—Mount Pleasant
Hal Crawley
Voice: 517-774-3975
E-mail: hcrawley@edcen.ehhs.cmich.edu
Modem: 517-774-3790
Telnet: edcen.ehhs.cmich.edu
Visitor login: visitor

Rural

Almont Expression—Almont
George Pratt
Voice: 810-798-8150
E-mail: gpratt@expression.org
Modem: 810-798-8290
Visitor login: Visitor (password: Visitor)

Great Lakes Free-Net—Battle Creek
Merritt W. Tumanis
Voice: 616-961-4166
E-mail: merritt_tumanis@fc1.glfn.org
Modem: 616-969-4536
Visitor login: visitor

Organizing Committees

Metro

Huron Valley Free-Net—Ann Arbor
Michael Todd Glazier
Voice: 313-662-8374
E-mail: michael.todd.glazier@umich.edu

Grand Rapids Free-Net—Grand Rapids
Andrew Bass
Voice: 616-459-6273
E-mail: andyb@bethany.org

Macatawa Area Free-Net—Holland
Richard Vander Broek
Voice: 616-396-2303, ext #24
E-mail: ad469@leo.nmc.edu

Capitol City Free-Net—Lansing
Whitney M. Johnson
Voice: 517-487-1516
E-mail: whit@jcn.com

MINNESOTA

Organizing Committees

Metro

Twin Cities Free-Net—Minneapolis
Scott Fritchie

Voice: 507-646-3407
E-mail: fritchie@stolaf.edu

Northfield Free-Net—Northfield
Andrea Christianson
Voice: 507-645-9301
E-mail: andreacris@aol.com

MISSISSIPPI
Organizing Committees
  Metro
    Magnolia Free-Net—Jackson
    Tom Lowe
    Voice: 601-354-1027
    E-mail: tlowe@ccaix.jsums.edu

    Meridian Area Free-Net—Meridian
    Ric Rogers
    Voice: 601-482-2000
    E-mail: ric4aardvark@delphi.com

MISSOURI
Affiliates
  Metro
    COIN—Columbia
    Elinor Barrett
    Voice: 314-443-3161 (ext. 350 for voice mail)
    E-mail: ebarrett@bigcat.missouri.edu
    Modem: 314-884-7000
    Telnet: bigcat.missouri.edu
    Visitor login: guest

    ORION—Springfield
    Annie Linnemeyer
    Voice: 417-837-5050, ext 15
    E-mail: annie@ozarks.sgcl.lib.mo.us
    Modem: 417-864-6100
    Telnet: ozarks.sgcl.lib.mo.us
    Visitor login: guest

Organizing Committees
  Metro
    Show-Me Free-Net—Cape Girardeau
    Larry Loos
    Voice: 314-334-9322
    E-mail: loos@mail.mac.cc.mo.us

    KC Free-Net—Kansas City
    James E. Osbourn
    Voice: 816-340-4228
    E-mail: josbourn@tyrell.net

MONTANA
Affiliates
  Metro
  Big Sky Telegraph—Dillon
  Frank Odasz
  Voice: 406-683-7338
  E-mail: franko@bigsky.dillon.mt.us
  Modem: 406-683-7680
  Telnet: 192.231.192.1
  Visitor login: bbs

NEBRASKA
Organizing Committees
  Metro
  Omaha Free-Net—Omaha
  Howard Lowe
  Voice: 402-554-2516
  E-mail: lowe@unomaha.edu

NEVADA
Organizing Committees
  Metro
  Las Vegas International Free-Net—Las Vegas
  Scott Susman
  Voice: 702-795-7267
  E-mail: scott@gate.vegas.com

NEW HAMPSHIRE
Organizing Committees
  Metro
  The Granite State Oracle—Manchester
  Quentin Lewis
  Voice: 508-442-0279
  E-mail: quentin.lewis@sun.com

NEW MEXICO
Organizing Committees
  Metro
  New Mexico Free-Net—Albuquerque
  Lewis R. Newby
  Voice: 505-277-8148
  E-mail: lnewby@unm.edu

  Santa Fe Metaverse—Santa Fe
  John R. Grizz Deal
  Voice: 505-989-7117
  E-mail: grizz@lanl.gov

NEW YORK
Affiliates
Metro

Buffalo Free-Net—Buffalo
James Finamore
Voice: 716-877-8800, ext 451
E-mail: finamore@ubvms.cc.buffalo.edu
Modem: 716-645-3085
Telnet: freenet.buffalo.edu
Visitor login: freeport

Capital Region Information Service—Albany
Norman D. Kurland
Voice: 518-442-3728
E-mail: nkurland@albnyvms.bitnet

Organizing Committees
Metro

CASSYnet—Corning
Tom Gabriele
Voice: 607-936-3713
E-mail: freenet@scccvb.corning-cc.edu

Southern Tier Free-Net—Endicott
Scott Cubic
Voice: 607-752-1201
E-mail: cubicsr@vnet.ibm.com

East Side House Free-Net—New York City (Bronx)
Robert Pondiscio
Voice: 212-522-5196
E-mail: rpondiscio@aol.com

Rochester Free-Net—Rochester
Jerry Seward
Voice: 716-594-0943
E-mail: jerry@rochgte.fidonet.org

NORTH CAROLINA
Organizing Committees
Metro

Mountain Area Information Network—Asheville
Ed Sheary
Voice: 704-255-5207
E-mail: abplnet@uncecs.edu
Triangle Free-Net—Chapel Hill
William R. Hutchins
Voice: 919-968-4292
E-mail: hutch@tfnet.ils.unc.edu

Charlotte's Web—Charlotte
Stephen H. Snow
Voice: 704-358-5245
E-mail: shsnow@vnet.net

Forsyth County Free-Net—Winston-Salem
John Annen
Voice: 919-727-2597, ext 3023
E-mail: annen@ledger.mis.co.forsyth.nc.us

NORTH DAKOTA
Affiliates
  Educational
SENDIT—Fargo
Gleason Sackman
Voice: 701-237-8109
E-mail: sackman@sendit.nodak.edu
Modem: 701-237-3283
Telnet: sendit.nodak.edu
Visitor login: bbs (password: sendit2me)

OHIO
Affiliates
  Metro
SEORF—Athens
Damien O. Bawn
Voice: Out of service temporarily
E-mail: bawn@oucsace.cs.ohiou.edu
Modem: 614-593-1136
Telnet: seorf.ohiou.edu
Visitor login: guest

Tristate Online—Cincinnati
Steve Shoemaker
Voice: <not available>
E-mail: sshoe@tso.uc.edu
Modem: 513-579-1990
Telnet: tso.uc.edu
Visitor login: visitor

Cleveland Free-Net—Cleveland
Jeff Gumpf
Voice: 216-368-2982
E-mail: jag@po.cwru.edu
Modem: 216-368-3888
Telnet: freenet-in-a.cwru.edu
Visitor login: Select #2 at first menu

Greater Columbus Free-Net—Columbus
Steven I. Gordon
Voice: 614-292-4132
E-mail: sgordon@freenet.columbus.oh.us
Modem: 614-292-7501
Telnet: freenet.columbus.oh.us
Visitor login: guest

Dayton Free-Net—Dayton
Patricia Vendt
Voice: 513-873-4035
E-mail: pvendt@desire.wright.edu
Modem: 513-229-4373
Telnet: 130.108.128.174
Visitor login: visitor

Lorain County Free-Net—Elyria
Thom Gould
Voice: 1-800-227-7113, ext. 2451; or 216-277-2451
E-mail: aa003@freenet.lorain.oberlin.edu
Modem: 216-366-9721
Telnet: freenet.lorain.oberlin.edu
Visitor login: guest

Youngstown Free-Net—Youngstown
Lou Anschuetz
Voice: 216-742-3075
E-mail: lou@yfn.ysu.edu
Modem: 216-742-3072
Telnet: yfn2.ysu.edu
Visitor login: visitor

Educational
Learning Village Cleveland—Cleveland
John Kurilec
Voice: 216-498-4050
E-mail: jmk@nptn.org
Modem: 216-498-4070
Telnet: nptn.org
Visitor login: visitor

Rural
Richland Free-Net—Mansfield
Ed Rebmann
Voice: 419-521-3111/3110
E-mail: earmrcpl@class.org
Modem: <service not available>
Telnet: <service not available>

Medina County Free-Net—Medina
Gary Linden
Voice: 216-725-1000 ext 2550
E-mail: aa013@nptn.org
Modem: 216-723-6732
Visitor login: visitor

Organizing Committees
Metro

Akron Regional Free-Net—Akron
Anne S. McFarland
Voice: 216-972-6352
E-mail: r1asm@vm1.cc.uakron.edu

Stark County Free-Net—Canton
Maureen Kilcullen
Voice: 216-499-9600, ext 322
E-mail: mkilcull@kentvm.kent.edu

Lima Free-Net—Lima
Paul Monas
Voice: 419-226-1218
E-mail: monaspa@olima.usaref.msnet.bp.com

OKLAHOMA
Organizing Committees
Metro

Ponca City/Pioneer Free-Net—Ponca City
Phil Abernathy
Voice: 405-762-0541
E-mail: pcok@ping.com

PENNSYLVANIA
Organizing Committees
Metro

Lehigh Valley Free-Net—Bethlehem
Timothy Lindgren
Voice: 610-758-4998
E-mail: tpl2@lehigh.edu

Erie County Free-Net—Erie
Steven Landon
Voice:
E-mail: srl115@psu.edu

Pittsburgh Free-Net—Pittsburgh
Dan Iddings
Voice: 412-622-6502
E-mail: iddingsd@clpgh.org

Mercer County Free-Net—Sharon
Scott Jones
Voice: 216-565-9526
E-mail: wr3g@aol.com

Chester County Interlink—West Chester
Jordan Seidel
Voice: 215-430-6621
E-mail: jseidel@locke.ccil.org

RHODE ISLAND
Affiliates
  Metro
    Ocean State Free-Net—Providence
    Howard Boksenbaum
    Voice: 401-277-2726
    E-mail: howardbm@dsl.rhilinet.gov
    Modem: 401-831-4640
    Telnet: 192.207.24.10

SOUTH CAROLINA
Organizing Committees
  Metro
    MidNet—Columbia
    Stephen Bajjaly
    Voice: 803-777-4825
    E-mail: bajjaly@univscvm.csd.scarolina.edu

    Greenet—Greenville
    Thompson R. Cummins
    Voice: 803-242-5000, ext 231
    E-mail: sgr002@sol1.solinet.net

    GreenCo-NET—Greenwood
    Kim Madden
    Voice: 803-223-8431

TENNESSEE
Affiliates
  Metro
    Jackson Area Free-Net—Jackson
    Donald Lewis
    Voice: 901-425-2640
    E-mail: dlewis@jackson.freenet.org
    Telnet: 198.146.108.99
    Modem: 901-427-4435
    Visitor login: guest

Organizing Committees
  Metro

Greater Knoxville Community Network—Knoxville
Greg Cole
Voice: 615-974-2908
E-mail: gcole@solar.rtd.utk.edu

TEXAS
Affiliates
  Metro

Rio Grande Free-Net—El Paso
Don Furth
Voice: 915-775-6077
E-mail: donf@laguna.epcc.edu
Modem: 915-775-5600
Telnet: rgfn.epcc.edu
Visitor login: visitor

Organizing Committees
  Metro

Big Country Free-Net—Abilene
J. David Bavousett
Voice: 915-674-6964
E-mail: davidb@alcon.acu.edu

Austin Free-Net—Austin
Jeff Evans
Voice: 512-462-0625
E-mail: jevans@versa.com

North Texas Free-Net—Dallas
Ken Loss-Cutler
Voice: 214-320-8915
E-mail: ntfnadm@ntfn.dcccd.edu

Tarrant County Free-Net—Fort Worth
Joseph Coles
Voice: 817-763-8437
E-mail: jcoles@pubcon.com

Houston Civnet—Houston
Joe Abernathy
Voice: 713-666-9250
E-mail: joe@starbase.neosoft.com

West Texas Free-Net—San Angelo
Timothy R. Elwell
Voice: 915-655-7161
E-mail: timelwell@delphi.com

San Antonio Free-Net—San Antonio
J. Carlos Santana
Voice: 210-498-1558
E-mail: santana@espsun.space.swri.edu

VERMONT
Organizing Committees
Metro
    Lamoille Net—Morrisville
    Balu Raman
    Voice: 802-888-2606
    E-mail: braman@world.std.com

VIRGINIA
Affiliates
Metro
    Central Virginia's Free-Net—Richmond
    Kenneth Guyre
    Voice: 804-828-6650
    E-mail: kguyre@cabell.vcu.edu
    Telnet: freenet.vcu.edu
    Visitor login: visitor
Educational
    VaPEN—Richmond
    Joe Aulino
    E-mail: jaulino@pen.k12.va.us
    http://www.pen.k12.va.us/

Organizing Committees
Metro
    SEVANET—Newport News
    Bill Winter
    Voice: 804-594-7092
    E-mail: bwinter@powhatan.cc.cnu.edu

    Blue Ridge Free-Net—Roanoke
    Cynthia Obrist
    Voice: 703-981-1424
    E-mail: cobrist@leo.vsla.edu

WASHINGTON
Affiliates
Metro
    Kitsap Free-Net—Bremerton
    Michael Schuyler
    Voice: 206-377-7601
    E-mail: michael@linknet.kitsap.lib.wa.us
    Modem: 360-698-4737

Telnet: 198.187.135.22
Visitor login: guest

Seattle Community Network—Seattle
Randy Groves
Voice: 206-865-3424
E-mail: randy@cpsr.org
Modem: 206-386-4140
Telnet: scn.org
Visitor login: visitor

Tri-Cities Free-Net—Tri-Cities
Bruce McComb
Voice: 509-586-6481
E-mail: tcfn@delphi.com
Modem: 509-375-1111
Telnet: tcfn.org
Visitor login: guest
Password: visit

Organizing Committees
  Metro
    OPEN—Port Angeles
    Larry Haas
    Voice: 206-417-9302
    E-mail: lhaas@aol.com

    TINCAN—Spokane
    Dr. Karen L. Michaelson
    Voice: 509-359-6567
    E-mail: kmichaelson@ewu.edu

    Clark County Free-Net—Vancouver
    Thomas E. Ryan
    Voice: 206-696-6846
    E-mail: tryan@netcom.com

WISCONSIN
Organizing Committees
  Metro
    Chippewa Valley Free-Net—Eau Claire
    Steve Marquardt
    Voice: 715-836-3715
    E-mail: smarquar@uwec.edu

    Community Access Network—Fond du Lac
    Philip Armstrong
    Voice: 414-922-4102

AUSTRALIA

VICTORIA

Organizing Committees

Metro

Melbourne Free-Net—Melbourne
Peter Bancroft
Voice: +61 3-652-0656
E-mail: pbancroft@ozonline.com.au

CANADA

ALBERTA

Organizing Committees

Metro

Calgary Free-Net—Calgary
David Elton
Voice: 403-264-9535
E-mail: delton@acs.ucalgary.ca

Edmonton Free-Net—Edmonton
Jon Hall
Voice: 403-421-1745
E-mail: postmaster@freenet.edmonton.ab.ca

Praxis Free-Net—Medicine Hat
Lawrence Chen
Voice: 403-529-2162
E-mail: dreamer@lhaven.uumh.ab.ca

BRITISH COLUMBIA

Affiliates

Metro

CIAO! Free-Net—Trail
Ken McClean
Voice: 604-368-2233
E-mail: kmcclean@ciao.trail.bc.ca
Modem: 604-368-5764
Telnet: 142.231.5.1
Visitor login: guest

Victoria Free-Net—Victoria
Gareth Shearman
Voice: 604-385-4302
E-mail: shearman@freenet.victoria.bc.ca
Modem: 604-595-2300
Telnet: freenet.victoria.bc.ca
Visitor login: guest

Organizing Committees
  Metro

Campbell River Free-Net—Campbell River
Pat Presidente
Voice: 604-286-0651
E-mail: ppreside@cln.etc.bc.ca

Prince George Free-Net—Prince George
Lynda J. Williams
Voice: 604-562-2131, loc 296
E-mail: williams@cnc.bc.ca

Vancouver Free-Net—Vancouver
Brian Campbell
Voice: 604-665-3579
E-mail: briancam@vpl.vancouver.bc.ca

MANITOBA
Organizing Committees
  Metro

Eastmanet—Pinawa
Doug Gehon
Voice: 204-753-2311, ext 2442
E-mail: gehond@wl.aecl.ca

SEARDEN Free-Net—Sprague
Larry Geller
Voice: 204-437-2016
E-mail: larry_geller@mbnet.mb.ca

Blue Sky Free-Net of Manitoba—Winnipeg
Betty Dearth
Voice: 204-945-1413
E-mail: bdearth@gateway.eitc.mb.ca

NEW BRUNSWICK
Organizing Committees
  Metro

York Sunbury Community Server—Fredericton
Michael MacDonald
Voice: 506-453-4566
E-mail: mikemac@unb.ca

NEWFOUNDLAND
Organizing Committees
  Metro

St. John's Free-Net—St. John's
Randy Dodge
Voice: 709-737-4594
E-mail: randy@kean.ucs.mun.ca

NOVA SCOTIA
Organizing Committees
  Metro
   Cape Breton Free-Net—Cape Breton
   Dan McMullin
   Voice: 902-862-6432
   E-mail: dmacmull@fox.nstn.ns.ca

   Chebucto Free-Net—Halifax
   Ellen L. Sherlock
   Voice: 902-425-2061
   E-mail: els@cs.dal.ca

ONTARIO
Affiliates
  Metro
   National Capital Free-Net—Ottawa
   David Sutherland
   Voice: 613-788-2600, ext 3701
   E-mail: aa001@freenet.carleton.ca
   Modem: 613-564-3600
   Telnet: freenet.carleton.ca
   Visitor login: guest

Organizing Committees
  Metro
   North Shore Free-Net—Elliot Lake
   Alan Wilson
   Voice: 705-848-5106
   E-mail: alanwils@village.ca

   Durham Free-Net—Oshawa
   John Norman
   Voice: 905-668-3390
   E-mail: john.norman@freenet.durham.org

   Niagara Free-Net—St. Catharines
   Jon Radue
   Voice: 416-688-5550 ext 3867
   E-mail: jradue@sandcastle.cosc.brocku.ca

   Thunder Bay Free-Net—Thunder Bay
   Don Watson
   Voice: 807-343-8354
   E-mail: dwatson@flash.lakeheadu.ca

   Toronto Free-Net—Toronto
   Rick Broadhead
   Voice: N/A
   E-mail: ysar1111@vm1.yorku.ca

QUEBEC
Organizing Committees
  Metro
    Free-Net du Montreal Metropolitain—Montreal
    Steven Sacks
    Voice: 514-278-9173
    E-mail: ssacks@cam.org

SASKATCHEWAN
Organizing Committees
  Metro
    Moose Jaw Free-Net—Moose Jaw
    Ron Locke
    Voice: 306-694-2510
    E-mail: locke@gdilib.unibase.sk.ca

    Great Plains Free-Net—Regina
    Robert Greenfield
    Voice: 306-584-9615
    E-mail: rhg@unibase.unibase.sk.ca

    Saskatoon Free-Net—Saskatoon
    Peter Scott
    Voice: 306-966-5920
    E-mail: scottp@herald.usask.ca

FINLAND

Affiliates
  Educational
    Finland Free-Net—Helsinki
    Heikki Korpinen
    Voice: +358-0-451-4007
    E-mail: korpinen@freenet.hut.fi
    Modem: 358-929292
    Telnet: 130.233.208.40
    Visitor login: visitor

GERMANY

Affiliates
  Metro
    Bayreuth Free-Net—Bayreuth
    Wolfgang Kiessling
    Voice: 0921/553134
    E-mail: Wolfgang.Kiessling@Uni-Bayreuth.de
    Telnet: freenet.uni-bayreuth.de

    Free-Net Erlangen Nuernburg-Fuerth—Erlangen
    Dr. Walter F. Kugemann
    Voice: +49-9131-85-4735

E-mail: walter.kugemann@fim.uni-erlangen.de
Modem: +49-9131-85-8111
Telnet: 131.188.192.11
Visitor login: gast

IRELAND

Organizing Committees
  Metro
    Connect-Ireland—Dublin
    Martin Maguire
    Voice: 6711687 (+353-1)
    E-mail: director@toppsi.gn.apc.org

ITALY

Organizing Committees
  Metro
    Venice Free-Net—Venice
    Corrado Petrucco
    Voice: 039-41-721900
    E-mail: conrad@cidoc.iuav.unive.it

NEW ZEALAND

Affiliates
  Metro
    Wellington Citynet—Wellington
    Richard Naylor
    Voice: +64-4-801-3303
    E-mail: rich@tosh.wcc.govt.nz
    Modem: +64-4-801-3060
    Telnet: kosmos.wcc.govt.nz

PHILIPPINES

Organizing Committees
  Metro
    PPTN—Quezon City
    Rommel P. Feria
    Voice: 632-931-5314
    E-mail: rferia@upd.edu.ph

SWEDEN

Organizing Committees
  Metro
    Medborgarnas Datanat—Norrkoping
    Kjell-Ove Martinsson
    Voice: +46-11-150000
    E-mail: kjm@norrk.pp.se

Number of Affiliates Online:	51
Community Systems:	37
Educational Systems:	8
RINs:	6
Number of Organizing Committees:	114
Community Systems:	114

U. S. Full-Service Dial-Up Providers

United States

The following is a list of full-access Internet providers, offering electronic mail, FTP, and Telnet, drawn from PDIAL and Barry R. Greene's excellent list. Immediately following it is a list of public access Unix sites, as found in the NixPub list.

A2I COMMUNICATIONS
1211 Park Avenue, Suite 202
San Jose, CA 95126
Voice: n/a
Dial-Up: 408-293-9010 (v.32, v.32 bis), 415-364-5652 (v.32bis) or 408-293-9020 (PEP). Use **guest** to log in.
Area codes: 408, 415
Local access: California: west and south San Francisco Bay area
Fees: $20/month or $45/3 months or $72/6 months.
E-mail: info@rahul.net

ACM NETWORK SERVICES
PO Box 21599, Waco, TX 76702
Voice: (817) 776-6876
Fax: (817) 751-7785
E-mail:: Account-Info@ACM.org

AIMNET CORPORATION
20410 Town Center Lane, Suite 290
Cupertino, CA 95014
Voice: 408-257-0900
Fax: 408-257-5452
E-mail: info@aimnet.com
Local Access: California: San Francisco Bay Area and Silicon Valley (408, 415, 410 area codes)

ALASKA, UNIVERSITY OF
Tundra Services
UAS Computing Services
11120 Glacier Highway
Juneau AK 99801
Voice: 907-465-6453
Dial-Up: 907-789-1314
Area Codes: 907

Local Access: Alaska: Anchorage, Barrow, Fairbanks, Homer, Juneau, Keni, Ketchikan, Kodiak, Kotzebue, Nome, Palmer, Sitka, Valdez
Fees: $20/month for individual accounts, discounts to public, government, and nonprofit organizations.
E-mail: jnjmb@acad1.alaska.edu

ALTERNET
3110 Fairview Park Drive, Suite 570
Falls Church, Va 22042
Voice: +1 800-488-6384 or +1 703-204-8000
Fax: +1 703-204-8001
E-mail: alternet-info@uunet.uu.net

AMERICA ONLINE, INC.
8619 Westwood Center Drive
Vienna, VA 22182-2285
Voice: 1-800-827-6364 or +1 703-8933-6288
E-mail: info@aol.com

ANOMALY—RHODE ISLAND'S GATEWAY TO THE INTERNET
Small Business Systems, Inc.
Box 17220, Route 104
Smithfield, RI 02917
Voice: 401-273-4669
Dial-Up: 401-331-3706 (v.32) or 401-455-0347 (PEP)
Area codes: 401, 508
Local Access: Rhode Island: Providence/Seekonk
Fees: $125/6 months or $200/year; education rates are $75 for 6 months or $125/yr.
E-mail: info@anomaly.sbs.risc.net

ANS CO+RE (ADVANCED NETWORK AND SERVICES, INC.)
1875 Campus Commons Drive, Suite 220
Reston, VA 22091-1552
Voice: 800-456-8267 or +1 703-758-7700
Fax: 703-758-7717
E-mail: info@ans.net

ANTERIOR TECHNOLOGY
P.O. Box 1206
Menlo Park, CA 94026-1206
Voice: +1 415-328-5615
Fax: +1 415-322-1753
E-mail: info@radiomail.net

APK PUBLIC ACCESS UNIX
19709 Mohican Ave
Cleveland, OH 44119
Voice: 216-481-9428

Fax: 216-481-9428
E-mail: zbig@wariat.org

AT&T MAIL
AT&T Mail Customer Assistance Center (ATTMAIL-DOM)
5000 Hadley Road
South Plainsfield, NJ 07080
Voice: (800) MAIL-672 or 1-800-367-7225; in Canada, 613-778-5815; in UK or the
republic of Ireland, 0800-289-403 or +44-527-67585; in Europe, +322-676-3737; in
Japan, 81-3-5561-3411; in the Pacific Rim, +852-846-2800; in Africa or the Americas, +908-658-6175
E-mail: POSTMASTER@ATTMAIL.COM

BARRNET (BAY AREA REGIONAL RESEARCH NETWORK)
Pine Hall Rm. 115
Stanford, CA 94305-4122
Voice: +1 415-723-3104
E-mail: info@barrnet.net

BIX
1030 Massachusetts Ave
Cambridge, MA 02138-5302
Voice: 800-695-4775
Dial-Up: 800-695-4882. Log in as **bix.** Enter **bix.news** at the Name? prompt. Complete the registration.
Area Codes: 617, PDN.
Local Access: USA nationwide
Fees: $20/month for 20 hours off-peak ($9 per hour prime time); $1.80/hour thereafter; $13/month membership fee. Or $9 per hour prime time, $3/hour off-peak
($2/hour direct dial or $1/hour via Telnet) plus $13/month fee.
E-mail: info@bix.com

THE BLACK BOX
PO Box 591822
Houston, TX 77259-1822
Voice: 713-480-2684
Dial-Up: 713-480-2686 (V32bis/V42bis)
Area Codes: 713
Local Access: Texas: Houston
Fees: $21.65 per month or $108.25 for 6 months
E-mail: info@blkbox.com

CAPCON LIBRARY NETWORK
1320 19th St. NW, Suite 400
Washington, DC 20036
Voice: 202-331-5771
Dial-Up: contact for number
Area Codes: 202, 301, 410, 703

Local Access: District of Columbia, suburban Maryland and northern Virginia. About to go nationwide.

Fees: $35 startup, plus $150/year plus $24/month for first account from an institution; $35 startup, plus $90/year, plus $15/month for additional users. 20 hours/month included; additional hours $2/hour. CAPCON member rates lower

E-mail: capcon@capcon.net

CERFNET (CALIFORNIA EDUCATION AND RESEARCH FEDERATION NETWORK)

P.O. Box 85608
San Diego, CA 92186-9784
Voice: +1 800-876-2373 or +1 619-455-3900
Fax: +1 619-455-3990
E-mail: help@cerf.net

CICNET (COMMITTEE ON INSTITUTIONAL COOPERATION NETWORK)

ITI Building
2901 Hubbard Drive, Pod G
Ann Arbor, MI 48105
Voice: +1 313-998-6102
E-mail: info@cic.net

CLARK INTERNET SERVICES, INC.

10600 Route 108
Ellicott City, MD 21042
Voice: Call 800-735-2258 then give 410-730-9764 (MD Relay Svc)
Dial-Up: 410-730-9786, 410-995-0271, 301-596-1626, 301-854-0446, 301-621-5216.
Log in as **guest.**
Area Codes: 202, 301, 410, 703
Fees: $23/month or $66/3 months or $126/6 months or $228/year
E-mail: info@clark.net

CLASS—COOPERATIVE LIBRARY AGENCY FOR SYSTEMS AND SERVICES

1415 Koll Circle, Suite 101
San Jose, CA 95112-4698
Voice: 800-488-4559
Dial-Up: Contact for number. CLASS serves libraries and information distributors only.
Area codes: Northern and southern California or anywhere 800 service is available.
Fees: $4.50/hour + $150/year for first account, plus $50/year each additional account, plus $135/year CLASS membership. Discounts available for multiple memberships.
E-mail: class@class.org

COLORADO SUPERNET

Colorado School of Mines
1500 Illinois
Golden, CO 80401

Voice: 303-273-3471
Dial-Up: Contact for number
Area codes: 303, 719, 800
Local Access: Colorado: Alamosa, Boulder/Denver, Colorado Springs, Durango, Fort Collins, Frisco, Glenwood Springs/Aspen, Grand Junction, Greeley, Gunnison, Pueblo, Telluride; anywhere 800 service is available
Fees: $1/hour off-peak, $3/hour peak ($250 max/month) + $20 signup, $5/hour surcharge for 800 use
E-mail: info@csn.org

COMMUNITY NEWS SERVICE
1715 Monterey Road
Colorado Springs, CO 80910
Voice: 719-579-9120
Dial-Up: 719-520-1700
Area codes: 303, 719, 800
Local Access: Colorado: Colorado Springs, Denver, and continental USA via 800 service
Fees: $2.75/hour; $10/month minimum, plus $35 signup
E-mail: klaus@cscns.com

COMPUSERVE INFORMATION SYSTEM
5000 Arlington Center Boulevard
P.O. Box 20212
Columbus, OH 43220
Voice: +1 614-457-0802 or +1 800-848-8990
E-mail: postmaster@csi.compuserve.com

CR LABORATORIES DIALUP INTERNET ACCESS
PO Box 326
Larkspur, CA 94977
Voice: 415-381-2800
Dial-Up: 415-389-8649
Area Codes: 213, 310, 404, 415, 510, 602, 707, 800
Local Access: California: San Francisco Bay area, plus San Rafael, Santa Rosa, Los Angeles, Orange County; Arizona: Phoenix, Scottsdale, Tempe, and Glendale; Georgia: Atlanta metro area; continental USA 800
Fees: $17.50/month plus $19.50 signup
E-mail: info@crl.com

CTS NETWORK SERVICES (CTSNET)
1274 Vista Del Monte Dr.
El Cajon, CA 92020-6830
Voice: 619-637-3637
Dial-Up: 619-637-3640 (HST), 619-637-3660 (V.32bis), 619-637-3680 (PEP); log in as **help.**
Area Codes: 619

Local Access: California: San Diego, Pt. Loma, La Jolla, La Mesa, El Cajon, Poway, Ramona, Chula Vista, National City, Mira Mesa, Alpine, East County, new North County numbers, Escondido, Oceanside, Vista
Fees: $10–$23/month flat depending on features, $15 startup; personal $20/month flat depending on features, $25 startup
E-mail: support@ctsnet.cts.com

CYBERGATE, INC.
662 S. Military Tr.
Deerfield Beach, FL, 33442
Voice: 305-428-4283
Dial-Up: 305-425-0200
Area Codes: 305, 407
Local Access: South Florida
Fees: $17.50/month on credit card; group discounts; SLIP/PPP: $17.50/month plus $2/hour
E-mail: info@gate.net or sales@gate.net

THE CYBERSPACE STATION
204 N. El Camino Real, Suite E626
Encinitas, CA 92024
Voice: n/a
Dial-Up: 619-634-1376; log in as **guest**
Area codes: 619
Local Access: California: San Diego
Fees: $15/month plus $10 startup or $60 for six months
E-mail: help@cyber.net

DASNET
DA Systems, Inc.
1053 East Campbell Avenue
Campbell, CA 95008
Voice: +1 408-559-7434

DELPHI INTERNET SERVICES CORPORATION
1030 Massachusetts Avenue
Cambridge, MA 02138
Voice: 800-544-4005
Dial-Up: 800-695-4002. Enter: **JOINDELPHI.** Password: FREE.
Area Codes: 617, PDN
Local Access: Massachusetts: Boston. Kansas: Kansas City.
Fees: $10/month for 4 hours or $20/month for 20 hours, plus $3/month for Internet Services.
E-mail: info@delphi.com

DIAL N' CERF, DIAL N' CERF AYC
P. O. Box 85608
San Diego, CA 92186-9784

Voice: 800-876-2373; 619-455-3900
Dial-Up: Contact for number
Area codes: 213, 310, 415, 510, 619, 714, 818
Local Access: California: Los Angeles, Oakland, San Diego, Irvine, Pasadena, Palo Alto
Fees: $5/hour ($3/hour on weekend), plus $20/month, plus $50 startup, or $250/month flat-rate for AYC
E-mail: help@cerf.net

DIAL N' CERF USA
PO Box 85608
San Diego, CA 92186-9784
Voice: 800-876-2373; 619-455-3900
Dial-Up: Contact for number
Area codes: 800
Local Access: Wherever 800 service is available
Fees: $10/hour ($8/hour on weekend), plus $20/month.
E-mail: help@cerf.net

DIGITAL EXPRESS GROUP
6006 Greenbelt Road, Suite 228
Greenbelt, MD 20770
Voice: 301-220-2020
Fax: 301-470-5215
E-mail: info@digex.net

DMCONNECTION
Doyle Munroe Consultants, Inc.
267 Cox St.
Hudson, MA 01749
Voice: 508-568-1618
Fax: 508-562-1133
E-mail: postmaster@dmc.com

EARTHLINK NETWORK, INC.
3171 Los Feliz Blvd., Suite 203
Los Angeles, CA 90039
Voice: 213-644-9500
Fax: 213-644-9510
E-mail: sales@earthlink.net

ECHO COMMUNICATIONS
97 Perry Street, Suite 13
New York, NY 10014
Voice: 212-255-3839
Dial-Up: 212-989-8411 (v.32, v.32 bis); log in as **newuser**
Area Codes: 212
Local Access: New York: Manhattan

Fees: Commercial: $19.95/month; students/seniors: $13.75/month
E-mail:horn@echonyc.com

ELECTROTEX, INC.
2300 Richmond
Houston, TX 77098
Voice: +1 713-526-3456, 1-800-460-1801
Fax: +1 713-639-6400
E-mail: info@electrotex.com

E & S SYSTEMS PUBLIC ACCESS *NIX
c/o Steve Froeschke
2817 Falvy Ave.
San Diego, CA 92111
Voice: 619-278-4641
Dial-Up: 619-278-8267 (V.32bis, TurboPEP), 619-278-8267 (V32), 619-278-9837
(PEP)
Area Codes: 619
Local Access: California: San Diego
Fees: BBS free; shell $30/3 months, $50/6 months, $80/9 months, $100/year
E-mail: steve@cg57.esnet.com

ESKIMO NORTH
PO Box 75284
Seattle, WA 98125-0284
Voice: 206-367-7457
Dial-Up: 206-367-3837 300-14.4k, 206-362-6731 for 9600/14.4k, 206-742-1150
World Blazer
Area Codes: 206
Local Access: Washington: Seattle, Everett
Fees: $10/month or $96/year
E-mail: nanook@eskimo.com

EVERGREEN INTERNET EXPRESS, INC.
5333 N. 7th Street, Suite B-220
Phoenix, Az. 85014
Voice: (602) 230-9330
Area Codes: 602
Local Access: Arizona
Fees: individual: $239/year; commercial: $479/year; special educational rates
E-mail: jennyu@libre.com

EXPRESS ACCESS—ONLINE COMMUNICATIONS SERVICE
6006 Greenbelt Rd. #228
Greenbelt, MD 20770
Voice: 301-220-2020, 800-969-9090
Dial-Up: 301-220-0462, 410-766-1855, 703-281-7997, 714-377-9784, 908-937-9481.
Log in as **new.**

Area codes: 202, 301, 410, 703, 714, 908
Local Access: Northern VA, Baltimore MD, Washington DC, New Brunswick NJ, Orange County CA
Fees: $25/month or $250/year
E-mail: info@digex.com

EZ-E-MAIL
Shecora Associates, Inc.
PO Box 7604
Nashua, NH 03060
Voice: +1 603-672-0736
E-mail: info@lemuria.sai.com

FREELANCE SYSTEMS PROGRAMMING
807 Saint Nicholas Avenue
Dayton, OH 45410
Voice: 513-254-7246
Dial-Up: 513-258-7745 to 14.4 Kbps
Area Codes: 513
Local Access: Ohio: Dayton
Fees: $20 startup and $1 per hour
E-mail: fsp@dayton.fsp.com

FULLFEED COMMUNICATIONS
359 Raven Lane
Madison, WI 53705
Voice: 608-246-4239
E-mail: info@fullfeed.com

GATEWAY TO THE WORLD
9715 West Broward Blvd., Suite 177
Plantation, FL 33324
Voice: 305-670-2930
Dial-Up: 305-670-2929
Area Codes: 305
Local Access: Florida: Dade County
E-mail: m.jansen@gate.com

GLAIDS NET
PO Box 20771
Seattle WA 98102
Voice: 206-323-7483
Dial-Up: 206-322-0621
Area Codes: 206
Local Access: Washington: Seattle
Fees: $10/month. Scholarships available. Free 7-day trial.
Visitors are welcome.
E-mail: tomh@glaids.wa.com

GLOBAL ENTERPRISE SERVICE, INC.
John von Neumann Center Network
6 von Neuman Hall
Princeton University
Princeton, NJ 08544
Voice: +1 609-258-2400 or +1 800-358-4437
E-mail: market@jvnc.net

HALCYON
PO Box 555
Grapeview, WA 98546
Voice: 206-426-9298
Dial-Up: 206-382-6245. Log in as **new**.
Area Codes: 206
Local Access: Washington: Seattle
Fees: $200/year or $60/quarter, plus $10 startup fee
E-mail: info@remote.halcyon.com

HOLONET
Information Access Technologies, Inc.
46 Shattuck Square, Suite 11
Berkeley, CA 94704-1152
Voice: 510-704-0160
Dial-Up: 510-704-1058
Area Codes: 510, PDN
Local Access: California: Berkeley
Fees: $2/hour off-peak, $4/hour peak; $6/month or $60/year minimum.
E-mail: info@holonet.net

IDS WORLD NETWORK
3 Franklin Road
East Greenwich, RI 02818
Voice: 401-884-7856
Dial-Up: 401-884-9002, 401-785-1067
Area Codes: 401
Local Access: Rhode Island: East Greenwich; northern RI
Fees: $10/month or $50/half year or $100/year
E-mail: info@ids.net

INET
University Computing Services
Wrubel Computing Center
Indiana University
750 N. State Rd. 46
Bloomington, IN 47405
Attn: Dick Ellis
Voice: +1 812-855-4240
E-mail: ellis@ucs.indiana.edu

INFINET, L.C.
Internet Communications Services
211 East City Hall Avenue, Suite 236
Norfolk, VA 23510
Voice: +1 804-622-4289
Fax: +1 804-622-7158
E-mail: rcork@infi.net

INFOLAN
Infonet Service Corporation
2100 East Grand Avenue
El Segundo, CA 90245
Attn: George Abe
Voice: 310-335-2600
Fax: +1 310-335-2876
E-mail: abe@infonet.com

**INSTITUTE FOR GLOBAL COMMUNICATIONS/IGC NETWORKS
(PEACENET, ECONET, CONFLICTNET, LABORNET, HOMEONET)**
18 De Boom St.
San Francisco, CA 94107
Voice: 415-442-0220
Dial-Up: 415-322-0284. Log in as **new**.
Area Codes: 415, 800, PDN
Local Access: California: Palo Alto, San Francisco
Fees: $10/month plus $3/hour after first hour
E-mail: support@igc.apc.org

INTERACCESS
9400 W. Foster Ave., Suite 111
Chicago, IL 60656
Voice: 708-671-0113
Dial-Up: 708-671-0237; log in as **guest**.
Area Codes: 708, 312, 815
Local Access: Chicagoland metropolitan area
Fees: $23/month shell, $26/month SLIP/PPP, plus $15 installation
E-mail: info@interaccess.com

INTERCON SYSTEMS CORP.
950 Herndon Parkway, Suite 420
Herndon, VA 22070
Voice: 703-709-5500, Ext. 551; 800-638-2968
Dial-Up: Contact for number.
Area Codes: PDN
Fees: $29/month, plus $29.95 one-time charge for software for WorldLink Basic
Service; $39/month for 9600 bps access.
E-mail: comment@intercon.com

INTERNET CONNECT SERVICES
202 West Goodwin
Victoria, TX 77901
Voice: 512-572-9987
Fax: +1 512-572-8193
E-mail: staff@icsi.net

INTERNET DIRECT, INC.
1366 N. Thomas Rd Suite 210
Phoenix, AZ 85014
Voice: 602-274-0100 (Phoenix), 602-324-0100 (Tucson)
Dial-Up: 602-274-9600 (Phoenix); 602-321-9600 (Tucson); log in as **guest**.
Area Codes: 602
Local Access: Arizona: Phoenix, Tucson
Fees: $20/month (personal); $30/month (business)
E-mail: info@indirect.com (automated); support@indirect.com (human)

INTERNEX INFORMATION SERVICES, INC.
1050 Chestnut St., Suite 202
Menlo Park, CA 94025
Voice: 415-473-3060
Fax: 415-473-3062
E-mail: info@internex.net

INTERPATH
PO Box 12800
Raleigh, NC 27605
Voice: 919-890-6305, 800-849-6305
Dial-Up: Call for number
Area Codes: 704, 919
Local Access: North Carolina statewide
Fees: $30/month; $35/month SLIP
E-mail: info@interpath.net

IWAY INTERNET SERVICES
140 N. Phillips, Suite 404
Sioux Falls, SD 57102
Voice: 800-386-IWAY, 605-331-4211
Fax: 605-335-3942
E-mail: info@iw.net

KAIWAN PUBLIC ACCESS INTERNET ONLINE SERVICES
12550 Brookhurst Street, Suite H
Garden Grove, CA 92640
Voice: 714-638-2139
Dial-Up: 714-539-5726, 310-527-7358
Area Codes: 213, 310, 714

Local Access: California: Los Angeles, Orange County
Fees: $15.00/signup, plus $15.00/month or $30.00/quarter (3 months) or
$11.00/month by credit card
E-mail: info@kaiwan.com

LavaNet, Inc.
733 Bishop St., Suite 1590
Honolulu, HI 96813
Voice: 808-545-5282
Fax: 808-545-7020
E-mail: info@lava.net

Los Nettos
University of Southern California
Information Sciences Institute
4676 Admiralty Way
Marina del Rey, CA 90292
Attn: Ann Westine Cooper
Voice: 310-822-1511
E-mail: los-nettos-request@isi.edu

Maestro
29 John St., Suite 1601
New York, NY 10038
Voice: 212-240-9600
Dial-Up: 212-240-9700. Log in as **newuser**.
Area Codes: 212, 718
Local Access: New York: New York City
Fees: $15/month or $150/year
E-mail: info@maestro.com; staff@maestro.com; rkelly@maestro.com, ksingh@
maestro.com

MCI Mail
1133 19th Street, NW
7th Floor
Washington, DC 20036
Voice: +1 800-444-6245 or +1 202-833-8484
E-mail: 2671163@mcimail.com

MCSNet
3217 N. Sheffield
Chicago, IL 60657
Voice: 312-248-8649
Dial-Up: 312-248-0900 V.32, 0970 V.32bis, 6295 (PEP), follow prompts
Area Codes: 312, 708, 815
Local Access: Illinois: Chicago
Fees: $25/month or $65/3 months; $30/3 months for 15 hours/month
E-mail: info@genesis.mcs.com

MERIT NETWORK, INC.—MICHNET PROJECT
University of Michigan, Institute of Science and Technology
2200 Bonisteel Ave.
Ann Arbor, MI 48109
Voice: 313-764-9430
Dial-Up: Contact for number, or Telnet hermes.merit.edu and type **help** at Which host? prompt.
Area Codes: 202, 301, 313, 517, 616, 703, 810, 906, PDN
Local Access: Michigan; Boston, MA; Wash. DC
Fees: $35/month, plus $40 signup
E-mail: info@merit.edu

THE META NETWORK
2000 N. 15th St., Suite 103
Arlington, VA 22201
Voice: 703-243-6622
Dial-Up: Contact for numbers.
Area Codes: 703, 202, 301, PDN
Local Access: Washington, DC metro area
Fees: $20/month, plus $15 signup/first month
E-mail: info@tmn.com

MIDNET
Midwestern States Network
29 WSEC
University of Nebraska
Lincoln, NE 68588
Voice: 402-472-5032
E-mail: nic@westie.mid.net

MILLENIUM ONLINE
Voice: 800-736-0122
Dial-Up: Contact for numbers.
Area Codes: PDN
Local Access: PDN private numbers available
Fees: $10 month/.10 per minute domestic, .30 international
E-mail: jjablow@mill.com

MILWAUKEE INTERNET X
Mix Communications
PO Box 17166
Milwaukee, WI 53217
Voice: 414-962-8172
E-mail: sysop@mixcom.com

MINDVOX
Phantom Access Technologies, Inc.
175 Fifth Avenue, Suite: 2614

New York, NY 10011
Voice: 212-989-2418
Dial-Up: 212-988-5030; log in as **mindvox** or **guest**.
Area Codes: 212, 718
Local Access: New York: New York City
Fees: Between $15–20/month. No startup fee.
E-mail: postmaster@phantom.com

MORDOR INTERNATIONAL BBS
409 Washington Street, #292
Hoboken, NJ 07030
Dial-Up: 201-432-0600; log in as **guest**.
Area codes: 201
Local Access: New York City and northern New Jersey.
E-mail: ritz@mordor.com

MRNET
Minnesota Regional Network
511 11th Avenue South, Box 212
Minneapolis, MN 55415
Voice: 612-342-2570
E-mail: info@mr.net

MSEN, INC.
628 Brooks St.
Ann Arbor, MI 48103
Voice: 313-998-4562
Dial-Up: Contact for number.
Area Codes: 313, 810
Local Access: All of SE Michigan (313, 810)
Fees: $20/month; $20 startup
E-mail: info@msen.com

MV COMMUNICATIONS, INC.
PO Box 4963
Manchester, NH 03108-4963
Voice: 603-429-2223
Dial-Up: Contact for numbers.
Area Codes: 603
Local Access: many New Hampshire communities
Fees: $5.00/month minimum, plus variable hourly rates.
E-mail: info@mv.com

NANDO
215 S. McDowell St.
Raleigh, NC 27602
Voice: 919-829-4500
Dial-Up: Call for number.

Area Codes: 704, 919
Local Access: North Carolina statewide
Fees: $30/month
E-mail: info@nando.net

NEARNET

10 Moulton St.
Cambridge, MA 02138
Voice: 617-873-8730
Dial-Up: Contact for number.
Area Codes: 508, 603, 617
Local Access: Massachusetts: Boston; New Hampshire: Nashua
Fees: $250/month
E-mail: nearnet-staff@nic.near.net

NEOSOFT'S SUGAR LAND UNIX

3408 Mangum
Houston, TX 77092
Voice: 713-684-5969
Dial-Up: 713-684-5900
Area Codes: 504, 713
Local Access: Texas: Houston metro area; Louisiana: New Orleans.
Fees: $29.95/month
E-mail: info@neosoft.com

NETCOM ONLINE COMMUNICATION SERVICES, INC.

PO Box 20774
San Jose, CA 95160
Voice: 408-554-8649, 800-501-8649
Dial-Up: 206-547-5992, 214-753-0045, 303-758-0101, 310-842-8835, 312-380-0340,
404-303-9765, 408-241-9760, 408-459-9851, 415-328-9940, 415-985-5650, 503-626-
6833, 510-274-2900, 510-426-6610, 510-865-9004, 617-237-8600, 619-234-0524,
703-255-5951, 714-708-3800, 818-585-3400, 916-965-1371
Area Codes: 206, 213, 214, 303, 310, 312, 404, 408, 415, 503, 510, 617, 619, 703,
714, 718, 818, 916
Local Access: California: Alameda, Irvine, Los Angeles, Palo Alto, Pasadena, Sacra-
mento, San Diego, San Francisco, San Jose, Santa Cruz, Walnut Creek; Colorado:
Denver; DC: Washington; Georgia: Atlanta; Illinois: Chicago; Massachusetts:
Boston; Oregon: Portland; Texas: Dallas; Washington: Seattle
Fees: $19.50/month, plus $20 signup
E-mail: info@netcom.com

NETILLINOIS

University of Illinois
Computing Services Office
1304 W. Springfield
Urbana, IL 61801

Attn: Joel L. Hartmann
Voice: 309-677-3100
E-mail: joel@bradley.bradley.edu

NETSYS COMMUNICATION SERVICES
992 San Antonio Rd.
Palo Alto, CA. 94303
Voice: 415-424-0384
E-mail: info@netsys.com

NEVADANET
University of Nevada System
Computing Services
4505 Maryland Parkway
Las Vegas, NV 89154
Attn: Don Zitter
Voice: 702-784-6133
E-mail: zitter@nevada.edu

NORTH SHORE ACCESS
145 Munroe St., Suite 405
Lynn, MA 01901
Voice: 617-593-3110
Dial-Up: 617-593-5774 (V.32, PEP). Log in as **new**.
Area Codes: 617, 508
Local Access: Massachusetts: Wakefield, Lynnfield, Lynn, Saugus, Revere, Peabody,
Salem, Marblehead, Swampscott
Fees: $10/month, includes 10 hours connect time; $1/hour thereafter
E-mail: info@northshore.ecosoft.com

NORTHWESTNET
Northwestern States Network
NorthWestNet
2435 233rd Place NE
Redmond, WA 98053
Voice: 206-562-3000
E-mail: nic@nwnet.net

NORTHWEST NEXUS INC.
PO Box 40597
Bellevue, WA 98015-4597
Voice: 206-455-3505
Dial-Up: Contact for numbers.
Area Codes: 206
Local Access: Washington: Seattle
Fees: $10/month for first 10 hours, plus $3/hour; $20 start-up
E-mail: info@nwnexus.wa.com

NovaLink
Voice: 800-274-2814
Dial-Up: 800-937-7644; log in as **new** or **info**, 508-754-4009 2400, 14400
Area Codes: 508, 617, PDN
Local Access: Massachusetts: Worcester, Cambridge, Marlboro, Boston
Fees: $12.95 signup (refundable and includes 2 hours), plus $9.95/month (includes 5 daytime hours), plus $1.80/hour
E-mail: info@novalink.com

NovaNet, Inc. On-Line Communication Services
2007 N. 15 St., Suite B-5
Arlington, VA 22201
Voice: 703-524-4800
Fax: 703-524-5510
E-mail: sales@novanet.com

Nuance Network Services
904 Bob Wallace Avenue, Suite 119
Huntsville, AL 35801
Voice: 205-533-4296 voice/recording
Dial-Up: Contact for number.
Area Codes: 205
Local Access: Alabama: Huntsville
Fees: personal $25/month, plus $35 startup; corporate: call for options.
E-mail: staff@nuance.com

NYSERnet
New York State State Education and Research Network
200 Elwood Davis Road
Liverpool, NY 13088-6147
Voice: 315-453-2912
Fax: 315-453-3052
E-mail: info@nysernet.org

OARnet
1224 Kinnear Rd.
Columbus, OH 43212
Voice: 614-292-8100
Dial-Up: Send e-mail to nic@oar.net
Area Codes: 614, 513, 419, 216, 800
Local Access: Ohio: Columbus, Cincinnati, Cleveland, Dayton; also 800 service
Fees: $4/hour to $330/month
E-mail: nic@oar.net

Old Colorado City Communications
2502 West Colorado Ave., Suite 203
Colorado Springs, CO 80904
Voice: 719-632-4848, 719-593-7575, 719-636-2040

Dial-Up: 719-632-4111; log in as **newuser**.
Area Codes: 719
Local Access: Colorado: Colorado Springs
Fees: $25/month
E-mail: dave@oldcolo.com; thefox@oldcolo.com

OLYMPUS—THE OLYMPIC PENINSULA'S GATEWAY TO THE INTERNET
Voice: 206-385-0464
Dial-Up: Contact voice number.
Area Codes: 206
Local Access: Washington: Olympic Peninsula/eastern Jefferson County
Fees: $25/month, plus $10 startup
E-mail: info@pt.olympus.net

OPUS ONE
1404 East Lind Road
Phoenix, AZ
Voice: 602-324-0494
Fax: +1 602-324-0495
E-mail: info@opus1.com

PACCOM
University of Hawaii
Department of ICS
2565 The Mall
Honolulu, HI 96822
Attn: Torben Nielsen
Tel: 808-949-6395
E-mail: torben@foralie.ics.hawaii.edu

PACIFIC SYSTEMS GROUP (RAINet)
9501 S.W. Westhaven
Portland, OR 97225
Voice: 503-297-8820
E-mail: rain-admin@psg.com

PAGESAT, INC.
8300 NE Underground Drive, Suite 430
Kansas City, MO 64161-9767
Voice: 800-989-7351
Fax: 816-741-5315
E-mail: root@tyrell.net

PANIX PUBLIC ACCESS UNIX
110 Riverside Dr.
New York, NY 10024
Voice: 212-877-4854
Dial-Up: 212-787-3100; log in as **newuser**.

Area Codes: 212, 718
Local Access: New York: New York City
Fees: $19/month or $208/year, plus $40 signup
E-mail: alexis@panix.com, jsb@panix.com

PATHWAYS
Pandora Systems
1903 Broderick #4
San Francisco, CA 94115
Voice: 415-346-4188
Area Codes: 415, PDN
Fees: $25 signup; $8/month, plus $8/hour peak, $5/hour off-peak, $3/hour via Internet, or $3/hour by direct dial modem access
E-mail: info@path.net

PEACESAT PAN PACIFIC EDUCATION AND COMMUNICATIONS EXPERIMENTS BY SATELLITE
Social Science Research Institute
University of Hawaii at Manoa
Old Engineering Quad, Building 31
Honolulu, HI 96822
Voice: 808-956-7794/8848
Fax: 808-956-2512
E-mail: peacesat@uhunix.uhcc.hawaii.edu

PERFORMANCE SYSTEMS INTERNATIONAL, INC. (PSI)
11800 Sunrise Valley Drive, Suite 1100
Reston, VA 22091
Voice: 703-620-6651
Dial-Up: Send e-mail to numbers-info@psi.com.
Local Access: Nationwide through PDN
E-mail: info@psi.com

PIONEER NEIGHBORHOOD
20 Moore St. #3
Somerville, MA 02144-2124
Voice: 617-646-4800
E-mail: admin@pn.com

THE PIPELINE
150 Broadway, Suite 1710
New York, NY 10038
Voice: 212-267-3636
Dial-Up: 212-267-8606; log in as **guest**.
Area Codes: 212, 718
Local Access: New York: New York City
Fees: $15/month (includes 5 hours) or $20/20 hours or $35 unlimited
E-mail: info@pipeline.com, staff@pipeline.com

THE PORTAL SYSTEM
20863 Stevens Creek Boulevard, Suite 200
Cupertino, CA 95014
Voice: 408-973-9111
Dial-Up: 408-973-8091 high speed; 408-725-0561 at 2400 bps; log in as **info**.
Area Codes: 408, 415, PDN
Local Access: California: Cupertino, Mountain View, San Jose
Fees: $19.95/month, plus $19.95 signup fee
E-mail: info@portal.com

PREPNET
305 S. Craig St., 2nd Floor
Pittsburgh, PA 15213
Voice: 412-268-7870
Dial-Up: Contact for number.
Area Codes: 215, 412, 717, 814
Local Access: Pennsylvania: Philadelphia, Pittsburgh, Harrisburg
Fees: $1,000/year membership; equipment: $325 one-time fee, plus $40/month
E-mail: twb+@andrew.cmu.edu

PROMETHEUS INFORMATION NETWORK GROUP, INC.
4514 Chamblee Dunwoody Road, Suite 284
Dunwoody, GA 30338
Voice: 404-818-6300
Fax: 404-458-8031
E-mail: questions@ping.com

PSCNET
Pittsburgh Supercomputing Center Network
Pittsburgh Supercomputing Center
4400 5th Avenue
Pittsburgh, PA 15213
Attn: Eugene Hastings
Voice: 412-268-4960
E-mail: pscnet-admin@psc.edu

RAINDROP LABORATORIES
Voice: n/a
Dial-Up: 503-293-1772 (2400); 503-293-2059 (v.32, v.32 bis); log in as **apply**.
Area Codes: 503
Local Access: Oregon: Portland, Beaverton, Hillsboro, Forest Grove, Gresham, Tigard, Lake Oswego, Oregon City, Tualatin, Wilsonville
Fees: $6/month (1 hour/day limit)
E-mail: info@agora.rain.com

REALTIME COMMUNICATIONS
6721 North Lamar, Suite 103
Austin, TX 78752

Voice: 512-451-0046
Dial-Up: 512-459-0604; log in as **new**.
Area Codes: 512
Local Access: Texas: Austin
Fees: $50/180 days. Monthly and quarterly rates available.
E-mail: hosts@bga.com

RISCNET
InteleCom Data Systems
11 Franklin Road
East Greenwich, RI 02818
Attn: Andy Green
Voice: 401-885-6855
E-mail: info@nic.risc.net

RUSTNET
6905 Telegraph Road, Suite 315
Bloomfield, MI 48301
Voice: 810-650-6812
E-mail: info@rust.net or help@rust.net

SATELLIFE
Associate Director of Operations
SatelLife-U.S.A.,
126 Rogers Street
Cambridge, MA 02142
Attn: Jon Metzger
Voice: 617-868-8522
Fax: 617-868-6647
E-mail: pnsatellife@igc.apc.org

SATELNET
2269 S. University Drive, Box 159
Davie, FL 33324
Voice: 305-434-7340
Fax: 305-680-9848
E-mail: root@satelnet.org

SDSCNET
San Diego Supercomputer Center Network
San Diego Supercomputer Center
PO Box 85608
San Diego, CA 92186-9784
Attn: Paul Love
Voice: +1 619-534-5043
E-mail: loveep@sds.sdsc.edu

SESQUINET
Texas Sesquicentennial Network
Office of Networking and Computing Systems
Rice University
Houston, TX 77251-1892
Voice: 713-527-4988
E-mail: info@sesqui.net

SIERRA-NET
PO Box 3709
Incline Village, NV 89450
Voice: 702-832-6911
E-mail: giles@sierra.net

SOUTH COAST COMPUTING SERVICES, INC.
PO Box 270355
Houston TX 77277-0355
Voice: 713-661-3301
Dial-Up: 713-661-8593 (v.32), 713-661-8595 (v.32bis)
Area Codes: 713
Local Access: Texas: Houston metro area
Fees: dialup: $3/hour; UUCP: $1.50/hour or $100/month unlimited; dedicated:
$120, unlimited access
E-mail: info@sccsi.com

SPEEDWAY FREE ACCESS
Voice: 503-520-2222
E-mail: info@speedway.net

SPRINTLINK
VARESA0115
12502 Sunrise Valley Dr.
Reston, VA 22096-0002
Voice: 800-817-7755
E-mail: info@sprintlink.net

STRUCTURED NETWORK SERVICES, INC.
15635 SE 114th Ave, Suite 201
Clackamas, OR 97015
Voice: 503-656-3530 or 800-881-0962
Fax: +1 503-656-3235
E-mail: info@structured.net (auto reply) or sales@structured.net

SSNET, INC.
1254 Lorewood Grove Road
Middletown, DE 19709
Voice: 302-378-1386, 800-331-1386

Dial-Up: Contact for info.
Area Codes: 302
Local Access: Delaware: Wilmington
Fees: full service, $25/month, plus $20/startup; personal SLIP/PPP $25/month, plus
$2/hour, $20/startup; dedicated SLIP/PPP, $150/month, $450/startup
E-mail: sharris@marlin.ssnet.com

SURANET SOUTHEASTERN UNIVERSITIES RESEARCH ASSOCIATION NETWORK
1353 Computer Science Center
University of Maryland
College Park, MD 20742-2411
Attn: Jack Hahn
Voice: 301-982-4600
E-mail: marketing@sura.net

TELEPORT
319 SW Washington, Suite 803
Portland, OR 97204
Voice: 503-223-4245
Dial-Up: 503-220-0636 (2400), 503-220-1016 (v.32, v.32 bis); log in as **new**.
Area Codes: 503
Local Access: Oregon: Portland, Beaverton, Hillsboro, Forest Grove, Gresham,
Tigard, Lake Oswego, Oregon City, Tualatin, Wilsonville
Fees: $10/month (1 hour/day limit)
E-mail: jamesd@teleport.com

TELERAMA
16 Southern Avenue
Pittsburgh, PA 15211
Voice: 412-481-3505
Dial-Up: 412-481-5302; log in as **new**.
Area codes: 412
Local Access: Pennsylvania: Pittsburgh
Fees: .66/hour 2400bps; $1.32/hour 14.4K bps; $6 minimum/month
E-mail: info@telerama.lm.com

TEXAS METRONET
860 Kinwest Pkwy., Suite 179
Irving, TX 75063-3440
Voice: 214-705-2900, 817-543-8756
Dial-Up: 214-705-2901/817-261-1127 (V.32bis), 214-705-2929(PEP); log in as **info**.
Or 214-705-2917/817-261-7687 (2400); log in as **signup**.
Area Codes: 214
Local Access: Texas: Dallas
Fees: $10–$50/month, plus $20–$30 startup fee
E-mail: info@metronet.com

THENET
Texas Higher Education Network
Computation Center
University of Texas
Austin, TX 78712
Voice: 512-471-2400
E-mail: info@nic.the.net

UNIVERSITY OF ALASKA TUNDRA SERVICES
Tundra Services Coordinator
UAS Computing Services
11120 Glacier Highway
Juneau, AK 99801
Voice: 907-465-6452
Fax: 907-465-6295
E-mail: JNJMB@acad1.alaska.edu

UUNET TECHNOLOGIES, INC.
3110 Fairview Park Drive, Suite 570
Falls Church, VA 22042
Voice: 800-488-6384
Fax: 703-204-8001
E-mail: info@uunet.uu.net

VERNET
Virginia Education and Research Network
Academic Computing Center
Gilmer Hall
University of Virginia
Charlottesville, VA 22903
Attn: James Jokl
Voice: 804-924-0616
E-mail: jaj@virginia.edu

VITA—VOLUNTEERS IN TECHNICAL ASSISTANCE
1600 Wilson Boulevard 5th Floor
Arlington, VA 22209
Voice: 703-276-1800
Fax: 703-243-1865
E-mail: vita@gmuvax.gmu.edu

VNET
PO Box 31474
Charlotte, NC, 28204
Voice: 800-377-3282
Dial-Up: 704-347-8839, 919-406-1544, 919-851-1526; log in as **new**.
Area Codes: 704, 919

Local Access: North Carolina: Charlotte, RTP, Raleigh, Durham, Chapel Hill, Winston-Salem/Greensboro
Fees: $25/month individual; $12.50 a month for Telnet-in-only. SLIP/PPP/UUCP starting at $25/month.
E-mail: info@vnet.net

WESTNET
Southwestern States Network
601 S. Howes, 6th Floor South
Colorado State University
Fort Collins, CO 80523
Attn: Pat Burns
Voice: 303-491-7260
E-mail: pburns@westnet.net

THE WHOLE EARTH 'LECTRONIC LINK (THE WELL)
27 Gate Five Road
Sausalito, CA 94965
Voice: 415-332-4335
Dial-Up: 415-332-6106; log in as **newuser**.
Area Codes: 415, PDN
Local Access: California: Sausalito
Fees: $15/month, plus $2/hour
E-mail: info@well.sf.ca.us

WISCNET
Madison Academic Computing Center
1210 W. Dayton Street
Madison, WI 53706
Voice: 608-262-8874
E-mail: wn-info@nic.wiscnet.net

THE WORLD
Software Tool and Die
1330 Beacon St.
Brookline, MA 02146
Voice: 617-739-0202
Dial-Up: 617-739-9753; log in as **new**.
Area Codes: 617, PDN
Local Access: Massachusetts: Boston
Fees: $5/month, plus $2/hour; or $20/month for 20 hours
E-mail: office@world.std.com

WVNET—WEST VIRGINIA NETWORK FOR EDUCATIONAL TELECOMPUTING
837 Chestnut Ridge Road
Morgantown, WV 26505
Attn: Harper Grimm

Voice: 304-293-5192
E-mail: cc011041@wvnvms.wvnet.edu

WYOMING.COM
312 S. 4th
Lander, WY 82520
Voice: +1 307-332-3030 or (800) WYO-I-NET
Fax: 307-332-5270
E-mail: info@wyoming.com

WYVERN TECHNOLOGIES, INC.
211 East City Hall Ave., Suite 236
Norfolk, VA 23510
Voice: 804-622-4289
Dial-Up: 804-627-1828 (Norfolk); 804-886-0662 (Penninsula)
Area Codes: 804
Local Access: Virginia: Norfolk, Virginia Beach, Portsmouth, Chesapeake, Newport
News, Hampton, Williamsburg
Fees: $15/month or $144/year, $10 startup
E-mail: system@wyvern.com

XLNET INFORMATION SYSTEMS
PO Box 1511
Lisle, IL 60532
Voice: 708-983-6064
Fax: 708-983-6879
E-mail: admin@xnet.com

XMISSION
PO Box 510063
Salt Lake City, UT 84151-0063
Voice: 801-539-0852
Fax: 801-539-0900
E-mail: support@xmission.com

XNET INFORMATION SYSTEMS
Voice: 708-983-6064
Dial-Up: 708-983-6435 V.32bis and TurboPEP
Area Codes: 312, 708, 815
Local Access: Illinois: Chicago, Naperville, Hoffman Estates
Fees: $45/3 months or $75/6 months
E-mail: info@xnet.com

U. S. Public Access Unix Sites by State

Here, as elsewhere in the Appendix, public access Unix sites are drawn from the NixPub list. The public access Unix sites are presented in the following format:

Updated Last	Telephone #	System Name	Location		Speed Range	Hours
09/93	602-274-9600	**indirect**	Phoenix	AZ	000300-FAST	24

Sun/SunOS + multiple 486/50's; Live internet, multiple lines (up to 14.4k); E-Mail/ USENET, 5mb disk quota, shell or menu system, multi-user games, off-line news readers (personal $20/mo, business $30/mo); UUCP feeds available ($20–$45/mo); SLIP/PPP connection at speeds up to 14.4k-demand/dedicated lines (leased line connections to 24kbps) (basic rates $150/mo).
Contact: info@indirect.com

| 03/93 | 602-293-3726 | **coyote** | Tucson | AZ | 300-FAST | 24 |

FTK-386, ISC 386/ix 2.0.2; Waffle BBS, devoted to embedded systems programming and u-controller development software; E-Mail/USENET; UUCP and limited USENET feeds available;
Contact: E.J. McKernan (ejm@datalog.com).
bbs: login: bbs (NO PWD)
uucp: login: nuucp (NO PWD)

| 09/93 | 602-321-9600 | **indirect** | Tucson | AZ | 300-FAST | 24 |

Refer to primary entry (Phoenix, AZ) for system/services details.

| 03/94 | 602-649-9099 | **telesys** | Mesa | AZ | 1200-FAST | 24 |

SCO Unix V/386 3.2.4; Telebit WorldBlazers; TeleSys-II Unix based BBS (no fee) login: bbs; Unix archives available via BBS or ANON UUCP; Shell Accounts available for full access USENET, email (fees); Phoenix Matchmaker with more than 9000 members (fees) login: bbs. Regional supplier of USENET Newsfeeds; uucp-anon: nuucp NOPWD;
Contact: kreed@tnet.com or . . . !ncar!noao!enuucp!telesys!kreed

| 02/94 | 602-991-5952 | **aa7bq** | Scottsdale | AZ | 300-2400 | 24 |

Sun 4, SunOS 4.1.2; NB bbs system; 900 meg online; Primarily Ham Radio related articles from usenet (Rec.radio.amateur.misc), complete Callsign Database, Radio and scanner modifications, frequency listings, shell access by permission, No fees, Free classified ads, Local e-mail only. Login: bbs (8N1) or Login: callsign for callsign database only. Don't use MNP!
For additional info contact: Fred.Lloyd@West.Sun.COM

| 01/95 | 213-962-8191 | **kitana** | Los Angeles | CA | 300-FAST | 24 |

LINUX; Internet E-mail, Usenet Newsgroups, MUD, Chat, Slackware Linux 1st-time downloading, Matchmaker (20K+ users). Pasadena number 818/793-9108. Contact: sysop@kitana.org; multi-lines V.32bis.

| 03/94 | 408-241-9760 | **netcom** | San Jose | CA | 1200-FAST | 24 |

Unix, Sun Network SunOS 4.1; Netcom-Online Communication Services; 70 Telebit lines V.32/V.42 9600/2400/; USENET (16 days), Lrg archive, News/Mail Feeds, Shell, Internet (ftp, telnet, irc), Slip Connections, Local access via CALNet San Jose, Palo Alto, Red Wd Cty, San Fran, Oklnd, Berkly, Alameda, Pleasanton, Los Angeles, and Santa Cruz; Fee $17.50/mo + Reg fee of $15.00. Login: guest (510)865-9004, (408)241-9760,

(408)459-9851, (310)842-8835, (415)424-0131, (510)426-6860;
Just Say No to connect fees, Login as guest (no password).

03/94   408-245-7726 **uuwest**   Sunnyvale   CA 300-FAST   24
SCO-XENIX, Waffle. No fee, USENET news (news.*, music, comics, telecom, etc) The
Dark Side of the Moon BBS. This system has been in operation since 1985. Login: new
Contact: (UUCP) ames!uuwest!request (Domain) request@darkside.com

03/94   408-249-9630 **quack**   Santa Clara   CA 300-FAST   24
Sun 4/75, SunOS 4.1.3; 3 lines: First two are Zyxel U-1496E (300-2400, v.32bis/v.42bis),
third is a Worldblazer (same and add PEP); Internet connectivity; Shell - $10/mo; New
users should login as 'guest';
Contact: postmaster@quack.kfu.com

06/94   408-293-9010 **a2i**   San Jose   CA 1200-FAST   24
Usenet/Email/Internet/SunOS (Unix). 20 lines. Dial 408-293-9010 (v.32bis, v.32) or 408-
293-9020 (PEP) and log in as "guest". $15/month for 6-month. Also available via telnet,
a2i.rahul.net, 192.160.13.1.
Contact: info@rahul.net [daemon response] or voice 408-293-8078

04/93   408-423-4810 **deeptht**   Santa Cruz   CA 300-FAST   24
4 dialin lines (2 2400 at 423-4810, 2 v32 at 423-1767), 486/40+32M, 2 GB disk space
including a large part of the uunet source archives, SCO Unix 3.2v4.1, C/Pascal/For-
tran/BASIC compilers, TinyMud, rn/trn.
Domain name: deeptht.armory.com (and alias armory.com).

02/94   408-423-9995 **cruzio**   Santa Cruz   CA 1200-2400   24
Tandy 4000, Xenix 2.3.*, Caucus 3.*; focus on Santa Cruz activity (ie directory of community and government organizations, events, . . .); USENET Support; Multiple lines;
no shell; fee: $15/quarter.
Contact: . . . !uunet!cruzio!chris

02/94   408-458-2289 **gorn**   Santa Cruz   CA 300-FAST   24
Everex 386, SCO xenix 2.3.2; 2 lines, -2837 telebit for PEP connects; Standard shell
access, games, email injection into the internet, up to date archive of scruz-sysops information, upload/download, usenet news including scruz.* hierarchy for santa cruz area
information; UUCP set up on as-requested; No charge, donations accepted; newuser: log
in as "gorn" and fill out online form.
Contact: falcon@gorn.echo.com

03/94   408-725-0561 **portal**   Cupertino   CA 300-FAST   24
Networked Suns (SunOS), multiple lines, shell or "online menu" access; Live Internet;
fees: $19.95/mn; conferencing, multi-user chats, computer special interest groups;
E-Mail/USENET; UUCP service also available.
Contact: Customer Service (cs@portal.com).

06/94   408-739-1520 **szebra**   Sunnyvale   CA 300-FAST   24
486PC, Linux; 4 lines, Telebit, V.FC, V32bis; Full Usenet News, email (Internet & UUCP),

first time users login: new, shell access/files storage/email, FTP, gopher, archie, WWW available (registration required); GNU, X11R4 and R5 source archives. viet-net/SCV and VNese files/software archives.
Contact: admin@szebra.Saigon.COM or {claris.zorch,sonyusa}!szebra!admin

03/94   415-332-6106 **well**   Sausalito   CA 1200-FAST   24
6-processor Sequent Symmetry (i386); Internet, UUCP and USENET access; multiple lines; access via CPN and Internet (well.sf.ca.us); PICOSPAN BBS; $15/mo + $2/hr (CPN or 9600 +$4/hr);
Contact (415) 332-4335

03/94   415-949-3133 **starnet**   Los Altos   CA 300-FAST   24
SunOS 4.1. 8-lines. MNP1-5 and v42/bis, or PEP on all lines. Shell access for all users. USENET—900+ groups. E-mail (feeds available). smart mail. Publically available software (pd/shareware). $12/mo.
Contact: admin@starnet.uucp or . . . !uunet!apple!starnet!admin

03/94   415-967-9443 **btr**   Mountain View CA 300-FAST   24
Sun (SunOS Unix), shell access, e-mail, netnews, uucp, can access by Telenet PC Pursuit, multiple lines, Telebit, flat rate: $12.50/month.
For sign-up information please send e-mail to Customer Service at cs@btr.com or ..![decwrl.fernwood,mips]!btr!cs or call 415-966-1429 Voice.

03/93   510-294-8591 **woodowl**   Livermore   CA 1200-FAST   24
Xenix/386 3.2.1. Waffle BBS, Usenet Access; Reasonable users welcome. No fee;
For more information contact: william@woodowl.UUCP, 111-winken!chumley! woodowl!william, or call and just sign up on system.

06/94   510-530-9682 **bdt**   Oakland   CA 1200-FAST   24
Sun 4, SunOS 4.1; BBS access to Usenet news, E-mail, with QWK support $35/year. Live Internet Access. Telnet to bdt.com. First time users login: bbs. SLIP/PPP starting at $20/month. Leased line connections, newsfeeds, POP3, domain mail services also available.
Contact: david@bdt.com

03/94   510-623-8652 **jack**   Fremont   CA 300-FAST   24
Sun 4/470 running Solaris 2.2 offers downloading of netnews archives and all uploaded software. Each user can log in as bbs or as the account which they create for themselves. This is a free Public Access Unix System that is part of a network of 4 machines. The primary phone line is on a rotary to five other lines.

02/94   510-704-1058 **HoloNet**   Berkeley   CA 1200-FAST   24
DECstations, ULTRIX; Commercial network, over 850 cities; Custom shell; Full Internet, IRC, telnet, USENET, USA Today Decisionline, games; $2/hr off-peak; Telnet: holonet.net, Info sever: info@holonet.net,
Contact: support@holonet.net

11/93   619-278-8267   **cg57**   San Diego   CA 1200-FAST   24
i386 Unix ISC 3.2 R4.0, UniBoard BBS Software (login as bbs); Worldblazer on dial-in,
-3905 Telebit Trailblazer Plus, -9837 Practical Peripherals (V32); BBS is free; Over 800
meg of downloadable software (Unix/FreeBSD/386BSD/Linux/NETBSD and DOS systems + Soundblaster files); Shell accounts available for $30 for 3 months with access to
ftp/telnet/irc/gopher/archie/etc. Full (USENET) news feed, and selected Fidonet uucp
accounts available. cg57.esnet.com is on the internet (198.180.239.3) Anonymous uucp
- login: nuucp (no password). Get file 1s-1R.Z for complete files listing.
Contact: steve@cg57.esnet.com

04/94   619-634-1376   **cyber**   Encinitas   CA 300-FAST   24
Equip ???; Multiple lines [HST16.8/V.32]; The Cyberspace Station; On the Internet (telnet to CYBER.NET [192.153.125.1]); A Public Access Unix service with full Internet
connectivity; E-Mail/USENET, International communications, hunting for files, and
interactive chatting; Login on as "guest" and send feedback (Don't forget to leave a
phone number where you can be reached).
Contact: info@cyber.net

03/94   619-637-3640   **crash**   San Diego   CA 12-FAST   24
CTSNET Public Access Unix. A network of 486-66/DX2 64mb+32mb, SCO Unix 3.2v4.1
machines, 41 lines; HST: 619-593-6400, 637-3640, 220-0836; V32/V32.bis: 619-593-7300,
637-3660, 220-0853; PEP: 619-593-9500, 637-3680, 220-0857. V42.bis most lines, All
modems at 38,400bps, Telebits at 19,200/38,400bps. 8N1 only. International Usenet
(6600+ groups), Clarinet News Service, Reuters News, worldwide email, shell and uucp
accounts. 3.5gb disk. Direct Internet T1 dedicated. Shell accounts $18 per month flat,
newfeeds, SLIP, PPP, other svcs.
Contact: bblue@crash.cts.com, support@ctsnet.cts.com, info@crash.cts.com

08/94   707-444-6614   **northcoast**   Eureka   CA 300-FAST   24
Northcoast Internet, 80486, Linux 1.0.1; 10 lines, full Internet, full USENET, chat,
UUCP. Cost: $20 a month for 20 hours . . . additional $1/hr. $25 sign-up fee.
Contact: info@northcoast.com (+1 707 443 8696 voice).

03/94   714-635-2863   **dhw68k**   Anaheim   CA 1200-FAST   24
Unistride 2.1; Trailblazer access; 2nd line -1915; No fee; USENET News; /bin/sh or
/bin/csh available

03/94   714-842-5851   **conexch**   Santa Ana   CA 300-2400   24
386 - SCO Xenix - Free Unix guest login and PC-DOS bbs login, one hour initial time
limit, USENET news, shell access granted on request & $25/quarter donation. Anon
uucp: ogin: nuucp NO PASSWD. List of available Unix files resides in /usr3/public/
FILES.

03/94   714-894-2246   **stanton**   Irvine   CA 300-2400   24
80386-25, SCO Xenix-386, 320mb disk, 2400/1200/300 MNP supported; E-Mail &
USENET; Fixed fee $20/yr; X11R4 archive and many packages ported to Xenix 386;
C development system (XENIX/MSDOS), PROCALC 1-2-3 clone, FOXBASE+; anon
uucp: login: nuucp, no word

11/94   818-287-5115 **abode**   El Monte   CA 2400-FAST   24
Unix SysVr4.2; 2400-9600 Baud (Telebit T1000 PEP); Fee of $40 per year; Users get
access to shell account, C compiler, email, usenet news, games, etc. For more information send email to contact name below or login as 'guest' with a password of 'password'.
Contact: eric@abode.ttank.com (cerritos.edu!ttank!abode!eric)

03/94   818-367-2142 **quake**   Sylmar   CA 300-FAST   24
ESIX/386 3.2D running Waffle; Telebit WorldBlazer on dial-in line, 818-362-6092 has
Telebit T2500; Usenet (1000+ groups), Email (registered as quake.sylmar.ca.us), UUCP/
UUPC connections; Rare Bird Advisories, Technomads, more; $5 a month if paid a year
at a time.
New users login as "bbs", then "new". One week free to new users.

08/94   818-997-7500 **amazing**   Los Angeles   CA 300-FAST   24
Equip ???, Linux; 2-1.8gb disk, 3 lines; E-mail/USENET; Custom BBS software; Live
Internet (via 28.8kbps SLIP) — telnet: amazing.cinenet.net;
Contact: david@amazing.cinenet.net.

03/94   916-649-0161 **sactoh0**   Sacramento   CA 1200-FAST   24
3B2/310 SYVR3.2; SAC_Unix, sactoh0.SAC.CA.US; $2/month; 3 lines, v.32 on 722-6519,
TB+ on 649-0161, 2400/1200 baud on 722-5068; USENET, E-Mail, some games; login: new
Contact: root@sactoh0.SAC.CA.US or . . . ames!pacbell!sactoh0!root

02/94   916-923-5013 **rgm**   Sacramento   CA 1200-FAST   24
486SX-25. 200mb. Coherent 386 v4.0.1; Dedicated incoming HST line. Full
Bourne/Korn shell access for all users. Internet mail, limited Usenet (requests encouraged). Mail & news feeds available. $2/mo. for light mail/news users. login: new;
Contact: root@rgm.com

03/94   303-871-3324 **nyx**   Denver   CO 300-FAST   24
A sort of "social experiment" aimed at providing Internet access to the public with minimal operational costs with a "friendly" front end (a home-made menu system). Completely donation and volunteer operated, no user fees at all. Log in as 'new' to create an
account. Equipment: Sun SparcServer II + Pyramid 90x, ~6Gb disk space, 16 phone
lines (+ network logins; usually ~50 users logged in). Public domain file area, private file
area, games, full USENET news, internet e-mail. Provides shell and more network
access with proof of identity.
Contact: Andrew Burt, aburt@nyx.cs.du.edu

05/94   719-520-1700 **cns**   Colorado Spring CO 300-2400   24
Sun 3/260, SunOS; 22 lines (on rollover); $35 signup fee, CNS has national 800 service
for $8/hr (incl Alaska, Hawaii, Virgin Islands and Puerto Rico), In Colo Springs/Denver
(719/303) and telnet: $2.75/hr; CNS offers dialup, uucp, slip, xwindows xremote; CNS
offers 56K and T1 access directly to the T3 ANS backbone nationally. Information at
1-800-748-1200 (voice) or write to info@cscns.com for automated response or write to
service@cscns.com for operator response

01/95   719-548-0782 **alphacm**   Colorado Spring CO 1200-FAST   24
386 - SCO-XENIX, no fee, Home of XBBS, 90 minute per login; dial-in has 3 Telebit
modems on rotory, -0757 has 3 v.fast modems on rotory.
Contact: Sanford <sandy> Zelkovitz (sandy@alphacm.rmii.com) +1 719 548 9971 uucp-
anon: login: nuucp NO PASSWD

05/94   719-632-4111 **oldcolo**   Colorado Spring CO 1200-FAST   24
386 - SCO-XENIX frontend, 2 CT Miniframes backend, e-mail conferencing, databases,
Naplps Graphics, USENET news; 7 lines 8N1, 2400 on -2906, USR Dual 9600 on -2658;
Self registering for limited free access (political, policy, marketplace) Subscriptions $10,
$15, $18 per month for full use.
Dave Hughes SYSOP.

04/94   203-230-4848 **colmiks**   Hamden   CT 2400-FAST   24
Linux. Public Access Unix site. Internet mail, Usenet news, FTP, Telnet, gopher, www,
wais, archie, etc. are all available. News becomes stale in one week. Low monthly fee; no
per hour connect charges and no setup fees. First two weeks free. Unix account with
choice of two shells and three news readers. In addition, members can select new Usenet
newsgroups that Colmik's is not currently receiving. Login as 'newuser'.
Contact: mps@colmiks.com.

03/93   203-661-1279 **admiral**   Greenwich   CT 300-FAST   24
SCO Unix 3.2.2. (HST/V32) 203-661-2873, (PEP/V32) 203-661-1279, (V32) 203-661-0450,
(MNP6) 203-661-2967. Magpie BBS for local conversation and Waffle for Internet
mail/Usenet news. Interactive chat and games. BBS name is "The Grid." Willing to give
newsfeeds and mail access. Shell (tcsh, ksh avail) accounts available at no charge. Direct
connect to Internet site (Yale) via UUCP. 230 megs disk space.
For more information contact uunet!admiral!doug (Doug Fields) or fields-doug@cs.
yale.edu.

06/94   305-587-1930 **satelnet**   Fort Lauderdale FL 300-FAST   24
MIPS RISCserver RC3260, Unix (RISCos 4.52). Login "new" for 1 week of free access.
Rates: $17/month or $60 for 4 months ($15/mo). Full internet access (telnet, ftp, gopher,
irc, etc), unix shell access, usenet (nn, tin, rn, trn), e-mail (elm, pine, mail). Any other PD
software installed upon request. UUCP and SLIP connections available.
Contact: root@sefl.satelnet.org

03/94   407-299-3661 **vicstoy**   Orlando   FL 1200-2400   24
ISC 386/ix 2.0.2. Partial USENET, e-mail (feeds available); Login as bbs, no passwd
(8N1); Free shell access; Orlando BBS list, games; cu to Minix 1.5.10 system (weather
permitting); USENET includes Unix/Minix source groups.
Contact: uunet!tarpit!bilver!vicstoy!vickde or vickde@vicstoy.UUCP (Vick De Giorgio).

11/94   407-324-9964 **gator**   Orlando   FL 300-FAST   2400
SVR4 4.0 - 6 lines, supporting v.32bis/v.42bis/v.FC/v.34/PEP/TurboPEP On the internet at
192.190.78.1 as gator.rn.com login as bbs, 9000 newsgroups, supports newsfeeds and
email forwarding. MX services are also available. The BBS is Uniaccess and is very easy
to use.

06/94   407-767-2583 **stardust**   Altamonte Sprin FL 300-FAST   24
80386DX-40 SCO XENIX 2.3.4; XBBS bulletin board & conferencing system, no fee,
login: bbs; partial Usenet newsfeed; amateur radio, H-P calculator, embedded controllers and electronic design forums and files.
Contact: kc4zvw@stardust.oau.org - David Billsbrough - 407/767-9310 (v)

03/93   904-456-2003 **amaranth**   Pensacola   FL 1200-FAST   24
ISC Unix V/386 2.2.1 TB+ on dialin. XBBS no fee. limited NEWS, E-mail
For more info: Jon Spelbring jsspelb@amaranth.UUCP

02/94   515-945-7000 **cyberspace** Jefferson   IA 300-FAST   24
SUNOS: FREE SERVICE, no time limits; T1 (1.536MB) Internet Link, Full News Feed,
Irc, Archie, Lynx, WWW, telnet ncftp, and more. FREE Unix Shell, PPP & Slip Accounts.

03/93   217-789-7888 **pallas**   Springfield   IL 300-FAST   24
AT&T 6386, 600 meg disk space; 4 lines w/ USRobotics Dual Standard modems; BBS
available at no fee (UBBS), shell access for $50/year; E-Mail, Usenet; "guest" login
available.

03/94   309-676-0409 **hcserv**   Peoria   IL 300-FAST   24
SGI 4d70 SysV and 386BSD - Public Access Unix Systems - Mult.Lines/ 1.8GB Access fee
structure based on usage and a $0.02 a minute connection with a cap of $20.00 a month.
Shells (sh,csh,bash,tcsh,zsh), Compilers C and Fortran, games, File and Pic. Libs.,
UUCP and USENET access with various news readers, U.S. Patent and USPS Stamp
databases, general timesharing and programmed on-line applications. Three gateways
including AT&T mail services with outgoing FAX. Self register.
Contact: Victoria Kee {uunet!hcserv!sysop sysop%hcserv@uunet.uu.net}

11/94   312-248-0900 **ddsw1**   Chicago   IL 300-FAST   24
Intel Machines, BSDI/DELL; guest users have free BBS access; fee for shell, Usenet,
Internet, unlimited use, and offsite mail; Authors of AKCS bbs; 6.5GB storage, fee varies
with service classification, V.32bis & PEP available. Newsfeeds and mail connections
available; Full Internet services including SLIP, PPP, and leased circuits
Contact: Karl Denninger (karl@MCS.COM) or voice/fax at 312-248-Unix

03/94   312-282-8606 **gagme**   Chicago   IL 300-FAST   24
80486 - Linux. World Wide Access (TM) Full Internet Access now available! Full netnews, E-mail, ftp, telnet, IRC, MUD, and so much more! Shell and BBS options. Multiple V.32bis and PEP lines. More lines added as needed. UUCP feeds also available.
Send mail to or finger info@wwa.com for more information.

03/94   312-283-0559 **chinet**   Chicago   IL 300-FAST   24
'386, SysVr3.2.1; Multiple lines including Telebit and HST; Picospan BBS (free),
USENET at $50/year (available to guests on weekends).

03/94   708-367-1871 **sashimi**   Vernon Hills   IL 300-FAST   24
80486 - SVR4. World Wide Access (TM) Full Internet Access now available! Full netnews, E-mail, ftp, telnet, IRC, MUD, and so much more! Shell and BBS options. Multi-

ple V.32bis lines. More lines added as needed. UUCP feeds also available.
Send mail to or finger info@wwa.com for more information.

03/93   708-425-8739 **oaknet**   Oak Lawn   IL 300-FAST   24
386 Clone running AT&T System V release 3.2.1, no access charges. Free shell accounts,
USENET news, and internet email . . .
Contact: jason@oaknet.chi.il.us, Jason Vanick (708)499-0905 (human).

03/94   708-833-8126 **vpnet**   Villa Park   IL 1200-FAST   24
386 Clone - Interactive Unix R2.2 (3.2), Akcs linked bbs FREE, including many selected
Usenet groups. Shells are available for a minimum $60/year contribution; under 22, $30.
Includes access to our FULL Usenet feed. Well connected. Five lines including three
Trailblazers. Two hunt groups - V.32 modems call 708-833-8127 (contributors only).
Contact: lisbon@vpnet.chi.il.us, Gerry Swetsky (708)833-8122 (human).

03/93   708-879-8633 **unixuser**   Batavia   IL 300-FAST   24
386, w/ Linux/Waffle; v.32[bis] support; Linux downloads; Limited free use; Paid subscribers get Internet mail access, some USENET groups; Subscription is $25/year;
CDROM disk available - changes monthly; Shell accounts are available.

03/93   708-983-5147 **wa9aek**   Lisle   IL 1200-FAST   24
80386, Unix V.3.2.3; XBBS for HAM radio enthusiasts; 1.5 Gigabytes online; Multiple
lines, dial in - USR HST DS V.32bis/42bis, 8138 - Tb T2500; Login as bbs (8-N-1).

11/93   815-874-3998 **maynard**   Rockford   IL 300-FAST   24
USL UnixWare SysVr4.2; Provides shell, USENET, E-Mail, uuftp sources, BBS, games,
chat and more. $5 Email only $10 Email USENET.. UUCP available
Contact: troy@maynard.chi.il.us

03/93   812-333-0450 **sir-alan**   Bloomington   IN 1200-FAST   24
SCO Unix 3.2; no fee; TB+ on 333-0450 (300-19.2K); archive site for comp.sources.
[games,misc,sun,unix,x], some alt.sources, XENIX(68K/286/386) uucp-anon: ogin:
nuucp password: anon-uucp uucp-anon directory: /u/pdsrc, /u/pubdir, /u/uunet, help in
/u/pubdir/HELP
Contact: miikes@iuvax.cs.indiana.edu (812-855-3974 days 812-333-6564 eves)

05/94   812-476-7564 **aquila**   Evansville   IN 2400-FAST   24
SCO Unix; Email/News provider to the Tri-State area; Supports regional BBSs; Has
satellite downlink for 2500+ Usenet newsgroups. No fee for mail, low fee for news; The
Aquila System, PO Box 4912, Evansville IN 47724-0912.
Contact: kilroy@aquila.nshore.org

08/94   502-968-5390 **iglou**   Louisville   KY 300-FAST   24
Equip ???, Solaris 2.x; Live Internet, multiple lines.
Contact: Dannie J. Gregoire (dannie@iglou.com) (+1 502 966 3848 voice)

03/93   606-233-2051 **lunatix**   Lexington   KY 300-2400   24
SCO Unix 3.2.2. 2 2400 baud lines. V32bis later in the fall. Home grown Pseudo BBS

software. Multiuser games, Full USENET Feed on tap, USENET Feeds available. Shells available, No Fees.

08/94   508-664-0149 **genesis**   North Reading MA 300-FAST   24
FreeBSD; Internet mail; Usenet news; No Fees; Gopher, lynx, IRC, FTP, telnet, etc; Shell access and menu system. Yes, this is a free Internet system.
Contact: steve1@genesis.nred.ma.us (steve belczyk). Automated reply: info@genesis.nred.ma.us

09/93   508-853-0340 **schunix**   Worcester   MA 2400-FAST   24
Sparc 2, 1.9GB; Email, Shell, Full UseNet, C/C++, over 11GB on CD's, $5/month $3/hr, $10/mn 5hrs incl. $2/hr, uucp-feeds call, login:guest for info, Free BBS inside of schunix, login:pbbs,
Contact: Robert Schultz (schu@schunix.com) 508-853-0258 SCHUNIX 8 Grove Heights Drive, Worcester, MA 01605

09/93   617-593-4557 **northshore** Lynn   MA 300-FAST   24
Sun SPARCstation, SunOS 4.1.3; Telebit Worldblazer modems (v.32bis, v.32, 2400, 1200 baud); Eco Software, Inc; GNU, archie, gopher, wais, etc. any software you need, we'll add it; $9/month for 10 hours connect time, 3 Mb disk quota (additional usage: connect - $1/hour, disk - $1/Mb/month); UUCP feeds available; Hours: 7 days/week, 24 hours/day (except Friday 15:00–18:00 for backups).
Contact: info@northshore.ecosoft.com (Voice: (617) 593-3110).

03/94   301-220-0462 **digex**   Greenbelt   MD 300-2400   24
Express Access Online Communications. Local to Washington, Baltimore, Annapolis and Northern Virginia (area code 703); Baltimore dialup 410-766-1855, Gaithersburg/Damascus 301-570-0001. SunOS shell, full Usenet, and e-mail $15/month or $150/year; Internet services incl. Telnet, FTP, IRC with news/mail $25/month or $250/year; includes unlimited usage 3am - 3pm and 1 hour between 3pm and 3am. Login as new (no password) for info and account application, major credit cards accepted.
Telnet to digex.com or mail to info@digex.com for more info; voice phone 800-969-9090 (or 301-220-2020).

01/95   410-661-2598 **wb3ffv**   Baltimore   MD 1200-FAST   24
Pentium-SMP, Unix V.4.2.x; UniBoard BBS for Amateur Radio enthusiasts; 5+ Gigabytes online; Full INTERNET including all features such as FTP, Telnet, Gopher, WWW, USENET, & Email to supporting members. Access to all local groups and Amateur Radio files for FREE. This system also supports Anonymous-UUCP and Anonymous-FTP, plus the BBS is Telnet accessible at the internet address of: wb3ffv1.sed.csc.com Multiple lines, dial in's -> USR V.34's on (410)-661-2475 hunt-group, Telebit WorldBlazer on (410)-661-2648 supporting V.32bis & Turbo-PEP.

12/93   410-893-4786 **magnus1**   Belair   MD 300-FAST   24
Equip Unisys S/Series, Unix 3.3.2; ksh, csh, sh; Multiple lines; $60.00/yr; E-Mail/ USENET,ftp, telnet,finger; 'C', Pascal, Fortran, Cobol, Basic development systems; Interactive chat and games; Files for download; USA Today, Online Magazines, Daily Busi-

ness News; PC Catalog; Local Online Forums as well; as Technical Help; Clarinet News; No limits.
Contact: cyndiw@magnus1.com

02/94   313-623-6309 **nucleus**   Clarkston   MI 1200-2400   24
AMI 80386 - ESIX 5.3.2, large online sources archive accessible by anonymous UUCP, login: nuucp, nucleus!/user/src/LISTING lists available public domain/shareware source code.
Contact: jeff@nucleus.mi.org

03/93   313-761-3000 **grex**   Ann Arbor   MI 300-FAST   24
Sun 2/170 with SunOS 3.2. Full Usenet feed, Internet e-mail, shell accounts, on-line games, PicoSpan, UUCP accounts. Voluntary donation ($6/month or $60/year) for coop membership and Usenet posting access. 6 lines, 300MB. Cooperatively owned & operated by Cyberspace Communications.
Contact: info@cyberspace.org

03/94   313-996-4644 **m-net**   Ann Arbor   MI 300-2400   24
486 - BSDI, open access; run by Arbornet, tax-exempt nonprofit; donations tax deductible; dues for extended access; user supported; 15 lines; Picospan conferencing; 500 MB disk; Internet e-mail; UUCP available; free shell access, C compiler, multiuser party, games (including nethack, empire, rotisserie baseball); M-Net 10 year anniversary in June, 1993! Access from the Internet: telnet m-net.ann-arbor.mi.us
Contact: help@m-net.ann-arbor.mi.us

03/93   517-789-5175 **anubis**   Jackson   MI 300-1200   24
Equip ???, OS ???; 1200 baud dial-in (planning on 19.2kbps); UUCP connections to the world, PicoSpan BBS software, Teleconferencing, C programming compiler, 3 public dial-in lines, Online games;
Contact: Matthew Rupert (root@anubis.mi.org).

03/93   616-457-1964 **wybbs**   Jenison   MI 300-FAST   24
386 - SCO-XENIX 2.3.2, two lines, XBBS for new users, mail in for shell access, usenet news, 150 meg storage, Telebit. Interests: ham radio, xenix AKA: Consultants Connection
Contact: danielw@wyn386.mi.org
Alternate phone #: 616-457-9909 (max 2400 baud). Anonymous UUCP available.

03/93   906-228-4399 **lopez**   Marquette   MI 1200-2400   24
80386, SCO Xenix 2.3.4; Running STARBASE II Software. Great White North UPLink, Inc. (Non Profit) 100+ local rooms, PLUS USENET, Multi Channel Chat, 5 ports, $30 yr, flat rate for full access to net news, mail. Upper Michigan's ORIGINAL BBS (since 1983)
Contact: Gary Bourgois . . . rutgers!sharkey!lopez!flash (flash@lopez.UUCP)

08/93   612-458-3889 **skypoint**   Newport   MN 300-FAST   24
Unixware System V R4.2. VGA Graphics BBS/OIS using Sentience BBS software from Cyberstore - Sentience uses the RIP graphics protocol; 4 lines are Courier 14.4 Modems, 1 Worldblazer; Full News Feed 7 day expire, Clarinet Feed Site, USA Today, Board

Watch, News Bytes, Internet Mail, Real time games and conferences; Unix, DOS, Windows and OS/2 source and binary archives on CDROMS and 2.1 Gigabytes of Disk; $45 dollars year basic services $85 dollars a year for full access, $100 a year for Unix shell account and access to full development tools; Will provide Clarinet and USENET News Feeds; Will add Fidonet and other networks in the near future; Login as 'guest'.
Contact: info@skypoint.com

03/94   612-473-2295 **pnet51**   Minneapolis   MN 300-2400   24
Equip ?, Xenix, multi-line, no fee, some Usenet news, email, multi-threaded conferencing, login: pnet id: new, PC Pursuitable UUCP: {rosevax, crash}!orbit!pnet51!admin

03/93   603-429-1735 **mv**   Litchfield   NH 1200-FAST   24
80386; ISC Unix; MV is on the Internet (mv.MV.COM, host 192.80.84.1); mail connections and news feeds via uucp; domain registrations; membership in "domain park" MV.COM; domain forwarding; archives of news and mail software for various platforms; mailing lists; area topics; $7/month for 1 hour/month; $20/month for 3 hours/month $2/hour thereafter; blocks of 30 hours for $20 month - First month free up to 20 hours.
Voice: 603-429-2223; USMail: MV Communications Inc, PO Box 4963 Manchester NH 03108; Or dial the modem and login as "info" or "rates".

03/93   603-448-5722 **tutor**   Lebanon   NH 300-FAST   24
Altos 386 w/ System V 3.1; Limited newsfeed; E-Mmail and USENET available via UUCP.
Contact: peter.schmitt@dartmouth.edu

08/94   201-236-8360 **nic**   Bergen County NJ 300-FAST   24
Solaris for x86, Pentium P-90 and Intel 486DX2-66, 32MB RAM each, 7.2GB total disk space, "big seven" and regional USENET news, rn, trn, nn, elm, pine, pico, emacs, vi, lynx, gopher, irc, gcc available to all users, unix shell or menu system, accounts from $10 per month. Local dialing area includes Wyckoff, Ridgwood, Ramsey, Upper Saddle River and Franklin Lakes, NJ.
Contact: info@nic.com (automated response), tel/fax 201-934-1445, or combes@nic.com

04/94   201-432-0060 **ritz**   Jersey City   NJ 300-FAST   24
Gateway2000 486/66 EISA, 28mb RAM, 1 gig FAST SCSI-2 disk space (with 2.1 gig of Barracuda FAST SCSI-2 disk on the way). BSDI/386 unix. 8 dialins, all support MNP 3-5 and v.42/v.42bis. 7 modems are AT&T Dataport (14.4kbps/v.32bis) and one is a Telebit T2000 (19.2kbps/PEP). Shells supported: ash, csh, ksh, tcsh. **Full Internet access.** Our IP number is 165.254.109.51. All user accounts have complete internet access (FTP,IRC,Archie,Lynx(WWW), Gopher,Telnet, and more!) Mailers supported: elm,pine. Full USENET feed. News readers supported: tin,trn, nn,rn. Editors supported: emacs,vi,jove, pico. RIP interface coming soon.
Contact: ritz@mordor.com

03/94   201-759-8450 **tronsbox**   Belleville   NJ 300-FAST   24
Generic 386, Unix 3.2; Provides shell for some users, USENET, E-mail (feeds available) at $15 a month flat; Multiple line (-8568 300 - 2400 baud).

08/94   609-896-3191   **njcc**   Lawrenceville   NJ 300-FAST   24
New Jersey Computer Connection. Linux, 5 lines, full usenet, and e-mail $7.95/month, $41.95/6 months, $79.95/year ($9.95 account setup fee - one time). Choice of shells, csh, tsch, bash, sh. Full internet services with Telnet, FTP, irc and news/mail, $14.95/month, $79.95/6 months, $149.95/year for unlimited use. ($9.95 account setup fee - one time). login as guest.
Contact: info@pluto.njcc.com (+1 609 896 2799 voice) (+1 609 896 2994 fax).

08/93   908-937-9481   **digex**   New Brunswick   NJ 300-FAST   24
Refer to primary entry (Greenbelt, MD) for system/services details.
Telnet to cnj.digex.com or mail to info@cnj.digex.com for more info; voice phone 1-800-969-9090.

03/94   212-420-0527   **magpie**   NYC   NY 300-FAST   24
? - Unix SYSV - 2, Magpie BBS, no fee, Authors: Magpie/Unix; No Shell; Muli-line (using Telebit Worldblazers) plus anonymous uucp;
Contact: Steve Manes, manes@magpie.com

03/94   212-675-7059   **marob**   NYC   NY 300-FAST   24
386 SCO-XENIX 2.2, XBBS, no fee, limit 60 min; Telebit Trailblazer (9600 PEP) only 212-675-8438;
Contact: {philabs|rutgers|cmc12}!phri!marob!clifford

03/94   212-787-3100   **panix**   New York City   NY 1200-FAST   24
2 Sparc10/40 & 2 Sparc2, 176MB RAM, 12GB disk, Cisco routers, Annex 64-port term servers. Use any of 6 shells or our own custom-written menu system. 119 dialins, all support MNP3-5 & V.42/V.42bis. 62 are V.32bis Zyxels (14.4kbps and higher), the rest 2400bps. We are a full internet site with high-speed (T1) line- telnet to panix.com (198.7.0.2). Full UseNet; (t)rn, nn, GNUs, Tin. Elm, Pine, MM, other mail readers. Vi, Emacs, Jove, Pico, other editors. Compile your own code (C/C++). $10/mn or 100/yr for basic, $9 per month add'l for telnet/ftp/gopher/www/etc. Feeds, domains, IP, more. NEW: SLIP or PPP service for only $35/month on 10 (soon 30) new lines. 24 local numbers in Long island (516) 626-7863. COMING SOON: Local numbers in N.J. (201) and Westchester (914). 4-processor CPU upgrade. And, as usual, more lines.
Contact: Alexis Rosen (alexis@panix.com) 212-877-4854, or Jim Baumbach (jsb@panix.com). Or email/finger info@panix.com, 212-787-6160.

08/94   212-989-1258   **interport**   NYC   NY 1200-FAST   24
Sparc 20/50, Solaris 1.1.1, 32 dialups. InterPort provides Internet access to the public. Subscription includes terminal session and SLIP/PPP connectivity. Terminal sessions provide an easy to use menu system or access to the Unix prompt. Extensive help system covering Unix, the Internet, and InterPort. We are connected to the Internet via a high speed T1 line: access e-mail, gopher, archie, WWW, internet news, telnet, ftp, wais, irc, talk, etc. Additional internet services added by user request. Diskettes provided for Windows and Mac SLIP software. Monthly subscription is $25/month - there is no startup fee. For more info, telnet to interport.net - login as "newuser" or e-mail/finger info@interport.net.

Contacts: accounts@interport.net, postal: InterPort, 1133 Broadway, NY, NY 10010, phone: 212-989-1128.

08/94   212-989-4141 **mindvox**   NYC   NY 1200-FAST   24
Sparc10/51, SparcServer, 2 TurboSparcs, 256MB Ram, 15GB Disk, 96 dialups, 32 additional Hayes V.FC modems @ 212-645-8065. More high-speed lines added every month. No startup fees. Conference-oriented system with CyberPunk/Creative Arts focus. Custom Interface. Wired, Mondo 2000, aXcess and others host online conferences. We are a full internet site with a high-speed leased line connection, telnet to phantom.com (198.67.3.2) and login as "guest" for a tour. Telnet, ftp, gopher, www, lynx, wais, irc, ddial, SLIP, PPP, newsfeeds, QWK, POP3. Prices go from $10–$17.50 per month for full access, discounts for pre-payment are available.
Contact: info@phantom.com, gopher phantom.com, or 800-MindVox

09/93   212-989-8411 **echo**   NYC   NY 300-FAST   24
Equip ???, OS ???; A full Internet site with a highspeed leased line: telnet to echonyc.com (198.67.15.1). Members have full access to shell, Usenet, telnet, ftp, gopher et al. $19.95/month, $13.95/month for students and seniors. We are a public computer conferencing system with 1500 members (40% female) and full Internet access.
Contact: horn@echonyc.com (Voice: (212) 255-3839)

06/93   516-586-4743 **kilowatt**   Deer Park   NY 2400-FAST   24
Consensys SVR4 running on a clone 80486-33. 516-586-4743 for Telebit World-Blazer, 516-667-6142 for a Boca V.32bis. Providing FREE USENET email/news to the general public. FREE feeds available with a selection of all of alt, biz, comp, rec, talk, sci, soc, and vmsnet newsgroups . . . using UUCP or QWK-packets. Contact: Arthur Krewat 516-253-2805 krewat@kilowatt.UUCP or krewat@kilowatt.linet.org Telnet/Ftp not available here, so don't even ask!

03/93   518-346-8033 **sixhub**   upstate   NY 300-2400   24
PC Designs GV386. hub machine of the upstate NY Unix users group (*IX) two line reserved for incoming, bbs no fee, news & email fee $15/year Smorgasboard of BBS systems, UNaXcess and XBBS online, Citadel BBS now in production. Contact: davidsen@sixhub.uucp.

03/93   716-634-6552 **exuco1**   Buffalo   NY 300-FAST   24
SGI Iris Indigo; 2 Lines, both Telebit WorldBlazers (on a hunt) [PEP Answer sequence last]; "The Buffalo Computer Society", Western New York's first Public Access Unix; Mon - Fri 6:00pm - 7:00am EST, 24 Hours on Weekends; No Fee; E-Mail/USENET Come March '93 — will be running on several DEC Vaxen running BSD 4.3, and MANY MANY MANY more lines.

04/94   718-252-6720 **intercom**   New York   NY 300-FAST   24
Dell Pentium/60, SVR4.2, 64MB RAM, 4.8 gigabytes disk space, all 16 dialups are Zyxel v.32bis, user-friendly menu system, 3000+ newsgroups, Internet mail, PINE, TIN, Games, DOS/Windows/OS2 CD-ROM with 5000+ files, PC/Mac/Amiga/Text Library,

Gopher, WWW, IRC, Hytelnet, Lynx, WAIS, MUD. Fees: starting $5/month (standard access) and $10/month (full access).
Contact: info@intercom.com

04/93   718-729-5018 **dorsai**   NYC   NY 300-FAST   24
80386, ISC 386/ix, Waffle bbs; Live Internet connection; 3 phone lines (V.32bis for contributors); no shell (yet); BBS with over 250 non-Usenet newsgroups, 1.2 gb of mac, ibm, amiga, cp-m, appleII, cbm files; BBS is free, $25/yr for UseNet access, (180 min/day), $50/yr for extended gold access (300 min/day); $?? for platinum access (i.e. ftp/telnet/irc/etc); Full news and mail feed from uupsi; login through bbs.
Contact: postmaster@dorsai.com

02/94   216-481-9445 **wariat**   Cleveland   OH 300-FAST   24
ISC Unix SysV/386; USR DS on 481-9445, T-3000 on 481-9425. Shell and UUCP/Internet mail access available. News and mail feeds are available; also, DOS and Unix files. Anonymous uucp: login: nuucp, no password; request /x/files/ls-lR.Z; nuucp account does not allow mail exchange; UnixBBS distribution point. BBS free (with e-mail) for shell/uucp/newsfeed donation requested.
For details, e-mail to: zbig@wariat.org (Zbigniew Tyrlik)

03/94   216-582-2460 **ncoast**   Cleveland   OH 1200-FAST   24
80386 Mylex, SCO Xenix; 600 meg. storage; XBBS and Shell; USENET (newsfeeds available), E-Mail; donations requested; login as "bbs" for BBS and "makeuser" for new users. Telebit used on 216-237-5486.

03/93   513-779-8209 **cinnet**   Cincinnati   OH 1200-FAST   24
80386, ISC 386/ix 2.02, Telebit access, 1 line; $7.50/Month; shell access, Usenet access; news feeds available; login: newacct password: new user to register for shell access

05/94   513-887-8855 **iac**   Cincinnati   OH 300-FAST   24
Multiple Sun systems, offering shell access, USENET, FTP, TELNET IRC, MAIL; Also offer SLIP/PPP/UUCP feeds; login: new
Contact: finger or mail info@iac.net for pricing and other info.

03/94   614-868-9980 **bluemoon**   Reynoldsburg OH 300-FAST   24
Sun 4/75, SunOS; 2.2gb; Leased line to the Internet; Multiple lines, HST Dual on -9980 & -9982, Telebit T2500 on -9984; 2gb disk space; Bluemoon BBS — supporting Unix, graphics, and general interest; Full USENET, gated Fidonet conferences, E-Mail;
Contact: grant@bluemoon.uucp (Grant DeLorean).

06/94   503-220-1016 **teleport**   Portland   OR 300-FAST   24
SPARCstations, SunOS 4.1.3, 10GB disk; 100+ lines and support PEP/V.32 and V.32bis; E-Mail/USENET; Shell access for $120 / year includes choice of shell, full news feed, complete internet (ftp, telnet, irc, mud, SLIP, PPP) access; now supporting UUCP connections and with locations in Salem, OR (503) 364-2028 and Vancouver, WA (206) 260-0330; apply with "new" or email info@teleport.com

11/94   503-227-1704 **hevanet**   Portland   OR 300-FAST   24
BSDI/386; $96/yr for full access; (E-mail, usenet news, ftp, www, irc, telnet, SLIP, and
shell access.) For info: http://www.hevanet.com
Contact: Craig Swift Voice: (503) 228-3520 E-mail: info@hevanet.com

03/94   503-293-1772 **agora**   Portland   OR 1200-FAST   24
Intel Unix V/386, $6/mo or $60/yr, news, mail, ftp, telnet, irc. Six lines with trunk-hunt,
all V.32bis. Agora is part of RAINet.
Contact: Alan Batie, batie@agora.rain.com

03/94   503-297-3211 **m2xenix**   Portland   OR 300-FAST   24
'386/20, Xenix 2.3. 2 Lines (-0935); Shell accounts available, NO BBS; No fee; E-mail,
USENET News, program development.
Contact: . . . !uunet!m2xenix!news or on Fido at 297-9145

03/94   503-632-7891 **bucket**   Portland   OR 300-FAST   24
Tektronix 6130, UTek 3.0(4.2bsd-derived). Bit Bucket BBS no longer online. Modem is
Telebit Trailblazer+ (PEP). Users interested in access to Unix should send EMail to
rickb@pail.rain.com. $30/year access fee includes USENET News, EMail (fast due to
local Internet access), and access to all tools/utilities/games. Internet 'ftp' available upon
request. UUCP connections (1200, 2400, 9600V.32, 9600PEP, 19200PEP) available
(through another local system which is not publically available) to sites which will poll
with reasonable regularity and reliability.

01/95   215-348-9727 **jabber**   Doylestown   PA 300-FAST   24
80486DX/33, Unixware 1.1.2; V.32[bis] on all dial-ins; Live Internet; Free services
include: Anonymous UUCP available for access to the latest nixpub lists, please see the
footer of this list for more details; Other services include: The "DataMill BBS" — providing E-Mail, USENET and IP style services to the user community, UUCP feeds for
access to Internet E-mail and USENET News (4100+ groups) from your home or office
computer; Contact us for pricing information;
Contact: Phil Eschallier (phil@bts.com) (+1 215 348 9721 voice).

03/94   412-481-5302 **telerama**   Pittsburgh   PA 300-FAST   24
Telerama Public Access Internet. 4.3 bsd. Multiple lines. Hourly fee includes telnet, ftp,
e-mail, Usenet, ClariNet/UPI, gopher, IRC, games, compilers, editors, shell or menu navigation and 1 meg disk quota. Also offering SLIP, UUCP and commercial accounts. Fees:
$20/mo (personal), $50/mo (commercial); Registration: login as new. FTP info from tel-
erama.pgh.pa.us; /info/telerama.info
Contact: Kristen McQuillin, info@telerama.pgh.pa.us. 412/481-3505 voice.

03/94   610-539-3043 **cellar**   Trooper/Oaks   PA 300-FAST   24
DTK 486/33, SCO Unix 3.2, Waffle BBS - The Cellar BBS, no shell; USR Dual-Standard
modems, five lines and growing. BBS is free; net news (full feed) and net mail by subscription. $10/mo, $55/6-mo, or $90/yr. Fancies itself to be more of a colorful "electronic
community" than the best plug into the net, and as such, it features a lively local mes-

sage base. But it also generally carries the latest Linux distribution, just to prove it hasn't forgotten its hacker roots.
Contact: Tony Shepps (toad@cellar.org).

03/93   814-353-0566 **cpumagic**   Bellefonte   PA 1200-FAST   24
80386, ESIX 4.0.3a (SVR4); Dual Standard (v.32/v.32bis/HST); The Centre Programmers Unit BBS, custom BBS software (Micro Magic); Files available: Unix, GNU, X, ESIX, MSDOS tools and libraries; No fee but up/download ratios enforced.
Contact: Mike Loewen at mloewen@cpumagic.scol.pa.us or . . . psuvax1!cpumagic!mloewen

03/93   401-455-0347 **anomaly**   Esmond   RI 300-FAST   24
Informtech 486 mongrel; SCO Open Desktop 1.1; Trailblazer+ (0347) and v.32 T2500 (401-331-3706) dialins. Directly connected to the Internet: IP Address: 155.212.2.2, or 'anomaly.sbs.risc.net'. Current fees: $15/mo. includes complete Internet access. Mail and USENET Newsfeeds available, limited feeds for non-PEP sites. SCO software archive site, anonymous UUCP login: xxcp, pass: xenix. Anonymous FTP also supported.
Software listing & download directions in anomaly!~/SOFTLIST

06/94   803-271-0688 **melanie**   Greenville   SC 2400-FAST   24
80386, 130MB Linux 0.99pl9; $1/hour connect time (minimum $10/month); Email and any USENET News group(s) requested. FREE: Will provide Waffle software and help setting it up within 50 miles of Greenville, SC. so you can get a feed at home or at work.
Contact: uunet!melanie!peter 803-271-4034

02/94   605-348-2738 **loft386**   Rapid City   SD 300-FAST   24
80386 SYS V/386 Rel 3.2, Usenet mail/news via UUNET, UUNET archive access. NO BBS! News feeds available. 400 meg hd. Fees: $10/month or $25/quarter. Call (605) 343-8760 and talk to Doug Ingraham to arrange an account or email uunet!loft386!dpi

03/93   615-288-3957 **medsys**   Kingsport   TN 1200-FAST   24
386 SCO-Unix 3.2, XBBS; No fee, limit 90 min; Telebit PEP, USENET, 600mb; login: bbs password: bbs anon uucp → medsys Any ACU (speed) 16152883957 Login: nuucp Request /u/xbbs/unix/BBSLIST.Z for files listing
Contact: laverne@medsys (LaVerne E. Olney)

03/94   214-248-9811 **sdf**   Dallas   TX 300-FAST   24
i386/25 isc 2.0.1; sdf.lonestar.org; 8-line rotary, 2400 bps, 14.4k, PEP; No Fees; Shell account and UUCP mail/news feeds available; Providing access to Internet E-Mail, 1600+ USENET newsgroups, online games, programming utilities and more. Login 'info' for registration information.
Contact: smj@sdf.lonestar.org

03/94   214-705-2901 **metronet**   Dallas   TX 300-FAST   24
HP-UX 8.07, HP 9000/705; Texas Metronet Communications Service.
10 14.4k dialups (7052901), 10 2400 dialups (7052917). Offers shell accounts w/ ftp, telnet, irc, UseNet, etc. Also UUCP and SLIP. Flat monthly fees from $10–$50, depending on service type. telnet connections to feenix.metronet.com welcome.

For more information login as info/info, or mail info@metronet.com, or call voice at 7052900.

03/94   512-346-2339 **bigtex**   Austin   TX FAST   24
SysVr3.2 i386, anonymous shell, no fee, anonymous uucp ONLY, Telebit 9600/PEP; Mail links available. Carries GNU software. anon uucp login: nuucp NO PASSWD, file list /usr3/index anon shell login: guest NO PASSWD, chroot'd to /usr3
Contact: james@bigtex.cactus.org

03/94   713-480-2686 **blkbox**   Houston   TX 300-FAST   24
486/33, SCO Open Desktop; 5 lines, all V32[bis]/V42[bis]; E-Mail/USENET (4500+ groups); 25 online adventure games, IRC, SLIP/PP; $21.65 / month for full shell access.
Contact: Marc Newman (mknewman@blkbox.com)

03/94   713-668-7176 **nuchat**   Houston   TX 300-FAST   24
i486/25, UHC Unix SVR4, 2.5 Gigs online, ** 56kb internet connection **, 7 lines (2 Trailblazers, 5 Worldblazers), full Usenet news feed, personal accounts ($3/hour), UUCP feeds (several options), dedicated lines available w/ unlimited usage @$120/month (SLIP or any protocol you like). Full internet access (ftp, telnet, gopher, archie),

08/94   713-684-5900 **neosoft**   Houston   TX 300-FAST   24
Multiple Pentium systems/BSDI, 96 lines for shell, 32 lines for PPP/SLIP, Clarinet, FTP, Telnet, IRC, Lynx, . . . WWW at www.neosoft.com, FTP at ftp.neosoft.com, rec.food.recipes archive site, NFS to wuarchive, shell access $19.95/mo, TCP $39.95/mo, Multiple T-1 links. POP in St Louis, New Orleans, Galveston . . . 713-684-5969 voice.

01/94   801-539-0900 **xmission**   Salt Lake City UT 300-FAST   24
Sun Sparc Classic, Solaris; T1 Connection into Internet Backbone; 10 (at the moment) incoming phone lines (ZyXEL 19.2K 1496E+ modems on all lines); tin, nn, rn news readers; gopher, lynx, www navigators; hytelnet, telnet, ncftp, ftp; zmodem, ymodem, xmodem, kermit protocols; PPP and UUCP connections with all accounts; gnu software and compilers; assisted "menus" or shell access; "Big Dummy's Guide to the Internet" hypertexted online; nethack, mdg, and robohunt multiplayer games.
$5 introductory rate for the first month . . . Individuals: $19/mn ($102/6mns), Small businesses: $29/mn ($162/6mns), BBS accounts: $39/mn ($216/6mns).
Voice Support at 801-539-0852

03/94   703-281-7997 **grebyn**   Vienna   VA 300-2400   24
Networked Vax/Ultrix. $30/month for 25 hours. $1.20 connect/hr after 25 hours. 1 MB disk quota. $2/MB/month additional quota. USENET News. Domain mail (grebyn.com). Full Internet IP connectivity expected in the summer of 1992.
Mail to info@grebyn.com, voice 703-281-2194.

04/93   703-528-4380 **sytex**   Arlington   VA 300-FAST   24
ISC Unix, UUCP, Waffle BBS, 5 lines. Login as "bbs". Mail, usenet news, ftp available via ftp-requests though UUnet. Serving Washington DC, Northern Virginia, Southern Maryland. First year startup Charter member accounts available for $120. Gives fullest access as the system develops.

06/93   703-551-0095 **ukelele**   Woodbridge   VA 300-FAST   24
Genuine Computing Resources. SVR4/386. Calling area includes District of Columbia, Fairfax Cty, Prince William Cty, Manassas, and Dumfries, VA. Shell, Full Usenet, Internet E-Mail. $15/month for access to (703)551 exchange, $10/month for (703)878 access. All lines V.32bis or higher. You get 1 hour/day connect time and 1.5MB disk storage. Direct Internet connectivity expected soon without rate increase for existing users. Login as 'guest' or send mail to info@gcr.com for further details. For human interaction send mail to cjl@gcr.com. News and mail feeds also considered.

08/94   703-720-4144 **unx**   Fredericksburg VA 300-FAST   24
80486 DX-2/66 - SCO Unix Enterprise 3.0. Online storage 2GB. 16 port RocketPort. AHOYnet Information Services featuring Coconet BBS high-resolution on-line graphics in client/server mode. UUCP/PPP feeds available. Internet email, Shell accounts. WWW and direct wire coming.
Contact: captain@ahoynet.com (+1 703 720 4048 voice).

03/94   703-803-0391 **tnc**   Fairfax Station VA 300-FAST   24
Zenith Z-386, SCO Xenix; 120 MB HDD; 12 lines, tb+ for UUCP only; "The Next Challenge"; Usenet, mail, Unique (sysop written) multi-user space game; No Shell; Free and user supported → No fee for light mail and usenet; Subscription required for game and unlimited mail and usenet at $25 / year;
Contact: Tom Buchsbaum (tom@tnc.UUCP or uunet!tnc!tom).

04/93   804-627-1828 **wyvern**   Norfolk   VA 1200-FAST   24
Multiple 486/66 networked, SVR4. Ten v.32bis lines. Shell accounts, mail, and news feeds available. Gigs of disk space with lots of games, programming languages, news. Modest fees. We provide full Internet services, including ftp, telnet, IRC, archie, etc. We can provide uucp email and news feeds, and can include your machine in our domain park. login as guest, no password, to register for full access.
Contact: Wyvern Technologies, Inc. at (804) 622-4289, or system@wyvern.wyvern.com (uunet!wyvern!system)

06/93   900-468-7727 **uunet**   Falls Church VA 300-FAST   24
Sequent S81, Dynix 3.0.17(9); UUNET Communication Services; No Shell; Anonymous UUCP, fee $0.40/min — billed by the telephone company, login: uucp (no passwd); Multiple lines, PEP and V.32 available; grab "uunet!~/help for more info" . . . Full internet mail and USENET access via subscriber UUCP accounts.
Contact: info@uunet.uu.net or call [voice] 703-204-8000.

03/94   206-367-3837 **eskimo**   Seattle   WA 300-FAST   24
Sun 3/180 SUN/OS 4.1.1_U1 - Everett Tel 206-742-1150 Fast 206-362-6731 14 Lines including TB World:lazer and TB-3000. Free 2-week trial account. Rates $10/month or $96/year. Everybody gets their choice of sh, csh, tcsh, ksh, bash, or zsh. Full Usenet News feed 7 day expire. Unique real-time conference, message and files system. UUCP mail and news feeds available. Home of the Western Washington BBS List. Many applications online. Lots of Unix source code archived online. Internet ftp/telnet coming soon!

03/94   206-382-6245 **halcyon**   Seattle   WA 300-FAST   24
ULTRIX 4.1, (PEP/V.32) 206-382-6245; monthly and annual fee schedules available.
56kBaud commercial Internet link to the T-3 backbone; NNTP news feed. Waffle bbs
available. Irc server, archie and gopher clients, hytelnet, spop; dialup or telnet: login as
'bbs' and provide account information.
For more information, contact: info@remote.halcyon.com, or call voice (PST, USA)
+1 206 426 9298

06/94   206-693-0325 **pacifier**   Vancouver   WA 300-FAST   24
ESIX 4.0.4, (V.32b) 206-693-0325; monthly and annual fee schedules available. 56kBaud
commercial Internet link; SLIP/PPP & shell access. IRC, FTP, TELNET, GOPHER, hytelnet, lynx; dialup or telnet: login as 'new' to register or for further information contact
register@pacifier.com or call voice (PST, USA) +1 206 693 2116

03/94   206-747-6397 **seanews**   Redmond   WA 1200-FAST   24
Xenix 386 2.3.2. SEANEWS is a free public service, providing access to Usenet and
Internet mail. There are no games, very limited files, etc. However SEANEWS does have
up-to-date Usenet news and excellent mail-handling capability.

03/93   414-321-9287 **solaria**   Milwaukee   WI 300-2400   24
Sun 3/60LE, SunOS 4.1. Internet E-mail, limited USENET news, shell access, Telebit
WorldBlazer soon. Feeds available. Donations requested, registration required. One hop
off of the Internet.
Contact: jgreco@solaria.mil.wi.us (Joe Greco) or log in as "help"

06/93   414-342-4847 **solaria**   Milwaukee   WI 300-FAST   24
Sun 3/60LE, SunOS 4.1. Internet E-mail, limited USENET news, shell access, feeds
available, donations requested, registration required. One hop off of the Internet.
Contact: jgreco@solaria.mil.wi.us (Joe Greco) or log in as "help"

01/95   414-351-1139 **mixcom**   Milwaukee   WI 1200-FAST   24
SVR4 Unix; Services and features: Email, Usenet, ftp, telnet, irc, supports QWK and Zip-
news off-line readers, easy to use menus; BBS, UUCP and personal SLIP/PPP services;
Info server: info@mixcom.com; Info account (call or telnet to mixcom.com): login as
"newuser";
Contact: Dean Roth (sysop@mixcom.com) [414-351-1868 voice].

06/93   414-734-2499 **edsi**   Appleton   WI 300-FAST   24
IBM PS/2 Model 55SX, SCO Xenix 2.3.2; Running STARBASE II Software. Enterprise
Data Systems Incorporated (Non-profit). 100+ local rooms, PLUS USENET, Multi Chan-
nel Chat, 9 ports, $15 yr, flat rate for full access to net news (no alternet yet), mail. The
Fox Valley's only public access Unix based BBS.
Contact: Chuck Tomasi (chuck@edsi.plexus.COM)

03/93   608-246-2701 **fullfeed**   Madison   WI FAST   24
Sun SPARC station SLC, 16Mb RAM, 1Gb disk, SunOS 4.1.1, Telebit WorldBlazers;
operated by FullFeed Communications; USENET/E-Mail, UUCP plus other digital communication services; login: fullfeed; UUCP starts at $24/month, shells cost $16/month;

No-cost, limited-term, evaluation accounts are setup over the telephone; FullFeed plans to offer Internet connections (SLIP, PPP, 56Kbps) within 6 months. Contact "SYSop@FullFeed.Com" or call +1-608-CHOICE-9 (voice).

03/93   608-273-2657   **madnix**   Madison   WI 300-2400   24
486, MST Unix SysV/386, shell, no fee required, USENET news, mail, login: bbs
Contact: ray@madnix.uucp

International Dial-Up Providers and Public Access Unix Sites

The increase in the number of dial-up service providers throughout the world in the past year has been startling. To track it more accurately, I have relied not only on Peter Kaminski's PDIAL and Phil Eschallier's NixPub lists, but I have also drawn from Barry Raveendran Greene's fine Network *Service Providers Around the World* document. References on how to obtain all these documents are provided at the beginning of this appendix. Perhaps the easiest way is to use this URL at The Internet Society:

```
http://www.isoc.org/~bgreene/nsp-c.html
```

Major network deficiencies still exist, particularly in Africa and South and Central America. To keep abreast of network developments in these areas, you may want to examine several specialized lists. Randy Bush's *Connectivity with Africa* document is the most detailed examination available. You can retrieve it by mail. Send to server@gopher.psg.com. The Subject: field should contain this message: **send pub/gopher-data/ networks/connect/africa.txt**. Or check the Gopher directly; the URL is gopher: //gopher.psg.com:70.

For Latin America and the Caribbean, take a look at the document *Network Service Providers in Latin America and Caribe*. You can retrieve it from a Gopher in Peru; the address is gopher://gopher.rcp.net.pe 70. Or send mail to Yuri Herrera at odi@rcp.net.pe.

ARGENTINA

ARNET (ARGENTINE SCIENCE NETWORK)
UNDP Project ARG-86-026
Ministerio de Relaciones Exteriores y Culto
Reconquista 1088 ler. Piso - Informatica
(1003) Capital Federal
Buenos Aires
Argentina
Attention: Jorge Marcelo Amodio
Voice: +54 1-313-8082
E-mail: pete@atina.ar or os@atina.ar

WAMANI
CCI
Talcahuano 325-3F
1013 Buenos Aires

Argentina
Voice: +54 1-382-6842
E-mail: apoyo@wamani.apc.org

AUSTRALIA

AARNET (THE AUSTRALIAN ACADEMIC AND RESEARCH NETWORK)
GPO Box 1142
Canberra ACT 2601
Australia
Voice: +61 6-249-3385
E-mail: aarnet@aarnet.edu.au

CONNECT.COM.AU PTY LTD.
129 Hawthorn Road
Caulfield Victoria 3161
Australia
Voice: +61 3-5282239
Dial-Up: Contact for number.
Area Codes: +61 3, +61 2
Local Access: Australia: Melbourne, Sydney
Fees: AUS $2000/year (1 hour/1 day), 10 percent discount for AUUG members;
other billing negotiable
E-mail: connect@connect.com.au

TMX—THE MESSAGE eXCHANGE PTY LTD.
2 King Street, 1st Fl
Newtown NSW 2042
Australia
Voice: +61 2-550-4448
Fax: +61 2-519-2551
E-mail: info@tmx.com.au

OTC ELECTRONIC TRADING
41 Mc Laren Street
North Sydney, NSW 2060
Australia
Voice: +61 2-954-3055
Fax: +61 2-957-1406

PACTOK
PO Box 284
Broadway 4006
Queensland
Australia
Voice: +61-7-257-1111
Fax: +61-7-257-1087
E-mail: pactok@peg.apc.org

PEGASUS NETWORKS
PO Box 284
Broadway 4006
Queensland
Australia
Voice: +61 7-257-1111
E-mail: support@peg.apc.org

TELEMEMO (TELECOM AUSTRALIA)
1/181 Victoria Parade
Collingwood, Victoria 3066
Australia
Voice: +61 3-4121539/4121535/4121078
Fax: +61 3-4121548/4121545/6637941

04/94   61-2-837-1183 **kralizec**   Sydney   AU 1200-FAST   24
Sun 3/50, SunOS 4.0 + 386/40, Linux; >1GB disk; V.32bis/V.42bis modems;
Dialup access to Full Internet services; 80 - 100 Mb software online for download. Full
C-shell access to all members; No joining fee, Usage fee $1/hr (min $10/mn) connect
time; Home of IXgate - Internet to Fidonet gateway - also Fido 713/602.
Contact: nick@kralizec.zeta.org.au

AUSTRIA

AUSTRIAN SCIENTIFIC DATA NETWORK
ACONET-Verein
Gusshausstrasse 25
A-1040 Wien
Austria
Attn: Florian Schnabel
Voice: +43 1-436111 or +43 222-58801-3605
E-mail: helpdesk@aco.net

EUnet EDV DIENSTLEISTUNGS GES.M.B.H
Dr. Michael Haberler
Thurngasse 8/16
A-1090 Vienna
Austria
Voice: +43 1-3174969
Fax: +43 1-3106926
E-mail: info@Austria.EU.net

BELGIUM

BELNET (BELGIAN RESEARCH NETWORK)
DPWB-SPPS
Wetenschapsstraat 8
B-1040 Brussels

Belgium
Voice: +32 2-238-3470
E-mail: helpdesk@belnet.be

EUNET BELGIUM NV/SA
Stapelhuisstraat 13
B-3000 Leuven
Belgium
Voice: +32 16-23-60-99
Fax: +32 16-23-20-79
E-mail: info@Belgium.EU.net

INNET NV
Postelarenweg 2
B-2400 MOL
Belgium
Voice: +32 14-319937
Fax: +32 14-319011
E-mail: info@inbe.net

BOLIVIA

UNBOL/BOLNET
Prof. Clifford Paravicini
Facultad de Ingenieria Electronica
Univ. Mayor de San Andres
La Paz
Boliva
E-mail: clifford@unbol.bo

BRAZIL

ALTERNEX
IBASE
Rua Vicente de Souza 29
22251 Rio de Janiero
Voice: +55 21-286-0348
E-mail: suporte@ax.apc.org

BULGARIA

DIGITAL SYSTEMS/EUNET BULGARIA
Neofit Bozveli 6
BG-9000 Varna
Bulgaria
Voice: +359 52-259135
Fax: +359 52-234540
E-mail: info@Bulgaria.EU.net

CANADA

AMT SOLUTIONS GROUP INC.—ISLAND NET
PO Box 6201 Depot 1
Victoria B.C. V8P 5L5
Voice: 604-727-6030
Local Access: Victoria and area, British Columbia
E-mail: mark@amtsgi.bc.ca

ARNET (ALBERTA RESEARCH NETWORK)
Director of Information Systems
Alberta Research Council
Box 8330, Station F
Edmonton, Alberta
Canada, T6H 5X2
Attn: RALPH PENNO
Voice: +1 403-450-5188
Fax: +1 403-461-2651
E-mail: arnet@arc.ab.ca

BCNET
BCnet Headquarters
515 West Hastings Street
Vancouver, British Columbia
Canada V6B 5K3
Attn: Mike Patterson
Voice: +1 604-291-5209
Fax: +1 604-291-5022
E-mail: Mike@bc.net

CA*NET
CA*net Information Centre
Computing Services
University of Toronto
4 Bancroft Ave., Rm 116
Toronto, Ontario
Canada, M5S 1A1
Attn: Eugene Siciunas
Voice: +1 416-978-5058
Fax: +1 416-978-6620
E-mail: info@CAnet.ca

CCI NETWORKS
4130-95 Street
Edmonton, AB,
T6E 6H5
Voice: +1 403-450-6787
Local Access: Alberta
E-mail: info@ccinet.ab.ca

COMMUNICATIONS ACCESSIBLES MONTREAL
2665 Ste-Cunegonde #002
Montreal, QC
H3J 2X3
Voice: +1 514-931-0749
Dial-Up: 514-281-5601 (v.32 bis, HST); 514-738-3664 (PEP); 514-466-0592 (v.32)
Area codes: 514
Local Access: Quebec: Montreal, Laval, South-Shore, West-Island
Fees: $25/month Canadian
E-mail: info@cam.org

HOOKUP COMMUNICATION CORPORATION
1075 North Service Road West, Suite 207
Oakville, Ontario, L6M 2G2
Voice: 905-847-8000
Dial-Up: Contact for number.
Area Codes: 800, PDN, 416, 519
Local Access: Canada: Ontario
Fees: Canadian $14.95/month for 5 hours; Canadian $34.95/month for 15 hours;
Canadian $59.95/month for 30 hrs; Canadian $300.00/year for 50 hours/month;
Canadian $299.00/month for unlimited usage
E-mail: info@hookup.net

INTERNEX ONLINE
1 Yonge Street Suite 1801
Toronto, Ontario
Canada
M5E 1W7
Voice: 416-363-8676 voice
Dial-Up: 416-363-4151
E-mail: vid@io.org

MBNET
Director, Computing Services
University of Manitoba
603 Engineering Building
Winnipeg, Manitoba
Canada, R3T 2N2
Attn: Gerry Miller
Voice: +1 204-474-8230
Fax: +1 204-275-5420
E-mail: miller@ccm.UManitoba.ca

NLNET
Newfoundland and Labrador Network
Department of Computing and Communications
Memorial University of Newfoundland
St. John's, Newfoundland

Canada, A1C 5S7
Attn: Wilf Bussey
Voice: +1 709-737-8329
Fax: +1 709-737-3514
E-mail: admin@nlnet.nf.ca

NSTN—Nova Scotia Technology Network
General Manager, NSTN Inc.
900 Windmill Road, Suite 107
Dartmouth, Nova Scotia
Canada, B3B 1P7
Attn: Mike Martineau
Voice: +1 902-468-6786
Fax: +1 902-468-3679
E-mail: martinea@hawk.nstn.ns.ca

ONet Computing Services
University of Toronto
4 Bancroft Avenue, Rm 116
Toronto, Ontario,
Canada, M5S 1A1
Attn: Eugene Siciunas
Voice: +1 416-978-5058
Fax: +1 416-978-6620
E-mail: eugene@vm.utcs.utoronto.ca

Prince Edward Island Network
University of Prince Edward Island
Computer Services
550 University Avenue
Charlottetown, P.E.I.
Canada, C1A 4P3
Voice: +1 902-566-0450
Fax: +1 902-566-0958
E-mail: hancock@upei.ca

PUCnet Computer Connections
10215 178th St.
Edmonton, AB T5S 1M3
Voice: 403-448-1901
Dial-Up: 403-484-5640 (v.32 bis). Log in as **guest**.
Area Codes: 403
Local Access: Alberta: Edmonton and surrounding communities in the extended
flat rate calling area
Fees: Canadian $20/month for 20 hours of connect time, plus $5/hour (for direct
Internet services such as FTP and Telnet), plus $10 signup
E-mail: info@pucnet.com or pwilson@pucnet.com

RISQ
Reseau Interordinateurs Scientifique Quebecois
Centre de Recherche Informatique de Montreal (CRIM)
3744, Jean-Brillant, Suite 500
Montreal, Quebec
Canada, H3T 1P1
Attn: Bernard Turcotte
Voice: +1 514-340-5700
Fax: +1 514-340-5777
E-mail: turcotte@crim.ca

SASKNET
Computing Services
56 Physics
University of Saskatchewan
Saskatoon, Saskatchewan
Canada, S7N 0W0
Attn: Dean Jones
Voice: +1 306-966-4860
Fax: +1 306-966-4938
E-mail: dean.jones@usask.ca

UUNET CANADA, INC.
1 Yonge Street
Suite 1801
Toronto, Ontario
Voice: 416-368-6621
Dial-Up: Contact for numbers.
Area Codes: 416, 905, 519, 613, 514, 604, 403
Local Access: Ontario: Toronto, Ottawa, Kitchener/Waterloo, London, Hamilton,
Quebec: Montreal; Alberta: Calgary; British Columbia: Vancouver
Fees: (All Canadian plus GST) TAC: $6/hour, UUCP: $20/month, plus $6/hour,
IP/UUCP: $50/month, plus $6/hour; ask for prices on other services
E-mail: info@uunet.ca

UUNORTH
3555 Don Mills Rd.
6-304 Willowdale, ON M2H 3N3
Voice: 416-225-8649
Dial-Up: Contact for numbers.
Area Codes: 416, 519, 613
Local Access: Ontario: Toronto
Fees: (In Canadian dollars) $20 startup, plus $25 for 20 hours off-peak, plus
$1.25/hour; or $40 up to 5 hour/day, plus $2/hour, or $3/hour
E-mail: uunorth@uunorth.north.net

WEB
Nirv Centre
401 Richmond Street West, Suite 104
Toronto, Ontario M5V 3A8
Canada
Voice: +1 416-596-0212
Fax: +1 416-974-9189
E-mail: support@web.apc.org

02/94   403-569-2882 **debug**   Calgary   AB 300-FAST   24
386, SCO-Xenix; Login: gdx; Telebit, HST, V.32bis, MNP-5 supported; 6 phone lines: (403) 569-2882, 569-2883, 569-2884, 569-2885, 569-2886; System runs modified GDX BBS software; Services: Usenet, Internet email, IRC, local-chat, 50+ games, legal-forms, programming, ftp-via-email, and much more; Fee: $10/month-3hrs/day to $25/month-24hrs/day; Visa & Amex accepted. Demo accounts with limited access are free.
Contact: Rob Franke root@debug.cuc.ab.ca

03/93   514-435-8896 **ichlibix**   Blainville Queb CA 300-FAST   24
80386, ISC 2.2.1; 2400 bps modem on dial in, HST DS on -2650; BBS program is Ubbs (RemoteAccess Clone) - named Soft Stuff, no shell; No fees required but are recommended for more access ($25 - $75/yr); Files for both dos and Unix + a lot of binaries for ISC; Possibility to send/receive UUCP mail from the BBS.

04/93   613-724-9817 **latour**   Ottawa   ON 300-FAST   24
Sun 3/60, SunOS 4.1, 8meg Ram, 660 meg of disk; 2nd line v.32[bis]; No BBS; Unix access rather than usenet; Login as guest for a shell (send mail to postmaster asking for an account); Anon uucp is login as 'anonuucp' (/bin/rmail is allowed) — Grab ~uucp/README[.Z] for an ls-1R.

03/93   613-837-3029 **micor**   Orleans   ON 300-FAST   24
386/25, 600 Meg, Xenix 2.3.2, USENET, email, 2 phone lines
fee required to get more than 15 mins/day of login and to access additional phone lines. Available: bbs accounts (waffle) or shell accounts.
Contact: michel@micor.ocunix.on.ca or michel@micor.uucp, Michel Cormier.

03/93   416-249-5366 **r-node**   Etobicoke   ON 300-FAST   24
80386, ISC SV386; SupraModem2400 on Dial-in line, Worldblazer and Cardinal2400 on other two lines; No fee services: Uniboard BBS for BBS users; shell access for those who ask; Fee services: access to subsequent lines, unlimited dl/ul access; full USENET News and International E-mail access through Usenet/Internet mail; Free UUCP connections.
Contact: Marc Fournier (marc@r-node.gts.org)

03/93   416-461-2608 **tmsoft**   Toronto   ON 300-FAST   24
NS32016, Sys5r2, shell; news+mail $30/mo, general-timesharing $60/mo All newsgroups. Willing to setup mail/news connections.
Archives:comp.sources.{unix,games,x,misc}
Contact: Dave Mason <mason@tmsoft> / Login: newuser

03/93   604-576-1214 **mindlink**   Vancouver   BC 300-FAST   24
80386 w/ SCO Xenix; 14 lines, 660 Meg disk space, TB+ & 9600 HST available; No shell; Fee of $45/year for BBS access; E-Mail, USENET, hundreds of megs of file downloads; Operating since 1986.

11/93   +31-1720-42580 **mugnet**   Alphen a/d Rijn NL 300-FAST   24
386 PC/AT, LINIX — Mugnet int. hobbyist network, Worldblazer 300-19.2k + V42bis + V32; No Fee services : all good stuff for Linux Fee services: UUCP feeds, internet E-mail mugnet domain.
SUITABLE FOR BUSINESS USE TOO Own distribution of Linux/Pro, supplied on disks/tape/removable pack or downloadable. Anonymous guest account. Bash Shell Access on Linux system, UUCP News and Mail Feeds.
Contact: root@nic.nl.mugnet.org, Voice +31 1720 40005, Fax: +31 1720 30979

COLOMBIA

COLNODO
Carrera 23 No. 39-82
Santafe de Bogota
Colombia
Voice: 57-2697181, 2444692, 2697202
E-mail: julian@colnodo.igc.apc.org

COSTA RICA

CRNET
National Academy of Sciences
Academia Nacional de Ciencias
San Jose
Costa Rica
Voice: 506-53-45-02
Local Access: Costa Rica (Acedemic, NGO, and R&D communities)
E-mail: gdeter@NS.CR

CROATIA

CARNET (CROATIAN ACADEMIC AND RESEARCH NETWORK)
J. Marohnica bb
41000 Zagreb
Croatia
Voice: +38 41-510-033
E-mail: helpdesk@carnet.hr

CZECH REPUBLIC

ECONNECT
Sdruzeni Pro Snadne Spojeni
Naovcinach 2 170 00 Prague 7,
Czech Republic
Voice: +42 02-66710366
E-mail: sysop@ecn.gn.apc.org

EUNET CZECHIA
COnet
Technicka 5
166 28 Prague 6
Czech Republic
Voice: +42 2-332-3242
Fax: +42 2-24310646
E-mail: info@Czechia.EU.net

DENMARK

DENET/EUNET (THE DANISH NETWORK FOR RESEARCH AND EDUCATION UNI-C)
The Danish Computing Centre for Research and Education
Building 305, DTH
DK-2800 Lyngby
Denmark
Attn: Jan P. Sorensen
Voice: +45 45-93-83-55
Fax: +45 45-93-02-20
E-mail: Jan.P.Sorensen@uni-c.dk

INTERNET CONSULT
abraxas dataselskab a/s
International House - Bella Center
2300 Koebenhavn S
Denmark
Voice: +45 32-47-33-55
E-mail: info@ic.dk

PINGNET
abraxas dataselskab a/s
International House, Bella Center
2300 Koebenhavn S
Denmark
Voice: +45 32-47-33-93
Fax: +45 32-47-30-16
E-mail: adm@ping.dk

DOMINICAN REPUBLIC

REDID
Asesor Cientifico Union Latina
APTD0 2972
Santo Domingo
Republic Dominicana
Attn: Daniel Pimienta
Voice: +1 809-689-4973 or +1 809-535-6614
Fax: +1 809-535-6646
E-mail: pimienta!daniel@redid.org.do

ECUADOR

ECUANEX
12 de Octubre, Of. 504
Casilla 17-12-566
Quito
Ecuador
Voice: +593 2-528-716
E-mail: intercom@ecuanex.apc.org

EGYPT

EUNET EGYPT
Egyptian National STI Network
101 Kasr El-Aini St, 12 floor
Cairo, Egypt. 11516
Ola Wagieh, Sherif Hassan, Maged Boulos, Dina Maher
Voice: +20 2-355-7253
Fax: +20 2-354-7807
E-mail: info@estinet.uucp

ESTONIA

BALTBONE
Ants Work
Deputy Director
Institute of Cybernetics
Estonian Academy of Sciences
Akadeemie tee 21
EE 0108 TALLINN
Estonia
Voice: +007 0142-525622
E-mail: ants@ioc.ee

ETHIOPIA

PADIS—PAN AFRICAN DEVELOPMENT INFORMATION SYSTEM
Box 3001
Addis Ababa, Ethiopia
Voice: +251 1-511-167
Fax: +251 1-514-416
E-mail: sysop@padis.gn.apc.org

FINLAND

CLINET LTD
PL 503 / Tekniikantie 17
02150 Espoo
Finland
Voice: +358 0-4375209
Fax: +358 0-455 5276
E-mail: clinet@clinet.fi

EUNET FINLAND OY
Punavuorenkatu 1
FI-00120 Helsinki
Finland
Voice: +358 0-400-2060
Fax: +358 0-622-2626
E-mail: info@Finland.EU.net

FUNET (FINNISH UNIVERSITY AND RESEARCH NETWORK)
PO Box 405
SF-02101 ESPOO
Finland
Voice: +358 0-457-2711
Fax: +358 0-457-2302
E-mail: Markus.Sadeniemi@funet.fi

TELECOM FINLAND
PO Box 228
Rautatienkatu 10
33101 TAMPERE
Finland
Attn: Seppo Noppari
Voice: +358 31-243-2242
E-mail: seppo.noppari@tele.fi

FRANCE

EARN (EUROPEAN ACADEMIC RESEARCH NETWORK)
BP 167
F-91403 Orsay CEDEX
France
Voice: +33 1-69-82-39-73
Fax: +33 1-69-28-52-73
E-mail: grange%frors12.bitnet@mitvma.mit.edu

EARN-FRANCE
European Academic Research Network, FRANCE
950 rue de Saint Priest
34184 Montpellier Cedex 4
France
Attn: Dominique Dumas
Voice: +33 67-14-14-14
Fax: +33 67-52-57-63
E-mail: BRUCH%FRMOP11.BITNET@pucc.Princeton.EDU

FNET, EUNET-FRANCE
Beatrice Closson
11 Rue Carnot

94270 Le Kremlin Bicetre
France
Voice: +33 1-45-21-02-04
Fax: +33 1-46-58-94-20
E-mail: contact@fnet.fr

INTERNET WAY
204 Blvd Bineau
92200 Neuilly sur Seine
France
Voice: +33 1-41-43-21-10
Fax: +33 1-41-43-21-11
E-mail: info@iway.fr

OLEANE
35 Boulevard de la Liberation
94300 Vincennes
France
Voice: 33 1-43-28-32-32
Fax: 33 1-43-28-46-21
E-mail: info-internet@oleane.net

ORSTOM—INSTITUT FRANCAIS DE RECHERCHE SCIENTIFIQUE POUR LE DEVELOPPEMENT EN COOPERATION SERVICE INFORMATIQUE
213, rue La Fayette
75480-PARIS-Cedex
France
Voice: +33 48-03-76-09 or +33 67-61-75-10
E-mail: renaud@paris.orstom.fr or michaux@orstom.fr

RED400
Serge Aumont
CICB
Campus de Beaulieu
35042 Rennes
France
Voice: +33 1-39-63-54-58
E-mail: contact-red@cicb.fr

GERMANY

COMLINK
Emil-Meyer-Str. 20
D-30165 Hannover
Germany
Voice: +49 511-350-1573
Local Access: Germany, Austria, Switzerland, Zagreb, Beograd
E-mail: support@oln.comlink.apc.org

DFN-Verein e. V.
Geschaeftsstelle
Pariser Strasse 44
D - 1000 Berlin 15
Germany
Voice: +49 30-88-42-99-22
Fax: +49 30-88-42-99-70
E-mail: dfn-verein@dfn.dbp.de

DPB
Research and Technology Centre,
Section T 34
PO Box 10 00 03
D-W-6100 DARMSTADT
Germany
Voice: +49 6151-83-5210
Fax: +49 6151-83-4639

EUnet Deutschland Gmb
Emil-Figge-Strasse 80
D-44227 Dortmund
Tel: +49 231-972-00
Fax: +49 231-972-1111
E-mail: info@germany.eu.net

GEONET
GeoNet Mailbox Systems
Voice: +49 6673-18881
E-mail: GmbH@geod.geonet.de

Individual Network e.V.
Geschaeftsstelle
Scheideweg 65
D-26121 Oldenburg
Germany
Voice: +49 441-9808556
Dial-Up: Contact for number.
Area Codes: +49
Local Access: Germany: Berlin, Oldenburg, Bremen, Hamburg, Krefeld, Kiel, Duisburg, Darmstadt, Dortmund, Hannover, Ruhrgebiet, Bonn, Magdeburg, Duesseldorf, Essen, Koeln, Paderborn, Bielefeld, Aachen, Saarbruecken, Frankfurt, Braunschweig, Dresden, Ulm, Erlangen, Nuernberg, Wuerzburg, Chemnitz, Muenchen, Muenster, Goettingen, Wuppertal, Schleswig, Giessen, Rostock, Leipzig and other cities
Fees: 15–30 DM/month (differs from region to region). Noncommercial use only.
E-mail: in-info@individual.net

INDIVIDUAL NETWORK—RHEIN-MAIN
c/o Oliver Boehmer
Linkstr. 15
65933 Frankfurt
Germany
Dial-Up: +49 69-39048414, +49 69-6312934
Area Codes: +49 069
Local Access: Frankfurt/Offenbach, Germany
Fees: SLIP/PPP/ISDN: 40 DM, 4 DM / Megabyte
E-mail: IN-Info@Individual.net

INS—INTER NETWORKING SYSTEMS
Voice: +49 2305-356505
Dial-Up: Contact for number.
Area Codes: +49 23
Local Access: Ruhr-Area, Germany
Fees: Fees for commercial institutions and any others: UUCP/e-mail,UUCP/USENET: $60/month; IP: $290/month minimum
E-mail: info@ins.net

MUC.DE E.V.
Frankfurter Ring 193a
D-80807 Muenchen
Voice: +49 89-324683-0
Area Codes: +49 089
Local Access: Munich/Bavaria, Germany
Fees: From DM 20.—(Mail only) up to DM 65.—(Full Account with PPP)
E-mail: postmaster@muc.de

NETMBX
Feuerbachstr. 47/49, D-12163 Berlin
Voice: +49 30-855-53-50
Fax: +49 30-855-53-95
E-mail: netmbx@netmbx.de

NTG/XLINK
Vincenz-Priessnitz-Str.3
D-76131 KARLSRUHE
Germany
Voice: +49 721-9652-0
Fax: +49 721-9652-210
E-mail: info@xlink.net

SEICOM COMPUTER GMBH/NO CARRIER E.V
PO Box 7165
72784 PFULLINGEN
Germany

Voice: +49 7121-9770-0
Fax: +49 7121-9770-19
E-mail: info@seicom.de or no-carrier@schwaben.de

11/94   49-30-694-60-55   **uropax**   Berlin   DE   300-FAST   24
80486/66, Solaris; 16 dial-in Lines (HST 14400/V.32bis/V.42bis and Zyxel plus Modems);
6GB archive (X11, Linux, MAC, WINDOS, Unix, etext, obi . . .) will distribute on tapes
(grab /src/TAPES for the order form, /src/SERVICE for info about support for Free Software). Dial-in accounts only for E-Mail, News, IRC, MUD.. (no direct internet access,
grab /src/BBS for info, or login as 'guest'); Login as 'archive' for x/y/z-modem and kermit
transfers; Anonymous UUCP available, grab /src/README for initial info;
SLIP/PPP-access with full internet access via analog and digital lines.
Contact: info@contrib.de (Thomas Kaulmann) anon uucp: ogin: nuucp word: nuucp

02/94   +49-40-4915655   **isys-hh**   Hamburg   DE   300-FAST   24
Intel 2*80486 >2GB Disk - Unix System V 3.2v4.2 & Linux 0.99PL14, multiple lines w/
V.32bis, ISDN +49-40-40192183, Shells: msh, sh, csh, ksh, bash; nn & tin for news read-
ers, ELM for mail, anon. UUCP: ogin: nuucp (no password) get ~/ls-lgR. [Z|z|F]
Contact: mike@isys-hh.hanse.de (Michael 'Mike' Loth)

04/93   +49-69-308265   **odbffm**   Frankfurt/Main   DE   300-FAST   24
Altos 386/2000, Telebit Modem, Public Access Unix; only shell accounts, no bbs soft-
ware. Mail and news access (currently via UUCP, Internet planned).
Contact: oli@odb.rhein-main.de, voice +49 69 331461, fax +49 69 307682

04/93   +49-30-694-61-82   **scuzzy**   Berlin   DE   300-FAST   24
80486/33, ISC 3.0; HST 14400/v.42bis on the first, HST 14400/V.32bis/V.42bis Modems
on other dial-in lines; Large library of source code including 386BSD, GNU, TeX, and
X11—will distribute on tapes (grab /src/TAPES for the order form, /src/SERVICE for
info about support for Free Software). Bulletin Board System with possible full Internet
access, i.e. email, USENET, IRC, FTP, telnet (grab /src/BBS for info, or login as 'guest');
Login as 'archive' for x/y/z-modem and kermit transfers; Anonymous UUCP available,
grab /src/README for initial info;
Contact: src@contrib.de (Heiko Blume) anon uucp: ogin: nuucp word: nuucp

GREECE

ARIADNE—GREEK ACADEMIC AND RESEARCH NETWORK
153 10 Attiki-Athens
Voice: +301 65-13-392
Dial-Up: +301 65-48-800 (1200-9600 bps)
Area Codes: +301
Local Access: Greece: Athens
Fees: 5900 drachmas per calendar quarter, 1 hour/day limit.
E-mail: dialup@leon.nrcps.ariadne-t.gr

EUNET GREECE
Stelios Sartzetakis
HERAKLIO central office/NOC:

Foundation of Research and Technology Hellas
FORTHnet/EUnetGR
36 Daidalou str.
PO Box 1385, Heraklion, Crete
Greece 71110
ATHENS Site:
Alwpekhs 8, Athina GR-10675
Local Access: Athens, Thessaloniki, Heraklio, and Patras
Voice: +30 1-7245324, 7245253, 7245313
Fax: +30 1-7245004
E-mail: info@Greece.EU.net

FORTHNET—INSTITUTE OF COMPUTER SCIENCE
Foundation for Research and Technology-Hellas (FORTH)
Vassilika Vouton, PO Box 1385
GR 711 10 Heraklion, Crete
Greece
Voice: +30 81-391200
Fax: +30 81-391201, 391601
E-mail: pr@forthnet.gr, noc@forthnet.gr

GUAM

KUENTOS COMMUNICATIONS, INC.
PO Box 26870
GMF Guam 96921
Voice: 671-637-5488
E-mail: pkelly@Kuentos.Guam.NET

HONG KONG

HONG KONG SUPERNET
HKUST Campus
Clear Water Bay, Kowloon
Hong Kong
Voice: +852 358-7924
E-mail: info@hk.super.net

HUNGARY

EUNET HUNGARY
Computer and Automation Institute of the Hungarian Academy of
Sciences
Krisztina Hollo
Victor Hugo str. 18-22
H-1132 Budapest
Hungary
Voice: +36 1-2698281
Fax: +36 1-2698288
E-mail: postmaster@Hungary.EU.net

HUNGARNET
Computer and Automation Institute
H-1132 Budapest
18-22 Victory Hugo
Hungary
Attn: Istvan Tetenyi
Voice: +36 11497352
E-mail: postmaster@ella.hu

PIROSKA GIESE
KFKI-Research Institute for Particle and Nuclear
Physics
H-1121 Budapest
Konkoly Thege ut 29-33
Hungary
Voice: 36 1-169-9499
Fax: 36 1-169-6567
E-mail: piroska.giese@rmki.kfki.hu

ICELAND

EUNET ICELAND/ISNET
Marius Olafsson
University of Iceland
Dunhaga 5
107 Reykjavik
Voice: 354 1-694747
Fax: 354 1-28801
E-mail: info@rhi.hi.is

INDIA

ERNET (EDUCATION AND RESEARCH COMMUNITY NETWORK)
Gulmohar Cross Road, Number 9
Juhu, Bombay 400 049
India
Voice: +91 22-436-1329
E-mail: usis@doe.ernet.in

INDIALINK BOMBAY
Praveen Rao, Indialink Coord. Bombay
c/o Maniben Kara Institute
Nagindas Chambers, 167 P.D'Mello Rd
Bombay - 400 038
Voice: 91-22-262-2388 or 261-2185
E-mail: mki@inbb.gn.apc.org

INDIALINK DELHI
Leo Fernandez, Coordinator Indialink
c/o Indian Social Institute

10 Institutional area, Lodiroad,
New Delhi
Voice: 91-11-463-5096 or 461-1745
E-mail: leo@unv.ernet.in

UUNET INDIA LIMITED
505B, Maitrivanam HUDA Complex
S.R. Nagar, Hyderabad
India
Attn: I Chandrashekar Rao or Narayan D Raju
Voice: +91 40-290933, 247787
E-mail: info@uunet.in

IRELAND

HEANET
Higher Education Authority
Fitzwilliam Square, Dublin
Ireland
Attn: Mike Norris or John Hayde
Voice: +353 1-612748 (Norris) +353 1-761545 (Hayden)
Fax: +353 1-610492
E-mail: Mnorris@hea.ie, jhayden@vax1.tcd.ie

IEUNET LTD,
Innovation Center, O'Reilly Institute
Trinity College
Dublin 2,
Ireland
Voice: +353 1-6719361
Fax: +353 1-6798039
E-mail: info@Ireland.EU.net

IRELAND ON-LINE
West Wing, Udaras Complex
Furbo
Galway, Ireland
Attn: Barry Flanagan
Voice: +353 91-92727
E-mail: postmaster@iol.ie

ISRAEL

ILAN ISRAELI ACADEMIC NETWORK INFORMATION CENTER
Computer Center
Tel Aviv University
Israel
Attn: Ramat Aviv
Voice: +972 3-6408309
E-mail: hank@vm.tau.ac.il

ITALY

EUNET ITALY/IUNET
IUnet S.p.A.
V.le Monza, 253
I-20126 Milano
Italy
Voice: +39 2-27002528
Fax: +39 2-27001322
E-mail: info@IUnet.it

GARR (GRUPPO ARMONIZZAZIONE DELLE RETI PER LA RICERCA)
c/o CNR, Istituto Cnuce
Via S.Maria, 36
56126 Pisa
Italy
Voice: +39 50-593360
Fax: +39 50-589354
E-mail: INFO@NIS.GARR.IT

ITALYNET
Via G.Taddei 3
Pisa, Italy
Voice: +39 5-57-6343
E-mail: cesare@gn.apc.org

LEGA PER L'AMBIENTE
via Salaria 280
I-00194 Roma
Italy
Voice: +39 6-844-2277
E-mail: legambiente@gn.apc.org

09/93   +39-541-27135   **nervous**   Rimini (Fo)   IT   300-FAST   24
386/33, 1GB, Unix System V; Menu driven BBS, no shell. This system is the official Uni-Board Development Site; latest UniBoard releases/fixes are available here. Also, lots of unix sources (& erotic images) as well as USENET & Fidonet conferences, are available on line.
Contact: pizzi@nervous.com. Foreign callers need to send email to the above address to gain access to most board options.

JAPAN

INETCLUB
2-1-15 Ohara Kamifukuoka-shi
Saitama 356
Japan
Voice: +81 492-66-7313

Fax: +81 492-66-7510
E-mail: kddlab.kddlabs.co.jp. Subject: help

INTERNET INITIATIVE JAPAN
Sanbancho Annex Bldg., 1-4 Sanban-cho,
Chiyoda-ku, Tokyo 102
Japan
Voice: +81 3-5276-6240
Fax: +81 3-5276-6239
E-mail: info@iij.ad.jp

AEGIS
Kyoto
Japan
E-mail: davidg@aegis.org

WIDE
c/o Prof. Jun Murai
KEIO University
5322 Endo, Fujisawa, 252
Japan
Voice: +81 466-47-5111, ext. 3330
E-mail: jun@wide.ad.jp

KENYA

ELCI
Box 72461
Nairobi
Kenya
Voice: +254 2-562-015 or +254 2-562-022
E-mail: sysop@elci.gn.apc.org

LATVIA

LATVIAN INTERNET CENTRE
University of Latvia, Institute of Computer Science
Rainis Blvd. 29
Riga LV-1459
Latvia
Voice: +371 2-224730 or +371 2-212427
E-mail: postmaster@mii.lu.lv

LVNET-TELEPORT
204 Brivibas str
Riga, LV-1039
Latvia
Voice: +371-2551133
E-mail: vit@lynx.riga.lv

LUXEMBURG

EUNET LUXEMBURG
Baerbel Ripplinger
CRP—Centre Universitaire
162a, Avenue de la Faiencerie
L-1511 Luxemburg
Voice: +352 47-02-61
Fax: +352 47-02-64
E-mail: info@crpcu.lu

RESTENA
6 Rue Coudenhove Kalergi
L-1359
Luxembourg
Attn: Antoine Barthel
Voice: +352 424409
E-mail: admin@restena.lu

MALAYSIA

JARING
MIMOS
7th Flr, Exchange Square
Off Jalan Semantan
50490 Kuala Lumpur
Malaysia
Voice: +60 3-254-9601 or +60 3-255-2700, ext 2101
E-mail: noc@jaring.my

MEXICO

ITESM
Depto. de Telecomunicaciones y Redes
ITESM Campus Monterrey
E. Garza Sada #2501
Monterrey, N.L., C.P. 64849
Mexico
Attn: Ing. Hugo E. Garcia Torres
Voice: +52-83-582-000, ext. 4130
Fax: +52 83-588-931
E-mail: hugo@mtecv1.mty.itesm.mx

LANETA
Tlalpan 1025, col. portales
Mexico, df. Mexico
Voice: 525-2774791, 525-5755395
Fax: 525-277-4791
E-mail: soporte@laneta.igc.apc.org

NETHERLANDS

ANTENNA
Box 1513
NL-6501 BM Nijmegen
Voice: +31 80-235372
Local Access: Netherlands
E-mail: support@antenna.nl

EBONE
c/o TERENA, Singel 466-68,
NL-1017 AW Amsterdam
Netherlands
Voice: +31 20639-1131
Fax: +31 20639-3289
E-mail: ebone@terena.nl

EUNET NETHERLANDS
Martijn Roos Lindgreen
Stichting NLnet
Kruislaan 413
1098 SJ Amsterdam
Netherlands
Voice: +31 20 592 5109
Fax: +31 20-592-5155
E-mail: info@EU.net

NLNET
Kruislaan 413
1098 SJ Amsterdam
Netherlands
Voice: +31 20-592-4245
E-mail: info@nl.net

RARE
RARE Secretariat
Singel 466-468
NL-1017 AW
Amsterdam
Netherlands
Voice: +31 20-639-1131
Fax: +31 20-639-3289
E-mail: raresec@rare.nl

SURFNET
PO Box 19035
NL-3501 DA Utrecht
Netherlands

Voice: +31 30310290
E-mail: info@surfnet.nl

11/93   +31-1720-42580 **mugnet**   Alphen a/d Rijn   NL   300-FAST   24
386 PC/AT, LINUX—Mugnet int. hobiest network, Worldblazer 300-19.2k + V42bis +
V32; No Fee services : all good stuff for Linux Fee services: UUCP feeds, internet E-mail
mugnet domain. SUITABLE FOR BUSINESS USE TOO. Own distribution of Linux/Pro,
supplied on disks/tape/removable pack or downloadable. Anonymous guest account.
Bash Shell Access on Linux system, UUCP News and Mail Feeds.
Contact: root@nic.nl.mugnet.org, Voice +31 1720 40005 , Fax: +31 1720 30979

New Zealand

Actrix Information Exchange
PO Box 11-410
Wellington
New Zealand
Voice: +64 4-499-1708
Fax: +64 4-389-6356
E-mail: john@actrix.gen.nz

04/93   +64-4-564-2314 **cavebbs**   Wellington   NZ   1200-FAST   24
AT&T 3B2/400 w/SysV 3.2; The Cave MegaBBS System. 144MB disk; 1 line. v32
MNP5/v42bis. Free access for paid users of the main Cave DOS-based system, 4 lines on
+64-4-564-3000. Shell accounts with elm mailer and rn/trn newsreaders. News and
email hub for local sites in the welly domain. The Cave runs using KiwiBoard s/w on a
386/33 to provide local messaging and 825MB of PC files;
Contact: clear@cavebbs.welly.gen.nz (Charlie Lear), Box 2009 Wellington, NZ,
phone/fax +64-4-564-5307

Nicaragua

CRIES
Iglesia Carmen
1 cuadra al lago
Apartado 3516
Managua
Nicaragua
Voice: +505 2-621-312
Fax: +505 2-621-244
E-mail: support@ni.apc.org

Norway

EUnet Norway
Arne Asplem
Forskningsparken
Gaustadallen 21
N-0371 Oslo
Norway

Voice: +47 22-958327
Fax: +47 22-604427
E-mail: aras@Norway.EU.net

OSLONETT Aksess
Gaustadalleen 21
N-0371 Oslo
Norway
Voice: +47 22-46-10-99
Fax: +47 22-46-45-28
E-mail: oslonett@oslonett.no

UNINETT
Postboks
6883 Elgeseter N-7002
Trondheim
Norway
Voice: +47 73-592980
Fax: +47 73-596450
E-mail: sekretariat@uninett.no

PHILIPPINES
EMAIL CENTRE
108 V. Luna Road, Sikatuna Village
Quezon City
Philippines
Voice: +632 921-5165
E-mail: postmaster@phil.gn.apc.org

POLAND
EUnet Poland
Michael Bielicki
PL-net sp. z o.o.
c/o Teatr Rozmaitosci
ul. Marszalkowska 8
PL-00-590 Warszawa
Poland
Voice: +48 90-21-85-712
Fax: +48 22-628-06-38
E-mail: info@Poland.EU.net

PORTUGAL
EUnet Portugal
EUnet Portugal Support Group
PUUG—Grupo Portugues de Utlizadores do Sistema UNIX
c/o UNINOVA
Quinta da Torre

2825 MONTE DA CAPARICA
Portugal
Voice: +351 1-294-28-44
Fax: +351 1 295-77-86
E-mail: info@Portugal.EU.net

RCCN Vasco Freitas
CCES
Universidade do Minho
Largo do Paco
P-4719 Braga Codex
Portugal
Attn: Dr. Vasco Freitas
Voice: +351 53-612257 or +351 53-604475
E-mail: ip-adm@rccn.net

Republic of China

TANet
Computer Center, Ministry of Education
12th Fl, No. 106
Sec. 2, Hoping E. Road
Taipei, Taiwan
Attn: Chen Wen-Sung
Voice: +886 2-7377010
Fax: +886 2-7377043
E-mail: nisc@twnmoe10.edu.tw

Romania

EUnet Romania
EUnet Romania SRL
Bd. Unirii 20, Bl.5C, Ap.14
R-76105, Bucharest
Romania
Voice: +40 1-3126886
Fax: +40 1-3126668
E-mail: info@Romania.EU.net

Russia

GlasNet
Ulitsa Sadovaya-Chernograizskaya
dom 4, Komnata 16, Third Floor
107078 Moscow
Russia
Voice: +7 095-207-0704
E-mail: support@glas.apc.org

RELCOM (RUSSIAN ELECTRONIC COMMUNICATION)
6/1 Ovchinnikovskaya nab.
113035 Moscow
Russia
Voice: +7 095-230-4022 or +7 095-233-0670
Fax: +7 095-233-5016
E-mail: info@hq.demos.su

SENEGAL

ENDA
BP 3370
Dakar
Senegal
Voice: +221 21-6027 or +221 22-4229
E-mail: sysop@endadak.gn.apc.org

SINGAPORE

SingNet
Singapore Telecommunications Limited
31 Exeter Road, #02-00, Podium Block
Comcentre, Singapore 0923
Voice: +65 730-8079
Fax: +65 732-1272
E-mail: sales@singnet.com.sg

TECHNET
National University of Singapore
10 Kent Ridge Crescent
Singapore 0511
Voice: +65 772-3119
E-mail: help@solomon.technet.sg

SLOVAKIA

EUNET SLOVAKIA
Gejza Buechler / Ivan Lescak
MFF UK, Computer Centre
Mlynska dolina
842 15 Bratislava
Slovakia
Voice: +42 7-377-434 or +42 7-725-306
Fax: +42 7-377-433 or +42 7-728-462
E-mail: info@Slovakia.EU.net

SANET (SLOVAK ACADEMIC NETWORK)
Vypoctove stredisko SAV
Dubravska cesta 9

842 35 Bratislava
Slovakia
Voice: +42 7-374422
E-mail: bobovsky@savba.cs

SLOVENIA
ARNES NETWORK
Jamova 39, Ljubljana
Slovenia
Attn: Marko Bonac
Voice: +38 61-159-199
Fax: +38 61-161-029
E-mail: helpdesk@ijs.si

HISTRIA (ABM-BBS)
Ziherlova 43 61
Ljubljana, Slovenia
Voice: + 38 61-211-553
E-mail: support@histria.apc.org

SINET
NIL Systems Integration and Consulting Ltd.
Leskoskova 4
61000 Ljubljana
Slovenia
Voice: +38 61-105-183
Fax: +38 61-105-381
E-mail: info@Slovenia.EU.net

YUNAC
Borka Jerman-Blazic, Secretary General
Jamova 39
61000 Ljubljana
Slovenia
Voice: +38 61-159-199
Fax: +38 61-161-029
E-mail: jerman-blazic@ijs.ac.mail.yu

SOUTH AFRICA
INCA
Internetworking Cape
PO Box 6844
Roggebaai 8012
South Africa
Voice: +27 21-4192690
E-mail: info@inca.za

INTERNET AFRICA
PO Box 44633
Claremont, 7735
South Africa
Voice: +27 21-6834370
Fax: +27 21-6834695
E-mail: info@iafrica.com

SANGONET
13th floor Longsbank Building
187 Bree Street
Johannesberg 2000
South Africa
Voice: +27 11-838-6944
Fax: +27 11-838-6310
E-mail: support@wn.apc.org

UNINET-ZA PROJECT
Foundation for Research Development
PO Box 2600
Pretoria 0001
South Africa
Attn: Mr. Vic Shaw
Voice: +27 12-841-3542
Fax: +27 12-804-2679
E-mail: uninet@frd.ac.za

SPAIN

EUNET SPAIN
Goya Servicios Telematicos S.A.
Clara del Rey 8, 1-7
E-28002 Madrid
Spain
Voice: +34 1-413-48-56
Fax: +34 1-413-49-01
E-mail: info@Spain.EU.net

RedIRIS
Secretaria RedIRIS
Fundesco
Alcala 61
28014 Madrid
Spain
Voice: +34 1-435-1214
Fax: +34 1-578-1773
E-mail: secretaria@rediris.es

SWEDEN

NordNet
Huvudskaersvaegen 13, nb
S-121 54 Johanneshov
Sweden
Voice: +46-8-6000331
Fax: +46-8-6000443
E-mail: support@pns.apc.org

NORDUNET
c/o SICS PO Box 1263
S-164 28 Kista
Sweden
Voice: +46 8-752-1563
Fax: +46 8-751-7230
E-mail: NORDUNET@sics.se

SUNET
UMDAC
S-901 87 Umea
Sweden
Attn: Hans Wallberg or Bjorn Eriksen
Voice: +46 90-16-56-45
Fax: +46 90-16-67-62
E-mail: postmaster@sunic.sunet.se

SwipNet AB
PO Box 62
S-164 94 KISTA
Sweden
Voice: +46 8-6324058
Fax: +46 8-6324200
E-mail: wallner@swip.net

TIPNet
Technical Sales and Support
MegaCom AB
Kjell Simenstad
121 80 Johanneshov
Stockholm
Sweden
Voice: +46 8-780-5616
Fax: +46 8-686-0213
E-mail: info@tip.net

SWITZERLAND

EUNET SWITZERLAND
CHUUG/EUnet Switzerland
Zweierstrasse 35
CH-8004 Zuerich
Switzerland
Voice: +41 1-291-45-80
Fax: +41 1-291-46-42
E-mail: info@Switzerland.EU.net

SWITCH
SWITCH Head Office
Limmatquai 138
CH-8001 Zurich
Switzerland
Voice: +41 1-256-54-54 or +41 1-268-15-15
Fax: +41 1-261-8133
E-mail: hostmaster@switch.ch

04/93　　+41-61-8115492　**ixgch**　　Kaiseraugst　　CH　300-FAST　　24
80386, SCO XENIX SV2.3.3, USR-DS (-V.32); Host: ixgch.xgp.spn.com (Ixgate Switzerland); Organization: XGP Switzerland & SPN Swiss Public Network; Public UI: PubSh (Public Shell), free!; Services among others: UUCP feeds for Internet Mail and Usenet News, Swiss BBS-List Service, Ixgate-Archive (RFCs,NIC-docs,non-comp-areas etc.), anonymous UUCP, CHAT conference, TALK software and more. BTW: V.32bis connections soon! General info: mail to service@spn.com (Subject: help).
Contact: sysadm@xgp.spn.com (. . . !gator!ixgch!sysadm)

THAILAND

CCAN (COMPUTER COMMUNICATION ACCESS FOR NGOs)
121/72 Soi Chalermla, Phya Thai Rd.,
Rajthevee, Bangkok 10400
Thailand
Voice: 66 2-255-5552, 251-0704
E-mail: ccan@peg.apc.org

TUNISIA

EUNET TUNISIA
Mondher Makni
IRSIT, BP 212
2 Rue Ibn Nadime
1082 Cite Mahrajane
Tunis
Tunisia

Voice: +216 1-787-757 / 289-853
Fax: +216 1-787-827
E-mail: info@Tunisia.EU.net

TURKEY

TUVAKA

Ege Universitesi
Bilgisayar Arastirma ve Uygulama Merkezi
Bornova, Izmir 35100
Turkey
Attn: Esra Delen
Voice: +90 51-887228
E-mail: Esra@ege.edu.tr

UGANDA

MUKLA

Makerere University
Kampala
Uganda
Voice: +256 41-532-479
E-mail: sysop@mukla.gn.apc.org

UKRAINE

GLUK—GLASNET-UKRAINE, LTD

14b Metrologicheskaya str.
Kiev, 252143
Ukraine
Voice: +7 044-266-9481
E-mail: support@gluk.apc.org

UNITED KINGDOM

DEMON INTERNET SYSTEMS (DIS)

42 Hendon Lane
Finchley
London N3 1TT
United Kingdom
Voice: +44 (0)81-349-0063
Dial-Up: +44 (0)81-343-4848
Area Codes: +44 (0)81
Local Access: London
Fees: GB Pounds 10.00/month; 132.50/yr (including 12.50 start-up charge). No on-line charges.
E-mail: internet@demon.co.uk

THE DIRECT CONNECTION

PO Box 931
London SE18 3PW

United Kingdom
Voice: +44 (0)81-317-0100
Dial-Up: +44 (0)81-317-2222
Area Codes: +44 (0)81
Local Access: London
Fees: GB Pounds 10/month and up. No on-line charges. GB Pounds 7.50 sign-up fee.
E-mail: helpdesk@dircon.co.uk

EuropaNET
DANTE (Delivery of Advanced Network
Technology to Europe Limited)
Lockton House
Clarendon Road
Cambridge, CB2 2BH
United Kingdom
Voice: +44 223-302-992
Fax: +44 223-303-005
E-mail: dante@dante.org.uk

EUnet GB/GBnet Ltd.
Kent R&D Business Centre,
Giles Lane,
Canterbury, Kent, CT2 7PB
United Kingdom
Voice: +44 227-475-497
Fax: +44 227-475-478
E-mail: info@Britain.EU.net

GreenNet
23 Bevenden Street
London N1 6BH
United Kingdom
Voice: +44 71-608-3040
E-mail: support@gn.apc.org

JANET (Joint Academic Network)
JANET Liaison Desk
c/o Rutherford Appleton Laboratory
GB-Oxon OX11 OQX
United Kingdom
Attn: Chilton Didcot
Voice: +44 235-5517
E-mail: JANET-LIAISON-DESK@jnt.ac.uk

JIPS Joint Network Team
c/o Rutherford Appleeton Laboratory
Chilton Didcot
Oxon OX11 0QX

United Kingdom
Attn: Dr. Bob Day
Tel: +44 235-44-5163
E-mail: r.a.day@jnt.ac.uk

PIPEX
Unipalm Ltd.
Voice: +44 223-424616
Fax: +44 223-426868
E-mail: pipex@unipalm.co.uk

UKNET
UKnet Support Group
Computing Laboratory
University of Kent
Canterbury
Kent CT2 7NF
United Kingdom
Voice: +44 227-475497, and +44 227-475415
Fax: +44 227-762811
E-mail: Postmaster@uknet.ac.uk

UK PC USER GROUP
Attn: Alan Jay or Matther Farwell
PO Box 360
Harrow HA1 4LQ
United Kingdom
Voice: +44 0-81-863-1191
Fax: +44 0-81-863-6095
E-mail: info@ibmpcug.co.uk
Dial-Up: +44 0-81-863-6646
Area Codes: +44 0-81
Local Access: London
Fees: GB Pounds 15.50/month or 160/year plus 10 startup (no time charges)
E-mail: info@ibmpcug.co.uk

08/93   +44-81-317-2222   **dircon**   London   UK 300-FAST   24
UNIX SysV3.2; The Direct Connection multi-user on-line service; Full Internet Connectivity (including TELNET, FTP, GOPHER, IRC, etc), USENET News conferencing with a choice of newsreaders, Internet electronic mail with an outgoing FAX gateway, 24 hour computer newswire, download areas, chat/talk facilities, personal file areas with access to a choice of shells (including Unix). UUCP and TCP-IP (PPP or SLIP) connections are also available. Login as 'demo' to sign-up.
EMAIL Contact: helpdesk@dircon.co.uk (+44-81-317 0100 [voice]).

03/94   +44 81 244 6677   **ExNet**   London   UK 300-2400   24
SunOS 4.1, V32/V42b soon. Mail, news and UNIX shell (/usr/ucb/mail, ream; rn; sh, csh, tcsh, bash) UK#5 per month. 500 USENET groups currently and expanding. All reason-

able mail and USENET use free. Beginner's pack available. Mail for contract and charges documents. One month free trial period possible. ***Mail and news feeds.*** ***SUITABLE FOR BUSINESS USE TOO.***
Contact: HelpEx@exnet.co.uk, or voice +44 81 244 0077 GMT 1300-2300.

04/93   +44 81 893 4088 **HelpEx**   London   UK   300-2400   24
SunOS 4.1, V32/V42b soon. Mail, news and UNIX shell (/usr/ucb/mail, ream; rn; sh, csh, tcsh, bash) UK#5 per month. 500 USENET groups currently and expanding. All reasonable mail and USENET use free. Beginner's pack available. Mail for contract and charges documents. One month free trial period possible. ***Mail and news feeds.*** ***SUITABLE FOR BUSINESS USE TOO.***
Contact: HelpEx@exnet.co.uk, or voice/FAX +44 81 755 0077 GMT 1300-2300.

04/93   +44-734-34-00-55 **infocom**   Berkshire   UK   300-FAST   24
80486, SCO UNIX 3.2.2; BBS, Teletext pages; 2nd line 32-00-55; Internet Mail/USENET at HOME using FSUUCP (DOS)/UUCP; Max 60.00 + V.A.T. per annum, this will also be the charge when internet access (i.e. ftp & telnet arrive shortly), this level includes UUCP Login & a BBS Login account, if you choose UUCP transfers this can save a lot of connection charges from those nasty telephone companies. File Upload & Download, no quotas; Some services are free and some are pay; login as 'new' (8-N-1) . . . on-line registration, password sent by mail;
Contact: sysop@infocom.co.uk or mail <information@infocom.co.uk> with "general" in the subject line or Fax +44 734 32 09 88

12/93   +44-81-863-6646 **WinNET**   London   UK   300-FAST   24
486 PC/AT, SCO Unix—IBM-PC User Group; Multiple lines, 300-19.2k + V42bis + V32; Fee: from 6.75 pounds sterling per month, (3.25 per hour) includes custom Windows 3.x Software; Software available for download vai anon ftp from ftp.ibmpcug.co.uk or via dial up link login as winnet (no password). Internet Access (optional FTP, Telnet and IRC) as well as News and Mail services via UUCP; Shell Access available as an option. UUCP News and Mail Feeds
Contact: info@ibmpcug.co.uk, or request@win-uk.net Voice +44 81 863 1191

URUGUAY

CHASQUE
Casilla Correo 1539
Montevideo 11000
Uruguay
Local Access: Uruguay and Paraguay
Voice: +598 2-496-192
E-mail: apoyo@chasque.apc.org

ZAMBIA

ZANGO
Zambia Association for Research and Development
Lusaka
Zambia

Voice: +260 1-252-507
E-mail: sysop@unza.gn.apc.org

ZIMBABWE

MANGO
PO Box 7069
Harare
Zimbabwe
Voice: +263 4-303-211, ext 1492
E-mail: sysop@mango.apc.org

Glossary

anonymous FTP   Entering **anonymous** as your login at an FTP site allows you to use resources that the system administrator has made available to the public. See FTP.

ANSI   American National Standards Institute. This body is responsible for standards like ASCII (q.v.).

archie   A system of distributed computers that tracks the holdings at FTP sites throughout the world. You can use archie to search for files.

ARPA   Advanced Research Projects Agency (formerly DARPA). This agency funded the original research that resulted in ARPANET, the network that validated the concept of packet switching through TCP/IP.

ARPANET   Funded by ARPA to study how to make computer networks secure in the event of nuclear war, this network later split its functions, with MILNET breaking off in 1983. ARPANET was retired in 1990.

ASCII   The American Standard Code for Information Interchange, which creates a standard for representing computer characters.

asynchronous   The transmission of information without reference to timing factors on the receiving end.

ATM   Asynchronous Transfer Mode. Perhaps the hottest news in network technology. Allows networks to move vast amounts of data, such as live video, on a switched, as opposed to a point-to-point, basis.

backbone   The system of high-speed connections that routes long-haul traffic, connecting to slower regional and local datapaths.

bandwidth   The size of the data pipeline; specifically, the amount of data that can be transmitted over a particular line in a given period of time. The higher the bandwidth, the faster information can flow. Bandwidth is commonly measured in bits per second (bps).

BBS   A bulletin board system. The term usually refers to a small, dial-up system designed for local users, although some BBSs are now widely available over public data networks.

BITNET   An academic network containing mailing lists on a wide variety of subjects, often populated by scholars and experts in their various fields. Uses a different protocol than the Internet to move its data. BITNET traffic now moves almost entirely over the Internet.

browser   A program used to navigate the World Wide Web. Browsers like Mosaic and Netscape allow you to click on a link to another document, and move to a different computer where that resource is stored.

CCIRN   The Coordinating Committee for Intercontinental Research Networks, which focuses on the growth of research in the global arena. Membership includes networking organizations in numerous countries.

ClariNet   A commercial service offering news and features in the form of USENET newsgroups.

Class A Network   A network with an IP number beginning 1 to 127. Used by universities, government organizations, and commercial organizations.

Class B Network   A network with an IP number beginning 128-191. Normally found at corporate sites and other large organizations.

Class C Network   A network with an IP number beginning 192-221. Normally used for service providers, small businesses, schools, and so on.

CNIDR   The Clearinghouse for Networked Information Discovery and Retrieval, in Research Triangle Park, North Carolina. Its mission is to support the development of network search tools.

client   Software that requests services from another computer (called the server). This model is known as client/server computing.

CMC   Computer Mediated Communication—an acronym you will occasionally encounter that refers to the entire range of networking activities.

compression   The process of squeezing data to eliminate redundancies and allow files to be stored in less disk space. In modems, data compression is used to provide higher transfer rates than would otherwise be possible.

CSLIP   A form of SLIP that compresses header information to improve performance.

CSO or CCSO   An acronym (Computing Services Office) for a system that allows you to search for students and faculty members at a given school. Now found as CCSO—Computing and Communications Service Office, following a name change at the site.

CWIS   Campus Wide Information Systems serve universities and colleges with local news, directories, library connections, and databases.

cyberspace   The universe of networked computers. Your electronic mail could be said to flow through cyberspace.

datagram   The standard format for a packet of data, as arranged by IP.

dial-up user   A person who accesses the Internet through a modem. This can refer either to a shell account from which the user connects to a machine that is on the Internet and uses its resources, rather than having his or her machine actually on the network; or a SLIP/PPP account (q.v.), in which the user's computer exchanges data packets directly with the Internet.

Domain Name System   The system that locates the IP addresses corresponding to named computers and domains. A DNS name consists of a sequence of information separated by dots. Thus mayer.hollywood.com. The Domain Name Service is a program that resolves domain names into IP addresses.

domain   A part of the DNS name. The domain to the far right is called the top-level domain. In the preceding example, this is .com.

downloading   Moving a file from one computer to another.

e-mail   Electronic mail involves sending and receiving messages over the network. You use a mail program like mail, pine, or Eudora to compose and read your messages.

emoticon   Another term for smiley (q.v.).

Ethernet   A network specification developed at Xerox Corporation's Palo Alto Research Center, and made into a network standard by Digital Equipment Corp., Intel Corp., and Xerox Corp. Connects computers in local area networks at speeds of 10 megabits per second.

FARNET   The Federation of Advanced Research Networks, a nonprofit corporation promoting networking in research and education.

FAQ   A Frequently Asked Questions list is a document that covers basic information from a particular USENET newsgroup or mailing list.

finger   A program that can display information about users on a particular system. Can also be used for other kinds of data.

flame   An angry response to a message posted on USENET or a mailing list. People get flamed for a variety of reasons, such as breaking Internet taboos against advertising over the network. Some newsgroups consist mostly of flames.

Free-Net   A community-based, volunteer-built network. Free-Nets are springing up in cities around the world, as citizens work to provide free access to selected network resources, and to make local information available on-line.

FSF   The Free Software Foundation is devoted to creating free software replacements for proprietary programs. Its operating system, GNU, is compatible with Unix.

FTP   File Transfer Protocol is your tool for moving files from any one of thousands of computer sites to your service provider's machine. From there, you can download them to your own computer.

FYI   The acronym for For Your Information. Refers to a series of Internet documents containing basic material for beginners.

gateway   A computer that handles moving data from one network to another.

Gopher   A tool developed at the University of Minnesota that creates menus that allow you to access network resources by moving an on-screen pointer. The idea behind Gopher is to simplify the process of using network information. Gopher can point to text files, Telnet sites, WAIS databases, and a wide range of other data.

Gopherspace   A play on cyberspace. Gopherspace is a whimsical term for the world wide system of Gophers.

header   A header appears as the first part of a data packet, and contains addressing information as well as providing provisions for error-checking. The word is also used to refer to the part of an e-mail message before the body of text.

hits   In network parlance, the term for results as applied to a database search. You might say, for example, that Veronica returned 65 hits when you searched under a particular keyword.

home directory   The directory on the service provider's computer that dial-up users are allocated for their account. This is the directory you are in when you log on.

host   A computer directly connected to the Internet.

host name   The name of a computer on the Internet. Could be almost anything that the system administrator can dream up.

hypertext   Data that provides links between key elements, allowing you to move through information nonsequentially.

HTML   Hypertext Markup Language. HTML is used to prepare documents that can be displayed by World Wide Web browsers. The document displays formatting, graphics, and links to other documents.

HTTP   Hypertext Transport Protocol. HTTP enables hypertextual browsing through the World Wide Web; the user clicks on links that are established in a Web document and moves to that document, even though it may be located on a different computer. HTTP provides for the specification of resources through Uniform Resource Locators, or URLs.

hypermedia   The ability to display a range of different media through hyperlinks. A World Wide Web page, for example, may contain photographs or drawings, textual formatting, and links to audio and video sources.

hypertext   Data that provides links between key elements, allowing you to move through information nonsequentially.

Internet   The worldwide matrix of connecting computers using the TCP/IP protocols. Does not include, but often moves traffic for, other networks like BITNET and UUCP. If you see the term internet (with a lowercase i), you are dealing with a TCP/IP network that is separate from the worldwide Internet.

Internet Architecture Board   Formerly the Internet Activities Board. Coordinates research and development of the TCP/IP protocols and oversees standards for the Internet Society.

Internet Engineering Task Force   A task force working as part of the IAB, which develops standards for protocols and architecture on the Internet.

Internet Society   Promotes the growth of the Internet and works to assist those groups involved in its use and evolution.

InterNIC   Internet Network Information Center. Your first place to ask questions about the network itself. Maintains a wide variety of data which it makes accessible to all users. Run by Network Solutions, Inc., AT&T, and General Atomics.

interoperability   The ability of diverse computer systems to work together by using common protocols. Without it, the Internet could not exist.

IP   Internet Protocol defines the packet structure of a datagram; it functions at the network layer of the protocol stack. IP also defines the addressing mechanism used to deliver data to its destination.

IP Address   A network address expressed in numbers.

ISO   The International Standards Organization. Creates standards for international use, not all of which take hold (see OSI).

Knowbot   A network tool that allows you to search several different databases consecutively to find network addresses and information.

latency   The delay that occurs as data moves through a series of routers to its destination. Latency is one more factor that affects how quickly we can manipulate data on the Internet.

LISTSERV   A program that manages mailing lists by responding automatically to e-mail requests and distributing new messages.

Local Area Network (LAN)   A network running, usually, in a business office, connecting multiple computers to a server computer.

MacTCP   The TCP/IP protocol stack for the Macintosh, as provided by Apple Computer, and included with System 7.5.

mailserver   A computer that responds to electronic mail requests for information. You could ask a mailserver, for example, to send you a particular file by giving a precise command, such as **send index**.

mailing list   A group discussion carried on through electronic mail. Mailing lists exist on a huge range of topics, often of a very specialized nature.

MBONE   The Multicast Backbone is a testbed for moving audio and visual information over the Internet.

metanetwork   A network that is made up of numerous other networks. The Internet is the prime example.

MILNET   A network run by the Department of Defense that serves the military. Split off from ARPANET in 1983.

MIME   Multipurpose Internet Mail Extensions; the system for providing graphics and other nontextual data through e-mail.

Mosaic   A graphical tool that allows you to access World Wide Web information in a point-and-click environment. Can be used only if you have direct network access; dial-up users use a SLIP/PPP account to make Mosaic work.

multicast   As opposed to broadcasting, which would send data to everyone, multicasting means moving data from one point to multiple, specified network points. The term is used in connection with the operational procedures of the MBONE.

nameserver   A computer that manages Internet names and numeric addresses. A nameserver turns a domain name into an IP address.

netfind   A network search tool that allows you to track down user information.

netiquette   The etiquette of using the network. Not a trivial issue, especially now that the rise in commercial Internet sites is raising questions about advertising and other business uses of the Net.

network   Computers connected together to communicate information.

newsgroup   A USENET discussion about a particular topic. Some 11 thousand newsgroups now exist.

NIC   Network Information Center. An organization charged with maintaining a particular network.

NNTP   Network News Transfer Protocol. The standard for the exchange of USENET messages across the Internet.

node   Any computer attached to a network can be called a node.

nixpub   A list of public access Unix systems compiled and maintained by Phil Eschallier.

nn   A software program used to read USENET messages. See trn.

NNTP   Network News Transfer Protocol. The standard for the exchange of USENET messages across the Internet.

node   Any computer attached to a network can be called a node.

NSFNET   The National Science Foundation Network, an essential part of the research networking infrastructure.

OSI   Open Systems Interconnection is a standard for networking developed by the ISO (q.v.). It is used much more heavily in Europe than in the United States, where TCP/IP prevails.

packet   The basic unit of Internet data. A message sent across the Net is assembled into packets, each marked with the address and other pertinent information, such as error-checking data. The TCP/IP protocols see to it that the packets are correctly routed and then rebuilt at their destination.

packet switching   The process of sending packets through the network, allowing for alternate routing if a particular network link fails.

PDIAL   A list of Internet dial-up providers maintained by Peter Kaminski.

pico   An easy-to-use text editor operating under Unix.

pine   A program used to read and create electronic mail. Uses the pico text editor and provides on-line help as well as an intuitive interface and an address book.

ping   A utility that lets you check whether a given host is reachable.

POP   Post Office Protocol allows electronic mail messages to be stored on your service provider's computer until you log in to retrieve them. The protocol then downloads the messages to your computer. You use a client program like Eudora or Pegasus Mail to read and reply to messages.

port   The designation identifying the location of a particular program on an Internet host computer.

postmaster   The person who takes care of the mail system at a given site. The postmaster responds to queries about users on the system and makes sure the mail gets through.

PPP   One of two methods (the other being SLIP) for exchanging data packets with the Internet over a telephone line. Point-to-Point Protocol offers data compression and error correction, and remains under active development.

protocol   A protocol defines how computers communicate; it is an agreement between different systems on how they will work together. The set of TCP/IP protocols defines how computers on the Internet exchange information (a set of protocols is commonly called a *suite*).

public data network   A network providing local numbers by which you can access computer services in different cities, using X.25 protocols to move data.

RARE   The Reseaux Associes pour la Recherche Europeenne, an association of network organizations in Europe. Serves a function similar to that of the IETF.

resolution   The process of translating an Internet name into its corresponding IP address.

RFCs   A series of documents that describes the protocols driving the Internet, along with diverse information about its operations.

RIPE   The Reseaux IP Europeens is an organization of European Internet providers. RIPE has now been incorporated into RARE.

router   A computer system that makes decisions about which path Internet traffic will take to reach its destination. IP determines how the router will direct a data packet to its destination.

server   A computer that provides a resource on the network. Client programs access servers to obtain data.

service provider   A company that offers access to the Internet. Dial-up users obtain an account on the service provider's system and use its computers to log on to the Net.

shell   A program that provides the interface users work with on Unix systems. A variety of shells are available.

shell account   A dial-up account to a Unix-based service provider's machine. Using a shell account, you use whatever resources the provider has made available on his or her machine, but do not exchange data packets directly with the Internet. You cannot run client programs like Netscape and Eudora over a shell account; they demand a SLIP/PPP connection.

signature   A short note, usually containing your name, address, and other information (and including, often, a favorite quotation), that appears at the end of mail or newsgroup messages you send. A signature is set up by creating a special file in your home directory.

SLIP   Serial Line Internet Protocol. As opposed to a shell account, a SLIP connection allows your computer to receive an IP address. FTP sessions are thus handled directly between remote computers and your system, without going through your service provider's computers first. A SLIP account also allows you to run graphical front-end programs like Mosaic and Netscape. Despite its widespread use, SLIP is not an official standard.

smiley   Also known as an emoticon. A group of ASCII characters that provide visual references to add commentary to text.

SMTP   Simple Mail Transfer Protocol is the Internet standard protocol for handling electronic mail messages between computers.

stack   A layered view of network operations, in which each layer is controlled by a particular protocol.

synchronous   The process of sending data communications at a fixed rate. Both sender and receiver must operate at the same rate to achieve synchronous communications.

T1   1.544 Mbps data transfer over a leased line.

T3   45 Mbps data transfer over a leased line.

tar   A method of file archiving.

TCP   Transmission Control Protocol. This is the part of the protocol stack that controls the transport of data, ensuring that it is delivered in its original form. TCP appears in the Internet's transport layer.

Telnet   An Internet protocol that allows you to log on to a remote computer. Used, for example, in searching remote databases.

terminal emulation   The process of communicating with a remote computer as if your computer were actually a terminal connected to that computer. By treating it as a terminal, the remote machine is seldom able to tap the full processing power built into your computer, thus limiting the interface you work with. VT-100 is the most common form of terminal emulation.

tn3270   Works like Telnet, but designed to handle IBM systems, which require full-screen operations.

URL   Uniform Resource Locator. A standard way to refer to resources. It specifies the type of service as well as the exact location of the directory or file in question.

UUCP   Unix to Unix Copy Program is a method of transferring files between computers, which includes electronic mail. Thousands of computers around the world use the UUCP network to exchange mail over dial-up telephone lines.

Unix   An operating system used by most service providers. Dial-up users usually encounter Unix when they log on to a service provider's system, and must use Unix commands to handle routine chores like file management. Berkeley Unix comes with the TCP/IP protocols already built in.

USENET   A worldwide network of newsgroups on thousands of subjects which can be accessed by newsreader programs like trn, WinVN, and Newswatcher.

WAIS   Wide Area Information Servers is a system that allows you to search databases by keyword and refine your search through relevance feedback techniques.

Wide Area Network (WAN)   A Wide Area Network can be any network whose components are geographically dispersed.

Winsock   A dynamic link library file, that contains the procedures for making Microsoft Windows work with TCP/IP. A Winsock is needed to run client programs like Mosaic or WinWAIS on a Windows-based system via SLIP/PPP.

workstation   Workstations are generally more powerful than desktop IBM-compatible or Apple computers, and usually run Unix as their operating system.

worm   A computer program that can make copies of itself. The Internet Worm was a program that caused network havoc in late 1988 when it duplicated itself at sites around the world.

Veronica   A program that allows you to search Gopher menus for particular keywords.

vi   A text editor with an inscrutable interface that is widely distributed over the Internet. pico is much easier to use.

VMS   An operating system used by Digital Equipment Corporation VAX computers. VMS systems sometimes require modifications to the way you handle FTP sessions, as discussed in Chapter 5.

WHOIS   A program that allows you to search a database for people or network addresses.

World Wide Web   A program that works through hypertext links to data, allowing you to explore network resources from multiple entry points.

X.25   A standard that defines how connection-based services operate. X.25 requires a connection to be made before data is transmitted.

X.500   A directory standard based on OSI (q.v.).

Bibliography

Abbott, Tony. *on Internet 94*. Westport, CT: Mecklermedia, 1994.

Abernathy, Joe. "What Is To Be Done?" *The Village Voice*, Dec. 22, 1992, p. 56.

———. "Creating the PBS of the Internet." *PC World*, vol. 13, no. 2, Feb. 1995, p. 62(2).

———. "The Internet: How to Get There from Here." *PC World*. vol. 13, no. 1, Jan. 1995, p. 130(10).

Anderson, Christopher. "The Rocky Road to a Data Highway." *Science*, May 21, 1993.

Angell, David and Brent Heslop. *The Elements of E-mail Style*. New York: Addison-Wesley Publishing Co., 1994.

———. *The Internet Business Companion*. Reading, MA: Addison-Wesley, 1995.

Anthes, Gary H. and Joanie M. Wexler. "Industry Looks to Clinton Regime to Accelerate Technology Highway." *ComputerWorld*, Jan. 25, 1993, p. 1.

Arms, Caroline R. "A New Information Infrastructure." *Online*, vol. 14, no. 5, Sept. 1990, p. 15.

———. "Using the National Networks: BITNET and the Internet." *Online*, vol. 14, no. 5, Sept. 1990, p. 24.

Aupperle, Eric M. "Changing Eras: Evolution of the NSFNET." *Internet Society News*. Winter 1993, p. 3.

———. "Internet and NSFNET's Evolution." *Internet Society News*, summer, 1992, pp. 2–3.

Ayre, Rick. "Connecting to the Web: New Twists." *PC Magazine*, vol. 14, no. 3, Feb. 7, 1995, p. 196(1).

Babcock, Charles. "The Shape of Things to Come." *Computerworld*, vol. 29, no. 6, Feb. 6, 1995, p. 8(1).

Banks, Michael A. *The Modem Reference*. 3rd Ed. New York: Brady Publishing, 1992.

Barlow, John Perry. "Crime and Puzzlement: Desperadoes of the DataSphere." *Whole Earth Review*, fall, 1990, pp. 45–57.

Beaver, David. "Pushing Beyond Paper." *MacUser*, vol. 9, no. 1, Jan. 1993, pp. 215–221.

Benedikt, Michael, ed. *Cyberspace: First Steps*. Cambridge, MA: MIT Press, 1991.

Berners-Lee, Tim. "A Summary of the WorldWideWeb System." *ConneXions: The Interoperability Report*, July, 1992, pp. 26–27.

Bernt, Phyllis and Martin Weiss. *International Telecommunications*. Carmel, IN: SAMS Publishing, 1993.

Bishop, Ann P. "The National Research and Education Network (NREN): Update 1991." *ERIC Digest*, Dec., 1991.

Booker, Ellis. "Net to Reshape Business." *Computerworld*, vol. 29, no. 11, March 13, 1995, p. 14(1).

Brandt, D. Scott. "Accessing Electronic Journals." *Academic and Library Computing*, vol. 9, no. 10, November/December 1992, pp. 17–20.

Branwyn, Gareth, et. al. *Internet Roadside Attractions*. Chapel Hill, NC: Ventana Press, 1995.

Braun, Eric. *The Internet Directory*. New York: Fawcett Columbine, 1994.

Browne, Steve. *The Internet via Mosaic and the World-Wide Web*. New York: Ziff-Davis Press, 1994.

Bulkeley, William M. "Hello World. Audible Chats on the Internet." *The Wall Street Journal*, p. B1 (W), p. B1 (E), col 6, Feb. 10, 1995.

Calem, Robert E. "The Network of All Networks." *New York Times*, Dec. 6, 1992, p. 12F.

Carroll, Jim. "Internet Expected to Be Backbone of Global Business." *Computing Canada*, vol. 21, no. 2, Jan. 18, 1995, p. 27(1).

Cerf, Vinton G. "Networks." *Scientific American*, September, 1991, pp. 72–81.

——. "The Internet's 25th Anniversary . . . We Think!" *Telecommunications*, vol. 29, no. 1, Jan. 1995, p. 23(2).

Christian, Kaare and Susan Richter. *The Unix Operating System*. New York: John Wiley & Sons, Inc., 1994.

Clements, Charles, M.D. "HealthNet Connects Africa to Vital Medical Data." *Satellite Communications*, Jan. 1992, pp. 18–21.

Comer, Douglas E. *Internetworking with TCP/IP Vol. I: Principles, Protocols and Architecture*. Englewood Cliffs, NJ: Prentice Hall, 1991.

——. *The Internet Book*. Englewood Cliffs, NJ: Prentice Hall, 1994.

Cortese, Amy. "Warding Off the Cyberspace Invaders." *Business Week*, no. 3415, March 13, 1995, p. 92(2).

Cronin, Mary J. *Doing Business on the Internet*. New York: Van Nostrand Reinhold, 1994.

Denning, Peter J. *Computers Under Attack: Intruders, Worms and Viruses*. Reading, MA: Addison-Wesley, 1990.

Derfler, Frank J., Jr. *PC Magazine Guide to Connectivity*. 2nd Ed. Emeryville, CA: Ziff-Davis Press, 1992.

Dern, Daniel P. *The Internet Guide for New Users*. New York: McGraw-Hill, 1993.

——. "Applying the Internet." *BYTE Magazine*, Feb. 1992, pp. 111–118.

——. "Kids! Earn Big Money Selling Grep!" *Internet World*, vol. 8, no. 1, Jan. 1995, p. 88(2).

——. "The Internet, Your Company, and You." *Network Computing*, vol. 5, no. 14, Nov. 15, 1994, p. 50(4).

——. "Painting the Right Picture." *Internet World*, vol. 5, no. 8, Nov.–Dec. 1994, p. 99(3).

——. "Casting for Internet Answers." *InfoWorld*, vol. 16, no. 43, Oct. 24, 1994, p. 84(1).

——. "Myth or Menace? A History of Business on the Net." *Internet World*, vol. 5, no. 5, July–Aug. 1994, p. 96(3).

Deutsch, Peter. "Resource Discovery in an Internet Environment—the archie Approach." *Electronic Networking: Research, Applications, and Policy,*" vol. 2, no. 1, spring, 1992, pp. 45–51.

Dougherty, Dale and Richard Koman. *The Mosaic Handbook for the Macintosh*. Sebastopol, CA: O'Reilly & Assoc, 1994.

Duncan, Ray. "Roaming the Internet." *Dr. Dobb's Journal*, Feb. 1993, pp. 131–32.

——. "Roaming the Internet, Part 2." *Dr. Dobb's Journal*, April, 1993, p. 127.

Ebersman, Paul. "Making the Internet Connection." *UnixWorld,* June, 1992.

Engst, Adam. "Making the Internet Connection." *MacUser,* May, 1995, p. 66.

Ellsworth, Jill and Matthew V. Ellsworth. *The Internet Business Book.* New York: John Wiley & Sons, Inc., 1994.

————. "Businesses on a Virtual Rush to the Virtual Mall. *PC Magazine,* vol. 14, no. 3, Feb. 7, 1995, p. 190(1).

————. "Three Routes to a Web Presence." *PC Magazine,* vol. 14, no. 9, May 16, 1995, p. 224(1).

————. "Boom Town." *Internet World,* vol. 6, no. 6, June, 1995, p. 324.

Engst, Adam C. *Internet Starter Kit.* Indianapolis, IN: Hayden Books, 1993.

Estrada, Susan. *Connecting to the Internet.* Sebastopol, CA: O'Reilly & Associates, 1994.

Falk, Bennett. *The Internet Roadmap.* San Francisco, CA: Sybex, 1994.

Fisher, Sharon. *Riding the Internet Highway.* Carmel, IN: New Riders Publishing, 1993.

————. "Whither NREN?" *BYTE Magazine,* July, 1991, pp. 181–189.

Fleishman, Glenn. "Looking for the Right Internet Connection." *InfoWorld,* vol. 17, no. 5, Jan. 30, 1995, p. 51(4).

Flynn, Charles E. *The Unofficial Macintosh Guide to America Online.* New York: John Wiley & Sons, Inc., 1995.

Fraase, Michael. *The Windows Internet Tour Guide: Cruising the Internet the Easy Way.* Chapel Hill, NC: Ventana Press, 1994.

————. *The PC Internet Tour Guide: Cruising the Internet the Easy Way.* Chapel Hill, NC: Ventana Press, 1994.

Franks, John. "What Is an Electronic Journal?" Posted on PACS-L mailing list, January 1993.

Frentzen, Jeff. "A Grab Bag of Internet Tools Worth Keeping." *PC Week,* vol. 12, no. 11, March 20, 1995, p. 13(1).

Frey, Donnalyn and Rick Adams. *!%@:: A Directory of Electronic Mail Addressing and Networks,* 3rd Edition. Sebastopol, CA: O'Reilly & Associates, Inc., 1993.

Gardner, James. *A DOS User's Guide to the Internet.* Englewood Cliffs, NJ: PTR Prentice Hall, 1994.

Gerber, Cheryl. "Booming Commercial Use Changes Face of Internet." *Infoworld.* April 12, 1993, p. 1.

Gibbs, Mark and Richard Smith. *Navigating the Internet.* Carmel, IN: SAMS Publishing, 1993.

Gibson, William. *Neuromancer.* New York: Ace Books, 1984.

Gonzalez, Sean. "HTML: Nothing but New." *PC Magazine,* vol. 14, no. 3, Feb 7, 1995, p. 156(2).

Goos, Anke and Daniel Karrenberg. *The European R&D E-Mail Directory.* Buntingford, United Kingdom: EurOpen, 1990.

Gore, Al. "Infrastructure for the Global Village." *Scientific American,* vol. 265, no. 3, September, 1991, pp. 150–153.

Graham, Ian. *The HTML Sourcebook.* New York: John Wiley & Sons, Inc., 1995.

Grundner, Tom. "Whose Internet Is It Anyway?—A Challenge." *Online,* July, 1992, pp. 6–10.

Gunn, Angela. "Law and Disorder on the Internet." *PC Magazine,* vol. 14, no. 5, March 14, 1995, p. 30(1).

Habegger, Jay. "Understanding the Technical and Administrative Organization of the Internet." *Telecommunications,* vol. 26, no. 4, April 1992, p. S12.

Hafner, Katie and John Markoff. *Cyberpunk.* New York: Simon & Schuster, 1991.

Hahn, Harley and Rick Stout. *The Internet Complete Reference.* New York: Osborne McGraw-Hill, 1994.

————. *The Internet Yellow Pages,* 2nd. Ed. New York: Osborne McGraw-Hill, 1995.

————. *Unix Unbound.* New York: Osborne McGraw-Hill, Inc., 1994.

Hardie, Edward T.L. and Vivian Neou. *Internet: Mailing Lists*. Englewood Cliffs, NJ: PTR Prentice Hall, 1993.

Harrison, Mark. *The USENET Handbook*. Sebastopol, CA: O'Reilly & Assoc., 1995.

Harrison, Teresa M., Timothy Stephen and James Winter. "Online Journals: Disciplinary Designs for Electronic Scholarship." *Public-Access Computer Systems Review*, vol. 2, no. 1, pp. 25–38. 1992.

Henderson, Harry. *Internet How-To*. Corte Madera, CA: The Waite Group, 1994.

Heslop, Brent and David Angell. *The Instant Internet Guide*. New York: Addison-Wesley Publishing Co., 1994.

Hoffman, Paul E. *Internet Instant Reference*. San Francisco, CA: Sybex, 1994.

Horvitz, Robert. "The USENET Underground." *Whole Earth Review*, no. 65, Winter, 1989, pp. 112–115.

Huber, Peter. "The Three Kings Take to the Net." *Forbes*, vol. 155, no. 2, Jan 16, 1995, p. 96(1).

Jackson, Mary E. "Document Delivery over the Internet." *Online*, vol. 17, no. 2, March, 1993, pp. 14–21.

Jacobsen, Ole J. "ConneXions—The Interoperability Report." *Internet Society News*, winter 1993.

Jennings, Edward M. "EJournal: An Account of the First Two Years." *Public-Access Computer Systems Review*, vol. 2, no. 1, pp. 91–110.

Jennings, Richard. "Who Needs the Internet?" *Byte*, vol. 20, no. 1, Jan. 1995, p. 296(1).

Johnson, Johna Till. "The Internet Opens Up to Commercial Use." *Data Communications*, March 1993, pp. 55–60.

———. "IP Addresses: Easing the Crunch." *Data Communications*, vol. 24, no. 1, Jan. 1995, p. 76(3).

Kahin, Brian, ed. *Building Information Infrastructure: Issues in the Development of the National Research and Education Network*. New York: McGraw-Hill Primis, 1992.

Kahle, Brewster. "WAIS: Wide Area Information Servers." *NSF Network News*, no. 11, March 1992, pp. 1–2.

Kahn, Scott. "Making Connections: Painless Path to the Internet." *PC Week*, vol. 12, no. 4, Jan. 30, 1995, p. 78(1).

Kapor, Mitch. "Civil Liberties in Cyberspace." *Scientific American*, vol. 265, no. 3, September, 1991, pp. 158–164.

Karraker, Roger. "Highways of the Mind." *Whole Earth Review*, no. 70, spring, 1991, pp. 4–11.

Kehoe, Brendan P. *Zen and the Art of the Internet: A Beginner's Guide to the Internet*, 2nd Edition. Englewood Cliffs, NJ: PTR Prentice Hall, 1994.

Killian, Crawford. "Why Teachers Fear the Internet." *Internet World*, vol. 5, no. 8, Nov.–Dec. 1994, p. 86(2).

Kilpatrick, Ian. "Why the Internet is Not Yet Ready for Business." *Computer Weekly*, Jan. 19, 1995, p. 28(1).

Knowles, Anne. "Improved Internet Security Enabling On-Line Commerce." *PC Week*, vol. 12, no. 11, March 20, 1995, p. 1(2).

Kochmer, Jonathan. *Internet Passport*. Bellevue, WA: NorthWestNet Academic Computing Consortium, Inc., 1993.

Korzeniowski, Paul. "Connections Are Everything in 1995." *Windows Magazine*, vol. 6, no. 1, Jan. 1995, p. 207(3).

Krol, Ed. *The Whole Internet User's Guide & Catalog*, 2nd Edition. Sebastopol, CA: O'Reilly & Associates, Inc., 1994.

———. "Delicate Balance Between Management, Control Is Needed." *Network World*, vol. 11, no. 49, Dec. 5, 1994, p. 41(1).

———. "Let Those Who Want More Security Pay for It." *Network World*, vol. 12, no. 10, March 6, 1995, p. 39(1).

Lambert, Steve and Walt Howe. *Internet Basics: Your Online Access to the Global Electronic Superhighway*. New York: Random House Electronic Publishing, 1993.

Landweber, Larry. "International Connectivity." *Internet Society News*, vol. 1, no. 2, spring, 1992, pp. 49–52.

Lane, Elizabeth S. and Craig A. Summerhill. *An Internet Primer for Information Professionals: A Basic Guide to Networking Technology*. Westport, CT: Meckler Corp., 1993.

LaQuey, Tracy L. with Jeanne C. Ryer. *The Internet Companion*, 2nd edition. New York: Addison-Wesley Publishing Co., 1994.

LaQuey, Tracy L. *The User's Directory of Computer Networks*. Burlington, MA: Digital Press, 1990.

Levin, Jayne. "Getting Caught Up in the Internet: More Area Firms are Plugging into the World's Largest Computer Network. *Washington Business*, May 17, 1993.

———. "The Internet Isn't an Academic Playground." *Computerworld*, vol. 28, no. 48, Nov. 28, 1994, p. 117(2).

Levine, John R. and Carol Baroudi. *The Internet for Dummies*. San Mateo, CA: IDG Books Worldwide, Inc., 1994.

Levy, Steven. *Hackers: Heroes of the Computer Revolution*. Garden City, NY: Anchor Press/Doubleday, 1984.

Lynch, Daniel C. and Marshall T. Rose. *Internet System Handbook*. New York: Addison-Wesley Publishing Co., 1993.

Malamud, Carl. *Exploring the Internet: A Technical Travelogue*. Englewood Cliffs, NJ: PTR Prentice Hall, 1992.

Malamud, Carl. *Stacks: Interoperability in Today's Computer Networks*. Englewood Cliffs, NJ: Prentice-Hall, 1992.

Malkin, Gary and April Marine. "FYI on Questions and Answers: Answers to Commonly Asked New Internet User Questions." RFC 1325 (FYI 4). May 1992.

Maloff, Joel. "The Business Value of Internetworking." *Internet World*, vol. 5, no. 5, July–August 1994, p. 34(5).

Marine, April. *Internet: Getting Started*. Englewood Cliffs, NJ: PTR Prentice Hall, 1993.

———. "Demystifying the Internet." *Open Systems Today*, Sept. 21, 1992, p. 86.

Markoff, John. "Turning the Desktop PC into a Talk Radio Medium." *New York Times*, March 4, 1993, p. A1.

———. "Building the Electronic Superhighway." *New York Times*, Jan. 24, 1993, Sec. 3, p. 1.

———. "The Staggering Scope of the Internet." *Digital Media: A Seybold Report*, vol. 1, no. 11, April 20, 1992, p. 19.

Maxwell, Christine and Czeslaw Jan Grycz. *New Rider's Official Internet Yellow Pages*. Indianapolis, IN: New Riders Publishing, 1994.

McCahill, Mark. "The Internet Gopher: A Distributed Server Information System." *ConneXions: The Interoperability Report*, vol. 6, no. 7, July 1992, pp. 10–14.

McCarthy, Shawn P. "NSF Bails on Internet: Regional Net Managers Throw Out Lifelines." *Government Computer News*, vol. 14, no. 4, Feb. 20, 1995, p. 44(2).

McClure, Charles R., Ann P. Bishop, Philip Doty, and Howard Rosenbaum. *The National Research and Education Network (NREN): Research and Policy Perspectives*. Norwood, NJ: Ablex Publishing Corp., 1991.

Meckler Publishing. *On Internet 1993*. Westport, CT: Meckler Publishing, 1993.

Meriwether, Dan. *The Macintosh Web Browser Kit*. New York: John Wiley & Sons, Inc., 1995.

Metcalfe, Bob. "Internet Digital Cash—Don't Leave Your Home Page without It." *InfoWorld*, vol. 17, no. 11, March 13, 1995, p. 55(1).

Mockapetris, Paul. "Domain Names—Concepts and Facilities." RFC 822.

Mohan, Suruchi. "Standards Body Pushes IP." *Computerworld*, vol. 29, no. 11, March 13, 1995, p. 87(1).

Moody, Glyn. "How the Internet Works and Why Nobody Runs It." *Computer Weekly*, Oct. 27, 1994, p. 57.

Moore, Michael A. and Ronald M. Sawey. *BITNET for VMS Users*. Burlington, MA: Digital Press, 1992.

Nickerson, Gord. "Computer Mediated Communication on BITNET." *Computers in Libraries*, Feb. 1992, pp. 33–36.

Norr, Henry. "Internet Links Fomenting Revolution from Below." *MacWEEK*, vol. 9, no. 13, March 27, 1995, p. 26(1).

NYSERNet Inc. *NYSERNet New User's Guide to Useful and Unique Resources on the Internet*. Syracuse, NY: NYSERNet, 1992.

Okerson, Ann. "The Electronic Journal: What, Whence, and When?" *Public-Access Computer Systems Review*, vol. 2, no. 1, pp. 5–24.

O'Neal-Patterson, Michael. "Ban Business Use of the Internet." *Computerworld*, vol. 28, no. 48, Nov. 28, 1994, p. 116(2).

Parkhurst, Carol A., ed. *Library Perspectives on NREN: The National Research and Education Network*. Chicago: LITA, 1990.

Peek, Jerry, Tim O'Reilly and Mike Loukides. *UNIX Power Tools*. Sebastopol, CA: O'Reilly & Associates/Bantam Books, 1993.

Pfaffenberger, Bryan. *Mosaic User's Guide*. New York: MIS Press, 1994.

———. *The World Wide Web Bible*. New York: MIS Press, 1994.

Quarterman, John. S. *The Internet Connection*. New York: Addison-Wesley Publishing Co., 1994.

———. *The Matrix—Computer Networks and Conferencing Systems Worldwide*. Burlington, MA: Digital Press, 1990.

———. "What Can Businesses Get Out of the Internet?" *ComputerWorld*, Feb. 22, 1993, pp. 81–83.

Que Development Group. *The Information Superhighway: Beyond the Internet*. Carmel, IN: QUE Corp., 1994.

Randall, Neil. "Find It and Do It On-line." *PC-Computing*, vol. 8, no. 3, March 1995, p. 112(2).

———. "The Net Connection." *PC-Computing*, vol. 8, no. 2, Feb. 1995, p. 170(2).

Raymond, Eric and Guy L. Steele, Jr. *The New Hacker's Dictionary*. Cambridge, MA: MIT Press, 1991.

Reichard, Kevin and Eric F. Johnson. *UNIX in Plain English*. New York: MIS Press, 1994.

Resnick, Rosalind. *The Internet Business Guide: Riding the Information Superhighway to Profit*. Indianapolis, IN: SAMS Publishing, 1994.

———. "Get Your Business on the Net." *Home Office Computing*, vol. 13, no. 2, Feb. 1995, p. 62(5).

Rittner, Don. *The Whole Earth Online Almanac*. New York: Brady, 1994.

Rose, Marshall T. *The Internet Message: Closing the Book with Electronic Mail*. Englewood Cliffs, NJ: PTR Prentice Hall, 1993.

Rutten, Peter, Albert F. Bayers III and Kelly Maloni. *netguide*. New York: Random House Electronic Publishing, 1994.

Sachs, David and Henry Stair. *Hands-On Internet*. Englewood Cliffs, NJ: PTR Prentice Hall, 1994.

Savetz, Kevin M. *Your Internet Consultant: The FAQs of Life Online.* Indianapolis, IN: SAMS Publishing, 1994.

Schneier, Bruce. *E-Mail Security: How to Keep Your Electronic Messages Private.* New York: John Wiley & Sons, Inc., 1995.

Schrage, Michael. "Betting Billions on a Long Shot to Boost U.S. Competitiveness." *Washington Post*, Feb. 26, 1993.

Schulman, Mark. *Introduction to UNIX.* Carmel, IN: Que Corp., 1992.

Schwartz, Michael F. "Which White Pages Service is Appropriate for My Site?" *Internet Society News*, vol. 1, no. 4, winter, 1993, pp. 19–21.

Seltzer, Larry. "The Future of TCP/IP." *Windows Sources*, vol. 3, no. 2, Feb. 1995, p. 108(1).

Semich, Jay William. "The World Wide Web: Internet Boomtown?" *Datamation*, vol. 41, no. 1, Jan. 15, 1995, p. 37(5).

Signell, Karl. "Upping the Ante: The Ins and Outs of SLIP/PPP." *Internet World*, vol. 6, no. 3, March 1995, p. 58(3).

Singleton, Andrew. "The Virtual Storefront." *Byte*, vol. 20, no. 1, Jan. 1995, p. 125(4).

Slater, Derke. "Keeping Secrets: E-Mail Privacy Products Are Still Scarce." *Computerworld*, vol. 29, no. 10, March 6, 1995, p. 101(1).

Snyder, Joel. "A Hard Look at Multimedia." *Internet World*, vol. 6, no. 3, March 1995, p. 86(2).

———. "Taming the Internet." *Macworld*, vol. 11, no. 12, Dec. 1994, p. 114(4).

———. "Internet: Going South." *Internet World*, vol. 5 no. 8, Nov.–Dec. 1994, p. 94(2).

Southerton, Alan and Edwin C. Perkins, Jr. *The Unix and X Command Compendium.* New York: John Wiley & Sons, Inc., 1994.

Stanton, Deirdre E. "Using Networked Information Sources: A Bibliography." Anonymous FTP from infolib.murdoch.edu.au.

Stark, Thom. "The Internet Protocol Suite: Understanding TCP/IP Helps Get You Where You Want to Go." *LAN Times*, vol. 12, no. 5, March 13, 1995, p. 91(2).

———. "The Constant of the Internet Is Change." *LAN Times*, vol. 12, no. 2, Jan. 23, 1995, p. 79(2).

———. "The Future of IP." *LAN Times*, vol. 11, no. 25, Dec. 19, 1994, p. 43(1).

Staten, James. "RealAudio to Bring Live Audio to Internet." *MacWEEK*, vol. 9, no. 18, May 1, 1995, p. 9(1).

Sterling, Bruce. *The Hacker Crackdown: Law and Disorder on the Electronic Frontier.* New York: Bantam, 1992.

Stoll, Clifford. *The Cuckoo's Egg: Tracking a Spy through the Maze of Computer Espionage.* New York: Doubleday, 1989.

———. *Silicon Snake Oil.* New York: Doubleday, 1995.

Strangelove, Michael. "Commercialization of the Internet: Catching the Ear of Ten Million Users." *Online Access*, June, 1993.

Strauss, Paul. "Just When You Thought IP Was Safe." *Datamation*, vol. 40, no. 21, Nov. 1, 1994, p. 71(2).

Streeter, April. "Don't Get Burned by the Internet." *LAN Times*, vol. 12, no. 3, Feb. 13, 1995, p. 58(3).

SURAnet Network Information Center. "SURAnet Guide to Selected Internet Resources." College Park, MD: SURAnet, 1993.

Swain, Michael. "Niceties of the Net." *MacUser*, vol. 11, no. 5, May 1995, p. 117.

———. "An Internet Hot List." *MacUser*, vol. 11, no. 2, Feb. 1995, p. 133(1).

Taschek, John. "Internet Browsing: It Keeps Getting Better." *PC-Computing*, vol. 8, no. 2, Feb. 1995, p. 133(1).

Taubes, Gary. "Publications by Electronic Mail Take Physics by Storm." *Science* 259, Feb. 26, 1993, pp. 1246–1248.

Tennant, Roy, John Ober and Anne G. Lipow. *Crossing the Internet Threshold: An Instructional Handbook.* Berkeley, CA: Library Solutions Press, 1993.

———. Tennant, Roy. "Internet Basics." *ERIC Digest,* September, 1992.

Todino, Grace, John Strang and Jerry Peek. *Learning the UNIX Operating System.* Sebastopol, CA: O'Reilly & Associates, 1994.

Tolhurst, William A., Mary Ann Pike, and Keith A. Blanton. *Using the Internet.* Indianapolis, IN: QUE Corporation, 1994.

Turlington, Shannon R. *Walking the World Wide Web.* Chapel Hill, NC: Ventana Press, 1995.

Ubois, Jeff. "What is Acceptable Internet Use?" *MacWEEK,* vol. 6, no. 34, Sept. 28, 1992, p. 30.

U.S. Congress. High-Performance Computing Act of 1991. Public Law 102-194. December 9, 1991. Washington, DC: U.S. Government Printing Office.

Various. *The Internet Unleashed.* Indianapolis, IN: SAMS Publishing, 1994.

Vaughan-Nichols, Steven J. "The Next On-line Wave." *Byte,* vol. 20, no. 1, Jan. 1995, p. 40(1).

———. "The Web Means Business." *Byte,* vol. 19, no. 11, Nov. 1994, p. 26(2).

Veljkov, Mark and George Hartnell. *Pocket Guides to the Internet. Volume 1. Telnetting.* Westport, CT: Mecklermedia, 1994.

———. *Pocket Guides to the Internet. Volume 2. Transferring Files with File Transfer Protocol (FTP).* Westport, CT: Mecklermedia, 1994.

———. *Pocket Guides to the Internet. Volume 3. Using and Navigating USENET.* Westport, CT: Mecklermedia, 1994.

———. *Pocket Guides to the Internet. Volume 4. The Internet E-Mail System.* Westport, CT: Mecklermedia, 1994.

———. *Pocket Guides to the Internet. Volume 5. Basic Internet Utilities.* Westport, CT: Mecklermedia, 1994.

———. *Pocket Guides to the Internet. Volume 6. Terminal Connections.* Westport, CT: Mecklermedia, 1994.

Vine, David. "Executive Edge: Using the Internet as a Strategic Business Tool." *Internet World,* vol. 8, no. 1, Jan. 1995, p. 44(5).

Vinge, Vernor. *A Fire Upon the Deep.* New York: TOR Books, 1992.

Weiser, Mark. "The Computer for the 21st Century." *Scientific American,* vol. 265, no. 3, Sept. 1991, pp. 94–104.

Weiss, Aaron. "Stretching the Mbone: The Internet Broadcasting Network." *Internet World,* vol. 6, no. 3, March 1995, p. 38(4).

Wilder, Clinton. "A Matter of Standards." *Information Week,* no. 518, March 13, 1995, p. 14(2).

———. "The Internet Pioneers." *Information Week,* no. 509, Jan. 9, 1995, p. 38(6).

———. "How Safe is the Internet?" *Information Week,* no. 505, Dec. 12, 1994, p. 12(3).

Wood, Lamont. *The Net After Dark.* New York: John Wiley & Sons, Inc., 1994.

Wygant, Leslie. "Voice Over the Internet." *PC Magazine,* vol. 14, no. 7, April 11, 1995, p. NE23(1).

Wylie, Margie. "Internet of the Future May Be a One-stop Information Shop." *MacWEEK,* Jan. 25, 1993, p. 22(2).

Index

The Internet
HOW TO REALLY DO IT!

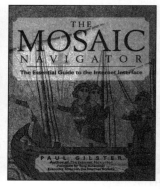

Finding It on the Internet

PAUL GILSTER

"...An excellent book for those who are already familiar with Internet strategies."
—*Compuserve Online Today*

In *Finding It on the Internet*, best-selling author Paul Gilster shows how to bring some measure of order to this chaotic situation. With clear discussions of how to formulate realistic, workable plans for gathering information, as well as step-by-step explanations of all the major Internet tools, the author describes the difference between search engines like WAIS, archie, and Veronica, and browsing tools like Gopher and World Wide Web, and much more.

ISBN# 0-471-03875-1
Paper 320 pp.
$19.95 US/$25.95 CAN

The HTML Sourcebook

IAN S. GRAHAM

"This is the best of the HTML cookbooks"
—*BYTE*

The HTML Sourcebook is an indispensable resource for authors, publishers, marketers, educators, and virtually anyone interested in publishing on the World Wide Web. It provides all the essentials for preparing character-based, as well as graphically based, hypertext documents for online publication. You will also quickly learn how to master all HTML commands and the URL syntax, create and edit HTML documents for Mosaic, Netscape, Lynx, and other WWW browsers, construct "cgi-bin" programs to create interactive documents, and more.

ISBN# 0-471-11849-4
Paper 432 pp.
$29.95 US/$41.95 CAN

The Mosaic Navigator

PAUL GILSTER

"Friendly comprehensive guide to the Internet Interface."
—*Computer Life*

Let best-selling author Paul Gilster show you how to use and customize the Web browser Mosaic, to surf the Net or build your own Home Page. *The Mosaic Navigator* describes the standard Internet tools available through Mosaic, such as Telnet, FTP, Gopher and Veronica.

ISBN# 0-471-11336-0
Paper 257 pp.
$16.95 US/$23.95 CAN

The SLIP/PPP Connection

PAUL GILSTER

You need this book to access the World Wide Web and to use graphical Internet tools! This is the first complete, step-by-step guide to getting, using, and maintaining a SLIP or PPP connection. Dozens of money saving coupons inside entitle you to free or reduced-rate SLIP accounts from leading service providers.

ISBN# 0-471-11712-9
Paper 480 pp.
$24.95 US/$32.50 CAN

WILEY
Publishers Since 1807

Available at Bookstores Everywhere
For more information **e-mail** - compbks@jwiley.com
or **Visit the Wiley Computer Book Web site at** http://www.wiley.com/CompBooks/CompBooks.html